Spring 1972

MODERN THEATRE PRACTICE

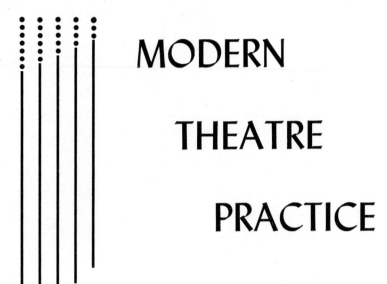

MODERN THEATRE PRACTICE

A Handbook of Play Production

HUBERT C. HEFFNER, *Indiana University*

SAMUEL SELDEN, *The University of North Carolina at Chapel Hill*

HUNTON D. SELLMAN, *San Diego State College*

With an Appendix on Costume and Make-up by

FAIRFAX PROUDFIT WALKUP

Fourth Edition

New York

APPLETON-CENTURY-CROFTS
EDUCATIONAL DIVISION
MEREDITH CORPORATION

6109-3

Library of Congress Card Number: 59-8109

For permission to use the selection from Clifford Odets' *Waiting for Lefty*, which appears on p. 91, we are indebted to Random House, Inc.

PRINTED IN THE UNITED STATES OF AMERICA
390-43101-X

PREFACE TO THE FIRST EDITION

THE LOVE of the theatre in the American people has given us today a pre-eminent position among nations of the world in the support of that institution and its art. Even in the early days of Colonial America, when fanatic Puritans damned it as the devil's drawing room and its actors as minions of Satan, it grew in popular favor year by year. Brought across the sea as a part of our English heritage, the theatre received its first welcome in the South, spread rapidly to the North, and followed the receding frontier westward into pioneer settlements and mining camps. Today we are among the most devoted theatre-going people in the world. Day after day, night after night, hundreds of thousands of city and country folk crowd into cinemas to satisfy their love of the theatre. The cinema is to these people what the popular theatres, the bear pits and bull rings, were to the Elizabethans, and the circus to the Romans. It has been said with sarcastic intent that the cinema is America's National Theatre. In part it is, but only in part. There is another part in our professional, our "Broadway" theatre, but a far larger part is in our nonprofessional or little theatres. Scattered throughout the length and breadth of this land, in cities, towns, hamlets, universities, high schools, churches, lodges, department stores, factories, settlement houses, rehabilitation camps, in every sort of community or organization where people are gathered together, there is a little theatre making life for men and women less drab, more bearable, extending the boundaries of living through the dreams raised with a few hours' traffic upon the stage. To the dull, prosaic commonplaceness of everyday living, to the hopeless tedium of poverty-stricken labor, to the satiety and boredom of wealthy idleness, this free theatre of the whole people has often brought a brief respite, a momentary lifting of the burden. This, the little or amateur theatre, is really the free, democratic National Theatre of America, amateur in the original sense of the word from which it derives—*amator,* lover.

Out of just such an amateur theatre developed the institution that bore and fostered the art of Aeschylus, Sophocles, Euripides, and Aristophanes. Out of such another amateur theatre in medieval Europe came the theatre and drama of Shakespeare and Molière; and out of the modern, free, amateur theatre in Europe and America have come the greatest contemporary playwrights, directors, actors, artists, and technicians—those who have produced a renascence in the theatre and brought forth a new conception of its art, a modern theatre practice.

This conception views the whole art of play production as a planned and orderly execution of a beautiful and effective design. Within this design all the elements of a performance—acting, scenery, lighting, properties, music, dancing—are harmonized and orchestrated toward producing in the audience an aesthetically satisfying emotional effect. Under this conception the performance of a play is to be compared to the performance of a symphony by a large and well-trained orchestra, under the guidance of a skilled conductor. No single musician, whatever instrument he plays, is unworthy of attention and training, or may be allowed to play out of harmony. Likewise in the modern theatre practice no single element in the production of a play may be left unconsidered or allowed to make an inharmonic disturbance in the symphonic effect of the whole. In this there is no question of relative importance; every element is important, for the play—the whole performance—is the thing.

To discuss thoroughly all of the problems of producing plays within a single volume is obviously an impossible task. To treat these problems superficially would be no novelty. In this volume the discussion is limited to three of the most important aspects of production: directing, scenery, and lighting, in order to cover each of these subjects more thoroughly than is often done in textbooks concerned with play production. At the same time the discussion in each case is elementary and comparatively brief, because the book has been planned as a textbook for college courses in play production. The material presented and the organization adopted will, however, make it useful as a reference book for directors and other workers in the nonprofessional theatre, and for high-school courses in dramatics. Toward those ends the basic fundamentals of directing and production have been treated in a simple and thorough manner. Again it may be repeated, the book is not intended to be a completely exhaustive treatment of directing, scenery, or lighting. Such a treatment would require many volumes.

Nor has it been the intent of the authors to write a manual that would supplant the teacher. The book should be used as a basis of class discussion and in conjunction with actual practical work in the theatre. In this way it may become a manual and guide to students in the theatre and workshop and a text serving as a basis for lectures and elucidations by the teacher in the classroom. The best results will be obtained when students are assigned practical projects in conjunction with portions of the text under study. Thus, when the class is studying the problems of play selection, each student should be required to prepare a program of plays that may be produced in the theatre and community with which he is familiar. In the study of the designing of the production, each student should be required to make a thorough study of an acceptable play, design a complete production of that play, and incorporate his results in a complete Prompt Book or Director's Copy. In the same way the study of the construction of a flat should be accompanied with the actual building of a standard flat. Used in this way the book becomes not a text to be memorized and recited, but an actual practical guide to be used in the theatre and shop. As such it was designed and written.

The authors have actively collaborated in the preparation of this volume. Each, however, is more definitely interested in, and has specialized in the teaching of, the subject matter in the main division of the book for which he is mainly responsible. Part One presents and discusses the nature of the task confronting the director of a theatre; Part Two, the method of designing and building the scenery for a production; and Part Three, the designing of the lighting equipment and the selection and use of the equipment in executing the design. Professor Heffner is primarily responsible for Part One, Professor Selden for Part Two, and Professor Sellman for Part Three.

The author of Part One wishes especially to acknowledge his indebtedness to Ruth Penny Heffner, without whose assistance this section could not have been finished in its present form. From the inception of this Part she has actively collaborated in its completion. He wishes, also, to thank Mr. Gilmor Brown, Supervising Director of the Pasadena Community Playhouse, and Professor Garrett H. Leverton, Director of the University Theatre, Northwestern University, for permission to reproduce photographs of their productions.

Acknowledgments for pictures and other material used in Part Two appear in the text.

The author of Part Three wishes to acknowledge his indebtedness to the following dealers in and manufacturers of lighting apparatus: General Radio Company, Century Lighting, Inc., Major Equipment Company, Kliegl Brothers, and Ward Electric Company. For permission to use photographs of productions he is indebted to Professor E. C. Mabie, Director of the University Theatre, University of Iowa. He wishes, also, to express his appreciation here for the assistance of Priscilla Morrison Sellman in the preparation of the manuscript. More than to any other person the writer is indebted to Professor Stanley R. McCandless of Yale University. Certain terminology, such as the term *instruments* instead of the more common term *units,* has been taken directly from his usage; but in a much larger way Professor McCandless has given the writer a greater breadth of vision in the whole field of stage lighting.

PREFACE TO THE FOURTH EDITION

In the preparation of this edition, Part I of the Third Edition has been reorganized into Parts I and II, enlarged with new materials, and the whole rewritten. An effort has been made to simplify the important subject of play analysis. For emphasis in instruction, certain important ideas and procedures have been repeated throughout Parts I and II. New exercises, problems, and questions have been supplied in these and other parts of the book. Additional material on color has been incorporated in Part III. Part IV has been revised to include new developments in stage lighting instruments, control boards, and sound effects, and to provide full instructions on their utilization. In bringing the Bibliography up to date, the authors have attempted to select judiciously from among the many books in each of the fields in order to provide the student who goes on to advanced work with a proper reference guide.

Our colleagues, and especially those in the academic theatre, have been most generous in supplying us with new illustrations for this edition. Acknowledgments of these appear in the text. We take this further opportunity to thank each of them.

For photographs and diagrams in Part IV, we are indebted to Kliegl Bros., Century Lighting Inc., Davis Mfg. Co., Ward Leonard Electric Co., Superior Electric Co., Major Equipment Co., General Electric Co., General Radio Corp., and Metropolitan Electric Co. For criticisms and suggestions concerning the chapter on sound in the theatre we wish to thank Professor Kenneth K. Jones, Jr. and Thomas G. Hays, Jr.

H.C.H.
S.S.
H.D.S.

CONTENTS

Part I: THE ARTS OF THEATRE AND DRAMA

Part II: THE DIRECTOR AND DIRECTING

Part III: STAGE SCENERY

APPENDIX ON COSTUME AND MAKE-UP

ILLUSTRATIONS

FIGURES

FIGURES

PART I

THE ARTS OF THEATRE AND DRAMA

By HUBERT C. HEFFNER

CHAPTER I

Theatre Arts

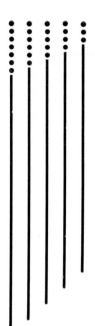

THEATRE IN ONE or more of its many forms has been a source of entertainment and enchantment for man throughout the course of civilization in the Western world. It has not only relieved the tedium and boredom of ordinary day-to-day living, in its ancient ritual aspects it also served man as a means of communion with whatever gods he worshiped and whatever spirits he feared. When the theatre became secular, it continued to hold for its spectators something of that awe and wonder which must have characterized ritualistic theatre. Within the confines of Broadway today entertainment and enchantment are frequently blended and sometimes wonder and awe are experienced.

But the theatre is not merely a place of entertainment, important as that is; it is also a place where meanings are rendered and significances are discovered. There masses of people come to know their fellow man in his commonplaceness, as well as in his strangeness and his amazing variety of character, disposition, emotion, and thought. There they come to understand what another person wants, what he believes in, what he will fight for and, if need be, die for. In this temple of entertainment we gain sympathetic comprehension of the emotions and feelings, the fears and griefs, the joys and sorrows, the happiness and misery of human beings not exactly like ourselves. We begin to see what gives life meaning for other people and thereby we begin to broaden our comprehension of its reality. Here, too, we discern the ludicrous in human nature and human action and learn to laugh with others at these comic aspects of man and his antics. That laughter is good for us, for it keeps us sane and normal. It helps to make our social culture seem cohesive and unified. It can aid in eradicating absurdities and abnormalities before they become dangerous evils. This theatre has persisted through the ages in an examination of good and evil, the ways in which these affect human character, and the ways these influence human behavior. In short, this theatre, especially in its production of plays, is continually engaged in revealing the nature of man and the meaning of man's life.

The theatre through its history has lent its services to many institutions and many causes. It has been the instrument of religion and religious teaching; it has served established governments and fought against them; it has been used for social preachments and social betterment; it has been employed in the task of education. But whatever causes it serves, or by whatever institutions it is employed, it must above all else be entertaining. Entertainment and enchantment are its primal functions. To fulfill these functions it must have within its ranks showmen who know the arts of theatre and who have skill in the manipulation of those arts. What are these arts? What are their components? How do they function?

1. THE VARIETY OF THEATRE ARTS

The arts of theatre antedate by many years, perhaps by centuries, the art of drama. Scholars hold that these arts, like those of drama, originated in religious ceremonials and were first fostered and developed by the officiators or "priests" of ancient primitive rites. It is known with considerably more accuracy of detail that many of the stage arts employed so effectively in the Renaissance theatres of Italy and elsewhere were developed in church ceremonials performed upon festal days in the medieval church. Records show that many of these were elaborately staged and involved miraculous representations of various kinds designed to fill the congregation with awe and wonder. Since their early origins in the primitive rites and ceremonials, the arts of theatre, which include the arts and techniques of showmanship, have undergone a variety of changes and developments but in a sense the essentials of these arts remain the same from age to age. That the arts of theatre are more inclusive than the art of drama is apparent when one considers that it is perfectly possible to stage a very good show without a play. The inclusiveness of these arts and the wide variety of ways in which they occur and are utilized in modern life and entertainment may be seen from a partial enumeration.

The arts of theatre are employed in the staging of variety shows, concerts, and nondramatic entertainments. They appear in circus performances, in motion pictures, including documentary films, and obviously they appear in radio and television performances of all kinds—even in news and educational programs. Most festivals and celebrations, commencements and founder's-day exercises in academic institutions, and many of our athletic events make wide use of certain of these arts and techniques. The organizing and staging of processions and parades depends in large measure upon showmanship, hence upon theatre arts. Anyone who has watched a national political convention or an inaugural ceremony is cognizant of the employment of arts and techniques of a theatric nature in these. Large formal banquets, dances, and night-club entertainments are similarly dependent upon these arts. Salesmanship is in a large measure a matter of showmanship, especially salesmanship through advertising. Theatre arts are, then, by no means confined to the staging of plays.

Though this book is primarily concerned with the techniques of presenting plays upon a stage, it will be useful at the outset to consider the arts and techniques of theatre in the broadest sense, since the art and technique of staging plays usually makes the fullest demand upon the arts of the theatre. The art of theatre does not merely impinge upon the art of drama, it conditions and determines that art in a variety of ways. The arts of the theatre may be considered from two different approaches:

1. They may be considered as a variety of techniques and devices with emphasis upon the ways and means of rendering these various arts;
2. They may be considered as effects upon an audience with emphasis upon the psychology of audiences and audience interest.

Actually the two approaches are interrelated, though in critical writings one or the other is apt to receive dominant emphasis. Details of those arts of theatre employed in the staging of plays will be presented in later chapters of this book. In this chapter the concern is with the general aspects of theatre arts and with ways in which they affect audiences.

A further understanding of the variety and complexity of these arts may be gained through a listing of the various types of theatrical-dramatic performances in which they are utilized. Such a list would include the following types of entertainment:

1. Performances of ancient and modern legitimate drama, staged in various styles and upon various types of stages;
2. Performances of musical dramas; including operas, operettas, comic operas, musical comedies, and other dramatic-musical pieces;
3. Performances of dance dramas, including ballets;
4. Performances of pantomimic pieces;
5. Performances of pageants, pageant-dramas, symphonic dramas, and other types of indoor and outdoor spectacular pieces;
6. Performances of variety, vaudeville, and minstrel shows;
7. Performances of carnival shows, including a wide variety of different kinds of acts.

This list could be enlarged, especially if it were extended back into history to include types of theatrical entertainments no longer extant.

Richard Wagner in his various critical treatises propounded the idea that the theatre was the "art of arts" because it included all of the other arts. If the various arts included in the seven types of performances listed above are detailed in a separate compilation, it may be seen that Wagner's contention indeed has validity. Supreme above each of the separate arts of the theatre is the art of showmanship. That art is essentially the art of affecting and moving audiences in predetermined ways. It is, however, an art utilized not only by theatre artists but by various others, including the expert in advertising, merchandising, and salesmanship. Specific arts of the theatre involved in one or more of the above enumerated types of performances would include the following arts and techniques:

1. Acting—pantomimic and vocal.
2. Singing.
3. Dancing.

4. Directing.
5. Design and construction of stage settings.
6. Design and construction of stage costume, including masks, wigs, and other articles of apparel and adornment.
7. Make-up.
8. The design of lighting effects and the manipulation of the requisite equipment.
9. The preparation and production of sound effects.
10. Stage and program management.
11. Playing of musical instruments.
12. Orchestral conducting.
13. Choreography.
14. Playwriting.

Some of these arts and techniques, such as orchestral conducting, are peripheral to theatre performances but often essential. Others, such as playwriting, though closely connected with theatre arts, may be considered as entirely separate arts which become theatre arts only under conditions of performance in a theatre. Moreover, each of these could be broken down into various types of arts and techniques but the list serves to show the variety of skills and techniques demanded in theatre performances. Even if the consideration of theatre arts is limited to the staging of legitimate plays of various types, as it will be in the later chapters of this book, the range is still broad and the combination complex. With few exceptions, all of the following arts and techniques will be involved in such ventures:

1. Acting
2. Directing
3. Scene design and construction
4. Costume design and construction
5. Stage lighting
6. Makeup

In certain plays yet other arts required are those of:

7. Music, vocal and instrumental
8. Dance
9. Sound effects

2. VISUAL AND AUDITORY ARTS

All art is in its primary effect sensuous in that it makes its first appeal and exercises its powers through one or more of the five senses. Each of the arts developed by man, cherished, and held in high regard utilizes only two of these, seeing and hearing. It is curious, though explicable, that there should be no cherished arts that are apprehended through the sense of feeling, tasting, or smelling. Seeing and hearing are the higher sense faculties of man and on these the various arts rely. Some arts are entirely visual; others are entirely tonal; and others, such as theatre art, are a combination of both the visual and the tonal.

The visual arts are also called space arts because they are arrangements in space. These arts include drawing, painting, and designs of various kinds; they include sculpture and carving; they include architecture and other structures, such as bridges. It is possible to perceive the space arts as a whole upon first sight and to feel their impact the moment the eye catches the image and conveys it to the mind. They have an immediacy, an instantaneity of effect not true of the auditory or time arts. The chief means which the space arts employ are:

1. Line
2. Mass
3. Color

These three means are so manipulated within the space to be occupied by their organization or arrangement as to form shapes, sometimes called space-forms or simply forms. Thus in some works on aesthetics both space and shape are themselves treated as means in the visual arts. Strictly speaking, space is the condition of the art-rendering and form is a major aspect of the object which the artist renders. In addition to the three means enumerated above, the artist so manipulates these as to give two other important media to his composition. These are light and shade. Indeed, mass itself, since it is made up of right use of line and color, should also be considered a similar subordinate aspect of the means of space composition. Thus, what the painter of a picture or the painter of a stage scene actually employs as the means in the composition of his design may be reduced to two: line and color. Out of these two he can create the effects of mass, light, and shade. Even texture, that surface quality of materials, which some works on aesthetics call a means, is actually only a composition of line and color. Texture, like movement, is an effect created by the artist through the skillful employment of the means of composition—line and color. No visual art has movement in a literal sense, since all visual art is fixed composition in space; yet in the way that line has extension which causes the eye to follow it, so may any visual design have a kind of horizontal, vertical, or inclined direction. In this sense, by analogy, it may be said to have a kind of movement in that it gives the effect of movement. In somewhat the same way the repetition of detail or motif in visual arts can give something of the sense of rhythm and the utilization of perspective can enhance the impression of movement. Through these devices artists have attempted to capture some of the effect of the time arts in visual arts; but visual arts have two predominate qualities: fixity and immediacy.

The auditory-time arts might better be called, when emphasis is placed upon means, the tonal-time arts. The supreme art in this area is, of course, music. Varied as music can be, it, nevertheless, like the visual arts, employs two dominant means:

1. Melody (or harmony)
2. Rhythm

Melody is the patterning of tone or sound; rhythm is the patterning of time. Rests, considered by some aestheticians as also a means in music, are simply the absence of tone or sound—the spaces, so to speak, of silence between tones. Rests as pauses in the time arts are so important in their effects that they have rightly received considerable attention in all major treatises on music. Music has been called the fundamental art because it is said to speak a universal language. Such a statement is at best a half truth, for most people of the Western world do not, when they first hear it, enjoy oriental music. Further, of the approximately 11,000 tones distinguishable by the human ear, musicians have chosen to make use of only about ninety; yet the possible combinations and arrangements of these ninety have by no means exhausted the resources of Western music.

All Western music is made up of a combination or succession of these ninety tones, or some of them, sounded tone by tone or in combination, as in a chord, with rests between. The succession and duration of the tones with the rests at determined intervals creates the rhythm; hence arises the dominant peculiarity of time in the tonal arts. No tonal art can be taken in as a whole with the immediacy of a visual art. It requires an interval of time for even the simplest and shortest melody to produce its effect. Just as the visual arts are arrangements in space, so are the tonal arts arrangements in time. The great virtue of the time arts is their ability to render motion; indeed they may be called the arts of movement. Since they are conditioned by time, all time arts are sequential and from their sequential nature arise certain of the principles of their composition. In these time arts, especially in music, in addition to rests, tone, pitch, duration, timbre or quality are so important as devices for producing their effects that these are also often considered as means. It will readily be seen that tone, pitch, and timbre are qualities of melody, and that pause and duration are qualities of rhythm.

3. COMBINED ARTS

Certain kinds of art combine the visual and the auditory. Perhaps in one sense the simplest of these is dance. Dance employs a single means—rhythm—and creates its effects entirely through the combination and manipulation of this means. Spectators tend to forget or overlook this simplicity of means in witnessing a dance, for dance is usually executed to music or in its execution (as in the tap or clog dance) is accompanied by the sound of the dancer's feet. In such instances we comprehend the dance through both seeing and hearing, that is, it is both visual and auditory. In essence it is essentially visual but, like music, it is sequential, a succession in time. In its visual aspect dance allies itself with the space arts; in its sequential aspect it joins the time arts. It is further and more completely allied with both arts when dance is elaborated into ballet and the related art of pantomime. So elaborated, it can render both character and story. Anyone who has seen the famous French pantomimist, Marcel Marceau, readily realizes how completely character and story may be effectively conveyed by silent pantomime alone. Those familiar with silent motion pictures will recognize in them an equally effective illustration.

In ballet and pantomime there is a close approach to yet another time art, literature, which in the forms of drama when presented in a theatre can readily be seen to combine the visual and the auditory, the space and the time characteristics. This kind of art, however, has not two but three means:

1. Melody
2. Rhythm
3. Discourse

Discourse, the patterning of words, is the dominant means of its rendering. Arts of this order are a "making with words." Words are not merely instruments for the conveying or carrying of sound —hence melody and rhythm—but they are even more importantly instruments for conveying meaning. The effectiveness of the literary arts is not merely sensuous and emotional; it is often chiefly intellectual. Certain literary arts, such as the lyric, can be and often are dominantly emotional and closely akin to music in their effects; whereas, other literary arts, such as the essay, may be almost completely intellectual in their effects, appealing not to emotions but to reason. The drama in its variety may range from the dominantly emotional, even lyrical, to the dominantly intellectual, even philosophical. It is safe to say, however, that even the most emotional drama conveys ideas in a way that music does not because it is rendered in discourse. It is equally safe to say that the most intellectual and philosophical drama produces its effects in no small measure through the sensuous and the emotional.

All of the literary arts are time arts in that a space of time, short or long, is required to comprehend their entirety. Even if a short lyric is rendering an emotion of a single instant, it requires an interval of time to take it in as a whole, to read it from beginning to end. The kinds of literature that belong to the body of narrative—epic, novel, short story, drama—are time arts in yet another sense. They are composed of incidents in a sequential pattern, either causally or chronologically ordered; hence they have, when properly ordered, a beginning, middle, and end. The pattern of their ordering is a time pattern. From this fundamental aspect arises some of the basic conditions and principles of their composition. Some of these principles as they apply to plays will be more fully explained in a succeeding chapter on drama.

Plays in performance are not merely heard; they are also seen.

The French people speak of going to hear a play; English and American people are more apt to speak of going to see a play. It is in the performance of drama that the combination of the visual and the auditory, of the principles of the space and the time arts, are most clearly combined. It is in this sense, then, that Wagner could also refer to the art of the theatre as the "art of arts." When this combination of arts is applied to the staging of plays, the resultant theatre art is highly complex. The result is not merely the complex situation which develops in the adding of one set of art principles to another. When principles of visual or space art are added to principles of tonal or time arts, they interact to modify each other, producing a complex art with its own complex principles.

4. SHOWMANSHIP

All art is conditioned by a number of considerations, one of the chief being the nature of the appeal which it is designed to make. Certain arts—a piece of music, a lyric, a dance, a painting—may be designed chiefly or entirely for the satisfaction and/or expression of the artist making the art. All theatre arts, which may be grouped under the general title of showmanship, are conditioned by being aimed to affect—not the artist who makes them nor even single individuals—but groups of individuals assembled as audiences. Though showmanship, if effective, works on each separate individual, it produces its effects upon that individual as a member of a mass audience. A knowledge of mass psychology, acquired or intuitive, therefore becomes essential to the showman. The showman must know, among other things, that when individuals are assembled in a mass audience, there is a consequent lowering of individual intellectual powers and a raising of emotional responses. This is in part due to the fact that emotional qualities within a mass can more readily communicate themselves to and affect individuals than can intellectual ideas. The general objectives of showmanship may be stated as follows:

1. To catch attention
2. To arouse interest
3. To increase and sustain interest
4. To satisfy interest

The variety of devices employed in the theatre, and especially in the complex art of staging plays, are so great that mere enumeration of these becomes almost an impossibility. Moreover, the levels of individual and audience interests vary so greatly that every theatrical performance must employ many devices on different levels. The attempt would be complicated further by the well-nigh impossible task of separating interests aroused by the play from interests in the performance. In fact in a good performance of a play the play and the performance become so fused as to become virtually one and the same for most of the audience.

Though a complete listing of all of the facets of interest which draw people into the theatre may be difficult, a partial list of some of the major interests in theatrical performances may prove helpful in further clarifying the nature of showmanship. People go to the theatre to see a performance for some of the following reasons:

1. To hear an intriguing story well told.
2. To become acquainted with various kinds of human characters.
3. To learn more about life.
4. To escape from the boredom or tedium of life.
5. To be in the "social swim."
6. To see an actor or performer of notable reputation.
7. To see a work by a well-known playwright.
8. To satisfy curiosity about a widely discussed performance or aspect of the performance.

Such a partial list reveals that proper showmanship requires the securing of a good show, an excellent performance of that show, and adequate publicity to make it known. To satisfy audience interest the showman must see to it that the audience sees and hears the show in comfort. Front-of-the-house management as well as back-stage management are, therefore, concerns of the showman.

Theatre arts are conditioned by the same considerations which condition other arts. Those considerations concern the following:

1. Selection
2. Arrangement
3. Variety
4. Emphasis
5. Completeness

Any show placed upon the stage, whether it be a variety show or the presentation of a play, requires exercise of judgment in making selections; in arranging the parts of the whole to build and sustain interest through variety; to give emphasis to the major parts; and, finally, to gain completeness for the whole by a fitting conclusion or ending. The governing considerations in this scheme are selection and arrangement. Variety, emphasis, and completeness are corollary principles to guide the artist in making the selection and arrangement of the parts. In the staging of a play certain prior selections and arrangements have already been made by the playwright; but many considerations of selection and arrangement remain for the stage artists. For example, the selection of the play, the selection of a cast of actors, the selection of a setting, the selection of costumes, the selection of a plan or scheme of lighting, are only a few of the most obvious exercises of judgment in selection that must be made. The arrangement of stage business for the actors, the arrangement of entrances and exits in the scenery and the arrangement of these for the actors, the arrangement of the furniture on the stage, the arrangement of shifts of scenery, arrangement of light cues, and arrangement of costume changes are again a few examples only of the exercise of judgment in arrangement.

The theatrical performance of a play, as has been remarked, involves the presentation of a story from an interest-provoking beginning to an interest-satisfying ending. Hence such a presentation, as a time art, must have an ordered progression. Progression is written into the play by the playwright and will be briefly commented upon in that respect later; but a variety show made up of various parts and elements is also more effective if it is arranged into some sort of progression. The mere performance of one part after another in such a show will, of course, give it a kind of progression; but it will be more effective if some kind of meaning emerges from the progression. The meaning which emerges can be logical or emotional or it can be both. The kind of meaning aimed at by the showman and the playwright determines the order and arrangement of the parts. To put this idea in other words, the kinds of effects which the playwright or the showman aims to create in audiences determine in considerable measure not only the selection of the parts, but also their arrangement. For example, if the effect aimed at is one of comedy, the creation of the feeling of risibility evidenced by laughter, that aim will dictate the inclusion of certain elements and the exclusion of others. Success in such an aim, as in others, involves a knowledge of audiences and a knowledge of techniques and devices of comedy.

The attainment of variety and emphasis in a stage performance involves two aspects or major considerations, the visual and the auditory. The visual aspects in the performance of a play include the following:

1. The setting or the environment of the action.
2. The costumes.
3. The make-up and other physical attributes (size, height) of the performers.
4. The lighting of the sets and the performers.
5. The gesture, movement, and pantomime of the performers.

In certain performances, such as those of the oriental theatre, it may also involve the changing of the settings, furniture, and costumes before the audience. These visual aspects as arrangements in space involve the following:

1. Line
2. Color
3. Mass or weight
4. Light and shade

In order to give variety and proper emphasis to these elements and to make them effective in rendering their meaning they should be arranged in accordance with certain principles. The principles which must be given consideration in arranging the space arts are:

1. Proportion
2. Balance
3. Symmetry

These principles are modified, as will appear later, when they are applied to the three-dimensional stage arts rather than to a two-dimensional painting. Yet the ways in which the painter employs them are suggestive and helpful to the stage artist. They are further modified in being combined with the time arts and the necessity for progression.

The auditory arts appear in a stage presentation of a play in the following elements or parts:

1. The spoken dialogue
2. The music
3. The sound effects (offstage noises, etc.)

The principles governing the time arts are:

1. Tone
2. Pitch
3. Rests or pauses
4. Time

The arrangement of the tonal pattern produces melody; pitch determines loudness or softness; rests and pauses are instruments of time; time includes rate, frequency, and repetition. All of these are determinants of variety and emphasis, as well as other stage effects. When these two types of arts are joined, as they most obviously are in the art of acting, they must be subtly combined and harmonized. The age-old advice repeated by Hamlet, "suit the action to the word, the word to the action," becomes not a mere mechanical act of joining two arts because the act of joining them is governed by the meaning which word and action must convey. The effects which the play is designed to produce become, then, the supreme control over the art of theatre artists.

In the stage presentation of plays the theatre artist is both an interpretative artist and a creative artist. He is an interpretative artist in that he must faithfully present for a specific audience the play as written by the playwright; hence he must be able to analyze and interpret plays. This aspect of his art will be more fully explained later. He is a creative artist in that he employs means quite other than those of the playwright for the producing of the proper effects upon the audience. These considerations and techniques of showmanship are the subject of chief consideration in this book.

5. ORGANIZATION FOR PRESENTATION

Every theatrical production requires an organization of some kind for its effectual presentation and this organization to some extent determines the nature of the performance. Theatre organization may be considered from two standpoints: the over-all organization of the theatre as a continuing institution and the organization of the various artists and workers within the institution for stage presentation. Both types of organization will be considered in detail later. At this point it is necessary merely to distinguish the components of organization for productional purposes. Such an organization has, of course, varied somewhat from age to age but, leaving aside the playwright who may or may not be allied to the organization, four essential components make up such an organization, as follows:

1. The producer
2. The director
3. The performers (actors)
4. The artists and technicians

Some comment upon each of these that will serve to reveal their relations to theatre arts is appropriate.

The producer is the individual, institution, or organization responsible for initiating and financing the production and for the management which puts the various components together in a smoothly operating organization. In ancient Athens the state was actually the producer of theatrical performances. It operated through the archons, officials of the city-state. In ancient Rome the Republic, and later the Empire, was the actual producer, operating, as in Athens, through officials called aediles. In the medieval period the church was first the producer, a function taken over later by the guilds and specially organized societies. In Shakespeare's day the various companies, such as the Lord Chamberlain's and the Lord Admiral's companies, were the producers; but in the Restoration period Charles II granted this function to two men, William Davenant and Charles Killigrew. Today on the Broadway stage the producer may be a single individual, a group of individuals brought together for this one production, or a continuing organization, such as the Theatre Guild or the Playwrights' Company. In the community theatre the theatre organization, usually under a board of directors, is the producer. In the academic theatre the department, the department head, or a theatrical society or organization may serve as producer. The producer obviously has control or a major voice in the play selected for presentation, the director and theatre artists chosen to produce it, and quite often has an important voice in the choice of performers. It should be understood that sometimes the function of the producer is combined with other functions, such as that of director. In the professional theatre the producer hires the scenic artists, the costumer, and often other artists and technicians; rents a theatre; arranges contracts; supervises publicity; books tryout performances; and settles points at issue during the process of production.

Though the director may also be in some instances the producer, his function as director is chiefly that of coaching and directing the performers. In the community and academic theatre he has to assume other functions and especially the function of co-ordinating the work of the other theatre artists and technicians. These other functions will be considered briefly later, but Part I of this book is primarily concerned with the arts and techniques of directing performers (actors) in the interpretation of plays. Though there has always been some individual within the production organization who assumed this function, the role of the director in the theatre is essentially a modern development. In ancient Greece, the playwright was usually his own director, though some of them, such as the young Aristophanes, turned to such experienced theatre artists as Callistratus for assistance in discharging this function. In Rome, Plautus, an experienced actor, probably directed his own plays; while Terence, without experience, turned to Ambivius Turpio. In later theatres the director was usually an experienced actor, though sometimes, as probably in the case of Shakespeare and certainly in the case of Molière, he was both playwright and actor. The term *stage manager* grew up in England in the eighteenth century to designate this position. In America the first significant theatre manager and stage manager who was not an actor was Augustin Daly, with whom one might say the history of directing in the United States begins.

The function of the performers (the actors) in the presentation of a play is so obvious that it needs no comment and illustration. In the realm of theatrical arts theirs is the central and indispensable art. History shows time after time, and especially in the well-known example of the Italian *commedia del' arte* or improvised comedy, that actors are entirely capable of producing shows without playwrights but a playwright cannot produce a performance before an audience without actors. The prime function of actors is to interpret the roles of the various agents in the action. Their art is a combination of both the visual and auditory in their most complete and complex relationships.

Though various aspects of the art of the actor are discussed later, this book is concerned with action only in relation to directing and is not intended to be a text for the training of actors.

The fourth category of production organization, the artists and technicians, may include a wide range of talents, depending upon the elaborateness of the production. It will certainly include some or all of the following:

1. Designers
2. Painters
3. Carpenters
4. Costumers (including seamstresses, mask and wig makers, jewelry and ornament makers, boot makers)
5. Musicians
6. Stage lighting technicians
7. Stage sound technicians
8. Technical director or stage manager
9. Dancers
10. Stage assistants and crew hands

This large group can be broken down into designers, costumers, and lighting artists who are concerned with the visual interpretation of the play; musicians and dancers who are also concerned with interpretation but in a more limited aspect; painters, carpenters, stage lighting and sound technicians, construction and stage crew hands of various skills; and the technical director or stage manager who co-ordinates the mechanical aspects of getting the show prepared and running the show during the performance.

Musicians and dancers appear in certain types of performances only; technicians of the third grouping appear in all performances, though not all that are enumerated above appear in every performance of a show. The activities of these technicians will be fully explained in Parts III and IV of this book. Those named in the first group—designers, costumers, and lighting artists—are also fully explained later. Here it remains to note only some general characteristics of their art. Each of these is concerned with the visual aspect of presentation; hence what has been said about the principles of visual art apply to their contributions to a show. That these principles must be modified by being combined with a time art becomes especially apparent in the artistry of stage lighting. Such considerations as light and shade, color or hue, and mass effects created by shadows show the relations of lighting to the visual arts; but the fact that it can be subtly and continuously changed to follow the varying mood of the action gives it an aspect of continuity that is a time element. Though the other visual elements employed in stage settings and stage costumes are more static, less plastic, than light and do not to the same degree as light exhibit both time and space principles, nevertheless, when they are employed in conjunction with time arts they are modified in a way that a painting, for example, is not. All of these visual arts are conditioned by aesthetic principles modified by the combination of time and space arts. In a stage performance they are further conditioned by other considerations, such as the following:

1. The form of the play.
2. The style of production adopted.
3. The type of stage on which the production is presented.
4. The size and shape of the auditorium.
5. The budget available for the production.

The form of the play and styles in production will be given later consideration. Budget is such a variable factor that it cannot readily be reduced to principles or rules. Moreover, it is rather a matter of business than of theatre art, though it is a powerful determinant of how theatre arts may be employed. Some further information must, however, be presented on Points 3 and 4 and this could perhaps best be done by consideration in historical order of certain major types of stages and theatres employed in the Western world. It must be understood that Point 3 above—type of stage—is assumed to include not merely the various architectural types of stage but also their equipment and methods of utilizing these elements. The student who would gain a thorough knowledge of theatre arts, and especially the student who anticipates the staging of a variety of plays from the past, must secure a detailed knowledge of the history and development of the physical theatre. Before a director can rightly make decisions about the staging of *Oedipus, The King,* for example, on a modern stage or on television, he must know as much as he can about how the play was staged in the theatre of its day. From that knowledge he will gain not only new insight into the play, but also suggestions for its most effective modern presentation. A number of the devices in Roman comedy become meaningless or difficult to understand to one who has no acquaintance with the Roman stage utilized by

Plautus and Terence. A knowledge of the typical stage of Shakespeare's day is a key to the contemporary interpretation of his plays. Information about stages of the past and methods of production on these stages is so readily accessible in numerous books that it is unnecessary to repeat it here. To show the bearing of different types of stages upon theatre arts it will suffice to limit this discussion to contemporary theatres.

6. CONTEMPORARY STAGES

Though there are a number of types of stages employed for theatrical presentations today, by far the most common is the proscenium or picture-frame stage. We can trace the evolution of this well-known modern stage through a series of changes from the seventeenth century. This evolution can be seen as a continuous process of withdrawing the stage and the performance behind a proscenium arch which separates these from the auditorium and the audience. With the enunciation and acceptance of the theory of illusion and with the triumph of realism (and later of naturalism) in theatre arts, the picture-frame stage became a necessity. The invention of the electric light and means for its control made that stage a suitable and subtle instrument for the presentation of realistic drama, the drama that gives the audience the illusion of actual people living in specific environments. Though the proscenium stage is architecturally not as flexible as certain other stages of the past, say the Elizabethan, it has utilized certain architectural and mechanical means, in addition to electric light, to attain flexibility. Among these are certain mechanical devices to expedite the changes of scenery; devices to aid in the arrangement, disposition, and grouping of the performers; devices for bringing exterior places and scenes within the confined space of the stage; and devices for bringing audiences and performers closer together. Examples of each of these types of devices can readily be enumerated by anyone familiar with our contemporary stage and its practices.

In this theatre the proscenium arch, which is seldom an arch, more often a rectangle, serves to divide the stage from the auditorium. Immediately in front of it will be found the footlights, if there are footlights, and immediately behind it will be found the fire curtain, the grand drape, and the act curtain. The stage and auditorium are further separated in many theatres by an orchestra pit immediately in front of the proscenium and the floor of the auditorium may be inclined upward to its back wall from the upper level of the orchestra pit. The stage is elevated above the front level of the auditorium floor. Back of the proscenium is a level stage floor, usually pierced in one or more places with traps. Some stage floors have a circular revolving area set within the floor; others have tracks traversing them on which wagons may be easily moved; still others have elevators which, when elevated or lowered, give different levels to the floor.

The stage house should be of ample depth to allow free passage behind the deepest set used on the stage. On both sides of the stage house there should also be ample room outside the visible stage area and behind the proscenium for the manipulation of scenery and properties. Above the whole stage area is a loft or gridiron, usually called a grid, for the flying of scenery, draperies, and lighting equipment. The grid to be properly effective should be somewhat more than twice the height of the proscenium, that is, if the proscenium opening is twenty-eight feet from the floor of the stage in height, the grid should be at least sixty feet high. Some stage technicians today advocate the elimination of the grid in favor of additional space at the sides of the stage, called the wings. In a number of the theatres built on college campuses this additional offstage space is acquired by building a scene-shop adjacent to one side of the stage, closing it off when necessary with large, sound-proof doors. Light-control equipment and sound equipment in many of these theatres are located on the back wall of the proscenium on one side of the stage, though many theatre technicians prefer to locate this equipment at the rear of the auditorium in a glass-enclosed, soundproof booth, where the operators have a full view of the stage. A further trend in modern theatre building is to provide a forestage or space (sometimes over the orchestra pit) for a forestage, with entrances on either side from behind the proscenium, and with ready access into the auditorium. Such a forestage makes the proscenium stage even more flexible and more easily adapted to the staging of ancient plays.

So equipped with a forestage, the proscenium stage, sometimes derisively called the "peep-hole" stage, becomes a combination of proscenium and platform stage. The platform stage in its strict form is seldom seen in modern theatre buildings, though it is rather widely used in modified forms. Such widely known theatres

Two scenes from John Patrick's *Teahouse of the August Moon* as produced at the Martin Beck Theatre, New York. Designed by Peter Larkin.

as those of the Oregon Shakespeare Festival, the Antioch College Drama Festival, and various outdoor pageant- and symphonic-dramas, such as *The Lost Colony,* employ this type of stage. The platform stage is best known to us through our acquaintance with the typical Elizabethan stage. Its chief feature is a bare platform which juts out into the auditorium and is, during performances, partially surrounded on three sides by the audience. Back of this platform is usually an inner stage, somewhat resembling a small proscenium stage, which may be cut off from the platform by curtains. Access to the platform is either through this inner stage or by means of entrance doors located on either side of the platform, in front of and to the left and right of the inner-stage opening. In the Elizabethan theatre there was an upper stage immediately above the inner stage, also curtained, and balconies located approximately above each of the large side-entrance doors. The balconies were likewise curtained. Back of the inner and upper stage was the "tiring house" where dressing rooms and other necessary behind-stage facilities were located. The Adams reconstruction, based on his study *The Globe Playhouse,* though subject to some minor questions of detail, gives us our best idea of the appearance of the Elizabethan platform theatre.

William Archer in his *The Old Drama and the New* argues that such a platform stage results in a "drama of rhetoric" rather than a drama of action in spectacle. Whatever the value of his argument, his analysis serves to show how influential the form and structure of the stage is upon the nature of the drama produced on it. Such a stage with its minor emphasis upon scenery allows for a free flow of scene upon scene and a rapidity of stage movement in the multiscene play. It de-emphasizes elements of environment which are of great importance in modern drama and in the stage settings of the modern theatre. In compensation for this loss it frequently utilizes colorful costumes, pageantry, crowd scenes, and battle scenes. When the localization of a particular scene or action becomes necessary, the poet or playwright has to provide it by means of description and allusion, instead of the stage artists. In general the action of drama written for this stage and the stage movements have to be on a broader sweep than those of the proscenium stage; yet it is capable of accommodating subtle meanings and subtle psychological significations. We have only to recall *Hamlet* to be reminded of this fact.

The third type of theatre employed in our age may be called that of the circus or arena stage. In this type of theatre the stage is usually located in the center of the theatre and is entirely surrounded by the audience. Sometimes, however, a modified type of arena stage, located against one wall of the theatre, with the audience on three sides, is employed. In such a modification the stage becomes essentially a platform stage. In the pure arena type the actors have to make their entrances and exits through the audience. Usually two to four aisles through the auditorium are provided for such purposes. In the arena theatre no scenery is employed. The audience is seated around the stage on raked platforms to give every spectator a full view of the stage. Furniture and properties are employed, though they are reduced to a bare minimum. At the beginning of the show and at the beginning of each act the lights are often lowered to allow the actors to take their places on the stage. Lighting equipment must be located overhead or high enough in the side walls to allow it to be angled down upon the actors without spilling across into the eyes of the audience.

Though this type of stage has been widely used, especially in colleges and universities, since Glenn Hughes made its advantages known at the University of Washington in the 1920s, thus far no significant plays have been written for it. Many plays written for the proscenium and platform stages have been successfully produced on this stage. What modifications, if any, it may bring in the technique of playwriting are not known. In the proscenium theatre the physical relationship of audience and actor remains fixed; in the arena theatre it is fluid. Hence it is obvious that production in the arena theatre requires a different kind of stage movement and stage business. In the arena theatre the audience-actor relationship is much more close and intimate; hence the techniques of projection must be modified. It would seem that certain types of plays dependent in part upon specific settings and specific mechanical effects could not be produced in the arena theatre; yet it is surprising to see how readily and satisfactorily an ingenious director can adapt a wide variety of plays, ancient and modern, to this stage. Usually, however, one-set shows whose action emphasizes the psychological relationships of the agents prove most successful. In de-emphasizing settings and in the close audience contact arena staging gains a compensating value in the subtlety with which it can render emotion, conflict, and personal reactions.

This brief discussion of the three types of stage—proscenium, platform, arena—must suffice to show how definitely theatre arts are conditioned by the physical stage. The actor, the director, the designer, the lighting artist, and the technician must know intimately the stage on which he is to work before he can begin to plan a show. This applies not only to the type of stage but also to its size and its equipment. Even the size of the auditorium and the audience will condition what these artists do and how they do it. A play suitable for a relatively small and intimate auditorium or an arena theatre might well be lost on a large stage with a huge auditorium. A style of acting suitable to a large auditorium would appear exaggerated, if not ridiculous, in a small theatre. Multiscene shows requiring large and elaborate sets, which play well in big theatres, cannot be accommodated on small stages without redesigning and adapting. The type, the size, and the equipment of a stage, as well as the size of the auditorium, affect every department of stage production and consequently are factors that must be considered in the mounting of shows.

7. STYLE IN STAGE PRODUCTION

Another important factor which influences and modifies theatre arts in stage production is style. Since style in relation to drama will be discussed in the chapter on the analysis of drama, it will be briefly examined here in relation to stage production. Even such a brief examination will involve some repetition. *Style* is a relatively difficult word to define because it has a variety of uses and meanings. Such variety makes it ambiguous and hard to pin down precisely when applied to theatre arts. Certain individuals employ the term, as in the verb form "to stylize," to mean any degree of departure from the realistic representation of normally perceived actuality. There are several objections to such an attempt to define style. Perhaps the major objection is that realism is itself a style and as a style may have degrees of variation. *Realism* is a relative term and is subject in practice to wide differences. Moreover, while some agreement might be obtained about what is meant by "normally perceived" when these words are applied to external and objective phenomena, wide areas of disagreement would appear when the terms refer to emotions, attitudes, reactions, thoughts, and other aspects of human personality. Perhaps a more fundamental approach to the problem will clarify the meaning of style.

In this discussion it has been discovered that every art employs a means or several means to render its object. Acting employs two basic means—voice and gesture or physical movement—to render its object. The object which the art of acting renders is a characterization of an agent in an action. In additon to means and object, every art has manner, the way in which the artist employs the means to render the object. Manner, then, is the way in which the means are joined to the object in a work of art. It is obviously dependent in part upon the way in which the artist, the actor, envisages the object which he is rendering. An actor, for example, in rendering the role of Iago might conceive of him as an evil gadfly or mosquito, darting in and out, shooting the venom of his poisoned word when and where they will cause the most pain and harm. The manner of such a rendering would condition the vocal delivery of lines and the gestures and stage movements of the actor. The way in which this conditioning is adopted and employed is what we refer to as style in acting. Fundamentally, then, style is the way in which manner is joined to means.

The usual object of a stage production as discussed in this book is a play which represents a complete action. The means of stage production of such objects are acting, settings, and lighting, though lighting might be considered a part of the settings. It would include offstage sound effects also. Acting would include the visual appearance of the actor, costume and make-up. The two means of stage production are, then, acting and settings. The style of the production would be controlled by a determination of how most effectively the emotional impact and meaning of the play, the object, could be rendered. *Hamlet,* for example, might be stylized as a modern realistic production in modern settings, modern costumes, and rendered in realistic acting. On the other hand, it might be considered more effective if it were stylized, not as a modern or Elizabethan piece, but as a story belonging to the late twelfth century, the era of Saxo Grammaticus' first narrative of the tale. The stylization of the play might be based, not upon period, but upon an interpretation of the meaning and significance of the play as a tragedy. Or the cue for style might come from an emphasis upon the mood and emotional effect of the piece. From whatever source the cue comes, the resultant style must determine, control, and guide all elements of the production. It will not only guide the actor, but also the designer of the scenery, the costumer, the lighting artist, and the director. When the results of their work are so guided, style becomes a unifying device in stage production.

8. THE SUMMIT OF THEATRE ARTS

When theatre arts are mentioned, the majority of people probably think of plays which they have seen on the stage. Such response is right, for, though the arts of theatre and the art of drama are separate, theatre arts attain their highest effectiveness when they are subordinated to the interpretation of great drama. This statement needs a word of explanation and emphasis. There has developed in the modern theatre, stemming from the theory and practice of Richard Wagner and enforced by such men as Max Reinhardt and Gordon Craig, the conception that theatre arts are not only distinct arts but are supreme. According to this conception the play is merely a script, a kind of scenario or rough outline, to be filled in and really created by the theatre artists. As a corollary, it is often said that a play is not a play until it is produced, just as a symphony is not a symphony until it is played by an orchestra. No great orchestra conductor would hold this point of view in the sense in which some theatre people have stated it. He knows that the symphony is there in the composition of the master and is not to be changed, rearranged, and reinterpreted at his whim. The idea that a play is a mere script to stimulate the creative imaginations of theatre artists is an example of egotism born of ignorance. The supreme art that has come out of the theatre is drama, a making with words, the creation of man in action by poets. Theatre reaches its highest artistry in the faithful interpretation of great plays. Drama is the enduring art that comes out of theatre. It is, as Jonson said of Shakespeare, not for an age but for all time. Its misinterpretation can but make the judicious grieve.

This book on modern theatre practice is centrally concerned with the staging of plays. The chief function of theatre artists in such an undertaking is right and effective interpretation of the play to be staged. That is not to say that there is *one* right interpretation only, for plays are separate creations that can have a variety of meanings and significancies. What one age sees in a play is not necessarily what the next age will find most significant. Like history itself, plays must be reinterpreted for each succeeding age. Moreover, once the meanings and significancies are thoroughly grasped, the theatre artist must then ask himself how these can be most effectively rendered for a specific audience. But "the play's the thing" in the sense that it is the play which really controls the production.

It follows, then, that for the director, who is the chief interpretative artist in the staging of a play, the understanding of drama is paramount. No matter how skilled he may be in the arts of theatre and the techniques of mounting a play, his production of any play will be strictly limited by his comprehension of the play. For that reason a book on directing must begin with drama and the analysis of plays, to which the next chapter, the longest in the book, is devoted.

A final word of warning must be sounded. Nothing is implied in any of the above statements about the insignificance of theatre arts. These the director must know. Specifically, to be an effective director he must know as much as he can about settings, lighting, costume, stage practices, and organization for production. He does not have to be himself an expert in scene design and construction or in the arts and techniques of costume but he does have to know these sufficiently well to be able to tell experts what he wants and to know if what he wants is possible. Only in the professional commercial theatre can the director expect to leave all of these stage arts to experts. In the academic and community theatre he may have to do all of them himself or instruct others in them.

QUESTIONS AND EXERCISES

1. Select an example of an effective television "commercial." Analyze it so as to show as fully as possible all of the elements of theatric arts and techniques employed in making the advertising effective.
2. What aspects of the theatric appeared in the last big football game which you witnessed?
3. How would you define the term *theatric* as used in the above question?

4. What arts can you name that are entirely space arts?
5. What arts can you name that are entirely time arts?
6. What arts can you name which are both space and time arts?
7. What aspects of the production of a play belong to the space arts?
8. What aspects belong to the time arts?
9. In terms of the brief statement about showmanship and what you can add to it, what would you call the essential characteristics of a good showman?
10. Can you give reasons why some degree of variety is essential to good showmanship?
11. Define as fully as you can (with the aid of dictionaries and other references) proportion, balance, and symmetry.
12. What is the difference between tone and pitch?
13. Can you name any Broadway directors who are also producers?
14. What outstanding Broadway producers can you name who are not also directors?
15. How many differences can you state between a proscenium stage and a platform stage?
16. What restrictions would an arena stage impose upon the production of a play that a proscenium stage would not?
17. State as fully as you can (using any references you can find on the subject) the meaning of the term *style*.

CHAPTER 2

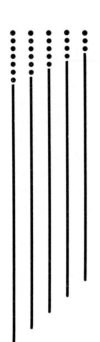

On Drama: Analysis of Plays

PART II OF THIS BOOK is devoted primarily to the director and his functions in the theatre and hence is concerned chiefly with the problems, methods, and procedures of directors in the staging of shows. Though the role of the director has become more differentiated and specific in the modern theatre, there has always been in the theatre from the days of the Greeks an individual whose responsibilities included the rehearsing of the actors and the supervision of the staging. Such an individual, especially in the presentation of plays, must be an interpreter, as well as a creative artist. He is a creative artist in that he employs all of the arts of theatre in the creation of unified, harmonious, and predetermined effects in audiences. He is an interpretative artist in the staging of plays in that his first aim must be to render for audiences the full meaning and effects of those plays which he directs. To accomplish this aim he must obviously know as much as he can about drama and especially about those plays which he chooses for production or is assigned to produce. Knowing how to direct will be of little value if the director does not know what he is to direct. For the director well acquainted with the nature, structure, and technique of drama the analysis and understanding of the more simple types of contemporary plays poses no great difficulty, but the more complex modern plays and great plays from the past often require considerable study. The late Louis Jouvet once said that he had put in over seven years in a careful study of Molière's *Tartuffe,* a play known to him since his student days, before he undertook to produce it. Jean Louis Barrault states that he spent two years in the study and preparation of the *Oresteia* of Aeschylus before he attempted its presentation. It is instructive to contrast the practice of such great directors with some directors, even in our academic theatres, who consider themselves quite capable of directing a play after they have read it over several times and jumped to some "bright" ideas about its staging.

What should a director know about drama? The answer to that question is everything that he can possibly know. Obviously that accomplishment will require years of study, experience, and the patient examination of plays. In addition to the text of plays, there are innumerable books and articles on the nature of drama, the techniques of play construction, and the interpretation of periods and of individual dramas that will prove helpful. Some of these are listed in the bibliography included in this book but the serious student of directing must not be content with the few books there listed. He should seek instruction in as many college courses in drama as are available to him but he must not be content with books and courses alone. He must see plays in performance. European students have an advantage over Americans in that the professional repertory companies of England, France, Germany, and other nations make available to their citizens a wide variety of theatrical performances. When professional performances of high artistic merit are not available, the less mature performances of the academic and community theatres can prove valuable. Then there is always television with, at times, some surprisingly good performances of worthy plays.

But where should the beginning director start in learning how to analyze plays for production and to understand drama? There is so much that he needs to know immediately before he can begin the direction of even a short play or scene that it seems everything about drama must be told him at once. But mere telling is not enough. The potential director must learn through practice, must acquire skill in play analysis, and must develop a method and procedure for himself. Fortunately he comes to his first training in directing, not like a child learning to read, but with some knowledge of drama at his command. One of the most obvious handicaps of students in directing is that this knowledge of drama is not wide enough. Consequently the answer to the question at the beginning of this paragraph is that he should begin with the reading of plays and constantly widen his acquaintance with plays.

1. HOW TO READ A PLAY

Plays cannot or should not be read as one reads the pages of this book or of any expository essay. Plays belong to the great body of narrative literature which includes novels, short stories, epics, and other types. Plays tell a story. A story is made up of a sequence of incidents in which people (agents) do and say things and have things happen to them. Certain stories, such as adventure stories, are chiefly concerned with incidents happening to people and what these people do about them; other types of stories may be almost entirely concerned with the ways people feel about what happens to them, the inner reactions and thoughts of the people. The stories of plays usually combine both external incidents and inner reactions and frequently the inner reactions and thoughts of the people cause the incidents. More correctly, past incidents and the thoughts and feelings of people about these produce present and future incidents. The whole sequence of these incidents form an action and a complete action represents a completed change in the lives of the principal people concerned in it. A dramatic story, then, has a beginning which leads through a series of incidents, reactions, and thoughts to an end.

The first objective in reading a play is to understand clearly the progress of its story from beginning to end. For many plays this is a relatively simple undertaking; for others, such as *King Lear* or Congreve's *The Way of the World,* it is more complex and difficult. The director, however, must read any play with a kinetic imagination. As he reads, he must see the action transpire, as it were, in his mind's eye. It must seem to be actually happening in the place of its occurrence. Such a reading is more difficult, at first, with plays than with novels, for the author of the novel supplies the reader with all kinds of descriptions and psychological analyses, telling the reader exactly what is going on in the minds and feelings of the people of the story. In a play, except for some comparatively short stage directions, there are no such guides. There is merely what the people (the agents characterized) say and do. The reader must infer from what they say what they are feeling and thinking. A play is much more cryptic than a novel but once a reader has really learned to read plays imaginatively, novels seem slow moving in comparison.

To read a play imaginatively the reader must first gain a clear conception of the characters in the play and of the environment in which it occurs. The cast of characters or dramatis personae should be examined and the characters' relations to each other carefully noted. Any clues to the kinds of people they are contained in descriptions or stage directions are important aids. Old plays, unless read in recently edited editions, will contain few such clues; modern playwrights are more concerned with a reading public and hence more generous. Sometimes one has to read well into a play before characters and their relationships become clear. In such instances considerable rereading becomes essential. Prior to the reading of the play, an effort must be made to comprehend the setting in which it occurs. For many older plays this likewise becomes difficult, for the settings are not described in preliminary stage directions by the author. The setting in many of Shakespeare's plays can be gleaned only from lines of the dialogue. Later editors of his plays have added brief statements of location to the scenes. In later plays, and especially in modern plays, the settings are more fully described. Before beginning the reading of the play, this description should be studied. It helps to draw a kind of pattern of the room or setting as it is described by the author. If the setting is a room, the fourth wall will, of course, be the curtain line at the proscenium opening. The location of doors, windows, fireplaces, pieces of furniture, and other objects should be indicated on the sketch and carefully studied. The reader should strive to see the setting as an actual room or place of the kind described. Pictures of former productions of the play, if available, are often helpful in this attempt. The young director should not let these be too constricting upon his imagination but should use them rather as a stimulation. Certain plays call for settings in places and localities with which the reader may have had no acquaintance; hence without pictures or extensive study, his imagination has nothing to work with. In a multiscene play the process here described of mastering the setting must be repeated.

With the setting visualized and the characters and their relations understood, the reader should begin the reading of the play. As he reads, in his mind's eye he should see the entrance of each character, his moves in the room or in the place of the action after he has entered, his reactions to other people and to what they say and do—in short, as he reads the play he should see what is on the pages as actually happening. The ability to do this requires repeated effort at first but soon becomes habitual. In fact it becomes so habitual that some directors make the mistake of assuming that they have grasped the whole play upon a first reading. It may be safely asserted that this is impossible with any director and with even the simplest plays.

First impressions based on an imaginative reading of a play are, however, important. Assuming that the director is a normal person, they are apt to be similar to the first impression of a normal audience. Hence the director should make careful note of these impressions. After he has read the play, he should put away the book and think about it and about his reactions to it. Assuming that he liked the play (and it is questionable whether he should attempt to direct it if he does not like it), he must try in an orderly way to arrive at a clear understanding of the facets of interest in it. Sometimes, of course, plays are so complex and difficult that these are not readily apparent. Analysis and study must be devoted to these before final answers are obtained but even with them first impressions are important. What are here called first impressions may not be really first impressions with an old, well-known play. They are first impressions after an imaginative rereading of the play.

The first question to be asked is why does this play arouse interest, sustain interest, and satisfy interest. The interest of the play may be largely in the exciting or absorbing story which it tells. It may be in the characters depicted; in the thought or ideas represented; in the emotions evoked; or it may be in all of these combined. Part of the interest in some plays, say a comedy by Noel Coward, arises from the cleverness and ingenuity with which the author manipulates incidents, characters, and emotions. In English Restoration comedy a considerable part of the interest arises from the wit and repartee of the dialogue. Whatever facets of interest are present, in any play a considerable portion of interest will arise out of the story. But the story is merely what happens to people, what they think, what they feel, and what they do. Hence if a play is to be interesting to an audience, its characters must be interesting. What is there about the people of this particular play that makes them in themselves interesting and makes the reader interested in what happens to them? Some of the characters will be sympathetic; others will be antipathetic. What in their natures and their actions causes the reader to sympathize with and feel antipathy toward certain of these characters? In certain plays there are characters that the reader will sympathize with and at the same time laugh at. What in their natures brings sympathy and what causes laughter? Yet other characters will arouse laughter and even ridicule without sympathy. It is a pleasure to see such characters get what they deserve in the end. Is that a source of interest in this particular play?

This discussion has already led to the next question to be asked: other than interest, what kind or kinds of emotional effects does this play produce? Every play is written to arouse certain feelings and produce certain effects upon reader and audience. These effects are what are called the powers of the play. It is quite proper, therefore, to speak of a play in production as an effect, or rather as a series of harmonious effects upon an audience. The arousal of interest is certainly one of the effects which a play must produce but the arousal of interest is a necessary effect of art in general and all plays in particular. The playwright uses the arousal of interest to lead to other more specific effects, which in turn add to audience or reader interest. These effects vary widely from play to play and even within plays. Yet each play has certain dominant effects, which are its peculiar powers. These may be as general as a sense of the pleasure of living and the satisfaction of obstacles overcome. They may involve fear for the safety and happiness of sympathetic people and the satisfaction of seeing the threats to their safety and happiness overcome. Mingled with suspense and fear for the well-being of a sympathetic person may be pity for his unmerited suffering and a fuller comprehension of his true worth as a human being. Or it may be dominantly pity at his falling short of that attainment and nobility of which he was potentially capable. The effect can combine suspense, fear, wonder, and awe in the realization of man's predicament. Such effects as those just described, along with others, are obviously serious. Mingled with them may be other effects which are essentially laugh provoking, that is, comic. Many modern plays, for example those of Luigi Pirandello, are a mingling of the serious and the comic effects.

The majority of the plays of the past and many modern plays are, however, dominantly serious or comic. In answering the question about the emotional effects produced by the play, the director must strive to determine as exactly as possible the dominant effect. What kind of total effect did the play at this first reading exert? The answer to this question might well provide a key to the kind of final effect that the play is designed to produce upon an audience. If it is dominantly comic, its effects may be chiefly those of good-natured laughter at individuals whose characters, actions, and speech render them in some measure ludicrous without making them unsympathetic. Such are the characters in *You Can't Take It With You* by Kaufman and Hart; in a somewhat different way such is the leading character in S. N. Behrman's *Biography,* Marion Froude, whom we wish to see triumph over her involvements and her too-tolerant disposition. The effects may be a mingling of laughter with ridicule and satire, such as we find in *Boy Meets Girl* by Bella and Samuel Spewack, or with a more savage intensity in Ben Jonson's *Volpone.* In trying to determine the effect or effects of the play, it will not suffice merely to say that they are serious or comic. It is important to the director to strive to determine as precisely as possible the explicit kind of seriousness or comicalness which the play produces. This is by no means an easy task and will not be accomplished after a first reading. It will often require intensive analysis but a first reading can give a guide to the effects.

The next question after this first reading is what are the big scenes of the play which stand out. Certain scenes in every play will impress the reader and remain with him. They may be primarily scenes of high emotional intensity; they may be scenes in which characters make important discoveries; they may be scenes in which reversals occur; or they may be scenes of spectacular stage effects. Other types of big scenes might be added and several of these might be combined. The scene of high emotional intensity might be combined with spectacular stage effects, as it is in the climax of the play within a play scene in *Hamlet,* or it might be a quiet scene largely without stage spectacle. Each of these big scenes should be examined to determine what kinds of effects they produce and how their effects are related to the total effects of the play. What leads up to the big scene and what does the big scene lead to? Answers to this question will serve to relate the big scenes to the play as a whole. It is important to discover these big scenes not only to understand the effects which they produce but also because they are instruments or elements in the organization of the play. These scenes represent climaxes in the plot of the play. Climax may be defined as any high point of interest. A play in production considered as an effect upon an audience must be considered as a series of climaxes, each leading into its successor and each building to the major climax. The potential director must learn to see plays as such a series of climaxes.

Is there a well-defined conflict in the action of the play? Since the publication of Ferdinand Brunetière's *La Loi du théâtre* (1894), it has been customary to conceive of drama in terms of conflict. Though it is doubtful that the so-called conflict theory of drama is adequate, conflict certainly does enter into dramatic situations. When a character reacts adversely to another and when a character makes a deliberate or an agonizing decision, the elements of conflict are present. In many modern plays, as well as some ancient ones, conflict is a central shaping force in the action of the play. *Hamlet* may be considered as a conflict between a murderer and an avenger of murder. It is more than that. It is a conflict within the soul of Hamlet himself, arising out of his nature and the obligation that is laid upon him. Many critics speak of the inner and the outer conflict in this play. If by so differentiating them critics imply that these are separate, they are wrong. In well-organized drama inner tensions and conflicts lead to outer struggles. Conflicts in plays in which they occur arise and develop in many different ways. In *A Doll's House* the conflict initially arises between Krogstad and Helmer before the play opens over the question of Krogstad's position in the bank. This conflict leads to a conflict between Krogstad and Nora, which leads to a conflict between Nora and Helmer, and then to a conflict within the soul of Nora herself. The conflict within the soul of Blanche Du Bois leads to conflict with her brother-in-law Stanley Kowalski and her sister Stella in Tennessee William's *A Streetcar Named Desire.* Willy Loman's conflict in *Death of a Salesman* arises in the struggle to keep his salesman's job now that he is growing old, which intensifies his big conflict with his sons, and especially with Biff. This conflict in turn reaches into the soul of Willy and challenges his salesman's philosophy of life. The conflict in S. N. Behrman's *Biography* arises initially out of Marion Froude's decision to write her biography for Richard Kurt's publication. This decision is not arrived at without conflict between Marion and Richard and it leads to conflict between Leander Nolan, her former lover, and Orrin Kinnicott, who is backing Leander for the Senate. These conflicts result in Marion's examination of herself, her standard of tolerance, and her final decision.

After a thoughtful first reading of a play, it is possible to state the nature of the conflict or conflicts, how these arise and evolve, and what they lead to or result in. It will not be possible without further analysis to state all of the nuances and implications of these conflicts. The more the play is studied, the more meaning and effectiveness may be seen in the conflicts utilized by the playwright. This attempt to examine the play upon first reading has, however, brought up two other aspects for questioning: progression and characters.

What is the nature of the plot progression? Every play to be satisfying to reader and audience must "get somewhere." That is, it must have some kind of progression from an initiation or beginning to an end. Plays "get somewhere" in a variety of ways. By arousing conflicts and finally resolving them a playwright may give progression to his story. Most plays in the early part of their action raise questions as a means of arousing interest. Whatever early questions are raised in the action, these gradually or rapidly lead to a main question. The chief involvements and conflicts in the action are around or related to this main question. When the main question is answered, the play has progressed to a satisfying ending. The question about progression can then be restated. What is the main question of the play and how is it answered? The reader must be well aware that the first questions raised in a play are not the main question, though they may and should lead into it. Moreover, the main question as first raised in the play is, in good plays, certain to grow and develop. The main question in *A Doll's House* is initially relatively simple. It is something like the following: Will Nora save Krogstad's position in the bank or will she fail and be exposed by him? Before the end of the play this question is answered but it has by that time developed into a much more profound question concerning Nora's integrity. Ibsen, being a highly skilled craftsman, has, before he raised the main question in its simple form at the end of Act One, led to it and prepared the audience to understand it by raising many smaller questions. Some of these will become apparent only after a more careful examination than is possible in a first reading. Yet a thoughtful consideration after a first reading should serve to show clearly the story line in terms of conflicts aroused and resolved and in terms of main questions raised and answered.

The progression of plays may be stated also in terms of complication, crisis, and denouement, that is, in terms of involvement and resolution. Technically this is known as the formal organization of the plot. Complication or involvement may be organized in different ways but often it is based upon entangling the main character or characters in more and more complexities. The tolerant and sophisticated Marion Froude in *Biography* becomes interested in an intolerant and angry young man, with a chip on his shoulder, Richard Kurt, and because of his attractiveness for her, she decides to write her biography for him. This is an involvement for Marion that leads to other complications. As soon as her decision becomes known, it brings her former, half-forgotten lover, Leander Nolan, to her place to protest against this venture. Leander fears that her revelations will endanger his race for the Senate. Thus Marion is further involved. But her attractiveness proves once again strong for Leander, and he becomes more deeply involved. Orrin Kinnicott, the physical culturist and man of wealth, father of Slade to whom Leander is now engaged, and backer of Leander for the Senate, comes with Leander to stop this biography before it can ruin their election race. Here are additional involvements for Marion and between the various characters. But Kinnicott too falls under the spell of Marion's attractions and the involvements become even more complicated. Slade sees Leander's awakened interest in Marion and this entangles the situation and the character relations all the more. Out of simple involvements at the beginning larger and more intense involvements grow. Eventually these reach a point, the crisis, where no further involvement is possible, where something must break.

This moment of crisis may come about through a discovery, through a decision of a main character, through a combination of these, or with other added devices. Then there occurs in complex plots a reversal. A simple type of reversal frequently found in comedy and melodrama and sometimes in tragedy is that of the tables turned. When the crisis occurs, the unwinding begins but the unwinding, the denouement, usually proceeds through stages of additional clarifying complications. Step by step the former entanglements are resolved until the final catastrophe, happy or unhappy, is reached. Thus complication leads through crisis and denouement to resolution, to an ending. This kind of progression is very important for the director, for on it hinges frequently much of the interest, suspense, and surprise for the audience. After a careful first reading of a play, it is possible for the thoughtful director to close the book and in memory recall and note the progress of the action in these terms.

The action of plays, of certain plays in particular, progresses in yet another way, in terms of the thought expressed. What is the nature of the thought expressed in the play and what is the course of its development? Every play, even the most trivial, says something. What a play says, its total meaning, may be quite simple, a platitude or proverb; or it may be highly complex, as in *Hamlet, King Lear,* the *Oresteia, Oedipus, The King.* The more these great plays are studied the deeper will their significancies and meanings appear. The great director is one who can grasp and render these deeper meanings for a modern audience. What upon first reading may appear to be a simple and clear meaning can often with further analysis be seen to be a complex and highly significant statement about the nature of man and the meaning of life. In this sense, then, a play may be considered as an argument. It proves its propositions in ways that differ from those of the logicians and debaters. Logicians and debaters arrive at their arguments through analyses of facts, types of rhetorical and logical proof, examination of hypotheses, syllogisms, deductions, and similar processes of reasoning. These processes appear in plays; but the chief instruments of the playwright in making his arguments are incidents and happenings, emotions and feelings, the nature or character of human beings, their involvements with each other, their desires and aspirations, and such like materials. A great play is like a segment of life, like an experience lived through. Many valid ideas, even lessons, may be deduced from it. Certain plays are strictly organized to demonstrate a thesis or teaching, which can often be stated in terms of a moral proposition.

When so strictly organized in terms of thesis, the play becomes primarily didactic. Its teaching or preachment may be moral, social, or political. Usually the thought of such plays, what they add up to, is not difficult to state. Sometimes, however, the real implications of the argument of even didactic plays are complex. On the surface the thought of *The Little Foxes,* for example, may seem relatively simple; but the argument of the play is built around the nature of predatory capitalism and shows the weakness of good and well-meaning people in the face of its ruthlessness. Shaw's comedies are built around a variety of arguments. *Man and Superman* revolves around the all-powerfulness of the Life Force even over an astute intellectual, Jack Tanner, who tries vainly to escape it. Thus as an argument the play may be considered as a progressive entrapment of Tanner in the forces which he fears, warns others against, and flees from. It is in this sense of an argument that modern critics maintain that every play has a theme or thesis. The use of this term *theme* has become dangerous because it leads to an oversimplification of the argument or thoughts of a play. Certain modern didactic plays are so tightly organized around a single proposition or preachment that their thought may be reduced to a single statement or theme. Such a reduction of the thought of great plays merely distorts them. These plays lead through human actions, human sufferings, human involvements, and human emotions, and through revelations of the nature of human characters to progressive ideas about man and life. Such ideas cannot always be reduced to simple platitudes.

Though the full comprehension of the meaning of a great play will require study, its chief ideas can become apparent upon contemplation after a first reading. It is these main ideas which are apt to strike an audience most forcefully. A grasping of these and their interrelations gives the director a unifying conception toward which to aim his production.

What is the order or progression of the action in terms of the incidents which occur? A play is a story. A story is composed of a sequence of incidents which have a beginning and a progression, one after another, in time. Through this sequence of incidents the lives of the characters change, the characters change, and a new condition or destiny may come upon them. Hamlet in a state of shock and grief is appraised of the murder of his father by his uncle. This incident in the play comes after other incidents which resulted in Hamlet being informed of the Ghost, his waiting for it to appear, and his following it when it did appear. Incident follows incident in a chronological order. In many modern plays this exact time order is clear and important; in other plays (*Hamlet*, for instance), though in general the reader is quite clear about which incident follows which, the precise time between certain main scenes is by no means exact and clear. In the modern plays, and even in some older plays, time as a determinant in the environment of the characters attains greater importance than it does in *Hamlet*. Whatever the importance of time in the action, the ordered sequence of the incidents is important and must be noted. A first reading easily reveals these.

What is the causal relation of the incidents? There is a much more important relationship of incident to incident in plays than that of mere chronology. That relationship is frequently called a causal relationship. More properly speaking, it is the relation of antecedents to consequences. The incident of the Ghost's appearance in *Hamlet* to Horatio and the companions of the watch, in Scene I, results in their decision to tell young Hamlet. As a consequence of that incident and that decision, they report what they have seen to Hamlet in Scene II. This incident in turn becomes the antecedent for Hamlet's watching with his friends in Scene IV. His watching and meeting with the Ghost is the consequence of the former incident. These incidents, in turn, stand as antecedents to the scene in which the Ghost reveals his murder and lays upon Hamlet a three-fold injunction. And so the plot progresses. Antecedents and consequences are a most potent way of organizing a plot for progression and for giving it unity and probability, as will appear later.

The antecedent-consequence relation of the incidents of a plot may be grasped upon a first thoughtful reading. It has become clear, however, that the sequence of incidents in a play, closely tied as they are to character, thought, and emotion, have more meaning than would a series of mere happenings in an adventure story. Not every incident in the sequence in a play is always so closely knit into the antecedent-consequence relation as those that have been noted in *Hamlet*. Note that the opening of Scene II breaks the sequence with an incident or several incidents centering around Claudius and his court and the opening of Scene III breaks the sequence again with the introducton of Polonius and his family. Both of these in turn become antecedents for later incidents in the play. Whole plays may be, in fact, composed of just such broken sequences which do not upon first reading seem to be causally related. Bertolt Brecht's so-called epic plays often have just such broken sequences. They are tied together in terms of the thought of the play and the sequences become elements of argument in the expounding of statements or ideas. Pageant dramas are often constructed in this manner.

It becomes apparent from this discussion that the ways in which plays "get somewhere" are not so simple. Intelligent questions about the progression of an action can lead to revelations and more penetrating interpretations. It has been mentioned above that plays also progress in terms of changes in the characters. That point will be mentioned further in connection with questions about the characters. In thinking about the various ways in which action progresses in a play, it is necessary for the director to arrive at some statement of the full change or the story line. Frequently this can be made clear in a figure or metaphor. Richard II supplies such a symbolic statement of the action of Shakespeare's play, *Richard II,* in comparing his and Bolingbroke's fortunes to two buckets on a rope over a well. As one ascends, the other descends. The story line in *Hamlet* may be likened to the chase of a murderer who, upon discovering his pursuer, turns upon him, and the pursued then pursues the pursuer. The end of their pursuits is death for both. Ibsen's *Ghosts* may be likened to the peeling away of layer upon layer of false illusions down to the stark, terrible kernel of life's meaning for Mrs. Alving. *Boy Meets Girl* reiterates its design in the formula: "Boy meets girl, boy loses girl, boy gets girl." Similar symbols or formulas will not always readily appear for all plays and not too much time should be spent in looking for such more or less apt condensations. For the director the important thing is to see clearly the story line, the way in which the action progresses and changes from a beginning to an end. The reason why it is important as a kind of skeleton on which to build a performance to see the clear line of progress is that plays are highly complex in their involvements. It is the director's duty as interpreter to see that this complexity does not become confusing.

What kinds of characters appear in the play? Plays are stories made up of incidents. An incident is an action which is caused or brought about by an agent or which happens to agents. When the incident happens to a human being, he is technically called the recipient or patient, rather than the agent. Human actions, which are the actions that plays are concerned with, are caused by human agents and suffered or experienced by human patients. The kinds of actions which a human being performs depend upon the kind of man he is; hence agents in plays are characterized. The way in which a human being will suffer an incident or happening, his reaction to it, will also depend upon the kind of man he is; hence again the necessity for characterization in drama. This type of analysis serves to show the intimate interrelation of character and action in drama.

A first thoughtful reading of a play will serve to reveal the kinds of characters in the action. Perhaps the very first question that should be asked about the characters is about their number. How many characters are in the play? How many men? How many women? In plays with large casts the reader may have to open the book and list the characters. Which of these are minor or subordinate characters and which play major roles in the action? Obviously these are important questions for a director who is considering the stage production of a play. Insofar as each of these characters is clearly characterized, what kind of man or woman is each? Though a full understanding of the characters must wait upon a more careful analysis than that of a first reading, a thoughtful first reading should serve to give a clear impression of the main characters in their more obvious aspects. These obvious aspects include sex, age, sometimes physical appearance, social status, chief desires or drives, and the main traits of their personalities. The director, like the actor, must strive to see each as an individual human being. Hence after the first reading he should thoughtfully recall all that he can remember about each.

What are the characters' relations to each other? Some will be joined together in familial ties; others will be united through such emotional ties as love and friendship; yet others will be related in terms of antipathy or hate. Since many plays are built in terms of conflict, it is important to understand clearly which characters are on which side of the conflict. Some of these characters will be sympathetic to reader and audience; others will arouse antipathy. What in the nature of the characters causes the arousal of sympathy or antipathy? The answer to this question will serve to reveal important traits of character. The alignments of the characters on different sides of the conflict and their associations with each other are important devices of characterization.

Whose play is it? Though there may be a number of important

characters in the action of a play, most plays are built centrally around one or two leading characters. When the action is built chiefly around a main leading character, this character is known as the protagonist. If he has a chief opponent, that opponent is the antagonist. Othello is protagonist and Iago is antagonist. Hamlet is protagonist and Claudius is antagonist. Lear, the protagonist, has several antagonists. The protagonist in a comedy of ridicule and exposure, such as Molière's *Tartuffe,* need not be a sympathetic character. Only in comedy that tends toward the romantic or toward the sentimental is the protagonist, or leading character, apt to be partly or wholly sympathetic. Sometimes in the comedy of manners, such as those of Philip Barry and S. N. Behrman, there are degrees of sympathy for the protagonist. The protagonist is, then, not always and necessarily the chief sympathetic character.

Whose play is it, about whom does the action revolve, are important questions for the director, for the answers determine which will be the lead in the show. In certain plays it can be settled in slightly different ways. In Sidney Howard's *They Knew What They Wanted* the protagonist is Tony but the play might be played with a strong actress as Amy's play. Robert E. Sherwood's *The Petrified Forest* has Alan Squier as protagonist but the roles of Gabby and Duke Mantee are both so strong that they might almost become the leads. Looked at from a somewhat romantic angle the lead in Somerset Maugham's *The Circle* is the young wife, Catherine; whereas, looked at as a somewhat satiric comedy it is the father-in-law, Clive Champion-Cheney. Obviously the shift in emphasis upon characters in this way will shift the meaning and effect of the plays concerned. Sometimes plays are almost equally balanced between two main characters. Witness *Romeo and Juliet,* for example. In Maugham's *The Circle* there are actually five main roles almost equally balanced and a sixth that is by no means insignificant. Contemplation of the play after reading will usually show distinctly whose play it is, if the action does center dominantly around a single role.

What are the apparent motives, drives, desires, and decisions of the chief characters? Contemplation after reading will also reveal these, though certain subtle motivations and character traits may remain hidden until further analysis. An old device for getting inside a character is to ask what he or she wants. What are his desires? What is he seeking? Sometimes characters are driven on by dominant passions, such as hate or infatuation. Yet others are driven by greed, the desire for power, and other such understandable and less admirable motives. Another key to understanding characters, especially characters in serious plays, lies in their decisions. It must be remembered in drama that failure to decide for a reason also constitutes dramatic decision. What decisions do the main characters make? What motivates these decisions?

Perhaps the questions raised are as far as a reader can go in the analysis of character from memory after careful reading. The attempt of the director and the actor from the start is to see each character as though he or she were a living personality, to see each as an individual. This procedure applies even to type characters, stylized characters, and exaggerated caricatures of characters. The typification, stylization, and exaggeration will be added in rehearsals after the character as a human being has been grasped. There are, of course, in drama some exceptions to the generally true statement that playwrights attempt to draw all of their characters so that they will be taken for living human beings. An extreme example is García Lorca's making a character out of the moon in *Blood Wedding*. Usually in drama, however, when animals and inanimate objects are personified, they are given human traits, moods, and attitudes or are made to comment upon these.

What kind of world does the play create? Every play creates its own realm, world, or picture of reality within which its characters and action are probable and credible. Many, probably most, modern plays attempt to create a realistic world of commonly known or commonly accepted external and objective reality. The world that they render may be the environment of sordid, depressed, underprivileged tenement dwellers, as in Elmer Rice's *Street Scene*. It may be the polished and sophisticated world of British upper-class society, as in Maugham's *The Circle*. It may be the ordinary world of typical young American city folk, as in Maxwell Anderson's *Saturday's Children*. It can be the world of a past time and place made convincing in modern terms, as in Anderson's *Valley Forge* or Shaw's *Joan of Arc*. It can be the world beyond life made in quite ordinary terms, as in Sutton Vane's *Outward Bound*.

On the other hand, the dramatist may leave the real world as it is conventionally known and carry his action into a realm of fantasy and imagination. Such a world may be a romanticized recreation of a past time and place, as in Rostand's *Cyrano de Bergerac* or *The Romancers*. Shakespeare creates idealized and romantic worlds for each of his comedies, rather than employing a depiction of the real world of contemporary London, as did Ben Jonson. The fantastic world of the play may be a kind of nightmarish dream world seen through a mediocre imagination, as it were, which is depicted in Elmer Rice's *The Adding Machine*. The world created may begin in the solidly real and progress into the realm of subconscious racial memory, as it does in O'Neill's *Emperor Jones*. It can be a kind of never-never land of romance and childish wonder, as in J. M. Barrie's *Peter Pan*. It can be the realm of a past age of wit, sophistication, and amorality, as in Congreve's *Way of the World*. Since every play creates its own climate of acceptance, this list could be extended indefinitely. Perhaps it is sufficient to illustrate the meaning of probability in drama.

Coleridge said that poetry required a "willing suspension of disbelief." So does drama. But both dramatist and director must go further than that. They must create a climate of belief, a basis of acceptance. If that acceptance is based upon some aspect of our conventionally accepted real and objective world, it must be written into the play and incorporated in the production. The human imagination is amazingly capable of acceptance on many levels. Often all that the artist has to do is to place a few subtle clues to the level of his projection to carry the audience with him. If interest is maintained, the audience will follow him. After a first reading of a play, it is usually quite clear as to the kind of realm of acceptance the playwright has created. In criticism this is rightly called his general scheme of probability. A thorough understanding of probability in all of its aspects will depend upon later analysis. Clear as the general scheme may be at first reading, it is by no means always easy to determine upon methods or devices to render it upon the stage. Much of the effectiveness of the director's interpretation will depend upon success in this endeavor.

What are the settings in which the action of the play occurs? This last question goes back to an earlier recommendation about how to read a play. It has been suggested that for clear and thoughtful reading of a play a kind of stage diagram of each set be made from the author's description to aid in visualizing the action of the play. If this has been done, the reader can now address his thoughts to the kinds of settings required by the probability of the action. The effort at this stage is not to solve stage problems but rather to imagine the exact room or place of the action with its proper mood and atmosphere. In addition to the creation of the right climate of acceptance, are the settings important in other ways to the action? What essential details cannot be omitted? How many different sets are necessary? Could one of the settings be eliminated without serious harm to the action? Are the settings so indefinite in the action that the designer could use an unlocalized setting and concentrate upon mood and atmosphere? Could the whole action be adapted to arena staging without settings, allowing furniture and costumes to make the proper suggestions of the environment? The answer to this last question is not always readily apparent from a first reading.

2. SUMMARY OF QUESTIONS ON PLAYS

For the young student of directing, unacquainted with plays in production and unaccustomed to wide reading of plays, these questions may seem overwhelming and impossible of answering upon a first thoughtful reading. That student should reread the play as often as is necessary for him to answer these questions and to support his answers with adequate arguments. The experienced director and reader of plays will be able to answer these questions after a thoughtful reading of the play. The only way for the immature student to gain experience is to see as many plays in production as possible and to read widely in drama, answering these questions about the play which he reads. It will be helpful as a guide if these questions are listed in the order in which they were discussed, though this is not necessarily a rigid order of questioning that must be applied to every play in exactly the sequence given.

The questions are:

1. Why does this play arouse interest, sustain interest, and satisfy interest?
2. What kind or kinds of emotional effects does the play produce?

3. Is the total effect dominantly serious, comic, or a mixture of the two? How explicitly can you state the dominant or total effect?
4. Which are the big scenes of the play, what is the nature of each, and what does each accomplish?
5. Is there a conflict in the play? What is its nature? How does it evolve? Who are concerned in it? Who are the chief characters on each side of the conflict? Is the conflict primarily within a single character?
6. What is the nature of the plot progression?
7. What is the main question of the play? How is it answered?
8. What are the complications in the action?
9. Where does the chief crisis of the plot occur?
10. What are the steps in the resolution after the crisis?
11. What is the argument of the play? What important thoughts are prominent in it?
12. What is the order of the incidents in the play? What is their sequence in time?
13. What is the causal relation of the incidents?
14. How would you describe the whole story line of the action?
15. What kinds of characters appear in the play? Who is the protagonist or lead? How many characters are there? What is the sex, age, and other prominent traits of each?
16. What are the characters' relations to each other?
17. Whose play is it? Is there more than one major role?
18. What are the apparent motives, drives, desires, and decisions of the chief characters?
19. What kind of world does the play create? How would you describe its general probability?
20. What are the settings in which the action of the play occurs? How many are required? Which could be eliminated? How should these settings appear to create the right mood and atmosphere? Could the play be staged without settings, arena style?

It must be regretfully admitted that some academic and community theatre directors cast plays and put them into rehearsal with no more knowledge of them than is indicated in these questions whose answers are based on a thoughtful reading. Such directors frequently depend upon the rehearsals to bring a fuller understanding of the play and to give them clues to its interpretation. Sometimes they depend upon their ingenuity and cleverness as a substitute for intelligent interpretation. Growth of understanding through rehearsals, ingenuity, and cleverness are all important in the directing of plays. The director who depends upon these, however, is apt to waste the time of his actors and theatre artists. It is this kind of directing that frequently accounts for so many of those shows that are hardly worth sitting through. The worthy director is one who brings to the process of staging a play a thoughtful and mature interpretation of the play, based upon study and analysis. Such study and analysis requires more than one thoughtful reading. It requires intelligent analysis. Such analysis can be made only by one who knows the structure and technique of drama. Such knowledge is acquired by wide reading and study of plays supplemented by equally wide study of books on the nature, structure, and technique of drama. To tell the director how to proceed in specific detail in the further analysis of plays after the first thoughtful reading and answering of questions would require detailed analyses of play after play—an obvious impossibility in limited space. Since no two plays are exactly alike, such analyses would have to cover the whole range of drama from the Greeks to the present and even then would not cover all possible contingencies. The remainder of this chapter will, therefore, be concerned with some general statements about drama, its structure and technique, which will serve as suggestions for further analyses of plays.

3. APPROACHES TO THE STUDY OF DRAMA

The study of drama may be approached in a variety of ways, as is indicated by the diverse scholarly and critical studies of drama. The study of drama may be considered a key means of understanding a period in the history of man, an age in the national life, social attitudes of a people at a given time, dominant ideas popular within certain periods, or moral attitudes of a time and a people. All such studies are worthwhile and the mature director will know how to use them and other studies of like nature. They certainly often contribute to one or both of the two major approaches which are most useful to the director. The two approaches most useful to the director are:

1. The study of drama in terms of its spirit or meaning.
2. The study of drama in terms of its construction.

Ideally these two approaches should go together but for various reasons they are not always linked in critical studies. There are numerous books, for example, on tragedy and comedy that are primarily concerned with the spirit of tragedy or comedy, with the nature of the tragic or the comic in human life, with the philosophy and meaning of one or both of these forms. Often the writers of such books seem hardly aware or are not chiefly concerned with tragedies and comedies as made things, as constructions put together through the artifice of makers. On the other hand, there are books on dramatic technique that seem equally unaware of the meaning and significance of drama. The director as interpreter of plays requires both approaches.

Plays may be written for many different reasons—to make money, to propound an idea, to reveal certain aspects about human conduct, to interpret something of life's meaning, to satisfy that creative desire that is in every artist, to expose an idea or attitude, to expound a philospohy of living, to reveal the shallowness or worth of certain human beings. The list could be extended indefinitely. Whatever the initial reason for its composition, every play, even the most trivial, makes some statement about life and about human nature. That statement may be trite and platitudinous or it may be profound. Plays are an interpretation of the meaning of life and the nature of man. They are means through which human beings may come to realize the rich variety of human existence, human thought, human emotions, and human nature. Great plays therefore add to the meaning of life for those who understand them. Tragedies aid man in understanding what is genuinely serious in life. Every tragedy asserts that life has meaning. At the same time it asserts that man has significance. His life is not merely an animal existence, of no more worth than that of a worm. Serious plays reveal and explore the meaning of goodness and evil in man's character and conduct. They aid us in seeing how character shapes destiny. They lead us to an appreciation of what is admirable in man. They show us how man can be a man in all the nobility of that conception. Sometimes they accomplish this by admirable example; in other instances they accomplish it by showing how man falls short of goodness and nobility.

Comedy, too, has its important significance. In one kind it reveals the ludicrous in human nature and human action. It shows that certain deviations in character and conduct are ridiculous and it teaches man to laugh at such ridiculousness. By

Above: *The Prescott Proposals* by Howard Lindsay and Russel Crouse, as produced by Leland Hayward. Setting by Donald Oenslager.

Below: *Tea and Sympathy* by Robert Anderson, as produced by the Playwrights Company. Setting by Jo Mielziner.

means of laughter and ridicule of such abnormalities in human character and conduct it purges these. Thus comedy serves to keep man sane and his society healthy, normal, and cohesive. The kind of comedy here described employs satire, mild or sharp.

There is another kind of comedy that shows the triumph of normal and sympathetic human beings over obstacles to happiness in life. Such are the romantic comedies of love triumphant. These comedies assert the happiness of life for normal human beings with normal characters. Audiences rejoice in the triumphs and ultimate happiness of such characters, especially after they have surmounted or escaped obstacles and impediments to happiness. The two kinds of comedy may well be combined in a single play. Shakespeare's comedies combine satire and ridicule with good-humored laughter and pleasure in the ultimate success of the sympathetic characters.

These general statements on the spirit and meaning of tragedy and comedy must suffice to indicate that approach. They should be supplemented by continuous reading on the subject. The bibliography is so extensive that a few suggestions about books with which to begin may prove helpful. As an introduction a short book by W. Macneil Dixon, entitled *Tragedy* (London: Edward Arnold & Co., 1924), which has been reprinted a number of times, will prove most helpful. On the interpretation and meaning of Greek tragedy the best book in English is H. D. F. Kitto's *Greek Tragedy,* reprinted with all the Greek passages translated in the Anchor Book series by Doubleday and Company, Inc., of Garden City, New York, in 1950. A. C. Bradley's *Shakespearean Tragedy* (London: Macmillan and Co., 1904), frequently reprinted and now issued in a paper-back edition, though an old work, is still an indispensable work for the interpreter of Shakespeare's tragedies. It should be supplemented by Harley Granville-Barker's *Prefaces to Shakespeare,* 5 vols. (London: Sidgwick & Jackson, Ltd., 1947) and Hugh Hunt's *Old Vic Prefaces* (London: Routledge & Paul, 1954), which are interpretations by directors of individual plays, tragedies and comedies. The most illuminating book in English on the tragedies of Corneille and Racine (and also on the comedies of Molière) is Martin Turnell's *The Classic Moment* (London: Hamilton Hamish, 1946). Though there are many books and essays on modern tragedy and modern drama, there is none that has the solidity and dependability of Kitto,

Bradley, and Turnell. Studies of the individual modern playwrights are usually more thorough and enlightening than are the general books.

Books on the nature of comedy are too often devoted to an explanation of one theory of why men laugh or what produces laughter. Two books of this sort which are nevertheless useful are Henri Bergson's *Laughter: An Essay on the Meaning of the Comic,* translated by C. Brereton and F. Rothwell (New York: The Macmillan Co., 1911) and Louis Kronenberger's *The Thread of Laughter* (New York: Alfred Knopf, 1952). Every student of comedy should know George Meredith's *The Idea of Comedy and the Uses of the Comic Spirit,* first delivered as a lecture in 1877 and published separately in 1897 by Charles Scribner's Sons in New York. Though Meredith's theory of comedy is too narrowly restricted, what he has to say is stimulating. A good general book on the types of comedy from the Greeks to the moderns is Henry Ten Eyck Perry's *Masters of Dramatic Comedy and Their Social Themes* (Cambridge: Harvard University Press, 1939). These books may serve as a beginning in gaining an understanding of the spirit and meaning of drama.

4. FORM IN DRAMA

In the study of plays the director is concerned with clarifying for himself the meanings of the play and the specific kinds of effects it can produce upon readers and audiences. Such a study requires analysis, that is, the breaking of the play down into its parts in order to discover how it is put together and how it creates its effects. Analysis is an intellectual procedure that can be dominantly mechanical and uninspired. As such its value would be limited for the director. Interpretative analysis of a high order requires, in addition to intellectual ability, imagination and an understanding of the nature of the thing analyzed. That is why this discussion of some aspects of structure and technique in drama has been preceded by a brief statement of meaning and significance in drama. Only certain aspects of structure and technique can be discussed. The student in directing must enhance his knowledge of these, ranging far beyond the few pages of this chapter that may be devoted to them.

For his use there are scores of worthwhile books, along with the study of which he must continue the reading and analysis of plays. A few of the more useful books only will be mentioned here. The student might well begin with Alan Reynolds Thompson's *The Anatomy of Drama* (Berkeley: University of California Press, 1942). The second edition of this book appeared in 1946. Two older books on the techniques of playwriting, both of which omit modern experiments in form and technique but are nevertheless useful, are William Archer's *Play-Making: A Manual of Craftsmanship* (New York and Boston: Small, Maynard Company, 1928; originally published in 1912) and George Pierce Baker's *Dramatic Technique* (Boston: Houghton Mifflin Company, 1919). To these should be added John Howard Lawson's *Theory and Technique of Playwriting* (New York: G. P. Putnam's Sons, 1936) which, though somewhat biased in approach, is useful; and Kenneth Thorpe Rowe's *Write That Play* (New York: Funk and Wagnalls, 1939) which demonstrates clearly and with examples a method of analyzing a play in terms of its craftsmanship. A more complete list of books on "General Criticism" may be found in the "Bibliography" appended to the third revised edition of John Gassner's *Masters of the Drama* (New York: Dover Publications, Inc., 1954), itself a useful book. Several of Gassner's other studies, such as *The Theatre in Our Times* (New York: Crown Publishers, Inc., 1954) and *Form and Idea in Modern Theatre* (New York: The Dryden Press, 1956) will be found useful and stimulating.

All art to be beautiful and effective must have form. Without form it would be chaotic, disorganized, incomprehensible. But arts do not have form in the same way, nor do they have beauty in the same way. The form of a symphony cannot be applied to a painting or to a drama, though the form of some dramas might be analogized to that of certain symphonies. Such an analogy could never be close or exact, for symphonies are made by different means out of different materials and in different organizations than those of drama. Form means "organization," the shape given to the materials out of which the object is made. To *form* means "to organize," to arrange, to dispose. To *form* is to *formalize* or formulate.

What is it that the dramatist formulates, organizes, or arranges? The principal thing that he organizes, orders, and arranges is human action, consisting of what goes on within human beings, what they think and feel, what they do, and what happens to them.

These actions make up what is called the incidents of the play and these, too, the dramatist organizes. These actions are performed or experienced by human beings as agents in them. What each agent does in the play is dependent in large part on the kind of man or woman he or she is, that is on character. The traits which characterize (give character to) the agents must also be organized and arranged by the playwright.

Human action means human change. Change becomes significant to an individual when it affects his happiness, his well-being, his destiny. The extreme change which may occur to a human being through his actions is a change from happiness to misery or from misery to happiness. The playwright may conceive the form of his action as one of these extremes, as tragedy or comedy; or he may conceive it and organize it as intermediate between these extremes. Modern drama has attempted to break the mold of form in this sense, asserting that life is neither comic nor tragic but is both. True as that is in life itself, it would seem, however, that when an artist attempts to order, organize, and formulate life in terms of human actions, his formulation, insofar as it has order and organization, falls into one of the two major classifications, tragedy or comedy, or into that third form, variously called melodrama, tragicomedy, *drame,* and dramatic romance. This conscious choice or determination of form affects the play as a whole in its powers; it also affects and helps to determine every element and part of the play. An action about human beings of worth and dignity that moves from happiness to misery would obviously be a serious action. Such an action well formulated has powers over or effects upon a reader or audience. To state the form of a play one must state the powers. Though it is possible to state generally the powers which belong to the categories of form in drama, it must be remembered that no two plays are exactly alike in form. *Hamlet, Macbeth,* and *Ghosts* are tragedies and in general have similar powers. But their effects are by no means alike. It is these individual powers or effects of specific plays that a director must strive to clarify before he can adequately interpret that play. To know the general or distinctive powers of each category of form will aid him in this task.

Tragedy requires a serious action, a genuinely, immutably serious action. For a human action to become serious it must fulfill certain requisites or conditions. It must be about a person or persons to whom we are not indifferent, for whom we can feel sympathy, understanding, and often admiration. It must involve a threat to the happiness of such a person. The kind of character and the magnitude of the threat will determine the importance of the effects. A threat to the financial security of sympathetic individuals may be comparatively serious but by no means as serious as a threat to their very existence, moral and physical. The operation of the threat serves to arouse our suspense, dread, and fear for the individual. As that individual struggles against the threat (that is, acts) and as he suffers defeats in his struggles, we pity him. Along with our pity may go admiration if he is humanly heroic in his struggles. Hence Aristotle's statement that the two distinctive powers of tragedy are the arousal of pity and fear and their purgation may be seen to arise out of the nature of a serious action fully formulated. The serious action gives fear and pity; the full formulation gives purgation.

Purgation, or catharsis, is a difficult term and has been given numerous interpretations. One of the difficulties arises because the term applies to what happens within the structure of the play (the purging or final working out of the threat) and to the effects of the whole action upon reader and audience (the powers of the play). Within the play the purgation consists in the orderly, convincing, step-by-step working out of the action to a meaningful conclusion or denouement. Such a working out consists in the right ordering of the incidents of the play, the proper building of the characters in relation to the incidents, and the arrangement of the dialogue and thought in a manner commensurate with the whole action. The last statement is another way of saying that the playwright gives form to drama. Obviously, before he can so formalize an action, he must have a conception of its meaning and significance, of what it adds up to. He must have a conception of the kinds of effects that will produce such meaning and significance. Perhaps his conception is that man's fate is determined for him and in spite of him by vast natural powers beyond his control. On the other hand, his conception may involve the conviction that what a man is does in a measure determine his fate. Whatever his controlling conception, his technique will involve the raising of questions and the arousing of emotions. As these questions are answered and as these emotions are allayed or reconciled, purgation occurs. Purgation in both senses, then, is not merely in the ending. It may occur throughout the play, and especially in that portion after the crisis. Purgation may be related to the arousing and satisfying of interest, provided the term *interest* is broadly enough interpreted.

Comedy is sometimes considered the antithesis of tragedy. This is wrong. Comedy and tragedy are complementary forms, not opposites. A comic action is one that is based upon an a-normality in character or conduct. The term *abnormality* may be substituted for *a-normality* provided the abnormality is not perceived as painful or harmful to normal human beings. The abnormality may be one of character, making such a character ludicrous or ridiculous. It can be very slight. Viola's only abnormality of character in *Twelfth Night* is the donning of boy's clothing, from whence arises many of her comic predicaments. When it is so slight or when the characters are dominantly normal, they remain sympathetic. If the abnormality is grosser and thereby approaches a threat to normal human beings, the character becomes ludicrous and even ridiculous. Our reaction to such a character is to laugh at him and his conduct, unless the abnormality becomes too definitely threatening. He then tends to arouse our antipathy so strongly that we consider him dangerous and even a villain. Tartuffe and Volpone are comic characters with abnormalities that approach the dangerous. The abnormality may be in human customs, social institutions and usages or manners of an age, with the characters for the most part normal. Our pleasure arises from seeing them work themselves out of predicaments caused by customs, social mores, manners, and the like.

The distinguishing powers of comedy, then, are the arousal of laughter and ridicule and their purgation. The purgation results in an assertion of the normal. Man's conception of the normal in human character and conduct depends upon his culture, his customs, mores, and manners. Hence all comedy is in a very real sense social comedy. The assertion of the normal may be accomplished in comedy in an indefinite variety of ways. It can result from merely making us see what is laughable or ridiculous in certain types of human character and conduct. It can result from an ultimate exposure of an a-normal individual. Molière's *Tartuffe* and Jonson's *Volpone* are among numerous examples. It may result from showing how love or other normative human attributes will triumph over the obstacles of custom and the impediments of older generations. Since comedy is normative and since it can deal with flaws in man and defects in society, its action may approach very closely to the serious in the making of its assertion of normality. The writing of great comedy demands a high vision of normal man and normal human actions. The range of the comic being broad, the varieties and types of comedy, like those of tragedy, are numerous. Among these are included farce, which is not a separate form but is a type of comedy.

Melodrama, sometimes called low tragedy, is not a type of tragedy but belongs to that third form of drama whose action and powers differ from tragedy. The action of melodrama is seemingly serious or temporarily serious. It poses a threat to a sympathetic individual or individuals and hence engenders fear for their happiness and well being. Usually that threat is initiated and manipulated by an antipathetic antagonist or villain whose machinations arouse hate. The distinctive powers of this third form are the arousal and purgation of fear and hate. Pity enters into our reaction usually in the form of pathos as a means of increasing the antipathy and hate and not as a distinctive power in itself. For the proper purgation the third form should have a double ending —reward for the sympathetic and punishment for the antipathetic individuals. The characters in this third form, unlike those in tragedy but like those in comedy, are static in that they have made their fundamental moral choices before the action begins. In the course of the action they do not make successive fundamental moral choices and hence do not grow and develop in the way that characters do in tragedy. Though we may learn successive new things about them, they do not change their fundamental natures. The hero remains essentially good and sympathetic throughout and the villain remains evil to the last. In the end of the play he may, as a part of his punishment, be convicted of his evil nature and ways and allowed to repent but the form is more satisfying if he is turned over to justice, beaten to death, or pumped full of lead. Melodrama should produce that relief of fear averted or escaped and that enjoyment of vengeance achieved. In its final effects it comes close to that of certain comedies. In fact this third form may be conceived as lying between tragedy and comedy and sharing some of the formal characteristics of both. It resembles comedy in that its characters are static, its final effects somewhat similar, and its structure may be loose and episodic. It resembles tragedy, among other ways, in that its action is for a time serious and one of its powers, fear, is the same as a power of tragedy.

There is a wide tendency to use the terms *tragedy* and *melodrama* in a prejudicative sense. This must be understood and guarded against in reading critical studies. Tragedy may be good tragedy or bad tragedy; melodrama may be good melodrama or bad. Simply because a tragedy is not in the ranks of the great masterpieces is no reason for obscuring an examination of its form by denying the name tragedy to it. Moreover, a good melodrama may be aesthetically better than a bad tragedy.

This discussion about the general aspects of form in the three major categories of drama should be helpful to the director when he is trying to determine as precisely as possible what effects a play should have on an audience. The mere attachment of a label such as tragedy, comedy, farce, or melodrama, to a play is relatively unimportant. What is important is the kinds of powers that are inherent in the form of the play. It cannot be repeated too often that these differ from play to play. In some instances it is not a simple matter to determine the form of a play. Is Elmer Rice's *The Adding Machine* a satiric and sardonic comedy or is it a tragedy of the little man? Are Luigi Pirandello's *Right You Are If You Think You Are* and *Six Characters in Search of an Author* comedies or tragedies? Obviously from the standpoint of one set of characters, the gossips and pryers, the first is a satiric comedy but from the point of view of another set, Signor Ponza, his wife, and Signora Frola, it is terribly serious. How then will the perceptive director interpret its effects upon an audience? Before he can adequately stage the play, he must answer this question. When he does so, he is determining an important, the major, aspect of its form.

5. UNITY IN DRAMA

To formulate is to order and organize, that is to unify. Every work of art to be comprehensible and effective must have unity. Unity means oneness but oneness may be achieved in a number of ways. We may say that a bushel of potatoes or a cord of wood has oneness. The oneness of a bushel or a cord is arbitrarily fixed by measurement and weight. No matter what the size and shape of the potatoes or of the pieces of wood, so long as they add up to a certain quantity they constitute the oneness of a bushel and a cord. This unity, a bushel or cord, is made up of parts but the size, shape, and arrangement of the parts are unimportant to the unity desired. The unity of an art object is also made up of parts but, unlike quantitative unity, arrangement in these is of utmost importance. For instance, take an example of useful arts, a shoe. It is made up of parts bound together. These parts cannot be switched around at random as can the parts that make up a bushel of potatoes. They may be put together badly or well but so long as they are put together in the right order we will recognize the object as a shoe. It will have the kind of unity, the kind of uniting that a shoe should have. Unity in art objects, which are similar to shoes in that they too are made things, consists in the orderly arrangements of the parts. The kind of unity the art object will have depends upon the kinds of parts of which it is made and upon the purpose in terms of powers and effects which the artist conceives. Thus the unity of a picture or painting will not be the same as the unity of a symphony or a poem.

Plays are time arts. They render or represent human actions. Actions have beginnings and lead through involvements to endings. The action might be quite simple, involving little complication; or it might well be highly complex, involving considerable complication before the ending. When an action is worked out (ordered and arranged) from a beginning through complications to an ending, it has completeness or wholeness. That is its unity.

A beginning of an action is the moment of its initiation. Plays that are made up of a complex series or strands of action have more than one beginning. In *Hamlet,* for example, one strand of action is initiated when the Ghost appears to Horatio and his companions and they decide to tell young Hamlet about it. This leads as a consequence to the action in which they tell Hamlet and his decision to watch with them. These actions become antecedents which lead to Hamlet's meeting with the Ghost and its three-fold command to him. Step by step other consequences follow from this beginning and its consequences. Another strand of the action begins in the scene in which first Laertes and then Polonius warns Ophelia about receiving attentions from Prince Hamlet. The consequences of this strand of action are developed but not so tightly arranged as are those of the former. Another beginning occurs when King Claudius determines to ferret out Hamlet's secret. Thus the beginnings in a play is not like the beginning of a road, in one place only. It appears throughout the involving action. When a beginning leads to complications, involvements, entanglements, it has developed into a middle. When it proceeds through crisis to resolution, it has come to an end. In well-constructed plays beginnings set up movements which lead to middles and through middles to endings. The kinds of endings, in turn, determine what kinds of beginnings the playwright will employ. Thus in drama beginnings and endings are causes of each other, though in different ways. The beginning is the effcient cause of the ending in that it sets up, puts in motion, that which will lead to or result in the ending. The ending is the final cause of the beginning in that the nature of the ending determines what form of beginning must be used. It can be seen from this analysis that the unity of a play is much more complex than the mere unity of a chronological succession of events.

A play may be unified in one or in all of three ways. More specifically, it can be said that the unity of a play may be based upon one of three different principles or may include the three. A play may be unified in terms of action. That is the type of unity that has been discussed thus far, a unity that proceeds from beginning through middle to end. Most plays are so unified. The action of a play can, however, be based upon the change which occurs within a character and the chief principle of unity may be the unity in character change. In the third place, a play may be unified in terms of thought. This is the kind of unity found in many of Bertolt Brecht's so-called epic plays and was to be found in the Living Newspapers produced by the Federal Theatre. In Brecht's *The Private Life of the Master Race* there is a series of disjunctive scenes which roughly sketch the fate of a German Panzer unit from its triumphant march through the Low Countries and France to its bogging down in Russia. Though some characters go through the whole and lend a rough continuity, different characters and incidents appear in the successive scenes and these scenes are not causally bound to each other. The unity of the whole is attained through thought, the gradual change of conceptions and ideas. This is also the dominant kind of unity in T. S. Eliot's *Murder in the Cathedral* and is important in all of his plays. In *King Lear* the three principles of unity are important.

The director in order to interpret a play must ask himself what kind of whole the play is. The answer to his question will lead him into an understanding of the powers and effects of the play. In order to be fully effective a play must have wholeness, completeness. This is not to say that every little strand must be resolved and neatly tied up, as in the well-made play of Scribe or Sardou. A play may end in a question or an enigma and still have completeness in that it has fulfilled the author's purpose in raising such questions or posing such enigmas. *A Doll's House* ends with a question and many of Pirandello's plays end in enigmas. Such plays can be puzzling and disappointing to audiences if the directors do not stage them with understanding. Such understanding comes in part from a comprehension of the way or ways in which the author unifies his play and from a comprehension of his purpose.

6. PROBABILITY IN DRAMA

The action of a play must not only have unity, it must also have probability. Probability as applied to drama is a technical term. It must not be confused with natural, mathematical, or statistical probability. There is a kind of probability in life that is based upon common sense and ordinary or average experience. Often in modern plays the probability of drama resembles this probability of life. But even when the probability of drama closely resembles the probability of life, the two must not be confused.

Probability in its simplest terms means believableness, credibility, convincingness. In terms of action it is that which within the realm of the possible is most likely to happen. The playwright first sets up the possibilities in his play. Say, for example, that the action is to occur in a space ship on a voyage to a distant planet. In this age of science fiction the author can very quickly establish just such a possibility. Examine the first scene of *Hamlet* and note the care and superb artistry with which Shakespeare establishes the possibility of the appearance of the Ghost. The time is just before midnight. The place is an eerie battlement in murky light and deep shadows. A guard whose movements and voice betray his disquiet and fear paces back and forth. His relief arrives and he assures Bernardo that he has had a quiet watch. When Horatio and Marcellus arrive, they ask if this *thing* has appeared again.

Horatio disbelieves what the others tell about the apparition but they insist upon what they have seen. Thus very quickly and dramatically Shakespeare establishes the possibility of the Ghost and then it appears. Thereafter each successive appearance is probable.

It becomes apparent, then, that the playwright is responsible for and makes the probabilities of the play. The probability which he establishes need not be naturally probable. The probability of the Ghost in *Hamlet* has nothing to do with natural probabilities and is not dependent upon Elizabethan beliefs about ghosts. The probability can be that of the fantastic world of fairyland, as in *A Midsummer Night's Dream;* it can be the romantic world of Theseus and Hippolita; or it can be the low and absurd world of Bottom the Weaver. Alice in *Alice in Wonderland* suddenly grows to nine feet tall and this is entirely probable in Lewis Carroll's story. It would not be probable in Steinbeck's *Grapes of Wrath* or Fielding's *Tom Jones.*

Every play is a made thing, an artifice put together by the artistry of a maker, an artificial, not a natural thing. Things in nature come about from an inner force which generates them—an acorn develops into an oak tree without any artificial maker. Its generative power puts together its own parts. Its generation, growth, maturity, and decay come from within. No art object has such generative power. All art objects are artificial, not natural. Their parts must be put together by a maker.

However much like real life a play may seem, it is nevertheless not real life. It is conventional and artificial. Examine it carefully and you will see the details that have been selected to give it the appearance or effect of real life. Earlier in this chapter it was said that every play creates its own world, the environment of its action. Strictly speaking, that should have been phrased as follows: Every play has its own probability created by the author who wrote the play. If he has done his task sufficiently well, the reader or audience will follow him imaginatively into the world which he has created. They will accept the probabilities of action, however fantastic, however unnatural in terms of common experience.

Probability is, then, the basis of dramatic illusion. Thus far it has been discussed largely in terms of the action or plot. But it relates to all of the parts and all of the parts may be used in establishing it. A setting may serve to make an action probable.

The modern drama with its emphasis upon the influence of environment in life and upon human nature has employed settings in various and subtle ways to establish probability. In certain instances nothing more than a costume is needed to establish the convincingness of a character's action. A policeman's uniform will sometimes suffice to establish an officer of the law. During the Second World War it was enough to establish an individual as a villain to give him Japanese features or a German accent. How often has an Irishman or a Southerner been established on the stage initially by an accent or idiom? Insofar as audiences generally accept certain attributes as belonging to Irishmen and Southerners, the accent or idiom will serve to make probable all of those conventional attributes of character in a role. These are low levels of probability but they frequently suffice for minor roles in plays.

On higher levels probability of character and action are established by thought and emotion, by the whole nature of the character, and by devices of action. When a playwright exhibits a certain character thinking about or contemplating a deed, that deed then becomes probable for that character, unless, of course, his very nature makes him reject it. When we see a character becoming more and more angry with another, his eventual striking of that other person becomes probable. A character who shows a growing interest in and attraction to another person will probably seek out that person. One who gradually becomes interested in another and in what he or she is saying or doing will probably pay attention to and even move toward that individual. It becomes apparent, from these examples, that probability is an important basis of the actor's character development and hence is of great importance to the director. The nature of a character, his desires and drives, his emotions and feelings, his deliberations and decisions determine and make probable what he does. His associations and his reactions to other people also have a share in this. Thus it is easy to see that character renders action probable.

Action may be made probable in terms of action. When one action follows another as its consequence, the latter action becomes probable. Antecedents and consequences are then a means of establishing probability. There is yet another way in which probability of action is established in drama. That is in terms of expectations. Every play in the beginning and through its development sets up certain expectations. In many of the modern comedies the playwright establishes an expectation that the boy will eventually get the girl. Molière's *Tartuffe* sets up an expectation that the clever Tartuffe will overreach himself. When these expectations lead to the anticipated outcomes, those outcomes seem probable. Playwrights establish their expectations in subtle ways, though often expectations are quite obviously planted. These are important devices for the director. Through them he can lead the audience to accept the play in the proper way.

Modern realistic theory has developed the doctrine of complete illusion in drama and theatre. According to this theory empathy is established between the characters and the audience. *Empathy* literally means the "imaginative projection of one's own consciousness into another being; especially sympathetic understanding of another human being." This psychological term has been extended by certain writers to include even a kind of antipathetic acceptance or identification with unsympathetic persons. It has been further extended to mean an imaginative acceptance of a setting, such as that of a specific room, to be the real room and not merely the symbol or conventional representation of it. Modern realistic drama, and especially modern naturalistic drama, has developed the doctrine of complete illusion and unbroken empathy. It has gone further and tied this illusion strictly to objective reality as literally experienced.

Obviously probability in drama is by no means so strict nor so prosaic. The human imagination is capable of wide adaptation. It will follow the playwright in his highest flights of fantasy so long as he gives the clues and establishes a sufficient probability. In reaction against the strict modern doctrine of illusion certain playwrights have rebelled in favor of theatricality and unreality. And audiences have followed them when they were good craftsmen. Thornton Wilder's *Our Town* with its stage manager as a kind of chorus and its lack of conventional settings is an example of the trend towards theatricality. Bertolt Brecht with his theory of "alienation" has gone even further. He deliberately breaks the illusion with all kinds of devices in order, he says, to force an audience to think rather than merely to feel and react. Probability in his plays, as was noted earlier, is largely based upon thought. The probability of drama and the imaginative potentialities of audiences must not, therefore, be conceived too narrowly by the director. Yet each play he stages will create the illusion of some kind of world with its own probabilities. He must find those probabilities in the play and translate them in terms of theatre.

7. SURPRISE IN DRAMA

Probably when the word *dramatic* is used to describe any event most people think of its chief element as surprise. Surprise is an important element in drama by means of which interest is sustained. Surprise is produced by the unexpected. It would therefore seem to be incompatible with probability and especially to probability developed on the basis of anticipations leading to outcomes. Surprise may arise out of chance. Contrary to some statements made about drama, chance does play an important role in the action of plays. It is chance that Oedipus should meet King Laius just at the time he did but it is probable that Oedipus being the man he was and Laius doing what he did Oedipus would kill him. It is chance that King Claudius is at prayer when Hamlet comes upon him after the Play-within-a-Play but it is probable that Hamlet would seek him and would find him. Chance is important in dramatic action but it must be properly used in relation to probability. When so used, it is an excellent device for surprise. But drama may also have surprise in an entirely probable series of events provided there is more than one probability within the series. When there are at least two lines of probability and one of these is partly hidden or seems up to the moment of surprise unimportant and when the surprising event suddenly occurs as a result of this seemingly unimportant probability, a dramatic action may then have both probability and surprise. This manipulation of the two is well known in detective stories, novels, and plays.

Surprise in drama must not be thought of as occurring merely in the events and incidents. It may appear in the stage spectacle. One has but to recall the numerous times in a theatre when the opening of a curtain revealed a setting that made the audience gasp with pleasure or even applaud to have an example of surprise from setting. Surprise may result from the turn of thought or the expression of feeling in a character. Or it may come from a decision. It may result from the dialogue, a turn of a phrase, a startling expression, or an unanticipated retort. The language of comedy is rich in such surprises. Read Oscar Wilde's *The Importance of Being Earnest* for an excellent illustration of a play whose dialogue is literally a fireworks of verbal surprises. Surprise in this play and in its dialogue often takes the form of paradox, an ancient dramatic device for securing surprise. But paradox and surprise are by no means limited to the language of comedy. They are employed in tragedy as well but in somewhat different ways. Comparisons, figures of speech, and especially metaphors are rich devices for securing surprise in dialogue. A metaphor which is a combination of the usual or expected and the unusual or unexpected is itself an illustration of surprise and probability.

8. STYLE IN DRAMA

The former discussion of style in theatre arts has served to give some indication of what is meant by style. In that discussion it was indicated that style is based upon the dramatist's conception of the world he is creating, that is on probability, and on the means which he manipulates. The determination of the kind of probability which the playwright has built into his play to make it believable becomes important to the director not only in the understanding of the play, but also in his decision about the appropriate style of the production. The style of drama and the style of theatre are not the same thing. More specifically, a play written in one style may be effectively interpreted in different styles. Probability as a determinant of style in drama is dependent upon the playwright's vision of man and reality, how he sees human beings and how he sees the universe which they inhabit. The way in which he imagines or envisions these will control his rendering of them. It will also control the form of the play which he puts together. Perhaps this is one reason why the terms *form* and *style* are often confused in writings about drama.

There are other factors which affect or control style. Hence style is discussed in different ways and from different points of view in books on drama. Perhaps it will aid in clarifying its meanings if some of the other factors are listed. Among these are the following:

1. The individual devices, characteristics, mannerisms, and eccentricities of the composition of the playwright.
2. His theories and conceptions of the structure of drama.

A setting designed in the style of old-fashioned painted scenery and one in modern outline. Above: *The Lion of the West,* produced by San Diego State College, designed by Don Powell and directed by Hunton D. Sellman. Below: O'Neill's *Desire Under the Elms,* at Stanford University, designed by Wendell Cole and directed by Nicholas Vardac.

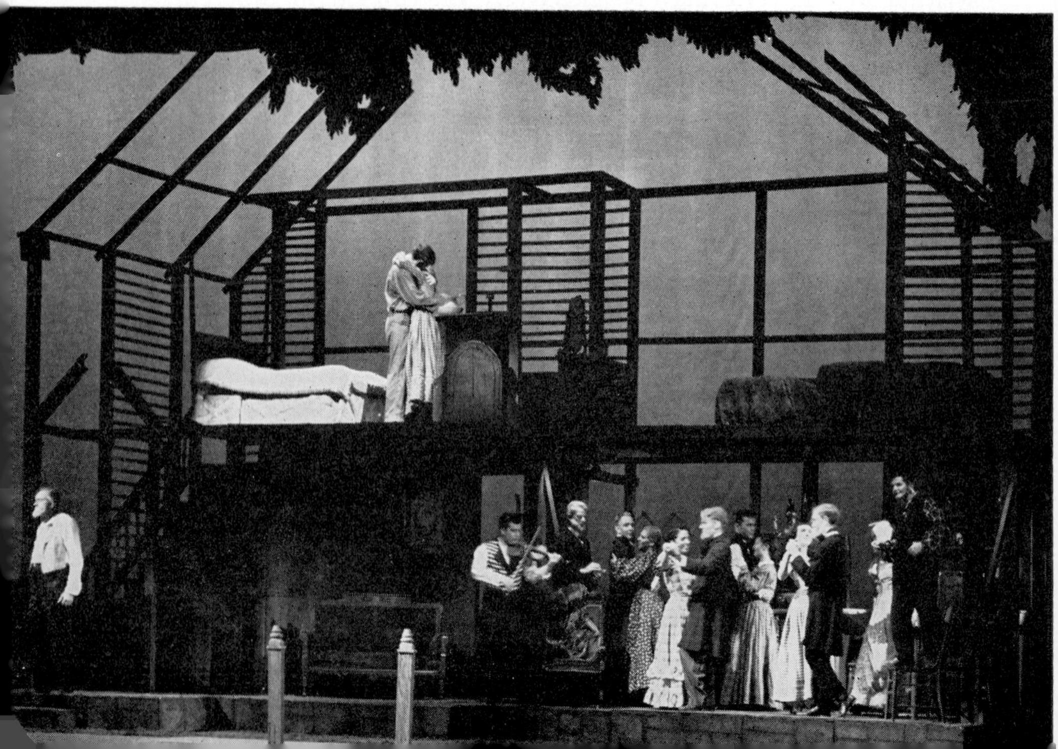

3. The physical stage and the methods of staging in the theatre for which he writes.

It is possible to discuss the style of Elizabethan or of Greek drama in general, emphasizing the philosophy of reality in that drama and the particular kind of performance for which it was designed. But the style of no two Elizabethan or Greek plays is exactly alike. We can differentiate among the styles of Aeschylus as compared to those of Sophocles, or those of Shakespeare compared to Ben Jonson. Shakespeare's theory of drama, as well as his individual mannerisms of composition, differ from those of Jonson. G. B. Shaw, J. M. Barrie, and Somerset Maugham are three English writers of comedy who were contemporaries; yet the style of their plays differs widely. Nevertheless, all that a director can learn about the style of drama in any period with which he is concerned will be helpful in the interpretation of a play from that period. To stage a Shakespearean play effectively in any style one needs to know as much as possible about Elizabethan style.

Plays may be interpreted on the stage in the style of the period in which they were written. Such presentations may be described as productions in historical style or period style. Actually they can be at their best only approximations of the original style. Even if a complete replica of an Elizabethan stage is built and the details right down to the pronunciation of the lines are as exact as possible, they will remain approximations because modern acting and modern audiences can never be exactly the same as those of former days. Since this is true, precise historical stylization is largely of only academic or antiquarian interest. In the staging of plays from the past the director has a two-fold obligation. He is obligated to render a faithful interpretation of the play and he is obligated in his rendering to make the play as effective as possible for an audience. Mere reproduction in strict historic terms might fulfill the first obligation and violate the second.

The majority of the plays that a director will be called upon to stage, unless he is employed in a theatre such as that of the Oregon Shakespeare Festival completely devoted to plays from the past, is apt to come from the modern repertory. That repertory is in a variety of styles, which perhaps can best be discussed in terms of schools. It has already become apparent that the dominant style of modern drama is realistic or naturalistic, a drama of illusion. Yet there are a number of trends in modern drama away from realism.

Some discussions of style in modern drama are based upon the idea that style is any departure from the natural or the realistic. That such a conception represents a false definition of style can easily be seen when it is remembered that realism and naturalism are themselves styles.

Realism is based upon the philosophy that objective reality as it is commonly experienced represents ultimate reality in life. It is, therefore, in one sense opposed to idealism which asserts that there is a reality beyond or behind the appearance of things. Certain realists can even accept this position of the idealists so long as the reality behind appearance is objective and scientifically verifiable. Realism places its emphasis upon sensory perception, upon things as they are perceived, upon the concrete, material universe.

Realism is a relative term. Euripides compared to Sophocles is in his depiction of human character and human actions a realist but in comparison with Shakespeare he is by no means as realistic. Yet Shakespeare, though he uses elements of realism, is by no means a realist. In Shakespeare's age Ben Jonson was considered much more of a realist than was his rival but Jonson's plays to the average reader today seem less realistic than Shakespeare's. Neither could really be called a realist in comparison with Ibsen or O'Neill. Realism is relative in yet another sense. Our vision of objective reality, though we do not usually realize it, is constantly changing. It changes from childhood to adulthood and it changes in adulthood. Anyone who has had the experience of going to a new and impressive place—say a city such as San Francisco or New Orleans, a Mexican village, an English village, or a French town—and living there for some time, will recall how strange and unusual the place seemed at first sight and how this view of the place gradually wore off as familiarity grew. Realism is relative in yet another sense. No two artists experience objective reality in exactly the same way. Finally, it is relative in another very important sense. Realism renders the artist vision with signs, devices, and symbols which in the period of their use stand for reality and evoke the proper responses toward reality in the perceiver. These symbols and devices are bound to change, just as the contemporary scene is bound to change. When they change and when the audience or viewer changes, the symbols will no longer mean what they originally meant. To audiences of 1852 and later

Uncle Tom's Cabin was a realistic and extremely moving work. Today, like many other melodramas of the past, it would seem entirely spurious, theatric in a bad sense, and laughable.

What, then, are the characteristics and devices of realism in drama? Realism places its emphasis upon the here and the now. It is primarily concerned with the contemporary scene, contemporary people, contemporary ideas and ideals, though realism may be used to render a past period. In depicting the here and the now, realism emphasizes the details. Realism is by no means unselective. Art must be selective. Realism differs from other styles in the kinds of details which the artist chooses to select. The view of the realist is that of the person completely familiar with what he is depicting. Realism can, however, be of the surface only. The famous realism of Belasco's stage settings and stage effects were of this nature. He would use a complete reproduction of a Childs' Restaurant or a setting from a poor-class rooming house to help make believable a sentimental and cheaply romantic action. The device of realism may be nothing more than the addition of a dialect or idiom to the diction of a character. It might even be merely the dress or costume of the character. It may go beyond these to involve the attitudes, emotions, and thinking of the character. Realism can affect the characterization, the dialogue, and the settings. The realism of many nineteenth-century dramatists, prior to the naturalistic movement, did not go beyond these effects.

Naturalism can be differentiated from realism, not as a method, but as a philosophy of life and literature. It developed in the nineteenth century after the Darwinian developments in biological science. Darwin's famous doctrine of evolution, the gradual evolvement of natural species through mutation, emphasized the absolute control of heredity and environment over the nature and development of living matter. The discoveries of other famous scientists seemed to make the Darwinian hypothesis a certainty. It was extended by other distinguished men into the realm of sociological phenomena and from this extension arose a mechanistic and materialistic philosophy known as determinism or positivism. This philosophy held that man was, like other animals, a completely determined being whose character and fate were shaped entirely by heredity and environment. Hippolyte Adolphe Taine (1828–1893) and Émile Zola (1840–1902) applied this philosophy to a theory of literature, which Zola named naturalism. It may be seen, therefore, that naturalism in the modern sense could not have influenced style in drama until after the middle of the nineteenth century. It became influential in the plays of Ibsen, Strindberg, Hauptmann, Galsworthy, and many succeeding writers.

Naturalism as a method or style extends and intensifies the methods of realism. The later naturalists were, however, somewhat scornful of the earlier realists, holding that their realism was a mere conventional and theatric realism that did not go below the surface. The naturalist turned to a depiction of man in his animal nature and as a product of his environment. With such ideas they naturally explored some of the more repulsive and animalistic aspects of human nature. Man's animal instincts were a dominant concern. In this attempt and in their seeking to show the influences of environment upon the shaping of human nature they turned to degraded and depressed humanity and to actions in sordid environments. The naturalists brought into literature and drama the new world of the proletariate, a world that had not appeared in drama before except as the subject for satiric and comic treatment.

With their philosophy of literature the naturalists developed a theory of art. Art should be an exact, objective, and faithful rendering of man, his environment, and his conduct. By faithful rendering they meant an analytically observed and scientific rendering, a rendering controlled by the latest scientific theories. Zola held that the writer, like the scientist, must be cold, dispassionate, analytical, observant. He has no right to moralize and draw conclusions. He must not himself organize and manipulate his materials toward predetermined arguments or outcomes. Actually Zola and most of the confirmed naturalists did exactly what they said the artist must not do in ordering and arranging their art to show that man was controlled by heredity and environment, that he was materialistically determined. In theory they held that a play must be a *tranche de vie,* a slice of life. Strictly speaking, the only organization that it should have was a chronological ordering, the natural time sequences observable in life. The artist is to be a trained observer and his art will be good only in terms of the accuracy of his observation and reporting. He must not impose upon the objects which he observes the theatric and dramatic organizations which characterize plays of the past. Obviously in its strict theory naturalism is a complete confusion of art and life. Equally obviously absolute naturalism would be an impossibility in drama and theatre. In this sense no great modern dramatist is a complete naturalist.

Naturalism turned the drama to scenes of humble and low life. It utilized scenes and characters from city tenements and the underworld, from industrial environment, from peasant life and folk life, from commerce and business. Since the social and political philosophy of Karl Marx and Friedrich Engles was based upon the same philosophic premises that underlay naturalism, Marxian socialism was to a considerable degree compatible with the thinking of many naturalists. Hence many of the naturalistic plays are proletarian drama. They often exhibit and defend the proletariate, revealing their exploitation, asking for sympathy toward their plight. Naturalism turned naturally to the exploration of modern industrial society. It advanced the realistic social thesis play, the folk and peasant plays, the problem play, and plays of discussion.

In method, it must be repeated, the naturalists intensified certain devices of the realists. They were, in their polemics if not always in their practices, violently opposed to the well-made plays of Scribe and Sardou. Shaw labeled these "Sardoodledom." They opposed these on the ground of their theatrical contrivance of their plots and their characters. Instead of incidents and characters contrived for theatric effectiveness, they argued for greater naturalness, even shockingness. André Antoine, to gain the shock of complete naturalness for a setting of one of his plays, moved a Paris butcher shop with its raw meat hanging about to his stage. Zola held that literature should give the veritable odor of a people. In their attempts to avoid so-called theatric contrivance of plot and yet to retain interest and meaning, the naturalists leaned heavily upon the juxtaposition of scene against scene, incident against incident. They soon learned, if they did not already know, that the plot of a play must have organization, that it cannot begin and end just anywhere. Hence many of the naturalists relied heavily upon thought to give order and meaning to their plots and hence many of their plays are primarily didactic. In their characterizations they brought in hitherto neglected attitudes and emotions, presented unidealistically. In dialogue they exploited a seemingly literal rendering of ordinary speech, with its circumlocutions, pauses, uncompleted thoughts. Slang, local accents and idioms, jargon, folk speech and dialects—the true language of the people—were widely employed. Hauptmann, for example, first wrote *The Weavers* in a Silesian dialect that had to be translated into standard German before it could be performed in Berlin.

If the theory of naturalism led to a serious confusion of art and nature and even if in practice naturalism could not be strictly followed, it did nevertheless influence modern drama in important ways. As a result of its influence a more incisive and effectual selective realism has evolved in drama and theatre. But the theory and practice of naturalism soon brought reactions. It was charged that naturalism was, after all, concerned merely with the superficial surface of reality and that the inner and meaningful nature of life and character could not be rendered by mere depiction of its external and objective appearance.

Among the chief revolters against naturalism were the neo-romanticists. Romanticism as a vision of life and as a style in drama is, like realism, constantly reappearing in drama. The romanticism of the late Greek romances is not like the romanticism of medieval romance. The romanticism of Renaissance and Elizabethan writers differs from the romanticism of the late-eighteenth and nineteenth centuries. Yet certain similarities of approach may be discerned in all of these. If realism depicts life from the standpoint of familiarity, romanticism depicts it from the standpoint of its strangeness. Romanticism tends to create an ideal dream world, a never-never land largely of the imagination. The persons who inhabit this world are equally idealized and colored by imagination. This idealization reaches in some romanticists to the extremes of sentimentalization. Thus it is often said that the romanticist sees life and this world through rose-colored glasses. The never-never land may be the forest of Arden, the seacoast of Bohemia, or that Elizabethan romanticized Italy of Shakespeare's comedies. It may be that "fairyland forlorn" in Keats vision of "magic casements opening upon perilous seas in fairyland forlorn." It may be an exotic South-Sea island of prewar romanticism (but try telling that to an old Marine who fought in those islands!). It might be the humble cottage of the shepherd or peasant. Whatever place, only its colorful, picturesque, and strange details are seen. It has no ordinary or sordid aspects or, if there are sordid aspects, these are colorful, strange, beautiful. There are, of course, the so-called decadent romanticists, such as the Pre-Raphaelites, who exploit the exotic appeal of the sordid, the fleshly, and the perverted. Byron even made a cult of the Satanic.

The romanticist places a primary emphasis upon emotion and feeling. Jean-Jacques Rousseau, the John-the-Baptist of nineteenth-century romanticism, said "I do wrong when I trust my head but I inevitably do right when I trust my heart." Human emotions and feelings transcend human actions; hence the prostitute with the heart of gold is somehow good whatever her actions. Byron's Don Juan and Schiller's Karl Moor show that even villainy, or what was formerly conceived as villainy, can from the romantic standpoint be admirable. There is, therefore, as Irving Babbitt charges in his *Rousseau and Romanticism,* a considerable confusion about moral values in some romanticists. Their characters are usually heroic, both in their goodness and their villainy. A Cyrano de Bergerac duels with a hundred men and comes off victorious. Within the soul of a Hernani there is a love and suffering far beyond the compass of ordinary humanity. Life for such characters is a high adventure.

There is no one technique for the romanticists, though they have since the late eighteenth century tended to borrow widely from Shakespeare. The romantic plays of Maxwell Anderson will attest to this, as well as the earlier romantic plays of Schiller, Hugo, and Rostand. Reality so conceived often is projected in verse but the romanticist by no means avoids prose. Witness the romantic Irish plays of J. M. Synge. When they employ prose for their dialogue, it is apt to be an elevated prose. Idiom and dialect are utilized for their strangeness.

Humble folk, lowly peasants, and common people are by no means absent from the writings of the romanticists. These are usually idealized in terms that analogize them to the "noble savage," a view of man based upon the idea that he was originally created perfect and that civilization and sophistication have robbed him of that original perfection. Through the utilizations of such characters and their habitats devices similar to those of realism often creep into romantic art. These devices also appear when the romanticist tries to recreate a past age and historic characters. The difference lies in the details selected and the emphasis given to them. The romanticist usually chooses the colorful and the strange, the realist the ordinary and the natural, even sometimes the drab. Romanticists are not averse to employing elements of the drab, the grotesque, and the ugly to heighten the convincingness and effectiveness of their art. Witness the grotesque scenes of Bottom the Weaver and his crew in *A Midsummer Night's Dream* and Cyrano's grotesquely ugly nose. On the basis of an analogy of art to nature and on the basis that life contains both the grotesque and the beautiful, the romanticists argue that drama should rightfully be a combination of comic and serious. Before the coming of the naturalists, they had aided in breaking down the ancient distinction of form in drama. Romanticism may be difficult to define accurately in general terms but the romantic elements of individual plays are usually not too difficult to determine.

Neoromanticism was by no means the only reaction in modern drama to realism and naturalism. One of the most important of the other reactions is generally known as expressionism. As a general term it should be taken to include Italian futurism and French impressionism. It, too, is difficult to define exactly, for there are various theories and practices to be taken into consideration. It had its important development in Germany after World War I, stemming in part from Strindberg's dream plays and from the new movement in the study of man which led to the depth-psychology of Freud and others. Its major tenet is that the true reality of man and things is an inner reality. This *geist,* spirit, or inner reality is all-important. Mere objective, outward appearance is important only as a symbol of this. Even the physical universe as we see it is actually an illusion. Man's real nature lies deep within him, often buried in his subconscious self. In dreams man frequently comes nearest to actual reality and the reality of human life is itself often dreamlike. The artist must search for the right symbols to expose and express this inner reality. The naturalists' preoccupation with observable and objective details is a preoccupation with surfaces which leaves the inner reality unexposed.

In a note on his *The Dream Play* Strindberg wrote the following:

> In this *Dream Play,* as in the previous *To Damascus,* the author has sought to imitate the disconnected, but apparently logical, form

> of the dream. Anything may happen; everything is possible and probable. Time and space do not exist; on an insignificant background of reality imagination spins threads and weaves new patterns: a mixture of memories, experiences, free fancies, absurdities, and improvisations. The characters split, double, multiply, evaporate, solidify, diffuse, clarify. But one consciousness reigns above them all—that of the dreamer; it knows no secrets, no incongruities, no scruples, no law.

Obviously the literal and complete fulfillment of such a prescription is impossible in the theatre, though much of it may be accomplished with trick photography in cinema. The expressionistic playwright's problem was to find symbols and devices to render his conceptions meaningful to audiences. He of necessity adapted many devices from former practices. In order to keep these from being taken in their old significancies, he added distortion, weird exaggerations, and guiding commentaries in the form of a prologue, a choral character, or asides and soliloquies.

Modern anthropology and psychology has revealed that a human being is actually a creature of multiple personalities and that he plays many roles in society. To exhibit this multiplicity the expressionists employed masks, the doubling of roles, and other devices. In O'Neill's *The Great God Brown* masks are used to represent the various aspects of the personalities; in his *Days Without End* two different actors represent the different aspects of John Loving's personality. In *Strange Interlude* the aside or "interior monologue" is employed for much the same purpose. In the *Emperor Jones* the subconscious racial memory of Brutus Jones, his real personality, is exposed through a series of tableaux from his past. In *The Hairy Ape* the conventionality and essential unrealness of the Fifth-Avenue Churchgoers is exposed by their exact similarity and their automaton-like movements. In Elmer Rice's *The Adding Machine* the nonentity of the protagonist is exposed in his name, Mr. Zero. That play employs the oft-used device of distortion in the setting to give the effect of unreality. It also employs the exact resemblance of characters, exaggeration, discordant sounds, and light effects for similar purposes. It succeeds in presenting the cock-eyed and terrible world of a nightmare, the world as a starved and conventionalized imagination would dream it.

The extremes of expressionism, especially as practiced by some of the postwar German dramatists, soon exhausted themselves and their audiences. Their devices became so exaggerated, so grotesque, so abstruse that they bewildered and confused, resulting in laughter and ridicule. Nevertheless, expressionism as a style has left marked influences upon later drama and theatre arts.

No important dramatist slavishly adheres to any one theory or style of drama. For him style is merely a means to an end. The competent dramatist employs any or all of these as they suit his purposes. Hence the sometimes expressed idea that a mingling of styles in drama is artistically impossible is a misconception. A play may begin in complete realism and gradually progress into romantic fantasy or into expressionism. The important procedure is for the playwright and the director so to lead the audience on to acceptance of whatever style is used or is desirable in the rendering of the meaning and effects of the play.

9. PARTS OF A PLAY

Form, unity, probability, surprise, and style are aspects of drama in general. To analyze a specific play requires the breaking down of that play into its parts. What are those parts? In many books on drama they will be stated as plot, character, theme, and dialogue. The vagueness of the term theme has been mentioned, though aside from its vagueness it is sometimes a useful term. A more exact and complete statement of the parts may be taken from Aristotle's *Poetics.* The parts of drama are therein defined as plot, character, thought, diction, music, and spectacle, and the exhaustiveness of these six parts is argued. Accepting the six parts for purposes of analysis without going into the argument for their exhaustiveness or their derivation, it will be more profitable to understand how these parts are causally related to each other.

Read down ↓		*Read up* ↑
Each is the formal cause of the one below it	Plot	Each is the material cause of the one above it
	Character	
	Thought	
	Diction	
	Music	
	Spectacle	

Plots are essentially made out of characters, what they do, think, and feel because they are the kinds of human beings who would do, think, and feel the kinds of things ascribed to them. Hence the material of plot is character and the material of character is thought in all of its aspects. But the kinds of characters that a playwright puts into a play are determined by the kinds of actions which they have to do throughout the play. The form of the characters is controlled by the plot. The thoughts that a character thinks and the feelings he exhibits are the bases of the kind of man he is. Thought is the material of character but the kinds of characters that the people of the play have determine the form of the thoughts and feelings expressed in the play. Diction is an ordering or arrangement of words. The thoughts and feelings in the play, expressed by the characters in what they say and do, are made of words arranged in meaningful patterns. Hence diction is the material of thought. Words vocally rendered are made up of sounds, represented by syllables. Sound that is expressive of thought and feeling takes on rhythm. Tone and rhythm may be called music, the material of diction—words meaningfully arranged. The material of sound is motion, as we know from physics. The visual aspect of the action, pantomimic action, is motion. Spectacle merely as motion can be seen to be the material of music. Spectacle is more complex than this, for it is the part of the play through which it is most immediately joined to theatre arts. This statement will become clearer in the discussion of spectacle.

The important point to see here is that a play is made up of parts and that the structure of the play is the ordering and organizing of these parts. The parts are not disjunctive. On the contrary, they are closely and intimately related in two causal aspects. Well-constructed plays are very intricate contrivances, not because the playwright has consciously thought out each detail of relationship in these terms, but because such an ogranic relationship will result from his visioning and rendering of a complete action in words. What has here been said about the order and relationship of the parts will become clearer if the parts are examined separately.

10. PLOT

The term *plot* is used in many modern critical works to mean merely the ordering of the incidents. Sometimes it is used to mean the arranging of devices and contrivances by which the playwright produces his effects. These are aspects of plot but not the only important aspects. Plot is the total arrangement of the play. It is the ordering of all the parts. Plot is the control through which the playwright determines how to arrange the other five parts—character, thought, diction, music, spectacle. Plot is the architectonic element in drama. It is the total ordering of the whole action and all of the parts of its rendering. Plot is the chief, the supreme part of drama. Some writers on modern drama speak of plotless plays, the plays of Chekov, for example. Actually there can be no plotless play. A plotless play would be a play without organization, a chaotic thing. The idea of a plotless play arises from a restricted use of the word *plot.*

When a playwright determines that his particular vision of a certain human action is serious, he is making a plot decision. That decision will determine the characterizations of agents in that action. Suppose that when Shakespeare sat down to revise the old Kydian *Hamlet* to compete, we may also suppose, with Ben Jonson's popular revision of the old Kydian *Spanish Tragedy,* Shakespeare had said to himself: "This old piece is trite and stale. How can I make it effective as a new play? Ah, I know. I will write a burlesque comedy on revenge plays." What would have happened to the characterization of Prince Hamlet in such a reworking? Until the playwright decides upon the organization of his whole action from beginning to end, he cannot know what characters he will need nor what kind of people they must be. When the playwright decides upon the effects to be created, the ordering of the climaxes, the kinds of progression in the action, the arrangements of complications, and such similar matters, he is plotting. Plot, then, is not merely the arrangement of the incidents, though this is part of plot. It is the over-all organization of the whole play. If plot is considered as the whole or complete ordering which the playwright is trying to achieve, the other five elements may be considered as parts of this whole. On the other hand, if plot is considered as the end which the playwright is striving to attain in his organization, the other five parts may be considered as means toward that end.

Plot taken alone, by itself as it were, can be analyzed in two ways in terms of its specific parts. Actually, of course, it is impossible, except analytically, to separate plot from other parts.

That is one reason why it is really quite difficult to state the plot of any play. Considered from the standpoint of its material elements, plot has three material causes. The first of these is what goes on inside the characters. Their feelings, emotions, thoughts, motivations from within constitute the basic materials of plot. Aristotle, writing of tragedy, called this suffering but the word *suffering* is used in a much more restrictive sense today. When we say a person is moved by anger or moved by pity, we are talking about the basic stuff of dramatic action. But characters may be moved by joy as well as by sorrow and this joy may be the real basis of a dramatic action, the material out of which it is generated. When the word *dramatic* is employed today, many people immediately think of great, sudden, outer, physical actions—an aeroplane miraculously escaping a crash, a train wreck in which two trains collide, all of the happenings in the collision of two ocean liners. These may or may not be truly dramatic. The real drama is first of all what happens within people. This is the first material element of plot and it is this that a director and an actor are striving to understand as they read and analyze plays.

Assume that a person is moved from within by uncertainty, apprehension, suspicion, and fear. It is obvious that if these inside conditions persist and he or she is sensible, he will try to find out what causes these, what basis there is for the feelings. If he persists in his efforts, he will eventually make discoveries. Discovery is the second material element in plot. It is the second device by which a playwright orders and organizes an action. In an earlier discussion it was pointed out that a dramatic action properly organized will lead to questions, that the early questions in a play will culminate in a major question, and that this major question may grow in the development of the action. Every time a question is answered in a play that answer, however simple, constitutes a discovery. A discovery is a passing from ignorance to knowledge; hence it is a form of change, a kind of action. The most effective dramatic discoveries are those that are made by characters moved from within. These discoveries by the characters, of course, become discoveries for the audience as well. There are discoveries that are not so intimately related to the action, such as discoveries about characters, about settings, even about motives which the playwright puts in his stage directions. These are important to the reader and the director as the basis for discoveries in the action. It can be said correctly that the art of formulating a play is the art of making and manipulating discoveries.

Just as there are various kinds of discoveries in a play, so are there various methods or ways of bringing these about. One person may recognize another person by a sign of some kind—his accent, the clothes he wears, a revealing mannerism, a mark of some kind. The author himself may make the discovery through having one character introduce another, through a stage direction which gives away the character and his motive, or through having one character tell about or discuss another. A character may discover the identity of another through remembrance of something in the past that links him to or identifies the second. Think of the numerous times in fiction that a faint whiff of perfume has brought up memories and led to the discovery of a woman's identity. A character puzzled about the true nature and identity of another, may attempt through memory and reasoning or through investigation to ascertain his identity. He may follow false leads and reason wrongly before the true discovery is made. Discovery through false reasoning is very powerful in the detective story and in drama. The discovery in *Othello* is built upon Othello's false reasoning about Desdemona. Clyde Fitch employs it with good effect in *The Girl with the Green Eyes*. Jinny's jealousy leads her through false reasoning to believe that Ruth Chester is in love with Jinny's husband, Jack. Through this false reasoning she eventually discovers that her cherished brother, Geoffrey, has contracted a bigamous marriage with Ruth. Finally, discovery can come about through the very course of the action itself. Such are the discoveries in *Oedipus Rex* and in *Hamlet,* as well as in many other plays. Discovery can be self-discovery. This is essentially what happens in the case of Oedipus, Mrs. Alving, and many characters in drama.

A director should make a careful list of the discoveries in the play he is analyzing and should ask himself just how these are brought about. This is important because discoveries represent the climaxes in the play, the high points of interest. Discoveries in well-built plays are cumulative. They lead into each other. Thus they build to higher and higher climaxes.

Plays may be built dominantly upon what happens within characters. They are usually more effective if they are built upon what happens inwardly to characters and upon discoveries that arise therefrom. Plays are usually most effective, however, when the discoveries lead to reversal—the third material part of plot. Add discoveries as clarifications one upon another and they often lead to a complete reversal, a change in the direction of the action. This process is simply illustrated in one kind of detective story. The detective puts clue upon clue, discovery upon discovery, until at last he knows the identity of the criminal. But in making his last discovery that reveals the true identity he gives himself away. Now the criminal knows who is pursuing him and he turns on the detective, trying to obliterate him. This turning constitutes a reversal of the action. Pursuer becomes pursued. Such is the situation in *Hamlet*. In the play scene Hamlet discovers that Claudius is truly guilty; but Claudius discovers that Hamlet knows of his guilt and determines to get rid of him. Pursuer becomes pursued. That is the reversal of the action in *Hamlet*. Reversal, then, requires a double discovery of the kind indicated. When the action of a play hinges upon a reversal, the discoveries are organized and manipulated in terms of this reversal. Reversal represents a complete change in the action. Hence it is the highest or most formal type of plot material.

Reversal constitutes the crisis or turning point in the action. Hence it can be seen that this highest material part of plot is directly related to the formal nature of plot as complication and denouement. Thus it may be said that plot has two formal parts. Actually plots are made up, as has been seen, of a series of complications and resolutions; thus there are a series of crises or reversals in plot. These are incidental or episodic reversals, that is, the whole line of action does not necessarily turn on them. The story line of a plot may turn on a discovery instead of a reversal and all of the reversals in it be mere episodic reversals. In such an organization the whole ordering of the elements is toward a big, final discovery that will bring about the resolution. In a plot of this order this big discovery constitutes the crisis, though it is not a full reversal. From this it can be seen that the playwright arranges or formulates the material parts of plot so that they are organized in terms of the formal parts—complication and denouement or involvement and resolution. These have already been discussed.

11. CHARACTER

It has become apparent that characters are formally determined by plot in a play and that plot is materially determined by characters. What is meant by character? A play is an action carried on or brought about by human agents. Insofar as those agents are conceived as mere functions in the action, they might theoretically be conceived as having no character. Whenever, however, one agent is differentiated from another agent, that differentiation serves to characterize. Thus man-agent *vs.* woman-agent is characterizing. The degree of characterization depends upon the culture pattern in which it occurs. Playwrights differentiate agents by ascribing to them traits. The traits which they ascribe to each depend upon the function and the role which each must play in the action. It also depends upon the kind and style of role which the playwright desires to create. If his objective is to create a fully-developed, complex, realistic modern individual, he will employ a wide variety of traits. If, on the other hand, his objective is to create a ridiculous portrait of a certain human trait, say jealousy or miserliness, he will select only those traits which harmonize completely with the dominant trait. The traits employed by writers to characterize may be arranged in an hierarchical order, as follows:

1. Biological traits
2. Physical traits
3. Bent, disposition, attitude
4. Traits of feeling, emotion, desire
5. Traits or characteristics of thinking
6. Decisions

In a well-organized characterization in which traits from all levels appear these traits lead into and help to determine each other. Thus feeling or desire may lead to thought and thought may lead to decision. Decision is characterization on its highest formal level, that is, it is the level at which character, so to speak, becomes action.

A character may be made believable or probable by an essential trait from one level only—a policeman's uniform, for example. This is characterization in terms of an acquired physical trait. It is all that the dramatist needs in certain minor roles. A character may be rendered largely in terms of disposition or attitude. Conventionally we say that Iago was born evil, that is, with an evil bent or disposition. Psychologists tell us today that an individual's bent or disposition is largely acquired in infancy and early childhood but it is still considered such a permanent impress upon his personality that we think of it as inherent. But bent as attitude may be acquired. The bent or disposition of the typical old maid, of the pedagog, of the miser, of the braggart warrior, of the acquisitive capitalist are examples well known in drama. Characterizations on this level are numerous in comedy but they also appear in serious drama.

Characterization in terms of feelings, emotions, and desires are basic to the chief roles in a dramatic action. On this level characterization joins to the basic element of plot—that which goes on within a character. Of course this is also true of attitude but attitude can be passive. Feelings and emotions formulated into desires are dynamic. They drive a character to do, to act. When feeling becomes more than passive, it leads to desires. What does the character want? What are his or her desires that he or she will try hard to attain? These are fundamental questions in character analysis for director and actor. In drama it is difficult to say where the feeling and desiring of the character leaves off and thinking begins. Actually the emotions of a character constitute a part of his thought in drama. But if a character is faced with difficulties in attaining his desires, a real conflict, he may be forced to deliberate.

True deliberation represents a rather high level in characterization. It can be of two kinds. Expedient deliberation is about ways and means of attaining a desire or objective. This kind can occur in comedy. Ethical deliberation, the second kind, concerns the good or evil of that which the character desires. When this kind of deliberation occurs, the character to that extent becomes serious. Deliberation in drama leads to choice. Choosing or not choosing for a reason is the highest level of character differentiation. Choice may also be either expedient or ethical. Expedient choice may occur in comedy but when the choice is in terms of the moral, it becomes serious. Fundamental moral choices determine the goodness or evilness of a character. That is the extreme range of separation of agent from agent that may occur in a dramatic action.

What decisions do the characters make? The answer to this question will help the director to determine the nature of the characters. It will also help him to determine the progress of the action. The plots of great tragedies move forward in terms of the decisions of the main characters. Expedient decisions may also be employed in comedy for similar purposes. Even burlesque moral decisions, such as occur in Falstaff's deliberation upon honor, may be employed for comedy. Decision may eventuate in one or in three ways: It may lead merely to a change of attitude on the part of the character; it may lead to words; or it may lead to physical deeds. The decision (or not deciding for a reason) is itself the dramatic action, however it eventuates. Usually it eventuates in the three ways listed.

12. THOUGHT

The thought in a play appears in all that the characters say and do. It is obvious, then, that it appears in the individual sayings and doings of specific characters and that it appears in the addition of all of these together. It has become apparent that thought on its basic level appears in the feelings and emotions of the characters and on the next level in their deliberations and decisions. Thought is thus seen to be the basic material out of which characters are made. A reader or audience adduces thought out of what the characters do, as well as out of what they say. The deliberations and decisions of the sympathetic characters may be considered the positive thought of the play when all that they say and do is combined and, as it were, added up. But this sum is modified and conditioned by the sayings and doings of the unsympathetic characters. That negative or antithetical thought helps to determine the whole thought of the play.

Thus every play may, in terms of meaning, be considered as a kind of argument. In that argument attitudes, emotions, desires, deliberations, decisions, sayings, and doings are the facts or materials of proof. A play is an argument by means of illustration rather than by means of abstract facts and logical proof. It is a dramatic argument by demonstration. A play may be thought of as adding up to a kind of proof or statement and in one sense that is its meaning. It may be quite simple, a mere proverb, rule of thumb, or piece of folk wisdom. It may be as profound as the meaning of Aeschylus *Oresteia* or Shakespeare's *King Lear*. In interpreting the play, the director is trying to get at, to comprehend this meaning. The more fully and completely he understands it, the more effective he can make his production.

Thought then appears in drama in three aspects:

1. As emotion and feeling
2. As deliberation
3. As the whole argument

It is rendered in three ways:

1. By what the characters say
2. By what the characters do
3. By the summation and balancing of the sayings and doings

13. DICTION

From the standpoint of the playwright the writing of a play is a making with words. Words are the central means of his art. All of the words which he may use appear in the dictionary to be freely used by anyone. Until an artist selects, combines, and arranges these words, they are mere denotations which may also carry connotations. When a playwright arranges or patterns these into diction or dialogue, they become the chief medium of his dramatic action. Diction may be simply defined as patterned words. How does the playwright know what pattern to give to these words from the dictionary? There are three major determinates of the pattern. The first is the thought to be expressed. Thus it can be seen that thought is the formal determinate of diction, just as diction is the material out of which thoughts are made in drama. The second determinate of diction is the nature of the character who speaks the words. The third is the kind of effect the words are expected to produce. Consider the following opening scene from Oscar Wilde's *Importance of Being Earnest:*

ALGERNON. Did you hear what I was playing, Lane?

LANE. I didn't think it polite to listen, sir.

ALGERNON. I am sorry for that, for your sake. I don't play accurately—but I play with wonderful expression. As far as the piano is concerned, sentiment is my forte. I keep science for Life.

LANE. Yes, sir.

ALGERNON. And, speaking of the science of Life, have you got the cucumber sandwiches cut for Lady Bracknell?

LANE. Yes, sir. (*Hands them on a salver*)

ALGERNON. (*Inspects them, takes two, and sits down on the sofa*) Oh! . . . by the way, Lane, I see from your book that on Thursday night, when Lord Shoreman and Mr. Worthing were dining with me, eight bottles of champagne are entered as having been consumed.

LANE. Yes, sir; eight bottles and a pint.

ALGERNON. Why is it that at a bachelor's establishment the servants invariably drink the champagne? I merely ask for information.

LANE. I attribute it to the superior quality of the wine, sir. I have often observed that in married households the champagne is rarely of a first-rate brand.

ALGERNON. Good heavens! Is marriage so demoralising as that?

LANE. I believe it *is* a very pleasant state, sir. I have had very little experience of it myself up to the present. I have only been married once. That was in consequence of a misunderstanding between myself and a young person.

ALGERNON. (*Languidly*) I don't know that I am much interested in your family life, Lane.

LANE. No, sir; it is not a very interesting subject. I never think of it myself.

ALGERNON. Very natural, I am sure. That will do, Lane, thank you.

LANE. Thank you, sir. (Lane *goes out*)

In this scene thought as the motivation of the characters and their diction is relatively unimportant. The characterization of the two men and especially the effect to be created are all important in the shaping of the dialogue. This being an opening scene, Wilde as a competent craftsman is especially concerned to establish the kind of effect which he wishes his play to produce.

The two dominant requisites of diction are that it must be clear and it must be interesting. Wilde obtains clarity, like any other dramatist, by employing commonly understood words in a sequence that is quite clear. Common words alone, while they would give clarity to diction, could lead to staleness and even boredom. Wilde obviates this undesirable contingency by the unusualness of the thought expressed by the diction. Algernon's statement about music and Lane's statement about marriage are unusual in their somewhat paradoxical meaning. Their resultant amusingness prevents the diction from being trite and uninteresting. Note, then, that even in a passage in which thought as a means of motivation of action is not prominent it does play an important part in shaping the diction.

Diction can be formally organized merely to give the impression or effect of natural speech. Most modern realistic playwrights are content with this degree of formalization. It can be highly effective, as may be seen from an examination of the colloquial dialogue in a play by Clifford Odets. Take, as example, the opening of *Waiting for Lefty:*

FATT. You're so wrong I ain't laughing. Any guy with eyes to read knows it. Look at the textile strike—out like lions and in like lambs. Take the San Francisco tie-up—starvation and broken heads. The steel boys wanted to walk out too, but they changed their minds. It's the trend of the times, that's what it is. All we workers got a good man behind us now. He's top man of the country—looking out for our interests—the man in the White House is the one I'm referrin' to. That's why the times ain't ripe for a strike. He's working day and night—

VOICE. (*from the audience*) For who? (*The* Gunman *stirs himself.*)

FATT. For you! The records prove it. If this was the Hoover regime, would I say don't go out, boys? Not on your tintype! But things is different now. You read the papers as well as me. You know it. And that's why I'm against the strike. Because we gotta stand behind the man who's standin' behind us! The whole country—

ANOTHER VOICE. Is on the blink (*The* Gunman *looks grave.*)

FATT. Stand up and show yourself, you damn red! Be a man, let's see what you look like! (*Waits in vain.*) Yellow from the word go! Red and yellow makes a dirty color, boys. I got my eyes on four or five of them in the union here. What the hell'll they do for you? Pull you out and run away when the trouble starts. Give those birds a chance and they'll have your sisters and wives in the whore houses, like they done in Russia. They'll tear Christ off his bleeding cross. They'll wreck your homes and throw your babies in the river. You think that's bunk. Read the papers! Now listen, we can't stay here all night. I gave you the facts in the case. You boys got hot suppers to go to and—

The effects of natural, ordinary speech in this passage, the short sentences, the slang, the figures of speech, the ellipses of words, the repetitions are artfully contrived by Odets to create just the effect of the character and the thought which he is aiming at. Note the way in which he manipulates the diction to reveal that Fatt is specious and sly in his argument. Here is an excellent example of the way in which thought not intended by the speaker is conveyed through diction. This allusive and suggestive element in modern prose diction is frequently used to compensate somewhat for the loss of expressiveness in the sacrificing of poetic diction.

Poetic diction is more highly, more formally, organized than prose diction. It is rendered probable by a higher degree of formalization of the whole action. When such formalization occurs, the probability of the play is based upon devices that do not require constant and ready reference to the natural and the ordinary. Poetic diction allows the fullest and most effective use of language as a means of drama. The narrowing restraints of realism do not operate in truly poetic drama to restrict the potentialities of the characters and their speech. Revelations of hidden and complex thoughts and of strong feelings become more fully probable in the poetic drama. The ways in which poetic diction operates in drama and its relations to the structure of tragedy have been competently explored in Moody E. Prior's *The Language of Tragedy* (New York: Columbia University Press, 1947). Here there is space enough for an example or two only.

For the finest examples of poetic diction we turn naturally to Shakespeare. Take the following example of passion in Lear's dispossession of Cordelia, Act I, Scene 1:

> For, by the sacred radiance of the sun,
> The mysteries of Hecate and the night,
> By all the operation of the orbs
> From whom we do exist and cease to be,
> Here I disclaim all my paternal care,
> Propinquity and property of blood,
> And as a stranger to my heart and me
> Hold thee, from this, for ever.

Prior points out: "Allusions to storms, to the procreative forces of nature, to the heavenly bodies diffused throughout the play give to the actions and sentiments not only a grandeur in scale but endow the specific events of the play with the widest possible kind of generality." It is the figures of speech, the comparisons in this passage that give it its strength as dramatic diction and its effectiveness as emotion. These point forward to similar figures in the play and join with them as a probability of the action and as a unification of the whole. Thus poetic diction can become an important device in the structure of a play. The dominant figures of speech in such a play can be a key to its meaning. A further illustration of language made colorful and interesting by the employment of comparison and figures and another illustration of the way in which diction can be made into anticipation appears in the following speeches from *Romeo and Juliet:*

> O, speak again, bright angel! for thou art
> As glorious to this night, being o'er my head,
> As is a wingèd messenger of heaven
> Unto the white-upturned wond'ring eyes
> Of mortals that fall back to gaze on him
> When he bestrides the lazy-pacing clouds
> And sails upon the bosom of the air. (II, 2)

The presagement of the future comes in the following passages:

> Although I joy in thee,
> I have no joy of this contract tonight;
> It is too rash, too unadvised, too sudden,
> Too like the lightning, which doth cease to be
> Ere one can say it lightens. (II, 2)

And following this speech by Juliet comes Romeo's similar presagement:

> O blessèd night! I am afeared,
> Being in night, all this is but a dream,
> Too flattering sweet to be substantial. (II, 2)

It is difficult to imagine a more perfect revelation in diction of the lightening-like intensity of their love which at the same time makes probable its tragic outcome. The manipulation of language for the full expression of high and intense passion requires poetic diction.

Diction is made clear by the use of ordinary and commonly understood words; it is made interesting by the employment of strange and unusual words. Idioms, dialect, slang, folk terms and sayings, and similar terms are widely employed in modern realistic prose dialogue for this purpose. Poetic diction employs strange and unusual words to create interest but its finest effect is created through the use of metaphor. Of all the figures of speech metaphor most effectively combines the usual and the clear with the unusual and strange. The following passage from the beginning of *Henry IV,* Part 1, illustrates the effectiveness of figures of speech, and especially of metaphor:

> So shaken as we are, so wan with care
> Find we a time for frighted peace to pant,

And breathe short-winded accents of new broils
To be commenced in strands afar remote.
No more the thirsty entrance of this soil
Shall daub her lips with her own children's blood;
No more shall trenching war channel her fields,
Nor bruise her flowerets with the armèd hoofs
Of hostile paces: those opposèd eyes,
Which, like the meteors of a troubled heaven,
All of one nature, of one substance bred,
Did lately meet in the intestine shock
And furious close of civil butchery,
Shall now, in mutual well-beseeming ranks,
March all one way and be no more opposed
Against acquaintance, kindred, and allies:
The edge of war, like an ill-sheathèd knife,
No more shall cut his master. Therefore, friends,
As far as to the sepulchre of Christ,
Whose soldiers now, under Whose blessèd Cross
We are impressèd and engaged to fight,
Forthwith a power of English shall we levy;
Whose arms were moulded in their mother's womb
To chase these pagans in those holy fields
Over whose acres walk'd those blessèd feet
Which fourteen hundred years ago were nail'd
For our advantage on the bitter Cross.
But this our purpose is now twelve month old,
And bootless 'tis to tell you we will go:
Therefore we meet not now.

From the standpoint of dramatic technique it is a rather daring gamble to open a play with a single speech of this length. The opening of a play should seize the interest of an audience as rapidly as possible. A long speech, unless it is masterfully done, is not best suited to this objective. In the above speech it is done with consumate mastery. The mastery lies largely in the diction. Note the numerous figures of speech employed by Henry. One of the secrets of these figures is their exact suitableness to the expression of Henry's ideas. Another is that they are picture-evoking. They raise in the imaginations of the audience a clear picture of warfare as it was conducted in those days. They successfully evoke something of the horror of civil war and what it does to a kingdom. Good poetic diction builds pictures in the mind.

Any examination of diction should always begin with the character of the speaker and the motivations behind his words, that is, the thought which gives rise to the words and which the words express. Henry IV is an astute, capable, and wily king. Hotspur later calls him a "vile politician," though that is a biased assessment. In this speech he is foreshadowing a policy often indulged in by strong rulers, embroilment in war abroad to cure civil dissentions. Another motivation for this projected holy war is Henry's guilty conscience. He usurped a throne and had a legitimate king killed. But note the last line of the speech which, up to that point, is seemingly a preliminary to a declaration of immediate departure for the Holy Land. Henry is dissembling. As we see later in the play, he well knows about Hotspur's refusal to deliver his prisoners before he launched upon this speech. He is astute enough to foresee this refusal as the initial step in another civil strife. It is against that background that the speech is made and the actor who delivers it must strive to indicate something of the subtle motivation. This he will have to do by the way he delivers the lines, for the clever Henry is endeavoring to conceal his real reasons in speaking. Probably Henry's dissembled anger at Hotspur and his artistry of concealment lend color to his diction and his delivery.

Note the figures of speech, especially metaphors, contained in the passage. There are several telling figures descriptive of civil war, which are arguments against further strife of brother against brother, kinsman against kinsman. Henry is consciously employing these for his purpose. A kind of startling climax occurs in the vivid "daub her lips with her own children's blood" and in the magnificently phrased "in the intestine shock/ And furious close of civil butchery . . ." Note how the consonant and vowels admirably fit this line to forceful delivery. Attention has already been called to the startling anticlimax in the last line. Rightly delivered, that should raise a question among the assembled lords, manifested in their looks and even mutterings of surprise, and should awaken also a question in the audience. In addition to the climaxes and surprises, there are quiet and smooth moments, admirably rendered in the meter, in which Henry is being wily. Note especially the passage beginning "Therefore, friends . . ." and ending with ". . . on the bitter Cross." This smooth, persuasive passage is followed by two very strong lines of expressed determination, prior to the anticlimax.

In that Henry is attempting to arouse his listeners in certain ways and to influence their attitudes, the whole speech, like many extended passages of dramatic diction (see, for example, the quarrel scene between Brutus and Cassius in the last act of *Julius Caesar*) becomes an argument. Dramatic diction reaches its highest effectiveness when it serves to arouse passion or emotion and to present argument. In both senses it expresses thought.

Now, after examining Henry's speech, turn to Hotspur's speech beginning "My liege, I did deny no prisoners," from Scene 3 of this play and note the way in which he evokes his condition at the end of the fight, the consummate picture of the "popinjay" who questions him, his extreme exasperations with the lady-like lord, and the manner in which he too is framing an argument. (For further discussion of this speech and the text see Chapter 7, Section 3.)

Apparently, to judge by the drama of past ages as well as that of the present, prose is more suited to comedy than to tragedy of high passion and deep significance. Ancient comedy was much more definitely about contemporary life and man than was tragedy. That is only one reason why comedy of the past was in prose. Today, except for a few experiments by playwrights such as Maxwell Anderson, T. S. Eliot, Christopher Fry, and others, drama both serious and comic is in prose. Modern writers have attempted to gain some of the color and effectiveness of poetic diction in their prose dialogue through various means. J. M. Synge in such plays as *Riders to the Sea* and *Playboy of the Western World* used Irish idioms and rhythms of speech for this purpose. Odets attempted to gain some of the same effects from a typical New York local speech. Tennessee Williams employs speech rhythm with considerable effect for the same purpose. O'Neill and other playwrights influenced by Expressionism have sought by different devices to break the narrow confines of realistic verisimilitude and to compensate by devices such as the "interior monologues" of *Strange Interlude* for the loss in imaginative language of modern realistic prose dialogue. They and other modern playwrights have attempted to make dialogue symbolic, allusive, and highly suggestive in order to give it a richness beyond mere bald and prosaic statement. That they have succeeded only partially is in considerable measure the reason for the widespread demand for the revival of poetic drama. Realistic prose dialogue at its best is severely restricted in comparison with the dialogue of poetic drama. Such dialogue is usually held to a strict verisimilitude and characters are allowed to utter nothing which could not be thought or felt within the completely natural, ordinary environment of their actions. Such a conception of character and speech restricts the variety of motive and emotion which may be projected in dialogue. Sometimes it will go so far as to make a shrug of the shoulder or a facial expression more highly effective than bald words. When this happens, diction, the central means of the playwright's art, has been reduced to a level of spectacle.

14. MUSIC

Dialogue is written to be spoken; therefore all dialogue has a tonal quality. A competent modern playwright with a good ear can, even when writing in prose, make this tonal quality highly effective. As stated above, Synge does this; so does Tennessee Williams. This tonal quality can be so highly formalized in drama that it demands or should have musical accompaniment. The choruses in Greek drama and the *cantica* in Latin comedy are formalized to this extent. So are the lyrics in Shakespeare's plays. These examples of diction highly formalized not only demand musical accompaniment; they also demand to be sung. The libretto of an opera is an example of this formalization of diction in terms of tonality throughout.

But dialogue need not be so highly formalized to have tonality. Indeed, every line of dialogue has it. Its effectiveness depends upon loudness or softness of utterance, stress and emphasis, timing and rhythm, and upon tone. These are the elements of music. The right employment of these elements can give both meaning and effectiveness to a line. Take, for example, the following prose line from Lady Macbeth's speech in the Sleep-Walking Scene, Act V, Scene 1:

> Yet who would have thought the old man to
> have had so much blood in him?

Speak the speech as a question, emphasizing "have had." Then speak it as a question, emphasizing "blood." Now, eliminate the question entirely from the speech and speak it as an exclamation. Next, speak it merely as a musing statement. In each instance the diction remains unchanged so far as the words go. The modification comes through the music.

This simple line can be modified in delivery even more widely than has been suggested and each modification will to some degree change the meaning. Each modification would certainly change the kind of effect which the actor produced in speaking it. Diction as the meaningful combination of words may, then, be conceived as basically a pattern of sound. Words are composed of vowels, consonants, and syllables. These are symbols of sound. In the well-organized play the playwright organizes the music, as well as the other parts. The director, and especially the actors, must be alert and sensitive to this part of drama. It might be said that music and spectacle are the parts of a play that join the art of drama to the art of theatre.

15. SPECTACLE

From the standpoint of the art of playwriting spectacle is the last and least important of the qualitative parts. From the standpoint of the art of theatre it becomes one of the most important elements. Spectacle as used to designate a part of a play does not necessarily mean spectacular. It means the visual element—the settings, the costume, the lighting, the make-up, and the pantomimic action of the characters. Any movement or physical action of a character on the stage is spectacle. As such it is highly important to the actor but not so important to the playwright as the lines spoken, the thought and emotion expressed, and the characterization. The actor makes spectacle an instrument or means for rendering thought, emotion, and character. The director likewise employs spectacle in arranging the physical actions (the business) of the characters, in their entrances and exits, in grouping them, in selecting or approving their costumes and make-up, and in the scenic environment selected to interpret the play. Spectacle is dominantly visual, a space art, but it can be symbolically rendered by sound. For example, the sound effects that signalize an approaching train or those that signalize a collision of automobiles really stand for spectacle. The function of the director might be described as the controlled rendering of a play in terms of music and spectacle.

Spectacle, like any of the other qualitative parts, can be em-

Plays presented at the Cleveland Play House. Above: J. B. Priestley's *An Inspector Calls*. Below: Arthur Miller's *All My Sons*. Both plays were directed by K. Elmer Lowe and set by William A. McCreary.

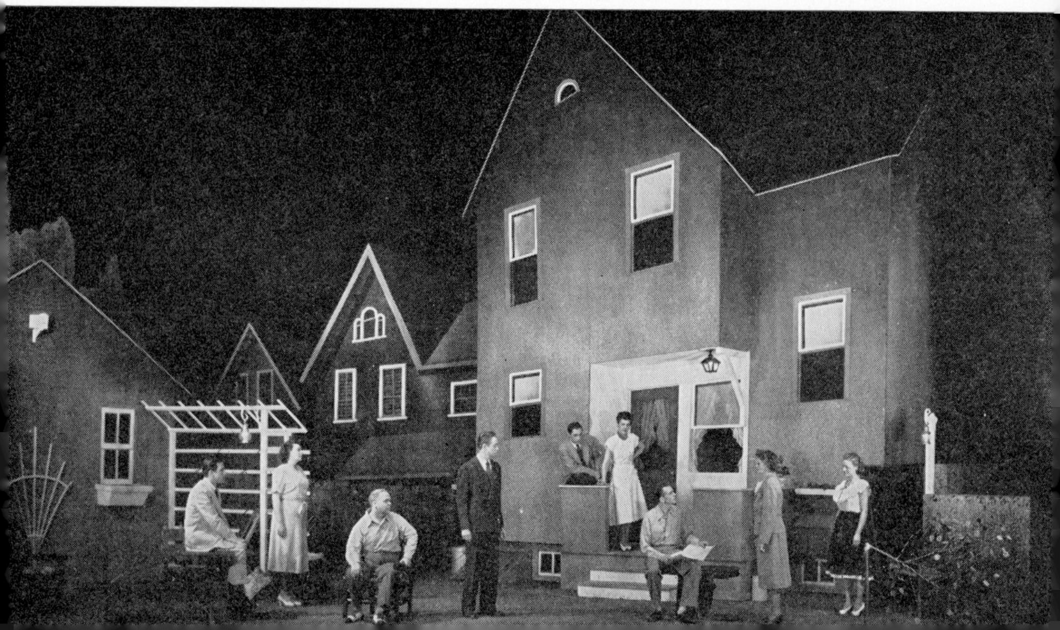

ployed to give probability to the action. The right kind of setting and lighting can help to make the Witches Scenes in *Macbeth* or the Ghost Scenes in *Hamlet* convincing to an audience. Settings and lighting can and should serve similar functions in the production of any play. A facial expression, a gesture, or a movement can aid in making effective and believable a line of dialogue. A costume can aid in identifying and making convincing a character. Spectacle can, as in the case of pantomime and the silent motion pictures, serve as a substitute for diction in telling the story. In some instances in the modern realistic drama it can become even more eloquent than words. Much of the spectacle that goes into the staging of a play is supplied by the director, the actors, and other artists of the theatre. Frequently the dramatist in writing his play does not bother to indicate in any detail in the stage directions the various elements of spectacle that belong to the play. These are often worked out in production and added to the manuscript before it is published.

16. THE MECHANICAL PARTS

The six parts that have been discussed—plot, character, thought, diction, music, spectacle—are qualitative parts through which by analysis the quality of a play may be determined. Plays are also divided into mechanical parts which may or may not have any relation to the structure. Greek drama was divided into choral odes and episodes, the dialogue part between choral odes. Probably from this division the five-act organization known to later Roman dramatists and utilized by Seneca was evolved. Insofar as Shakespeare utilized mechanical divisions in the writing of his plays, he thought largely in terms of scenes. With possibly a few exceptions, the act divisions in his plays were supplied by later editors. Corneille and Racine, adhering closely to the mechanical rules of neoclassicism, observed the five-act organization and in these dramatists the act divisions do bear a relation to the structure of their plays. The Romantic movement, though it broke down much of the neoclassical practice, did not abandon the five-act division. In the popular theatre of the eighteenth and nineteenth centuries, especially in comic opera, there evolved a three-act organization, later taken over to a large extent by the modern drama. Though the modern drama frequently utilizes a three-act organization, it is by no means as definitely tied to this organization as was the neoclassic drama to the five acts. It employs a variety of act and scene divisions. With the advent of the picture-frame stage and the drama of illusion, act divisions attained a certain structural significance.

The opening of a play, be it the opening of the first scene or the first act, may be designed to accomplish the following:

1. Focus the attention of the audience.
2. Catch the interest of the audience.
3. Lead the audience interest forward.
4. Set the mood of the play, that is, tell the audience how to take it.

All openings may not accomplish all of these four; they should accomplish the first two. Great openings, such as the opening of *Agamemnon* and of *Hamlet,* accomplish all of these. The focusing of attention in the modern theatre is easily accomplished. The lowering of the house lights, raising of the stage lights, and opening of the curtain suffices for the first step and the playwright, if he is a competent craftsman, has provided the succeeding steps. He has also largely provided the means of catching the audience interest. Usually he accomplishes this by various devices but chiefly by raising questions. Once a question is raised in the consciousness of an individual, he is interested to the extent of an answer. The raising of interest by means of questions naturally leads forward but the forward movement can be made even more substantial by making it apparent that whatever happens in the opening is antecedent to a consequence. Not all opening scenes set the whole tone or mood of the play, as do the opening scenes of *Agamemnon* and *Hamlet.* When the playwright has written such an effect into the opening, it is a highly useful device for the director. Its importance is especially appreciated in comedy. If a laugh can be secured from the audience early in the play, the comic mood thereby established helps to sustain the right audience acceptance of the play and enhances the interest.

The ends of acts in modern plays are usually built to a climax. These climaxes at the end of each act prior to the last should be sufficiently intense and should raise a sufficiently momentous question to carry the audience interest through the intermission. These act climaxes are best when they are antecedents that obviously anticipate consequences. In the well-constructed play the playwright builds these into the structure of the play but the director can often enhance them. To accomplish this he must known how they are built in order to know what spectacle or stage business will appropriately interpret them.

A further clarification of the word *scene* needs to be made. The word has been used largely thus far in this discussion to mean a change of setting. Playwrights frequently use it in another sense, sometimes called scene in the French sense. When so used it means any new combination of characters on the stage. Thus the entrance of a new character or the departure of a character from a group will constitute a new scene. Any act, though it occurs within a single setting, will be composed of a number of scenes, some short, others longer. Scene in this sense is very important in the analysis of a play for production. When two congenial individuals are together, they create a psychological atmosphere in which they converse and act. Introduce a third uncongenial person into this group and the whole complex of atmosphere, attitude, and feeling changes. This is subtly true of the alteration of any combination of characters on the stage; hence scene in the French sense is a mechanical division of drama of great importance to actors and directors. Actually it is more than a mechanical division since it determines to some extent what goes on within people and therefore affects the structure. The number of characters within a scene affects the composition of the stage picture and the stage business. Scene in this sense likewise involves the problem of entrances and exits.

There is one final point that may be discussed in connection with mechanical parts, although it is not really a mechanical part. That is the endings of plays. The ending of a play must satisfy audience interests. This is accomplished in a number of ways by the playwright. When a series of complications work themselves out to a complete conclusion, a satisfying ending results. When a series of antecedents and consequences result in a final consequence, say the death of the protagonist as in *Hamlet,* there is completion and in that sense a satisfaction of interest. It has become clear that a play raises a major question, which may grow and change. When that question is finally answered, there is satisfaction of interest. Of course certain plays, and especially didactic plays, may end upon a question. To an extent *A Doll's House* ends in this way. So do a number of Pirandello's plays. The action with which *A Doll's House* is concerned, the awakening of Nora, is, however, completed. The question at the end serves Ibsen's purpose in that he is hoping the audience will ask themselves about the future status of women as self-determining individuals. In the same way Pirandello's purpose is to raise certain questions about the nature of reality, about what human personality really is, and his purpose is best accomplished by leaving the question up to the audience. The immediate action of such plays as *Right You Are If You Think You Are* and *Six Characters in Search of an Author* is so arranged and organized as to lead to a big question. They are so arranged as to lead to a kind of enigma at the end. It is this enigma that Pirandello wishes to leave with the audience. While drama must solve its dramatic problems, it need not resolve all philosophical problems. In a drama of thought designed to raise questions or issues the "and-they-lived-happily-ever-after" conclusion is not always the best resolution.

QUESTIONS AND EXERCISES

1. Because of the relative simplicity of structure and meaning the young student of directing will do well to begin his training in the analysis of drama with the one-act play; but he should not neglect, at the same time, the reading and study of longer plays. Eugene O'Neill's one-act play, *Ile,* because it is a well-built serious play, and James Barrie's one-act play, *The Twelve-Pound Look,* because it is an equally well-built comic play, will repay study and analysis and serve as excellent beginning models. Taking *Ile* first, after very careful reading and study, try to state the "spire of meaning" or the "soul" of the play. What was O'Neill trying to put over to an audience? What are the main ideas in the play? How are these ideas related in terms of the controlling, or over-all, tragic conception?
2. The above questions cannot, of course, be completely answered until a thorough analysis of the play has been made. To begin that analysis, note that the play is composed of two major complications: the mutiny of the sailors; and the mutiny of Mrs. Keeney, though quite a different mutiny is the latter. What is the initiation, or beginning, of the first complication? Where does its crisis come? Where is its resolution? Where does the so-called mutiny of Mrs. Keeney begin? Where is its crisis? Where is its ending? Note that the mutiny of the sailors produces outer or external conflicts; whereas the mutiny of Mrs. Keeney, though presented

in outer conflict between the Captain and his wife, is largely concerned with inner conflict, especially the inner conflict of the Captain. With this understanding of the two separate complications well established, examine and make note of the various ways in which the two are woven together to make a unity of the play.

3. Now turn back to the beginning of the play and note each moment of emotional expression in it. Which of these are truly climactic within themselves? How is the climax built? Which moments of climactic emotion are built primarily by means of spectacle? Examine the ways in which the climaxes themselves are built throughout the play in an ascending or climactic order.
4. Examine the scenes of argument between two or more characters. Trace the course of each argument in order to reveal the deliberation of each character—wherever deliberation appears. Which of these lead clearly to decisions? What is the relation of each decision to the action (and to the meaning) of the play? What does each decision reveal about the character or characters making that decision?
5. What devices are used to make probable the revolt of the sailors? What devices are used to make probable Captain Keeney's decision to grant his wife's plea to go home? What devices are used to make probable his reversal of that decision?
6. Turn to the first scene (the opening scene of the Steward alone on the stage) and list each question that may be raised in the minds of an audience watching the scene. Where, later in the play, is each of these questions answered? In similar manner list each question raised in the second scene between Ben the Cabin Boy and the Steward. Where, later in the play, is each of these answered? Each of these represents a discovery. List all of the other important discoveries in the play.
7. State the major question of the play in the first form in which it appears. Where does it first appear? State the major question in its full form and full implication for the play as a whole.
8. Note each instance of reversal in the play. Is there a major plot reversal in the full sense?
9. How does the opening of the play tell the audience that this is a serious action?
10. Turning now to the characters, what device does O'Neill employ to characterize the Steward? Note the contrast between the Steward and Ben. What other examples of character contrast are specifically utilized in the play? How is the Captain characterized? In what respects is he heroic or "noble"? How is Mrs. Keeney char-

acterized? Whose play is it, that is, who is the protagonist? Would it make any difference in the effect and meaning of the play if you interpreted it as Mrs. Keeney's tragedy rather than that of the Captain?

11. Note the emotional relationships of the characters. Especially note the kinship (the emotional tying together) of the Captain and Mrs. Keeney. Suppose that Mrs. Keeney were not the Captain's wife and that he did not love her, what difference would it make to the play as a whole? Note, too, the kinship between the Captain and the Second Mate, especially the difference between that kinship and the kinship existing between the Captain and his wife. Are the sailors antipathetic characters? What is the effectiveness of dressing those who accompany Joe the Harpooner alike?
12. What difference would it make in the effect and meaning of the play if the Steward were played as an outright comic figure?
13. Note how certain of the lines of dialogue are so phrased as to raise questions (e.g. Ben's ". . . before she got like she is"). Note the inarticulateness of the Captain. What effect has this inarticulateness in characterizing him? Contrast the diction of the Captain with that of his wife. Pick out those lines which you consider most effectively expressive. Try to deliver them with different intonations, different music. Note the difference made in their effectiveness by different vocal renderings.
14. After this analysis, make a ground (or floor) plan of the setting for the staging of the play on the stage on which you work (see directions for floor plans in the next Chapter and in Part III).
15. State as clearly as you can the style of *Ile.*
16. Prepare a full statement of the director's approach to or interpretation of this play.
17. After a careful reading of *The Twelve-Pound Look,* state the central comic meaning of the play. For Barrie what is the "spire of meaning" or the "soul" of his play? Certain other of the above questions should likewise be applied to the analysis of this play.
18. Ordinarily a wife's leaving her husband and breaking up a home are not comic matters. How does Barrie keep them comic in this play? Note, in answering this question, the lack of emotional involvement between characters. Comedy, unlike tragedy, does not require the kinship of the central characters.
19. What are the major plot complications in this play? How are they tied together?
20. What are the chief discoveries (questions asked and answered)?
21. Is there a major plot reversal? If so, where does it come?

22. What are the ludicrous or ridiculous aspects of each of the comic characters in the play? Is anyone of these "cured" of ridiculousness by the end of the play? Which?
23. Is there a normative character?
24. With these matters determined, state what Barrie is satirizing.
25. Turn now to the superb opening scene and note by what devices it is made funny. What questions are raised in this scene?
26. What structural purpose does the scene between Kate and Lady Sims serve? Why is it placed here before the meeting between Kate and Sims? What relation does it bear to the ending?
27. Where is the crisis of the play? Note the effective relation of crisis and resolution or conclusion in this play.
28. What major devices are employed to keep the action moving forward in this play? Do you note any difference between these and the devices of plot progression in *Ile?*
29. What devices of complication are employed throughout the play and within each of the scenes?
30. Note the ways in which line after line of the dialogue in this play are made funny within themselves. The dialogue itself is comic in conformity to the form of the whole play. Note, too, the way in which Barrie gives his comic lines their "sting in the tail," as it were, making them effective for delivery upon the stage and the raising of audience laughter.
31. Choose several of the most amusing speeches from the scene between Kate and Harry Sims and note the ways in which intonation contributes to or kills the comic effectiveness of these lines.
32. Follow for this play the instructions given above in Questions 14, 15, and 16.
33. Prepare a procedure for the analysis of Ibsen's *A Doll's House.* This full-length play is more complex and of greater magnitude than is either of the two one-act plays examined above. To aid you in preparing your procedure, consult the analysis of *A Doll's House* contained in Kenneth Thorpe Rowe's *Write That Play.*
34. After your plan of procedure has been approved, study and make a complete analysis of *A Doll's House.*

PART II

THE DIRECTOR AND DIRECTING

By HUBERT C. HEFFNER

CHAPTER 3

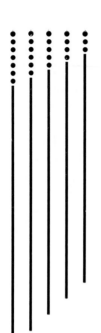

The Director as Organizer and Manager

The variety of theatres operating in the United States is such that some differentiation needs to be made before attempting a discussion of the director in the theatre. At the apex of the American theatre structure there is the commercial or Broadway theatre, which, at its best, ranks among the leading theatres of the world. It is, unfortunately, very restricted geographically and hence available to only a very small percentage of American citizens. In that theatre, though a few producing organizations such as the Playwrights' Company and the Theatre Guild continue from year to year, the producing organization assembled for each play lasts only for the life of that play at most. Actually when the play opens some of the artists—scene designer, costumer, and director in some instances—have completed their associations with the production. In this theatre the production of each separate play is an entity in itself, separately financed and separately incorporated. For a production of each play a new staff and a new cast of actors are assembled. When the play finishes its run or when it fails, the whole organization, including the actors, is disbanded. The settings, costumes, properties, lighting equipment assembled for the production are disposed of. There is neither accumulated equipment nor accumulated group productional experience in our commercial theatre. In this theatre the director is hired to direct and mount a single play. In some instances the producer may hire the director merely to direct the actors, with little voice in the mounting of the play beyond the actual physical requirements of the action.

Another category of theatre in New York City, whose development has accelerated greatly since the close of World War II, is the so-called Off-Broadway theatre. These are located in remade cinema houses, in the recreation rooms of churches, in lofts, in basements, wherever a room may be found that will accommodate some kind of stage and an audience of varying numbers up to 190. Fire laws and union regulations become more stringent when the seating capacity is above 190; thus the Phoenix Theatre, located at Second Avenue and Twelfth Street and organized by Norris Houghton and T. Edward Hambleton, is comparable in seating capacity to the regular Broadway theatres and must therefore observe the stringent fire code and operate in strict accordance with Equity practices. The unions have made substantial concessions to the little theatres in this group. In the season of 1955–56, if appearances of foreign artists and companies are eliminated, the Off-Broadway theatres mounted more productions than did Broadway. By 1959 there were over a score of these theatres in operation. Some of the best known include Circle-in-the-Square, which takes its name from its modified arena staging and its location at Sheridan Square; Theatre de Lys, on Christopher Street, first organized by William de Lys from Denver in the made over Hudson Movie Theatre; Fourth Street Theatre, organized by David Ross on Fourth Street; the Cherry Lane Theatre in the Village, in which Noel Belm and Robert Kimlot are the moving spirits. Yet another well-known group that has played in different theatres is the Shakespearewrights. The Greenwich Mews Theatre is located in the basement of the Village Presbyterian Church and Brotherhood Synagogue located on West Thirteenth Street; while the Rooftop Theatre is on the top of St. Marks Palace, a building located on Houston Street which rents rooms for public meetings. The various operators of these theatres have formed the Off-Broadway Producers Organization. Their administrative organization varies widely. Some, such as The Phoenix and others, have continued operations for a number of years, while many that spring up each year are unable to survive for a single season. The main incentive in their development is the high cost of production in the commercial Broadway theatre and the resultant high admission prices. The production costs of an average play on Broadway run around $100,000; whereas the Off-Broadway theatre seldom allows a total production budget to run as high as $10,000 or $12,000. Most of their production budgets are well under these figures. In other respects the production operations are sufficiently similar to those of the Broadway theatre that additional explanations may be omitted.

Another type of American theatre, not so numerous now as formerly, is the road show or touring company. After the transcontinental development of the railroads, following the Civil War, the touring company rapidly replaced the old local stock company. From approximately 1890 to the Great Depression in 1929 the touring company reached into every important town and city in America. During the Depression in the 1930s, this type of theatre declined rapidly and is today no more than a skeleton of its former self. Yet most American cities are dependent for professional commercial theatre upon the relatively few shows that go on the road. Most road shows stem from Broadway, though occasionally, especially on the West Coast, a touring show will come out of Hollywood. The organization of the touring show differs radically from that of the Broadway theatre. Usually these shows represent successful Broadway productions sent on the road after their close or, in certain instances, during their Broadway runs. In the latter case, a new cast must be recruited, along with a skeleton production and managerial group. The show is booked through a central booking agent for one or more performances in the cities in which it is to appear prior to its departure from New York. Stage and house crews are furnished by the local theatre manager on a contract arrangement with the agency or business manager of the touring company. Since the road show does not represent a producing organization doing new shows, it need not further concern us here.

Yet another important type of theatre is the summer theatre or summer stock. Though the first theatre of this type seems to have originated in Denver, Colorado, the summer theatre had its first important development in New England and to some extent in Pennsylvania. Now summer theatres are to be found in every state of the Union. Originally the summer theatre was a stock repertory theatre, often located in a renovated barn, church, town hall, or any other suitable building. Many successful summer theatres operate in tents. The company organization was much like that of the community theatre, though designed to operate for the summer months only. It differed from most community theatres in that from its early days it sought apprentices and students. In fact, originally it was thought of as something of a tryout theatre for plays and artists. Numerous summer theatres also operated schools in conjunction with their production programs. Originally the whole repertory of plays was performed by the resident company but as the summer theatre grew more and more attractive, visiting stars from Broadway and Hollywood were brought in to enhance audience appeal. After World War II, the booking of "package shows," a complete or largely complete company with a play ready to perform, developed so rapidly that today many summer theatres are mere booking houses for such touring shows. Under these circumstances, the summer theatres have to a considerable extent lost their former value as tryout theatres. A somewhat different type of summer theatre is the festival theatre, such as the Oregon Shakespeare Festival, the American Shakespeare Festival of Stratford, Connecticut, the Festival Theatre of Stratford, Ontario, Canada, and the outdoors pageant dramas, such as *The Lost Colony* on Roanoke Island and *Unto These Hills* in western North Carolina. These are complete organizations operating through the summer months. Many of them draw heavily upon the academic theatre for their artists and technicians.

In the other two major types of American theatres are found relatively permanent organizations devoted to continous operation. In the community theatre the director has important duties other than the direction of plays. In the academic theatre he is a member of a faculty engaged in teaching drama or literature courses as well as in directing plays. In this theatre it almost never happens that a young man or woman is hired merely in terms of his competence as a director. The young person hired directly after the completion of his academic training is seldom given immediately extensive opportunities to direct unless he accepts a position in a small institution. In the larger institutions and community theatres he is fortunate if he gets an opportunity to direct one or at most two productions in a year. In such larger establishments he often must first prove himself and his abilities in the direction of "studio or experimental productions" before he is allowed to direct a major production. One of the most important assets of the young person seeking a position in an academic or community theatre is a thorough command of the arts and techniques of stage production. Designer-technicians are seemingly always in demand and such an equipment is an invaluable asset to a potential director. Further clarification of the position of the director in these theatres and the kinds of qualifications he should have may be presented through an examination of the duties of such directors.

1. DUTIES OF THE DIRECTOR

In the academic and community theatres the director, in addition to directing the plays produced, usually also assumes many of the responsibilities which are undertaken by the producer in the Broadway theatre. The exact duties and responsibilities will vary from one organization to another. As was noted above, the academic theatre director will usually have a program of teaching in addition to his directing; the community theatre director will have community responsibilities not shared by the academic theatre director. A large community theatre, such as The Pasadena Playhouse or the Cleveland Playhouse, and large departments in major universities will have several directors on their staffs. In such institutions the *Director* of the whole theatre may be primarily an executive who seldom or never has time to stage plays. The word *director* thus appears in a dual sense, corresponding to the two-fold obligation of directors in academic and community theatres. These duties may be stated as follows:

1. The director's duties in the selecting, casting, rehearsing, and presenting of a play or program of plays.
2. The director's duties as the organizer, manager, promoter, business agent, press agent, and chief representative of an academic unit or community enterprise.

Though Part I of this book is primarily concerned with the first category of duties listed above, the second category cannot be dismissed as unimportant. A frequent complaint heard from experienced community theatre directors is that the young people whom they hire from colleges and universities, though often well equipped in stage arts, really know nothing about organization and management. These directors have often called for course instruction in this area.

Frequently a high school or small college will hire a young person as the "Director of Dramatics" and in some instances he is the only member of the faculty with training in theatre arts. All of the duties of directing and staging plays, as well as the full duties of organization and management, will fall upon his shoulders. The success with which he accomplishes the second category of duties will tell as much in the making of his reputation as will his effectiveness in the first.

In yet another situation community groups frequently hire a director to stage a single show for them. If it is successful and if the group continues to succeed, it will soon be looking to a more permanent organization and for a full-time director. When this happens, there is a new and potentially splendid opportunity for some energetic man or woman with training and vision. Such an individual will have to be mature enough and ready to assume some degree of community leadership. He may have to guide the building of a community institution from its infancy. Some of the things which he will assuredly have to do will include the wise and judicious promotion of the community theatre; the selection of plays which will satisfy community interests and receive community approval; the selection of casts for these plays from eager volunteers (always a delicate undertaking); the careful business management of the organization; the preparation of news stories and press releases; the development of a backstage producing organization; the establishment of morale in the supporters of the theatre and among its participants; and many other tasks, varying from community to community. In some or all of these he may have the aid of trained staff members eventually and he should certainly seek from the beginning to enlist competent local individuals and committees. In the initial years the chief burden will fall upon him. In either the community or the academic situation he will find ample scope for any qualities of leadership which he may possess. He will require tact, diplomacy, and organizing ability.

2. ORGANIZATION AND MANAGEMENT

Certain artists—poets, painters, sculptors, some musicians—may create their arts in complete independence of other persons. Other arts, and especially theatre, are group arts which require the organization of a number of individuals into a cohesive group for their rendering. Organization, therefore, is not merely important to the theatre and theatre artists, it is absolutely essential if theatre is to operate at all. Organization and co-operation are basic necessities without which there can be no theatre and no theatre production. The competent, efficient director must be an organizer. However difficult organization and advanced planning may be for him initially, he must become proficient in both if he is to succeed. The director may be concerned in two different types of organization and planning:

1. The organization of the theatre as a whole and the general and business management of its affairs.
2. The organization of the production staff and the management of a show through its production and performances.

The first type has to do with the setup of the theatre as an institution and may be briefly discussed first.

The organization of any theatre as an institution will depend upon its function, its location, and its history or development. A community theatre with its own specific purposes and situation will differ from an academic theatre located in a college or university and serving needs which a community theatre may never have to consider. The primary objective of an academic theatre is the training and education of students. The major aim of the community theatre is the recreation and entertainment of the citizens of the community which supports it. No two academic theatres and no two community theatres will conceive of their objectives in exactly the same way nor have the same kind of locale in which to operate. An equally strong shaping force in the form of the theatre organization is the way in which it originated and the changes that have occurred to it in its development. Though the patterns differ, some of their general aspects or characteristics may be specified.

In the college or university the producing organization is often either a dramatic society or a department. When the staging of plays is largely an extracurricular activity, the producing organization is usually a student society or continuing group. When the productions are closely co-ordinated with instruction, the producing organization is usually a department. In some instances the instruction and the accompanying theatre activities are carried on within a department of English, with a member of the faculty of that department having the title of director of dramatics. In other institutions the program is ogranized into a separate department or school; while in yet others it is associated with courses in speech.

Some departments set up producing organizations within the department with the members of the faculty engaged in theatre work forming the governing committee. In others in which the chairman or head of the department is himself a theatre man he serves as the governor or co-ordinator and is essentially the producer, acting, of course, for the department. Usually he calls upon other members of the faculty to participate in decisions, though he may reserve the final decision about finances, selection of plays, and assignment of functions and positions. A young man or woman coming into an academic theatre should learn as quickly as possible the organization and operation of the theatre which he is joining. His objective should be to fit himself into an existing organization and to learn an established procedure. Until he has accomplished that and has established himself, he will merely injure his career by attempting to reorganize an established group and institute new procedures.

In the academic theatre with large staffs men are usually hired in terms of their competence for specific tasks. Their tasks in the production organization are frequently correlated with their teaching assignments. The expert in stage lighting or stage costume teaches the courses offered in those areas and is responsible for the lighting or costuming of the plays produced. His mission is to train students in his specialty both through instruction in classes and through practical experience. The abilities and maturity of the student will determine the degree of responsibility which he is given in a stage production. Thus in the academic theatre, faculty and students work closely together. In the small college or the high school where there may be only a single trained member of the faculty, the more experienced students will have to be organized into a production staff. If there is not already a well-organized dramatic society, they will also have to be utilized in positions of organizational responsibility. The duties which they may have to perform will become clearer in the following discussion of community theatre organization.

A community theatre sufficiently well-established to employ a full-time director usually operates under a governing board. In some theatres this board is called a Board of Directors; in others it is called an Executive Committee. Often it is elected by the members of the community theatre. However selected, it is the major policy making body. It has the responsibility of selecting and hiring the director, who may or may not be a member of the board. He may be given authority by the board to hire any other authorized staff assistants, though often these are hired by the board upon the recommendation of the director.

This board, however designated, chosen, and constituted, is responsible for the whole theatre as a continuing institution. If the organization owns its own theatre and equipment, the board is responsible for it and its upkeep, though they may delegate this authority to a superintendent, the director, or to a special committee. It is responsible for the finances, though again it may delegate this function to an individual or a committee. The board has the obligation to appoint or approve all committees. It is concerned with the welfare of the theatre in the community, its good reputation, and its service to the community. The types and quality of the shows produced are definitely its concern. If the board consists of a large membership, it may wisely delegate its executive function to a subcommittee or to an individual. In most community theatres it carries on its duties through other committees whose membership the board selects or approves. The governing board should be a support to and a safeguard of the director. The successful community theatre director is one who has learned how to work in harmony with a governing board. Often the board delegates to an experienced director large responsibilities, including selection of members of certain committees. In some of our community theatres the director is in the happy position of being the foremost leader in the community theatre.

The committees and their duties found in most American community theatres will become clear from a listing of these. Those committees are:

1. A house committee responsible for the box office and the front of the house.
2. A play-reading committee responsible for recommending plays for production.
3. A casting committee responsible for aiding the director in the selection of casts.
4. A publicity committee responsible for publicizing the theatre and the shows.

When the financial operations are extensive and complex, to these four may be added, as has been said, a finance committee. The preparation of the program, especially when local advertising is included, is often entrusted to a member or members of the publicity committee. This task becomes a heavy burden upon a director if extensive advertising must be solicited. In certain theatres in which season tickets are sold a special committee is set up for this. There are community theatres in the United States whose operations are so large and complex that their committee structure is far more extensive and complicated than is here indicated. These committees, however, are the ones which function in most theatre organizations operated on the committee principle. The student of directing should acquaint himself as fully as possible with theatre organization, operation, and problems of management.

3. ORGANIZATION FOR PRODUCTION

Just as the success of a theatre as an institution depends upon effective organization, so does successful production likewise require adequate organization. In order to prepare a play for presentation before an audience, a director is going to have to call upon the following artists and technicians to assist him:

1. One who can design the settings (and perhaps also the costumes) for the play.
2. One who can costume the play (perhaps including the designing and construction).
3. One who can plan the lighting effects, install the implements, and manipulate these during dress rehearsals and performances.
4. One who can secure or build the necessary furniture and other properties for the play.
5. One who can do the make-up for the actors (if they cannot do their own and if the costumer cannot undertake this).

6. One who can supervise the technical construction and painting of settings and properties, can aid in planning the efficient shifting of these, and supervise the stage management during the performances (tasks sometimes combined with those of scene designer).

In addition to these individuals, the following crews will have to be recruited and organized, either by the director or the technical director (mentioned in No. 6 above):

1. A construction crew for scenery and properties.
2. A paint crew for scenery and properties.
3. A stage crew for the shifting of scenery and properties during performances and dress rehearsals.
4. A lighting crew to handle the lighting and the sound.
5. A costume construction crew (if costumes are made).
6. A costume crew for changes before and during performances.
7. A make-up crew (often a part of the costume crew).

These crews will vary in accordance with the demands of the show. Insofar as they are necessary, experienced individuals will have to be secured to serve as crew heads. If there is no technical director or designer-technical director on the staff to co-ordinate their work, then perforce the director will have to do it. Any number of directors have at the outset of their careers in small institutions served as designer-technician, costumer, property man, make-up artist, and technical director; worked on the construction and painting of scenery and the building or securing of costumes and properties, in addition to directing the show. Such an exacting undertaking is by no means desirable. When a director finds himself in such a position, he must seek volunteer assistance from students or from citizens of the community. In so doing, his powers as a leader and organizer come into play and his success may well depend upon the extent to which he possesses such powers. Here, again, it becomes clear that training in all of the arts of theatre is of great importance to a director. Some of the problems which the director must solve in the planning and co-ordination of the work of these various individuals will be considered in the chapter on designing the production. Here some further clarification of the duties of each individual will serve further to clarify problems of organization.

Sometimes in the Broadway theatre a designer creates the designs for the whole show, including scenery, lighting, and costumes. The scenery is then built and painted by a commercial firm and the costumes are made by an expert of known reputation. Often, too, in the academic and community theatre one individual likewise designs the whole show and with the help of volunteers supervises its construction. In many academic theatres one individual is responsible for the designing of the scenery or the scenery and the lighting, while another is in charge of costume design and construction. In these theatres, moreover, there are usually trained or partly-trained students who can serve on the essential crews, thereby gaining additional experience in their theatre training. Assuming that there are separate individuals for each function, the duties of the scene designer are to provide adequate sketches, models, and working drawings of the settings of the play for their construction and painting. If the scene designer is not himself supervising the construction and painting, a mere sketch of the separate sets will not suffice. The designer will need then to provide sketches and elevation either in color or with a color chart, and adequate construction blueprints to show all except the usual details of construction. This task will obviously require prior conferences with the director and with other members of the production staff.

In academic and community theatres which possess a stock of flats and other pieces of scenery, the director must be familiar with these and determine which may be utilized. This is done through consultation with the technical director. In planning the color of his sets he must know how they may be lighted; hence he must confer with the man in charge of lighting. Sets and costumes must not clash and kill each other; hence the scene designer must confer with the person in charge of the costumes. The responsibility for initiating these conferences between members of the production staff falls usually upon the director. Until he decides certain questions about the kind of production he plans to give to the play, the members of the production staff obviously cannot begin work. The work of the production staff must be initiated well in advance of tryouts and rehearsals; hence the necessity on the part of the director for advanced study and analysis of the play.

The duty of the costumer is to provide the necessary clothes and accessories for the actors. When it is a contemporary play in modern dress that is being staged, these can often be provided from the wardrobes of the actors or borrowed. In many cities dress shops have lent articles of clothing for the production in return for proper acknowledgment on the program. Such borrowings are at best difficult and sometimes risky. The period play must be costumed either through rental or construction. When the dress is to be constructed, the costumer should supply costume sketches for each of the major roles and an indication of the kinds of dress worn by the minor characters. An adequate costume sketch will show the lines and flow of the garment, as well as its color. Color often has to be a matter of compromise in terms of material available. Many costumers prefer to use neutral materials of the right weight and texture and resort to dyeing for the appropriate colors. Such a task takes advanced planning, time, and work, requiring considerable assistance from seamstresses and costume crew members. A good costumer in the academic and community theatres really has to be a tailor as well as a designer.

The duties of the individual in charge of lighting the show may not be quite as exacting as those of the costumer but they are equally essential. His first task in conference with the scene designer and the costumer, after the director has outlined the production, is to plan the lighting for each scene. He cannot do this in any detail until he knows the business of the play. He must be prepared to make alterations in his detailed plans in the technical and dress rehearsals. If he does not plan in advance, however, he will not be able to install the lighting equipment, angle, and focus it, until the last minute.

In some theatres the man in charge of stage lighting has also the duties of the technical director, though the position may not always be so designated. The person who assumes these duties, whether he is called technical director or by some other title, must co-ordinate and supervise all aspects of technical production in the mounting of plays. With or without salaried assistants, he is responsible for the supervision of the shop work in the building and painting of scenery and properties; for the rigging of the stage; for the making of schedules to guide the preparation and completions of elements of production; for the supervision of the technical-production rehearsals, and for the backstage running of the show during dress rehearsals and performances. In many instances he delegates this last-named duty to a stage manager, working under his direction and supervision.

The following individuals constitute the production staff:

1. Scene designer
2. Costumer
3. Stage lighting artist
4. Technical director

Whether one or more of these offices are combined, the individuals holding them constitute the director's production staff and are ultimately responsible to him. If there are three or four individuals on this staff and if one of these is a competent technical director, the director will do well to establish the technical director's authority over the production procedures. The wise director will conceive of the whole production as a joint undertaking and will encourage each of these staff members to make his full contribution to the planning and development of the show. If questions arise that concern the manner of production, the director as co-ordinator of the whole undertaking and as interpreter of the play must have the final authority. Obviously, in order that the members of his production staff may work intelligently and efficiently, the director must convey to them as fully as possible the manner and style of the projected show. For this purpose he will need to hold a series of conferences and discussions. These should be held as early as is practicable, though the time of their scheduling will depend upon the general program of the theatre.

In order to do creative thinking about a forthcoming production, the members of the production staff must be relatively free of those arduous and time-consuming duties which occupy them fully when construction work begins. In the academic theatre and in some community theatres where plays are chosen in advance for a whole season, and especially where there are several directors involved, there is no reason why preliminary production discussions should not be held months in advance of the casting of a play. These preliminary conferences will vary in accordance with the play to be produced but will include, among other items, the following:

1. The director's interpretation of the play and the style which he conceives will best project that interpretation to the audience.
2. The settings of the play, including the number, how each may be designed to conform to the style of the production, scenery available, scenery to be built, costs.
3. The costumes for each character in the play, including much the same series of items mentioned above under scenery.

4. The lighting of the various scenes in the play and how the lighting may most effectively contribute to the interpretation chosen.
5. Sound or other unusual effects needed.
6. The production budget.
7. The production schedule, including the schedule for scene and costume construction, for scene painting, for securing and/or building properties, and other details in the preparation of the mounting of the play.
8. The rehearsal schedule, especially the time of the technical and dress rehearsals.

These items need not necessarily be considered in the order given. The rehearsal schedule, for example, must be kept in mind from the initial planning of the production. Other items, such as budget, may also be fixed by authority above that of the director and his staff.

When the conferences have gone far enough to establish the basic pattern of interpretation, the designers can then go to work. Frequently the director and the designer or designers have prepared a series of preliminary discussions so that he or they may come to the first full conference with sketches of settings and costumes. Some directors prefer to work with each staff member in turn on an individual basis. The obvious disadvantages of the director working in this manner is that it takes much more time, robs the production of the group contribution in its early stages of conception and planning, and does not enhance group morale. Nevertheless, many excellent shows have been done on this man-to-man basis.

As soon as the conferences have progressed far enough, the various staff members then confer, in turn, with the crew head or heads working directly under them. Each designer or staff member passes on to the crew heads information about the construction of scenery, the painting, the construction of costumes, the assembling and/or making of properties, and such other instructions as they will need to work effectively. With the crew heads the staff member plans a schedule of work related to the crew members available and in terms of the time of the first technical rehearsal. Often in the community theatre his first major task will be the securing of enough assistants to make a crew. Frequently the designer-technician must himself undertake all of the production tasks with only one or a very few reliable helpers. Such a contingency must be foreseen and the planning in the production conferences must be done in terms of it. Obviously the kind of conferences that have been discussed cannot be undertaken until the director himself has completely worked out his stage interpretation of the play—as far as it can be worked out prior to casting and rehearsals. Moreover, the other staff members must know the play thoroughly if they are to make contributions to the production discussions.

4. THE FRONT OF THE HOUSE

In many theatres the director has yet another problem of organization and management, that of the "front of the house." The "front of the house" refers to the whole process of the theatre's contact with the public in the selling of tickets, admitting the audience to the theatre, seating the audience, and looking after their comfort and safety. If the theatre is well established and large enough to afford a business manager on its staff, these duties will fall to him. Frequently in the academic theatre an advanced and responsible student is intrusted with this position or with the position of house manager. In some community theatres the board or the director sets up a committee to take charge of these.

The duties of this committee or the individual in charge may include manning the box office, providing adequate ticket takers for each entrance to the theatre and for each night of performance, assigning ushers to seat the audience and give them programs, assuming responsibility for the opening in proper time of the auditorium of the theatre, seeing that the temperature of the building is comfortable at the opening and through the performances, checking on fire control and fire regulations, and handling the audience during intermissions. Simple as these duties may appear, they are of considerable importance in establishing and maintaining the right audience attitude. A surly box office attendant or a thoughtless or discourteous usher may partially spoil the pleasure of theatre-going and help to drive individuals away from academic and community theatres, as they undoubtedly have in the professional commercial theatre.

In the academic and community theatres these positions are filled by students and volunteers. Usually they change each night because the students and volunteers cannot afford to give more time to these tasks. Their services are, because of that condition, going to be at best indifferently performed unless the house manager works out in advance a precise plan of operation in each position, calls his assistants together before the appearance of the audience, and carefully instructs them in their duties. They should be made aware of the importance of these duties and told that they have a considerable part in the success of the show through their contributions to the enjoyment of the audience. Neatness in appearance, courtesy in manner, and strict attention to duty must be stressed. Here, as in all other departments of theatre work, morale is of greatest importance. The capable house manager can build such a morale.

In addition to knowing how to organize his staff of assistants, train them, win their enthusiastic participation, and quickly instruct each in his duties, the house manager must be aware of certain other matters that make for the comfort of the audience and the smooth running of the show. He must insist that the performance begin as nearly on the time advertised as is possible but he must not let the stage manager ring up the curtain until the audience is in the house. Nothing is so annoying to an audience as to have the first part of a play ruined by the attempts to seat late-comers in the dark. Stragglers will always pose a problem and there is actually no entirely satisfactory way to deal with them. In small theatres they can become such a nuisance to the bulk of the audience that the theatre has to adopt and advertise a policy of admissions only at scene or act breaks. For a popular play with a considerable last-minute rush of patrons it may, therefore, be necessary to hold the curtain as much as ten minutes beyond curtain time. Such delays unfortunately condition audiences to expect them. A wait of as much as ten minutes will seem excessive to the prompt members of the audience unless there is some kind of satisfactory "prologue music."

Well-chosen music of this kind, "canned" or live, can be an asset to the play. In community theatres where talented musicians are available, it can also be a device for tying these gifted people into the organization. When they are used, they should be recognized on the program. Another problem which the house manager must anticipate, especially during the winter months, is that of wraps, overcoats, overshoes, and umbrellas. If there is a checkroom, it must be manned for a rapid handling of patrons.

The temperature of the auditorium poses another problem. The house manager must see that the auditorium is properly warmed in cold weather and properly cooled in warm. He must remember that a large audience in a room will raise the temperature within an hour or less by many degrees; therefore he must keep a constant check. He is responsible, also, for seeing that the house lights are neither too bright nor too dim at the beginning and during intermissions. It is his duty to see that smoking and fire regulations are carefully observed. Finally, he must agree with the stage manager about signals for the starting of the play and the termination of intermissions. Some means of giving the audience ample warning of the ending of an intermission must be provided so that they can return to their seats before the house lights are dimmed. No two theatres pose exactly the same problems in house management and the duties here outlined must be adapted to special conditions.

This summary outline of theatre organization and management will suffice amply to demonstrate the statement that the director must be an organizer and a manager. The duties here outlined by no means exhaust his functions in organization and management. He will have to employ these in a variety of additional ways but especially in the arranging of procedures in the casting of plays and in the planning of rehearsals. A student of directing, in his eagerness to learn the arts of theatre and the techniques of directing, is apt to overlook the importance of acquainting himself as thoroughly as possible with management. He should seek through his reading and especially through serving on the "front-of-the-house" staff to inform himself and to gain experience in this area.

Finally, a brief word must be said about the cultural responsibilities of the director of a community or academic theatre. Thus far through these pages emphasis has been placed upon the director building up an audience for his theatre and giving the audience the kind of fare that will bring him approval and support. Obviously he must start here but every director worth his salt longs to do better and better plays. It is probable that an astute director, on whatever level he has to begin his career, can eventually satisfy that desire if he works patiently and skillfully. Audiences can be built both in numbers and quality of appreciation, but it takes time, patience, and good productions to establish them. Though the theatre is first, last, and always a place of entertainment, it need not remain a place of mere diversion of low calibre. Entertainment can descend to the level of the "strip-tease" or it can ascend to the level of high comedy and high tragedy. Some human beings can find pleasure only in the lower, baser appetites; others gain their pleasures chiefly on the level of refined taste and intellectual enjoyment. There is a wide gamut between these two. The theatre is unquestionably the home of entertainment but it is also a cultural institution devoted to revealing man to himself.

A director who consistently lowers the moral tone of a community or an institution by constantly pandering to baser taste is, no matter how financially successful he may be, a detriment to the community or the institution. Perhaps certain audiences will never respond in enthusiastic number to Shakespeare's plays or to Greek tragedy but that does not mean that they are incapable of enjoying anything more meritorious than *Abie's Irish Rose* or *Time Out for Ginger*. And what is wrong with a good production of either of these plays or others like them? The theatre which did nothing but these light farces season after season would certainly be betraying its obligations to extend and develop the potentialities and possibilities inherent in any American audience. The director as leader has an obligation toward his audience that includes the advancement of these inherent potentialities. Little by little he should extend the range of the repertory to include plays that will challenge thought and feeling.

Drama is a meaningful art; it says something. What it says may be extremely trivial or it may be most profound. Plays can be produced to challenge audiences and audiences developed to respond to such challenges. What is being said in this discussion must not be construed for an argument in favor of *avant-garde* plays over the heads of audiences or antagonistic to them. Rather, the contention is that in the whole range of drama there is a cultural heritage which it is the responsibility of directors to give to audiences and to lead them to appreciate what is rightfully theirs. Obviously, the director unacquainted with the vast range of drama is unequipped to fulfill this duty.

5. THE PROGRAM

A further concern of the director as organizer and planner is the assembling of the materials and the writing of the copy for the printed program. Though he may delegate all or a part of this task, he must see that it is completed well in advance of the first performance (at least two weeks) so that it may be sent to the printer. The content and format of programs used in academic and community theatres vary widely. Some are very simple one-sheet affairs, while others are elaborate. Each of these is so well known that nothing more than a brief summary of their content need be included. The standard theatre program may be said to consist of four sections:

1. The heading or title page;
2. The cast of characters, followed by place and time;
3. The production organization and acknowledgments;
4. Editorial comment (optional).

The heading or title page tells who, what, when, where, either in that or some other order. The "who" is the organization or producer (often with the director's name included); the "what" is the play or performance to be presented, with the author's name; the "when" is the date or dates of performance and often also the time; and the "where" is the theatre or place in which the performances occur. The title page may also include an ornament, emblem, or signet. A word of caution is necessary about the "who." If programs are to be used for later publicity and are to be mailed out of town and if the name of the producing organization is something like "The Community Players" or "The Sock and Buskin Society" without a place name, then the town or institution in which the organization is located should be included with the name. Item 2 in the above list is so obvious as to need little comment. In this section of the program should be a clear indication of intermissions. As for item 3, in the listing of the membership of the production staff, including members of all crews (some programs include also the officials of the permanent organization), the director should be certain that every member of a crew who has worked on the show is named. This credit and their enjoyment in the work are often their only rewards. Unlike the actors, they do not appear on the stage to receive the plaudits of the audiences.

Item 4, editorial comment, includes all types of program notes. In some programs these are extensive, including statements about the play and its interpretation, a brief biographical note about the author, and in some community theatre programs biographical sketches of the performers. The latter are useful in building organizational morale and developing interest in the theatre. Many directors, especially in college and university theatres, utilize program notes to inform audiences about the aims and goals of their programs and to influence the interest and appreciation of the audiences in the kinds of plays which they are presenting. The inclusion of program notes increases the expenses of the program but are justified by many theatres as a kind of public relations. They are certainly one means through which directors can encourage and even influence audience interest. In general, however, program costs should be carefully guarded and kept to a minimum.

6. FINAL PERFORMANCES

In this Chapter on organization and management may be included as a conclusion some necessary considerations about final performances. As the date for the opening performance approaches, the wise director, busy as he is with the preparation of the production, will do well to keep himself informed about the advance ticket sale, even though he may have a competent business manager to look after the details. If the sale is lagging, increased publicity may be indicated. Moreover, prior to the opening performance, the director should check with the house manager (or have his business manager check) to see that all details of the front-of-the-house organization and operation have been attended to.

In the larger organizations directors frequently turn the responsibilities for the running of the show over to the technical director or stage manager from the time of the technical and dress rehearsals (see Chapter 6, Sections 11 and 12) through final performances. Others, and especially those in the smaller organizations, find it advisable or prefer to keep a hand upon the details even through final performances. In any case, it is advisable for the director to free himself of backstage operations to the extent that he may be able to watch the opening and even subsequent performances from the auditorium. Many directors like to keep notes of errors made and opportunities missed for later conferences with the cast and with the crew, especially when there are to be subsequent performances. If the errors are numerous, it may be wise to call a brush-up rehearsal before the second performance. In the Broadway theatre out-of-town performances are usually scheduled prior to the Broadway opening for this purpose of polishing the production in terms of the actors' performances and the audience response. Extensive rewriting of the script and restaging are common practices in these out-of-town tryouts. Unfortunately, the academic and community theatres have no such opportunities even with productions of original plays. Hence, as will be noted later, they must utilize the dress rehearsals for this purpose. It is equally unfortunate that the academic and community theatres are unable usually to play a production into which has gone so much work for more than a very limited number of performances.

Because of the latter condition and because he is dealing with inexperienced actors, the director should not attempt in the academic and community theatre extensive alterations after the first performance. At most he should correct the gross errors and show the cast how to take advantage of opportunities missed. It is safe to say that with almost every cast one of his problems (discussed in subsequent chapters) will be that of projection. Another, which will occur in the performances of comedy, will be that of the actors playing into audience laughs, thereby killing the laugh and causing the audience to lose the lines. Yet another will concern missed cues on the part of the actors and also of the backstage crew. There will be others, varying from play to play and cast to cast.

In the correction of these errors, the director must be especially careful not to weaken the morale of the cast and crew. Scolding or fault-finding will do exactly that. His approach must be that of the helper and guide who is building up certainty and confidence. Elimination of errors, not condemnation of them, is the goal. Critical post-mortems, which are helpful teaching devices in the academic theatre, should be postponed until after the run of the show. In the building of morale and confidence some directors find a "pep-talk" prior to the opening performance useful; others prefer to inject their "pep-talks" into the finishing rehearsals. Whatever the method, the director will find that one of the secrets of success is the constant encouragement of actors, artists, and technicians working under his direction.

QUESTIONS AND EXERCISES

1. Make a study of the organization of your local academic theatre. Include in your written report on this organization a chart or plan of it. Be sure to include all committees that function in the organization.
2. Make a similar study of the backstage organization for production in your local or community theatre.
3. Make a list of the functions or responsibilities of the director of the local academic or community theatre which he must perform in addition to the direction of the stage productions.
4. If there is a technical director in the organization, find out as precisely as you can what his duties and responsibilities are. If there is no member of the staff who has this title, find out who performs the duties and functions of technical director and make a comprehensive list of these.
5. Examine the "front-of-the-house" organization in your theatre. How effective is it? Could it be improved? In what ways?

CHAPTER 4

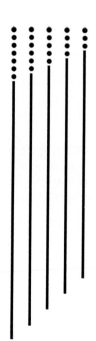

Selecting and Casting Plays

THE DIRECTOR's primary task is so to interpret the play in production that it will cause audiences in large numbers to want to see it and will entertain and please them when they do see it. But no matter how large his potential audience, how well disposed they are to the theatre, or how excellent his theatre plant, equipment, and technical assistants, unless a director can secure a good play and an excellent cast, he will fail measurably in his primary task, despite his professional qualifications. This matter of play selection and of the casting of plays is, then, of major concern to every director. It is, as has been said, another aspect of his managerial duties. In both the academic and the community theatre the director who is to direct the play should have a voice in its choice and in the cast selected for it. It becomes apparent again that the director and whatever committee he may co-operate with must be familiar with a wide number of plays, must continually read plays of the past and the present, and must know the general tastes of the community. Even before he or his committee can make a final selection of a play, they must have a good idea of the acting talent available.

1. SELECTING PLAYS

The considerations governing the choice of plays for an academic theatre differ from those in the community theatre. Usually in the academic theatre the choice of the plays is directly related to the instructional program. In both theatres the available acting talent, the nature of the theatre and its equipment, and the general tastes of the community are further considerations. In various articles, notably several that have appeared in the *Quarterly Journal of Speech,* and in innumerable talks at theatre conferences and annual conventions the American community theatres have been accused of producing largely "warmed-over Broadway hits to the exclusion of many other perhaps more worthy plays." The statistics of community theatre productions would seem to bear out this charge, nor are the academic theatres entirely immune. The matter is not quite so simple as some writers and speakers would have it appear. Two questions will make that apparent. First, what exactly is wrong with the reproduction of a Broadway hit? Secondly, what ought the community theatres to be producing instead of those Broadway hits which their audiences want to see?

Examine the repertories of theatres of any past age and you will find that their dominant offerings consisted of plays from the immediate past. Prior to about 1900 the United States had a far-flung system of local stock companies, corresponding roughly to the community theatres of today. It is true that those stock companies included in their repertories, especially prior to the Civil War, a considerable number of old plays, popular favorites from the past. But the major number of their productions consisted of plays from the metropolitan areas that had been recent successes. With the coming of the railroads and with changes in the American theatre, the road shows or touring companies replaced the local stock companies, especially after 1900. These touring companies were, for the most part, playing the recent popular plays of New York theatres to communities remote from that center of theatrical entertainment. Today the touring company has almost disappeared. If audiences in the "hinterland," as Broadway says, are to see the recent plays in performance, the community theatres and the academic theatres must largely supply them. It is a part of their duty to their audiences to do so.

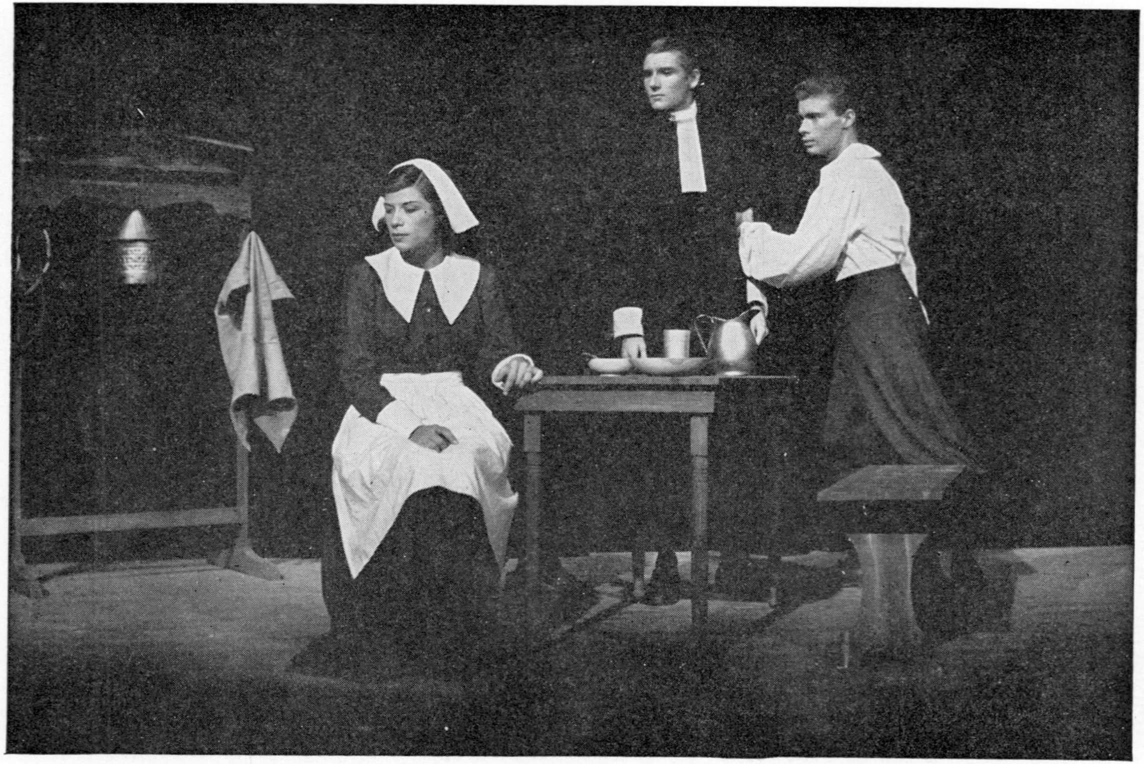

Attention compelled by the direction of eyes. Arthur Miller's *The Crucible,* at Tulane University, directed by Paul Hostetter.

Thus in this question of play selection the function of the theatre comes to the fore. What is the function of a theatre, any theatre? This subject has been debated since the days of the Greeks. It has remained an important issue since then. The function of the theatre in Soviet Russia has been strictly formulated by the Communist Party. The function of the theatre in France has been to a large extent determined by the history and cultural heritage of the nation. England has, from time to time since the Tudor period, taken official governmental cognizance of the function of the theatre and has, since World War II, established an Arts Council to aid in the formulation and encouragement of the theatre in its cultural and educational functions. In the United States there has never been any official formulation of policy with regard to theatre. The nearest approach to it thus far is contained in the Congressional Charter granted to the American National Theatre and Academy in 1935. From the early beginning each American theatre organization has formulated its own functions and policies.

Diverse and complex as these are, it is possible to state simply the general function and purpose of community theatres. That purpose is to give pleasure through theatrical entertainment to as many people as possible and thereby establish and develop the theatre as an enduring community institution. Arguments have been advanced that the mere reproduction, season after season, of popular Broadway shows does little to advance the taste of the community and to promote a better American drama; that such a schedule of production stultifies the artistic abilities of a director; and that the community theatres should be promoting American drama by presenting new plays by new playwrights and raising the cultural caliber of the theatre by presenting outstanding masterpieces, the classics, of the past. All of these worthy aims are legitimate functions of any community theatre but only if such productions can give pleasure and satisfaction to the majority of the theatre's audiences. No community theatre is under any obligation whatever to produce any play, old or new, that will not be acceptable to and enjoyed by its audiences. No theatre can survive that consistently flouts in the choice of plays the level of taste prevailing in a community. But the average or level of taste does not consistently have to be measured in terms of the lowest. Experienced directors know that they can to a considerable degree influence audience taste and thus can over the years shape the kind of audience for the types of programs which the theatre as a stable institution should be giving for its community.

The first question, then, in the process of selecting plays for production concerns the audience appeal of the play. How will it go over? That question confronts every producer in every theatre when he contemplates the presentation of any play. The full answer to the question, however astute the producer may be, is never finally given until the play is actually performed before an audience. On Broadway, where the losses are financially great if the play fails, the percentage of failures in each season for many years past has never been less than 60 per cent of the total and is usually higher. These failures result, of course, with new and hitherto unproduced plays. With the reproduction of plays already tried out no such percentage of failures need ever occur. Indeed no community theatre or academic theatre could survive a single season with so many failures. Nevertheless, in these theatres also the final verdict is never known until the production is actually on the boards before an audience. The appeal of any play varies from audience to audience, from community to community; nevertheless, what is proving popular in a number of American communities at any given time is likely to find favor in another community. The experienced production group or director will therefore try to keep up with trends in other theatres, try to keep informed on what communities are finding successful. Likewise the experienced director will take every means to know and to respond to the tastes of the community in which he is working. He will know that to persist in presenting plays that run counter to the likes and tastes of his audience is to court complete failure.

Every community has its mores, prejudices, beliefs, or accepted dogmas which the director there dares not disregard. Restrictions of this nature in some of the sectarian and smaller institutions and in some of the less fortunate communities are notorious. Even in the larger institutions and more cosmopolitan communities there are groups, sects, and opinions of which the director must be cognizant and take into account. Some sad and some amusing situations have arisen from the director's violation of local taboos and mores. An amusing one arose in a Western state university when a well-known religious sect protested the presentation some years ago of Jesse Lynch Williams' comedy, *Why Marry?*, solely on the basis of its title; and an even more amusing situation arose in a Southern community when a women's patriotic organization attempted to prevent a production of *Uncle Tom's Cabin* by a group in a state-supported institution. In both instances the attendant general controversy and newspaper publicity so excited the interest of the respective communities that both productions were completely sold out and the director was laughingly accused of instigating each of the protests. The performances were given in each of these cases because the director carefully judged his community and knew that the protesting groups represented a minority opinion. Nevertheless, such situations are fraught with danger to the theatre and must be handled with caution and diplomacy.

Restrictions and dislikes of the nature mentioned above are usually rather obvious and are easily met by the director who has the good will of his community. Without that good will, he should move to a new locality as soon as possible. A director who takes a position in an academic institution which makes its restrictions known to him is in a sense honor-bound to abide by those restrictions cheerfully and gracefully. Communities cannot so simply and easily make their restrictions known; the director himself must usually discover these. More difficult than this determination, however, is the finding out of exactly what the audience in a given community does want. This is difficult, first, because members of the audience themselves do not know what their range of dramatic interest is. The director has to deduce this range through various means. Obviously his first means is an examination of the list of plays that have previously succeeded or failed in the community, with an attempt to determine the causes. Sometimes the failures can be even more instructive than the successes, especially if poor production, conflict of other public events, and inadequate promotion can be ruled out as causes. Next, the director must turn to a careful study of the community in which he works in an effort to obtain a wide and intimate acquaintance with all aspects which will influence his program and his theatre. Attention to the local items in the newspapers, to the programs of clubs and churches, information as to the kinds of books drawn from the local library or sold in the bookstores—in short, a systematic study of the whole social activity of the community will yield many suggestions.

There is yet another aspect of this matter of selecting plays in terms of audience appeal over which the director does have considerable control. That is the question of his own interpretation of the play. Some directors can see appeal in plays which seem sure audience borers to others. Certain community theatre directors will staunchly insist that Shakespeare and Ibsen are sure death to any community enterprise; yet Angus Bowmer has steadily increased his audiences season after season since 1935 with nothing but Shakespeare at the Oregon Shakespeare Festival Theatre. At least three major community theatres have reported for a number of years that Ibsen represents one of their best box-office attractions.

An instance of the writer's own obtuseness will further illustrate the point. When he was in charge of the theatre at Biarritz American University, operated by the United States Army in France, Mordecai Gorelik, chief scene designer on the staff, approached him several times with the request that Ben Jonson's *Volpone* be presented. He confidently assured Mr. Gorelik that this play would not succeed with a G.I. audience, even though the men at Biarritz were carefully and rigorously selected. Later, when the request was repeated, *Volpone* was scheduled and, as produced by Mordecai Gorelik and Anthony Ceferatti, proved both at Biarritz and after on tour through Germany and Austria to be one of the Army's most successful productions.

Perhaps it would be safe to say that almost any really good play in the hands of a competent and discerning director, with an adequate cast and production facilities, can be made to appeal to most audiences in most theatres. When a director says, therefore, that any play that has proved widely popular with audiences elsewhere will not appeal to his particular audience, he should examine his reasons for this statement with the greatest care to see if they cannot actually be reduced to the simple statement that he does not know how so to interpret that play as to make it go over with an audience. Perhaps his reason for making such a statement is that he personally does not care for the play or the author. That is a legitimate reason for his not undertaking production of the works of that author. If, however, the author is such a major one as Ibsen or Shakespeare, it is also reason for him to examine his own taste in and understanding of drama. Like the conductor of an orchestra, the ambitious director must be constantly studying new plays for interpretation.

2. FACTORS IN CHOOSING A SEASON'S PROGRAM

Another important aspect in the selection of a play for production is its relationship to the whole season's program. Many academic theatres and some community theatres announce their entire season of productions in advance, using such publicity as a means for advertising their season subscription ticket. Such a procedure offers some obvious advantages. It allows greater opportunity for a more co-ordinated as well as a more varied program than does the show-by-show choice. It gives an opportunity for balancing the whole program so as not to overload the season with too many productions of a similar nature, allowing an easy distribution of plays in modern dress, plays in costume, plays in traditional styles, plays in so-called "experimental" styles, modern plays, and plays from the past. It allows the production staff to calculate properly their whole season of work so as not to overload any single department. Such a methodical planning of the whole program obviates last-minute hurry in the selection, which may result in the frantic acceptance of any play in order to get it into rehearsal. It allows a calculated distribution of the total anticipated budget over the whole season and a more balanced proportioning of the budget between production departments. It further makes possible a better balancing of royalty with nonroyalty plays. In organizations which employ the annual season ticket sale, this system gives the business manager or the membership committee a much better opportunity for advertising and promoting a successful campaign.

Perhaps of most importance, it makes it possible for the director and his staff to engage in a proper study of the play and long-range planning of its interpretation. Against these advantages for many organizations may be urged the following disadvantages: Such a procedure, if rigidly adhered to, may lose the theatre the advantage of most recent releases of new plays. It may prevent the director from being able to employ a new and talented actor or actress who has just appeared in the organization or community and is especially adept in certain roles.

It may not allow the immediate opportunity of responding to a change of interest in the community, though such rapid changes will seldom occur. Finally, some directors who have operated for a long time on the pick-as-you-go system do not like such long-range planning.

Yet another significant set of factors in the choice of plays for production is the type of theatre building, the stage on which they are to be presented, and the equipment available. A subtle, psychological drama, with little spectacle, can be entirely lost on a large stage in a big auditorium. Conversely, to attempt to crowd a spectacular piece with massive scenery, many changes, and crowds of supers on a small stage in a theatre seating two hundred or less is to court failure. A play that depends upon numerous and elaborate settings and a variety of lighting effects should not be selected for center-stage production. On the other hand, it is amazing to examine the large number and different kinds of plays that have been effectively adapted to center-stage production by ingenious directors. Equally amazing are the effects that a clever director and a skilled designer can produce on a small stage. Nevertheless, these factors of the physical plant and its equipment must be taken into account. Fully adequate lighting equipment will render possible the staging of some plays that cannot be undertaken with makeshift equipment. It will, for example, make possible the employment of projected scenery, widely used in Germany and Scandinavian countries but thus far not adequately employed in the American academic and community theatres.

Whatever the choice of plays, the production must be paid for; hence budget is a weighty item in the selections of a season's program. The normal costs which go into the preparation of a budget for any production include front-of-the-house costs and expenses for the production departments. In the first category must be included royalties, advertising, salaries (if any), theatre rentals and charges, the printing of programs and similar items. Some theatres, especially community theatres, cover or more than cover the cost of printing the programs by selling local advertising included therein. There are arguments for and against this practice, which is usually deemed undesirable in the academic theatre.

In addition to royalties, advertising, and programs, other costs, such as the hiring of box-office attendants, staff salaries for any other members, fixed interest on bond charges or mortgages on the theatre, may have to be included. Whether or not these latter charges are included in the budget of each production will depend upon the system of accounting established for each theatre. Certainly the first three items must be included.

In the second category of production costs will come the total cost for scenery construction, scene painting, costume construction, stage lighting, sound effects, properties, and make-up. Once a theatre has acquired a stock of units of scenery and adequate lighting equipment, these costs will be very reasonable. Upkeep and replacement in each department must not be overlooked however. Since each of these production items is fully discussed in later chapters of this book, additional comment is unnecessary here. The point here is that production costs are an important consideration in the choice of plays.

Perhaps, however, since the matter is not discussed later, a few remarks upon the question of royalties may not be amiss. No self-respecting director will or can afford to make himself party to the dishonest stratagems and subterfuges sometimes practiced by a few community theatres to escape the payment of royalties. A laborer is worthy of his hire, and such practices of depriving the playwright of his just and due return is no less than thievery. It is a misdemeanor punishable by heavy fines if the playwright's agent cares to prosecute. Under no circumstances does an intelligent director need to stoop to such dishonesty. With the whole range of dramatic literature to choose from, European and American, ancient and modern, that director must be ignorant indeed who cannot build programs season after season without an undue load of royalty payments. It would be no more dishonest to steal the lumber, cloth, and paint that go into making the scenery than to steal the play produced. Any director who does engage in such practices nowadays soon becomes known to the agents and subsequently finds it difficult to do business with them.

The royalty charge on plays varies from $5 to $50, or more, for each performance. Agents will usually quote special rates for long runs, for small theatres, for theatres in localities remote from professional stock-company centers, and for regular customers. It is always advisable to write for quotations on royalties, giving full information in each letter about the size of the house, the number of performances, and the nature of the performance planned. On the other hand, it is useless to appeal to agents for royalty reductions because the play is planned as a benefit for a worthy local charity. The playwrights and their agents are under no obligations to support all the local charities throughout the nation or all the worthy causes.

Often recent plays are not available to academic or community theatres within the drawing range of a stock-company center or on the regular road-company circuit, despite the fact that stock companies are extremely rare in America and the road-show or touring-show business has all but disappeared. Within a radius of fifty or seventy-five miles of San Francisco, for example, it is impossible to get permission to do any really popular Broadway success long after other sections of the nation have presented the play time and again. On the theory that some stock company or professional group might possibly be organized in Hollywood at some unknown future date to produce a particular play, and might want to bring it to San Francisco, agents keep it out of circulation, sometimes for years. Frequently these unintelligent stock restrictions are made to apply to communities that have not had a stock company within their boundaries for decades. It is such senseless practices as these that have caused the profession of commercial theatre as it was once known in this nation to decline to its present alarming state.

Actually the production of a play in the local academic or community theatre does not in the least harm the run of that play later when produced by an adequate company of professional actors. The exact contrary is true, as has been demonstrated time and again by revivals. But with this restrictive practice in operation, the director must ascertain if the play under consideration has been released for production in his community and at what royalty when he and his organization are considering the inclusion of recently written and produced plays on their programs. This same restriction applies to older plays still under royalty protection that are revived on Broadway. For example, in 1952, when *The Male Animal* was successfully revived on Broadway, it was taken out of the available category.

The matter of available acting talent as a consideration in the selection of plays has already been mentioned but some further points in that regard bear mentioning. It is dangerous to select a play that depends upon the successful interpretation of a major role if the director is quite unsure of the availability of an actor or actress who can fill that role. It would be foolish, for example, to include *Hedda Gabler* in any season's program if an actress known to be capable of playing Hedda were not readily available. Conversely, when a director can call upon an actress of such capabilities, certain plays might be selected to exploit her talents and drawing powers. To carry the illustration further, however much a director may desire to produce *Hamlet* and however eager a community is to see a good production of that play, obviously it cannot be done without a Hamlet. But it would be just as foolish to attempt to produce the play with only a good actor for Hamlet available and not enough competent actors of sufficient maturity to fill the other roles. There must be available actors of sufficient maturity and ability to give authoritative interpretations to the middle-aged roles of Claudius and Gertrude and the old-aged Polonius. For these roles actors who are obviously as youthful as those playing Hamlet, Ophelia, Horatio, and Laertes would make the selection of this play highly questionable.

The potential acting talent is, then, another significant factor in the choice of plays; but there is a reservation which should go with the advice to consider available actors when choosing plays for production. That is, can the play be cast without utilizing actors in roles similar to those which they have played *ad nauseam* before the same audiences? This matter of repeating the same casting in play after play and thus coming to depend upon a relatively few actors can make, perhaps, for better acted plays but at the same time can so restrict the theatre activity as to kill it. All directors, community and academic alike, must be on guard against the latter situation.

3. AIDS IN PLAY SELECTION

In their hunt for plays the directors and the theatre organizations fortunately have a great number of aids to assist them. As has been said, the best resource for any director is a wide and intimate acquaintance with the vast body of dramatic literature, European and American, ancient and modern. To guide him and his organization in their consideration of plays for production there are a number of bibliographies and play lists available, some of which are included in the bibliography appended to this book. A more complete bibliography of play lists may be found in Blanch M.

Baker's *Dramatic Bibliography,* published by The H. W. Wilson Company, New York City, in 1933, and in the revised and enlarged edition of that work, entitled *Theatre and Allied Arts,* published by the same company in 1952. *Bibliography of Speech Education,* compiled by Lester Thonssen and Elizabeth Fatherson, with the assistance of Dorothea Thonssen, and published by the same company in 1939; and the revised Supplement, compiled by the Thonssens and Mary Margaret Robb, published by The H. W. Wilson Company in 1952, contain, perhaps, the most complete bibliography of play lists available. Of course every organization and every director must have ready access to the catalogues of the chief publishers and play agents, and especially those of the following: Dramatists Play Service, Inc., 14 East 38th Street, New York City; Samuel French, 25 West 45th Street, New York City, and 811 West 7th Street, Los Angeles, California; Baker's Plays, 569 Boylston Street, Boston 16, Massachusetts, and Denver 2, Colorado; The Dramatic Publishing Company, 59 East Van Buren Street, Chicago, Illinois; Row, Peterson and Company, 1911 Ridge Avenue, Evanston, Illinois; Longmans, Green and Company, 55 Fifth Avenue, New York City, and 215 Victoria Street, Toronto 1, Canada. These publishers and agents will be glad to send copies of their catalogues to theatre organizations and established directors.

In order to keep abreast of what is being produced in academic and community theatres, the director should consult regularly the *Educational Theatre Journal, The Quarterly Journal of Speech,* and *Theatre Arts.* The first is the official publication of the American Educational Theatre Association and the second is the official publication of the Speech Association of America. In addition to articles on the academic and community theatres included from time to time, each journal carries a section of news in which appear frequently the titles of plays presented through the nation. Two other journals devoted to academic theatre are *Players Magazine,* Box 339, Gainesville, Florida, the official publication of the National Collegiate Players Honorary Dramatic Fraternity; and *Dramatics,* College Hill Station, Cincinnati 24, Ohio, the official publication of the National Thespian Society. The last-named journal is aimed primarily at the high schools and the Thespian Troupes in those schools. It is especially valuable in keeping one informed of what the high schools are producing.

Unfortunately we have no journal in the United States devoted primarily to the community theatre; hence there is no one source that will aid the director in keeping up with what these theatres are doing. The exchange of programs among directors and community theatres is a valuable means of information. In the May, 1953, issue of *Educational Theatre Journal* was published "A Directory of Nonprofessional Community Theatres in the United States," which, while by no means complete, will give names and addresses of some four hundred of these. *A Guide to Play Selection,* revised edition, compiled by Joseph Mersand and published by Appleton-Century-Crofts in 1959 should be known to all directors.

Keeping up with productions on Broadway is, of course, a much simpler task. Most directors are probably familiar with the theatre reviews that appear regularly in the newspapers of New York City. These reviews are also distributed by Critics Theatre Reviews, Inc., 235 East 22nd Street, New York City 10, in a publication known as *New York Theatre Critics' Reviews.* Three journals which are most useful are the two trade weeklies, *Variety,* 152 West 46th Street, New York City 36; and *Billboard,* 2160 Patterson Street, Cincinnati 22, Ohio; and the already mentioned *Theatre Arts,* 130 West 56th Street, New York City 19. A full listing of similar periodicals may be found in *Simon's Directory of Theatrical Materials, Services, & Information,* published by Bernard Simon, 247 West 46th Street, New York City 36. One of the most useful publications in the field is the annual volume entitled *Best Plays,* originally edited by Burns Mantle and published each year since 1920. Burns Mantle and Garrison P. Sherwood edited a supplementary volume covering the ten-year period from 1909 to 1919 and entitled *Best Plays of 1909–1919, and the Yearbook of Drama in America;* this volume was published by Dodd, Mead & Company, New York City, the publishers of the whole series, in 1933. In 1944, Mantle and Sherwood brought out *Best Plays of 1899–1909,* thus giving us a continuous bibliography of American plays appearing during this century. In 1950, Lydia Sears Mantle compiled and published an *Index to the Best Plays Series, 1899–1950.* The usefulness of these volumes cannot be overestimated. After the death of Burns Mantle in 1948, the annual volume was compiled until 1953 by another New York drama critic, John Chapman. Louis Kronenberger took over the task in 1954. Anyone interested in the earlier American plays should consult Arthur Hobson Quinn's *A History of the American Drama from the Beginning to the Civil War,* second edition, 1943, *A History of the American Drama from the Civil War to the Present Day,* revised edition, 1936, and his collection *Representative American Plays,* seventh edition, 1953—all published by Appleton-Century-Crofts, Inc., New York City.

Guides to Shakespeare's works and those of the older European dramatists are so numerous that any attempt at naming even the most important would occupy far too much space. Blanch M. Baker's *Theatre and Allied Arts,* mentioned above, will prove a useful initial guide to these more specialized works. Anyone engaged in the production of Shakespeare's plays should be familiar with Walther Ebisch and Levin L. Schücking's *A Shakespeare Bibliography,* New York City: Oxford University Press, 1931; and the *Supplement for the Years 1930–1935,* published by the same firm in 1937. Annual Shakespeare bibliographies will be found in *The Shakespeare Association Bulletin,* published in New York by the Shakespeare Association of America, Inc. Allardyce Nicoll's *British Drama: An Historical Survey from the Beginnings to the Present Time* (New York: Thomas Y. Crowell Company, 1935) is a ready one-volume reference to the whole of British drama prior to World War II. John Gassner's *Masters of the Drama,* third revised and enlarged edition (New York: Dover Publications, Inc., 1954), is a good reference for drama in general. Contemporary productions in the world theatres of those nations belonging to the International Theatre Institute are regularly listed in *World Premières: Monthly Bulletin of the International Theatre Institute,* distributed in the United States through ANTA, 1545 Broadway, New York City 36.

There are specialized theatre groups, such as those of the high schools, those of the churches, and the center-stage or arena theatres, whose problems in the choice of plays are in part determined by this special nature of their organization and/or operation. On the subject of plays for the high schools the Committee on Theatre and Drama in the Secondary Schools of the American Educational Theatre Association is constantly preparing lists and materials. A special subcommittee of this group published in *Educational Theatre Journal,* I (December 1949), 131–35, "Directors' Choice: 70 Long Plays for High Schools; 24 Seldom Produced Favorites," a list with comments and information, including publishers and agents. The plays in this bibliography have been widely produced in the high schools throughout the United States. A continuation of the list, "Directors' Choice: 80 One-Act Plays for High Schools," appears in the same journal, Volume II (October, 1950), pp. 218–21. A somewhat similar list of plays for production in the churches may be obtained from the Extension Service Office of the Chicago Theological Seminar, 5757 University Avenue, Chicago 37, by sending the office 10 cents to cover the cost of mailing.

Many lists of plays for children's theatres have been published. Expert information on these lists may be obtained from the Children's Theatre Division of the American Educational Theatre Association. As for arena or center-stage plays, some excellent suggestions for their production will be found in Glenn Hughes' *The Penthouse Theatre: Its History and Technique,* published by Samuel French, New York City; in Walden Boyle's *Central and Flexible Staging: A New Theatre in the Making,* published by the University of California Press at Berkeley; and in the numerous articles on center-stage production in *Educational Theatre Journal, Dramatics,* and *The Players' Magazine.* This type of production has become so extensive throughout the United States that the Stage and Arena Guild of America, 140 West 55th Street, New York City 19, was formed to supply on a percentage basis plays for these arena groups. As has been said, almost any play which does not directly depend upon settings and elaborate stage machinery may be presented in the arena manner by an ingenious director; hence all of the aids to play selection mentioned above are of value to the director of an arena-stage theatre.

4. SELECTING THE CAST

In some respects the matter of choosing a cast for a play is even more momentous and is often more difficult than selecting plays for production. Of course no director is in a position to choose a cast for a play until he has mastered that play and worked out his interpretation of it. Prior to casting, he must especially concentrate his study upon the characters in relation to the whole play and as individuals. He must know precisely how many speaking roles there are in the play, which of these are roles for men and which are for women, how many can be effectively doubled if necessary, how many supers or walk-on actors are needed, and how many actors will be needed for crowds and mobs. The number needed for the last category will vary according to the size of the stage and the setting.

In addition to these general considerations, there are a number of specific aspects of each role which the director must determine. The first of these is the kind of personality depicted by the playwright in the role. In determining this conception of the personality, the director must keep that conception liberal, realizing that no two actors will render exactly the same interpretation of any role and that therefore the personality of any character can, like the personality of a human being, be only generally stated and variously understood. He must see the possibilities of several different actor-interpretations of each role that might be consonant with his general interpretation of the whole play. To see a role, for example, only as it has been done by some favorite actor or actress on the stage or in the motion pictures is to limit casting severely and such a conception will almost inevitably lead to poor directing. Along with this determination of personality go such things as size, coloring, age, and voice quality requisite to the role. The latter consideration is of great importance, too, in terms of the ensemble of voices which the director wishes to utilize in his interpretation. One point which must not be overlooked is the emotional range of the character. Finally, any special qualifications, such as the ability to sing or to dance, must also be noted.

In the casting of plays the director may himself select the actors or may employ, as is often done, a committee to work with him. The committee method has certain definite advantages, especially in the community theatre, in that it does not leave the director to bear singly the full responsibilities and criticisms in connection with the choice of individuals for the roles. Moreover, a committee of several members offers the director some means of getting potentially diverse reactions to different actors and thus gives him something of the variety that will be found in an audience, though on a much smaller scale, of course. It will aid him, in other words, to guard himself, as he will constantly be trying to do, from his own individual preferences and responses which will probably be more definitely oriented towards the aesthetic than will those of the average audience. If a director does employ a committee to aid in casting, he himself must nevertheless maintain the final decision in each selection. Toward this end it may be better to have the committee select two or three potential actors for each role, leaving the final selection to the director.

5. METHODS OF CASTING

Whether or not he utilizes the services of a committee, every director has three major methods for the casting of a play, which he may employ separately or in combination. The first method is simply to cast the play from among actors whose abilities, personalities, and range of roles are known. Every director who has worked in a community or in an institution for any length of time uses his knowledge of available actors who have demonstrated their abilities in former productions. Even while he is studying the play, he often thinks of certain roles as specifically suited to certain actors and designs his interpretation of the play, in part at least, with these individuals in mind. When he gets ready to cast the play, he simply calls these actors in, if they are available, and assigns roles to them. This is the method that is most frequently used on the Broadway stage, especially in the casting of leading roles. Indeed, some of the playwrights write roles especially designed for specific actors, a practice that certainly goes back to Shakespeare's time and is probably as old as our written drama. This method of casting is the most economical and efficient of the three, but, if used exclusively in an academic or community theatre which is meant to serve many people and dependent upon the general esteem of its participants, it is more apt to give rise to charges of favoritism than is the open tryout method. Moreover, it does not alone give the director a method of finding constantly new talent; therefore, other methods should be combined with it, at least from time to time.

For his major productions the director may use this method exclusively or in combination with the interview method if he provides other means for the selection of new actors. Some directors accomplish this aim of building up a corps of available actors through interviews and through public tryouts held from time to time. The aspiring actors selected in these ways are used as rapidly as possible in minor roles until they have demonstrated their abilities, and then are given important roles in major productions.

An even better scheme, widely employed, is to run a series of small or studio productions designed to give new actors an opportunity to demonstrate their abilities and to receive training which may fit them to play in the major productions. These studio productions are open to any new actor and may be cast either by the interview or the open tryout method. This scheme of supplementary productions requires a staff of assistant directors, to whom it gives training as well. In the academic theatre, it is rather easily managed through the courses in acting and directing offered in the curriculum. Here the teacher-director himself supervises the work of the student directors. In the community theatre it offers opportunities for the members of the theatre who have had training and/or experience in directing, though in small theatres it can throw an extremely heavy burden upon an already overworked director.

In some professional productions and in some college or community theatres, where the open tryout method would be impracticable, the director employs a system of appointment to roles based upon information obtained through interviews with prospective actors. Usually the interview is a kind of private tryout in which the actor demonstrates for the director his abilities in reading lines, singing, dancing, or other requisites of the particular role. In such an interview the director probably begins by ascertaining the previous experience of the actor if this has not already been supplied to him in writing. His aim is to "size up" the actor—to note his appearance, his manner, his type of personality, his voice, his movement, and other qualifying traits or qualities. Usually it is wise to make an orderly record of all of this information, along with the address, telephone number, and the times of availability for rehearsals and performance. Some directors request a photograph or snapshot to be included with this record. Such records should be kept up to date by adding the new roles played by actors employed and by noting changes of address. Some such records as these are important to every college and community theatre no matter what the method of tryouts. Though the community be an old and established one, individuals are constantly coming and going in this country, and in academic institutions the personnel upon which the director may call is always changing. By means of these interviews, the director builds up a group of actors within the organization upon whom he may call to tryout for specific roles in his productions.

The open tryout method may be used to select individual actors for specific roles in any one production or it may be employed to build up the pool or group of actors from which the director may appoint actors to specific roles in future performances. The employment of the open tryout method for the casting of each new production is time-consuming and perhaps never as efficient as either of the other methods; but it has certain other advantages which fully justify a considerable expenditure of time in utilizing it. Requiring the prospective actor to demonstrate his ability through a reading, private or in open tryouts, affords the director an opportunity to see the contestant in the role to be filled. Whatever the method of casting used in the academic or community theatre, it is unwise to assign a role "finally" to any actor who has not an established professional reputation without some opportunity to see him in the part for which he is being considered. Further, open tryouts give the actor some opportunity to demonstrate his abilities to play to an audience. Usually the audience consists of the director, members of his tryout committee (if he employs a committee), and other prospective candidates for the roles. Some directors prefer, however, to take the contestants one at a time and not have the whole group hear all of the readings. These are matters of individual preference.

In academic institutions where dramatic work is an activity of the whole student body or any large segment thereof, as well as in the community theatre, the open tryout method with a committee to aid in selection should be used at stated intervals, if not for each individual play. One of the greatest assets that a teacher-director can have in the dealing with students is a reputation for scrupulous fairness and impartiality in all phases of his work. The open tryout method, especially if used with a committee, will aid in establishing this reputation. Perhaps one of the surest way of planting the seeds of destruction in any community or academic theatre organization is through the playing of favorites in the work.

The method of conducting open tryouts is relatively simple. As far in advance of the tryouts as possible the director places copies of the play in accessible public places, such as the library, where prospective candidates for the roles may have an opportunity to read and study it. If these are general tryouts, rather than tryouts for a specific play, the director should select a variety of scenes involving two or more actors, announce his selections publicly, and see that books or scripts are readily available. The scenes should be chosen for range of emotional effect, as well as for variety. The director then announces the time and place of the tryouts and makes certain that this announcement is kept before the public by means of news stories or any other publicity devices, in order to secure a large number of contestants for each role in the play.

Each contestant should make application for a tryout by filling out a prepared card or form and presenting this at the theatre office prior to the tryouts. Sometimes this application form is dispensed with or is filled out at the tryouts. Upon the card should be written the name and address of the candidate and a list of the roles which he may wish to read. Some organizations have cards printed or mimeographed for this purpose which contain a statement of the conditions under which roles are filled and to which the contestant agrees when he presents the application. These forms may be made of further service as records if space is allowed for the listing of roles played in previous productions. A supply of these cards or forms should be available at the time and place of the tryouts for those contestants who have not previously had time to secure them. In the meantime the director selects a committee (if this committee has not been appointed by the governing board). The members of this committee may be of use prior to the tryouts in calling various individuals to inform them of the tryouts but, if they do this, they must be cautioned against placing the committee under obligation to any applicant prior to the actual tryouts.

It is often desirable to conduct the tryouts in the theatre or in a large hall so that the power and range of the voice of each contestant may be properly appraised. Before the tryouts begin, the director may need to instruct his tryout committee carefully. He certainly will need to communicate to them his projected interpretation of the play as a whole and of each major role. If any members of the committee are inexperienced, he may have to take some time in explaining to them exactly what he is seeking in each role and what he is looking for in the applicants for these. When the contestants assemble, a similar interpretation of the play and a very brief statement of the nature of each role may prove useful. This explanation may have to be repeated, for if a large number of contestants apply for parts, or the play contains a large cast requiring numerous tryout scenes, the tryouts may extend over several days. In that case the schedule of specific roles to be tried at each session should be announced and the announcement repeated at the first session of tryouts.

These preliminaries completed, the director has an assistant call the names of applicants who are trying the roles in, say, the first scene to be read or to call up all applicants for two of the parts in it. These applicants are assembled behind the stage or near the front of the auditorium, so that they may take their turns upon the stage without undue delay and disturbance and one by one show their abilities in reading the parts. When the first group of actors has finished reading, a second group is called, and so on until all the applicants have had an opportunity to read the roles that have been selected for particular scenes. The scenes must of necessity be short but not too short to give the contestants a fair chance. Ordinarily applicants should not be permitted to read a large number of roles but should be carefully informed that the tryouts are of a general nature as well as for specific roles.

On the other hand, the director or the committee members should not hesitate to request any contestant in whom they see potentialities for any additional role to read for this, or to repeat his previous reading. This repetition or additional reading can usually be done without too much delay because the unequal number of applicants for the various parts will make some repetition necessary. It may be repeated again that it should be made clear to all contestants that they may be cast in parts for which they did not originally apply, provided always, of course, they wish to accept such roles. Some directors in conducting tryouts prefer not to admit into the auditorium or room any candidates other than those in the scene being read, because a crowd tends to create disturbances and also because those who observed previous contestants are apt to imitate their interpretations of the roles. Perhaps the fact of imitation is significant in making selection, and certainly there is some advantage in having an audience.

At the conclusion of each session, the next session should be announced and a statement made about when and where the selections for the cast will be finally announced.

6. WHAT IS SOUGHT IN TRYOUTS

To state exactly what the director and members of the committee are looking for when they hear applicants read parts would be difficult because this decision varies with every role and with its interpretation. Nevertheless, a general statement about the criteria may be made. They are seeking to determine the adaptability of individuals to the interpretation of the roles in a play in harmony with the aims of the design for its production. It is entirely conceivable that an actor may be excellently equipped to give one specific kind of interpretation of a single role in a play but cannot be used in the contemplated production. Yet more specific general statements may be made about what the director or members of the committee should consider as they hear various applicants read. Perhaps these considerations may be sharpened if they are put in the nature of questions, as follows:

a. *Is the applicant physically adapted to the role?* Is he of approximately the build and complexion that the role demands? Will he effectively pair off with other individuals being considered for other roles in the play? For example, if he is the young hero and lover of this play, is he tall enough to play opposite the person cast as the heroine?

b. *Has the applicant an effective voice for the role?* The voice must be strong, pleasing, and trained, as well as harmoniously expressive of the character. It must also be in harmony with the ensemble of voices. Care must be exercised in selecting two individuals who play opposite each other to avoid the confusing and unpleasant effect their voices will have if they are so similar in tone and pitch as to render them difficult to distinguish. The last consideration is of the highest importance in the casting of plays for radio presentation; in fact, it becomes almost the major voice consideration. It is not to be neglected in casting stage and television productions.

c. *Does the applicant possess, or does he have the ability to assume, the necessary special traits or characteristics of the role?* This consideration includes the mannerisms and idiosyncrasies, the peculiar features and physical size, the distinguishing qualities and characteristics, and the acquired abilities of the character. For example, can the applicant portray the characteristics of old age in posture, walk, and gesture, as well as voice? Does he have features similar to, or can he be dressed and made up to give the appearance of, the character? Can he sing, play a musical instrument, dance, or speak a dialect, or readily learn to do these things skillfully, in accordance with the demands of the role?

d. *Has the applicant a conception of, or is he capable of developing and projecting a conception of, the role?* This question involves both his understanding of the character and his amenability to direction. An actor lacking in imagination, into whom the director has to pour every idea of the part as well as train in the execution, is a detriment to any cast. It is sometimes difficult in an open tryout with many applicants wishing to read parts to assess the individual's imaginative equipment and response to direction. Frequently this must be done through subsequent readings. There are actors, too, who display in tryouts a facile if shallow perception of the role but who are not capable of developing a deeper understanding or taking direction in rehearsals. Usually any actor gives himself away in the way in which he reads lines; though there are actors who cannot really develop a role until they are able to discard the script.

These four major questions with their subsidiary questions are about all, perhaps more than, the director will be able to discover at tryouts. An important question, the reliability of each applicant, cannot be discovered through tryouts but must be obtained through previous acquaintance with his work and through working with the applicant. Whether or not he will work harmoniously with a cast and with a director are likewise matters that can be deduced only from his past career and from actual experience. Sometimes members of the committee or the director himself will have knowledge of the contestants, or some of them, but often the director will have to cast his roles without such knowledge.

A statement on "type casting" may not be irrelevant, especially since the subject has evoked considerable discussion, much of it meaningless, in the past. Much of the argument has been occasioned by the confusion of the meaning of the term *type* as applied to roles in plays. Throughout the eighteenth and much of the nineteenth century, when many of the plays were written with specific type characters—such as the stage Irishman, the stage Yankee, etc.—and when companies were composed of actors who specialized in playing these type roles, roles were automatically assigned to actors in the company according to the type system. The companies were composed of a leading man and a leading lady, a juvenile lead, an *ingenue*, a soubrette, first business, second business, a heavy, a low comedian, and so on. In the casting of plays in these old companies, the various roles of characters in the play fell by right to the actors who had played those types previously. In this sense no director today casts plays according to the type system.

But every director, in the sense that he seeks for each part an actor that exemplifies the specific physical qualities, the mannerisms, and the characteristics of the role, may select his cast according to type. He does not place an actor with a pronounced serious, quiet, and reflective disposition in a part for a vivacious, sparkling, comic character. Only in the case of so-called psychodrama or sociodrama ("educational dramatics" or "corrective dramatics") in which the aim is placed primarily upon the correcting of a maladjusted personality or on the development of certain characteristics in a personality would he cast a play in such a manner. In theatre production for the public, he seeks a type of actor that will fit the role. In successfully accomplishing this, his greatest asset is a knowledge of his actors and of the success they have had in previous roles and productions.

To the inexperienced director tryouts may at first be a bewildering confusion, but experience will soon teach him how to select actors. It will teach him also to choose them for potentialities and development rather than immediate skill in performance. Some applicants, it may be repeated, will display their full abilities in the tryout, while others may give merely an indication of how they may develop through rehearsals. To differentiate between these will always remain difficult. For that reason it is wise to cast several individuals in the chief roles at the beginning and to eliminate through additional rehearsal-readings. In the process of making selections, it is best to begin first with the leading roles and to eliminate all of the obviously unacceptable contestants, reserving for further consideration and discussion (if there is a committee) all of the potentially acceptable ones. Having narrowed the selection in this way, the director and the committee then proceed by the same process of comparing and balancing each of the remaining contestants further to reduce the applicants for each role.

Sometimes, when there are a number of promising candidates for one or more of the major roles, a further reading may be held for these alone; or they are permitted to attend the first rehearsal and all are given there an additional opportunity to read. Ideally each role should be cast with an actor and an understudy but it is often difficult to get many of the understudies to attend any rehearsals. Sometimes in the educational theatre there is a double casting of the play and each cast is given opportunity to perform before the public. This system is excellent in that it offers double the number of opportunities for training to the students but a director must either have ample time for his rehearsals or must have a co-director who works in the closest harmony with him. As soon as the cast and the understudies have been selected, they should be announced, along with an announcement of the rehearsal schedule, and a call for the first rehearsal. It may bear repeating again that not until rehearsals have shown conclusively the fitness of an inexperienced actor for the role in which he is cast should he be allowed to consider that role definitely his own. In the professional Broadway theatre all actors are on trial for the first two weeks. After that time they must be paid severance pay if they are dismissed but up to that time they are still, in a sense, trying out for the part.

QUESTIONS AND EXERCISES

1. If you were invited to assume the duties of director of the community theatre in your home town and were asked by the governing board to select eight popular plays for production which would entice your local audience into the theatre, what eight legitimate plays would you produce?
2. If you were invited by the president of your college or university to take over the duties of director of your school theatre and had to select eight plays for the season, which plays would you select?
3. Secure a copy of the latest edition of *Best Plays* and examine carefully the legitimate plays produced on Broadway during the season represented. Then examine the "Ten Best Plays" included in the volume. Do you detect any pattern of general interest apparent during the season? Which of the ten plays given in synoptic form

would you wish to produce in your community or college theatre? Which would you not care to produce? Why?

4. One of the problems which the director is often facing is that of the best English version of a foreign play. There are numerous guides to help him with which he should form acquaintance. For the classical drama of Greece and Rome see Philip W. Harsh, *A Handbook of Classical Drama*. For modern continental drama of Europe appearing prior to 1931, see the play bibliography in Frank W. Chandler, *Modern Continental Playwrights*. For more recent years the *Index Translatorum* is invaluable.
5. Make an analysis of the cast requirements of one of the one-act plays which you have studied. If you had available only that acting talent represented in your class or group, how would you cast that one-act play?
6. Listen to three different news commentators over the radio. Write a description of your conception of the appearance and personality of each commentator as suggested by the voice. Try to discover just what qualities gave you your impression of the appearance and personality.
7. Note carefully the facial appearance, build, posture, walk, and voice of the members of your class or group and decide which of these could be cast to play roles older than the individuals themselves.

CHAPTER 5

Planning the Whole Production

To what extent can a director plan a production of a play in advance? It is unquestionably true that some directors have with only the briefest reading of a script cast it and put it into rehearsal, working out, insofar as they were worked out, the problems of interpretation and staging as the rehearsals progressed. Some kind of a show can be put on in that manner, especially if there is available a cast of actors with a fair degree of competence. In fact, in such a situation, there is very little need for a director. An efficient prompter who will take some responsibility for coordinating the various departments of production will do as well. It is a tribute to the effectiveness of drama and of actors or a condemnation of the audience's standards of judgment that plays so produced seem to satisfy certain audiences. In such a situation the director, if he may be called such, is certainly not the interpreter of the play. Under such circumstances he has abrogated his chief function and the theatre which employs him will do well to replace him as soon as possible.

The answer to the above question varies, however, for the serious and worthy director. There are circumstances under which he may have all too little time for advance study and preparation of the play. Sometimes, as in summer stock, directors are caught with a last-minute, rush assignment and must make up in concentration for the time not at their disposal. Such quick preparation requires a maturity and a method in interpretation. To describe this method it is best to assume that the director has ample time prior to the actual process of production for the planning. In college and community theatres where a season's program is announced in advance, time is available.

It has been pointed out that the director has two major governing responsibilities in the staging of plays:

1. His responsibility to the play
2. His responsibility to the audience

It is conceivable that an erudite stage interpretation of a play might be over the heads of certain audiences. Conversely, it is easy to stage a play in such a way that its staging will so misinterpret the author's work as to cause the judicious to grieve. Hugh Hunt has dealt admirably with this dual responsibility of the director in his *The Director in the Theatre* (London: Routledge and Kegan Paul, 1954), a series of lectures delivered for the Department of Drama at the University of Bristol. Unless a director has lived or worked in a community for some time, he cannot know the audience as intimately as he might wish. Fortunately, however, though audiences do vary widely from community to community, there is a degree of homogeneity among the inhabitants of the United States. What appeals to theatre audiences in one part of the nation is apt to appeal in much the same degree in other parts. The staging of contemporary plays seldom presents perplexing questions on the score of audience appeal because the playwright has written his plays in terms of the audience interests of the present. The question of whether the contemporary play is too "advanced" or too shocking for a particular community may arise. Restrictions of this nature have been noted in the discussion of choice of plays. The real problem of adapting an interpretation to an audience arises with plays from the past. Just how best to present a Greek play, a Shakespearean play, or a play by Molière so that an audience will most fully appreciate it is a question that the director must attempt to answer in his planning. The answer will require a knowledge of the play and a knowledge of the audience.

In addition to the kind of play which he is to present, there are other considerations which affect a director's planning of a production. Some of these have already become apparent but may be summarized as follows:

1. The physical structure of the stage
2. The potentially available cast
3. The equipment and the budget
4. The time available for rehearsals and mounting
5. The production staff
6. The size of the production to be attempted

A director in a community or academic theatre who is thoroughly familiar with his theatre, staff, equipment, time schedule, and potential acting talent has an advantage in planning over the director who is not so blessed. Even the latter, however, can study and make preliminary plans for plays which he would, when the opportunity offers, like to direct. Such study and planning are done constantly by the most able directors on both sides of the Atlantic.

1. THE DIRECTOR'S INTERPRETATION

After a study and analysis of the play, such as that outlined in Chapter 2, the director should have arrived at some kind of conception of the dominant effect and an understanding of what Hugh Hunt calls the soul of the play. The latter may not be as quickly determined as the former. Every play gives up some of the secrets of its effects upon first reading. These effects, as became apparent in the discussion of drama, arise from the form. A comedy produces laughter and ridicule but what a wide variation there is in such responses! The hearty, robustious, unthinking laughter elicited by the skillful clowns or comedians in low comedy differs markedly as an effect and a response from the sophisticated smile of Shavian comedy. Both Shaw's *Man and Superman* and Samuel and Bella Spewack's *Boy Meets Girl* are comic; both occasionally in performance produce hearty laughter; both satisfy audiences in the way that comedy should.

Boy Meets Girl produces its laughter largely through its zany exposure of the topsy-turvy world of Hollywood and the codes of conduct artificially bred by that environment. Exaggerated human eccentricities and the extremely ludicrous situations in which such people embroil themselves within this cock-eyed world of motion pictures are the chief sources of laughter. The effect remains close to the farcical throughout. Shaw's play, on the other hand, is much more sophisticated, producing its laughter largely through the paradoxical exposure of ideas and conventional attitudes. Even the seemingly sympathetic central character, Jack Tanner, the intellectual revolutionist, is comically trapped into marriage in the end through the pursuit of the female under a compulsion far more powerful than that of intellect, the Life Force. Though there are many hilarious and ludicrous situations in *Man and Superman,* it is dominantly a comedy of ideas; hence much of the fun comes from the wit of the dialogue. Both plays contain ideas that are shown up, exposed, and ridiculed; but the Shaw play is more largely concerned with the exposure of normally accepted ideas among intelligent people of respectable society. This analysis by no means exhausts the comic effects of either play, but it is sufficient to show that two comedies differ in the nature and sources of such effects. To probe more thoroughly for these effects it is necessary for the director to consider the play scene by scene, situation by situation, character by character, and often line by line. Often in comedy the effect lies in the right phrasing of a line, as in the passage previously quoted from Oscar Wilde's *Importance of Being Earnest.*

Serious plays, too, differ in their effects. Consider Arthur Miller's *Death of a Salesman* and Shakespeare's *Macbeth,* both serious plays productive of fear and pity, though by no means of equal quality as tragedy. For many people Miller's play will be only the extremely pathetic story of the "little guy" who got himself so involved and befuddled that death was the only way out. Sympathy for Willy Loman will draw such spectators very close to him, so close that they are apt to miss other meanings and effects of the play. There is here, however, the tragedy of a man failing to realize his potentialities as a man. Through the worship of the prevalent doctrine of success, he falls short of human nobility, loses direction, creates false illusions, and perverts his values and his sons. In our sympathetic understanding of Willy, we feel suspense for his future and pity him. Macbeth, too, arouses our sympathy, suspense, and pity but the play allows us to stand farther off, as it were. Hence there is less pathos and more tragic pity in it. Here, likewise, we see a man choosing the path of evil, but he is a man of immeasurably greater potentialities and far keener intellect than is Willy. As a result, he has a much more developed conscience and knows evil to be evil. His choices are made with this knowledge and against his conscience. Despite the Witches, he is not as much a victim of blind fate as is Willy. Willy is a rather blind victim of a capitalistic doctrine of success, whose adherence to a salesmanship philosophy of life creates complete bewilderment as to all values. Willy hardly has any choices; hence is essentially pathetic. Macbeth, despite the Witches, has a succession of choices; hence more definitely determines his own fate. The temptation to succeed through choosing evil becomes Macbeth's tragedy. We sympathize, pity, and understand. Though there are obvious similarities in the effects of the two plays, the differences are far greater than the resemblances.

If this examination of the effects of different comedies and tragedies were extended to include examples from all periods and types, it could occupy the entire book. Melodramas differ in similar ways from each other. But plays produce their effects not only by their emotional impacts but also by their meaning or significance. Galsworthy, an exponent of naturalism, believed that plays should build up to a spire of meaning. Hunt speaks of the significance of a play as its soul. Modern plays since Ibsen, tending as they do toward a drama of ideas, do build up to a spire of meaning in Galsworthy's sense perhaps more obviously than do older plays. Nevertheless, as was explained in Chapter 2, all plays do have an argument in the sense of a significance and many plays have a theme or thesis.

One approach to an understanding of how to interpret the play is to discover its meaning, significance, argument, thesis, or soul. Shaw's comedy has an argument about an idea, the Life Force. That Life Force is bent upon the process of creative evolution in an attempt to bring forth the superman or to make human beings supermen. That Force traps even the intellectual Jack Tanner whose eyes are open to its operation, just as it manipulates Ann in her lies, coquettry, and pursuit of Jack. The comedy of human beings so manipulated is the central argument of the play. It could be the tragedy of that manipulation if Shaw did not conceive of all-powerful creative evolution as essentially beneficient. The argument in *A Doll's House* amounts almost to a thesis. In that play Ibsen expounds the necessity for every human being, in this case a woman, to be an independent, self-determining individual in the sense of intelligently choosing values and making decisions. But each of these plays can be so interpreted as to emphasize other meanings. For example, *Man and Superman* might be seen merely as the comedy of an attractive woman pursuing and capturing her man. *A Doll's House* might be seen merely as the awakening disillusionment of a wife. Shaw's play might be played merely as a comic satire on conventional middle-class attitudes and mores. Ibsen's play might be viewed as a satire upon a pompous, self-important husband and head of the household. Each of these ideas is to some extent to be found in the respective plays. What they will become in production will depend to a measurable extent on what the director sees in them and emphasizes.

But a play may have meaning without being so definitely an argument to a thesis. Shakespeare's *Twelfth Night* is essentially a play about love. In it there is, first, the Elizabethan, romantic, sonnet-sequence conception of love, exemplified by the Duke's love for Olivia. That is a highly artificial, conventional conception of love. Actually the Duke is more in love with being in love than with Olivia. More accurately, he is in love with his picture of himself as an ideal lover. Since this is an artificial love, it is gently ridiculed in the play, even though it is beautifully rendered. A normal and true love, made comic by the predicament of her dress, her disguise, is Viola's love for the Duke. This same disguise that produces her comic predicament causes Olivia to fall absurdly in love with a maid on the assumption that he is a youth. Olivia's love is not in itself as ridiculous or rather as artificial as that of the Duke, hence it can be transferred to the twin youth, Sebastian, as true love. In the object on which it is manifested, however, it does involve Olivia in a ridiculous plight, a sort of punishment for her former too-great absorption in love for a brother. But these by no means exhaust the love involvements of the comedy. There are the ridiculous burlesques of love in the absurd idea that Sir Andrew Auguecheek might pay court to Olivia and especially in the self love of Malvolio. That variety of love gains Shakespeare's harshest ridicule. Finally, there is the earthy love of Sir Toby and Maria, a kind of normal, commonsense love of relatively unsophisticated people. All of these love complications take place in a romantic world of the imagination, an artificial, never-never land, the Sea Coast of Illyria. Even love as friendship between Antonio and Sebastian finds a place in this comedy of love.

From another view, it might be seen as the comedy of disguise and unmasking. The Duke disguises his true self in a convention. Viola disguises herself in boy's clothing. Olivia hides from real love behind the disguise of love for a brother. Malvolio deludes himself with the guise of a man of importance. Feste is really a wise man in the guise of a fool and Sir Andrew is a fool in the guise of a knight of importance. In the end comes the unmasking and stripping away of disguise. Such a meaning is in the play and is important to its effect but it probably is subsidiary to the love argument.

There is yet another approach to the determination of the effect of a play, along with its meaning. That is through trying to ascertain its interest. Every play exerts an effect when it interests a reader or audience and every play has a variety of sources of interest. The playwright's objective has been said to be to arouse interest, to sustain and increase interest, and to satisfy interest. How does he do these things? He may accomplish this purpose through an absorbing story, whose entanglements, involvements, and suspense carry the reader or audience forward to their ultimate resolution. Every play has something of this kind of interest. He may do it through a character or group of characters who are in themselves, and for various reasons, unusual, exciting, interesting. All plays to an extent employ this method of arousing interest. The playwright may depend upon the exposition of ideas to catch and hold audience interest. Again, all plays to some extent utilize this method.

There are subordinate but none-the-less significant interest-compelling elements and devices in plays, but plot, character, and thought are the elements of interest to consider first. Sidney Kingsley's *Darkness at Noon,* based on Arthur Koestler's book, exploits essentially the interest in its situation or tense story. There is interest in idea and interest in character in it but the chief interest comes from the story. *You Can't Take It with You,* though it arouses interest in its comic situations and predicaments, derives its chief interest from its eccentric characters. The *Don Juan in Hell* epilogue to Shaw's *Man and Superman* depends primarily for its interest upon a clever exposition of ideas. In general, the more appealing plays include these three interests

A modern setting for a classical play, *The Trojan Women,* directed by Walden P. Boyle and designed by Nordstrom C. Whited for the production by the Department of Theater Arts, University of California at Los Angeles.

with the dominant interest in plot and character. Nevertheless, many modern dramatists, Shaw and Ibsen in particular, depended upon a certain shockingness of their ideas to arouse interest. An attempt to state the sources of interest in a play can become an effective key to a statement of its interpretation.

Some such statement must be prepared by the director before he can explain his interpretation to members of the production staff and to the cast. Yet another consideration, the style of the production, must go into that statement, especially if it is to be an effective guide to designers. One may gain a rather profound student's knowledge of a play, especially plays of the past that have been widely analyzed and discussed, and yet have quite a problem in determining how most effectively to present these to modern audiences.

It is possible to learn as much as is known about *Oedipus, The King* as Sophocles wrote it and as the Greeks must have viewed it in their Theatre of Dionysus without even considering its modern production in a contemporary theatre. Such a knowledge will be of the greatest aid in helping one to decide what not to do and it will contribute some suggestions about what to do. It may be produced by simulating as far as possible the ancient Greek stage, as we think we know it, and attempting to render the choral odes with music and expressive movement. Such an antiquarian approach might be quite proper in an academic theatre. Whether it would bring the full impact of the drama to a modern heterogeneous theatre audience is doubtful.

One might conceive of a production set, not in the fifth-century Athenian theatre, but in the dim antiquity of the half-barbarous legend itself. With the assistance of archeological and anthropological materials, one might create massive, semibarbaric settings and costumes such as might have belonged to the ancient age of the myth. Such a rendering might be impressive, though certainly not consonant with the intellectual meaning and depth of the tragedy.

As a third alternative, a director might decide to modernize the interpretation as far as possible, cutting the chorus to three rather realistic courtiers and reducing the choral odes to their talk among themselves. The other characters would have to be in similar realistic key and their costumes would have to be modified to suit. The setting would be tied down to a definite palace or house, perhaps only faintly Grecian. If the emphasis in the interpretation is upon the universality of meaning within the play, perhaps the best interpretation might be to avoid all localization, giving the piece an imaginative, "stylized" rendering that would make it largely symbolic. Any number of cues for such stylization may be found within the play. For example, the frequent emphasis upon blindness and sight in their various senses might lead one to begin the play in a kind of shrouding fog or misty light that gradually clarifies and becomes more revealing. A setting of platforms and three-dimensional pieces, symbolically conceived, and enveloped in a vast sky cyclorama might provide the environment.

Finally, one might go so far as to rewrite the piece almost entirely with an almost complete modernization of its meaning. It should not then be advertised as Sophocles' *Oedipus, The King*. These different approaches obviously represent different styles of production. Which style will be adapted in a production of any play depends upon what the director sees in the play and how he thinks what he sees may be best communicated to an audience.

In this attempt to indicate various styles in which plays may be produced, period and place have had to be considered as determinates. Period and place not only affect the style of production. They also help to determine the kind of effect the play will produce upon audiences and they have a bearing upon problems of mounting. Period and place are matters which a director can decide from a study of the play and are important matters to be communicated to members of the production staff. *A Doll's House* may be presented in the costumes and settings of 1879 or in contemporary dress and settings. *Hamlet* may be played in Renaissance or Elizabethan costume with an Elizabethan stage setting or, with a different effect, in modern costume and an attempt toward settings of realistic style. It can be wholly unlocalized in time and place and given a more symbolic, more "stylized" rendering.

In general, period staging lends a kind of aesthetic distance to a performance; that is, period costumes and settings alter somewhat the probability of the play and its acceptance by an audience. Certain plays with realistic reference to contemporary events and things are difficult to translate into contemporary costumes and settings. *The Show-Off*, for example, with its references to Mellon as Secretary of the Treasury and its allusions to wireless headphones, automobiles of a definite period, as well as other allusions definitely place the action in the 1920s. Perhaps it is still contemporary enough in tone and effect to allow for a change in period by merely changing these allusions. This is a question for the director to decide in determining his approach.

The change in the place of the action, on the other hand, is usually in modern realistic plays a far more difficult matter because the place in which the action occurs can be highly important in establishing its probability. Even in a romantic play, such as *Marco Millions,* it would be impossible to shift the oriental scenes to occidental settings. There is a certain feeling, a mood and atmosphere, belonging to the whole play that would be unacceptable in another time and place. The playwright usually fully realizes this when he chooses the time and place of his action. The director, therefore, should have weighty reasons if he changes these in his interpretation.

Prior to the modern drama, there was not that conception of the shaping influence of environment and time upon character which is so widely accepted today. The action of Shakespeare's *Hamlet* takes place presumably in Denmark in some past period but the environment, insofar as this enters the play, is largely that of Elizabethan London. *Lear* presumably occurs in ancient Britain but again the mood of the play is Elizabethan. *Macbeth* is set in Scotland and is based on Holinshed's account of incidents that occurred in the mid-eleventh century but in point of view it more nearly belongs to London of about 1611. Molière's plays belong largely to Paris of the mid-seventeenth century but they are no more strictly tied to time and place than are those of Shakespeare. In plays of this nature the director in a sense has a greater freedom of choice in his interpretation, especially with regard to the elements of style dictated by time and place. In the interpretation of any one of these, however, he must make some decision about time and about locale. His decision may be to make these definite and precise or it may be to keep these essentially vague and not too definitely localized. In either event, the decision will affect the style of settings, costumes, and acting.

Whatever his decision as to effects, meaning, style, time, and place, he must communicate these to members of the production staff and eventually to the cast. It is worth repeating here that no two directors will necessarily interpret any play in exactly the same way; indeed, it is doubtful if two different directors could render precisely the same interpretation of a play. To the extent that a director succeeds in communicating his interpretation of the play, to that extent will he potentially unify its production. It is wise, therefore, for him to prepare with care his statements of interpretation. What might be called the director's approach may be illustrated with an example. This example was prepared by Director Charles Vance for the production conferences on his presentation of O'Neill's *Marco Millions,* as performed by the Stanford Players. Incidentally, he was both designer and director of this show; hence his written statement, accompanied by a variety of illustrations in color of sets and costumes, was relatively brief. It follows:

> The show, in my estimation, is primarily a satiric comedy within a romantic setting against a background of colorful, oriental spectacle (see attached time- and place-chart of scenes). It satirizes the American business man, or any man, who closes his eyes to eternal truth, beauty, and love in his acquisitive quest for gold. At the same time, the play is romantic spectacle or at least it partakes of many elements of the spectacular. There is, therefore, a definite clash between the romantic and the satiric, between the emotional and the satiric-comic, which offers difficult problems in interpretation. Part of this difficulty is resolved in the play in that the satire is directed against the unromantic. A clue to the solution of the difficulties, so far as production is concerned, lies in the definitely fantastic nature of several of the scenes. Even though the play is satiric, the probability is on a level of fantasy. The play must be presented in a stylized form which will harmoniously combine the romantic and realistic elements.
>
> I shall, therefore, direct the play for these values:
>
> 1. To bring out the element of satire.
> 2. To play up and enhance the fantasy and spectacle.
> 3. To present the action and characters in a stylized form but, because of the satiric element, to employ a stylization rooted in realism.

This general statement of his approach was supplemented with designs of costumes and sets; charts of time and place, of lighting changes, of characters and character relations, of color symbolism; and lists of characters with the number of costumes for each, of properties, and of set changes. With such a fully worked-out plan of production to guide them, members of the staff were able to proceed with the construction of the settings and with the selection of materials for costumes well in advance of casting. Since his supplementary charts and lists carried full information on time and place, these were not mentioned in Vance's statement. This statement later became the basis of his first talk to the cast in which he explained clearly his interpretation of the play.

2. ADVANCE PLANNING OF PRODUCTION ELEMENTS

Having determined his approach to the interpretation of the play, there are other aspects of the production which the director can and should plan in advance. Some of these might be planned in consultation with the designers and the technical director or might even be left to these individuals. The thoughtful director usually prefers to work out all or most of these himself as he is working out his interpretation. In the production editions of modern plays many of these have been included in the appendix. These usually include a floor plan of each set, a furniture and properties list, a list of characters and their necessary costumes, and sometimes a list of sound effects and a lighting chart. These are usually given as they were prepared for the commercial professional production of the play and may or may not suffice for the show as the director plans it for his theatre. For older plays of which no production book is available, these must be planned from the text and from the kind of production contemplated. What, then, can the director plan in advance which his production staff will need to know? That will, in general, depend somewhat upon the play but the following list will prove suggestive:

1. The number and nature of the sets.
2. The number of scene changes requiring set changes.
3. Requisite furnishing for each set.
4. The time of action of each separate scene, especially those which require lighting changes.
5. The number of characters, divided into men and women and into major and minor.
6. A list of essential costume changes, with the total number of costumes.
7. Any special sound effects required for the interpretation or called for in the action, including music and musical accompaniments.

Sometimes a multiscened show may be planned to eliminate one set or to be staged within a single set. Without resorting to an Elizabethan setting, a director may stage a Shakespeare play upon an architectural setting, consisting of platforms, steps, ramps, and set pieces. These may remain permanent and the only changes are those accomplished by means of lighting. Or a kind of inner stage that may be changed for certain scenes may be provided. For some audiences the permanent architectural set becomes uninteresting, even boring, as the play progresses. This lack of interest in the setting can often be compensated for with colorful costumes, pageantry, and exciting stage business, including a rapid flow of the action. These are decisions which the director must make and communicate to his designers and technicians.

Obviously he cannot fully plan the settings without knowing the physical action, the business or spectacle, of the play. Stage business cannot be fully planned until the play is put into rehearsal but the gross stage business can be preplanned. For example, the director may start with the entrances and exits. Some of these may be minor, require only the expeditious getting of an actor on or off stage. Others may be highly important to the action and dramatically effective, if properly executed. For their effective execution the door- and entrance-ways must be carefully thought out and properly placed. A piece of business, such as Marc Antony's funeral oration, may require an elevation or platform upon the set. It is uneconomical and bad planning to put such an elevation within a permanent set for this one speech merely; hence it must be planned in terms of its full utilization. The problems of utilizing and placing stage business upon the stage will be more fully discussed in Chapter 8. At this point the director is concerned with stage business only insofar as it can be worked out in advance and is necessary to the designers in planning sets in particular. Obviously, before a designer can make an adequate plan for a set, he must know any special requirements of action within that set. If there is to be a stairway showing, just where is it located, how, and to what extent utilized? If there are windows, are they practicable, that is, can they be opened and closed? Must there be a fireplace or can that be dispensed with? If there is, just where is it located so that the action around it can be most effective? Other scenic elements, such as views into hallways or other rooms, vistas of the outdoors, and similar considerations must be given thought and determined. The director likewise must decide upon the architectural style and the period of the furnishings. For exteriors, he must determine the kind of scenic view which will most effectively enhance the action. These are matters that will depend upon the kinds of dramatic values he finds in the play and the ways in which he plans to interpret these.

The set changes, the furnishings, and the time scheme of the action are matters that may often be conveyed merely by a listing or a chart. Sometimes, however, the furnishing must be more amply described. Such is especially true when the style is symbolic and not directly related to an era or a period, as for example in Elmer Rice's *The Adding Machine*. The problem of choice in such instances becomes more difficult than in those instances in which definite period furnishings may be used. More imagination is necessary to visualize the forms of the furnishings consonant with such stylized interpretations. That the furnishings must be chosen in harmony with the style of interpretation should be clear. These, in turn, must harmonize with settings, other aspects of the mounting, and with the acting.

In the study and early planning of the production the director must come to a full understanding of the separate characters. Ways of accomplishing this will be discussed in Chapter 7. Until he attains this understanding, the director cannot choose a cast and cannot tell a costume designer what kinds of clothing the characters must have. The sex, age, and essential physical characteristics of each character need to be noted. Any special qualifications or accomplishments, such as the ability to sing or to dance, should be included in the notes. Sometimes minor roles may be doubled in casting, giving two or more roles to a single actor. In some plays several roles of a minor nature may be telescoped into a single role. If either doubling or telescoping is to be done, the director must scrutinize the roles carefully to see that the process will work in production.

In these minor roles the director may sometimes change a male character into a female, or vice versa, depending upon whether male or female actors of abilities are more readily available. For the major roles he must first clarify their exact functions in the action, determining whose play it is and which characters are supporting leads. Then the nature of each of the major roles should be determined as precisely as possible. In this process, special acting requirements, such as abilities in certain lines of comedy, will become apparent. All of these clues and interpretations of the characters are helpful to the designer of the costumes and should be communicated to that individual. In this study of the characters, it is wise to make a chart of the major groupings of characters in the important scenes for later rehearsal purposes.

If music or other sound effects are to be utilized in the production, they must be planned. The script may call for the leading lady to play the piano but the actress most suitable for the role is not a pianist. The piano playing will then have to be faked with a piano off stage. This necessity will affect the placement of the piano on stage. Shakespeare's plays often call for trumpets, drums, and other sound effects. These can be produced today artificially with sound records played over the sound system but they must be planned and later rehearsed. If these elements are not included in the early planning, they will not be ready when needed in rehearsal. In certain plays a character or characters are called upon to sing, to dance, to fence, accomplishments which the individual actor cast in the role may or may not possess. When he is not, for example, a singer but must sing a song in the play, it will be necessary to provide training for him. In certain instances either the song or the music for the song must be provided. Arrangements must be made with a competent person to train him in singing the song. The same applies to dancing and fencing. In the case of fencing, there will be a need to secure early the necessary fencing instruments, as well as to arrange regular instruction.

In this study and planning the director should note carefully the climaxes of the action, the high points of interest in the play. He should examine the play carefully to see how these are built. Sometimes they will be scenes of quiet intensity; at others they will rise to their heights through sound and spectacle. At least two questions arise in connection with these. Just how are they built? Where within the set do they occur? The playwright himself has built these climaxes but it is the director's task to render them effective in stage action. Sometimes he must invent devices of business to accomplish this and these devices may require properties. Just where within the set these high moments occur is a clue to the placing of the action on the stage. One of these may indicate the advantage of a platform or elevation. All of them will be helpful to the man in charge of lighting in that their placement within the set tells him what areas must be especially lighted. This working out of the acting areas, discussed more fully in Chapter 8, must to an extent be planned in advance for the sake of both scene designer and lighting man.

It cannot be fully done without businessing the entire script. Stage business is dependent upon the abilities of actors to execute it; hence final planning of business must wait upon the business rehearsals. Nevertheless, a trained director can plan in advance the gross business for a play. Beginning with the first entrance of a character, he can visualize the movements of that actor about the stage and the entrances, exits, and movements of subsequent actors. Thus he can go through the play, making notes of positions, movements, and groupings. It is wise, especially when the director plans a production well in advance, to set all of these matters down (in pencil) in a director's production book (see instructions on preparing a prompt copy in Section 8 of this chapter). Only by some such planning of the gross business can he tell the designer of the set where to locate doors, windows, fireplaces, elevations, stairways, and similar units that will be utilized in the physical action. Further, only by such planning can he indicate to the lighting technician the important acting areas that must be specially lighted.

Some directors go well beyond what has here been suggested as essential in the prior planning of a show. In Europe, where repertory is usual in the theatre, it is the general practice for directors to work out shows well in advance of production. In doing this, they utilize the whole body of writings on the author and on the play, searching especially in the history of past productions for suggestions about what not to do as well as for ideas that will kindle their imaginations. There are, for example, prompt books of many of Molière's plays that go back almost to the days of the dramatist in the library of the Comédie Française. Most of these have been published in one form or another. These establish a tradition, honored often in the breach, which a competent director will insist upon knowing, whether he plans to observe or depart from this tradition. Likewise, there are large numbers of prompt books of Shakespeare's plays, dating from Garrick's day, which help to establish something of a Shakespearean tradition. Fortunately, thanks to the many investigations by competent scholars, the materials of these widely scattered prompt books are readily accessible in such important works as George C. Odell's two volumes, *Shakespeare from Betterton to Irving* (New York: Charles Scribner's Sons, 1920), many similar studies, and kept somewhat up to date in the annual *Shakespeare Survey,* published in Cambridge, England, by the Cambridge University Press. Similar studies on the staging of Greek plays are not readily available but on the interpretations of the tragedies H. D. F. Kitto's admirable *Greek Tragedy,* published in a paper-back edition in the Doubleday Anchor Books (Garden City, N.Y.: Doubleday & Company, 1955) should be consulted.

3. PLANNING THE SETTINGS

When the director has acquainted himself to the extent indicated with the business requirements of the play, he is ready to tackle the task of planning the settings. Whether or not the director is his own scenery designer, he nevertheless has a definite responsibility for the settings, especially in academic and community theatres. As the interpreter of the play he is responsible for all of the elements of production. The ideal director would probably know how to design all of these, but the design and execution of all elements in a production in a season's program is much too heavy a burden to place upon a director with all of his other duties. The director, therefore, needs a staff of artists and technicians to help him. With such a staff he will have to formulate some definite program of production conferences. A plan for such conferences is given in Section 9 of this chapter.

A number of relatively obvious considerations govern the planning and preparation of scenery for a show. Among these are the following:

1. The requirements of the play.
2. The type of stage on which the production will be presented.
3. The style of interpretation.
4. The available budget.
5. The available technicians and crew members.
6. The time available for the necessary preparation.

Scenery is merely the environmental background of the action. It may range from complete Belasco-like realism, complete in every detail, through selective or skeletonized realism, to a bare-platform type of production, such as is utilized in arena staging.

Some plays, notably nineteenth-century melodramas, depend to a considerable extent upon scenery and machinery. The big scenes of these plays, such as approaching trains, burning buildings, shipwrecks, and similar spectacular episodes, depended upon a high degree of mechanical and scenic realism. Settings for many modern plays, developed under the influence of Naturalism and perfected by such innovators as André Antoine in his *Théâtre Libre,* relied upon a similar completeness and accuracy of detail. This development gave dominance on the modern stage to the box set with its three relatively solid walls, practical doors and windows, and fidelity to the environment of the action. Such a setting attempts to create scenically a complete illusion of the actual place of the action. The modern drama with its emphasis upon the effects of environment upon character and conduct often demands such settings. When there is this strong emphasis in the play upon the environmental factors, such a completely realistic setting will probably most effectively serve. Such settings are costly and time consuming in their preparation. Furniture and other details of mounting must correspond to the completely realistic style and the direction and acting must be likewise governed. The curtain line in such a setting becomes a kind of fourth wall and the play is, as it were, overheard or spied upon by the audience.

This style of complete verisimilitude has its disadvantages. It confines the action within a solid cage, so to speak. Direct contact between audience and actor is out of place usually. Passion, emotion, and speech must be toned down to the ordinary. Complete realism can become a cramping restriction upon drama. There has, consequently, been a variety of reactions against this style of drama and production almost from the days of its origin. These departures from realism, represented in drama by revivals of romantic and poetic drama, by expressionism and similar stylizations, and by selective realism, have had their influences upon stage settings. One of the earliest reactions against the realism of Antoine was led by Jacques Copeau, who established his *Theatre de Vieux-Colombier* in 1913, where he instituted major reforms in scenic design which became very influencial in Europe and America. On his architectural stage he simplified scenery to the point of symbolism.

Many realistic plays may be adequately staged in settings of simplified or selective realism. In such staging the scenery may be reduced to a mere skeleton of essential pieces, consisting of doors, windows, and enough flats to suggest the demarcations of the room or place. Such a simplified setting was excellently employed by Mordecai Gorelik for the staging in 1956 of the naturalistic play about dope addiction, *A Hatful of Rain,* by Michael V. Gazzo. The action of this play occurred in a remodeled apartment on New York's Lower East Side. The visible room represented the combination bed-kitchen-living room of Johnny and Celia Pope. The stage at the rear was closed in with a blue sky-cloth. In front of this, upstage left was a rather large window flat. Farther forward and to the right was set a pair of flats with a door flat, the door leading to Polo Pope's offstage bedroom. Continuing at right angles to this partial rear wall was another partial wall, consisting of several flats and a door flat, leading to the outside hallway, partially visible because the right wall extended only a little way down stage. On the downstage right was a long ladder, presumably leading to an upper story or to the roof. Black drapes well off from the scenery were used to mask downstage on either side and to mask the hallway. Such a simplified setting, consisting of a window flat, two door flats, and several plain flats, with drapes, was entirely adequate both for the New York and the road-show productions. The kitchen portion of the set was on a raked ramp. Upstage to the left of the inner-bedroom door was a large refrigerator that aided in the masking. It is remarkable how completely such a well-designed skeleton set can suggest the room that it is supposed to represent.

A variety of similar simplifications of realistic settings may be worked out by the imaginative director. Settings so simplified can save both time and money. In considering the question of settings for realistic plays, the director must not overlook such a possibility.

Numerous modern playwrights, dissatisfied with the restrictions of realism, have turned to a variety of other devices to escape these. Thornton Wilder discarded scenery entirely in *Our Town,* 1938, and used a kind of architectural or permanent set for *The Skin of Our Teeth,* 1942. Both Tennessee Williams and Arthur Miller have attempted to push out the restraining boundaries of realistic settings. In *Death of a Salesman,* 1949, Miller combines realism with a kind of expressionistic stylization, which served to reveal various areas and levels for action. Williams frequently calls for both interior and exterior scenes shown simultaneously in his settings, thus precluding the tight confinement of the box set.

Older plays, especially those of Shakespeare and the Greek dramatists, are, as has been noted, not so dependent upon exact locale as are modern naturalistic dramas. The creation of the environment of their action, as with Shakespearean production in the nineteenth century, can veer toward the realistic and the spectacular. Such heavy mountings are largely out of favor today. The trend seems to be toward an architectural unit set, made as flexible as possible with levels, ramps, and various acting areas.

Settings should be regarded as an unobtrusive and silent actor in the play. Inexperienced theatre people tend to become enchanted with elaborate settings and mechanical effects for their own sake. It can be stated as almost axiomatic that when any settings, part of a setting, or mechanical stage device calls attention to itself, it is therefore bad. There are exceptions, of course. Many nineteenth-century melodramas, to repeat an example, are based upon a series of just such big effects and many children's theatre plays utilize these. British Christmas pantomimes exploit them beautifully and shamelessly. In the majority of plays, however, the settings should, without blatantly "hogging the show," provide an unobtrusive background for the action that aids in creating the proper mood and effect. The cue for the setting, then, comes from the play and from the director's interpretation of the kind of effect it should produce in an audience. The director must define for the designer as precisely as possible this effect. A helpful aid in doing this is to define the level of probability which the interpretation aims at. Some designers can find imaginative incitement by trying to get at the spirit of the whole play; others consider plays as moods of feeling and utilize these as cues to proper settings. Some individuals find it helpful to consider the play as a metaphor or symbol as the key to the right design. Whatever the method of approach, in a multiset show the various settings should harmonize, though this harmony may, if the play demands, be built upon contrasts.

Settings can be an important source of interest in a production. They need not be overelaborate to create this interest. Highly expressive and interesting settings can be designed and constructed by good and ingenious artists out of few and inexpensive materials. In general, simplification without sacrifice of expressiveness should be the aim. Perhaps it would be helpful, in conclusion, to state in outline what settings may accomplish:

1. Provide a mask or enclosure for the action.
2. Provide acting areas and levels.
3. Aid in establishing the atmosphere, mood, and effect of the play.
4. Add to the interest of the spectacle.
5. Indicate the general or exact locale of the action.
6. Aid in establishing the social status of the characters.
7. Indicate the taste and attitudes of characters.
8. Help to establish period or time.

All settings do not, of course, accomplish all of these and certain settings may accomplish other effects.

4. PLANNING THE LIGHTING

The lighting and the settings should be planned together, for the settings depend in large measure upon the lighting for their effectiveness. Indeed, in a sense the term *setting* might be used to include the scenery, lighting, furniture, and draperies of the stage. In the so-called space-stage technique of mounting a play, scenery as it has thus far been discussed may, with the exception of some masking drapes, platforms, and levels, be entirely eliminated and lighting alone utilized to indicate environment and change of scene. When the designers begin work on the designs of scenery, they must co-ordinate that work with the lighting. The functions and techniques of lighting are fully discussed in Part IV of this book; here we are concerned with the director's awareness of the lighting demands of the production. The first function of lighting is to make the action on the stage visible to the audience. If the technician in charge of the lighting is to accomplish that, he must know the important areas of the stage in which action occurs. Beyond mere visibility, lighting can accomplish a range of functions. It too can act with the actors. It can aid in establishing tone, mood, atmosphere. It can reveal the time of day. By such uses and the proper employment of light and shadows it can aid the play in creating its effect upon an audience. Comedy calls for a brightness and brilliance of lighting not always adapted to tragedy. Serious drama may employ a range of "mood lighting" not compatible with comedy. The director must, therefore, supply certain definite information to the artist in charge of the lighting. Among these are:

1. The important acting areas in each set.
2. The effects aimed at in the play as a whole.
3. The changes in mood from scene to scene.
4. A time scheme of the action.
5. Any special lighting effects, such as fire in the fireplace, offstage hallway lighting, horizon or back-drop lighting, stars, moon, etc.
6. Projections, if they are to be used.

This list could be extended if certain plays and their lighting effects were taken into account. A casual examination of it will readily indicate the previously stated necessity for the scene designer and lighting artist to work together. Neither can proceed until he knows definitely what the director is aiming toward in his interpretation.

5. SELECTING THE PROPERTIES

As was pointed out above, the furniture and set properties are really a part of the setting, and what has thus far been said of settings applies with proper limitations to this phase of production. Furniture and draperies, books and bric-a-brac, all articles of ornament and adornment—usually classed together as properties or set properties—can, when chosen with taste and intelligence, become a subtle and expressive means of revealing character and environment. They can be a definite aid in creating the effects of the play. Perhaps the script calls for a table. What kind of a table? Not just any table will do, for this table must accomplish more than its mere utilitarian purpose of serving as a repository for articles or a stand for a lamp. Those things which people live with for long reveal the personalities of those people, for such things seem to take on something of the very coloring of the owner's character. Everyone has seen at one time or another a room in which a single thing or combination of things, a picture, a vase, lamp, or chair, established the whole tone and character of the entire room, and marked it as eminently belonging to the occupant. It may have been not only the thing itself that did it; it may have been the peculiar way in which it was fitted into the room. It is just such an effect that a director should aim to accomplish with the chief pieces of furniture or properties that he uses.

Sometimes the furniture or properties called for in a script are of such a nature that they cannot be found in a community, and hence cannot be borrowed or rented. The oriental burial cart called for in the opening scene of *Marco Millions,* as well as other properties required in that play, are examples of articles not readily available. They must, therefore, be designed and made for the production. Often, however, the exact property called for in the script or an adequate substitute can be found. Archaeological or antiquarian exactness is not a necessary requisite for stage properties. The director and the designer are seeking the effect, the proper effect, and not historical accuracy in selecting properties. Nevertheless, a study of the historically accurate is necessary before the director can say just what effect must be striven for in a substitute. A piece of modern chrome-and-plastic office furniture would certainly ruin a setting in Shaw's *Saint Joan.* The director and the designer must know what kind of furnishings were to be found in the period and time in which the action occurs but they do not have to have available antique fifteenth-century French furniture before they can stage *Saint Joan.* Whatever they employ as substitutes, however, must be in harmony with the effect of the play and with the forms of that period. At least it must be sufficiently ancient in form and appearance and sufficiently appropriate to the action that it does not destroy the illusion, the probability, for the general audience.

Furniture must be appropriate to place as well as to period. French and English furniture of the fifteenth century, for example, differed. Moreover, furniture that might be wholly appropriate to a fifteenth-century cathedral room would be entirely out of keeping in the public room of an inn. The furnishings for Arthur Miller's *The Crucible* must suggest seventeenth-century colonial America. The furnishing of a Mexican hovel in southern Arizona would be completely inappropriate in a Negro shanty in Alabama. If the director is staging a series of period plays and modern plays of varying locales, he cannot know all of the details of period and local furnishings. He must, however, know where to find the information and either he or a member of his staff must seek it out. The conscientious director will not be satisfied until he himself has the information on good authority, at least in a general way.

The arrangement as well as the selection of the furnishings

aids in the expression of the characters, the mood, and the atmosphere. Arrangements help to create the effects. The disordered, cluttered tenant farmer's dirty living-room, with clothing hanging about on nails in the walls, no curtains in the windows, a rag stuffed in a broken windowpane, the mantlepiece littered with all kinds of small objects and trash, speaks eloquently of the people who live there and of the kind of life they lead. The arrangement of furniture on the stage involves a number of considerations that pertain to principles of direction, to be discussed in Chapter 8. Here the concern is merely with the effects of arrangement upon selection.

Modern drama with its emphasis upon the influence of environment in the shaping of character and conduct requires a large and specific list of properties. The premodern drama, by contrast, is economical in this respect. The few furnishings and properties required for these earlier plays must, however, be made. Fortunately the historical and archeological explorations of past eras have been so extensive that the director has readily available in any reference library ample illustrative materials. For Shakespearean plays these illustrations have been gathered together in numerous books and manuals. One of the best references which the director and the designers may consult on Elizabethan houses, furnishings, manners, and customs is *The Pageant of Elizabethan England* by Elizabeth Burton and profusely illustrated by Felix Kelly, published in 1958 by Charles Scribner's Sons.

6. THE PROPERTY LIST

It has been noted that most acting editions of plays, especially of modern plays, contain property lists. These may or may not suffice for the interpretation of the play which the director chooses. If they do not, or if he is producing an older play, he will have to prepare, or have prepared, a complete list of properties. Whether or not the director himself prepares the list, he must determine the nature and fitness of the properties used. Properties should be divided into "set props" and "hand props." Set props are any pieces of furniture, draperies, curtains, books, pictures, ornaments and bric-a-brac that remain permanently through an act or set. Hand props are any articles which the actors themselves bring on or take off the set. Even articles of clothing not worn by them but carried on by actors are hand props. Letters, bags, canes, purses, money, umbrellas, a tea service, and similar articles carried on stage by actors come in this category. All properties are under the custody of the property man, though in some instances the costumer takes responsibility for certain articles of clothing that are really props.

As the director studies the script, he makes a list of these. Most of them will be called for in the stage directions of the script or in the action of the play. These are a minimum essential for the business of the play. The first task is to list the items of furniture and properties requisite to the business of the play. But he must go beyond this first essential. A mere list will not suffice. As he makes the list, or after making it, he must specify exactly what is wanted. The more fully descriptive the list is, the more serviceable it will prove to the property man and the more time it will save both director and property man. Only the director who makes a full study of the play is in a position to know or to determine exactly what is wanted and needed. In addition to the essential properties called for by the business of the play, the designer may, and probably will, wish to include properties, such as window curtains, pictures, and similar objects, to dress the sets. These properties of adornment must be added to the property list. When the property list is completed, it is included in the prompt copy of the play and duplicate copies are suppied to the property man, the designer, the technical director, and the costumer—if that individual is involved in supplying certain properties.

There is one other property list, the rehearsal props, which the director must prepare. Before the business rehearsals of a play utilizing furniture and properties can be undertaken, certain essential articles must be provided. These need not be the real props of the play nor even authentic substitutes. For example, a bench will suffice for a sofa and any kind of chairs may be utilized for rehearsals. Even several chairs placed together may substitute for the sofa. Two sticks may in the beginning substitute for foils or swords. Any table not too large or too small will suffice for rehearsals. Nevertheless, the director must make a list of these essential rehearsal properties and furnishings so that they can be provided in ample time.

7. COSTUME AND MAKE-UP

The director may have on his staff a costumer who will design and make the costumes for the show, but it is the director's duty to inform that costumer as to the exact requirements. The determination of the kind of costume to be worn by an actor in a play is based on an intimate understanding of the kind of character he is, his function in the action, and the style of the interpretation. Again, the director is responsible for supplying this information to the consumer. A detailed treatment of costume and make-up will be found in the section on those subjects in this book; here we are concerned with them as they enter the director's planning of the whole production.

Appearances are not deceiving on the stage. There a man is what he seems to be. In life, clothes may not make the man, but on the stage they certainly help to portray his character. They may help also to focus attention upon him. The first control, then, in the selection or design of a costume is the nature of the character for whom the costume is chosen or made. The dominant characteristics, even the mood and attitude of an individual, may be accentuated and highlighted by the clothing he wears. Hamlet's "customary coat of inky black" is a key to his mood and his personality. Often costume is a badge or sign of character, such as ministerial garb, a policeman's uniform, and similar distinctive dress. Some of these may be indications of function as much as, or even more than, of character. To the extent that dominant roles are made to stand out by the kind of dress given them, all costuming is indicative of function. The dress may also indicate the tone of the play, whether it is serious or gay, and thereby aid in its effect. In this way it is a suggestion of the probability aimed at but it may go even further in establishing the level of probability. The costume can readily tell the audience that the play is one of ordinary, contemporary life, or that it is about life in a past era. It can help to reveal that the probability is on the level of the fantastic, the bizzare, the unreal, or the distorted.

Probability, the way in which the character is to be taken or accepted by the audience, is a key to the character's costume. It has previously become apparent that probability is likewise an important basis of style in the interpretation; so it is in the costumes also. Costumes and settings must, of course, be designed in a unified style. If the interpretation is styled in terms of period, the costumes must likewise be in terms of period. Should the approach to the style be in terms of a departure from realism, that same departure should be observed in the dress. The designers of the settings and of the costumes, if they are two separate individuals, must keep in close touch in their work, not only in terms of style but also in terms of color. The colors in a setting can kill a costume and clashing colors in costumes can adversely affect settings. The costumer can also employ color, emblems, lines, and other identifying elements to reveal alignments and groupings of characters. An obvious illustration occurs in the costuming of *Romeo and Juliet,* with the Capulets given one type of similarity in costume and the Montagues another. From what has been said it is apparent that the director must furnish guidance to the costumer concerning the interpretation of the play and the characters. Finally, the director or his assistant will need to make regular engagements with the actors for costume measurements and costume fittings.

Much that has been said of costume as interpretative of the various characters can equally well be said of make-up. Trained actors usually do their own make-ups for the legitimate stage. When the make-up is done by a crew, that crew should work directly under the supervision of the costumer. In addition to facial make-up, there are such things as masks, wigs, and certain types of beards which are prepared by the costumer or under the supervision of that person. All make-ups for a show must be done in terms of the stage lighting and the size of the auditorium. The type of lighting employed, the intensity, and the color must be taken into consideration. Again, co-ordination in the planning becomes important.

8. PREPARING THE PROMPT BOOK

The results of the planning of the whole production are incorporated in a Director's Copy, which becomes the basis of the Prompt Copy. Some directors who prefer to retain a Director's Copy of each play which they stage have a separate Prompt Copy prepared; others use one copy for both purposes. The Prompt Copy will form when finished a complete and accurate acting and staging version of the play and a detailed analysis of the particular production. There is no single system or method of preparing this copy, no set style to be used, nor unvarying content to be included. The method and content vary from director to director and from play to play. In general, however, the practices adopted by publishers of plays, based as these usually are upon professional stage versions, are followed in most theatres.

The first step is the preparation of the book itself. If the text of the play is to be typed on regular letter-size paper (8½ x 11), wide margins for notes and directions should be observed. The actual making of the book would then include the mounting of these in a binder, along with the floor plans, drawings, pictures, various lists, and records. If a printed text is used, one of two methods may be followed. A space in the center of the regular letter-size paper sufficiently large to accommodate the actual text but not large enough to prevent the margins from being pasted in is cut. Into this square space the text of each leaf is carefully pasted onto the letter-size paper. Thus the text of each side of the page can be read and the margins of the letter-size paper can be used for notes and directions. This type of mounting takes time.

The second method is more expeditious. For this method two copies of the text will be needed. Carefully unbind each of the copies and glue the pages on the sheets of paper of the desired size (not smaller than 8½ x 11). The sheets on which the text is mounted should be of good-grade paper, heavy and durable. Beginning with the title page, mount each leaf of the copy. When page one of the first printed copy is pasted face up on the sheet of paper, page two, printed on the reverse side, is entirely hidden. The operation is repeated with the first leaf of the second printed copy, with page two of the text showing. In this manner both copies of the printed text are used to make a single prompt copy. Though this method requires an additional printed copy, it is more rapid than is the first method. Floor plans may be drawn, pictures mounted, and lists typed on separate sheets of the same size as those used for mounting the text. When the sheets are thoroughly dry after the text is pasted in, all are perforated for inclusion in a loose-leaf binder. The binding holes will need reinforcing. The book should not be permanently bound, at least not until after the final performances and all materials to be included are inserted.

The book so prepared is ready to receive the director's notes of interpretation. The Prompt Book will include, in addition to the text, all directions for stage business, floor plans of all settings, complete property lists, light plots, designs or sketches of the sets and costumes (often included after the performance to make the book a complete record), the rehearsal schedule, a summary of the budget, and any other records pertaining to the production that the director may desire to include. On the margin of the text the director writes the directions for the stage business. Beginning with the first line, or the rise of the curtain, he indicates every entrance or exit, every cross or movement, every effect used in interpreting the play. Some of these directions may be indicated in the printed stage directions of the text, which are retained. Printed stage directions not used will be crossed out. All of these notes and directions must be written in pencil, *not in ink*. They are subject to change right up to and including the dress rehearsals.

Frequently, especially to indicate complex groupings or complicated movements, the director will draw in the margins miniature floor plans of the scene and indicate the character groupings by means of symbols for each character and the intricate crosses by arrow-pointed lines. Into the book he will insert notes on interpretations of lines, indications of words to be stressed, indications of tempo, and such other matters. These interpretative directions and signs some directors prefer to write in blue, using a black pencil for business on stage. Off-stage effects with warnings for their execution will go into the book in red. Thus into the book, either written in red pencil or underlined in red, will go the directions for "curtain," "fast curtain," "blackout," "bell rings," "a baby cries," and opposite the stage direction, "he turns on the lights," will appear in red "lights up . . ." Two minutes before any of these occur, a warning will have been given to the proper person by the prompter through an assistant. Thus at the proper place in the text (approximately two minutes running time before the end) will occur in red "warn curtain," and before the entrance of Nora in *A Doll's House* will occur "call Nora." In this way the Prompt Book is made a guide for the performance as well as a record by which the rehearsals are conducted.

In order to save space and time the director and the prompter employ a number of abbreviations in writing the directions in the book. Some of the old stage-direction symbols so common in nineteenth-century plays, such as R.E. for right entrance, L.E. for left entrance, R.U.E. and L.U.E. for right and left upper entrance, L.1.E. for left first entrance, P.S. for prompter's side of the stage, and O.P. for opposite prompter are generally used today. Other symbols or abbreviations, such as "Xing" for crossing, or "John X. D. L." for "John crosses down left," are employed, varying somewhat from director to director. Those used are a matter of choice, so long as they convey a clear and accurate record to the people concerned. In the same way, the use of colored pencils is entirely optional; they are a convenience, not a necessity. In the majority of modern plays, unless otherwise stated, "right" and "left" are used in stage directions to mean stage right and left from the actor's point of view. "Downstage" means toward the footlights and "upstage" means away from the footlights toward the rear wall. In entering stage directions in the prompt book, and in all stage usage, these terms should be consistently employed in the sense here stated. They apply, of course, to the proscenium-arch stage and are not appropriate to center staging.

After the performances, the Prompt Book may be retained as a permanent record of the production to be brought forth and used again in case the play is revived. For this purpose many directors like to make the record as accurate and as complete as possible. Exact descriptions, designs (when not on too large a scale), photographs of sets, costumes, properties, make-up, and outstanding scenes in the action as played are included. Some directors like to include records of the run of the play, financial accounts, a copy of the printed program, and reviews in this permanent record. In this way the director and the organization can build up year by year a valuable collection which makes revivals comparatively easy. Such records are historically valuable.

9. PRODUCTION CONFERENCES

Throughout this discussion of planning reference has been repeatedly made to production conferences. When a Director works with a production staff composed of several individuals, such conferences become imperative. It is wise to schedule them in a regular program and to conduct them in an orderly manner. In these conferences there is opportunity for the Director to present his interpretation of the play and his ideas for the production; there is opportunity for the Designers to present designs, estimates of materials and work, various methods of accomplishing given ends, budgets, and other matters pertinent to production; and, perhaps, of equal importance, there is opportunity for full discussion of the production, the exchange of ideas and interpretations, and the arriving at a unified point of view or approach. The schedule of conferences here given is based upon the practice followed in several university theatres and is suggestive rather than definitive. Naturally it must be adapted to the whole program, time available, working conditions, and other factors.

SCHEDULE OF PRODUCTION CONFERENCES

FIRST CONFERENCE—8 weeks prior to the opening of the show.
The Director's Meeting

The Director outlines his approach to the show—his interpretation—explains as clearly as possible the style to be used, outlines the dramatic values he sees in the script which he is seeking to project in production, and discusses the meaning and emphasis which he wishes to convey.

I. The Director gives to the Scene Designer:
   1. A full statement of the scenic requirements, including the number of sets, acting areas in each, entrances, levels, etc.
   2. A complete property list (to be passed on to the property man).
   3. A list of properties needed for the rehearsals.
   4. A full statement of the lighting requirements.
   5. A complete rehearsal schedule, including technical and dress rehearsals.
   6. A statement of scenery needed for rehearsals, including levels, steps, etc.
      (If there is a Technical Director separate from the scene designer, items 2 to 6 inclusive would go to that individual.)

II. The Director gives to the Costume Designer:
   1. A complete analytical list of all characters to be used in the play.
   2. A statement of costume requirements, including period, type, changes for each character where required, etc.
   3. A statement of acting requirements of costumes; for example, practical pockets, special reinforcement for violent use, etc.

4. Costume accessories as required by each character.
5. Make-up requirements.
6. A complete rehearsal schedule, including technical and dress rehearsals.
7. A list of costumes required for rehearsal prior to dress rehearsal.

SECOND CONFERENCE—6 weeks prior to the opening of the show.
The Designers' Meeting

I. The Scene Designer submits:
   1. Ground or floor plans of each set, showing entrances, stairways, levels, etc.
   2. Preliminary sketches of each set (these should be sufficiently comprehensive and complete enough to allow final decisions to be made about the settings—or to allow adequate suggestions of alterations).
   3. Property sketches if essential.
   4. The preliminary lighting plan (which may have been worked out by a separate individual in charge of lighting and in consultation with the Designer and the Costumer).
   5. The working schedule of the various construction crews (prepared by the Technical Director).
   6. A schedule for stage crew rehearsals (prepared by the Technical Director).
   7. A descriptive list of properties, including set props and hand props (prepared by the Property Man under the Technical Director).
   8. The complete scenery, property, and lighting budget for the show.
   Items 5 to 8 inclusive are presented by the Technical Director if that individual is not also the Scene Designer.

II. The Costume Designer submits:
   1. Costume sketches in color for each costume. Duplicates are merely listed, with indications of color variations.
   2. A working schedule, including periods for appointments with actors for measurements, etc.
   3. A complete list of costume properties, including handkerchiefs, fans, cigarette cases, hand bags, etc.
   4. Make-up sketches or pictures where necessary.
   (If masks and wigs are involved, they would be submitted as part of the make-up.)
   5. The budget for costumes and make-up.

THIRD CONFERENCE—5 weeks prior to the opening of the show.
The Business Manager's Meeting

I. The Director summarizes whatever changes have been agreed upon in the production, reports on casting, and aids in adjusting any differences.

II. The Scene Designer submits:
   1. Any changes in set designs.
   2. Any changes in arrangements of the stage or in the work schedule.
   3. Secures final approval of the budget for his department (if there is a Technical Director in addition, he submits the budget for sets, lighting, properties).

III. The Costume Designer submits:
   1. Any changes in costume designs.
   2. Any changes in costume or make-up arrangements.
   3. The approved budget for his department.

IV. The Business Manager submits:
   1. A complete advertising campaign.
      a. Posters, cards, banners, direct mail, etc., and their distribution.
      b. News stories, interviews, newspaper advertising, picture displays, etc., and their distribution.
   2. Methods of handling ticket sales when necessary for discussion.
   3. A plan of house management for all performances, if departures from established practices are involved.
   4. The preparation of the program copy, including necessary statements of credits.
   5. Any schedule or arrangements for the making of pictures and photographs.
   6. A summary of the total budget for the production.

Some such schedule of production conferences as the above makes for co-ordinated staff effort and for high morale in the process of production. It will, of course, need to be supplemented with frequent talks between the Director and the individual members of the staff. For example, the Designers of sets and of costumes cannot submit at the first production conference the sketches called for unless they have been in close consultation with the Director. In some theatres these consultations between individuals are substituted for the more formal production conferences. While such consultations are effective, they are time consuming and they do not aid in building morale to the extent that the production conferences do. A theatre staff, however, must adopt whatever orderly process best suits its needs and conditions.

QUESTIONS AND EXERCISES

1. Choose a one-act play which appeals to you and which you think the audience in your community would enjoy. Prepare a complete director's interpretation of the play.
2. Choose a Shakespearean play other than *Twelfth Night* and state several possible approaches to its meaningful interpretation. Hugh Hunt's *Old Vic Prefaces* and Harley Granville-Barker's *Shakespeare Prefaces* will be helpful to you in this exercise.
3. Plan an architectural stage setting for the Shakespeare play you have chosen.
4. Make a list of the essential stage properties for the play.
5. Outline the time scheme of the play. Do changes in time indicate any important changes in lighting effects?
6. If you were staging this Shakespeare play on an architectural stage in your local theatre for the usual audience that comes to that theatre, what style of interpretation do you think would be most effective? State this conception of style as clearly as possible.
7. In terms of the style adopted, what kinds of costumes would you use for the chief roles? Prepare a statement about these for the costume designer to follow.
8. If you were staging this play in your local theatre with the regular staff of artists and technicians (with the exception that you are substituting for the director), what production conferences would you find necessary? What would you plan to accomplish at each?

CHAPTER 6

Rehearsals

THE REHEARSALS of a play are designed to prepare it for presentations to audiences in such a way as to create desired and predetermined effects. In this preparation certain specific things are to be accomplished within a limited period of time; therefore, rehearsals must be conducted according to an orderly and well-planned schedule. If such a schedule is not prepared and adhered to, the director may find the date of the opening performance upon him and the last act not ready for presentation, or he may find much of the preparation of the play left unfinished to be crowded into the last few rehearsals. There have been, of course, plays "put on" by "torch-bearer" directors by merely placing scripts in the hands of a cast and beginning rehearsals without any kind of plan other than that of proceeding from act to act until the date of performance arrives. Such muddling procedure supplies the bulk of the 90 per cent of amateur performances that are said not to be worth sitting through. If they "go over" at all, it is because they are performed for uncritical audiences, or because fortunately the cast includes some competent actors. Under either of these circumstances they are no credit to a director.

1. THE FUNCTION OF REHEARSALS

There may be said to be seven major aims in conducting rehearsals. These are:

1. Imparting to the cast a clear and definite understanding of the play, including each line, scene, act, and role.
2. Interpreting the play in pantomimic action.
3. Characterizing the roles.
4. Perfecting the speaking of the lines.
5. Co-ordinating and orchestrating the various elements into a smooth and unified whole.
6. Perfecting the manipulation of the settings, lighting, sound effects, uses and changes of properties, wearing of costumes, and co-ordinating these production elements with a smooth and expeditious running of the show.
7. Trying out the whole production.

The group of corresponding rehearsals in the schedule, for purposes of discussion, may be named as follows:

1. Reading rehearsals.
2. Business or blocking rehearsals.
3. Characterization rehearsals.
4. Line interpretation rehearsals.
5. Finishing rehearsals.
6. Technical rehearsals.
7. Dress rehearsals.

While these are divided into groups for clearness in discussion, certain of the functions must be accomplished together, as will become apparent later. The reason they are usually separated into definite groups by directors is to allow the director and the actors to concentrate upon a specific task or problem to be mastered. For best results it is advisable to break down the work to be accomplished into some such units as those listed above. If a director at the outset attempts to accomplish several of these functions simultaneously, he may succeed merely in confusing the actors and end each rehearsal period with relatively small results. Rehearsals are a learning process and the director is in the fullest sense of the term a teacher. As an instructor, he knows that in the mastery of any complicated problem or process it is necessary to break it down into its major components or units.

2. ALLOTMENT OF TIME FOR REHEARSALS

The number of rehearsals to be allotted to each of the seven groups listed above will depend upon the nature of the play and the amount of time available for the production. Some plays involving intricate pantomimic action will require a relatively large number of business rehearsals, while others, because of their nature, will require a large emphasis upon characterization and lines. Certain plays dependent upon stage and mechanical effects will require a number of technical rehearsals, while others not so dependent may be satisfactorily perfected with two or three such rehearsals. The director, sometimes in consultation with his production staff, must use his judgment in blocking out the rehearsal groups on the rehearsal schedule. Opinions vary greatly, too, as to the ideal amount of time that should be devoted to the whole rehearsal schedule.

There are directors, influenced no doubt by Equity ruling, who maintain that four weeks are ample for the production of the average play. Indeed some are so partial to this period that they assert that a cast is apt to "go stale" if required to rehearse for a longer time. Perhaps they have failed to remember that only dead things which are no longer growing go stale. As long as a cast is learning and developing, there is no danger of staleness. A trained and talented director with an intelligent and gifted cast can continue this process of growth toward perfection indefinitely. The argument of professional precedent is of no validity when applied to a nonprofessional cast. The professional cast is made up of trained and experienced actors who presumably do not need to be taught the rudiments of their art. Further, acting is their profession, to which they can devote their major energies and a large portion of their time. In their work they are under an economic compulsion not felt by the nonprofessional actors, who are usually engaged in the art as an avocation. The major energies of the latter and most of their time must go into other occupations. Only in exceptional cases are they thoroughly trained in the art of acting. With many of them, in addition to the rehearsal periods, the director may have to spend long hours in drill on basic fundamentals. It is, then, an optimistic director indeed who expects to accomplish in four weeks with nonprofessional actors what most professional companies do none too well in the same length of time. There is, however, some danger from "staleness" with young and inexperienced actors. After they have perfected a characterization and business to the extent of their present capabilities, constant additional rehearsals may tend to render their performances mechanical.

Frequent repetitions over a considerable period of time are requisite for the nonprofessional actor to master a role, learn to execute the business with ease and naturalness, learn to speak lines effectively, and acquire all of the other accomplishments necessary for a finished performance. The answer then to the question of how much time the director should allot to the rehearsals of a play is as much time as it is possible to allow, and this will more frequently be too little rather than too much. In academic institutions the schedule and calendar of campus and school events will effectively curtail this time, to say nothing of holidays, examination schedules, and opening and closing dates. In the community theatre the amount of time that the actors are willing to or can afford to allot to the undertaking will prove a no less effectual barrier to the undue extension of the time factor.

Compromising, as he must, with all of these, the director should attempt to secure at least five weeks of rehearsals for the average modern play, and a proportionately longer time for the revival of period plays and modern plays that offer unusual difficulties. Often he may have to crowd the production into a shorter time. In certain summer-theatre schedules he may be fortunate to secure two full weeks. Plays for such productions must be chosen with care and with full cognizance of the limitations of time. Plays with large casts and many scenes, and difficult period plays, such as those of Shakespeare, should, if possible, have at least eight weeks of rehearsals. Certainly that does not appear excessive when we recall that one of the best productions the Moscow Art Theatre ever gave was rehearsed for two years. The records do not reveal any sign of staleness on the part of the actors in that production.

3. THE REHEARSAL PERIOD

These recommendations concerning the length of time for preparing a production have been based on the assumption of one rehearsal each day for six days of each week (with the addition of any drill periods that may be necessary, which will be discussed later). In some community theatres and in a few academic theatres rehearsals on Saturdays and Sundays are not usually or always possible. If such is the case, due allowance in the rehearsal schedule must be made. Another time factor which the director must consider is the length of each of these daily rehearsal periods. This factor, too, is frequently conditioned by demands made upon the members of the cast in their various other pursuits. Because of such demands, it is somewhat difficult, especially in community theatres, to schedule a consecutive series of rehearsals with the full cast. But in view of the fact that a great portion of the director's time must be spent in instructing and drilling individuals in their specific roles and small groups in difficult scenes, this limitation need not prove too irksome if rehearsal and drill periods are properly scheduled in advance. In both the drill rehearsals and in the regular rehearsals with the fuller cast, as has been said, the director is engaged in teaching and the cast in learning. In this, as in all other learning processes, the element of fatigue enters. When rehearsals are continued for too long a period, this element greatly diminishes their value. Experience has shown that two rehearsal periods of three hours each are often more effective than a single period of six hours. We learn more readily by repetition after intervals of rest than we do in a single long, tiring effort. The rehearsal period should rarely be continued beyond three and a half hours, and then only in exceptional instances, such as that of the first reading or study rehearsal, some of the technical rehearsals, and the first dress rehearsal.

On the other hand, if the period is only an hour in length and if corrections and repetitions are frequent, it will not be possible to complete the rehearsal of a full act or any large segment of the play. Considering each of these, directors have found three-hour periods about the right length of time for most rehearsals. Frequently not all of the actors in the cast need to be called for the full three-hour period. When an actor does not appear until the middle or latter portion of an act, it is a waste of his time to require him to report at the beginning of the rehearsal period and merely sit for half the period until time for his appearance. Such idleness and wasting of time produces bad morale. The director can easily avoid it by careful attention to the rehearsal schedule and the making of calls for rehearsals. If the director is considerate of the time of his actors, they usually will reciprocate by showing him consideration.

Through his study of the play, the director has discovered the scenes or segments into which it may be divided. Many scenes in plays really concern only two characters. Moreover, these two characters often have several such duologue scenes scattered through the play. As soon as the blocking or business rehearsals have been completed, these scenes involving two actors only may be grouped for one or more rehearsal periods, or portions of rehearsal periods. It is not necessary, nor is it desirable, to keep six or eight other actors sitting by while these two actors are being trained. Careful attention must, then, be given to the units which compose the play and to the combinations of characters within these units.

4. DRILL PERIODS

Even when these regular rehearsals are accurately planned and properly conducted they are usually not sufficient for all of the training that must be accomplished. There are few full-length plays that can be adequately prepared with nonprofessional casts in thirty rehearsals of three hours duration. It becomes necessary, therefore, to supplement these regular rehearsal periods with periods of intensive drill. Even in instances in which a greater length of time than five weeks is available for rehearsals, these drill periods are still desirable in training inexperienced actors. These periods may range in time from fifteen minutes to a full hour, and may be scheduled at any time to suit the convenience of the actors and the director. Sometimes these drill periods, as in the case of singing, dancing, and fencing, may be scheduled with an instructor other than the director. Scenes of complicated action and business, such as the fencing scene in *Hamlet* in which Hamlet and Laertes must exchange swords, or the scene in *A Doll's House* in which Nora dances the tarantella, can be much more readily perfected in several short periods of repeated drill under direction, where entire attention is focused upon one thing, than in the longer rehearsals devoted to larger units. In the same way, individual characters and speeches can be given the benefit of more intensive drill. Every important scene in each act should be perfected in short drill periods given over exclusively to the single scene. An actor who needs coaching in the use of his voice, the characterization of his role, or in the enactment of any big scene may be given more effective instruction in a series of such drill periods.

In the beginning of this intensive instruction, the scene, character, speech, or piece of business should be thoroughly analyzed, broken into its parts, laid out step by step, and then by repeated drill made so much a part of the actor that its execution becomes automatic. Only by such a process as this will these difficult and troublesome elements acquire a smoothness of execution that gives professional finish to the whole. Almost all nonprofessional and many professional actors need these periods of more intensive work. In them the director can teach the actor how to make his entrance or exit, how to walk and stand on the stage, how to sit down and rise gracefully in character, how to handle properties, how to secure volume and project his words; in them he has opportunity to teach the fundamentals of the actor's art which the individual must employ in the interpretation of his role. The regular rehearsal period does not allow time for all of this; if it did, it would be at the expense of others in the cast not concerned. Such a schedule of drill periods should begin as soon as the play is put into rehearsal and the needs of individual members of the cast become apparent. They should continue over a period of time adequate to accomplish their purposes. They will greatly relieve the burden of the regular rehearsals and aid in making these more valuable and pleasant for everyone. The nature and number of these drill periods will vary according to the nature of the play and the abilities of the cast.

5. THE SCHEDULE OF REGULAR REHEARSALS

Similar variations occur in the scheduling of regular rehearsals, as has been pointed out, but for purposes of discussion an outline of rehearsal periods that may be alloted to each group of rehearsals is indicated below. In planning similar schedules for different plays, the director will have to consider the total time available, the characteristics of the play to be produced, and the kind of production projected. Assuming that the play is to be produced with five full weeks of regular rehearsals, six rehearsal periods plus necessary drill periods each week, and that it is a modern full-length play offering only average difficulties, such as *A Doll's House, Biography,* or *Detective Story,* the schedule may be planned as follows:

A REHEARSAL SCHEDULE

1st Rehearsal Period *2nd Rehearsal Period* *3rd Rehearsal Period*	Reading rehearsals of the whole play, and intensive study of the first act.		
4th Rehearsal Period *5th Rehearsal Period* *6th Rehearsal Period* *7th Rehearsal Period*	Blocking or business rehearsals of the first act.		
8th Rehearsal Period	Reading rehearsal of the second act.		
9th Rehearsal Period *10th Rehearsal Period*	Characterization and line rehearsals for the first act.		
11th Rehearsal Period	Run-through of the whole first act.		
12th Rehearsal Period *13th Rehearsal Period* *14th Rehearsal Period*	Blocking or business rehearsals for the second act.		
15th Rehearsal Period	Characterization and line rehearsal of the second act.		
16th Rehearsal Period *17th Rehearsal Period*	Run-through of the first and second acts consecutively.		
19th Rehearsal Period *20th Rehearsal Period*	Blocking or business rehearsals of the third act.		
21st Rehearsal Period	Run-through of the first and second acts consecutively.		
22nd Rehearsal Period	Characterization and line rehearsal of the third act.		
23rd Rehearsal Period *24th Rehearsal Period* *25th Rehearsal Period* *26th Rehearsal Period*	Rehearsals of the whole play	Orchestrating rehearsals of the whole play for perfecting movement, tempo, rhythm and timing.	The finishing rehearsals
27th Rehearsal Period *28th Rehearsal Period*	Technical rehearsals.		
29th Rehearsal Period *30th Rehearsal Period*	Dress rehearsals—try-outs of play.		

Such a schedule of rehearsals requires some further explanation. According to the above outline, work on the second act begins before the first is completed, and on the third before the second is completed. The director who waits until his first act is completely finished before beginning work on the second and insists upon a similar finishing before beginning on the third will be apt to find little time left for finishing the third act or for polishing the whole play. Such a procedure is apt to result in a finished first act and a ragged second and third.

After business rehearsals are started on the second act, the first act should not be neglected. It should be run through from time to time at the beginning or end of the rehearsal period. As soon as the second act shapes up, the first and second should be run through together from time to time, as intensive work proceeds on the third. Adjustments must be made in the schedule and order of rehearsals to accommodate these run-throughs.

Two technical rehearsals, followed by two dress rehearsals, will usually suffice for the play of average difficulties. Of course more are desirable if they can be secured. Technical rehearsals are usually trying for the cast and sometimes seem a waste of time to them. If the technical director and the stage manager have watched the show through several of the latter rehearsals, they should be able through careful planning and advance preparation to save time and avoid much of the tedium of the technical rehearsals. All of the production elements of the show should be ready by the beginning of the fifth week so that lights may be hung, sound effects tried out, and settings moved on stage prior to the technical rehearsals. If this procedure is followed, the stage crew can gain some experience in striking and setting the various scenes even prior to the technical rehearsals.

Costumes likewise should be ready by the beginning of the fifth week (in a five-weeks production schedule). If period dress is required, the actors should be encouraged to wear these well in advance of the dress rehearsals so that they may become thoroughly familiar with them. If the technical rehearsals are properly planned and conducted and if the dress rehearsals are equally well planned and prepared for, they need not be the confusing and exhausting ordeals which they appear to be in many productions. Even with the most careful planning, dress rehearsals will be something of a strain. Without careful planning and advance preparation, they can become so chaotic as to be almost useless. With advance planning and proper preparation they can become true tryout performances.

6. CONDUCTING REHEARSALS

In the conduct of rehearsals the personality and abilities of the director are of paramount importance. He must be a manager, a teacher, and a leader, as well as an artist. In fact, no matter how good an individual artist he may be, if he is not a good manager, teacher, and leader, he will never become a very good director. In rehearsals his job is not merely to interpret a play but also to handle people, induce them to work together, and inspire them to bring out of themselves their best abilities. Only the director lacking in personality and leadership, unsure of his abilities, resorts to screaming at his cast or employs biting sarcasm. Most nonprofessional actors are working without remuneration for the love of their work and the training they may derive, but the training and pleasure are not worth the disagreeableness of working under such a director. If the director knows his work, conducts his rehearsals in a systematic and orderly manner, and develops a proper morale in his staff and cast, he will find no necessity for recourse to discourtesy or abuse. Strict attention to the business in hand, firmness, tact, impartiality, and courtesy will aid any director in building up a devoted following in his organization.

Frequently the statement has been made with some justification that amateur dramatics is nothing but a waste of time. The trained director who organizes and schedules his rehearsals and drill periods in an orderly way and conducts his work in a systematic fashion will do much to obviate this criticism. Rehearsals should invariably begin and end exactly on time. No director should permit any requisite member of a cast to be absent or tardy from rehearsals. If an Irish bull may be permitted, no member of a cast should ever be permitted to be absent and should be excused for tardiness only in cases of illness, hasty marriage, or sudden death; and if any of these happen too often, he should be dropped. A director can much better afford to lose a good actor than countenance the loss of morale in the whole cast. Firmness in this respect will save the director and the cast many hours of irritation and waste.

After the dismissal of one or two offenders, there will be little to complain of in the matter of punctuality and attendance, provided the director holds himself to the same stringent requirements. These requirements should be clearly outlined at the very first rehearsal and all members of the cast told then and there that if for any reasons they cannot live up to these requirements they should relinquish their parts at the outset. This announcement can be made diplomatically and firmly, without offense. Coupled with it should be a statement about the schedule, indicating that the actor's time will not be wasted. What was said above about arrangements to conserve the time of actors applies to regular rehearsals and drill periods and might aid in the building of morale if summarized at the first rehearsal for the whole cast.

The rehearsal periods should at all times be devoted strictly to the work in hand. They should be as serious and as intensive as are periods of drill upon the football field. Concentration is absolutely necessary for effective achievement. Inattention to duty and undue levity at rehearsals must not be countenanced. There are plenty of opportunities for fun and enjoyment in the theatre, but they must not be permitted to undermine the serious nature of artistic work. This is by no means to say that rehearsals must be a grind; they can and should be a pleasure. When the director and every member of the cast are working harmoniously together as artists for the achievement of a production which will reflect credit upon all who are engaged in it, the work may be exacting but it will be enjoyable.

The theory underlying rehearsals is the theory of learning by intelligent and concentrated repetition. As has been said, this repetition must not continue to the point at which fatigue decidedly diminishes the returns, but must be so frequent that what has been accomplished in one rehearsal will not be forgotten before the next. Select limited segments of a play or an act for drill and rehearsal and devote the period or the portion of the period to one aspect of their rendering. When actors tend to become fatigued with rehearsing the business of a scene or series of scenes, move on to a new scene or sequence. The change will lessen the fatigue. Do not try to cram everything—business, characterization, interpretation of lines, etc.—into one early rehearsal. Proceed in orderly manner from task to task. Anything once acquired by repetition is difficult to unlearn and replace by something else. Business and interpretation of lines should not, therefore, be set by repetition in rehearsals if they are not correct and to be retained.

7. THE READING REHEARSALS

In order that the whole interpretation may be correct from the beginning, the director begins the rehearsals of a play with reading rehearsals, in which business, character, lines, and all other elements in the production may be clearly explained and discussed with the cast. For some directors the reading rehearsal or rehearsals are nothing more than the first perfunctory reading through of the play by the whole cast. These rehearsals can be much more than that and can save considerable valuable time. For these rehearsals the entire cast, including understudies and alternates, should be assembled in a large room or on stage. The stage is not at all necessary. A large room with comfortable chairs, a large table, and a blackboard, is preferable. In these early rehearsals the director attempts to impart to the cast the kind of interpretation of the play which he is aiming at in its production. Many directors prefer to begin these reading rehearsals with an explanation of the following:

1. The effects or powers aimed at in the production.
2. The dramatic values in the script.
3. The meaning or significance of the play as a whole.
4. The style of production adopted to bring these most forcefully to an audience.

Sketches of sets and costumes may be helpful in these explanations. From these points, the director proceeds to a discussion of the characters, explaining the function of each in the action and elucidating the nature of each. Dominant characterizing traits, typical or habitual actions, and other devices of characterization should be pointed out. If the dialogue is in any way unusual, it should be noted in this general discussion of the play. The director has several objectives in this preliminary discussion. He is, first, attempting to make the actors see clearly just what is aimed at. Secondly, he is attempting to fire the imaginations of the actors, to make them see the roles which they are to play as living human beings, interesting personalities. He is trying to bring the play to life, to make it seem worth doing and interesting. He is not attempting to force his exact interpretation in minute detail upon the actors, though he is stating explicitly the general effects aimed at. The more he can kindle the imaginations and interests of the actors, the more successful will his preliminary discussion be.

With the play thus explained and brought to life, the first reading can begin. Before the reading of each act, the director should fully and minutely describe and explain the setting, using sketches, diagrams, and blackboard drawings. If a model of the set has been made, it will prove most useful. The placement of furniture and the stage props should be clearly described and their positions carefully indicated. The objective is to familiarize each member of the cast with the appearance of the set and the location of acting areas and properties which they will use. If they are to visualize these completely, sketches and models are almost essential. When this has been accomplished and after each actor has been supplied with a copy of the script and a pencil, the actual reading can begin. Some directors prefer to read the play to the cast; others object to this on the score that it tends to produce imitation. It would seem that imitation would occur to any dangerous degree only with very immature actors, and then only with those who had little or no imagination of their own. Indeed, the question may be asked: What is wrong with imitation anyway in the beginning of an artistic endeavor? Apparently all great artists and all great art began by imitation. It is only when art continues to be a mere copying that it becomes valueless and dangerous. If the director is capable of it, and if by that means he can best induce conceptions of the characters that fire the imaginations of the actors, let him enact every role in turn through these first rehearsals, provided always that he never permits an actor to continue rehearsal after rehearsal in a mere repetition of his portrayal. Some directors have the cast give the first reading of the play, because when this is done, the director is left free to correct and explain errors and omissions during the reading. In this, once again, the method employed rests entirely with the director, and he may vary it from play to play. The entire play should be gone through at the first reading, in whatever way chosen.

In order to complete the reading rehearsal in a reasonable time, too much comment and explanation cannot be injected into the reading of the play. The main idea at the first reading rehearsal is to clarify the interpretation of the whole play. Any cuttings and changes in the script should be clearly indicated here and the actors instructed to cross out the cuts and make the changes in their copies. Little attention can be given in this first reading to the details of stage business, characterization, and lines. Important entrances and exits may be indicated and major acting areas pointed out but the major objective is to read through the whole play, act by act, for its general interpretation. If time permits of the inclusion of more than the three reading rehearsals, dividends may be reaped by a thorough analysis and discussion of the play, especially of those plays of more than usual depth and significance. The minimum aim in the first or early readings is to clarify the interpretation of the play as a whole, to attain a solid understanding of the nature of the leading characters, and to clarify the meaning and significance of any obscure lines of dialogue. In these early readings the directors should keep clearly before the cast the dominant effects aimed at.

With these general matters of interpretation clarified, the director may in the second reading rehearsal or second series turn to the problems of stage business. Beginning with the first act, members of the cast, along with any alternates retained, should read it through, aided by the director's explanations and suggestions. Every important speech in the act should be thoroughly explained and discussed, so that the actor sees what emotion motivates it, what it means, what place it has in the scene, and what effects it is designed to arouse. At the same time, every piece of business, all necessary actions accompanying the dialogue or occurring in any scene should be fully indicated and described. It goes without saying that much of this action will have to be worked out in detail, modified, and new action added in the business rehearsals. In these reading rehearsals the important gross stage movement, as a minimum, is to be clarified. To clarify all complicated business, and to point out entrances, exits, and crosses, references should be constantly made to the floor plan of the set.

Each member of the cast should be required to write into his copy of the script clear directions for all actions, business, and stage movements—crossing out, of course, any printed stage directions for such as are to be discarded. Those retained directions must become a part of his study of the script to be associated always with the dialogue. The director should at these reading rehearsals make it clear that certain modifications may be necessary and certain new pieces of business added during the business rehearsals. Therefore, the actors should write all directions for business into the scripts in pencil. Along with these matters of concern at the early reading rehearsals, any ideas as to how and what to study in mastering the character should be given. Novels or stories containing similar characters, individuals in real life known to the director and actors, essays and commentaries on the character or on former interpretations, and pictures and illustrations can prove useful. The deeper, fuller, and richer the actor's insight into the character, the more brilliant will be his possible portrayal of the role.

In the beginning, it should be insisted that every part in the play, even the smallest role, can be made an effective characterization if the actor has the imagination and makes the effort to do it. The actor's task is to bring to life upon the stage a real human being. Toward that end, it is dangerous for him to give too much emphasis to his role as a type. His aim, especially in the chief roles, is to individualize the character. Even the most unsympathetic role in the play must be looked upon by the actor in that role with a sympathetic imagination. As that character, he must proceed to build up a justification for himself and his actions; he must begin to feel in the role as that character would feel in real life. Indeed, for the time being the situation of the play must be "real life" for the cast. Only in this way can the director and the actors attain that sincerity of character portrayal that somewhat compensates for the lack of professional skill and professional finish on the part of the actors.

After the director and the cast have worked their way through the first act, scene by scene, even line by line—if necessary—then the act should be read through once again by the cast with the barest minimum of interruptions by the director. In this way, clarifications arrived at in the analysis will be more firmly fixed. If several actors have been retained for a single role, each of these should be given opportunity at this time to read. In this way the director will be able to single out, perhaps, the one actor whom he wishes to retain for the role. Certainly, by the end of the reading rehearsals the director should make his final choice of actors for each of the roles.

Sometimes he has to resort to elimination tryouts or additional readings by those actors retained for each of the roles before he can arrive at a final decision. If it has not become apparent in the process of the reading rehearsals of the whole play that certain actors are best suited to certain roles, the elimination tryouts or readings of roles should be held after the whole play has been completely analyzed and run through in the reading rehearsals. By scheduling these after the reading rehearsals each contestant will have derived the benefits of the analyses, interpretations, and clarifications of these readings.

Perhaps a final word of caution on casting will not be amiss. The director should make it quite clear to the actors that he retains the right for the good of the show to replace an inadequate actor even after rehearsals have been in progress for some time—a policy that is strictly limited if he is working with an Equity cast under Equity rules.

The procedures outlined for the reading rehearsals of the first act should be followed in the reading of the remaining acts or divisions. The time given over to reading rehearsals will be limited if the rehearsal schedule confines the director and cast to four weeks of preparation. If time is available, it can be used most profitably with the more intricate dramas and with plays from the past. The more obvious plays, on the other hand, usually can be easily explored and explained in three reading rehearsals. Any additional time available for the rehearsal of such plays can perhaps more profitably be spent in other types of rehearsals, especially in the polishing and finishing rehearsals. It is apparent, therefore, that the proper planning of a rehearsal schedule requires judgment and experience on the part of the director. With reading rehearsals, as with other types, there is a point of diminishing returns when it is wise to stop them and turn to the next step or stage in the preparation.

8. BUSINESS REHEARSALS

With a clear conception gained from the reading rehearsals of the play, the effect aimed at in its production, the style in which

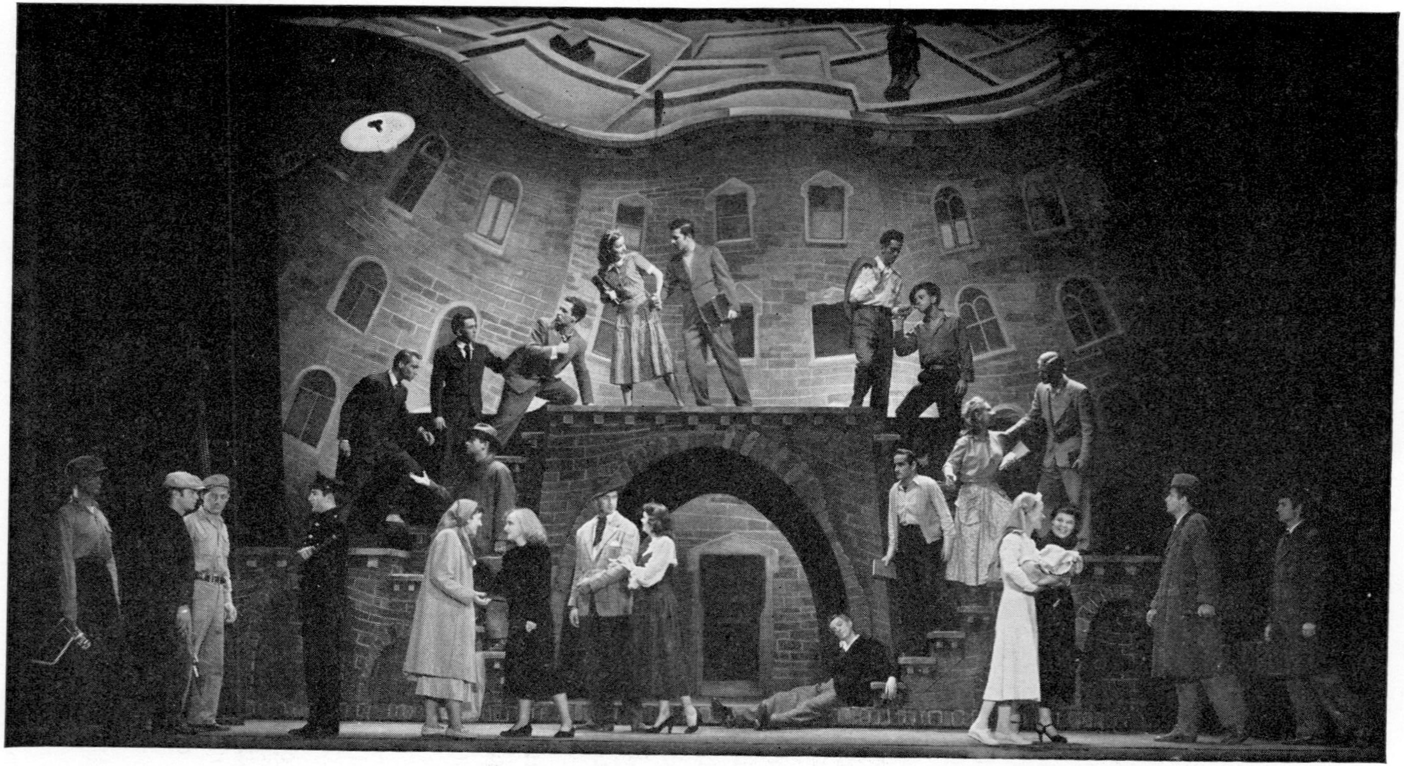

Frank Sundstrom's adaptation of *The Trial* as produced by the Pasadena Playhouse. Directed by Mr. Sundstrom and designed by Scott McLean.

it is to be interpreted, the essential nature and function of the characters, the layout of each setting, and with a general idea of the business as the director has planned it, the cast is ready to begin the business rehearsals. The director's objective in these rehearsals is to perfect the composition of the business, to teach it to the cast, and by means of repetition and direction to train the actors in its execution. As has been repeatedly stressed, the design of the business as previously planned may undergo considerable modification in the course of these rehearsals. The gross, essential business may remain largely unmodified but it is probable that many details will be added to it and a considerable amount of supplementary business not at first in the director's plan will be included. Certain pieces of business may have to be modified or even replaced because the actor in the role or roles involved simply cannot effectively execute that business as originally planned. The experienced actor will himself, as he grows in his role, add bits of characterizing business.

The purpose of these business rehearsals is not the perfection and final finish of execution of each piece of business; rather that purpose is to establish the business, set it in relation to the lines which it accompanies and illustrates, relate it to the characters who are involved and whose personalities it reveals, to accommodate it to its environment, and to fix the style of its execution. Polishing and finishing will come later. In the first business rehearsals the director is concerned to "get the play on its feet," so to speak. Since business is intimately tied into dialogue and character, as well as into other elements of presentation, the conduct of business rehearsals will of necessity involve these other matters. Consideration of them should, at this time, be kept to the minimum necessary to clarify the business and the primary attention centered upon the movement of the whole play from beginning to end in pantomimic action. Yet, since a play in performance is an organic whole if rightly done, all of the elements of interpretation will come to the fore in the businessing of the script. That is one of the reasons why the director must know the play thoroughly and must plan the production in advance of rehearsals. By conveying this plan of interpretation to the whole cast during the reading rehearsals, he makes it possible for each actor thereafter to work on his role with intelligent understanding of the aims and effects to be achieved.

What is business? It may be said to be the physical action and movements used by the actors to characterize their roles and to project the dramatic action of the play. Business is that part of spectacle of a production executed by the actors. It is a part of the visual aspect of performance. It supplements and enforces the diction and, at times, actually replaces diction by substituting for it. An old maxim says "actions speak louder than words." In certain dramatic situations, especially when such situations are built up to with words, actions do speak with a power that words would dwarf. Business includes the pantomimic dramatization of the emotions of characters which underlie and motivate their actions; it includes also the visual representation of the events that occur—the telling of the story through spectacle; it therefore includes all of the movements of the actors on the stage—their entrances and exits, their standing and sitting, their crosses, their joining in groups and separating, their employment of hand props and utilization of furniture. Broadly speaking, it includes, too, their posture, gesture, and their facial expression used to convey emotions and meanings.

Business might be further defined and its nature clarified by arbitrarily dividing it into types but it must be remembered that such a division is arbitrary and for analytical purposes only. All business might, first, be divided into requisite business and supplementary business. By requisite business is meant all of that movement called for in the script and often detailed in stage directions. A most obvious example of requisite business will be found in the entrances and exits of the characters. It includes all movements on the stage made clearly necessary in the action, though these may not be indicated by stage directions—as they often are not in Shakespeare's plays. It includes all necessary handling of properties and utilization of furniture, such, for example, as Nora's showing the stockings to Dr. Rank while they are seated together or of Torvald's opening and reading of his letter. The dialogue and action of the play makes necessary the showing of the stockings and the reading of the letter.

It includes, further, such special business as Nora's dancing of the tarantella or the duel between Hamlet and Laertes, likewise demanded by the script. Requisite business, especially, is the business that the director will have planned in advance. The script will tell him what this requisite business is but it will not tell him specifically and explicitly how he must have it performed in accordance with his specific interpretation and style of production. The exact way in which the business is done is the problem of the actor and the director, guided by the effect which they are seeking to create.

Supplementary business is all of that business not specifically commanded by the script but invented by the actor and the director to enhance the effect and meaning striven for. It includes all of the business added by the actor to individualize and project his characterization. Thus it includes his posture, his walk, his facial expression, and all of his visual mannerisms. Though it does not include the entrance or exit itself, it might include the special way in which the actor makes either. The actor invents supplementary business to characterize his role and to convey and enhance the emotion which he is projecting. That business may be nothing more than the intense way in which he listens to another or, conversely, the way his attention wanders while another is speaking. It may be the shrug of a shoulder that accompanies a line, a gesture of assent or negation, a facial grimace, or a smile.

It is by means of this supplementary business, at least in part, that an actor brings a character to life and individualizes him. The director's duty is to encourage each actor to be inventive in devising this kind of characterizing business. If the actor is not imaginatively inventive, the director should aid him with suggestions and pieces of business—provided, of course, that the actor makes the business thought up by the director his own. Such business mechanically performed, not made to seem an actual part of the character portrayed, can destroy the probability of characterization.

For purposes of clarification, business may be divided into two other types or categories, which overlap the two types just discussed. The two additional types are story-telling business and compositional business. (Before proceeding with a discussion of these, the reader is advised to turn back to Chapter 2 and read again the discussion of "Spectacle"; to turn to Chapter 5 and read again the discussion of the planning of business; and to turn to Chapter 8 and read the materials therein on pantomimic dramatization and the principle involved in placing action on the stage.)

The story of any play is told, first of all, in the lines of dialogue.

Some of the action and movement that accompany the dialogue, but by no means all, is indicated in the stage directions. In a novel these brief descriptions or indications of action would be expanded and often minutely narrated; the emotions which the characters are undergoing would, as they spoke and did their deed, be described and even carefully analyzed; their motivations for their conduct would be fully examined; and what happens to them in their actions and as a result of their actions, along with the effects of the happenings upon their characters, would be made clear to the reader by the author. Novels are, therefore, much easier to read than are plays.

In the play much that is conveyed to the reader directly by the author is merely implicit in the lines. The director must invent ways of making this explicit for an audience. He must enhance the story of the lines by businessing the script, by projecting the implicit action in visual spectacle. This is in part the problem of pantomimic dramatization, to be discussed in Chapter 8. If the story-telling business has been well worked out and well acted, a spectator can, though entirely unfamiliar with the language of the play, follow and feel the effects of the drama to a remarkable degree. Stage business is thus a kind of universal language, another reason for its importance.

To turn to compositional business, a play, as was made apparent in Chapter 2, is composed of a sequence of character groupings, called scenes, representing a variety of psychological relationships. Sometimes these scenes are made up of long sections of uninterrupted dialogue between two characters which can become static or uninteresting if the actors are merely allowed to sit or stand and deliver lines. Often the director must invent supplementary compositional business to break up such scenes. Wherever possible, of course, that business should be story-telling business which reveals the subtle variations between the two characters.

Such invented business is also compositional in that it must be devised to give maximum pictorial effectiveness to the grouping of the two characters. The need for compositional business becomes often even more compelling in groupings involving more than two characters. Such groupings are constantly changing with the progress of the story and the flow of the action. To keep the groupings balanced and pictorially effective the director must from time to time invent pieces of business to change the positions of actors in the grouping. Sometimes he must devise a cross for an actor to maintain the proper focus in the scene. He devises unobtrusive business to move a character out of focus who is not for the moment prominent or a piece of business to move a character in a position to receive the focus of attention that is shortly coming to him. Frequently the director or the actor must think up a piece of business that will move a character into the right position for an effective exit, for the speaking of a significant line, or for the doing of a necessary deed. These examples of compositional business, by no means exhaustive, will serve to illustrate the meaning and reveal the director's responsibility. Some of the principles governing their usage will be presented in Chapter 8. Here the intent is merely to clarify the nature of business to the extent necessary to a discussion of business rehearsals.

For the conducting of business rehearsals and all subsequent rehearsals (with the exception of additional reading rehearsals and perhaps some line rehearsals), the stage or a large rehearsal room is needed. If a large rehearsal room is used, it should be of a size to accommodate a layout in exact dimensions of the setting. On the floor of the stage or room should be marked in chalk in right dimensions the floor plan of the setting for the act to be rehearsed. It is highly important for the rehearsing of business that this plan be in exact dimensions and that doors be indicated in their proper width. The positions and dimensions of all important pieces of furniture should likewise be chalked out within the set. Substitute pieces of approximate dimensions may be employed for rehearsals if the exact dimensions are indicated for the actors. If this procedure is not followed, the director may find when he comes to place the action within the real setting that entrances and exits have been rehearsed to occur where no doors are provided, that carefully planned and timed crosses have been learned with too many or too few steps, and even executed through tables, over sofas, or into other furniture.

For the same reason, important hand props or substitutes should be provided, so that business in which they play a part can be properly learned from the beginning. By these suggestions it is not meant to imply that actors cannot learn to act a part without the actual articles which will be used in performance. It has been said that an actor who could not in rehearsal, while sitting on an upturned box, portray a king on his throne would never become a good actor. True as this may be, there is nothing to be gained in subjecting either inexperienced or trained actors to extra hardship and hazards in the mastering of their parts, when they have so much to learn in a brief period.

There is a further requirement for the rehearsing of business, or at least a question concerning a requirement, the memorizing of lines, which needs to be presented. Some directors request actors to "have lines" before the business rehearsals begin, for, as they say, an actor cannot fully concentrate upon the learning and execution of a piece of business when he is glued to the script. There is truth in this, but, on the other hand, lines and business should be learned together. The actor must "suit the action to the word and the word to the action" if either is to be convincing and effective. No matter how exactly and minutely each piece of business has been explained and diagramed in the reading rehearsals, as each should be, an actor does not "get the feel of it" until he has walked through the business and to some extent mastered the way it is to be done. Most directors, therefore, prefer to give the order "have lines" only after the cast has had enough business rehearsals to set the business of the act. In the early stages of the business rehearsals attention should be called to the necessity for studying lines and business together, and for the memorizing of lines outside the rehearsal periods.

If the director has properly planned his production in advance and if adequate explanation has been given to essential business during the reading rehearsals, the procedure in conducting business rehearsals is relatively simple. The work should begin with a walking rehearsal of the act. After the director has explained the layout of the set chalked upon the floor and made any additional comments on the business of the act, the directions for which the actors have written in their scripts at the reading rehearsals, the actors then go upon the stage, and begin to walk through the business as they read their lines. In the walking rehearsals the actors learn where and how they enter, how they move from place to place as the action may require, where and how they stand and sit, and where and how they make their exits. In the early walking rehearsals the emphasis is upon the requisite business, with only incidental attention upon supplementary business that time may allow at this point. As soon as this requisite business has been blocked out and established by walking through it, it should then be repeated as often as necessary to set it.

When the requisite business is set and the actors have "the feel" of it, lines should be memorized for the remaining business rehearsals. These rehearsals are devoted to the addition and mastery of supplementary business and to the polishing of all business. This cannot be accomplished as long as the actors are encumbered with scripts in their hands and eyes glued to a page. Nor can the speaking of lines and execution of business be harmonized with such a handicap. The exact measurement of every piece of business must be made, that is, the approximate number of steps in a cross or an entrance must be learned and made to fit the line or lines that accompany them. Large and complicated pieces of business must be broken into parts, learned step by step, put together into a whole, and the execution made through repetition almost automatic and absolutely smooth. A complicated stage action will never acquire professional finish unless it is initially broken down into its simplest details and mastered with the precision of a well-executed military drill. Only after this drilled precision has been attained, can such complicated spectacle be given the appearance of naturalness and improvisation.

After the gross requisite business and the essential supplementary business have been blocked out and established, in the process of drilling the cast in its execution, certain details must be constantly watched. Actors must be taught to balance, uncover, and point in group scenes (see Chapters 7 and 8). They must be constantly required to co-operate in the execution of all business, not only in what they do and say, but also in reaction to what others do and say. A piece of business well executed by an actor can be totally spoiled in its effect if the other actor toward whom it is aimed fails to react. Teaching actors to react is an important part of the director's task in business rehearsals. Reaction includes the ability to give the impression of listening to another with close attention and concentration. To anticipate what will later be stressed in the discussion of acting, reaction may be shown in facial expression, body posture, gesture or business, speech, or in all of these employed together. In the delivery of dialogue such reactions should slightly precede speeches in reply, as they do in life. That is, the actor must "register" first, and then speak. From the end of the walking rehearsals through the dress rehearsals the director must insist upon every actor in every part registering during each moment that he is on stage. These matters will be given further attention in Chapter 7.

Plays of complicated action rendered in pantomime and spectacle, or certain scenes in otherwise regular plays having these characteristics, will require separate pantomime rehearsals. One way of conducting such rehearsals is to have the prompter or the assistant director read the lines at the normal rate and rhythm and to allow the actors to concentrate entirely upon the business. Another method is to have the actors say their lines themselves but in an undertone or whisper. Some directors like to hold at least one complete pantomime rehearsal of each act of a play, running through the whole act in pantomime from the first entrance to the curtain. Other directors hold that unless young actors are accustomed to pantomimic exercises they are too self-conscious in such rehearsals to profit by them. These directors prefer to rely entirely upon repeated drills with each separate piece of business. Each director must use the method that works best for his cast and for him.

9. CHARACTERIZATION AND LINE REHEARSALS

Business rehearsals, as has been repeatedly noticed, will inevitably and of necessity involve both characterization and the speaking of lines. A piece of business to be executed effectively must be done in character and must be co-ordinated with the delivery of lines. In a well-planned rehearsal schedule which runs smoothly and according to plan (a contingency that does not always occur), the director's emphasis gradually shifts to characterization and delivery of lines as the business is established and increasingly mastered by the actors. The techniques of characterizing a role and of speaking lines are considered in the next chapter. At this point the concern is with the director's problems and procedures in conducting such rehearsals.

The director's first task in characterization is to aid the actor to attain a conception of the individuality of his role, to see the role that he is playing as a kind of genuine and living personality. Some plays and some roles offer little difficulty in this respect. The characters are clear-cut, sometimes obvious, and are meant to be so. In other plays the problems and difficulties are preplexing in the extreme. Sometimes minor roles, such as those of Rosencrantz and Guildenstern in *Hamlet,* are harder to differentiate and individualize than are the major roles. One editor finds the superb effectiveness of Rosencrantz and Guildenstern to lie in their lack of personal individualization, saying that they are as alike as two peas in a pod. Hence the King can say, "Thanks, Rosencrantz and gentle Guildenstern"; and the Queen can echo, "Thanks, Guildenstern and gentle Rosencrantz." Such utter similarity might be put to advantage by actors and director; or the director may, as Hugh Hunt did, seek some differentiation. Hunt thought he discerned a greater stupidity in Guildenstern than in Rosencrantz, who must come to the rescue of his fellow student when the former upon several occasions gets in over his head, and on that built the differentiation.

Whatever the clues and traits are, the director must aid the actor in finding these and in assimilating them into a composite portrait. The best procedure is to utilize stimulating suggestions, to lead the actor on to his own imaginative conception. Sometimes it aids a young actor to describe for him the chief traits of the role and then to ask him if he has ever known an individual like that in life. If he has, he can perhaps take that individual as the basis of his characterization, as a kind of skeleton or framework on which to build. Upon occasions the director must take the character line by line, scene by scene, and show the actor exactly what that character is feeling and thinking. In other instances, especially with certain big emotional scenes, he must describe, depict, analyze, and expatiate upon the emotions the character is supposed to feel. With some actors, especially inexperienced actors, it is necessary for the director to illustrate the characterization by himself attempting to act portions of the role. Such a device is perfectly legitimate if it gets the desired results and if the actor does not merely continue to imitate the director's portrayal. The building of a characterization may begin in mere mimicry if it proceeds to imaginative creation.

For many actors it is best to begin the characterization with the posture, walk, and any other individual mannerisms of body and voice which serve to distinguish the character. There are, of course, any number of "straight" characters that have no particular or noticeable idiosyncrasies and these are often hardest for the inexperienced actor to characterize, especially if they are somewhat near his own age and social status. Often it helps such an actor to find or to have the director suggest some typical mannerism for the role as a kind of key to the character. The inexperienced actor may be aided in the creation of a straight role by calling to mind an individual somewhat similar to the character in the play and basing his characterization upon an imitation of that known individual.

There is danger in this practice, however, if the immature actor bases his characterization upon mimicry of some well-known motion picture or television performer. It is frequently helpful to the untrained actor in the beginning characterization of a character role to encourage him to exaggerate the mannerisms and idiosyncrasies of the role. Eventually these exaggerations must be toned down and smoothed into a finished characterization. In the initial stages such exaggerations help many actors to overcome a certain shyness in giving breadth to character qualities and, if the qualities exaggerated are central to the role, helps them to gain a firm grasp of the part they are to play. For other aspects of characterization and further details on the nature of character in drama, turn to the section on characterization in Part I, Chapter 2 and to Chapter 7. The objective of the director in these rehearsals is to stimulate the actor to identify himself with the character he is creating and to stimulate the actor's imagination in the creation of the role.

The process of characterizing will necessarily involve problems of the vocal rendering of lines. Hence the rehearsals devoted to characterization, especially in the later stages, must also be concerned with the speaking of lines. Character is revealed on the stage not only by what a person does and what he says, but also by how he says what he is uttering. The inarticulateness, the inability to verbalize his feelings and points of view are distinct qualities of the character of Captain Keeney in O'Neill's *Ile*. As such they are keys to the nature of the man. But the actor playing Captain Keeney must be articulately inarticulate. This ability requires a technique of vocal expression acquired only through training and experience. Most inexperienced actors and many with considerable experience do not possess this technique and this training. The director who thinks that he can impart these within the limited periods of rehearsals is doomed to defeat. If he can add a series of drill periods to the rehearsals, he will accomplish more.

The immature actor thinks of his first task as that of memorizing lines. In a sense that *is* his first task but he will be aided greatly in it and in later mastery of the role if he will first make sure that he fully understands each line and each word of each line before he sets about committing it to memory. Into this understanding must go a full comprehension of the thinking and feeling of the character underlying the words that he utters. Mention has already been made of the importance of associating business and lines. When there is full comprehension of the lines and a complete awareness of the business which accompany them, it is easier to commit them to memory.

Individuals vary, however, in their abilities to memorize but whatever the ability memorization is a matter of repetition. From the very beginning, the director should make it clear that the rehearsal periods are not the time for line mastery but that these must be memorized by the actors on their own time. The young actor must also be warned to memorize the cue with the line. To memorize a role, the actor should first break down his part into a series of separate scenes and, where these are long, into separate sequences within the scene. Then by reading aloud and rereading the first six or eight speeches he will find these becoming fixed in his memory. Little by little he quits reading these from the pages and depends upon his memory, referring to the printed page only when memory fails. He must be aware from the outset of committing these to memory exactly as they are written —unless, of course, cuts and alterations have been indicated in the reading rehearsals.

The director's first problem in the matter of lines is to see that they are spoken in character with the right shade of meaning, emphasis, and effect. In this, speaking lines is a part of the characterization rehearsals. Sometimes an actor will seem incapable of rendering a given word or line with the right inflection and emphasis. Even though he repeats it over and over, he gives it the wrong inflection or emphasis. This constant repetition of error results from his inability to hear himself as he speaks. Sometimes he can be made to hear what he is saying if the director can imitate him successfully and immediately after speak the line or word as it should be rendered. It is even more helpful to record on a tape or wire recorder the actor's speaking of the lines and play those back for him.

As soon as the actor has acquired some abilities in speaking his lines in character and with effective meaning and emotion, the director should then turn attention to any faults of delivery that may appear. Perhaps the most common faults for which he should be on guard are faults of:

1. Pronunciation
2. Enunciation
3. Projection

Faults of pronunciation are by no means as frequently encountered on the stage as are the others but when they do occur, especially in a play of sophisticated people, they are glaring and ludicrous. Unless standard stage English is employed, Webster's *Unabridged Dictionary* should be the guide. Sometimes actors have difficulties with foreign names and with the names in classical Greek drama. Many of these can be solved by reference to dictionaries but occasionally, as with contemporary foreign names, one has to seek linguistically competent authority in the community. Mispronunciations occasionally occur in standard English on the part of actors brought up in a local idiom. These, too, must be corrected.

Of far greater seriousness and frequency are the faults of enunciation and of projection. Americans as a whole are probably no worse and no better than any other nationality in the matter of speech but American actors are without question far behind their European colleagues in the speaking of lines. There are various reasons for this. The almost completely realistic nature of our performances has led to the "mumble-and-mutter" school of acting. That is perhaps a chief reason for the faulty diction on our stage. But another reason can be traced to the lack of importance given to speech in the United States. In England, perhaps with undue stress, speech is definitely a distinguishing social badge. An Englishman can tell the social position of another Englishman almost exactly as soon as he hears him speak. Hence in the best English preparatory schools every teacher is to some extent a teacher of speech. Few Americans get such careful checking up in their speech habits. In consequence many of our American actors are defective in their speech abilities.

If this defectiveness is reprehensibly observable in the professional commercial theatre, as it is, it is ten times worse in the nonprofessional theatre. Very few amateurs have been properly trained in pronunciation, enunciation, projection, and in the making of points in their speaking of lines. Consequently, from the outset of rehearsals, the director must place emphasis upon these matters and continue that stress throughout the preparation of the production. Every good director of nonprofessional productions must therefore be a teacher of speech. He must be on his guard against certain difficulties which he will encounter.

From his standpoint the first of these, perhaps, will be his own familiarity with the spoken lines and hence the tendency to think that the actors are enunciating and projecting when such is not the case. Another is that rehearsals are usually conducted in a room that is much smaller and with different acoustical properties than those of the theatre or auditorium in which the final productions will be presented. Under such conditions even the actor trained in the speaking of lines is liable to fall into lazy habits. In the early stages of rehearsals it is wise to concentrate upon the reading of lines for meaning and for effective enunciation.

With these matters mastered, the problems of projection should be constantly watched through the remaining rehearsals. Sometimes the difficulties of projection are a lack of sufficient force and loudness. Voices of certain qualities, especially those of women, encounter these problems. More often, however, the problems of projection are a mere matter of technique. The inexperienced actor is prone to deliver his lines to the floor or to the back and sides of the set, rather than out front to the audience. An experienced actor who must speak a line with his back to his audience automatically delivers that line with added enunciation and special attention to projection but the inexperienced actor must be coached in such techniques. The beginning actor should be made aware of the great importance of eye contact with audiences. The director can often spot a possible bad projection by watching the eyes of his actors as well as listening to their lines. Teach the immature actors to play to the first row of the balcony, even though there may be no balcony in the theatre. It is helpful to the director and to these immature actors to hold as many rehearsals as possible in the theatre in which the production is to be presented prior to the dress rehearsals. Even if the theatre is not available for full rehearsals, it may often be utilized in brief periods for separate scenes in which the director may concentrate upon matters of projection. Other matters of rendering lines upon the stage are discussed in the following chapter.

10. FINISHING REHEARSALS

After the play has been rehearsed and mastered in its separate parts, elements, scenes, and acts, it must then be put together and perfected as a whole. It is not wise to leave this perfecting of the whole to the dress rehearsals, especially when there are immature actors in the cast. Any production will benefit by a number of finishing rehearsals devoted to running through the whole play. Moreover, time will be saved for the technical and dress rehearsals if such finishing rehearsals have been properly conducted in advance of these. The first objective in the finishing rehearsals is the important one of timing. Each act and the show as a whole must be timed to see that it is not running too long. Of course the final timing of the show cannot be done until after the technical rehearsals have been completed, for such matters of production as the change of settings will play an important part in the timing of the whole show. Nevertheless, the director can settle many of his questions of timing as they pertain to the acting of the play in the finishing rehearsals. If the sets and properties are ready or sufficiently ready for use, they will be decidedly helpful in these rehearsals but are not absolutely essential.

Another matter of timing which may be determined at these rehearsals is that of the show dragging because of lack of speed in business and the delivery of lines. These rehearsals give opportunity for the exact timing of entrances, exits, crosses, the serving of food and drink, and other types of business. Often a scene or scenes must be speeded up; less often a scene of important psychological action or deeply developing emotion needs to be slowed down. Yet other matters, such as the timing of climaxes, of punch and laugh lines, and of the introduction of songs and music, can be and should be given attention in these rehearsals.

These matters of timing raise the question of rhythm. Every good production has a rhythmic pattern of its own. Some directors go so far as to look upon their productions as a kind of dance pattern amenable to choreographic orchestration. Everyone knows that the tempo of comedy is generally faster than that of tragedy and consequently has a different rhythmic pattern. In order to set the right tempo and rhythmic pattern Richard Whorf once rehearsed regularly the scenes of *Richard II* to the accompaniment of a drum. Thus he was from the early stages of his rehearsals able to establish the right rhythmic pattern for his particular production.

It takes a considerable maturity of experience to be able to determine in advance the right rhythmic pattern for a play and to rehearse it from the beginning to attain this pattern through the variations in the vocal and visual elements. The beginning director will probably have to sense the desirable rhythmic pattern as his rehearsals proceed but he can enhance the sensing of this pattern if he consciously strives to discern it. Rhythm comes in a production through alternation in the tempo of parts and scenes. A simple rhythm may be attained through the alternation of relatively slow scenes with more rapid ones but very few plays lend themselves to such a simple and fixed rhythm.

Rhythm is also attained through the proper utilization of climaxes in the action. A scene of relatively slow pace which gradually accelerates to a moment of climax is common to the majority of plays. Conscious attention to the placement and utilization of these will aid the director in determining and effecting the rhythmic movement. Certain stylized plays, such as Maeterlinck's *Pelléas and Mélisande* or Lorca's *Blood Wedding,* depend heavily upon rhythmic movement for their effectiveness but even the most naturalistic play can be enhanced in production by the employment of a right and consciously planned rhythm.

In addition to pace, tempo, and rhythm, the finishing rehearsals are also to be utilized to give a smoothness and final finish to all other elements of the acting. For that purpose it is essential to have adequate costumes and hand properties and it is highly desirable to hold these rehearsals on the stage of the theatre if it is at all available. Assuming that each of the separate pieces of business has been completely mastered prior to these rehearsals, they now provide the opportunity to put these separate parts together in a smooth, constantly moving, free-flowing action. In the early stages of the finishing rehearsals the actors may have to be stopped occasionally and required to repeat a scene or piece of business but in the later stages the acts should be run through without interruptions. Only in this way can the director and the cast begin to realize that cumulative and smooth build of a play toward which they are striving. The director or his assistant should, during these latter stages, make notes of changes and improvements and communicate these to the cast at the end of an act or at the end of the rehearsal period. If in these latter stages a scene or a piece of business should obviously need considerable separate polishing, that part should be taken separately at a time conveniently arranged but should not hold up the run-through of a finishing rehearsal. These drill periods have already been explained.

11. TECHNICAL REHEARSALS

The technical rehearsals are those rehearsals devoted to the perfecting of the technical details of the production, including the shifting of the scenes between acts, the adjustment of the lighting, the cuing-in of sound effects, the exact timing of offstage effects, the manipulation of properties, and other such details. These rehearsals are usually trying times for the cast, and inexperienced actors need to be impressed with their importance. The technical rehearsals are properly under the direction of the technical director or of stage manager if there is no technical director in the organization. If the director and the technical director have worked together from the beginning of the production and have properly planned the technical aspects of the production, much of the tediousness and fatigue may be removed from these rehearsals. Lights may then be roughly adjusted, sound and light cues planned, and the shifting of sets perfected in advance of the actual rehearsals.

If little or none of this advanced planning has been done, these rehearsals will be long and tedious. Under such circumstances the technical director must train his crews and technicians in the handling of the production entirely within the rehearsal periods. If, however, the crew members and technicians have been carefully instructed and rehearsed in their duties prior to the actual technical rehearsals, these can then become what they should be, finishing rehearsals for the technical personnel.

In the first technical rehearsal the technical director and the director should not hesitate to repeat the manipulation of any technical element until it is properly mastered. If there is a difficult or tricky cue in the lighting, it should be gone over time after time until completely mastered. If there is a rather intricate problem of getting just the right lighting effect or scenic effect of other kinds, these should be rehearsed until the technicians have fully mastered them. The cuing and timing of a change of light, say from daylight to dusk or from dark to dawn, often becomes highly important in the effectiveness of a scene. It must be carefully worked out and repeated until it is fully mastered. Then the lighting technician must be sure to record the exact readings so that he can henceforth repeat the effect. The second and subsequent technical rehearsals may then be run through without interruptions or largely without interruptions. Such slight changes and corrections as are to be made may be conveyed to the technicians at the end of an act or at the end of the rehearsal from notes kept by the technical director or his assistant.

12. DRESS REHEARSALS

If the finishing and technical rehearsals have been properly conducted in the manner indicated, the dress rehearsals may then become, as they rightly should, tryout presentations of the play. If, on the other hand, many of the details of finishing the show and many of the technical details have been left incomplete, the dress rehearsals are apt to become something of a nightmare. The experienced director plans against such an eventuality. When it occurs frequently in a theatrical organization, it is a clear indication of an inefficient director who, however brilliant he may be in other respects, probably will find difficulty in holding a permanent position. Upon occasions, however, the best organizers find that because of circumstances beyond their control they must utilize the dress rehearsals for the finishing of the play and the completion of the technical aspects. At these final rehearsals the show in all of its details just as it is to be given to audiences must be presented. This is the last chance of the director, technical director, cast, and technicians to perfect the show upon which their reputations will depend.

Assuming that the finishing and technical rehearsals have been properly and successfully completed, the director should call his actors sufficiently in advance of curtain time for them to get into costume and make-up. If the cast is large and a number of the actors are not capable of doing their own make-up, some of them may have to report at least an hour in advance of curtain time. Should the costume and make-up crew be limited, this interval of time may have to be increased. There are also in certain productions intricate make-ups which require additional time. The director and the costumer should anticipate these and should arrange for rehearsals of these make-ups prior to the dress rehearsals.

In the same way, any difficult or time-consuming costume changes should be worked out and rehearsed in advance of the dress rehearsals. For productions involving large casts in theatres with limited dressing-room facilities it sometimes becomes advisable to call actors to appear at different times. Thus the actors appearing in the first part of the show report early and those who do not come on until later report after these actors are taken care of or are nearly ready to go on. A proper schedule of calls should be carefully worked out and communicated to actors and also to technicians.

The dress rehearsals should be run exactly as a performance will be run. Some directors like to have an invited audience, limited in number, for these dress rehearsals. Such an audience may be helpful in their reactions to the actors and may also be helpful to the director. If, however, the dress rehearsals are not ready to be run as a tryout performance, an invited audience may be a distraction and not desirable in terms of word-of-mouth publicity for the production. For the sake of the cast, the crew, and later performances dress rehearsals should be run through with interruptions at a minimum. The last dress rehearsal, at least, should be run as nearly like a finished performance as is possible, even though the earlier ones may have been occasionally stopped for corrections.

Some amateurs console themselves with a completely false statement to the effect that a bad dress rehearsal means a good performance. Nothing could be farther from the truth if by a bad dress rehearsal is meant one of confusion and lack of ordered planning. At times amateur and experienced professional actors do under the stimulus of a receptive audience rise above the kind of acting performances that they have exhibited in rehearsals but only if they have been thoroughly trained in the potentialities of their roles. Technicians and stage-crew members do not have such direct-contact stimulus and must rely upon careful planning and thorough drill. Hence the wise director shapes his program of rehearsals so that his dress rehearsals are tryout performances.

From what has been said it is obvious that the proper rehearsal of a play involves more than merely the assembling of a cast and the reading of lines on the stage. A rightly planned rehearsal schedule represents a series of progressive stages in the learning and mastery of a production; hence the director must know from adequate advance preparation exactly what is to be accomplished at each stage. He cannot, of course, know the full capacities of his cast until he has worked with them as individuals and as a group; hence he must adjust his rehearsal schedule, including the drill periods, as the rehearsals proceed. The experienced director can nevertheless plan the stages of the preparation, can know what must be accomplished in the interpretation and production of a script well in advance of the selection of a cast. Intelligent planning is the secret to the orderly and progressive development of a production. No matter how much originality and inspiration the director may have, these will not substitute for orderly planning. The director must be, along with other qualifications, a thinker and a planner.

QUESTIONS AND EXERCISES

1. The Bristol Old Vic Theatre opens the production of each new play in its season on Tuesday evening, plays that play for the remainder of that week and for the two succeeding weeks each evening, except Sunday, and includes two matinee performances in each of the three weeks. Thus they have for the rehearsal of each new production after the season opens ten days of full time and six days of half time, with no evening possible except on Sundays and on the one Monday of dress rehearsal, when the theatre is dark. Replan the rehearsal schedule given in this chapter to fit the Bristol Old Vic program. (Assume that the play to be prepared is the Shakespeare play which you used in Chapter 3.)
2. Utilizing the one-act play which you have chosen in fulfillment of Assignment 1 in the last chapter, make a floor plan of the setting which you would use on your stage and block out all requisite business.
3. Assuming that you had three weeks of rehearsal time with a com-

petent cast of amateur actors for the presentation of this play, how many rehearsals would you give to business?

4. What special problems of characterization and speaking of lines would you anticipate in the preparation of this play?
5. Are there any special problems of co-ordination that must be anticipated?
6. Assume that as Director of Dramatics in your local high school you must prepare the presentation of the senior-class play within an eight-weeks period. You can have your cast for rehearsals for a thirty-minute period each morning and for an hour-and-a-half each afternoon, Monday through Friday. Replan the rehearsal schedule given in this chapter to fit these conditions in the preparation of a specific high-school play assigned to you.

CHAPTER 7

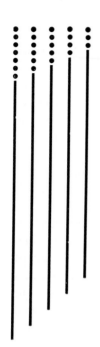

The Director and the Actor

THE DIRECTOR, especially in the noncommercial theatre, is concerned with every individual who has any responsible part in the production of a show, but he spends a major part of his time with and energies on actors. The good director in the Broadway theatre, in the community theatre, and in the academic theatre is a teacher of acting and a coach of actors. A director must, therefore, know the art and technique of acting and must know how to impart this information to others in such a way as to draw from them their best efforts.

In the community and academic theatre the director must aid the actor not only in the creation of character but also in the acquiring and mastering of acting techniques by which the character is rendered. Since a considerable part of a director's time and energy will go into the teaching of the art and technique of acting and the coaching of actors in those techniques, the subject must be explored in any general treatment of directing. That this exploration cannot be a thorough discussion of acting in all of its aspects perhaps goes without saying; nevertheless, the basic problems of a director's relations to and work with actors must be summarized. His work will naturally vary from actor to actor and will depend upon the actor's training and experience, his role in the show, and upon his personality and attitude. A teacher cannot deal successfully with every student in exactly the same way.

The art and technique of acting is complex and requires, in addition to aptitude, years of training and experience. In the short period of rehearsals the director cannot hope to teach the whole art to an inexperienced person. He must, therefore, concentrate with each individual actor upon those techniques essential to the role and essential to overcoming faults in the actor's performance.

In the modern realistic theatre and especially on the American stage and in motion pictures the techniques of acting have been all but submerged and discarded, to be replaced with a kind of exhibitionism. In the casting of plays and pictures an individual with exactly the right physique, features, and personality is sought for each role and the individual, once found, is simply coached in the rendering of his own peculiarities and eccentricities. If a tough gangster is wanted, someone with features and characteristics similar to those of the late Humphrey Bogart is sought. If an elderly man with polite and polished manners is required, such an individual is found. Sometimes these people, admirably suited by appearance and temperament to a single role, have had no previous training or acting experience whatever. If they make a success in the role, they will probably go on playing that role in show after show and picture after picture. They are, in other words, constantly playing themselves and would be total failures if required to interpret a character from a play by Molière or Shakespeare. Casting of this kind and acting of this type can at times and in certain plays be compellingly convincing and highly successful. Every director in seeking actors for a show employs such casting procedures to some extent. But such casting and such acting will not produce a versatile actor in full command of his art and with such casting it is difficult, if not impossible, to develop that ensemble acting requisite to the interpretation of the classics for which the French and English stages are noted. An exhibitionist of personal characteristic could not ordinarily adapt himself to the varying styles of characterization in Greek drama, Shakespeare, Molière, Sheridan, and Ibsen.

The artist-actor, on the other hand, with his complete training in and thorough mastery of technique is equipped to interpret within a range a variety of characters in many different styles. Even within the restricted range of realism, technique is important and essential to good acting. To succeed in role after role the exhibitionist-actor must learn the means and methods of the actor's craft. Those many little devices and techniques by which certainty, smoothness, and effectiveness are given to the interpretation of a role are acquired only through constant training and experience. There is no one key to the actor's art, no one "method" that assures success.

In addition to the foundation techniques, the great actor must acquire an actor's imagination, if he does not already have it in some measure, and must, if he has it, constantly develop it. An actor's imagination is, first of all, an ability to enter intuitively into the personalities of many different individuals; an actor's technique is the means or devices which he selects and perfects in order to render the intuitively imagined personality of the role. Along with this intuitive imagination in the great actor is found a sense of style in characterization which can grasp and discriminate the differences, say, between Duke Orsino in *Twelfth Night* and Alceste in *The Misanthrope*.

Acting as it is discussed in this chapter may be defined as the art of rendering a character through vocal and visual means upon the stage in such a way as to convince and move audiences. The two instruments of the stage actor's art are voice and body. In motion-picture acting there is another instrument, the camera, which serves to differentiate that acting somewhat and the same differentiation applies, though somewhat differently, to television acting. Acting in radio plays eliminates the visual entirely and forces the actor to rely upon a single instrument, the voice. It is apparent, then, that in stage acting there are two categories of techniques, voice and body, which the actor must master. As the camera is a determinant in motion-picture acting, so are the theatre and the audiences determinants in the acting of an experienced actor. Such an actor does not merely play a role; he likewise "sizes" his interpretation to the requisites of a specific theatre and he plays an audience. An actor who plays a character within the same Broadway theatre throughout its run or who always plays in the same community or academic theatre may not realize the degree to which an interpretation of a role must be "sized" to the theatre. If, however, he goes on tour, playing in different theatres from week to week, he soon becomes cognizant of the influence of theatre size upon his techniques. The intimate and delicate techniques suitable to the projection of a role in a small central-stage theatre would be completely lost in a large theatre seating three thousand.

One of the factors that keeps an experienced actor fresh in his interpretation night after night in the long run of a play is his knowledge of and exhilaration in playing audiences as well as a role. In this he may be likened to the skilled angler playing a big trout with a light rod and tackle. Such a fisherman knows that no two fish and no two bodies of water may be handled in exactly the same way. Some are easy, while others require all of his skill, alertness, and resourcefulness. In similar manner, without letting them know he is doing so, the actor watches his audiences, guides their reactions, and utilizes those reactions to build further effects. Such an actor feels his audiences in much the same way that a skilled public speaker feels his audience. This playing of an audience and sensing their reactions are a great stimulation to the seasoned actor. The lack of this ability is one of the factors which differentiates the amateur from the professional. The beginning actor has so many problems in the mere interpretation of his role and in his stage business that he is apt to forget his audience entirely if the director does not constantly remind him to play to the audience.

In the previous chapter it was noted that one of the chief causes of lack of projection was the almost universal tendency of the inexperienced actor to play to the floor or to the walls of the set. It is this same tendency that defeats visual as well as vocal contact. From the beginning of rehearsals the director must insist upon all actors playing to the audience. They must be taught to have that same greediness, so to speak, for audience contact, that desire for the center-stage spotlight, that marks the experienced professional. As a general rule, the actor should play directly to the first row of the balcony or just above the heads of the audience in the main auditorium.

1. MASTERING A CHARACTERIZATION

The actor's first task is to master the character which he is to play and to make that character seem like a living personality. In

James Riley's setting for Kermit Hunter's *Darkening Shore* as produced by The Carolina Playmakers of the University of North Carolina. Above: the artist's sketch. Below: the scenery made from this.

terms of specific characterizing traits a role in a play may be very limited; yet it is the actor's job to bring that limited characterization upon the stage as a living, convincing individual. To do this he must build in his imagination an image of the kind of individual he is portraying and identify himself with that individual. Actors vary widely in their methods of doing this. Some are highly intuitive and work best from suggestions rather than from direct analysis; others are more intellectual and must first analyze the role they are to play in all of its details before putting it together.

The director can be helpful to each of these by making as clear as possible the kind of character demanded in the action of the play. He can point out the specific traits with which the playwright has endowed the character and made his actions probable. As he comes to know his actor, he can suggest subsidiary traits and mannerisms that may enhance the characterization and aid in bringing it to life upon the stage. He must be careful, however, not to impose a too rigid interpretation upon the role but must encourage the actor to develop the character as he grows into it.

The external and visible traits of a character—age, size, posture, walk, dress, mannerisms of gesture, etc.—are relatively easy to analyze and state and are not too difficult to master. It is the inner aspects of attitude, emotion, thought, and decision that are more difficult to discern and to render. A good device for getting inside a character, so to speak, is, as already suggested, to ask what he wants. What are his desires? What is he after? What drives or wants impell him? Sometimes this desire or inner drive is easily stated but is complex and difficult to identify with. The example of Racine's Phaedra, driven by a guilty lust for her stepson, illustrates the point. Her guilty desire, like the ambition of Macbeth, leads to a terrible inner turmoil.

In certain instances, especially with minor characters, the desire or inner drive is not the central factor in the characterization. Sometimes it aids an actor to imagine an inner drive for such a role. Of course the inner drive given to the character must be consistent with the role in the play. In other instances, as with Nora in *A Doll's House,* the inner drive emerges slowly and changes with the development of the action. In certain roles the character is not fully conscious of the nature of his inner drive. Nina Leeds in *Strange Interlude* is impelled through her life by a romantic illusion about love. She has made her unconsummated love for Gordon into an image which dominates her. Captain Keeney in *Ile* can explain his inner drive by the ineffectual statement, "I've got to get the ile," but getting the whale oil obviously means far more than he is able to state. Blanche Du Bois in *A Streetcar Named Desire* is impelled by a desire for the refinement of a past aristocratic culture with which she attempts to compensate for her shabby past of alcoholism and prostitution. Her image of herself as a cultured lady is in direct conflict with her past and present state. In the light of her circumstances her desires are pathetically ludicrous, just as are those of Amanda in *The Glass Menagerie*. The desires of characters in comedies, especially in farces, are often simple, clear, and ludicrous, without the element of pathos. Molière's chief comic characters are, for the most part, impelled by an excessive and narrow desire that becomes antisocial. In lesser comedies the impelling desire of the hero is often merely to win the heroine.

Another device for the mastering and getting inside of a character is the building up or inventing of a biography for the character. The imaginative director or actor may easily construct a suitable outline of the previous life of any character, though that previous life appears little or not at all in the play. We know that certain playwrights, including Ibsen, worked in this manner in developing their characters. By drawing upon acquaintances, characters in books and novels, and upon free imagination the actor can surround his role with a host of details that serve to give that character stature, breadth, and reality. This device should be encouraged so long as the details of the imagined biography are completely consonant with the role in the play. The objective is to make the character in the play come to life upon the stage in all of his or her fullness.

Another device which aids the actor in realizing the character is to determine and identify with the character's attitudes and with his reactions to other characters in the play. Toward some he may be completely indifferent; toward others he may be openly or secretly hostile; toward yet others he will have friendly or sympathetic feelings of varying degrees. The actor must sense these varying relationships even though at times it is difficult to state in explicit terms just why one person reacts to another as he does. These reactions of human being to human being are a basic material out of which drama is built; hence the actor must understand or feel them and utilize them. He has a variety of means—the tone of his voice, the choice of his words, the way in which he looks at another person, the shrug of his shoulder, the gesture of his hands, the posture of his body—by which he may convey to the audience his attitude toward another but he must first feel that attitude.

In this process of reaction to others the actor must build up in his role a kind of self-justification. Even though he may be playing the role of an out-and-out villain, an Iago say, he must see the attitudes and reactions through Iago's eyes. He must not view Iago primarily through the eyes of the objective reader of the play. He must seek to feel Iago's hatred of Othello and Iago's pleasure in ensnaring him. To play Iago without this identification and self-justification is to play him externally. However technically perfect such a portrayal, it will lack greatness and full convincingness. In this, as in other devices for the mastering of a character, the director can be of great aid, especially to the inexperienced actor. Throughout the rehearsals he can repeatedly emphasize the actors' reactions to each other.

Yet another device in characterization is, in its beginning, purely external. It often aids an actor to get into a character by practicing his walk, his mannerisms of posture, gesture, and voice, and by dressing like the character. One can begin to get the feel of a role by standing, walking, and talking as that character would in life. We can glean from Joseph Jefferson's *Autobiography* that this was his first step in the mastery of any role that he played. Hundreds of other actors have employed it. But the actor must not be satisfied with the mere externals of the character. He must make these lead to the inner nature of a personality.

Immature actors may have some difficulties in knowing how to proceed in the examination of a characterization in a play. These difficulties may be lessened for them in most modern plays with their full stage directions, which include descriptions of characters. No such stage directions will be found in older plays unless these have been carefully edited for reading and production. Clues to the nature of each of the characters, especially the chief characters, are fully embodied in the lines and actions of the play. A diligent examination with proper questioning will serve to reveal these. Perhaps an orderly series of questions to be asked will serve to reveal a method of uncovering the nature of a character. Answers to some of these questions will be immediately obvious; others will be obtained with more difficulty; and in some instances certain questions may not apply.

1. What is the sex, the age, and the physical appearance of the character?
2. What is his social status or position?
3. What is his habitual attitude or disposition?
4. What emotions does he exhibit through the lines and action of the play?
5. What does he desire and what does he strive for? What are his inner drives?
6. What are his relations with other characters? To which is he drawn and to which is he antipathetic?
7. What do other characters think of him? What attitudes are taken toward him?
8. How does he think? What examples of deliberation appear in his role? Does his thinking and his feeling lead directly to decision and action?
9. What decisions does he make? Are these decisions moral or merely expedient?
10. Is he a sympathetic or an antipathetic character? Is he partly both?
11. Is he essentially a noble, admirable character; ordinary, though admirable; or is he essentially a ludicrous, comic character? Is he a combination of the serious and the comic?

Since every significant characterization in drama differs in some degree from all others, a sustained attempt to answer these questions about any one character will probably raise other questions of direct import to that specific character. A clear understanding of the answers to these questions should give a firm basis upon which the actor may imaginatively build a convincing physical embodiment of the character.

2. MEMORIZING LINES

After the actor has some clear grasp of the role he is to play, he should then set about memorizing the lines he is to speak. Some actors are "slow studies"; others are quick in committing lines to memory. The beginning actor, unpracticed in the technique of committing lines to memory, may profit by some suggestions. Before attempting to memorize lines, the actor should read the whole play through a number of times to be sure he fully understands the play and his role. He should then, as has been said, gain a clear understanding of the character he is to play and begin intuitively to identify himself with that character. With this task well under way, and as a part of it, he should examine each line he is to speak with care to be sure that he understands the meaning of the line. Just what does it say? For example, just what does Hamlet mean by this portion of a speech appearing in Act I, Scene iv:

> So, oft it chances in particular men,
> That for some vicious mole of nature in them,
> As, in their birth—wherein they are not guilty,
> Since nature cannot choose his origin—
> By the o'ergrowth of some complexion,
> Oft breaking down the pales and forts of reason,
> Or by some habit that too much o'er-leavens
> The form of plausive manners, that these men,
> Carrying, I say, the stamp of one defect,
> Being nature's livery, or fortune's star,—
> Their virtues else—be they as pure as grace,
> As infinite as man may undergo—
> Shall from that particular fault: the dram of eale
> Doth all the noble substance of a doubt
> To his own scandal.

Commentators may disagree and scholars argue over this speech; but the actor who speaks it must arrive at some decision as to the meaning he is to convey with it. Until that meaning is understood and clearly determined, the speech will be difficult to memorize.

But a speech may have more than exact meaning, its denotation; it may have also overtones and connotations. It has emotional color in several senses. Often it is the direct result of feeling; in turn, it conveys the emotion of the speaker; and, finally, it arouses feelings in others. Dramatically this connotative aspect of speech is of as much, even more, significance than is the denotative. The understanding of the lines of a role includes the comprehension of this aspect and an appreciation of the full effectiveness of a line. To acquire this comprehension necessitates a reading and rereading of the play and especially of the lines of the role.

This understanding and constant reading of the play will in themselves help to fix the lines of the role in the memory. The next step is to break down the role into its separate segments, the scenes in which the role appears. If these scenes are of any length, they should be broken down into separate sequences and only a single sequence attempted at a time. Read the sequence through time and again to get its coherence and the consecutive nature of the speeches. Carefully note and memorize the cue to each speech along with the speech. After a sufficient number of readings, the lines will begin to stick in the memory. Then close the book and attempt to repeat as many as possible from memory, opening the book and reading when memory fails. When the first segment is committed in this manner, proceed to the next. Be sure not to attempt too large segments. After three or four small consecutive segments have been memorized in this manner, repeat the whole series from beginning to end. Proceed slowly at first. Attempts to rush the memorizing of lines will result in faulty commitment. When these faults are fixed in the memory, they are very difficult to correct. This matter of memorizing lines has been discussed further in Chapter 6.

3. SPEAKING LINES

An actor has a double instrument or a dual means of his art, his voice and his body, which he must use as a co-ordinated unit in the effective presentation of a character. As instruments both voice and body need patient and careful training. It is not appropriate here to undertake a discussion of voice training. That is a matter which should be supervised by a trained and experienced teacher and every potential actor should seek such a teacher. Since, however, the director will be called upon for some guidance of actors in the use of their voices, he must certainly know the essentials of the subject. He cannot learn these merely from a book but a good book on the subject can prove suggestive and helpful. One of the best is Virgil A. Anderson's *Training the Speaking Voice* (New York: Oxford University Press, 1942). Valuable as the reading of this book is for any director, it must be emphasized that the director who has extensive training in voice has a distinct advantage over his colleague without that training.

Actors obviously vary greatly in their vocal abilities. Some are endowed with clear, beautiful, resonant voices; others through natural environment or through right training have acquired good vocal abilities and admirable diction. The majority of individuals, however, mumble and mutter, using their voices in the laziest possible manner. Many are handicapped with localisms and intonations that will mark them for life. The director in the academic and community theatres is constantly faced with such problems in his casts. The more serious problems cannot be dealt with in the short period of rehearsals. Actors with such handicaps must be advised to seek assistance from trained teachers if they are at all interested in the art of acting. There are certain other problems, however, in the speaking of lines with which the director must deal. Probably the director can eliminate some of these if he will select his cast in terms of vocal as well as visual effectiveness.

Probably the first and most persistent of these problems is that of effective projection, already discussed. Projection involves not only adequate force, loudness, and proper direction of speech, but also pitch, rate, and phrasing. High-pitched voices are usually more difficult to understand than are those of lower pitch; hence women and men with voices of this caliber must be trained to take special care in the phonation and phrasing of their lines. When an actor elevates his voice in an emotional speech and especially when he raises the pitch in conveying excitement and emotion, this problem of projection almost always enters. Words screamed by an actor must be especially well enunciated and phrased to be understood. It is the failure to do these things that makes most high-pitched emotional scenes in amateur productions largely unintelligible. Hence a director must always be on guard against unintelligibility in such scenes.

Phrasing is as important to the understanding of lines as is enunciation. Any extended speech can become largely meaningless, even unintelligible, if it is not properly phrased by means of pauses and alterations in pitch. In order to keep a play from dragging, actors must usually speak, especially in comedies, at a rate that is more rapid than normal speech. To attain this rapidity the inexperienced actor often sacrifices the proper phrasing of the words in the speech.

Proper phrasing is a matter of emphasis involving the grouping of the words, indicated by changes in pitch or by pauses, and involving the stressing of certain key words.

The stressing of these key words was called in the old school of acting "making points." In the stock-company system every young actor was drilled in the making of points, the picking out and stressing of the key words in a speech. If these key words are rightly selected and if they come over effectively, the audience will be able to follow the whole speech even though the other words in the speech are delivered at a rapid rate. Phrasing and emphasis not only aid in conveying the denotative meaning of a speech, they are also important in conveying its emotional connotation. Sometimes a young and inexperienced actor will give a completely misleading or wrong implication to a speech by stressing the wrong word. The following simple illustration will serve to show what stress as emphasis may do with three words:

Close the door.
  (*Speak this as a simple statement with about equal stress on each word.*)
Close the door?
  (*Make the words a clear question.*)
Close the door.
  (*Close it; do not open it.*)
Close the *door.*
  (*Close the door, not the window.*)
Close the *door.*
  (*Speak this as a stern demand.*)
Close the door!
  (*Speak this with astonishment at the request.*)
Close the *door.*
  (*Speak this as an angry, exasperated request.*)

Of course loudness, pitch, and other qualities of voice, in addition to stress, will appear in these exercises. Some such exercise as this will often aid an inexperienced actor to see why he is giving a wrong emphasis to his speech, especially if the director will use the speech itself for the exercise.

The introduction of the above exercise has carried the discussion of speaking lines beyond the matter of intelligibility into the realm of emotional connotation. Drama is basically a matter of feelings and emotions, a matter of what goes on inside characters. This inner feeling is conveyed not only by what is said but also by how it is said. This *how* has been discussed in Chapter 2 as the music of drama, the vocalization of the lines of a play. In the seven examples of the above illustration the three words, "close the door," remain the same. In terms of the dictionary they do not change their meaning but the meaning of the whole speech changes greatly. The examples could be extended beyond the seven given.

To be able to act effectively upon the stage an individual must be capable of producing a wide variety of effects with three simple words or with a single word. That ability demands a trained voice that is fully under control. But the actor must go beyond the mechanics of voice training and become a trained interpretative reader. In this, as in voice training, books will not alone suffice but may prove helpful. There are a number of good books on interpretative reading. One of the best is by Charles H. Woolbert and Severina E. Nelson, *Art of Interpretative Speech: Principles and Practices of Effective Reading,* Fourth edition (New York: Appleton-Century-Crofts, Inc., 1956). There are two additional books on the art and technique of oral interpretation, both by a distinguished teacher in the field, that are especially important for the actor and the director. These are Cornelius Carman Cunningham's *Literature as a Fine Art* (New York: The Ronald Press Company, 1941) and *Making Words Come Alive* (Dubuque, Iowa: William C. Brown Company, 1951).

From the discussion thus far it has already become evident that the effective speaking of lines on the stage involves more than an intellectual comprehension of their meaning. It involves an understanding and feeling for the emotional meaning of the words and also the emotions and situation which motivate the words. A line of dialogue in a play is usually a response to another person and a situation. The kind of response that other person and that situation will evoke depends, in turn, upon the character reacting to it. Illustration will again prove useful.

(*You have just escaped along with a companion into a room from a pursuing enemy, bent upon your death. You hear the approach of the enemy and in agonized terror you shout*):

Close the door.

(*You and the one you love, seeking to be alone, have stolen away from companions and entered a room. You whisper to your beloved*):

Close the door.

The different situations, the different emotions back of the words, and the different individuals to whom they are addressed will color and change the delivery of the two speeches. Thus the actor must sense all that lies behind a speech, as well as understand its meaning. When he does understand its denotation and senses its full connotation and when he delivers the speech effectively, it then becomes a right cue for another speech by another actor. This is what actors mean when they speak of fellow actors giving them something to play to or against.

A further fault often observed in the inexperienced actor is the speaking of lines exactly as though he were reading them from the printed page. Such delivery lacks life-likeness and spontaneity. Every speech should be spoken as though it were the exact and immediate reaction of a specific individual to a direct motivation. One of the reasons for this mechanical reading of lines will be found in the intonation; another will be found in the failure of the offending actor to react. If he reacts in body and voice to the stimulus which calls forth the line, he will find it impossible to read the line mechanically.

Every speech should be spoken as though it were the first time that character had said those words, as though the words came as an immediate response to a stimulus. The amateur actor often fails to attain this naturalness because he mechanically recites lines without pause, schoolboy fashion. In addition to intonation, the pause is one of the most powerful elements of naturalness. A pause at the right place in the line with the right intonation preceding and following it is a major means for giving emphasis to a word, group of words, or idea, and for making the speech seem perfectly natural. It gives the effect, so to speak, of the character feeling his way through his ideas and their expression.

Every character in a play, as in life, has his own peculiar or individual rhythm which in the projection of that character the actor must catch and fix. This rhythm is exhibited in every movement the actor makes but is perhaps most obvious in his delivery of lines. Rhythm as applied to the speaking of lines means the "movement of the uttered words as marked by the succession and alternation of long and short, accented and unaccented syllables and by the position of the pauses." Rhythm is dependent upon the nature of the character and the emotional stimulus motivating the speech.

Excitement or anger may cause an individual of extremely slow natural rhythm to speak rapidly and tensely; conversely, rapidity and tensity may be used to convey excitement and anger. Shakespeare has splendidly illustrated this acceleration of tempo under excitement in Act I of *Hamlet,* in the scene in which Horatio reveals to Hamlet the appearance of the Ghost. Following this revelation is a scene of dialogue made up of questions by Hamlet and answers by Horatio. The click, click, click of the rhythm in this scene reveals Hamlet's excitement and pulls up the attention of the audience. The tempo of the speeches is in marked contrast to that which precedes the revelation by Horatio. It is this change in tempo and the consequent altering of the rhythm of the scene that really catches audience attention. Everyone is aware of how quickly a slow speaker with a monotonous rhythm will put an audience literally to sleep. By contrast, the speaker with a rapid delivery and a lively, changing rhythm gains attention and elicits interest.

The tempo and rhythm of a speech is not only dependent upon the nature of the character and the emotional stimulus; it must also be harmonized with the tempo and rhythm of the scene and the play. Any effective interpretation of a play on a stage is characterized by a distinct rhythmic pattern. In general comedy must be played at a more rapid rate than is tragedy but a comedy such as *The Importance of Being Earnest* requires a different rhythm from, say, *Tartuffe.* Much of this rhythmic pattern of the production as a whole derives from the rhythm of the lines but the rhythm of the stage movement likewise contributes to it. Rhythm of line and movement must be harmonized. In fact it is difficult for most individuals to move in one rhythmic pattern and speak in another. To do so is comic, an old piece of comic business that goes back to the "running slave" of Roman comedy. Occasionally an inexperienced actor who has learned a certain rhythmic pattern of speech will incongruously continue to move and gesture in another habitual pattern. The director must be on guard against such failures in co-ordination of speech and movement.

The tempo of a scene is not only dependent upon each actor's rate of delivery, but often more largely upon the proper taking of cues. One of the chief reasons why many amateur productions drag is that the untrained actors do not pick up their cues. Such an actor waits until the actor speaking opposite him has entirely finished speaking and his voice has died away before he begins his response. This creates a pause between each speech. When that pause is used purposefully and with meaning, it can be effective but when it is merely an habitual wait, it slows down the scene and drags the performance. When no meaningful pause or stage business intervenes, actors must be drilled into the snapping of their lines the split second the cue word is out of the mouth of the individual playing opposite them. Often it becomes necessary for the director to schedule special line drills for actors untrained in the snapping of cues.

Another fault quite as general among the untrained as the failure to pick up cues is the dropping of endings. The amateur tends to let his voice trail out and fade away on the end of his speech. This practice renders him ineffective and makes it hard for the audience to understand his lines. This dropping of the voice on the end of a speech is so general that the director can expect it with all untrained actors. It is bad in all performances and fatal in the playing of bright, witty comedy. It, like the failure to pick up cues, contributes to the slow, dragging effect in a performance. Constant drill is again the only remedy.

Another technique in the picking up of cues is that of "topping." The tendency of the untrained actor is to begin his speech in much the same tone in which the preceding speech ended. This practice makes for monotony and dullness. In a climatic scene of consecutive lines uninterrupted by extensive business the practice of topping will aid in overcoming this fault and in the effect of snapping cues. That is, the actor in beginning a speech in such a scene must top the conclusion of the speech which serves as his cue. His tone must be pitched differently and his force must be a trifle stronger than that of the actor who has spoken the cue. This gives a scene an effect of building, which is absolutely essential in the development of a climax. The practice is equally important in the playing of bright, witty comedy. The technique is useful likewise in building a quarrel scene or other scene of tense emotion. Something similar to this effect is to be observed in a real scene from life in which two angry people cut and thrust at each other with words. In that instance, however, the practice may lead to shouting on the part of each as they strive to top each other. This is avoided on the stage by the subtle variations of tone within the speech itself and by the skillful balancing of scenes of rising intensity with those of a calmer and quieter nature.

Faulty delivery often arises from a misconception of the nature of dramatic dialogue. It is too often thought of as set speeches to be spoken, rather than as spontaneous conversation. Such a false conception leads to the attitude and practice that may best be described as the "I speak my speech; now, you speak your speech; now, you have spoken your speech, and I will speak my next speech." Such a conception inevitably leads to a mechanical and stilted delivery. Dramatic dialogue rightly viewed is not such a set series of speeches to be spoken by reciters. It is conversation in which individuals say what they say because they are what they are and because they respond to other individuals and the situation they are in. What they say is not a recitation or a harangue to an audience. So far as they are concerned as characters in a realistic play (but not as actors) there is no audience.

The words of one character make another angry, happy, or puzzled and, being the kind of individual he is, he replies as he does. If you watch the angered one closely, you see his expression change, his body stiffen, his hands clinch perhaps, and then the words come. Always the action, or rather reaction, will precede his words, unless he deliberately conceals his reaction. He is not then reciting speeches; he is living and words are called from him by the situation in which he finds himself, and by his thoughts and feelings. It is thus that lines must be spoken on the stage. The actor is not merely acting; he is living the character; he is the character. But the actor is after all playing for an audience and he and the director must see that his acting carries over to and produces the desired effect upon that audience. This takes techniques in addition to imaginative identification.

What has been said up to this point about the delivery of lines has been largely in terms of the speaking of realistic prose dialogue, though the techniques discussed apply likewise to the delivery of poetic dialogue. Some considerations governing the speaking of poetry on the stage must be presented, although the subject is too large and complex to be examined thoroughly in a brief discussion. Without question drama as an oral art reaches its epitome in poetic plays. Most of the great drama prior to the modern period was written in verse; hence the actor who plays roles from plays of the past must gain some comprehension of poetic dialogue. One of the best books on the nature of poetry in drama is Moody Prior's *The Language of Tragedy* (New York:

Columbia University Press, 1947), though this book does not deal with the oral delivery of poetic dialogue. One of the great pleasures of attending the theatre is the hearing of beautiful and meaningful language beautifully spoken. The hearing of sound eloquently wedded to sense gives a thrilling experience akin to that of great music. To produce this thrilling effect the actor must have not only a trained and controlled voice, but must also have a comprehension of and feeling for metrical and poetic devices. Metrics involve not only length and accent, but also all of the devices of sound utilized by the poet to produce meaning, especially emotional meaning. Examine again the passages quoted in the discussion of Diction in Part I, Chapter 2 in terms of the sound effects which give meaning to the lines or note in the same terms the following speech by Hotspur from *Henry IV,* Part I, Act I, Scene iii:

> My liege, I did deny no prisoners.
> But I remember, when the fight was done,
> When I was dry with rage and extreme toil,
> Breathless and faint, leaning upon my sword,
> Came there a certain lord, neat, and trimly dress'd,
> Fresh as a bridegroom; and his chin new reap'd
> Show'd like a stubble-land at harvest home;
> He was perfumed like a milliner;
> And 'twixt his finger and his thumb he held
> A pouncet-box, which ever and anon
> He gave his nose and took't away again;
> Who therewith angry, when it came next there,
> Took it in snuff; and still he smiled and talk'd,
> And as soldiers bore dead bodies by,
> He call'd them untaught knaves, unmannerly,
> To bring a slovenly unhandsome corse
> Betwixt the wind and his nobility.
> With many holiday and lady terms
> He question'd me; amongst the rest, demanded
> My prisoners in your Majesty's behalf.
> I then, all smarting with my wounds being cold,
> To be so pester'd with a popinjay,
> Out of my grief and my impatience,
> Answer'd neglectingly I know not what,
> He should, or he should not; for he made me mad
> To see him shine so brisk and smell so sweet

And talk so like a waiting-gentlewoman
Of guns and drums and wounds—God save the mark!—
And telling me the sovereign'st thing on earth
Was Parmaceti for an inward bruise;
And that it was a great pity, so it was,
This villainous saltpetre should be digg'd
Out of the bowels of the harmless earth,
Which many a good tall fellow had destroy'd
So cowardly; and but for these vile guns,
He would himself have been a soldier.
This bald unjointed chat of his, my lord,
I answer'd indirectly, as I said;
And I beseech you, let not his report
Come current for an accusation
Betwixt my love and your high Majesty.

Note the strength of the beginning of the speech and the relative calmness of the speaker. The dominant consonant sounds in the first two lines may be employed to give power to Hotspur's denial. As he launches into his description of the popinjay, his indignation mounts and the consonant sounds may be employed to express his scorn. Indignation reaches an explosive stage in the plosive sounds of the line "To be so pester'd with a popinjay." This indignation bursts out into violent anger with the line "Of guns and drums and wounds—God save the mark!—" and again the consonant and vowel sounds express and support the emotion. In the next line, after this angry explosion, indignant scorn takes over again and the consonant sounds carry it. Finally, with the lines beginning "This bald unjointed chat . . . ," reasonable argument and forthright statement are the objective and the sounds are again suited to the purpose. This speech may not represent the epitome of great poetry but it represents one of the great speeches in verse in drama. The brief series of examining statements above by no means exhausts the metrical effects of the passage but should serve to illustrate some of the great vocal effects in verse dialogue.

In the discussion of Diction in Part I, Chapter 2, Section 13, comment was made about the image-evoking power of poetic dialogue. Hotspur's speech quoted above evokes a marvelous image of the popinjay. Here the image is called up through the descriptive powers of Hotspur; usually in poetic dialogue they result from the figures of speech. Poetry is figurative language which by its music creates emotion and by its figures creates pictures in the imagination. The actor who would effectively utilize its picture-producing power must study its figures of speech, of which the greatest is metaphor.

4. ACTING AS PANTOMIME

Thus far in the presentation of the director's concern with the actor the discussion of acting has been largely concerned with acting as a rendering of lines, that is in its aural aspects. Acting is, however, quite as much a visual as an aural art. Indeed it may be, as in the silent motion pictures and in pantomimic performances, entirely visual. The enactment of a role in a play, though it requires the combination of voice and body movement, may be as definitely pantomimic as is the performance in a silent motion picture. Anyone who has had the experience of seeing trained actors performing in a foreign language which the spectator does not comprehend, knows how effective the pantomimic interpretation of a role may be and anyone who has seen a performance by such a brilliant actor as Marcel Marceau knows how completely a character may be rendered in pantomime alone.

If acting is to be effective, the actor must act quite as definitely with his body as with his voice. Time and again in the former pages it has been indicated that the character's reaction must appear in his body before he gives voice to his thoughts and feelings. This motivating body reaction is what many directors mean when they say to actors, "act the part; don't just recite the lines." The pantomimic dramatization of the whole play is a problem for the director and the entire cast. As such it will be discussed in the next chapter. The pantomimic dramatization of the single role is the problem of the individual actor under the guidance of the director. For effective pantomimic interpretation the actor must have a fully trained body which, like that of the dancer, is completely responsive to his will. Hence body training is as important as voice training for the actor. Today that training of the body can probably be best secured through instruction and drill in dance.

The pantomimic interpretation of a role requires that the actor imaginatively identify himself with the character which he is playing. As was said earlier in this chapter, that imaginative identification probably begins most easily for actors with the visual aspects of the role. It helps many actors to assume the character of their role by getting into the costume representative of the character. Joseph Jefferson's account of his building of the role of Rip Van Winkle illustrates the point. Along with the wearing of the costume should go the assumption of the body posture of the role. For example, in playing an old man or old woman well past middle age, it helps to get the feel of the character's body by letting the stomach muscles and the shoulders sag. With this sagging of the shoulders and relaxing of the stomach muscles comes a curvature of the back. There are, of course, old men and old women who stand straight as a ramrod. The body posture depends upon the nature of the character.

As the posture is mastered, the actor should develop the characterizing walk distinctive of the role. Assuming the posture will aid in developing the walk and the walk should help to fix the posture. The carriage of the head and the use of the arms and hands must be harmonized with posture and walk. A quick, alert turning of the head or gesture in an absent-minded, somnolent old man will be incongruous and will destroy the probability of the character.

Once an actor has mastered the posture, walk, gesture, and other visual physical attributes of his role, he must then proceed to a pantomimic dramatization of that role. This involves the full expression of the inner feelings, emotions, and thoughts of the character through physical, visual means. It involves the obvious emotional reactions demanded of the role as well as the character's reactions to those around him. For example, an actor may express dislike of another character by the way in which he draws away from and avoids him, and by the way he looks at him. Repulsion is usually expressed by drawing away from, attraction by drawing toward another person. These responses to other characters must be made visual, must be put over to the audience, not only in what is said but also in the body and movement of the actor. Likewise the whole gamut of emotions and thoughts which move the actor must be pantomimically dramatized. For example, what another person in the play says to a character may arouse fear in him, make him angry, or merely puzzle him. The actor playing the character should be able to show each of these reactions through his body alone. Finally, every role in a play is a means of telling the story of the play; hence the actor must master the pantomimic dramatization of his deeds and actions.

With these requisites in mind, the necessity for economy on the part of the actor would seem obvious. He cannot afford to use a gesture or a movement that does not have motivation and meaning. Moreover, there is so much that he must express that he must employ the most economical means of visually realizing each factor of his role. When a shrug of the shoulder or a nod of the head is sufficient to express his reaction, he must not elaborate the bodily expression beyond these. If his role is an important one in the action, there will be reactions and scenes which he must elaborate. Proper emphasis and proper development will require such elaboration. But to elaborate the pantomimic dramatization of every reaction and every deed called for by the role is to "ham" the part.

Thus, to repeat, acting requires body techniques which are dependent upon a trained body. Some of these techniques which concern the director in the training of the single actor are standard and are required in all plays. We must now turn to a consideration of some of the most important among these.

5. STANDING AND WALKING

The first problem of the young actor is to learn how to stand on the stage. Of course the way he stands, his body posture, will be dictated by the role which he is interpreting, but he must learn how to stand still in correct posture. The usual tendency of all of us when standing still is to sag and relax the muscles. In correct posture the body should be erect, the feet aligned—fairly close together for women, not so close for men—the knees pulled back, the abdominal muscles pulled in, the diaphragm lifted, chest expanded, shoulders back, head lifted, and neck lengthened. The weight should be on the balls of the feet so that it can be easily shifted to either foot for movement. With practice, this posture can be free and easy, not the stiff military posture of the soldier at attention. The feeling should be one of the body lifted up to its full height. The arms and hands should hang freely at the side, not pressed in rigidly against the body.

To move forward from this position, first shift the body weight to one foot and then move out the free foot, with the free foot straight—not turned in or out. Start the walk from the hips, not from the knees, thus taking the weight of the body forward. Keep the head up and the eyes front. With the step-out, shift the weight to the forward foot and bring the second foot forward in a straight line in front of the former. Try practicing this walk on a straight line drawn upon the floor. Keep the head and chest up, eyes front, and the abdominal muscles drawn in. As you step forward, say with the right foot, at the same time swing the left shoulder forward, not in an exaggerated manner, as a balance of the body weight. At the same time swing the left hand forward with the shoulder. Keep the fingers of the hands together, though not rigid, while walking.

The effectiveness of polite drawing-room comedy can be largely killed by actors slouching in their posture and ragged in their walk. The smoothness of movement on the stage depends, first, in the actor's ability to stand and walk correctly. Having acquired that ability, he can then vary and adapt it to the specific demands of the role. Posture and walk are two important assets in the revelation of character. The possibilities of their utilization are far too extensive to enumerate here.

6. SITTING AND RISING

Assume that an actor is required to move from upstage center to downstage left and sit in a chair that faces right front. He should walk in a straight line to the chair, in front of it, pivot so that the calf of his left leg touches the side of the chair to the left, past the center. Thus he is assured of sitting in the chair and not on its edge when he lowers himself into it. After lowering himself into the chair, he brings his right foot back in line with, but apart from, the left. A woman should draw both feet together in the center. Reverse the technique if the chair is on the right. The movement will be smoother, especially for women, if the out foot is drawn into line with the foot nearest the edge of the chair before she lowers herself into the chair. Unless the characterization requires it, do not slouch in the chair. Keep the body upright but relaxed. If a woman should cross her legs while sitting, she should slide one leg under the other, not throw one across the other as a man does. Place the hands on the lap. Bring forward slightly the shoulder opposite to the crossed knee, not vice versa.

In rising from a sitting position, bring the body weight forward, move the upstage foot outward (unless the rise precedes a direct upstage cross), and lift the body weight upward by means of the hips and knees. Let the hands fall naturally and easily to the sides. All of these, like all stage movement, should be done with economy. Other things being equal, the fewer the motions the better. The director must be on guard against the tendency of amateurs to fall out of character while standing still, or sitting, or rising, and especially against their tendency to indulge in little random gestures and movements that distract.

7. THE HEAD AND THE EYES

One of the most noticeable failings of the untrained actor is the tendency to drop the head and look at the floor. The head and the eyes are among the most expressive instruments at the actor's command; yet the young actor usually uses them as though he expected to produce his chief effects upon the floor of the stage rather than upon the audience. A trained actor knows that he must not lose a moment's eye contact with his audience, unless, of course, there is a specific requirement that he look upstage. Even then, he will compensate for that momentary loss of eye contact by trying to make some other part of his body more than usually expressive. To digress for a moment, no trained actor would allow a piece of furniture or another actor to block him off from his audience contact, unless, again, the specific demands of the scene so required. If he were so covered by another actor or a piece of furniture, he would quietly uncover at the first opportunity.

To return to the head, it is the heaviest part of the body, but the part which, when correctly carried, gives great strength and dignity. Part of this upright carriage of the head is achieved by the right use of the eyes. Downcast eyes aid in giving the appearance of a drooping head; eyes uplifted raise the head. On the other hand, trained actors never stare directly at their audiences. They look just above their heads at approximately where the floor of the first balcony appears. Clowns and comics, however, sometimes gain a humorous effect by playing directly into the faces of the audience.

To make the young actor keep his head and eyes up and play

front will be one of the most difficult tasks confronting the director. He must insist upon it from the very beginning of the rehearsals. He must make himself conscious of and sensitive to these vices of the young actor by noticing in each amateur performance he attends how often the effectiveness of the performance is marred by the actors looking at the floor, turning away from the audience, and speaking lines upstage.

At the same time, a young actor must be taught to look at the actor to whom he is speaking. This may require a quarter turn—perhaps as much as a half turn—away from the audience. But an actor can give the impression of looking directly at another actor who is slightly upstage of him and yet actually not lose eye contact with his audience and not speak his lines upstage. These are problems of grouping, of the position and placements of more than one actor on the stage, to be considered later. An actor plays an audience as well as a role. That playing of an audience is as important as the playing of the role. He cannot play an audience with whom he has no contact. His first method of contact is through the eyes. The eyes are in many respects his most expressive instrument. They help him to convey the emotions of his role and to direct the attention of the audience. The way in which an actor turns and looks at another actor or an object will serve to focus the attention of the audience upon that other actor or object, as well as upon the first actor himself. The director should make his actors keep their eyes off the floor with their heads up. He should make them face one quarter from full front, unless requirements are specifically otherwise, and deliver their lines to the audience, not to the back wall of the set.

This matter of keeping open contact with the audience is involved also in making gestures, shaking hands, embracing, and handling properties. An actor playing on the right or left side of the stage who gestures to others opposite and upstage may cover his expression and reaction from the audience unless he is cautioned. If he shakes hands with one who is slightly upstage of him, he may also lose direct audience contact. Of course, if the other actor has the scene (and he should probably not be in the upstage position if he did not), then the momentary loss of contact by the downstage actor on the right is not objectionable. Here, however, we are into the problem of the placement of two actors, not a single actor, in the action. In general an actor, facing front, should not take a letter or other object by reaching across his body. He should so place himself that such covering is not necessary.

Since the subject of gesture has of necessity arisen at this point, another aspect of the subject of concern to the director of amateur actors might be introduced here, though related more specifically to the uses of arms and hands rather than the head and the eyes. One of the reasons why amateur performances seem so ragged and unfinished can be traced to the angularity in gesture of those actors. The ragged, chopping effect of hands and arms results from a lack of technique. The inexperienced actor is apt to gesture from the wrist or from the elbow, seldom or never using the whole arm from the shoulder in the broad, sweeping, finished gesture that looks well from the stage.

Unless indecisiveness is to be conveyed, a gesture should have a definite beginning and a conclusive ending. If it is an arm gesture, swing the whole arm out from the shoulder; or, if the gesture is one of pointing, bring it up and out from the side. Actors with faults in gesturing should be given instructions and then told to practice before a mirror. Such broad gestures as are here recommended are especially necessary in Shakespearean plays but even in modern realistic drama, especially in plays about cultured and sophisticated people, awkwardness of gesture can do much to decrease probability, call attention to the amateurishness of the actors, and rob audiences of pleasure.

8. ENTRANCES, CROSSES, EXITS

There is an old half-truth that says first appearances are lasting. Certainly they often are on the stage. Any entrance, and especially the first entrance, is significant in the establishment of the character. It must be carefully planned and executed with finish. Entrances likewise help to tell the story, a matter to be considered later. Every entrance in a play, as we have seen, represents a new psychological grouping and creates a new scene. An actor must know exactly why the character he is enacting makes his entrance and must go directly to the completion of that purpose. At the same time, he must be aware of the new psychological state established by his entrance and must play his appropriate role in that emotional state. Thus the first requisite of any entrance is that it be made in character. Nothing so ruins

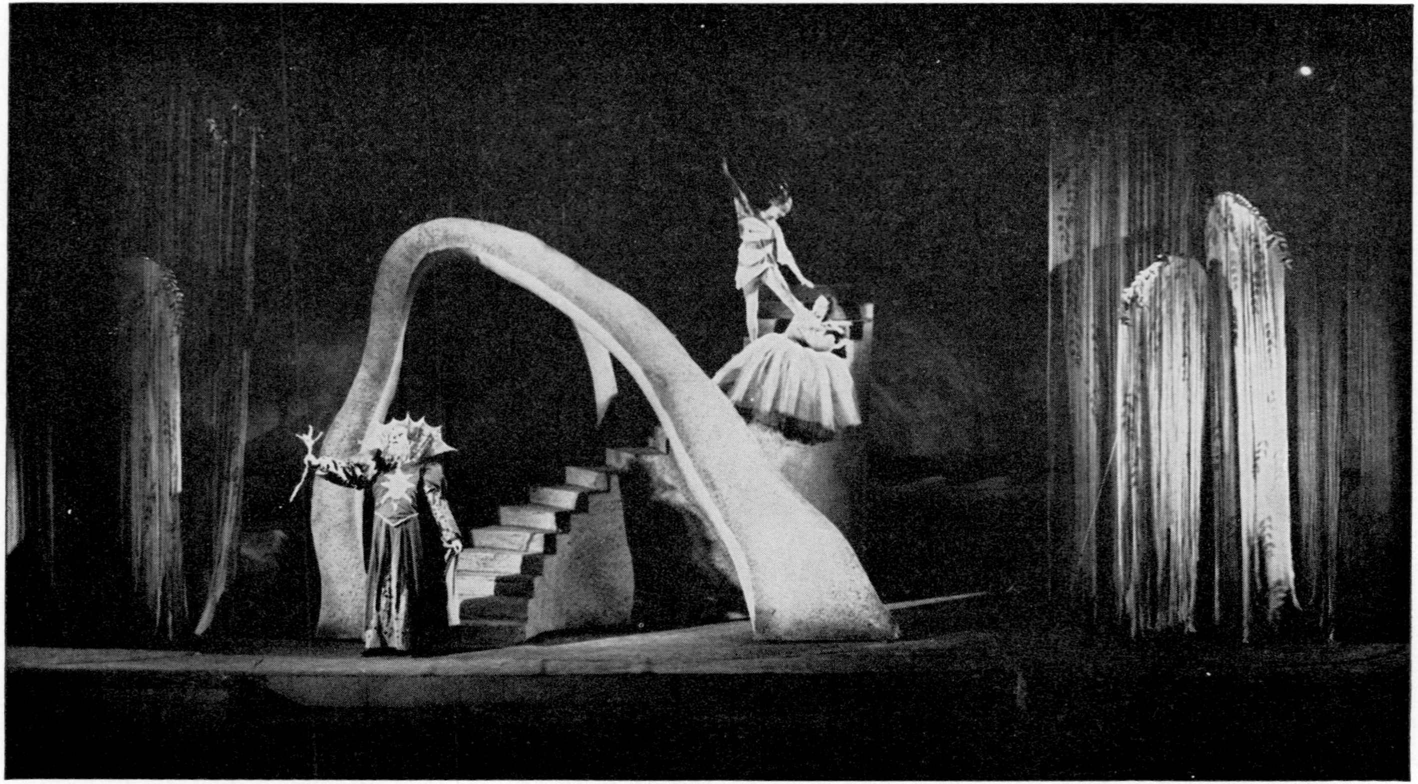

The Tempest, directed by Foster Fitz-Simons and set by Lynn Gault. Produced by The Carolina Playmakers at the University of North Carolina.

the probability of a scene than for an actor to enter the stage and then visibly assume his character before the eyes of the audience. To guard against this fatality, the actor should assume his character some steps and some seconds—minutes would be better—offstage before he makes his entrance. Then the entrance should be executed with proper finish.

If the entrance is from upstage center, the actor should grasp the door knob with his right hand (if the door swings to the right and opens on stage), open the door, and enter on his left foot. Reverse the procedure if the door swings to the left. If the door is in the left wall and swings downstage, he should grasp the door knob with his left hand, open the door, and enter on his right (upstage) foot. This causes him to enter facing the audience. If the door swings upstage, he will grasp the door knob with his right hand, open the door, and enter upon his right (upstage) foot. If the door is in the right wall, reverse the procedures. After the entrance from stage left, close the door with the left hand on the door knob; if the entrance is on the right, close it with the right hand.

The objective is to keep as full a view as possible to the audience. After the entrance, do not hesitate at the door (unless the business requires doing so) but go directly to the purpose or objective of the entrance. When two characters enter together and one of them is speaking, the one speaking should ordinarily enter last, thus allowing him to continue to address the other actor and still face the audience. The nature of the entrance and the relationships of the two characters will demand variations in this procedure.

Keep the head up and the eyes off the floor when making an entrance. An actor entering an unfamiliar room can convey his unfamiliarity with it by the way in which he looks around and finds his bearings. Conversely, an actor entering a familiar room can convey his familiarity by the way in which he goes directly to his objective. Similarly a character shows by his reaction upon entrance whether he is acquainted or unacquainted, friendly or unfriendly, with other characters present. This reaction to environment and to other characters is part of the process of keeping in character when making an entrance.

Master playwrights build the entrances of their characters, especially of their key characters, with great care. Almost any good play will show examples of this attention to the technique of an entrance. Two examples will suffice. Molière carefully builds up the character of Tartuffe for nearly three acts before he brings him onstage and then brings him on with a superb entrance of which Louis Jouvet took full advantage in his production in Paris in 1950. The first entrance of Cyrano de Bergerac, on the other hand, is a covered one but equally masterly in its technique. That character is also carefully built up before he suddenly appears in the midst of the theatre crowd. Entrances so built, when properly executed, are an important part of the theatrical effectiveness of every play. They must be analyzed by the director, carefully designed, and repeatedly rehearsed.

Exits can be no less effective. Both exits and entrances involve crosses, to be more fully considered presently. In general an actor should make his exit on his own line, thus avoiding a stage wait while he is going out. Sometimes, however, just such a stage wait is the very device of emphasizing an exit which warrants such emphasis. Examples often occur in the old melodramas when the villain delivers his denunciation and challenge like a thunderbolt to his victims from center stage, turns his back on them disdainfully, and stalks out, leaving them in fear and despair. In this instance, the halting of the flow of the scene and the registering of various emotions by the remaining characters is part of the pantomimic dramatization of the action and is used for special dramatic purposes. Many other instances of such exists, not involving villains, occur in modern drama.

Where the scene must flow on in smooth transition to the succeeding scene, however, the actor must so plan his business as to make the cross preceding his exit in such a way as not to cause a wait between scenes. Often the last part of his line can be delivered at the door immediately prior to his exit. If the door is in the right wall, he will grasp the door knob in his right hand; if it is in the left wall, with his left hand (varied in accordance with the swinging of the door). In this way he faces his audience to the last. Exits and entrances on stairways must be planned in relation to lines so as not to keep the scene waiting. They, too, of course, must be made part of the pantomimic dramatization of the action.

Entrances, exits, and crosses on the stage, from one point of view, are mere utilitarian devices for getting actors on- and offstage and for getting them from one stage area to another. From another point of view, that of the pantomimic dramatization of the action of the play, they represent dramatic action on its most elementary level, that of physical movement. Both the utilitarian and the dramatic objective must be kept in mind by the director and the actor at all times. Therefore, in the execution of a cross an actor must know his objective in two senses: He must know the exact physical spot to which he is going in making the cross, and he must know the emotional implications and dramatic effect of the cross. It should go without saying, then, that an actor must know how to walk on the stage and how to walk in character in order to make an effective cross.

The first principle of crosses that young actors must learn is that he must make his crosses on his own lines. The reason for this is that, presumably, while he is speaking he has the stage—commands the major attention of the audience. An audience's attention may be held by sound but is more powerfully attracted by motion; hence, as we have previously seen, the audience's attention always tends to gravitate to the object in motion. If a silent actor makes a cross while another is speaking, his cross tends to distract audience attention from that speech and that actor, makes the audience miss the line spoken, and makes it wrongfully place its attention away from the dramatic meaning of the action in progress. The violation of this principle makes many amateur shows difficult to listen to.

There are certainly instances in the progress of a scene in which this principle may be violated for good and compelling reasons. An actor may quietly and unobtrusively move to one side while another is speaking in order to uncover. He may, indeed, deliberately and obviously cross on another's line if that serves the psychological intent of the scene and if he is so directed by the director. In such instances, the speech of the speaking character is not the major focus of interest. If it is, that speech must be delivered with extra care and the speaking actor should have the upstage position. He may be given some counter move to aid in holding attention.

On the stage, as in geometry, the shortest distance between two points is a straight line. In general every stage cross should be made in a straight line. If an object lies between the actor and his objective, he should break his cross into two lines at angles to each other. Unless there is an intent to give indecisiveness and wavering to the motion, an actor should never walk in curved patterns. Pick out your exact objective and go straight to it. This device helps to give finish and smoothness to the physical movement on the stage.

In general, too, crosses should be made in front of any physical object lying in the path of the movement in order not to conceal the actor, even in part, from his audience. This injunction cannot always be followed but the director must always plan the placement of the action on the stage and the placement of the furniture so that the furniture does not conceal the action. Further, in the planning of crosses they must be timed exactly. Thus the actor must know how many steps and how many words he has to take him from his position to his objective. "Suit the action to the word and the word to the action" applies in this, as well as in all that the actor does. This fitting of the words to the movement will, after the first walk-through rehearsals, occupy much of the time of the business rehearsals. Actors must be drilled carefully in the exact co-ordination of lines and stage movement. Obedience to this injunction involves the matter of both tempo and rhythm, determined by the tempo and rhythm of the character and of the scene.

Sometimes actors are required to make entrances and exits and to execute crosses when the one actor alone occupies the stage (see the first scene of Eugene O'Neill's *Ile*). So far our consideration has been largely confined to this type of business. More often, however, when entrances, exits, or crosses are made by an actor on a stage, that stage is also occupied by other actors. Thus these pieces of business affect the pantomimic dramatization and equally affect the composition of the stage business, matters to be more fully considered later. Here we must consider some matters of balance and pictorial composition as related to the single actor. When an actor makes a cross to another actor, he should not approach too close to him and thereby crowd their scene together. If this happens, the director must request them to open up; that is, to separate so as to play the full audience.

Of course there are pieces of business that require the approaching actor to come in full bodily contact with another. The stage embrace is an example. When more than two actors are playing a scene and one actor moves away from another and toward a third, the second actor must counterbalance the scene. That is, he must move away from his position slightly, in a direction opposite to that of the first actor. This balancing serves to maintain the composition of the scene within the playing area. Actors must acquire a feeling for this kind of balance of the scene and must open up or balance unobtrusively through the action.

Similarly, entrances and exits require a new balancing of the stage grouping. What is said here is in a sense a violation of what was said above about actors moving on their own lines only. If this balancing of the grouping is done obviously, it will be a violation and will make for raggedness in the flow of the action. It is perfectly possible for the actor to learn how to balance a scene or grouping by unobtrusively stepping aside, forward, or backward without undue distraction of audience attention. Without training in stage movement, however, the young actor will not acquire this ability.

9. TWO-ACTOR SCENES

What has been said thus far about the director in relation to the actor has been focused primarily upon the training of the single actor, though in the last section and elsewhere the consideration has involved more than one actor. Some further attention must be given to the handling of actors in groups, though that subject will be largely reserved for discussion in the next chapter. Repeatedly through the discussion in this and preceding chapters stress has been placed upon the importance of reaction. When two or more actors are playing a scene together, the effectiveness of the scene will depend as much upon their reactions as characters to each other as upon their individual vocal and pantomimic renderings of their characterizations. One of the first problems in reaction which the inexperienced actor must master is that of listening in character to another. Unless the business specifically calls for inattention on the part of certain characters, each actor on the stage must give at all times the effect of complete and full attention to the character speaking. But reaction requires more than mere attention. Each in terms of his character must register. His posture, gesture, facial expression—even his movements—must indicate the effects that the words and deeds of another have upon him. It is this visible registering of responses that should precede speech. That is what an actor means when he says of another, "he gives me something to play to or against." With amateur actors a considerable portion of the business rehearsals, as well as subsequent rehearsals, may have to be devoted to teaching them to register.

Perhaps enough has already been said about the tendency of inexperienced actors to huddle together and to play too close to each other. Certain scenes may demand such close proximity, even bodily contact between characters. In most groupings, however, the director must teach the actors how to open up. The technique is essentially the same as that mentioned in connection with one actor balancing another. When an actor senses that a grouping is too close, or when the director orders "open up," the actors unobtrusively move away from each other by "cheating." They quietly, with small steps, move their bodies so that there is a greater distance between them.

In the same manner an actor must be taught to "take stage." In this instance he may deliberately move out on his own lines from the group so as to assume a more dominant stage position or so that in his crosses accompanying his lines he may traverse more of the stage area. Such a taking of stage may be made more effective if the other actors counter by moving a step or two in the opposite direction to the direction of the actor taking stage. There are, of course, scenes and psychological situations in which such countering movements would not be suitable. As in opening up a grouping, such counter movements must be done expeditiously and unobtrusively.

Certain situations, on the other hand, may require an actor to follow the actor who is taking stage, especially if the actor following is imploring, begging, beseeching, or pleading with the first actor. In such actions care must be exercised to avoid the old comedy routine of parallel movement. Taking stage is part of the problem of playing the whole stage, to be mentioned in the next chapter. The director must be alert to the tendency of many amateur actors to root themselves in one spot and tend to play all of their scenes from that place. It is these actors that need to be taught to take stage. In certain big scenes, impressive speeches, and strong moments nothing can be quite so effective in enhancing these as a bold swing across stage. Such a big movement, on the other hand, must go with big moments in the role and the play. Of course they must always go with the character. A timid, restrained person is not likely ever to indulge in such large movements.

It has been noted before that many plays are made up in large part of duologues, scenes between two actors, and that such scenes can become static and thus lose interest. One of the devices of keeping them alive and fluid is through business between the two actors. At moments when the roles are about evenly balanced in the scene the two actors may play on a level with each other, that is, they may play opposite each other about an equal distance from the footlights.

Often, however, one or the other character has the dominant position in the scene, a relationship that may vary several times within a long scene. Examine the second act of Eugene O'Neill's *Mourning Becomes Electra,* in which Lavinia and Christine alternate in holding the whip hand, for a superb piece of craftsmanship in the art of constructing such a scene. In these scenes the dominant character should take and hold the upstage position so long as he or she is dominating the scene. As the roles change in terms of dominance, so must the positions. The upstage actor in the dominant position should be allowed the freer movements—should take stage. Often a "twosome," as a two-actor scene is frequently labeled, is played on a sofa or chairs. Such a scene can be as interestingly varied as a standing scene by an imaginative director and experienced actors. Again the dominant character must be given the chief responsibility for movement—unless, of course, the dominance arises from a very quiet intensity and power in the character. The variety of positions which two actors on a sofa may assume, or the variety of arrangements of two actors and a chair, are so diverse that it would take lengthy descriptions to spell them out. Such spelling out is not necessary for any imaginative student of directing.

Here, however, is an opportune moment to make some observations on playing with furniture. Amateur actors must be cautioned—unless, of course, their characterizations call for such actions—not to lean against or slouch upon the furnishings. On the other hand, they must be coached in the actual use of furnishings, especially in modern realistic plays. Furniture and other properties are there to be used and the actors should use them. Little pieces of business, such as the setting straight of a chair or the picking up of a picture or object from a table, glancing at it or examining it carefully, and replacing it, the straightening of a picture on the wall, and many other such simple actions can add verisimilitude to the scene and become potent devices for revealing character. Such pieces of business must never be allowed to hold up or interfere with the flow of the scene. They must be worked in naturally in that flow. Hand props carried on by the actor—such as umbrellas, handbags, hats, books, etc.—can be similarly utilized and are frequent aids in overcoming the embarrassment and awkwardness of inexperienced actors. The director must be on guard, however, to see that such "fiddling with" properties does not become a distraction.

10. SCENES WITH MORE THAN TWO ACTORS

Scenes of two actors, and especially scenes involving more than two actors, become problems in the composition of grouping, to be discussed in the next chapter. Some other aspects of the handling of groups of actors must be presented here. The director's chief problem with a number of actors on stage is to see that the minor characters stay in character while the major characters are largely carrying the scene. For some inexperienced actors it is extremely difficult to stand still and remain in character, with no lines to deliver. As has been previously observed, the director's first task is to teach these how to listen. If they are allowed to fall out of character or to move about, they will distract attention from the central focus. Each of them should be told his or her characteristic reactions to what is being said and is happening. Thus they can be shown how they can, without lines or major business, make a contribution to the effects.

Scenes involving three actors can be most easily and effectively patterned in terms of the triangle. The actor who is dominant in the scene is given the apex position upstage and the other two actors play downstage right and left of him, about three-quarter face to audience. Such a position can be easily changed as one or the other of the two actors assumes dominance and moves to the apex of the triangle. Such a triangular grouping may be widely varied. It need not be in the upstage-downstage plane but may be arranged across stage—left to right or right to left. It can be further varied with platforms and elevations.

The triangular pattern is likewise an excellent device for arranging group and mob scenes. Such scenes to be fully effective require detailed planning and careful drill. With amateur actors it is wise for the director to give each participant in the group or mob a definite characterization to assume. Bits of business to be executed on cue, such as a laugh, a shout, the shaking of a fist, etc., should be assigned. Unless a drill effect is sought, straight lines and movements in unison should be avoided. With a mob scene some milling about is desirable but must be introduced on cue at moments when it will be least distracting. In a mob scene, such as that in *Julius Caesar,* a good entrance effect can be attained by having one or two shouting characters run on first, followed by three or four, and then by masses.

Another excellent effect can be created by having little pieces of business between two or three characters within the mob executed during the mob scene and varied from group to group. Often a mob, such as that in Hauptmann's *The Weavers,* has an obvious leader, who should be given the prominent apex position when the mob is relatively static in its grouping. *Ad lib* shouts from the mob must be carefully planned and assigned to individual actors. If the mob takes up the cry, a building effect can be obtained by having one person shout, followed by three or four taking it up, then by several more joining in, until the whole mob is shouting. Similarly, in the dying away of the shouting, it is often effective to have it die away to a final single shout. Sometimes, of course, a precision and drill-effect is aimed at, rather than that of a spontaneous mob.

Though mob scenes often occur in musical plays, there is another routine—that of the chorus—that is more frequent. Choral routines are usually precise and drill-like. In some instances they are designed for stiff, manikin-like movements; in others a greater naturalness within the group routine is desirable. Since the effectiveness of choral routines often depends upon precision and exact similarity of execution, individual characterizations within the choral group are avoided. The members are costumed and made up to resemble each other as nearly as possible. Similarity in height or gradations in height are utilized. Choral routines, like dance patterns, are more strictly the province of the choreographer or dancing master, rather than the director. But the director who is called upon to stage musical plays and operas will have to become something of a choreographer. In fact, choreography is a distinct asset to any director, for in a sense the businessing of any play is a problem in choreography. In certain highly stylized plays the movements of the actors can closely approach those of dancers.

This discussion has carried somewhat beyond the problems of the director as a coach of actors but should suffice to show the range of the director's responsibilities in training members of casts. For further information, the director should turn to the numerous good books on acting. Three helpful books on techniques of acting, among the many that might be mentioned, are F. Cowles Strickland, *The Technique of Acting* (New York: McGraw-Hill Book Company, 1956); E. B. (Zeke) Colvan, *Face the Footlights! A New and Practical Approach to Acting* (New York: McGraw-Hill Book Company, 1940); and Florence Lutz, *The Technique of Pantomime* (Berkeley, California: The Sather Gate Book Shop, 1927). While acting cannot be learned from a book, any more than can directing, the above-named books will prove helpful and stimulating to the director who has had some previous training in acting.

11. STYLES IN ACTING

The discussion throughout this chapter has been about acting in general, though the emphasis has been upon realistic acting. Different styles of drama require different styles of acting. The completely natural style of acting suitable for many modern plays would not be appropriate to the interpretation of a role in a Greek tragedy, a Shakespearean play, a Restoration comedy, or a play by Molière. Obviously it is not fitting in this chapter nor in this book to enter into an elaborate discussion of styles in acting. Such a subject pertains to the advanced study of acting. Nevertheless, the director must be cognizant of the different stylistic demands of various plays and in planning the style of a production must include the acting.

Style, as we have seen, depends ultimately upon the particular and special view of the artist, the way in which he sees what he is rendering. This view, in turn, determines the kind of probability which the dramatist will give to his rendering of his materials. Thus, it is perfectly possible for an O'Neill to view class-stratified human beings as automaton-like manikins, as he does in the Fifth-

Avenue scene of *The Hairy Ape,* while at other times and in other plays he might view these same kinds of human beings differently. Yank in this same play is characterized fundamentally in a naturalistic style but is also meant to represent a symbol. The actors who play the Fifth-Avenue churchgoers cannot play their roles in the same style as that of Yank. The manikins are characterized in terms of Yank's vision of them and are therefore rightly rendered in an expressionistic style. The actor who plays Yank might give an effective performance by concentrating upon the naturalistic rendering of Yank but his performance will become more meaningful and significant if he sees the devices by which O'Neill has made him a symbol and incorporates these into his characterization. They will influence the naturalism of style. Long in that same play represents yet a somewhat different style. He, too, is basically naturalistic but is conceived in terms of a class, the Socialist agitator. What has been said should suffice to show that even in modern plays, and especially in those that have been influenced by styles other than realism, there is a range of styles in the characterizations.

Older plays more obviously differ from modern realistic drama in their stylistic characterizations. While we may speak generally of the style of characterization in Greek tragedy, the characterizations of the three great tragic dramatists are distinctly different. All of the characters in those tragedies demand a dignity, stateliness, and selective restraint in their rendering but the characters of Euripides are far more "realistic" and emotional than are those of the other two tragedians.

Shakespeare's plays differ subtly in style from play to play and his characterizations within a single play vary. The low-comedy characters in *Twelfth Night,* for example, differ stylistically from the chief characters, though the styles of characterization of the two groups are harmonious. Sir Toby, Sir Andrew, and their crew are more Jonsonian, more Elizabethanly realistic, than are the chief characters. Malvolio originally belonged to the low-comedy style but is attempting to ape his betters. Similar discriminations could be indicated in Restoration comedy and in the plays of Molière but those here given should serve to illustrate the requirements and something of the procedure.

The actor's first obligation is to make the role which he is playing convincing to an audience. Though convincingness may be attained on different levels of probability, for the beginning actor it is perhaps wise if he first approaches his role as though the character were a real, living personality. When he has mastered the character in this way, he can then proceed to such stylization as is requisite. The requisite stylization will be determined, first, by the general style of the whole production and, second, by the kind of probability which the playwright has employed in creating the role. Style is the way in which means are related to manner. In acting the manner is the imaginative embodiment and rendering of a personality. The means are the visual and vocal traits and devices which serve to individualize that personality. Style, then, is varied in terms of the selection and utilization of the two types of traits. After the amateur actor has mastered a role as a real, living character, he can then, under the guidance of a director, eliminate certain traits and highlight others in a way that will give the desired stylization.

QUESTIONS AND EXERCISES

I. *Exercises in Characterization:*

1. Entirely by means of pantomime render each of the following characters:
   A. A seventy-year-old, somewhat infirm, proud, and arrogant retired army officer.
   B. A seventy-year-old, infirm, rheumatic, dirty, and ragged beggar.
   C. For women: Change A above to an old dowager, formerly a leader in society. Change B to a beggar woman.
   D. A twelve-year-old boy (girl) aimlessly strolling home from school on a warm spring day.
   E. A middle-aged business leader (club woman) and solid citizen.
2. Examine O'Neill's *Ile* for every suggestion which you can discover concerning the characterization of Mr. Slocum, the Second Mate. On the basis of the traits which you have found, add other appropriate and consistent traits, utilizing the scheme of questions given in Section 1 to stimulate your imagination. When you have developed the character fully, render him pantomimically.
3. For women: Take the character of Lady Sims in *The Twelve-Pound Look* and follow the instructions given in No. 2, above.
4. For the protagonist of the Shakespearean play which you have

been using in other exercises prepare a complete and orderly character analysis. Go first to the text and find every indication of character therein. Then utilize any commentaries or discussions of the role which will aid in stimulating your imaginative conception.

II. *Vocal Interpretations of Character and Speaking Lines:*

1. Imitate the vocal mannerisms of a child of five.
2. Imitate the vocal mannerisms of the most dignified, precise, somewhat pompous individual that you know.
3. Imitate the vocal mannerisms of a giggling, teen-age girl.
4. After you have formed a definite conception of the character of Fatt as he appears in the first scene of Odet's *Waiting for Lefty,* read each of his speeches so as fully to render his character.
5. Having acquainted yourself fully with the character of Hotspur in *Henry IV,* memorize the speech quoted in the text on the Popinjay and render it in character.

III. *Some Exercises in Single-Actor Techniques:*

1. Read carefully the instructions on how to walk on the stage. Practice these until you have mastered the walk. Observe that posture, body carriage, and position of the head are important in this walk.
2. Follow the instructions given in the text for sitting and rising, practicing these until you have perfected them.
3. By means of facial expression and use of the eyes render the following: Your attention is caught; curiosity is aroused; you look intently; you are startled; this changes to amusement; and ends in hearty laughter.
4. By means of facial expression, eyes, hands, and arms render the following: Your attention is caught; you are startled; this changes to fear; fear becomes horror.
5. What gestures are essential or useful in your rendering of Hotspur's speech, as indicated in II, 5, above?

IV. *Some Exercises for Two Actors:*

1. Render the following entirely in pantomime: Boy enters room. Is surprised to find his girl friend there. The girl friend is miffed over a broken date and somewhat angry. Boy friend tries to find out what is wrong and is finally told. He explains and pleads with the girl. Finally she relents and forgives him.
2. Stage the same scene but in this staging utilize a sofa.
3. Stage the same scene but end it in a rousing quarrel and separation.
4. Plan, rehearse, and present a quarrel scene between two characters in which the dominant position changes several times.

Be sure to characterize distinctly each role. Utilize stage positions, stage movements, crosses, and gestures economically but for full effectiveness.

V. *Some Exercises for Three Actors:*

1. Render the following in pantomime: Two congenial friends are talking together intimately. Enter a third person whom neither likes. They want the third person to leave but he (she) is quite unaware of this. At last the two have to leave themselves.
2. Two individuals are gossiping about a third person, when to their surprise and confusion that person enters. The third person senses their confusion and becomes suspicious. This leads to questions, denials, guilty looks, accusations, and finally to the third person discovering and denouncing the two.
3. Restage the scene outlined in No. 2, utilizing a table.
4. Three individuals are playing cards. First one, then the other, begins to suspect the third of cheating. They watch him carefully and eventually trap him.
5. Two lovers are sitting together in earnest conversation when they are surprised by the entrance of the irate father (or mother). who objects strongly to the boy's attentions to the daughter. A quarrel results. The girl, at first afraid, eventually joins in on the side of the boy. The boy restrains the parent from chastizing the girl. When the parent is finally calmed down a bit, boy and girl announce that they are already married.

CHAPTER 8

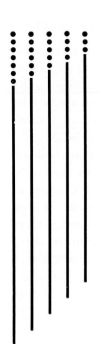

Some Principles and Practices in Directing

THE ART OF DIRECTING is the art of interpreting a play for a specific audience through the means of theatre arts. Just as there is no one and only interpretation of a play, so is there no one single method of directing. Yet there are certain principles and certain practices which can be stated, learned, and applied widely to the stage interpretation of various plays. But the art of directing, like that of playwriting or any other art, cannot be learned merely from reading a book about it or from hearing lectures on it. Both books and lectures are highly important to teach the learner principles and methods which he must apply in practice but his learning is incomplete if he does not go on to practice, preferably under the guidance of an experienced director-teacher. The director in transferring the action of a play from printed word symbols on paper to action on a stage before an audience has a task which demands that he exercise several functions. For clarity we must again list these functions.

His first function, as we have seen, is that of interpreting the play by study and analysis. In the exercise of this function he resembles the scholar in method, though their aims may not coincide. The scholar's aim is the full and complete interpretation of the play in terms of its authorship, sources, and the age that gave it birth; whereas, the director's aim is an imaginative interpretation of the play so that it will affect and have meaning for a contemporary audience. To the director a play is a script to be brought to life upon a stage, not a document whose study will illuminate a past age or aid in the understanding of an author. Much of what the scholar discovers and presents will be directly or indirectly useful to the director and some of his methods of analysis will be helpful. Accordingly, this function of the study and analysis of drama has been rather fully explored in Chapter 2.

The second function of the director is that of a teacher. When, through study and analysis, he has arrived at a stimulating interpretation of the play, he must convey that interpretation to others and train them in executing it. He must teach and coach actors in the interpretations of their roles. The less the technical training of the actors cast in the production, the more prominent this function becomes. In directing with untrained casts, this function of teaching actors to act becomes so large that it often threatens to overshadow other functions. But the teaching function appears in all stage productions, even in those that employ the most highly trained professional actors. Problems connected with the exercising of this function have been discussed in Chapters 6 and 7.

Every director, then, enhances his directorial abilities in proportion as he acquires pedagogical abilities. The director cannot present his interpretation of a play directly to audiences himself. He must rely on other artists, including actors, to put that interpretation over; hence his success will be conditioned by his ability to inform these others about the interpretation and to train them in presenting it with maximum effectiveness. This teaching function of the director is worthy of far more detailed examination than space will permit, but what has already been said about the conduct of rehearsals and the training of the actor will serve further to elucidate it.

The third function of the director is that of the co-ordinator of the arts of the theatre and the work of the other co-operating theatre artists, outlined in some detail in Chapter 1. The exercise of this function requires not only teaching ability, but also diplomacy and leadership. It goes without saying that it also requires a considerable knowledge of all the arts of theatre. The ability to deal with other people harmoniously, with tact, with diplomacy, and with leadership, is an asset that comes partly by inheritance but largely by training. These qualifications may be acquired to some extent in the study and practice of directing provided that study and practice is under the guidance of a wise teacher.

The fourth function of the director is the actual production of plays, that is, it is the application of the principles and practices of directing to the staging of various kinds and types of drama. This function is the special subject of this chapter. It has been placed fourth as a kind of summit of the director's functions and because its successful fulfillment depends upon the right execution of the other functions.

This fourth function merits further general clarification before proceeding to an examination of its details. Note the use of the qualifying term "some" in the title of this chapter. Though the body of our information on the art of directing is extensive, it is as yet not sufficiently complete to allow any authority to claim to present *all* the principles and practices in logical order. We need considerably more research before any complete aesthetics of directing can be written. The complexity of the subject is apparent from the above listing of the four functions and a discussion of any one function is constantly complicated by the necessary inclusion of principles and practices belonging to the other functions. These are considerations, however, for the more advanced student of directing who has already acquired extensive knowledge of and wide experience in the large body of known principles and practices.

Throughout these pages we have insisted that the primal function of the director is the faithful interpretation of a script for a specific audience, a contemporary audience, in such a way as to make the play interesting and meaningful to that audience. In this sense he is primarily an interpretive artist. In what sense is he also a creative artist? In the sense that he employs means quite other than the means of the playwright to form an artistically effective and meaningful representation for that audience; in that sense the director is a creative artist, as well as an interpretive artist. The means which he employs are the arts of the theatre.

The primal art of the theatre, and that with which the director is first concerned, is the art of acting. The subsidiary arts include those of stage setting, lighting, costume, stage properties, sometimes music—the whole investiture of the action. Their combination for a presentation is often called the mounting of a production. These arts were discussed in Chapter 1. The director's function is to unify, co-ordinate, and weld these together with the acting of the actors into a whole composition. When he does this in such a way as to bring the written script to life upon the stage, he is a creative artist. The mere reproduction of a former staging of the play, ancient or modern, will not suffice for this distinction. Insofar as the director creates a new production, however traditional it may be, thus far is he a creative artist.

1. PANTOMIMIC DRAMATIZATION

In the former chapter, in order to discuss the techniques of the actor, considerable attention has already been given to the subject of pantomime and the pantomimic dramatization of a role. Of necessity some repetition will occur as we turn attention to the director's concern with the pantomimic dramatization of the whole play. Such overlappings are inevitable in any discussion of stage presentation, for the presentation is not made up of separate units mechanically put together. To digress for a moment, it is worth noting that motion-picture acting and editing have become just such a mechanical putting together of pieces. By pantomimic dramatization we mean here the visually meaningful interpretation of the whole play by actors. It is the representation of the complete drama by means of spectacle. It is the director's and the actors' translation of an art of words symbolizing sounds into a space art with visual symbols. This is a chief way in which the director interprets what the playwright has expressed; hence the importance of a director acquiring the ability to read a play with a kinetic imagination. Spectacle, the least important of the six qualitative parts of a play as a poetic composition, becomes a major part of the play as a stage representation. Spectacle is a fundamental union of the written play to its stage interpretation.

For the untrained, inexperienced reader plays are cryptic compositions, much more difficult to read than are novels. So much that the novel includes and elucidates is left out by the playwright, or rather included merely by implication. To sense these implications and imaginatively expand them is beyond the abilities of the inexperienced. The overtones, nuances, intonations, and shadings that give wide implications to an otherwise simple speech or bald statement, which the trained actor almost instinctively grasps as he masters a characterization, are missed by the general reader. The facial expression, the shrug of the shoulder, the gesture of revulsion, which the actor and the director use with the bald spoken words bring them to life in a way that the printed text of the play cannot. The illuminating responses and reactions of one character to another which truly vivify the effects and meanings of a scene are, if at all, only tersely indicated in printed stage directions. These are but a few examples of some of the effects, inherent in a script, which actors and directors render for audiences. By so doing they supply what the untrained and inexperienced reader would miss in a mere silent reading of the play.

Hence it is that their interpretation of that play usually becomes for the inexperienced, when they first see the drama in production, the only and fixed interpretation for them. For example, a student once reported that he had seen a production of Ibsen's *Ghosts* in which the leading actor of the company played the role of Oswald and made the play Oswald's play. Since then he has had great difficulty in seeing that play in any other way, though he now knows that Ibsen was primarily concerned with Mrs. Alving's tragedy and that she is the protagonist. Though the trained actor and director is capable of seeing with his mimetic imagination much of the effectiveness of a play upon a first reading, for its full interpretation he needs to be able to dig into it and add to that comprehension. That is why a chapter on drama and the analysis of drama becomes highly important in a book on directing.

Pantomimic dramatization is by no means esoteric or unusual. All of us indulge in it to some degree regularly. The person who expresses his amusement—an inner feeling—by smiling or by laughing aloud is dramatizing that inner feeling. The mother who frowns as she admonishes her child, the individual who shakes his head in disbelief, the woman who wrings her hand in grief are all engaging in pantomimic dramatization. It is the outward rendering of these inner states that we have already discussed in connection with the actor's pantomimic dramatization of his characterization.

In life, too, all or most of us are given to some visual expression of our reactions to other human beings. We smile fondly at one we love; we shrink away from one whom we fear as he threatens us; we show our delight in an embrace at seeing a loved one who has been long absent. We tend to move toward those who attract us and move away from those who repel us. We put a finger to our lips to silence a friend about to make an indiscreet public disclosure. We hold up a hand, palm out, to stop a person from advancing and occasionally we may shake a fist at one who has aroused our anger. These are acquired gestures and learned behavior which in our culture have become signs of general or universal significance. It is these that the actor and the director utilize in pantomimically dramatizing emotions and feelings, character reactions to others, character relationships, thoughts and ideas, and deeds and actions.

Much of the study of a role by an actor and of a script by a director is devoted to discovering just what in these can be made more effective through such visual rendering. For example, the actor who plays the bit-part of Francisco in the first scene of *Hamlet* can greatly enhance that role and the opening of the play if he realizes that because of recent past experiences this guard would be extremely nervous as he walks his post. He could convey that nervousness, even fear, to the audience by the manner in which he moved, used his body, and by the nervous manner in which he issues his challenge. Such a pantomimic dramatization of the inner state of Francisco would communicate that state to the audience and serve to arouse their interest by raising a question. What is this man afraid of? It does not take a great imagination nor much ingenuity for actors and a director to work up this opening scene of changing the guard into an interest-producing scene of emotion and unanswered questions. To do so means that more than a mere recitation of the lines must be given to the audience. That more will come largely through pantomimic dramatization.

In a similar way something of the character of Hamlet—his separation, aloneness, melancholy, and brooding disposition—may be indicated in the second scene by the placement of the Prince on the stage in relation to the court group and by his posture. A further illustration may be drawn from the scene in which Hamlet meets his old schoolfellows, Rosencrantz and Guildenstern (Act II, Scene ii). When Hamlet first sees them, he hails them happily and heartily and they engage in a scene of friendly schoolboy banter. Hamlet calls them "my excellent good friends" and tells them how glad he is to see them. He hospitably invites them to go along on equal terms with him into his castle.

Then suddenly he turns upon them and questions them as spies. Why this sudden turn? How can it be handled convincingly on the stage? To illustrate a method through pantomimic dramatization, several lines must be quoted.

> ROSENCRANTZ } We'll wait upon you.
> GUILDENSTERN }
>
> HAMLET. No such matter: I will not sort you with the rest of my servants, for, to speak to you like an honest man, I am most dreadfully attended. But, in the beaten way of friendship, what make you at Elsinore?
>
> ROS. To visit you, my lord; no other occasion.
>
> HAM. Beggar that I am, I am even poor in thanks; but I thank you: and sure, dear friends, my thanks are too dear a halfpenny. Were you not sent for? Is it your own inclining? Is it a free visitation? Come, deal justly with me: come, come; nay, speak.
>
> GUIL. What should we say, my lord?
>
> HAM. Why, any thing, but to the purpose. You were sent for; and there is a kind of confession in your looks which your modesties have not craft enough to colour: I know the good king and queen have sent for you.

This obvious change in Hamlet's attitude must be visually rendered and must be made probable. How? If Rosencrantz in his speech "To visit you, my lord; *no other occasion,*" emphasized a bit too strongly the "no other occasion," this could immediately give to the sensitive and keen Hamlet the information that there is another occasion and his lightning-like intellect could see at once the whole scheme.

The actor playing Hamlet must, therefore, so react to that portion of Rosencrantz's speech as to show the audience what is occurring in his mind. That effect can be produced in a number of ways. In an intimate theatre a turn of the head, a facial expression, and the way he looks at Rosencrantz could help to do it. Then a pause as he takes it in and contemplates it, followed by his dissembling opening of his next speech to put the two schoolfellows off guard. As they relax, he lets them have it in the bold "Were you not sent for?" Surprised, they give themselves away and Hamlet follows up with the remainder of his speech. In a large theatre Hamlet's reaction to the "no other occasion" part of the speech might have to be as broad as a full turn toward the two as he suddenly comprehends the significance of the stress upon those words. The audience effect from what is here suggested is obviously a result from both vocal and visual means and not merely from pantomimic dramatization. As in most scenes, the two must go together and support each other.

Before a director can begin to build a pantomimic dramatization of any scene, he must first determine what the scene means in terms of audience effect, what it adds up to, what are the varying attitudes of the characters in it toward each other, and what is the progress of their feelings, emotions, and thoughts. On such a basis the variety of scenes which appear in drama are so great that it would probably be a hopeless task to attempt to organize these into types. Some scenes are included merely to give exposition of past action; others are included merely as transitional scenes. To overdramatize these would throw the play out of focus; yet they must be given sufficient pantomimic dramatization to make them clear and interesting.

In every play there are certain big scenes, however, which need to be given strong pantomimic dramatization. Two categories of such scenes might be called love scenes and quarrel scenes. In love scenes might be included any scenes of affection and friendship among characters and extended to include scenes of the most passionate kind between a boy and a girl or a man and a woman. Quarrel scenes likewise might range from scenes of mere disagreement to fight scenes involving physical conflict. Both categories of scenes can be written in many different ways. It is well known that a love scene may be written as a quarrel scene. In fact, that is essentially what the Benedick-Beatrice quarrel scenes in *Much Ado about Nothing* are. As has been indicated, a love scene represents an attraction which gradually draws the characters closer and closer together; whereas a quarrel scene represents a repulsion which pushes them apart. But at the climax of a quarrel scene when mutual hate or anger impels the characters to do bodily harm to each other, that passion may draw them violently together. Every extended scene of the kind here indicated builds its effects gradually or rapidly toward a climax, a high point of interest. That process of building, as well as the climax, must be worked out in the pantomimic dramatization.

In this building of effects the movements of two characters in relation to each other are revealing. As stated, their movements toward or away from each other can be expressive of their feelings toward each other. If a person is startled or afraid, he will draw back or away from the object which startled him. Pity, on the other hand, draws one toward the object of that pity. Contempt, disdain, and loathing cause a sense of withdrawal; just as interest, curiosity, and friendliness cause one to approach. When one is suddenly startled, he tends to freeze in his track—to stand still. Then, if the startling turns into fear, the individuals want to escape or flee. Other examples of the expressiveness of movement may readily be added to those here suggested.

Of course it is not the movement alone which conveys the emotional effect. The entire body, including the eyes, the head, the nostrils, the lips and jaws, the torso, the hands and arms, and the legs, must be utilized by the actors. For example, in the case of fear the eyes would probably be greatly enlarged and would move from side to side in a restless manner and even rotated; the lips would be relaxed and the mouth open wide, with probably a trembling of the lips; the hand may be expanded, palms down, and opened and closed convulsively. The head would probably be lifted in a strained manner; the torso would expand and contract quickly to the quickened breathing. If the fear were great, the body would tremble. Some of these expressive reactions would not be compatible with fleeing; others would.

Those utilized by the actor would depend upon the character he was portraying. By use of his experience, observation, and imagination, the student can work out similar expressive pantomimic dramatizations of other emotions and reactions. Florence Lutz, formerly Instructor of Pantomime in The American Academy of Dramatic Arts, has worked out and set down in her previously-mentioned book, *The Technique of Pantomime,* many suggestive procedures for the visual expression of a wide variety of feelings, emotions, and attitudes. Similar suggestions may be found in most of the good books on pantomime.

Other things being equal, downstage movements (movements toward the audience) are stronger than upstage movements; yet the haughty retreat upstage of a dissenting leader from his rebellious downstage followers can be made very strong by devices other than the direction of the movement. The mounting threat of one character to another can be powerfully portrayed by his step-by-step approach toward the character threatened. In the quarrel scene between Brutus and Cassius in *Julius Caesar,* the growing dissention between them can be effectively portrayed by their gradual separation, just as their reconciliation can be dramatized by their coming together again in the conclusion of the scene.

A quarrel scene, such as that referred to in the second act of *Mourning Becomes Electra,* in which the contestants are equal, or nearly equal, would probably be most effective with movements across stage, left to right or *vice versa.* Such movements could be varied with upstage retreats as either Lavinia or Christine became the weaker, and with strong downstage movements on the part of the one in the position of dominance. In some quarrel scenes involving two characters, one of the two is the aggressor throughout. In others, such as the one cited above, the position of dominance changes through the scene from character to character. The latter tend to be more exciting if they are properly staged and dramatized to bring out this shifting dominance. Such scenes involve the problem of shifting focus, to be discussed later.

Properties and furniture can also be used expressively in pantomimic dramatization. The spectacle of an enraged person bearing down upon another and that other dodging the enraged one by taking refuge behind a sofa is an illustration of one such usage. The darting behind the sofa can serve to reveal the fear of the character. It also maximizes the threat of the enraged one. Imagine two young men seated at a table engaged in a friendly talk. The talk gradually grows into an argument and the argument into a quarrel. Note how you may represent a stage in the disagreement by one or both rising; how the progress of the quarrel can be revealed by their drawing apart; and how intense and angry separation can be aided with the table between them. Then let the quarrel subside and a *rapprochement* occur. Note again the use of the table in their coming together. The old comic device of the boy hitching his chair closer and closer to the girl of his attention is another illustration of the use of furniture in telling the story. Imagine, now, a young girl entering her room, discovering a package upon her table, finding that it is addressed to her, opening it, discovering that it is a gift from the boy she loves, and that it is a box of candy. A skillful actress can tell this whole story with many shades of emotion through pantomime alone. She can make it entirely comic or partly comic and partly serious. Next, imagine the same situation but in this instance the package is a wrapped basket containing a kitten. Note the different business that must be utilized to tell us that the package contains a kitten.

These scenes will serve to show, not only the uses of properties and furniture in pantomime, but also that pantomimic dramatization can be made to tell the story. In some respects that is its major function in stage production. Perhaps it is worth saying again that acting is not, as some amateurs seem to suppose, merely the reciting of memorized lines. It is the pantomimic dramatization of inner feelings and emotions, of the thoughts and ideas, of the attitudes and reactions of individual to individual, and of the deeds of characters. Out of these and as a result of these come the words. The whole story may be told in the pantomime alone—note, again, the effectiveness in this respect of the old, silent motion pictures. The businessing of a play, then, by director and actors is not merely the planning and rehearsing of entrances, exits, and crosses, of sitting and rising at the proper times, or of shaking hands with or knocking another person down. This gross business is important and minimal. But if the play is to come to life, every role and its whole story must be pantomimically dramatized. To accomplish this, the actors must know their characters in all of their changing feelings and attitudes and the director must know exactly what each scene involves and accomplishes.

2. FOCUS

In the writing and staging of plays focus is important as a means of directing attention and attaining emphasis. Certain scenes in plays may be described as wide-focus scenes, others as narrow-focus. A wide-focus scene is one which occupies the whole stage or a major portion of it; a narrow-focus scene is one which occurs in a more specific and confined area. Since a play is a fluid, moving progression of scenes, these are, of course, constantly flowing into each other. Scenes of narrow focus may open up and occupy more of the stage area; whereas, scenes of wide focus may in their progression narrow to a more restricted area. Shakespeare's plays offer many illustrations of this duality of focus and of this merging of focus. The second scene of the first act of *Hamlet,* representing the king and queen on their thrones and the assembled courtiers and officials, may, like the Play-within-a-play

Experimental minimal settings. Above: scenery by Gordon Bennett for Eugene Wiggins's *They Shall Take Up Serpents,* directed by Robert Eberle. Below: Donald Treat's setting for Nancy Henderson's *Lo, the Angel* directed by Thomas Patterson. Both produced by The Carolina Playmakers.

scene, be presented most effectively as a wide-focus scene. The scene of Hamlet visiting his mother in her closet after the play would demand a narrow focus and the scene of Hamlet's soliloquy, "To be or not to be," represents a complete narrowing of the focus to a single area. In *Candida* the scene in the beginning of the last act of Eugene and Candida sitting by the fire is a narrow-focus scene, which opens up to a wide focus as Morell and the other characters return from the meeting.

Focus in the sense discussed above is rather obvious. There are, however, problems of focus within each type of scene that are not so obvious. To determine these, the director must decide who has the scene—which character is the dominant center of focus. In the Christine-Lavinia scene from *Mourning Becomes Electra* the focus changes as the dominance changes. An easy method of revealing this dominance is to give the dominating character the upstage position. We have already seen how the triangle may be employed to focus attention on a character. But in such a grouping the focus may be distorted or ruined if the participating characters do not point, that is, do not turn toward, look at, or seem to be looking in the direction of the dominant character. Pointing as a focusing of attention is a perfectly natural human procedure that may be observed time and again in our daily lives. When utilized on the stage it must be made to seem equally natural. It is such an important device in the directing of audience attention, that is in focusing, that further illustration may be helpful.

Imagine on the stage a large room in which a considerable number of people are gathered. This crowd is in groups of varying sizes, with the larger number massed downstage, talking excitedly. They represent angry, rebellious citizens. Suddenly the large door upstage center is flung open and the king appears, shouting silence. Every face turns toward him and every pair of startled eyes is focused upon him. The audience likewise must follow the pointing of the crowd. Place the upstage door on an elevation at the top of a flight of stairs and the king's entrance is given even more dominance and the emphasis upon him is greater. Or, as another device, as the king enters and commands silence, let the crowd in amazement fall back from the center of the stage toward each side, leaving an open avenue up the center of the stage to the king. This avenue, especially if shaped in a triangle with the king at the apex, helps to point to the center of the focus.

The pointing need not be so obvious as the examples described in order to direct audience attention. Any centering of interest by one or more characters upon another, by whatever device the centering of interest is indicated, will serve to focus upon the character arousing interest. An actor can focus audience attention upon an object by letting the audience see the object casually catch his attention, then seize it more strongly, and finally draw him toward it. Unless there are counter attractions on the stage, audience interest will naturally follow that of the actor. By this point in the discussion, it has become evident that the whole matter of focus is a problem in the directing of audience attention and interest. Pointing is a device for attaining focus. Audience attention may be distracted in a number of undesirable ways, often observable in amateur performances. Obviously the failure of one or more actors to point properly will to an extent divert audience interest. An actor may spoil the focus by upstaging the actor who is supposed to be the center of interest, especially if the upstage actor moves when the attention is not supposed to be focused on him. In life our attention tends to seek out objects at some distance toward the horizon.

In the proscenium theatre with an elevated stage the audience attention tends to gravitate towards the upstage figures. On the other hand, a moving object tends to receive more attention than a fixed one; hence an actor free to move about in a downstage area may draw attention away from still persons in the upstage areas, especially if the attention of those persons is focused upon the moving character. This is why, as was indicated in the last chapter, it is very important for actors to learn to stand still and to pay attention.

3. ACTING AREAS

In order to plan the stage business, locate it properly on the stage, and light it effectively, the stage must be divided into areas. These areas or portions, often called acting areas, may be represented differently by different divisions of the whole stage. It is customary to divide the stage into six areas, three upstage and three downstage, according to the following chart:

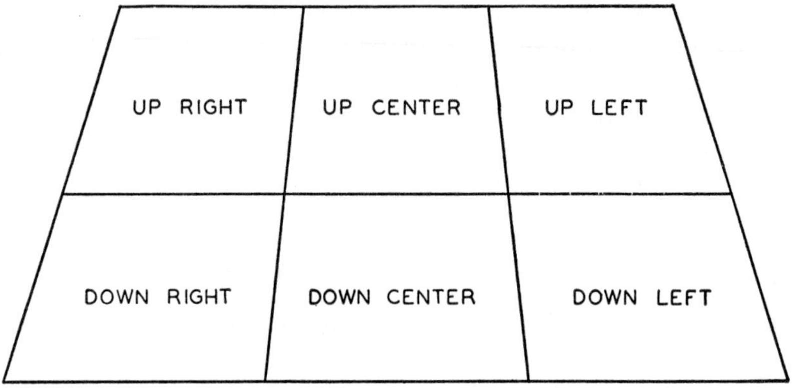

FIG. 1. A chart of acting areas.

It is obvious that in our fan-shaped theatres the strongest focus of attention would be upon the centerstage areas. An actor playing or a scene located in these areas would ordinarily, therefore, carry great emphasis. Further, it is clear that the upstage positions, left and right, are remote and relatively ineffective; hence ordinarily would not be used for scenes of power and importance. Francisco might, in the opening scene of *Hamlet,* walk his beat in one of these areas or in the three upstage areas, and the Ghost might later appear in one of them; but when the scene of Horatio and his companions and their talk about ghosts comes up, that group of characters should be pulled downstage into one of the other areas. The reason for this is simple: They will receive more attention in a downstage area, for there they can be better seen and better heard.

Alexander Dean in working out his theory and practice of directing held that these stage areas could each be differentiated in terms of strength and that, further, each had a distinct mood value. Insofar as Dean's theory is helpful as a procedure for locating scenes in different areas of the stage, it is justifiable. Literally in terms of sound theory it is questionable. Obviously quarrels, fights, crises, and climaxes will receive a maximum of attention and effectiveness if they are played in the downstage center area but that is not to say that such scenes may not be located in one of several other areas.

Often other considerations, such as pantomimic dramatization and variety, are of more importance in the determination of the location of the action on the stage than is any theoretical assignment of values to stage areas. Moreover, an area may be given added value in terms of emphasis by the utilization of elevations. Dean's theory remains valuable, however, as a stimulus to the imagination in the planning of stage action, however susceptible to question it might be. In arena staging, if not entirely inapplicable, it loses much of whatever value it may have.

4. PLACING FURNITURE ON THE STAGE

Clearly, before the director can plan the stage action, he must arrange the furnishings of the stage, including the selection and the arrangement. The problem of selection enters, not only as a matter of probability and style, but also in terms of suitability to the action. A sofa with too high a back may block an important action behind it. A table that is too large may interfere with the movements on stage. A piece of furniture may be so ornate and so colorful that it distracts attention. The color of the draperies may clash with the color of the set or of the costumes. Such considerations are obvious but, unless the director makes them clear to the technical director, designer, or crew head, he may come to his dress rehearsal and find that much of the furniture must be discarded and replaced.

When the selection is judiciously made in terms of the play's requirements, the nature and style of the production, and the arrangement of the action, the director can proceed to the important question of arrangement and composition. In a modern realistic play the first demand in the arrangement of furniture is to simulate the probabilities of a real and specific room or scene. The various pieces of furniture in a room must be so grouped that from the audience they seem to be the kind of arrangement that a person or a family occupying this room would utilize. In this task the author's stage directions in which he describes the room as he visualized it represents the starting point. These, of course, need not be literally followed. Each production insofar as it has a style of its own will require selection and arrangement in terms of that style.

Here it might be mentioned that books on interior decoration can be of considerable aid to the student of directing in the planning of interiors in particular, just as they are to the scene designer. The task of the director and scene designer differs from that of the interior decorator. Their settings must merely seem to be real and must leave ample space for the movements of the actors. Pieces of furniture must not be allowed to block or mask important entrances. If such pieces stand in the way of a very important cross, they may have to be rearranged or even discarded. It becomes clear, therefore, that the arrangement of the furniture must go along with the planning of the business.

In the arrangement questions of pictorial composition, to be discussed next, are important. When the style is primarily expressionistic or symbolic, or when the techniques of space staging are employed, composition becomes the chief consideration.

5. PICTORIAL COMPOSITION

Every production on the stage may be considered as a succession of scenes. A few scenes in certain plays may be bare-stage scenes in that they contain no actors. Such a scene occurs at the opening of Eugene O'Neill's *Ile,* for example. Occasionally a scene will involve a single actor only. These two types of scenes are relatively brief when they occur. Most scenes include two or more actors and the business of those scenes raises problems of pictorial composition. Certain of these scenes, notably the "tableau scenes" from nineteenth-century plays and scenes such as the court scene of Act I, Scene ii, of *Hamlet* and the courtroom trial of Shylock in *Merchant of Venice,* gain much of their audience effectiveness through composition. Such scenes, which are for a moment static, require the careful posing and arrangement of the actors in relation to the settings and the stage space. That posing and arranging is what is meant by composition. No scene, even such obviously pictorial scenes, remains static in drama for more than a moment. Drama is the rendering of an action and that action is constantly changing the arrangement of the agents in the scenes. It must change, progress, and flow. But even in scenes of changing movement questions of composition enter.

Every work of art insofar as it has form and meaning involves questions of ordering, organizing, and arranging its parts. That is what is meant by composition. In Chapter 1 we discovered that theatre arts include both time and space arts. Every scene in a production likewise involves arrangements in space and arrangements in time. These interact to modify each other; hence the pictorial composition of a scene on stage cannot be treated in exactly the same manner that one would treat a pictorial composition on canvas. Yet the student of directing may learn much about the art of composition from a study of paintings. In this discussion of stage scenes, for the sake of clearness, we will ignore much of the time factor and treat these scenes largely as visual, space arrangements.

We have already learned that one of the chief devices in good composition is that of balance. Balance simply means the equal weight of things opposite each other. To be more specific, physical balance is the weight times the distance on one side of a fulcrum offsetting (or balanced against) the weight times the distance on the other side of the fulcrum. Complete physical balance is beautifully illustrated by the precision balance scales seen in laboratories and in pharmacies. That scale has a beam or lever suspended in its exact center, with two scales or pans hanging from the end of either arm. Such precise balance gives a state of equipoise or equilibrium and hence is not dynamic nor dramatic. Exact balance of this nature is sometimes employed in abstract design when complete symmetry is desirable.

Designers and directors are often concerned with symmetrical balance; but, because of the different values of the various elements with which they are working and because of varying emphases, they are more likely to utilize asymmetrical balance. Asymmetrical balance is attained, as has previously been indicated, without the exact bilateral proportion observable in symmetrical balance, which is apt to become monotonous if sustained too long or resorted to with frequency upon the stage. Thus the designer and the director must constantly exercise artistic judgment in attaining balance in their compositions.

Balance applies to the design of the setting, arrangement of the furniture, and groupings of characters. Perfect balance represents complete symmetry and an equilibrium. A set that had a large door in the exact center of the back wall, a window on each side of that door equidistant from it and of the same size, and a door of the same size and shape and in the same position in the right and left walls would, assuming no other upsetting factors, be exactly balanced and monotonous.

If, on the other hand, within a stage setting we placed all of the large and massive pieces of furniture on the left side of the stage with no proportionate balance on the right, it would be as though the stage tipped up on the right and down on the left. An example of perfect balance in grouping may be attained by arranging three actors in an equilateral triangle upon the stage, with the dominant actor at the apex of the triangle upstage and the other two downstage, right and left. Such perfect balance is often useful in settings and in groupings but if indulged in too frequently tends to lessen interest. Hence the artists are constantly seeking devices for introducing variety into their compositions without destroying balance.

Balance is important not only as a means of making a pictorial effect pleasing but also as a means of giving it clarity and emphasis. The center of balance in a grouping of characters is the center of focus and hence the center of emphasis. It is also a means of unifying an arrangement.

In order that balance may not create monotony, the director and scenic artist employ variety in attaining balance. Different things may weigh equally against each other and thus create balance. A large fireplace with a striking picture hung over the mantlepiece on stage left may be balanced with a colorful tapestry on stage right. A powerful character on a platform upstage right may balance a whole mob of people grouped downstage left. A striking color may be utilized to balance mass. Light and shadow may be used to aid balance and give variety. Variations in the arrangements of the groupings are an excellent method of varying the balance. The equilateral triangle may merge into an isosceles and then into a right angled triangle. The apex of the equilateral or isosceles triangle may even be inverted and the dominant actor placed in the downstage center position. Such a grouping might be very strong and meaningful if the dominant character were, say, turning his back upon his comrades and resisting their pleadings. It thus appears that the meaning of the grouping, what it is supposed to say to an audience, determines its arrangement. That is why pantomimic dramatization was discussed first among the important principles of directing.

The necessity for variety applies not merely to pictorial composition but also to the entire planning of stage business. Conceivably it could be highly effective in a scene with a certain kind of character to have that character upon every entrance make straight for a specific chair, say downstage left by the fireplace, and sit throughout his scene in that position. Other means would then have to be found to secure variety. Ordinarily, however, the repetition of a piece of business is to be avoided.

It must be remembered, along with the preceding injunction, that repetition is an excellent device of emphasis and is highly effective in comedy. Even repetitive business can be ingeniously varied in little details to add to its effectiveness. When repetition has a meaning or produces a desired effect, use it; when it is merely repetition, avoid it. The progressive flow of the action in most plays usually provides enough change to avoid monotony in groupings if the action is adequately dramatized.

Yet there are often scenes of some length between two characters, say, which may become largely static in grouping if the director does not seek to vary them. Two scenes from *A Doll's House* will serve to illustrate these. In Act One Mrs. Linde and Nora have a rather long scene together. Two mighty competent and powerful actresses might conceivably play this scene with great effectiveness while sitting in the same positions throughout. In the hands of less competent actors, it would be wise for the director to vary the grouping by inventing some appropriate business that would break it up. In Act Two Nora and Dr. Rank have a similar scene together that could also become static with inexperienced actors if not carefully businessed.

Here a word of warning might be inserted. The tendency of the inexperienced director or even of experienced directors with inexperienced actors is to "overbusiness" a script. While too little business can become static and monotonous, too much business can be very distracting. Usually this tendency to introduce too much business, too many distracting movements, arises because the director or the actor does not trust the power of the spoken words. If the words are properly and effectively rendered, and if the actors have pantomimically dramatized their characters, emotions, and thoughts, the two scenes referred to from *A Doll's House* may be played without the actors moving about the stage.

Often all that is needed to give necessary variety to such scenes is that the actors intensely play into the scene. A leaning forward in the chair in strained attention or a turning away from the character opposite may be all that is required to vary the scene. Gestures, facial expression, and body posture, in addition to locomotion, are means of attaining variety in such groupings. It is in intimate scenes, such as the two cited, in which the psychological relationships of two characters are highly important, that overbusinessing can be a very serious detriment. On the other hand, experienced directors have learned that in such scenes ingenious introduction of business can help to cover the deficiencies in characterization and delivery of lines by inexperienced actors.

In Chapter 2 we discovered that every play has a sequence of big scenes that are usually climactic and often involve a number of characters and a considerable physical activity. In planning these and arranging their groupings, the director must consider the question of their location on the stage, that is, the area in which each will be staged. The problem of variety and the problem of emphasis enter here, as they do in other arrangements of business and character groupings. A key scene which the audience must grasp in order to follow the development of the action obviously might lose much if staged in a remote upstage area and might gain much if placed in a downstage area. On the other hand, it is perfectly possible for accomplished actors to overcome much of the disadvantage of the remote area by good pantomimic dramatization and by effective vocal means.

Unless variety and the meaning conveyed by the scene demand it, however, even the mature and experienced actors should not be handicapped by the location of their scene. With some ingenious planning and a careful consideration of the meanings and effectiveness of different scenes, the director can utilize the whole stage and secure the necessary variety through the location of succeeding scenes without sacrificing the power of big and climactic scenes. Utilize the less advantageous areas for scenes that are purely or largely concerned with the mere mechanics, such as introductory and transitional scenes, and save the more advantageous areas for the significant scenes. Do not overlook the fact, however, that an entrance scene, which is introductory, can also be climactic and of great significance. In general, comedy scenes which depend to a considerable extent upon intimate audience contact are more effective if played downstage, while scenes of strong emotion and serious scenes may be located farther upstage.

In summary, it should have become clear from the foregoing discussion that the planning of business and the arranging of groups on the stage require a clear comprehension of the meaning and effect of the scene in which the action and grouping occur. Group arrangements on the stage are not executed merely as pretty pictures posed by living actors; composition is utilized to express meanings and create effects that belong to the scenes of the drama. It is another means or medium through which plays in production become effects upon audiences. In order that these group arrangements may have maximum effectiveness, the following principles, devices, or considerations are used in pictorial composition:

1. The acting area in which the scene is located.
2. Balance in the whole composition.
3. The center of emphasis in the composition.
4. Variety within the arrangement and among different arrangements.

We have said that in the mastery of pictorial composition the student of directing will find considerable aid from the study of paintings, especially paintings involving groups of characters. In these he will find excellent illustrations of balance and the ways of achieving balance; of focus upon the center of interest and the ways of achieving emphasis; of variety in details; and of the ways in which varying details are made to harmonize. In these will also be found many excellent suggestions for the employment of light and shadow and for the employment of color as a means in the composition.

The director, however, as has been said, is not a painter working merely in space; rather his task is more analogous to that of the choreographer. Though he is composing pictures, he is composing moving pictures. Some competent directors see the choreographic function as a main part of their task in directing and tend to view the stage interpretation of any play as a problem in dance drama. Such an approach is more suited to some plays than to others. Maeterlinck's *Pelléas and Mélisande,* for example, might profit from such an interpretation and the Fifth-Avenue scene in O'Neill's *The Hairy Ape* could definitely be enhanced by such an approach. In these the symbolism is highly important and removes them from the realistic to the abstract. Completely realistic plays are less amenable to such an approach. Nevertheless, every play involves some aspects of choreography in that it is made up of a series of pictures or scenes arranged, not merely as pictorial compositions, but also as a progression.

A production of a Greek tragedy or comedy invites elaborate employment of choreography, not only in the staging of the choral portions but also in the staging of the episodes. The comedies of Molière, as well as the mannered comedies of the English Restoration period, may profit from a high degree of stylization in the business and groupings. In each type of play the groupings should be arranged and styled to give meaning. In a similar manner, groupings in realistic play should be composed in terms of their effects, though the choreographic aspect is not so readily apparent.

6. PACE, TIMING, AND RHYTHM

Choreographic considerations raise questions of pace, time, and rhythm and thus serve as a transition from the discussion of visual and space aspects of staging to those pertaining to drama as a time art. These considerations have been introduced before in other connections but must be here related to the principles of directing. Just as characters have a pace and rhythm which aids in distinguishing them, so do plays and scenes within plays have their own distinctive pace and rhythm.

By pace is meant the rate—rapidity or slowness—involved in the execution of business and speaking of lines. Comedies, comic scenes, scenes of excitement, and scenes of tension require in general a more rapid rate than do tragedies, serious scenes, and scenes that are relatively without tension. Light comedies and farces are far more effective if played at a rapid rate. Such plays as *Boy Meets Girl, Personal Appearance,* and *The Male Animal* lose much of their effectiveness and seem to drag if not played at a rapid rate; they demand a machine-gun pace. On the other hand, psychological dramas and serious plays would lose in effectiveness if played at such a pace. Even these plays can, of course, be performed at such a slow pace that they drag—a greater evil than that of playing them too rapidly. Often directors of amateurs attempt to compensate for shortcomings in acting abilities by increasing the pace of the performance and sometimes that is the only resort left to them. In general, however, the director should determine the most effective pace for the interpretation of the play or the scene and attempt to attain that rate.

While we may properly speak of the pace of the whole play, this is not to imply that every scene in any play is played at exactly the same rate. Different scenes must be paced differently in terms of their effect. For example, a scene of mounting tension can be made to convey that effect by the gradual or rapid increase of the rate. Quarrel scenes often gain effectiveness by increase in tempo. This effectiveness becomes even more marked if the quarrel scene develops out of a scene of relatively slower pace. Such variations in pace have an electrifying effect upon the attention of the audience. The first encounter between Beatrice and Benedick in Act I, Scene i, of *Much Ado About Nothing* and the first encounter between Katherine and Petruchio in *The Taming of the Shrew* are examples of scenes that demand this electrifying effect of rapid pace. Conversely, scenes of deliberation or scenes in which a character is trying to explain to and convince another person, such as the scene in the first act of *Ghosts* in which Mrs. Alving attempts to make Parson Manders understand her position, would lose in effectiveness if played at a breathless rate. It is evident, then, that pace may be utilized to aid in bringing out the meaning of a scene and in aiding that scene to create its proper effects.

Pace is a matter of timing but questions of timing enter into many aspects of stage production. To take the more obvious examples first, there are numerous mechanical effects in a performance that must be properly timed. When an actor turns on a light on stage, the controlboard operation must be exactly timed and synchronized to the business so that the light comes up at the right moment. Incidentally, in such instances the actor should be instructed to hold his hand on the light switch until the stage lights are fully up. Similarly, in lighting a candle or a lamp, the match or flame should be held to the wick until the stage lights are fully up. Offstage sound effects of all kinds must be similarly timed to cue. The closing and opening of the main curtain must also be properly timed. Stage effects, involving lighting and machinery, must be exactly timed and synchronized to the action. Every piece of stage business, be it a simple cross or an elaborate duel scene, requires precise timing. Often these must be first rehearsed in slow motion to get the time and movement pattern set and then speeded up to the proper tempo and rhythm. It often aids actors with defective co-ordination to count out the exact number of steps in a cross or the successive movements in a pantomime. These will, of course, be mechanically executed when so done but after the exact movements have been acquired they can then be finished and made natural.

Timing is extremely important in the actor's art, not only in elaborate pantomime but even in the smallest and simplest reaction. Not merely the way in which an actor reacts, but also the moment at which he reacts can be revealing. It is important in all acting and absolutely indispensable in the playing of comedy. Much of the comedian's effectiveness depends upon the exact timing of business and lines. This is one of the reasons why the old vaudeville stage offered a superb training for comic actors. There is an exact moment in the scene when the lifting of an eyebrow, the shrugging of a shoulder, or the dropping of a jaw will set the audience off into gales of laughter. Miss that moment, play the business or gesture too soon or too late, and much of the comic effect is blunted. It becomes apparent from this illustration that comic actors must constantly play audiences as well as roles.

The timing of lines is equally as important as the timing of business in all acting and completely indispensable in comic acting. Take, as one example, a line from O'Neill's *Ile.* In the first scene with the Steward and Ben the conversation progresses to the subject of Mrs. Keeney, whom the Steward has heard weeping behind the closed door of her cabin. Ben, the Cabin Boy, says of her:

> (*Sadly.*) She uster be awful nice to me before—(*His eyes grow wide and frightened.*) she got—like she is.

Let an actor say this line rapidly and glibly and it loses its effectiveness. If he pauses after the word "before," indicated by the long dash, and after the word "got," again indicated by the dash, and says the last two groupings of words with a kind of fearful reluctance, the effect of the line becomes powerful. It raises an audience question as to just how Mrs. Keeney is. It surrounds her condition with mystery.

Another example, this time from *Twelfth Night,* may be used to show the use of timing for comic effect. Viola, disguised in boy's clothing, in her first encounter with Olivia (Act I, Scene v), makes quite an impression upon the Countess and is even granted her desire to speak with Olivia alone. When she fulfills her mission to speak for Orsino and Olivia is about to dismiss her, curiosity gets the best of her and she begs to see Olivia's face. Olivia smilingly points out that she is now out of her role as Orsino's messenger but grants her request, asking ". . . is't not well done?" Upon which Viola, stung by her gentle scorn or raillery and perhaps by a touch of jealousy, replies:

> Excellently done, if God did all.

The right inflection, coupled with just the right pause before the last modifying clause helps to create and heighten the comic effect. An actor who rushes through the line without the significant pause will kill its effectiveness almost completely.

Illustrations of ways in which tempo and rate enhance meaning and increase effectiveness can be found in every play. Those given above must serve as suggestive samples only. These stage effects are analogous to effects which all of us have observed among our fellowmen. Everyone is aware that excitement and tension will cause an individual to move and speak with increasing rapidity. Conversely, other emotions, such as fear, may well tend to slow down the rate. Puzzlement, hesitancy, and thoughtfulness likewise tend to slow down tempo of movement and speech.

These instances from common experience reveal how timing may be utilized in both speech and action to convey meanings and create effects. In such devices the rate of movement and speech is important but of equal importance is the change of rate and the breaking of rate. Change of rate gives rhythm, to be briefly examined later. Breaking of rate may mean a complete stop or a pause. The illustrative lines previously cited serve to indicate the importance of pause in speech. It can be equally important in business and movement. As in speech, it may be employed to give emphasis. Imagine a character entering a room in which there are several other individuals. The entering character comes on briskly but upon seeing one of those already present pauses, then strides purposefully toward that character, grasps him roughly by the shoulder and swings him about. The pause in his movement toward the group as he catches sight of the disturbing character helps to set off and emphasize the succeeding action. It can also convey an element of surprise upon seeing the disturbing character in this environment. It could show that the entering character is startled upon seeing the other person. Thus, in addition to lending emphasis, the pause may be also an aid in conveying emotion and meaning.

Rhythm, as was made clear in Chapter 2, is a patterning of time and therefore applies to both speech and movement. We have also discovered that each character in a play may have a distinctive rhythm that aids in characterizing him. Scenes likewise have their rhythmic patterns and in certain scenes the rhythm becomes important as a means of producing the right effect. That is, in such scenes a considerable part of the effect depends upon the rhythm, while in other scenes, though rhythm is present, it is not so definitely observable as a means.

There are, for example, scenes in Greek tragedy that are composed of stichomythic dialogue (one-line antithetical dialogue) and there are scenes between characters or between a character and the chorus that are completely lyrical. Rhythm obviously comes to the fore in such scenes as a very important means of creating their effects. Analogous scenes may be observed in modern plays. Oscar Wilde's *The Importance of Being Earnest* offers us a number of examples of balanced, antithetical dialogue similar to, though not the same as, stichomythia. So do any number of other plays. Any quarrel scene in which two characters cut and thrust at each other with words or any scene of comic repartee will offer examples analogous to stichomythia in which the rhythm becomes highly important. But rhythm appears from scene to scene in less obvious, more subtle ways in many modern plays.

Expressionistic and symbolist playwrights especially have employed it with telling effects. Maeterlinck's atmospheric plays, so-called static drama, are greatly dependent upon it for their audience effect. Even a first reading of *Pelléas and Mélisande* will reveal the importance of rhythms in that piece. Rhythm is so obvious in this play as a major means that it cries out to be played to music and, as expected, music has been composed for it. In a similar manner Ibsen has employed rhythms to give mood and effect to many of the scenes of *Peer Gynt.* A less obvious but equally effective employment of rhythm appears in Sean O'Casey's *Juno and the Paycock,* a tragi-comedy in which rhythm aids in differentiating the serious and the comic scenes. Some of the rhythmic patterns in the O'Casey play are obvious from scene to scene; others must be arrived at only after careful study. It is this variation in rhythmic pattern, especially as the play is played by the Abbey Theatre company, that accounts for much of its powerful effect. A play in performance, then, may be considered as, not only a design in choreography, but also as a symphony of rhythms.

7. BUILDING CLIMAXES

These considerations of tempo and rhythm have brought us several times to the discussion once again of the matter of climaxes, previously discussed in other relations. In Chapter 2 it was stated that climax may be defined as any high point of interest and that playwrights in writing plays are concerned with ordering and building climaxes. A play may be, therefore, looked at as an arrangement or composition of climaxes. The playwright must resolve several problems in the handling of climax. First, he must determine where in the scene or action the climaxes come; second, he must find or devise means for developing and sustaining climaxes. He faces a third problem in the ordering of the climaxes in a cumulative manner so that, say, a climax in the middle of Act One is topped by a bigger climax at the end of that act. The director's task is, first, through a study of the script, to determine what the climaxes are and where they come—often not a very difficult undertaking—and, second, to find out just how the playwright has built each. His third task is to find means, visual and auditory, for building and sustaining climaxes.

Drama is the art of intensification; hence many of the climaxes in plays result from a mounting tension between characters. We have already seen how an increase in the rate of movement and of dialogue can suggest and convey this increased tension. Conversely, a slowing down of tempo can indicate a decrease in tension. Similarly a gradual increase in the loudness of sound can aid in the building of a climax, observed often, along with increased tempo, in quarrel scenes. Climax also occurs in drama as the result of discovery. A discovery may come about gradually and hence build to its high point, or it may be made suddenly.

An example of the latter type occurs in *Ghosts,* when Mrs. Alving and Parson Manders overhear Oswald and Regina in the conservatory. As a result of overhearing Regina's speech, Mrs. Alving suddenly discovers the presence of ghosts. Ibsen carefully prepares for this discovery but the climax, coming suddenly, is not built. Coming at the place it does in the action and as an antecedent leading to future consequence, it does not require to be sustained for any length of time. Each important scene in the action of a play contains a major climax and scenes of any extended duration often contain several climaxes arranged in a cumulative manner. The arrangements of these climaxes within scenes vary greatly, depending upon the nature of the scene and the functions of the separate climaxes. An extended speech, such as Hotspur's speech about the Popinjay, may likewise have more than one climax.

Certain onstage climaxes may be enhanced with offstage effects. Such enhancements may be either visual or auditory and in some instances may embrace both. An example of auditory build occurs in the mob-scene of the fourth act in Gerhart Hauptmann's *The Weavers*. The noise of the approaching mob is at first merely a low murmur, which grows in volume and distinctness until the separate shouts and cries can be distinctly heard within Dreissiger's private room. In the last scene of O'Neill's *Beyond the Horizon* the building of the final climax is accompanied and assisted by the coming of dawn, culminating with the rising of the sun above the horizon.

The Play-within-a-play in *Hamlet* offers an excellent opportunity for the employment of sound, visual effects, and movement for the building of the climax which comes with the King's cry, "Give me some light: away!" The director's problem in such a scene is complex. He must maintain focus and right emphasis with the building of tension and he must devise ways, largely visual on the part of the King and Hamlet, of revealing the mounting tensions to the audience. Then, when the climactic moment comes, he must work out movements that will reveal and sustain the climax. The courtiers must sense the King's agitation and distress and must mirror it in their movements. The cumulation of the climax in the appearance of the called-for lights, a cry which others may take up, aids in sustaining the climax. The climactic point must be sustained a sufficient time for it to register properly with the audience. In this case, as in others, the director and the actors must invent means of holding the climax for a sufficient duration. If the climax comes tardily off or if sustained too long, it becomes anticlimactic and probably ludicrous. Thus the importance of timing in the handling of climax becomes apparent.

In summary, the director's task is, first, to ascertain what climaxes the playwright has utilized and how he has handled these.

His next task is to invent additional visual and auditory means of making each of these climaxes effective with audiences. His cue for what he invents comes through his understanding of what the playwright has done. Often, as in Hauptmann's stage directions accompanying the scene cited, the playwright has rather fully indicated the means to be employed in staging the climax. Whether or not such is the case, the additions which the director makes must be appropriate to the scene and consistent with such means as the playwright has indicated. Thus, once again, the importance of analysis of drama in the direction of stage performances becomes apparent.

8. CENTER STAGING

Within recent years, and especially since the close of World War II, there has been a great revival in the United States of arena or center staging of plays. Led by Professor Glenn Hughes of the University of Washington, and by others, this revival of an old method of presenting plays has proved a boon to many organizations and institutions which may not own elaborate conventional theatre plants and has demonstrated once again, even in those institutions and organizations with modern and elaborate plants, that audiences can be captured and held by the play and the acting.

In one sense this revival is a reaction against the trend apparent throughout the nineteenth century toward more and more elaborate stage spectacle, a trend which culminated, so Dr. Nicholas Vardac argues in his book, *Stage to Screen,* in making necessary the invention of the cinema in order to satisfy this demand for increased spectacle and enhanced realism. Some staunch defenders of arena staging employ it in their discussion as a device for attacking conventional proscenium-arch staging, referring to the latter as the "peep-hole" stage method.

There is no need for such partisanship in a discussion of the merits of the two types of staging and it must be avoided if a levelheaded assessment of their respective merits is to be made. Both arena staging and proscenium-arch staging are instruments that theatre artists may wisely employ with profit. Certain plays that are dependent upon effects of spectacle, notably nineteenth-century melodramas, are difficult, if not impossible, to present by the arena method. On the other hand, almost any play whose effects are largely in terms of the psychological involvements of the characters and are conveyed largely through the diction are fitting vehicles for center or arena staging. Most of Shakespeare's plays can be very effectively rendered in this manner. In fact one eminent critic, Professor Leslie Hotson, has argued in an article, published in the *Sewanee Review* in 1954, that this method of staging was probably largely employed by the Elizabethans.

Whether or not Hotson is correct in his contentions, a matter of no great importance to this discussion, arena staging does offer certain advantages to the community and academic theatre. Indeed, these advantages are so obvious that various commercial theatre groups in New York and throughout the nation have adopted this method of staging.

The first and most obvious advantage is the economic one of less cost. An arena stage may be easily erected in any large room or, as has often been done, in a tent. The cost of such a theatre lies largely in the cost of ramps for the seats, the seats themselves, a framework for the lighting equipment, and that lighting equipment. Since scenery is eliminated from this type of staging, production costs are likewise more economical than they are on a proscenium-arch stage.

Another advantage of the arena stage is the closer juxtaposition of audience and actor made possible by that manner of production. In some proscenium-arch theatres the distance from the downstage acting area to the first row of seats across a large orchestra pit and to the rear row is great and proves a serious handicap to the young actor. This handicap becomes especially noticeable in the performance of light comedy or in a quiet, serious psychological drama in which the interaction of the characters is highly important. On the other hand, the very proximity of audience and actor can prove an embarrassment. Most dramatic action needs aesthetic distance between audience and actor in order to render its proper effect. Certain scenes can become downright embarrassing to an audience when played too near to them.

In arena staging the director must realize this fact and, when dealing with such scenes, must compensate for the lack of distance by placing a careful restraint upon the rendering of the scene. Still another advantage of the arena method is the relative ease of projection in such staging. A considerable portion of a director's time is given to this matter of projection in rehearsals for ordinary staging. Indeed, young actors acquire the techniques of projection and of audience contact with considerable difficulty. But the director must not think for a moment that there is no problem of projection in the arena theatre, though that problem is more easily solved than it might be in some proscenium-arch theatres. The arts of acting and directing apply as specifically to arena staging as they do to conventional staging. What is said about these in this book can, therefore, be adapted to arena staging with proper modifications.

The most obvious modifications are those which the director must make in designing his production. His first compromise, or modification, will come, of course, when he chooses the play for production. However much he may wish to do Barrie's *Peter Pan,* since the very meaning of that play is tied up with the flying of Peter Pan and the children, he may not be able to adapt this play for arena staging. In many plays, however, the stage business is not so inextricably tied into the effectiveness of the play itself. Many modifications or substitutions may be found for business written into the script and employed in conventional staging. The ingenious arena director will be on the lookout for just such possible substitutions as he reads plays in search of scripts to produce on his stage.

At first glance one might think that Sheridan's *School for Scandal* with its important screen scene might not be a happy choice for center staging; yet there was a very effective center-stage production of this play in Washington, D. C. The director imaginatively utilized the perturbations of Mrs. Teazle to hold the audience interest of those members who were partially cut off by the screen from watching Sir Peter. In another instance, in the staging of a play in which considerable business of importance transpires about a doorway, a director set a real door frame at the entry to the stage area. Purists in arena methods sometimes object to such mixture of devices. The test for or against such inclusion should be entirely on the basis of their effectiveness and not on the basis of any abstract theory.

In his reading and study of the play selected for production the director must translate most of the devices of stage spectacle, however, into other devices that can be utilized on a stage without scenery. Most plays, especially plays written since the seventeenth century, have been written specifically for the proscenium stage; yet it is amazing how many of these can, with a little ingenuity, be adapted to center staging.

Having made his major decisions with respect to modifications and adaptations of the chief spectacular devices of the play, the arena director's next major task is the businessing of the script. He knows that he is going to have to break his script up with considerable stage movement in order that the actors may play the whole house. There is a tendency, as we have noted, on the part of young and inexperienced directors to overbusiness a script for conventional stage presentation because they are afraid to rely on the word. In arena staging this overbusinessing of the script becomes essential because of the necessity of constantly changing the focus of the stage groupings. It is, in fact, inaccurate to call this enhancing of the stage movements of the actors overbusinessing in arena production.

Static positions in grouping on the arena stage, such as a long scene of two characters sitting in the same position on a sofa, will deprive more than half of the audience of a proper view of the actors and the action. Hence the director in his study of the script must find every opportunity for the breaking up of each scene with a variety of stage movements and actor positions. In this search the director is looking for action lines, those lines which demand stage movement or at least permit stage movement in their projection. All that is said in previous discussion of acting and pantomimic dramatization applies with special emphasis to the rendering of stage movement on the arena stage.

It is in the transferring of the spectacle of the play, as represented by the stage movement of actors, that the director will find the greatest difference between arena staging and conventional staging. In arena staging all acting areas are of equal importance and the business must be so planned that no one acting area is utilized for an overlong period. The planning of the placement of the stage movement on the arena stage may be facilitated by laying out the stage in conventional acting areas, provided it is remembered that all are of equal importance and that all must be constantly utilized. In general it is wise to avoid the extreme outer edges of the acting areas without, however, bunching all of the action in the middle of the stage.

The planning of the action is somewhat conditioned by the

selection and placement of the furniture but it is unwise in arena staging to tie down a piece of stage business too strictly to a single piece of furniture if it is possible to avoid doing so. Of course a table scene with characters eating, such as occurs in *You Can't Take It With You,* requires that the characters sit at the table and simulate the eating of a meal. But even such scenes can be broken up with characters getting up, moving about, and sitting again. A love scene on a sofa can easily be broken up into varying positions. Even a single long speech allows many opportunities to the inventive actor and director for changes of position. It should go without saying that all of this stage business must be as carefully planned, plotted for the various areas, and rehearsed for the arena stage as for the picture-frame stage.

Entrances and exits are sometimes rather difficult in this type of staging, since they must be made through the audience when the full arena stage is employed. All that has been said about the method of making entrances and exits, with the exception of the handling of doors, applies even more strictly to arena staging. In the full arena staging there are four area-ways to the stage through the audience, though all four are not employed in every act.

Since the audience sees the character from the moment he appears in the theatre, the placement of entrances and the careful planning of the way in which each actor makes his entrances are of great importance. Knocks or other signals announcing the approach of a character should usually be done offstage (and usually by the actor himself) before the actor appears within view of the audience. What was said about actors making their exits on their own lines applies with special rigorousness to arena acting. When a play or an act opens with characters already on the stage, the lights can be dimmed out and brought up again after the actors have entered and taken their places. In similar fashion, a blackout may serve in lieu of a curtain at the end of an act or a play.

Mention has already been made concerning the selection of properties, especially furniture, for the arena stage. One final word might be added in that respect. Obviously high pieces of furniture, such as a large upright piano, should be avoided. Such pieces conceal too much of the action from certain parts of the house. For the same reason, high-back sofas and chairs must also be eliminated. Furniture and properties must be kept to a minimum.

Plays requiring changes of scene, which in arena staging means resetting of the furniture, should especially be played with the simplest furnishings possible. It is helpful to costume the stage hands who change the furniture in view of the audience.

Arena staging does not necessarily require the full arena method with the audience seated on all sides of the stage. It may be modified to place the audience on three sides only. When this type of staging is utilized, with the stage placed on one side of a square room, that stage becomes in effect a platform stage and the direction of action upon it becomes more nearly like that of the proscenium stage. It still requires a breaking up of the action pattern to allow the actors to play an audience on three sides rather than directly in front.

Some directors have combined the arena method with a simultaneous stage technique, using several different stages set about the room to represent the various localities of the action. These and other modifications of the arena method are perfectly legitimate devices for the effective presentation of plays. With such modifications as are suggested in this Section all that is said about directing in this discussion may be applied to these modifications as well as to full arena staging.

There are a number of good books available on arena staging. One of the first to be published is Glenn Hughes' *The Penthouse Theatre: Its History and Technique* (New York: Samuel French, 1942), which gives an account of the development of this type of staging at the University of Washington by the foremost pioneer in its development. It includes a discussion of techniques employed in such staging. A later book on the subject of arena staging is Walden P. Boyle's *Central and Flexible Staging* (Berkeley, California: University of California Press, 1956). Boyle discusses not only the pure arena method but also other methods of the flexible staging of plays. His explorations of techniques and devices and his illustrations are well presented. With such books easily available, a trained director can readily adapt the techniques and methods which he has mastered to this type of staging. Further discussion of the methods of such adaptation would result in needless repetition.

QUESTIONS AND EXERCISES

Pantomimic Dramatization (without words)

1. Make an entrance into a room in such a way as to show that this is your room in which you live and with which you are thoroughly familiar.
2. Make an entrance into a room in such a way as to show that this is a strange room to you.
3. Make an entrance into a room in such a way as to show that you are surprised to find a crowd of people in it.
4. Make an entrance into a room with another actor in such a way as to show that you are friends. Change the entrance to show that you are quarreling.
5. Continue the quarrel to a climax and the angry departure of the second actor.
6. Continue the quarrel to a climax which involves a discovery that leads to a reconciliation.
7. Develop and pantomimically dramatize the following situation, building as much suspense and interest as possible: Two close friends, a man and a woman, are playing cards at a table. One is cheating. The other suspects and finally discovers the cheating. A quarrel results and the discoverer leaves.

   Change the casting to two men and replan the scene.
8. Pantomimically dramatize the following: A man and a woman are seated on a sofa. He is telling her a secret that seriously affects her happiness. Build the scene through the climactic revelation and her distress upon hearing it.

   Vary the scene according to the following relationships:
   a. They are close friends and trust each other.
   b. The man is really her enemy but she does not know it.
   c. They are mere acquaintances.
   d. Plan a different relationship between the two and reveal that relationship to the audience through the pantomime without telling it in words.
9. Replan the above sequence of scenes with the woman telling the secret.
10. Using the same characters, replan the situation so that it is comic and pantomimically dramatize the various suggested scenes for comic effects. Note the changes that must be made.
11. Pantomimically dramatize the following: Two characters onstage are deeply absorbed in conversation when a third character enters. Show that the third character, antipathetic to both, is the subject of their conversation. Show that the third character, sympathetic

to both, is the subject of their conversation. Show that the third character, ludicrous to both, is the subject of their conversation. Show that the third character suspects that he (or she) is the subject of their conversation and forces the two to admit it.

Stage Grouping, Stage Movement, Climax

Several of the foregoing exercises will involve questions of movement, focus, balance, and pictorial grouping. Note the problems involved and make the proper applications.

12. Vary the entrance of the third character in Exercise 11, as follows:
    a. upstage center
    b. left stage center
    c. right stage center
    d. downstage right
    e. downstage left

    Plan the groupings in each scene and the necessary movements in accordance with the most effective pantomimic dramatization in each.
13. Each of the major scenes in O'Neill's *Ile,* with the exception of the scene involving Joe the Harpooner and his sailor companions, is a scene of two characters. Utilizing the floor plan previously prepared for this play, plan the stage business for the scene between the Steward and Ben, the scene between Captain Keeney and the Second Mate, and the scene between Captain and Mrs. Keeney. Consider areas to be utilized, focus, relative positions, movements toward and away from each other, and the cumulative relationships of these three scenes to each other.
14. Plan in a similar manner the stage business for the scene between the Captain, the Mate, and the sailors led by Joe, assuming that Joe is accompanied by two companions. How would you change your arrangements if Joe is to be accompanied by five companions?
15. Analyze the step-by-step developments in the scene between the Captain and Mrs. Keeney so as to bring out the successive psychological relations between the two characters and the audience effects to be produced by each relationship. How would you utilize relative positions between the two to aid in projecting the relations and effects?
16. In addition to factual information, what are the chief emotional effects in the scene between Captain Keeney and the Mate? How can the positions of the characters on stage and with respect to each other be utilized to aid these emotional effects? What stage movements would be similarly effective?
17. Assume that three characters are involved in a scene and are arranged on stage in an equilateral triangle, with character A in

the dominant position upstage center, and characters B and C downstage, left and right. As the scene progresses, first, character B and, later, character C become dominant. Plan the successive stage movements to give each in turn the proper position. (This exercise will be more meaningful and effective if combined with Exercise 11 above.) What would happen if the grouping were arranged in terms of a right-angle triangle?

18. Assume that the three actors enter together, with actor A talking and receiving the focus. Plan the entrances from several different positions, upstage center, right and left center, and downstage right and left.
19. After a study and analysis of J. M. Barrie's *The Twelve-Pound Look,* make a floor plan for the staging of the play on the stage with which you are familiar. What are the values or effects to be created by the first scene? Plan the stage business for this scene.
20. Determine the values and plan the business for each of the successive scenes.
21. Assume, next, that you are to stage this play on an arena stage. What changes in planning must you make?
22. Select a scene from a play involving more than three characters. (The opening scene of *Boy Meets Girl* will serve as an example.) After a study of the play, analyze the scene for its values and effects. State these as explicitly as you can. What important pieces of business, movements, and stage groupings might be utilized to aid in rendering these? What changes in dominance or changes in focus occur within the scene? How might these be indicated in changes in the grouping?
23. Utilizing the two speeches from *Henry IV* (King Henry's opening speech and Hotspur's Popinjay speech), determine the climax or climaxes in each speech. What function does each climax serve? How might the actor build each?
24. Examine the scene between Kate and Sims in *The Twelve-Pound Look* and find the climaxes. How is each made comic? How may each be built by the actors?
25. Work out two different plans for the staging of the Play-within-a-play in *Hamlet*. Include in your two plans different groupings, as much different business as is allowable, and a different way of handling the climax.
26. Such plays as Noel Coward's *Hay Fever* have been often and effectively staged by the arena method. Select this or a similarly adaptable play and, after a study of it, indicate what major changes in the gross business must be made to present it on an arena stage.

Tempo and Rhythm

All of the above exercises will involve problems of tempo and rhythm. Though these elements are usually more obvious in exercises and scenes that include spoken dialogue, they must also be considered in scenes without diction.

27. Name a character from any play known to you in which tempo and rhythm are obvious elements in the rendering of his nature. Define these elements as precisely as you can, that is, tell what tempo and rhythm belong to the character. What evidence from the play can you cite to support your employment of these specific rates and rhythms?
28. Examine the scene between Captain Keeney and Mrs. Keeney to determine the differences, if any, in rate and rhythm required of the two characters.
29. Chart the rhythmic pattern of the scene, determining especially which speeches require a slow or accelerated rate.
30. Name a contemporary play in which tempo and rhythm are obviously highly important to its success, as they are in Maeterlinck's plays. Explain as clearly as you can why these elements are important to that play.
31. Examine the first act of a full-length play known to you to determine what changes in rate are required from scene to scene and within scenes. Why are these changes in rate necessary? What may they accomplish?
32. From an examination of the scene between Kate and Sims in *The Twelve-Pound Look* show where and how rate and variations in rate may contribute to the comic effect.
33. Explain how a slowing down of rate may contribute to suspense. Cite an example from a play to illustrate the effect.
34. Explain how an acceleration of rate may increase excitement. Cite an example from a play to illustrate the effect.
35. In the examples cited in the two previous questions, is tempo alone sufficient to produce the effects? If not, what other elements contribute?
36. In the two different stagings of the Play-within-a-play from *Hamlet* which you have planned, what variations in tempo have you utilized? What effects did you propose to secure from such variations?
37. In general, comedy demands a faster pace than does tragedy. Explain reasons for this difference.

PART III

STAGE SCENERY

By SAMUEL SELDEN

CHAPTER 9

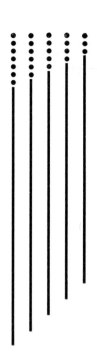

The Purpose of Scenery

THE ART OF THE STAGE is the art of Presence. Presence in the theatre is the enkindling influence exerted by a personality of superior radiance. The personality may be that of a man or a woman, or it may belong to an inanimate object which, because of its association with human action, takes on a living quality. A rug, a wall, a chair, a dress, or a snatch of song may have "presence."

The supreme stage presence is, of course, the actor's. Because he is the most direct and intimate embodiment of the playwright's vision, his radiant influence dominates all the others. In fact, in many periods of theatre history the actor has had to assume not only the chief part of, but all the responsibility for creating dramatic presence. And he has done it successfully. The early Greek players performed the tragedies of Aeschylus, Sophocles, and Euripides before the simplest of façades. The actors of Shakespeare's time performed an even greater variety of scenes on an open wooden structure with two levels. Molière often played on the barest type of platform with the help of no other scenic properties than a plain table and a pair of neutral chairs. It mattered little to Molière and his fellow actors whether they moved in front of the mirrored walls of a palace ballroom or the brick walls of a tennis court, or whether they walked on carpets or uncovered boards, because they were able to establish by their words and actions the atmosphere, or presence, of their surroundings.

Since Molière other artists have contributed to the effects of a stage performance. This is particularly true of the scenic artists. Sometimes, overeager to create surrounding forms which would exert upon the audience the influence of their own pictorial personalities, they have nearly destroyed the influence of the acting. Only in comparatively recent times has much thought been given to the efficient blending of the two arts. The guiding theories of the so-called "new stagecraft" became clearly defined only around the turn of the present century. In accordance with them, the actor's presence remains—or becomes again—the center of the dramatic design, but the "presences" of the scenic forms (walls, furniture, and lights) which surround him become increasingly important in creating the right mood for the player's actions, supporting the force of his influence on the audience.

Modern dramatists, striving for greater economy by omitting from their plays the long passages of description and exposition which slowed the action of older plays, depend more and more on the effects produced by stage settings to describe their characters and to project their stories. The significance they attach to the scenic environment of the dramatic action is indicated by the careful specifications they place in their stage directions.

Loretto Carroll Bailey begins her one-act play of frustrated desire, *Cloey,* in this way:

> *When the curtain rises,* JOSEPH HALL *is sitting at a little walnut desk in* MRS. MOTSINGER'S *living room, busily chewing a pencil, and writing at intervals.* JOSEPH *is a rather good-looking man of thirty-five, pleasing—often appealing—but somewhat ineffectual. He fits rather nicely in the dim sitting room on the edge of "Germantown." It is a quaint, musty little room, with a great fireplace in the middle of the back wall, and shallow alcoves on either side of it. The light filters through small diamond-paned windows at the back of the alcoves, falling on dim and dusty books in the shelves, bringing faint color to the portrait above the fireplace—the portrait of a girl with a pretty, spirited face. . . .*[1]

A full appreciation of the story of Joseph's ineffectual hope to better himself, of Cloey's wistful longing for release, and of Mrs.

[1] *Carolina Folk Comedies.* Edited by Frederick H. Koch. Reprinted by permission of Samuel French, New York.

Motsinger's peculiar ordering of their lives would be impossible without that musty, dimly lighted little room. Before the play is over, nearly every visible object takes some part in the action—the table in the center of the room, the high-backed chair by the fireplace, the curtains on the alcoved windows, the silver candlesticks on the mantel, and, above all the others, the portrait of Cloey's mother on the wall. *Cloey* is a play of presences.

To perform Paul Green's *The House of Connelly* convincingly would be impossible without the interior of the proud old Connelly mansion, with its high, Georgian-paneled walls cracked and stained, and the portraits of the ancestors moldering in their frames. The decaying dining room, decorated with ivy by the Connelly girls in a pathetic effort to recapture a little of the lost glory of Christmas, Mr. Green describes with great care. Before the scene in the old mansion, there is another scene laid in the fields near the house. The author sets the whole tone of his play in the opening paragraph of his stage directions:

A late winter afternoon is over the fields, and across the land to the west a murky cloud creeps up the sky, lighted along its edge by a bluish tinge from the hidden sun. The air is raw and has the feel of snow in it. A rail fence grown up with an unkempt hedgerow of dead fennel weeds, poke stalks, and sassafras bushes crosses the foreground, rotten and spraddled, with a disused stile near the center. Close beyond it in the field, three stack-poles now empty and gaunt, stand up like black gallows-trees, with ragged wisps of hay clinging to the cross-pieces above. The decaying stalks and weeded hedge exude the rot of death into the air, and the mood of a heavy loneliness is over the earth.[2]

No play illustrates the important part scenery plays in modern drama better than Eugene O'Neill's *Beyond the Horizon.* Two views of the sitting room in their farmhouse effectively exhibit the deterioration of the Mayo family. In the second scene of Act 1 the affairs of the Mayo family are in good order, and the playwright notes:

Everything in the room is clean, well kept, and in its exact place, yet there is no suggestion of primness about the whole. Rather the atmosphere is one of the orderly comfort of a simple, hard-earned prosperity, enjoyed and maintained by the family as a unit.[3]

[2] *The House of Connelly and Other Plays.* Reprinted by permission of Samuel French, New York.

[3] Reprinted by permission of Random House, New York.

By the beginning of the third act the impractical Robert has failed. He has lost his idealism, the greater part of his property, his child, and his health. Both he and his wife have long since given up all hope of material betterment and have sunk into an attitude of dull despair. Before a line is spoken, Mr. O'Neill gives his audience an understanding of changed conditions by revealing an altered room. He describes in detail the smoky chimney on the oil lamp, the torn and dirty curtains in the window, the blotches of dampness which disfigure the wallpaper, the faded carpet, and the broken rocker. The playwright sums up by saying:

> *The whole atmosphere of the room, contrasted with that of former years, is one of habitual poverty too hopelessly resigned to be any longer ashamed or even conscious of itself.*[4]

The modern stage setting, it will be observed, not only describes character and creates mood for action, but also helps the player tell a story. If we should attempt to give an informal definition of scenery from the point of view of a modern designer in the theatre, we should say, perhaps, that it is the living *environment* of the actor. The able artist enters into close communion with the author and the director of a play, and then, with the design of the acting clearly in mind, conceives for it surrounding forms which project its meaning and intensify its effects. The walls, the doorways, the rugs, the tables, the chairs, and—above all else—the lights which he plans, will be not simply architecture, furniture, and illumination, but objects possessing an animate, vibrant presence, exerting an influence which, blended with and through the acting, makes the audience understand and enjoy the play to the highest extent.

QUESTIONS AND EXERCISES

1. What is the dramatic purpose of stage scenery?
2. How may scenery describe human character?
3. How may scenery create a mood for action?
4. How may scenery help the actor tell a story?
5. Where does the scenic artist look for the first ideas of each new design?

[4] Reprinted by permission of Random House, New York.

CHAPTER 10

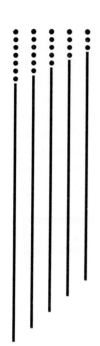

The Form of Scenery

1. THE TOPOGRAPHY OF THE STAGE

BEFORE THE ARTIST and his partner, the technician (the two men in the nonprofessional theatre are frequently one), can begin to plan, build, or paint workable settings for plays, they must know what are the principal structural features of a theatre, and what is the fundamental "anatomy" of scenic forms.

A modern playhouse, viewed as a lesser field for conquest than the Gaul described by Caesar, may conveniently be divided into two parts, the *front of the house* and the *back of the house*. In the "front" part are usually located the auditorium, the lobby, the patrons' lounges, the box office, and all other business offices. In the "back" part are situated the stage, the dressing rooms, the Green Room (if any), and all shops and storerooms.

The transverse wall dividing the auditorium from the stage is the *proscenium* (Figures 2 and 3). The opening in this wall, whether rounded or square at the top, through which one sees the stage, is called the *proscenium opening*. The architecture of this opening is the *proscenium arch*. Behind the proscenium wall, the spaces offstage to each side are the *wings*—that to the right, facing the audience, the *right wing*, that to the left, the *left wing*. Here are located the exit to dressing rooms, the loading door through which scenery is brought in and taken out, often a door to a special property room, the control board (usually in older theatres), the counterweight system—if the equipment includes this (Chapter 12, Section 7)—stacks of scenery, properties, lighting apparatus, safety devices, a clock, and the stage manager's prompt desk. The floor of the stage is of softwood boarding, usually tongue-and-groove fir or yellow pine, laid parallel to the proscenium from the front to the back wall. It is frequently pieced by *traps* that open into the basement to permit the use of sunken stair-

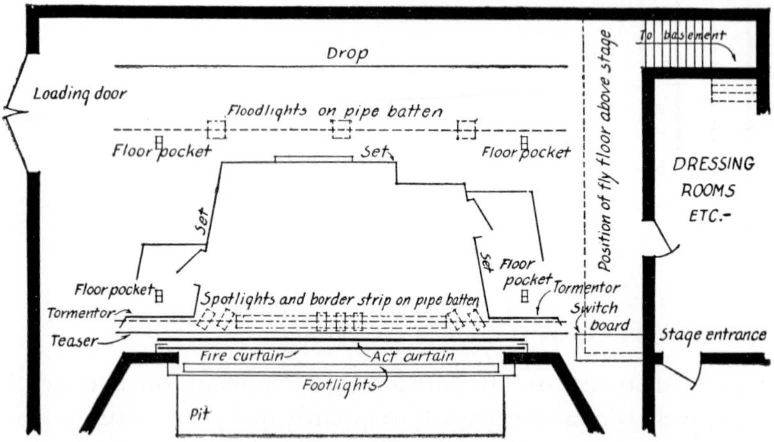

FIG. 2. Plan of a typical stage, showing the usual positions of the fire and act curtains, the teaser, tormentors, footlight trough, overhead lighting instruments, loading door, fly door, and other features, and a set of scenery in place. This stage is 52 feet wide and 28 feet deep with a proscenium opening of 28 feet. Commonly the front of the stage extends out a little beyond the curtain line in the form of an apron. (See Fig. 3.)

ways, and so forth, and is usually covered during a performance by a large piece of heavy waterproof duck called a *ground cloth.* The *footlight trough* is located along the edge of the stage floor nearest the audience.

At the top of the space above the proscenium, known as the *flies,* is the *gridiron* or *grid,* a steel or wooden framework of open beams placed five to ten feet below the roof, forty to a hundred or more feet above the stage, and extending over the entire working area. From this frame is suspended all the hanging scenery such as drops, borders, and tree trunks, as well as certain lighting units. *Sets of lines* are attached to each hanging piece, passed over

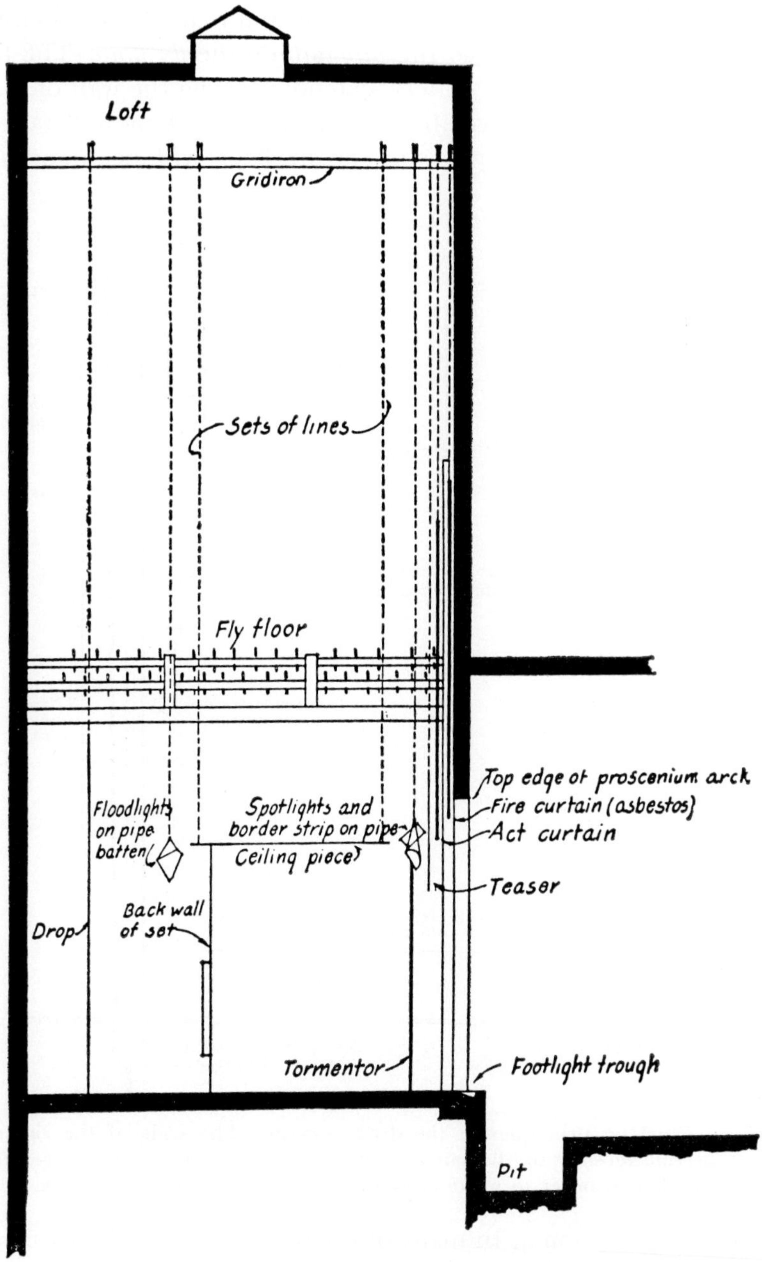

FIG. 3. Vertical section of a typical stage, showing the position of the fire and act curtains, teaser, one tormentor, footlight trough, overhead lighting units, fly floor, gridiron, and other features, and a set of scenery in place. This stage is 28 feet deep (from the curtain line), and the gridiron is 60 feet above the floor. (See Fig. 2.)

pulley blocks in the grid, brought down, and tied off on a double row of belaying pins, called the *pin rail,* on the *fly floor.* The fly floor is a shelf, or narrow gallery, extending along the wall of one of the wings some distance above the main floor. A more detailed description of the gridiron and the fly floor will be found in

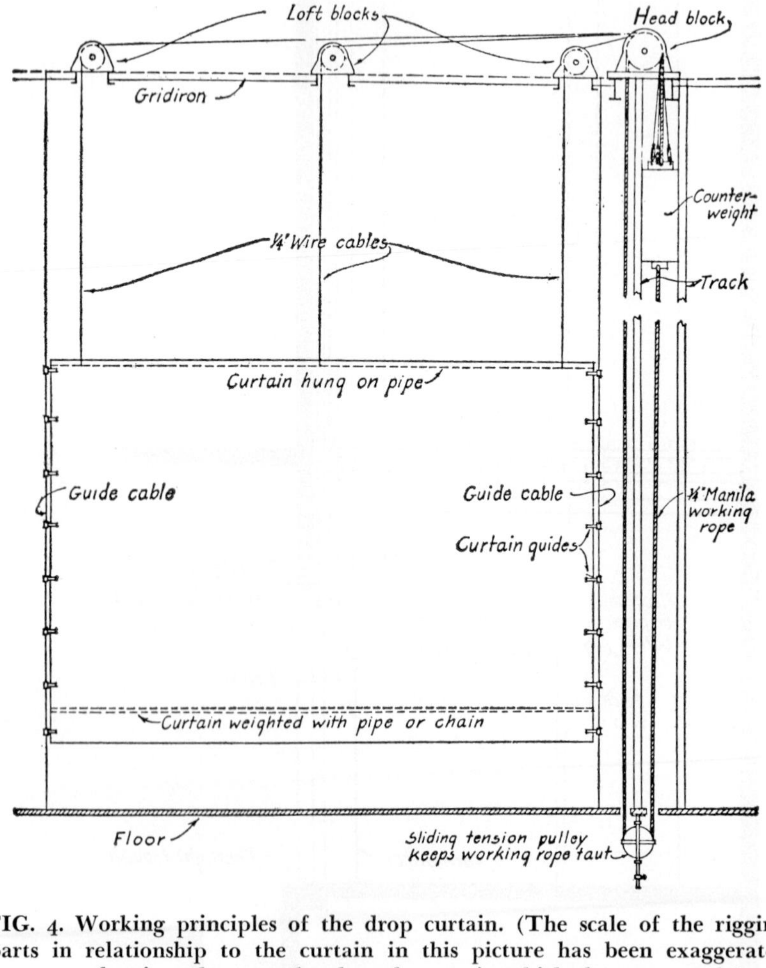

FIG. 4. Working principles of the drop curtain. (The scale of the rigging parts in relationship to the curtain in this picture has been exaggerated somewhat in order to make clear the way in which the parts work.)

Chapter 12, Section 4. In many of the newer theatres the fly floor, with its pin rail, has been omitted and all hanging scenery is handled with a *counterweight system* operated from the floor. This method is described in Chapter 12, Section 7.

We have just considered the stage and some of the permanent, built-in equipment. Now let us look at the principal adjustable "masking pieces." Returning to the proscenium opening—the two perpendicular and movable screens that mask from the audience the spaces on each side between the downstage edges of a set and the proscenium arch are the *tormentors*. These, together with the

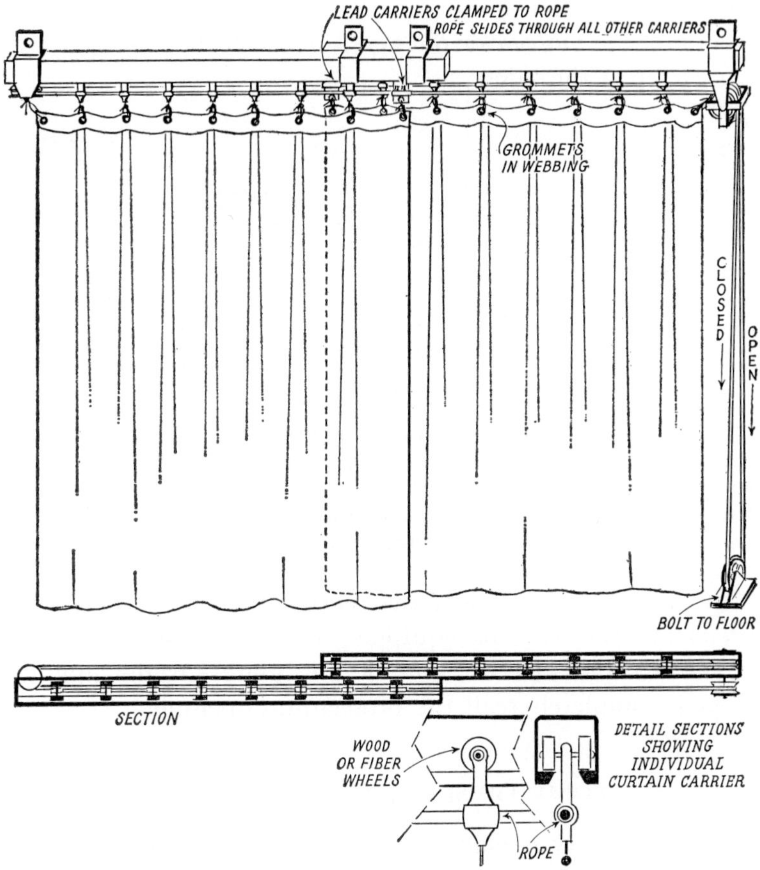

FIG. 5. Draw curtain on a traveller. The path of the drawline through the traveller is indicated in the diagram below the curtain.

horizontal screen or mask known as the *teaser*—usually a simple, dark-colored border or piece of drapery suspended above, between the arch and the tormentors—form an adjustable inner frame for the stage picture. The *act curtain,* or *house curtain,* closes the proscenium opening between the arch and this inner frame. On most larger stages the curtain is of the *drop type* (Figure 4), suspended from the gridiron and rigged, balanced, and operated by an endless rope on the same general principle as a unit of the counterweight system. Other common curtains, used more frequently on small stages, are the *draw* type (Figure 5), in which two sections, parting in the middle and tied to a number of wooden or fiber wheels, moving in a slotted track called a *traveller*, are pulled on and off without raising or lowering the curtain as a whole; and the *tableau* or *tab* type, in which the two sections are gathered up at the sides.

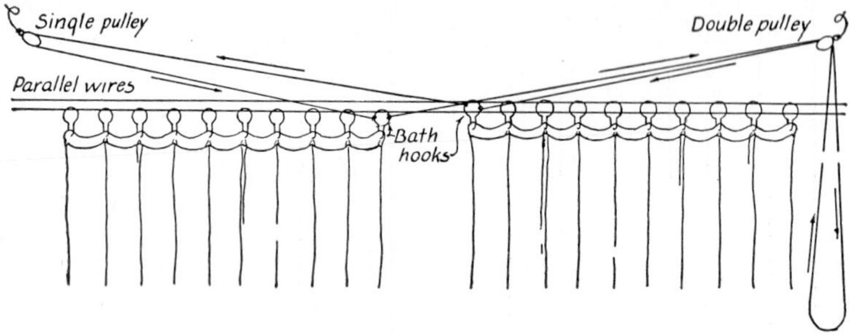

FIG. 6. Simple homemade draw curtain on wires. The two wires are fastened to the side walls of the stage at the same level and drawn taut by means of turnbuckles. The two pulleys are shown raised so that the path of the operating rope will be seen clearly. In practice the pulleys should be attached to the walls on a line with the wires.

Fire regulations in most cities require that every theatre, commercial or otherwise, be equipped also with a steel or asbestos *fire curtain.* It hangs in front of the house curtain and, when dropped, completely seals the proscenium opening.

2. THE ANATOMY OF SCENERY

A set of scenery is made up of a number of wood and canvas screens, platforms, and other light-framed pieces, which are so designed that they may be assembled or taken apart simply and quickly. Standard-made units, whatever their length, have a maximum width of only 5 feet 9 inches. Frames of this size are easy to construct and cover (Chapter 11, Sections 6 and 7), and they are convenient to handle and to pack away (Chapter 12, Section 9).

The most common forms of unit scenery may be grouped under five general headings:

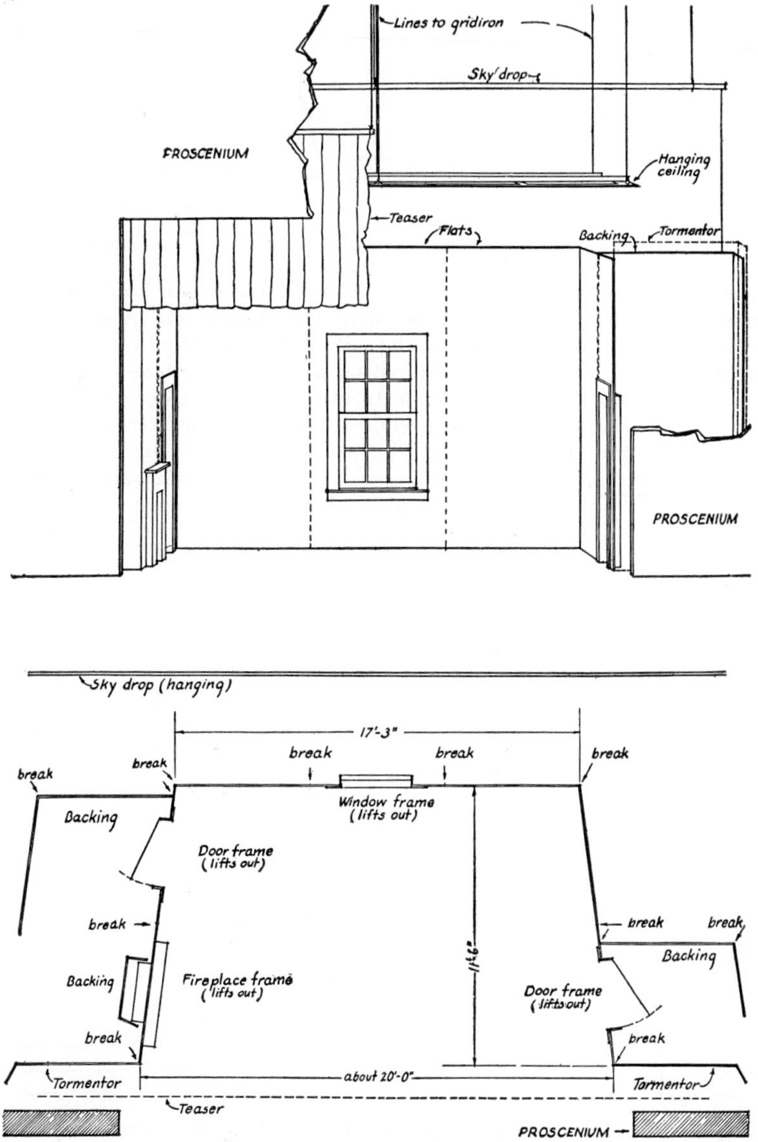

FIG. 7. Small box set in front view and plan, showing a typical arrangement of walls, door, window and fireplace units, ceiling, sky drop, backings and front masking pieces.

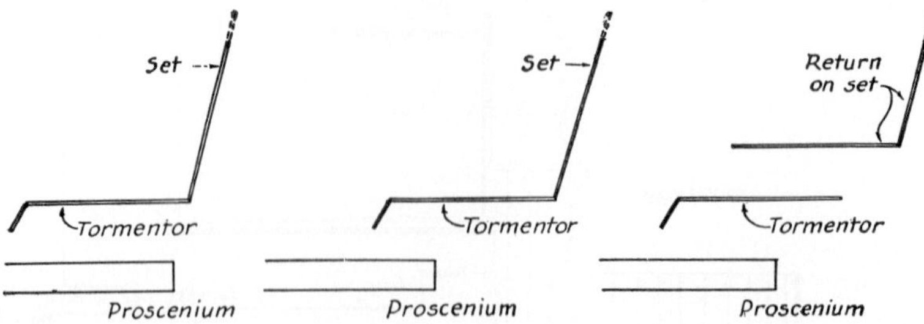

FIG. 8. The tormentor and the return. These diagrams show how the proscenium opening may be opened out or narrowed on each side by shifting the position of the tormentor, or by making use of an additional return. If side lighting units on standards are required on a set they are frequently placed between the tormentor and the return. In this case a 12-inch or 18-inch thickness is usually placed on the onstage edge of the tormentor to shield the light from the audience, and the return is pulled back to allow the lighting unit to be angled freely onto the set. A teaser (see Fig. 7) serves as an adjustable masking piece above.

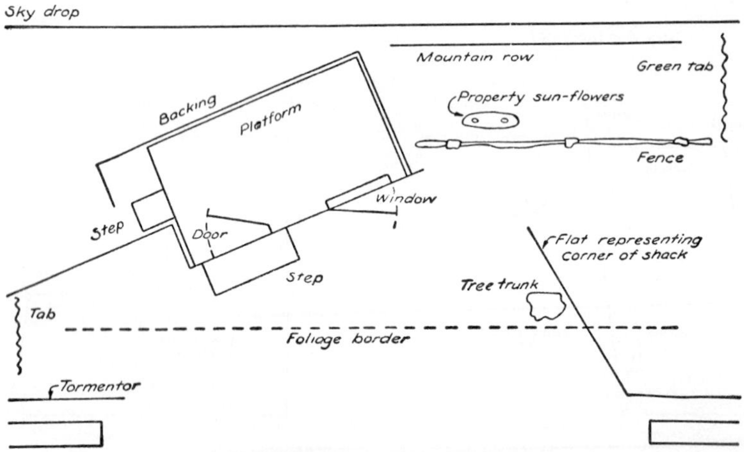

FIG. 9. Floor plan of an exterior setting, including the front of a small country store, and a view of distant mountains against the sky.

A. Standing Units:

flat (plain)—A tall screen made of wood and canvas, with a standard width of 5′ 9″, but no standard height, used as a section of a wall. (Figure 19)

door flat—a flat with an opening for a door frame. (Figure 21)

window flat—a flat with an opening for a window frame. Figure 21)

fireplace flat—a flat with an opening for a fireplace frame. (Figure 21)

two-fold—two flats hinged together to fold inward, face to face. (Figure 20)

three-fold—three flats hinged in the same way. (Figure 20)

door frame unit—a solid wood door frame made to fit in a flat designed for it. (Figure 22)

window frame unit—a solid wood window frame made for a similar purpose. (Figure 24)

fireplace unit—a fireplace frame, not always solid, made for a similar purpose. (Figure 26)

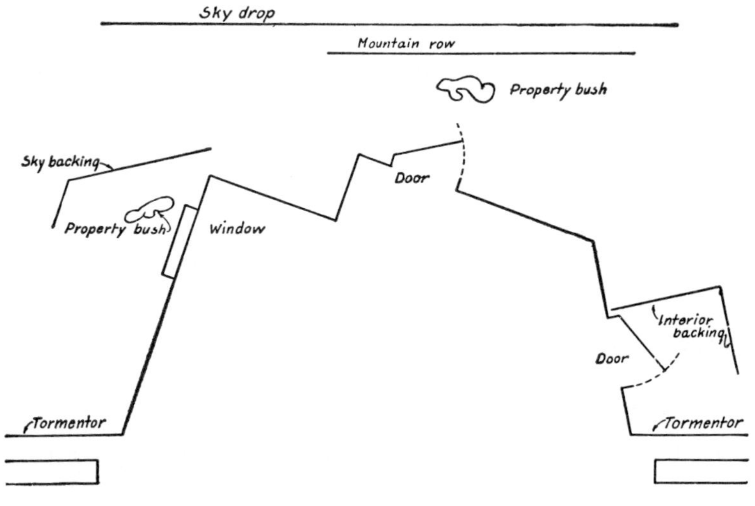

FIG. 10. Floor plan of an interior setting, showing a room with doors leading to the outside and to another part of the house.

B. Hanging Units:

ceiling—a large, horizontal, canvas-covered frame, suspended by a set of lines from the grid, used to close the top of an interior scene. (Figure 27)

drop—a large sheet of canvas, partly or fully framed, suspended

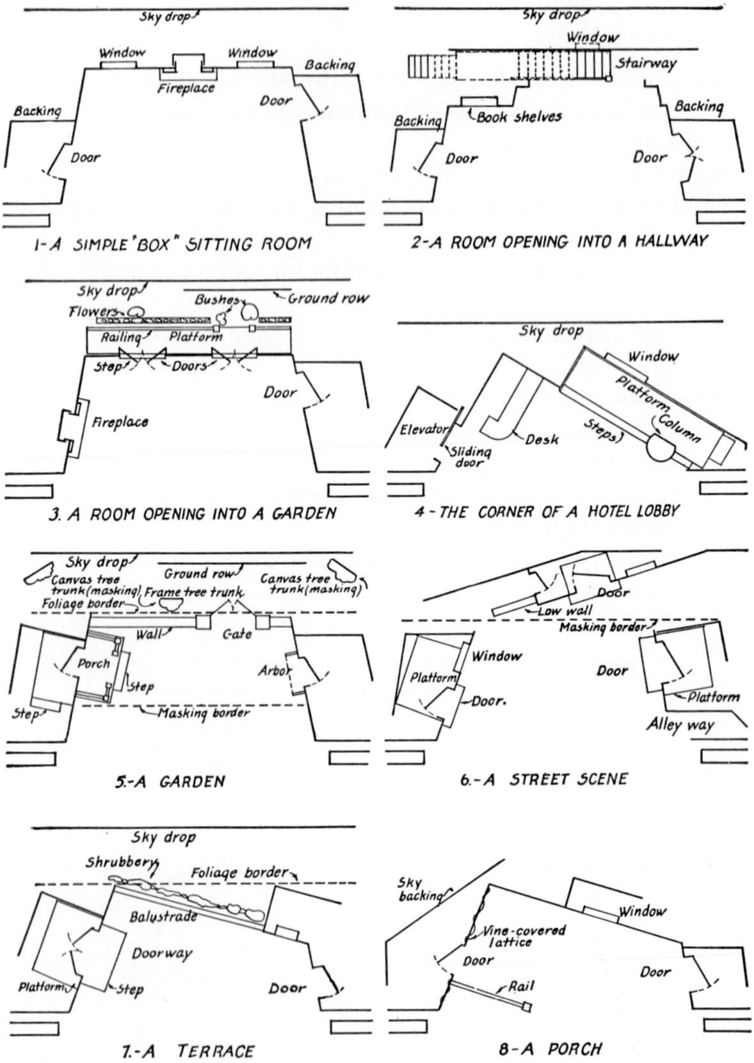

FIG. 11. Floor plans of several different types of interior and exterior settings.

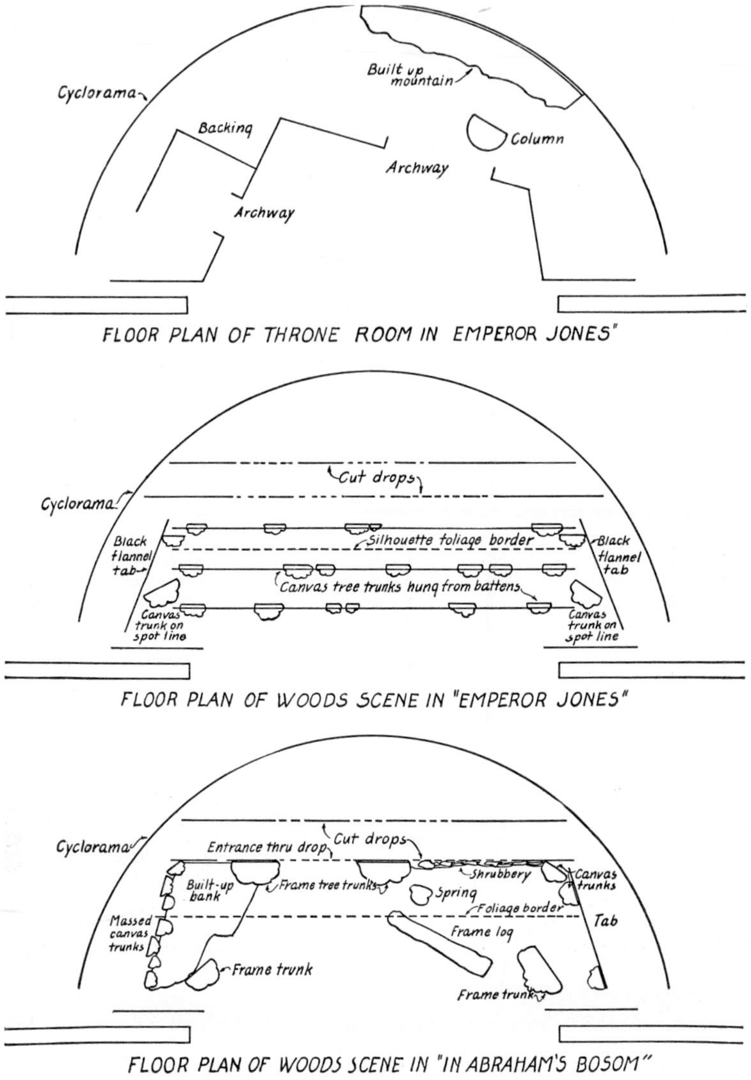

FIG. 12. Floor plans of three settings which make use of the sky cyclorama. The three settings were designed by Cleon Throckmorton for productions at the Provincetown Playhouse, New York.

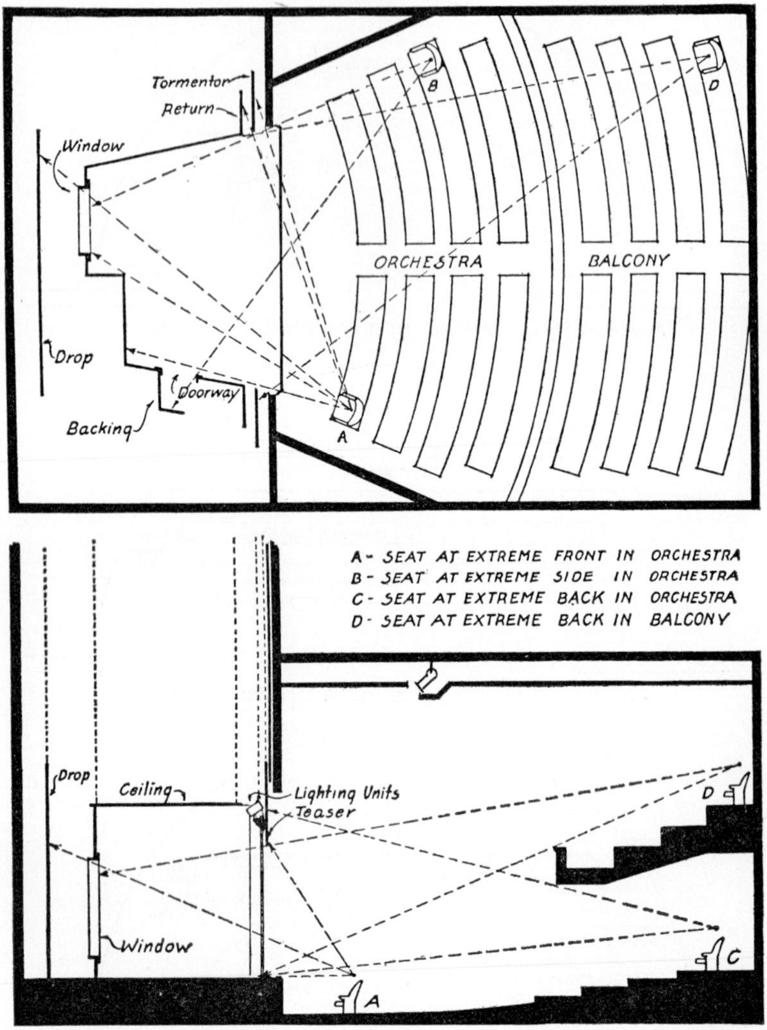

FIG. 13. Sight lines. Good lines of vision to the stage from the auditorium require (1) the full visibility of the acting area and the chief features of its setting, and (2) the adequate backing of door, window, and fireplace openings in the setting, and the complete masking of lighting units and stage machinery for every position in the house (except, occasionally, a few of the first row seats, if too close to the stage).

vertically on a set of lines from the grid—commonly used to represent the sky. (Figure 29)

border—an abbreviated drop, occasionally used to represent foliage or to mask the flies. (Figure 29)

cyclorama—a large curtain of canvas, or other material, hung from a horizontal U-shaped wood or metal frame suspended by a set of lines from the grid—commonly used to represent the sky in exterior scenes, as well as for a number of other purposes. (Figure 31)

C. Built Units:

platform—a collapsible and portable frame platform constructed in unit sections. (Figure 33) Some small platforms are rigid.

steps—a light, portable run of steps contructed in unit sections. (Figure 34)

column—a light frame or canvas column. (Figure 35)

tree—a light frame or canvas tree trunk. (Figure 35)

rock—a light, irregular frame-and-canvas imitation of a rock, made in unit sections. (Figure 36)

built-up ground—a similar imitation of a bank of earth.

D. Set Units:

ground row—a flat profile of a bank of earth, or a distant mountain, painted on thin three-ply veneer board, cut out, framed behind, and made to stand up independently on the floor. (Figure 37)

fence or wall—a frame imitation of a fence or wall, designed to stand up independent of other units on the floor. (Figure 38)

E. Draperies:

Under this head may be listed a variety of curtain units, largely unframed.

These twenty-one units do not represent all of the "standard parts" of scenery. They are, however, some of the principal ones. The number of designs into which these parts may be assembled is almost limitless. Flats, door, window, and fireplace units, ceilings, drops, and frequently steps, columns, and other units, may be combined to represent indoor scenes in a wide variety of shapes and styles; while drops or cycloramas, trees, fences, ground rows, and frequently flats, columns, and other units, may be put together to suggest outdoor scenes in an equal variety of forms.

These or other units, again, may be united to make formal, poetic, or expressionistic backgrounds.

There is no standard arrangement of standard parts. Certain arrangements are, however, fairly characteristic of some of the more common classes of scenes. Several examples typical of their kind—realistic interior and exterior settings, and formal drapery-cyclorama settings—are illustrated in floor plans in Figures 9–12.

QUESTIONS AND EXERCISES

1. What is the "topography" of a stage?
2. Compare the "front of the house" with the "back of the house" in a typical modern playhouse.
3. Distinguish between, *proscenium, proscenium opening,* and *proscenium arch.*
4. What are the right and left *wings?* What is commonly found in them?
5. Identify *flies, gridiron, sets of lines, fly floor, pin rail.*
6. Identify *tormentor, teaser, house curtain, fire curtain.*
7. Name the most common units of standing scenery.
8. Name the most common units of hanging scenery.
9. Name the most common units of built-up scenery.
10. Name two or three typical units of set scenery.
11. What types of scenery may be grouped under the general term *draperies?*
12. Draw a floor plan of a typical interior setting for a stage with a proscenium opening of 30′. Label the various units of scenery which compose the set.
13. Draw a floor plan of a typical exterior setting for the same stage, and label the different scenic parts. (Keep your drawing simple.)

CHAPTER 11

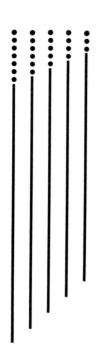

The Construction of Scenery

A. GENERAL PRACTICE

1. PRACTICAL REQUIREMENTS OF SCENERY

Scenery constructed for the stage must fulfill a number of practical requirements.

First, scenery must be designed for easy and rapid construction. The plan of production most frequently adopted by both professional and nonprofessional producing groups allows from three to five weeks only for the complete preparation of a play. Within this brief period the stage designer, the technical director, and his staff and crew, must design, draft, build, paint, and fit to the stage usually two or three—frequently more—complete sets of scenery. It is absolutely necessary, therefore, that this scenery be planned for the simplest and quickest possible methods of construction.

Second, scenery must be designed for economical construction. Unless great care is exercised, the item of scenery on the final expense sheet of a production is apt to be a large one. It should be the purpose of the designer and his technical colleagues, therefore, to keep down costs by choosing materials wisely, by adopting efficient methods of building and, above all, by avoiding waste.

Third, scenery must be designed for quick and silent shifting. That is, it must be constructed in light, well-shaped units which can be handled efficiently by a minimum number of stagehands.

Fourth, scenery must be strong. It must be able to resist considerable strain in the course of being handled by stagehands and actors, especially when it is to be placed in service for performances night after night. It must be firmly put together and well joined.

Fifth, scenery must be well assembled. The methods of fastening together the various units must be such that it will be unnecessary to drive a nail during the performance. Nothing sounds more amateurish to the audience during a scene shift than hammering on the stage. The assembling and taking apart of the units should be handled during the shifts quickly and silently.

Sixth, scenery must be designed for easy storage. It must be so planned and constructed that when it is not in use it may be packed away on the stage or in a storeroom in a minimum amount of space. That is, large flat units, like drops, flats over 5′ 9″ wide (Section 9), and ceilings must be capable of being rolled or folded; three-dimensional frame units, like platforms, must be collapsible; wide thicknesses on archways and other flats must be removable; and other bulky, awkward units, must be made either to be folded or to be taken apart in sections. Scenery which is to be sent on tour and must be planned for storage in a crowded boxcar or truck must be planned to fulfill these requirements especially.

How the practical requirements of scenery construction here indicated may be met is discussed in the following sections of this chapter, and in the next chapter.

2. WOOD MATERIALS

The following materials are essential for scenery construction:

Because all frames must be light and strong, only particular grades of lumber may be used. Requirements of shop and stage demand that the lumber be soft enough for easy working, light enough for easy handling, yet tough enough to stand considerable strain and wear. It must not splinter readily, it must not warp, it must be straight-grained and free from any large blemishes, and it must be well seasoned. By far the best wood for general scenic construction is good grade Northern or Idaho white pine. It is the standard. Sugar pine is the best substitute. Douglas fir, yellow pine, and certain other soft woods also may be substituted; but none of these can approach the efficiency of white pine. (The choice of lumber will depend to a great extent on the section of the country in which the shop is located.)

For ordinary purposes, the lumber should be ordered in strips 1″ x 2″, 1″ x 3″, and 1″ x 4″, by 12 feet to 20 feet long, dressed and surfaced. The first two widths are used in building flats, the last in building ceilings, door frames, and so forth. In surfacing a strip at the yard, about ⅛ inch is planed off the thickness and about ¼ inch off the width, making a so-called 1″ x 2″ strip actually ⅞″ x 1¾″, and so on. This makes no difference except that proper allowances must be made in measurements during construction.[1] If the lumberman is obliging, he will prepare the strips[2] with a thickness of ⅞ inch to accommodate theatrical hardware designed for it and, at the same time, with widths in even inches, to facilitate the work of the carpenter.

Another useful wood material is veneer board of fir, basswood, or whitewood (or other wood, preferably soft) in three or more plies, called *plywood* or *plyboard* or, sometimes in stage work, *profile board*. It comes in 4′ x 8′ sheets in several thicknesses (the most practicable of which are the ¼ inch and ¾ inch), and is useful for all semi-rigid parts requiring lightness and toughness combined with flexibility. A strip of plywood can be bent into a fairly small circle without cracking. It is employed to advantage in various kinds of light facings, such as risers for steps, curved backs of benches, ground rows, silhouettes, cutouts, and so forth.

A good substitute for plywood where strength is not of primary importance is Upson board or Teakwood, which is considerably cheaper than plywood.

[1] Because mills vary a little in the amount of wood they remove in dressing a strip of lumber, this loss in width and thickness will not be taken into account at all (unless it is specifically stated otherwise) in the discussion of cutting lengths of lumber in this and the following chapter. That is, 1″ x 3″ batten will be assumed, in the specifications, to be actually 1 inch thick and 3 inches wide. Each building carpenter, with the dressed size of his own lumber in mind, can make allowances wherever necessary.

[2] In the following chapters the common term *batten* will be used as a synonym for *strip*.

3. COVERING MATERIALS

Scenery is usually covered with either *canvas* or *muslin*. Flame-proofed linen canvas is the best, but it is now too expensive for general use. Duck canvas is very serviceable, while muslin is cheaper and comes in various weights. Heavyweight muslin should be picked for covering large frames. Lightweight cloth can be used to advantage on small frames only. If necessary, two 36-inch strips may be seamed together to make a 72-inch width. Drill, also, is a good covering material.

4. HARDWARE MATERIALS

The following hardware must be ordered from some theatrical supply house:

Lash cleats—small hooks on the frame of a flat over which a lash line is thrown to bind one flat to another
Lash-line eyes—metal eyes to which the lash line is attached
Brace cleats—small plates into which stage braces are hooked to prop flats
Ceiling plates—plates for bolting together and hanging ceiling frames
Hanging irons—hardward for hanging scenery
Foot irons—hardware for securing scenery to the floor
Stage picture-frame hooks and sockets—hardware for hanging or otherwise attaching light scenery units to other units
Corner blocks and keystones—small triangular and keystone-shaped pieces of ¼-inch plywood used to reinforce joints

The following hardware may be secured from a local dealer:

Screws—No. 9 wood screws (¾-inch and 1½ inches)
No. 8 wood screws (¾-inch and 2 inches)
Corrugated fasteners—No. 5 (¾-inch)
Nails—Cement coated wire nails (4, 6, and 10 penny)
Finishing nails (assorted)
1¼-inch lath nails
1¼-inch clout nails
Tacks—No. 4, No. 6, and No. 8 carpet tacks
Hinges—2-inch tight-pin back flaps (each flap 2 inches)
2-inch loose-pin back flaps (each flap 2 inches)
6-inch strap hinges (each flap 6 inches)
Butt hinges—(for lightweight doors)

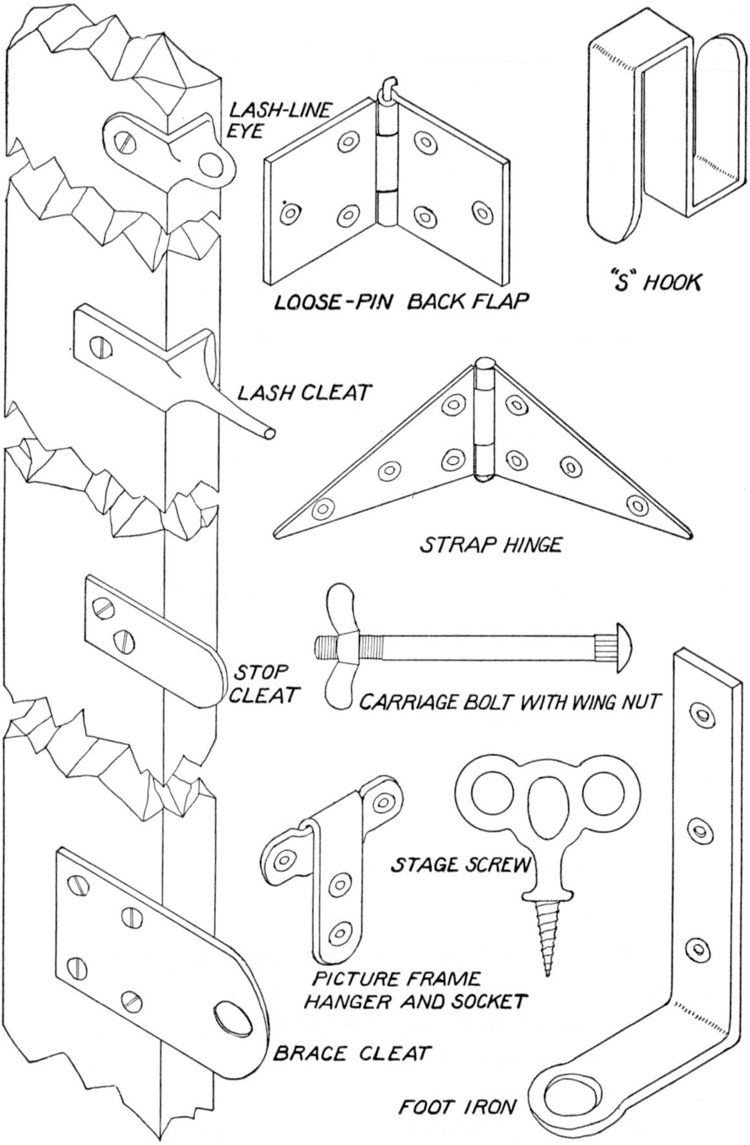

FIG. 14. Common pieces of hardware.

Bolts—3/16″ x 2″ stove bolts
3/8″ x 2″ to 6″ carriage bolts with wing nuts
Door knobs and rim locks
Angle irons and flat corner braces—assorted sizes
Pulleys—assorted sizes
Sash cord—No. 8 (used for lash lines)
Strap iron—3/16″ x 7/8″ strips to be made into saddle irons

There are some materials which the stage carpenter will not use so often but with which he should be familiar.

Burlap, rep, and monkscloth—coarse-textured fabrics which are useful for hangings, tapestries, and curtains
Plasterer's burlap—a loosely woven material which can be used for surfacing rocks, mounds, and tree trunks
Bobbinet and linen scrim—fine gauzes used for creating hazy effects and transformations ("vision" scenes)
Netting—for holding together painted flat foliage sections
Hansen gauze—a durable, heavy gauze with a smooth side and a ribbed side, suitable for painting when transparent or semitransparent effects are desired
Velour—a heavy fabric resembling velvet, used in the making of drapery cycloramas, and occasionally for covering scenery when a surface with a nap is required
Duvetyn—similar to velour, but cheaper
Pearl screening—used in place of glass in windows

5. CONSTRUCTION PROCEDURE

Before starting even the first steps in building, the whole plan of a set of scenery should be carefully drafted on paper. This plan is made up of what are called the "working drawings" (Chapter 14, Section 5) and is usually supplied to the carpenter by the artist who designs the set. It includes complete diagrams—plan, elevation, and, where necessary, cross sections and details—of each unit to show beyond any question the exact construction of every part. In order to prevent any possible waste of materials and time (not to mention patience) caused by the finished product's failure to check with the artist's original idea, a good carpenter demands to know in advance, to the fraction of an inch, just what he is supposed to do. If the carpenter is a man of experience, certain standard arrangements of joints, braces, and hardware may be omitted from the drawings, but enough detail must be included to make the plans clear.

With the working drawings before him, the carpenter is ready to start. He checks them over and decides what materials are required. From stock he selects lumber of the right widths and thicknesses in lengths that will leave the least waste. He examines each piece for straightness and absence of flaws. He sets the best pieces aside for use in parts that require the greatest strength and trueness, such as the stiles of a flat, while he places any slightly blemished pieces in another pile for making toggle rails, cross braces, and so on. Before cutting the lumber, he removes the raw edges (the sharp corners, called appropriately by stagehands the "curse") from each strip with a plane. This eliminates the hazard of splinters. A sixteenth of an inch is all that needs to be shaved off. This is done by running the plane the length of each edge once, with the grain.

Now the carpenter proceeds:

a. He measures carefully, cuts, and marks the pieces of lumber to be used in the frame under construction. Accuracy here conserves both material, time, and temper.

b. He assembles the frame.

c. He covers the frame.

6. JOINTING

The joint most commonly used on the stage—at least, in nonprofessional construction work—is the simple butt or right-angle joint, reinforced with a corner block or keystone (Figures 15 and 16). The two pieces to be joined are placed squarely together, one at right angles to the other, and two ¾-inch No. 5 corrugated fasteners (if these are used) are driven in edgewise (teeth down), flush with the wood, across the seam. The corner block or keystone (small triangular or keystone-shaped piece of ¼-inch plywood is laid above this and secured by a number of 1¼-inch lath or clout nails. (When clout nails are used they should be inserted with their flat edge at right angles to the grain so that they will not split the wood.) Since the combined thickness of the ⅞-inch batten and the ¼-inch block is 1⅛ inches, the ⅛ inch of the point of the nail which protrudes must be turned by holding a

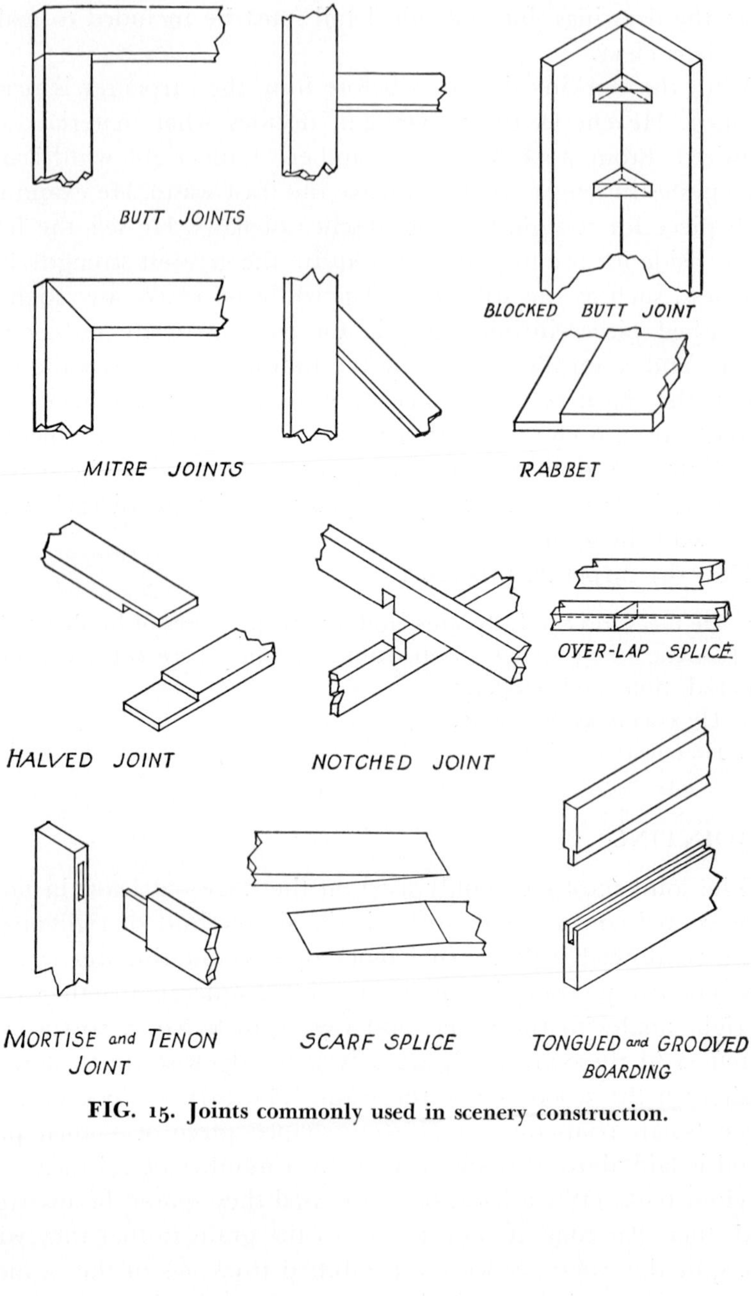

FIG. 15. Joints commonly used in scenery construction.

flat, heavy piece of iron, called a *clinching iron*, against the under side of the batten while driving the point of the nail. The easiest method is to drive all the nails part way in at first, while the frame is flat on the template, to keep the parts from slipping; then to lift the corner, place the iron underneath, and drive the nails in the rest of the way. If iron plates are built into the corners of the template, it is, of course, unnecessary to use an additional plate. The clinching helps to hold the joint rigid (Figure 16).

Corner blocks and keystones should be set in ¾ inches from the outer edge of the piece of scenery to which they are attached in order to make them fit the edges of other flats which may be butted up against them from behind.

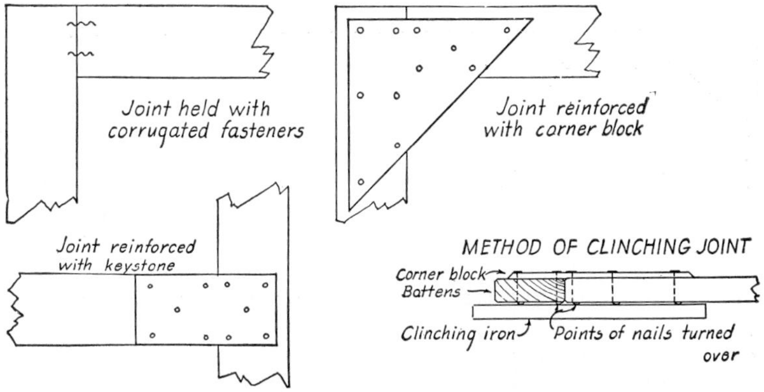

FIG. 16. Corner block and keystone reinforcements. The plyboard plates shown here are of the smaller, homemade, type. (See Sect. 8 and Fig. 33.)

The regular corner blocks and keystones mentioned above are rather expensive when secured from theatrical firms. Substitutes can be made easily at home from ¼-inch plywood. Corner blocks should be cut in triangles about 8″ x 8″ and keystones in rectangles 6″ x 3″. Sizes may be varied to suit needs. Composition board, such as beaver board, however, because it is not very tough, is of little use for reinforcing joints.

Screws hold more firmly than nails. Where real strength is required in joints which cannot be reinforced by corner blocks and keystones, such as those used to put door and window frames together, only screws should be used.

During the process of construction it is important to keep the frame absolutely square at all times. Corners should be tested frequently with the steel square. A flat that is even half an inch out of line will cause trouble when placed in the set.

After the jointing is completed, the frame is ready for covering and the application of the lashing hardware. It does not make much difference which is done first, although the usual practice is to apply the hardware before covering (Sections 7 and 8 and Figures 17 and 18).

7. COVERING

Covering is the term applied to the process of attaching a canvas face or surface to a frame. The method of covering a flat will be used to illustrate the steps in this process.

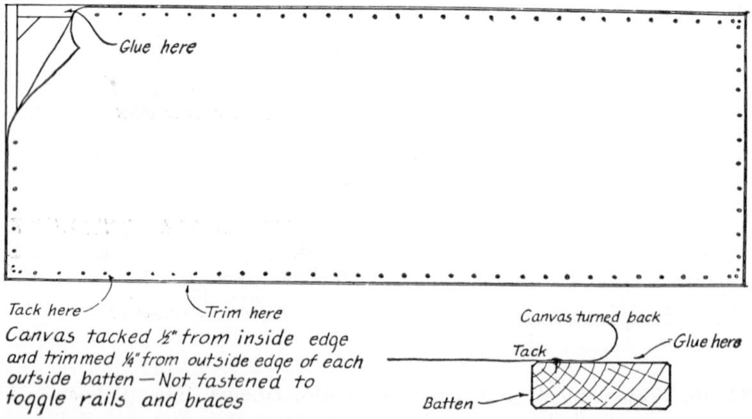

FIG. 17. Covering the frame. The canvas is stretched, tacked, and glued on the face of the frame, the other side from that on which the plywood reinforcements and hardware are placed.

a. Turn the frame over on its back so that the smooth side—the side without corner blocks and hardware—is facing up. Lay the canvas or muslin, which has been cut the proper length plus 2 inches or 3 inches, over this. The frame is presumably 69 inches (5′ 9″) wide while the cloth is 72 inches wide. Divide the difference, so that about 1½ inches extends over the frame all around. Stretch the canvas and fasten each corner with a No. 8 carpet tack, driven in part way only.

b. Now tack the canvas to the wood a half an inch from the inner edge of the frame all the way around. Keep the cloth pulled evenly. A good plan is to tack one end first, and to walk to the other end and stretch the canvas from the first row of tacks while driving in the second row. Repeat this process on the sides. It is unnecessary to draw the cloth extremely tight in covering because the first coat of paint will shrink it somewhat. Do not fasten the cloth to the toggle rail and the braces. Space the tacks about 6 inches apart.[3]

c. Remove the four temporary tacks in the corners and lay back the loose cloth. If the canvas has been properly secured to the wood, there should be a free flap about 4 inches wide all the way around. Two and one-half inches of this is pasted to the frame. To prepare an adhesive agent for this purpose mix 1 pound of flake or ground glue in 2 quarts of water in a pail, and cook this on a stove until it is thoroughly dissolved. Be careful that it does not burn. When glue burns, anyone two blocks away is aware of it. For safety's sake, it is well to put the vessel inside another containing a little water, in the double boiler manner, with a small block at the bottom of the larger vessel to prevent the inside pail from touching bottom. When the glue has completely dissolved, stir 1 pound of whiting into it.[4] Turn back the flap of muslin on the frame and apply the mixture, while it is still hot, evenly and generously to the wood with an old brush. Do not place any over the edge; apply to one surface only. If the paste seems thin, let it dry for a moment before applying the cloth to it. Use the edge of a keystone, covered with a rag dipped into warm water and wrung out, to rub over the glued area in order to make sure that the canvas sticks smoothly everywhere. Drive a couple of tacks into each corner, and trim the excess canvas with a sharp knife ¼ inch from the outer edge of the flat. This forces the cut edge into the wood, and prevents fraying when the set is handled.

Because wood does not take scene paint as well as cloth, all large wood surfaces, such as those on columns and steps, should likewise be covered with canvas. Brush the hot glue and whiting preparation over the surface to be covered and spread the canvas over it carefully; then pull the canvas tight, rub it down and tack it, trim the edges, and allow the glue to harden before painting.

[3] Some stage carpenters prefer to use, in place of hammer and tacks, the hand-operated compression stapler.

[4] An alternate mixture is made of flour (wallpaper) paste, sometimes reinforced with a little glue.

8. FASTENING THE UNITS TOGETHER

There are three principal ways by which one unit may be fastened to another: (1) by a lash line, (2) by a loose-pin hinge, and (3) by a carriage bolt (Figure 18).

1. Flat, standing scenery, and occasionally tall built pieces, are tied together by the lash line method. This method uses a piece of No. 8 sash cord, called the lash line, and a series of small metal plates or hooks, called lash cleats, placed parallel to each other near two adjacent edges. The lash line, attached to the upper-right-

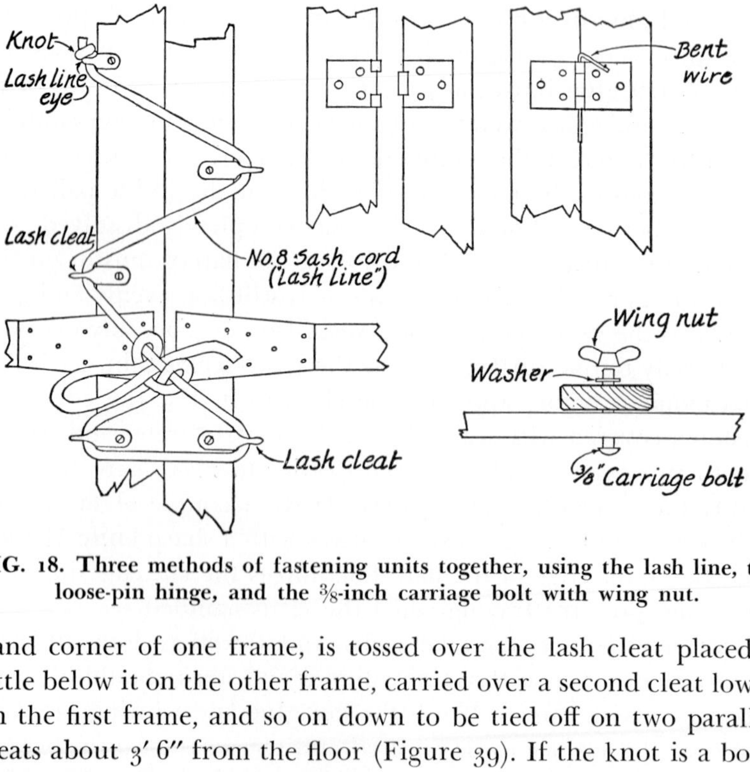

FIG. 18. Three methods of fastening units together, using the lash line, the loose-pin hinge, and the ⅜-inch carriage bolt with wing nut.

hand corner of one frame, is tossed over the lash cleat placed a little below it on the other frame, carried over a second cleat lower on the first frame, and so on down to be tied off on two parallel cleats about 3′ 6″ from the floor (Figure 39). If the knot is a bow, it may be quickly untied when the scene is struck (Chapter 12, Section 9). This method of lacing two flats or other large units together works very efficiently.

2. Certain small pieces, as well as most of the heavier units, such as platforms and stairs, are fastened to each other by what is commonly called the *pin-hinge*. The full title of this humble piece of hardware, however, is a "2-inch loose-pin back flap." One

half of the hinge is screwed to the edge of each unit and fastenings and unfastenings are made simply by inserting or removing the pin (Figure 18). As the regular pin fits so snugly that it is sometimes difficult to put it in and take it out quickly, a short piece of heavy annealed wire (a little smaller than the pin) is commonly used in its place. The top of the wire is bent over to prevent it from falling through.

3. Many structural units, particularly those designed to bear some weight or strain, such as stretchers and temporary braces for platforms and imitation beams, are fastened in place with ⅜-inch carriage bolts put through holes bored in the frames to be joined, and drawn tight with a wing nut over a washer (Figure 18).

B. SPECIFIC PRACTICE

9. FLATS—SINGLE FLATS AND WINGS

The height of a flat (Figure 19), which depends upon the size of the stage and the demands of the set for which it is designed, may be of practically any size (though seldom over 20 feet), but its width is usually not more than the standard 5′ 9″. This width is generally found to be the most satisfactory. It makes the flat easy to construct and cover, easy to handle, and easy to store (see Section 1).

For a flat 12 feet high, one should cut from white pine or other softwood stock (Section 2) the following:

2	battens	1″ x 3″ by 11′ 6″	with square ends	(stiles)
2	"	1″ x 3″ by 5′ 9″	" " "	(top and bottom rails)
1	"	1″ x 3″ by 5′ 3″	" " "	(toggle rail)
2	"	1″ x 2″ by 3′ 6″	with mitred ends	(corner braces)

Place the first four pieces on the template or the floor and put them together in the form of a rectangle, with the two 5′ 9″ rails lapping the two 11′ 6″ stiles, as illustrated in Figure 19. Making sure that the corners are absolutely square, first secure each joint by driving a couple of corrugated fasteners [5] across the seam, then reinforce it with a corner block in the manner which is described in Section 6. Place the 1″ x 3″ by 5′ 3″ piece (the toggle rail) be-

[5] There is a growing tendency in school and community theatre shops to omit the use of corrugated fasteners. If the joint must be held rigid before the clout nails are driven in, two or three thin wire nails can be used.

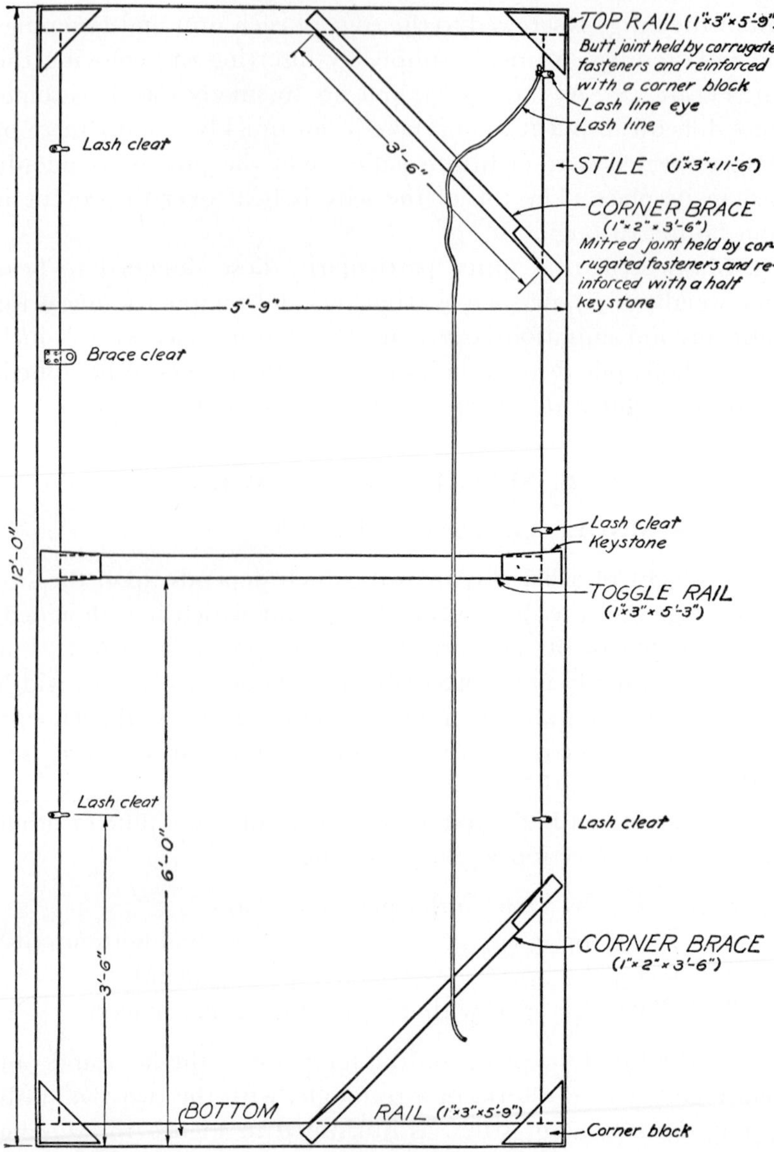

FIG. 19. Plain flat, rear elevation. The plywood reinforcements shown here are of the larger professional size. (See Chap. 4, Sect. 8.) Scale ½" = 1'.

tween the stiles 6′ from the bottom, and the two mitred 1″ x 2″ by 3′ 6″ pieces (corner braces) in the upper- and lower-right-hand corners. Secure the corner braces with corrugated fasteners but reinforce the joints with keystones (which fit better here) instead of with corner blocks. If one wishes to take the time, the edges of the blocks and keystones may be beveled off with a plane. If one flat is to be butted up against the back of another, to make a corner, the corner blocks and keystones along one edge of one of the flats should be set back ¾ inch (about the thickness of a batten) in order to permit making a snug joint (Section 6). If the flat is over 12 feet high, one or more additional toggle rails will be necessary. Toggles in the frame should not be more than 6 feet apart. They may be less.

Apply the hardware. Place a lash-line eye, or a screw eye with a ½-inch hole, in the upper-right-hand corner, a lash cleat just above the toggle rail on the same side, another one on the left side opposite a point halfway between the first two plates, and two more, one on each side, 3′ 6″ from the bottom of the bottom rail. If the frame is over 12 or 14 feet, of course additional lash cleats are required. Attach brace cleats only to flats which need special propping up by stage braces, such as those occupying a position in the center of a long straight wall, or those holding door frames. In an emergency, 6-penny finishing nails may be substituted for lash cleats, and screw eyes with 1-inch holes for brace cleats. It should be understood, however, that the use of this emergency hardware is distinctly makeshift.

Cut a length of No. 8 sash cord long enough to reach from the lash-line eye to within 3 inches of the floor, put one end through the hole in the hardware, and knot it to prevent it from pulling through. The method of lashing two flats together is described in Section 8.

When the hardware has been applied, turn the frame over and cover it with canvas on the smooth side, that is, the side without corner blocks and keystones (see Section 7).

A jog, a narrow flat, is constructed in the same general way as the larger unit.

A two-fold, a combination of two flats, is hinged so that the members fold face to face. Three or more 2-inch tight-pin back flaps are used to fasten the two frames together; and a 5-inch strip of canvas is glued and tacked carefully over the crack to prevent light from shining between the flats when the two-fold is set up. A three-fold is built in the same way, except that an extra 2-inch batten, called a *tumbler,* must be hinged between No. 2 and No. 3 flats to allow the latter to fold over the edge of No. 1 when the combination is closed and packed away. In this way whole walls are often constructed in one piece.

The special construction of flats for doors, windows, and fireplaces is shown in Figure 21.

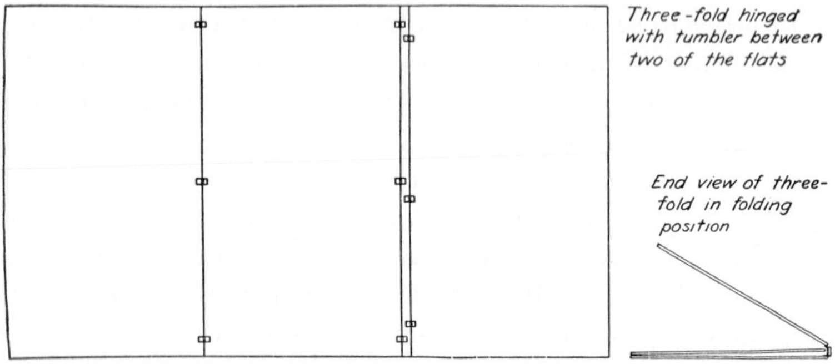

FIG. 20. The three-fold.

10. DOORWAYS

A door frame unit (Figure 22) consists of a solid *shutter* hung in a frame *casing,* built usually of 1″ x 4″ to 6″ white pine stock and plywood. A section of the casing itself (Figure 25) includes a box, or *thickness,* the part that fits into the wall; and a facing, or *trim,* parallel to the surface of the wall at right angles to the thickness. The door is set back in the casing, so that when the door is closed it shows the thickness; the door is commonly hinged in such a way that when it is opened it swings off and upstage.

Because the casing can be constructed to fit the shutter more easily than the shutter can be made to fit the casing, it is wise to build the shutter first. The most common form of door is the paneled one. It is made by fastening (by means of ¾-inch No. 9 screws) a sheet of plywood to the back of a light skeleton of 1″ x 4″ to 6″ stock, as illustrated in the drawing. The skeleton which represents the raised framework of the paneling should, if possible, be fastened together by means of mortise-and-tenon joints (glued and nailed without keystones). If tools for making this type of joint are not available, the 1″ x 4″ (to 6″) pieces may be attached

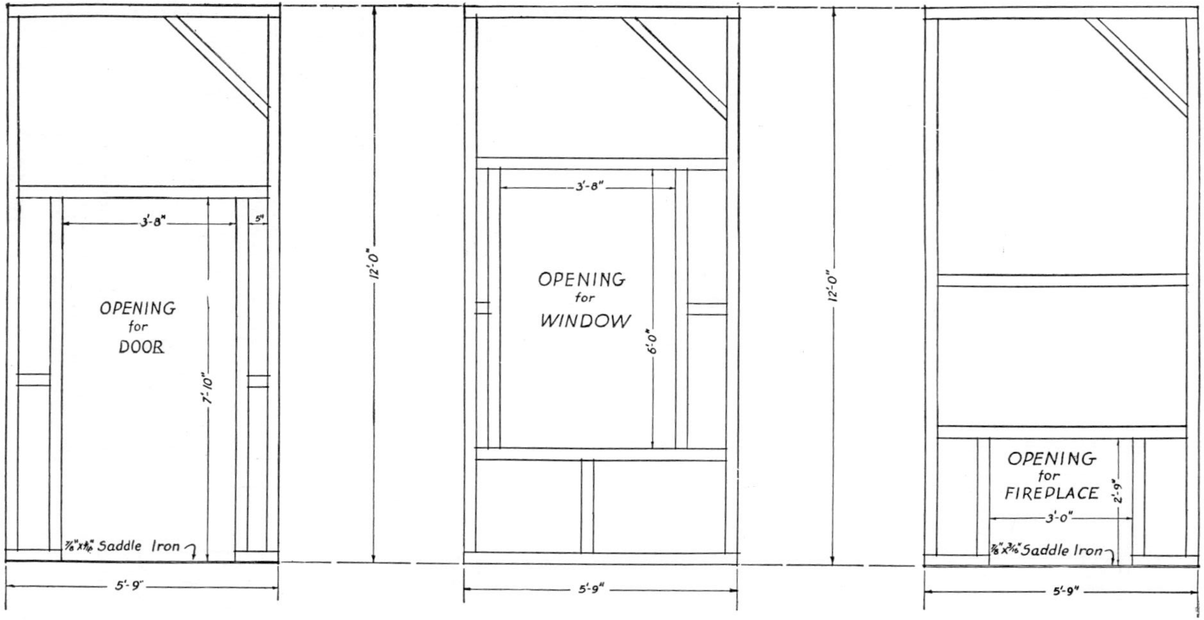

FIG. 21. Flats for a door, a window, and a fireplace, rear elevation. All joints are reinforced with corner blocks and keystones. Scale 1/4" = 1'.

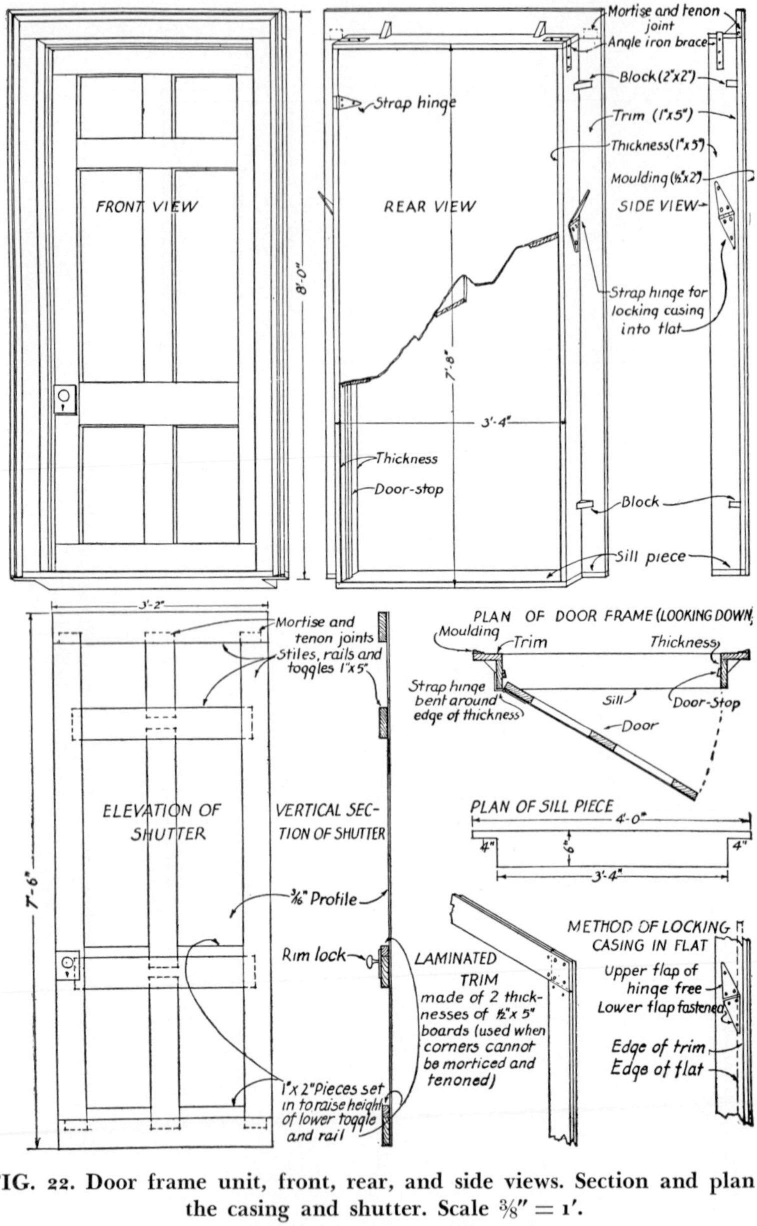

FIG. 22. Door frame unit, front, rear, and side views. Section and plan of the casing and shutter. Scale 3/8" = 1'.

directly to the plywood. Fasten each piece of the heavier wood to this board with a couple of nails, then turn the door over and secure all the pieces with screws. If the latter method of building a shutter is employed, be certain that the sheet of plywood selected for the back is absolutely flat, and heavy enough to keep the shutter hanging true. If a door of any size is to be made this way, it is wise to use plywood of ½″ thickness, instead of the usual lighter wood. Good ready-build shutters can often be picked up quite reasonably at the lumberyard. The only disadvantage of stock doors is that, being built for long wear, they are apt to be heavy.

The casing, as has already been stated, is built in two parts—a thickness and a trim. The thickness, made just large enough to fit the shutter comfortably, is constructed first. Out of 1″ x 4″ (to 6″) stock (or heavier if the door unit is to be large) cut three straight pieces for the two sides and the top, and a winged piece for the bottom. The width of the last piece should be that of the others, plus the width of the trim. Put the four pieces together with right-angle box (butt) joints held by 1½-inch No. 9 screws. Wood splits very easily when long screws are driven into it. To prevent this from happening, first make a hole by using a hand drill with a ⅛-inch bit or by driving in and drawing out a 6-penny nail, and then inserting the screw. The head and the sill should lap the edges of the jambs. The sill is attached in such a way that its extra width extends to the front. The trim is fastened with screws to the thickness, at right angles to the latter, all the way around except across the bottom. Its lower edges meet the two narrow wings on the sill. The latter is secured to the former by means of 1¾-inch No. 9 screws put through from below. The sill piece (sometimes called the *saddle*) will sit more steadily on the saddle iron of the flat into which the door frame is placed if a shallow groove is cut in the bottom of the sill.

Use mortise-and-tenon joints, if possible, for fastening together the three members composing the trim. If this cannot be done, build the trim out of two layers of ½-inch stock and lap the corners. That is, cut the three pieces for the first layer so that the two side pieces will extend the full height of the trim and the top piece will fit between them, and cut the three pieces for the second layer so that the top piece will extend the full width, and the side pieces will fit below it. Firm corner joints will be obtained if the second layer is bound to the first by a number of screws, or by

1¼″ lath nails driven through and clinched on the under side (Section 6, and Figure 16). For further strengthening, a few 2″ x 2″, or larger, rectangular or triangular blocks may be placed in the angle formed by the meeting of the thickness and the trim.

The shutter is hung in the casing by means of two 6-inch strap hinges usually placed on the outside. One flap of each hinge is fastened to the shutter, and the other flap is carried over the edge of the thickness, bent, and attached to the side of the latter. Small strips of ¾″ x ⅜″ wood, called door stops, are nailed around the inside of the casing to prevent the door from swinging the wrong way.

The appearance of a door unit is usually very much improved by the addition of a little molding.

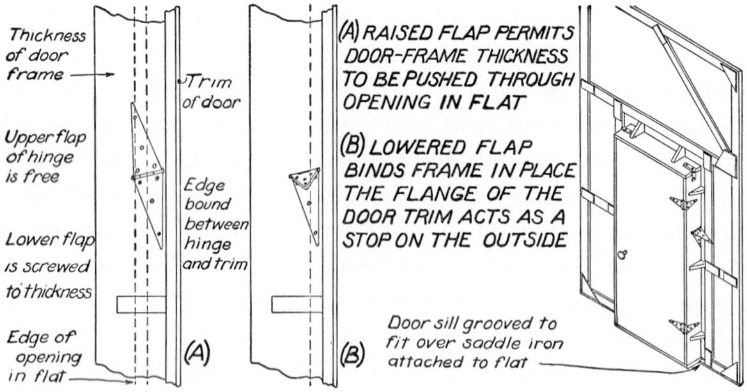

FIG. 23. Strap hinge method of locking door, window, and fireplace frames into their flats.

Both door and window units are contrived to lock into their respective flats. To make this possible the 6-inch strap hinge is again brought into use. One of these hinges is fastened to the thickness, part way up, on each side (Figures 22 and 23). It is set at an angle, as illustrated, and only the lower flap is screwed to the wood, the upper flap remaining free. In setting the scene the free flaps are raised, the thickness part of the frame is put through the opening in the flat, and the free flaps of the hinges are lowered to bind the door and casing against the 1″ x 3″ upright battens of the flat that form the sides of the opening. The trim, resting against the surface of the flat on the inside, prevents the frame from falling out.

In order to permit room for the strap hinges and the little rectangular reinforcement blocks in the angle of the trim and thickness on the casing, and to make it possible to lift door and window frames out and in easily, the openings in the flats should be a little larger than the height and width of the thicknesses. Allow about 2½ inches clearance all the way around. That is, if the over-all measurement of the part of the door frame that comes through it is 7′ 8″ x 3′ 4″, the opening in the flat should be 7′ 10½″ x 3′ 9″. If the little rectangular reinforcement blocks are not used on the casing, a clearance of 1 inch all the way around will be ample.

If a door unit is to be left in a flat through the whole of a performance and set or flied with the flat (as is often done), the door unit may be fastened in place by means of two or four ⅜-inch bolts (put through the trim of the door unit and the frame of the flat), instead of the strap hinges.

A door unit should be well made. If it is loosely put together, it will sag after a little use, and the shutter will bind against the casing. A firmly constructed unit, on the other hand, will last for years.

The construction of a flat designed to hold a door frame is illustrated in Figure 21. Notice that the usual toggle rail is raised to form the top of the opening and two extra uprights are placed between this and the bottom rail. The part of the bottom rail between the uprights is cut away. In order to prevent the two legs from racking, a 5-foot, 9-inch piece of ⅞″ x 3⁄16″ soft steel called a "saddle iron," drilled and countersunk to accommodate No. 9 wood screws, is fastened to the bottom edge.

11. WINDOWS

A typical double-hung window unit (Figure 24) consists of two sash frames sliding between ¼″ x ¾″ and ¾″ x ⅜″ strips of wood (called a window stop and a parting strip) in a casing which is similar to that used with the door (see Figure 25). The general plan of construction for both units is the same. Sash weights and other hardware are seldom used on windows. If one sash must be raised, it can be held in place temporarily by means of a nail, or some other simple fastening. Because real glass is shattered so easily, it is desirable to use in its place galvanized wire screening

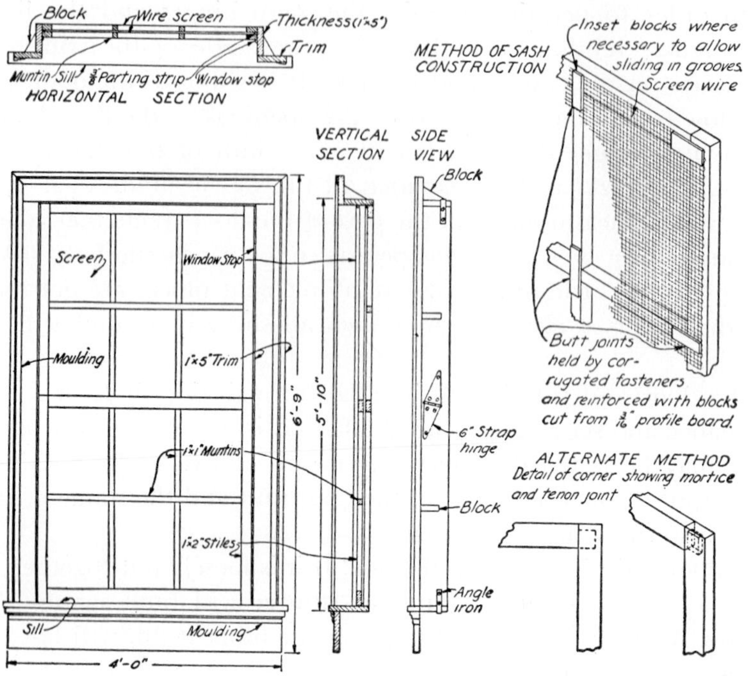

FIG. 24. Window frame unit, front and side elevations. Plan and section of a double-hung window. Scale ⅜″ = 1′.

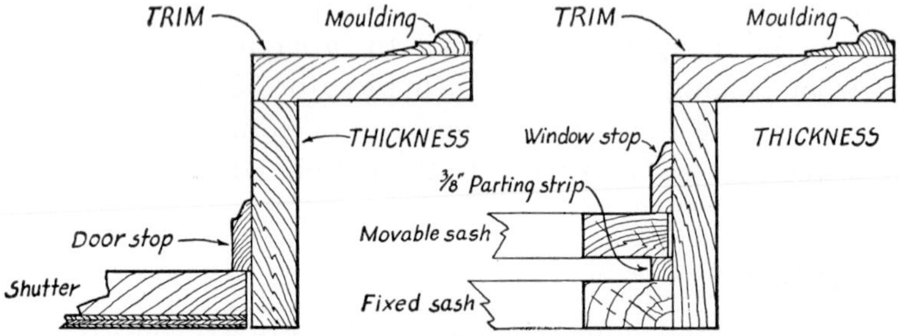

FIG. 25. Door and window casings. A comparison of the two jambs in cross section. Scale 2″ = 1′.

(or pearl screening, or translucent plastic sheet) tacked to the back of each sash.

The unit is said to be *practical* if it can be opened, *impractical* if it is permanently closed. The window casing is fastened into its flat by either the strap-hinges or the bolt method described in the preceding section.

12. FIREPLACES

A fireplace is constructed by nailing or screwing plywood over a light framework of 1″ x 3″ battens (Figure 26). After a mantel cut from 1″ x 8″ or 10″ stock is fastened in place, the unit is dressed up with molding and any additional woodwork desired.

The fireplace is used with a flat cut for it (Figure 21). If the fireplace is of the type that extends out a few inches from the wall, it will stand safely by itself, especially if its bottom is given a slight rake so that it leans backwards. If it is of the other type, however, such as the one pictured, it is safer to construct it with a 6-inch permanent thickness, and to mount on the outer sides of this two 6-inch strap hinges, to clamp the frame into the flat in the same manner as door and window frames.

A small three-fold screen daubed with gray and black serves as a backing for the opening. If the thickness described above is used, it must be painted to match this.

13. CEILINGS

In old-fashioned interiors the space above the wings or flats was masked by a series of vertical cloth strips called *borders.* Modern practice, however, uses the more realistic ceiling piece to close in the set above. Attached to two or three sets of lines, it is raised and lowered horizontally.

The more common type for small stages is the *roll ceiling* (Figure 27). Its construction is simple. A large sheet of canvas, made by sewing together several widths, with seams running lengthwise, is tacked and glued to two long 1″ x 4″ battens, one at the upstage edge and one at the down. If the ceiling is to be of any length—over 20 or 22 feet, for instance—each of these battens may be made of two shorter lengths spliced together with a scarf splice (Figure 15). Three or more 1″ x 3″ battens, called *stretchers,* cut the width of the ceiling minus 8 inches (the combined width of the two longitudinal battens), are laid across between the longitudinal battens and bolted to them. A ceiling plate, one half of which is attached to an end of each stretcher by means of ¾-inch No. 9 screws (reinforced with 3/16-inch stove bolts if the ceiling is heavy), laps the edge of the longitudinal batten and is fastened to the latter by a ⅜-inch carriage bolt, which passes

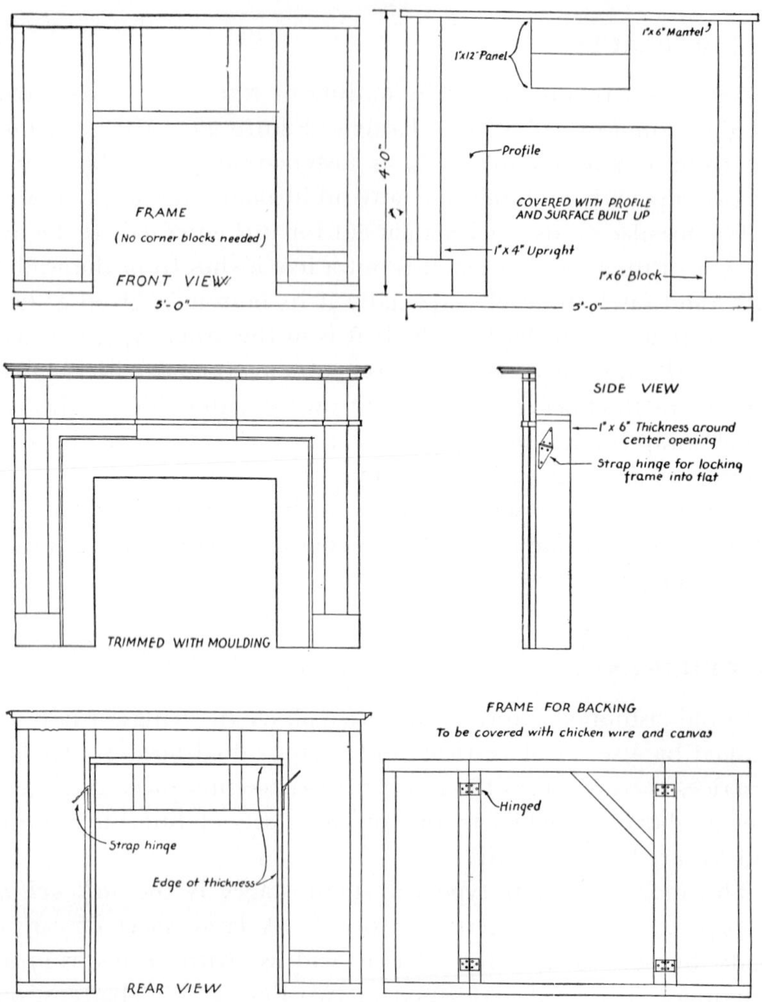

FIG. 26. Fireplace unit, showing the method of building it up from a flat frame. Also a hinged backing. (The "profile" indicated in the second drawing at the top is plywood. Scale 3/8" = 1'.)

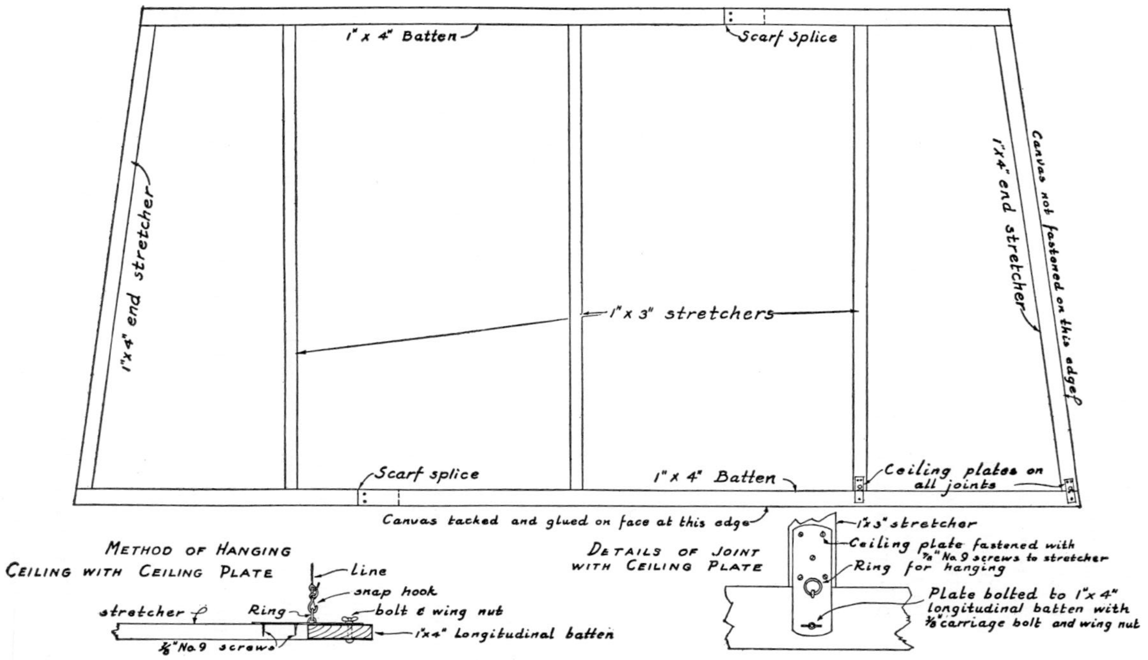

FIG. 27. Plan for a roll ceiling, looking down from above. When the stretchers are removed this type of ceiling may be rolled up on the longitudinal battens. Very large or heavy ceilings may be braced on the back with 1" x 3" stiffeners fastened on edge to the stretchers by means of loose-pin hinges. Scale ¼" = 1'.

through a hole in the wood and is drawn up tight with a wing nut above the plate. Stretchers are not attached to the canvas. Therefore, they should be long enough to make a snug fit, and so prevent a sag in the cloth. The outer edge of this canvas at the sides can be fastened temporarily to the last two stretchers by a few tacks driven in part way.

If the ceiling is very wide, two stiffeners (1″ x 3″ battens on edge) may be pin-hinged across the stretchers to prevent sagging.

To fly the ceiling, two sets of lines with snap hooks are lowered and attached to rings in the plates. When the frame is in use, it is handled in a horizontal position. When it is not in use, one set

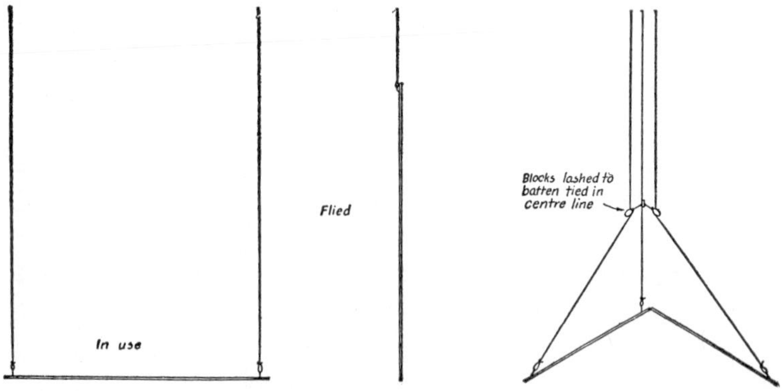

FIG. 28. Roll and book ceilings, the methods by which they are hung and flied. End view.

of lines is detached and it is flied out of the way vertically like a drop. When the ceiling is taken on tour, it is lowered, the stretchers are removed, and the canvas is rolled up on the two long battens.

Three virtues which should exist in every good ceiling are: lightness, tautness, and size sufficient to cover the whole set (except the backings) comfortably.

14. DROPS AND BORDERS

If possible, drops (Figure 29) should be made of good duck or linen canvas, not muslin, because the material must be strong enough to support itself without the aid of a frame. To prevent wrinkling in hanging, seam the cloth horizontally. Use single

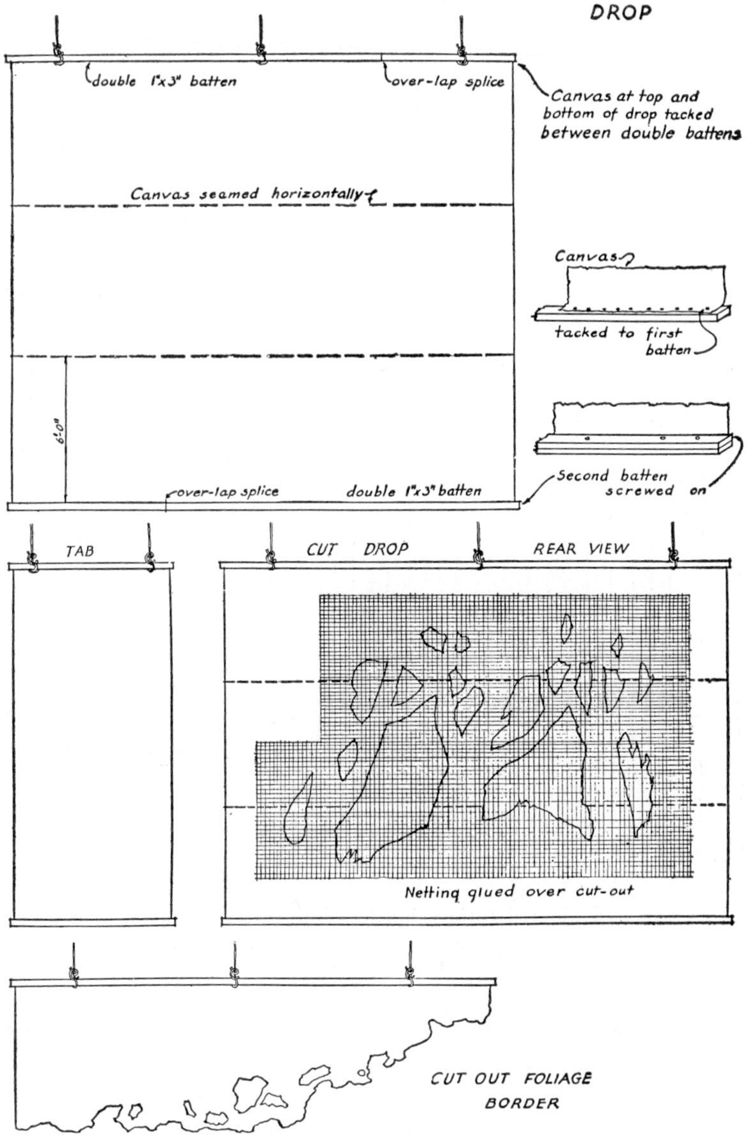

FIG. 29. Plain and cut drops, a cut border, and a tab. The units shown here are considerably smaller in scale than those in general use on full-size stages. Scale 1/8" = 1'.

straight seams and keep all the selvage edges on the back. Tack the cloth between double 1″ x 3″ or 4″ battens at the top and bottom, taking great care to avoid puckers. The battens are fastened together with 1½-inch No. 9 screws. If the wood strips are not long enough to reach the full width of the drop, they may be spliced with the usual scarf splice, or an overlap splice, but preferably the former (Figure 15).

Tapering the drop slightly, that is, making the top two feet longer than the bottom, will cause the side edges to hang straighter.

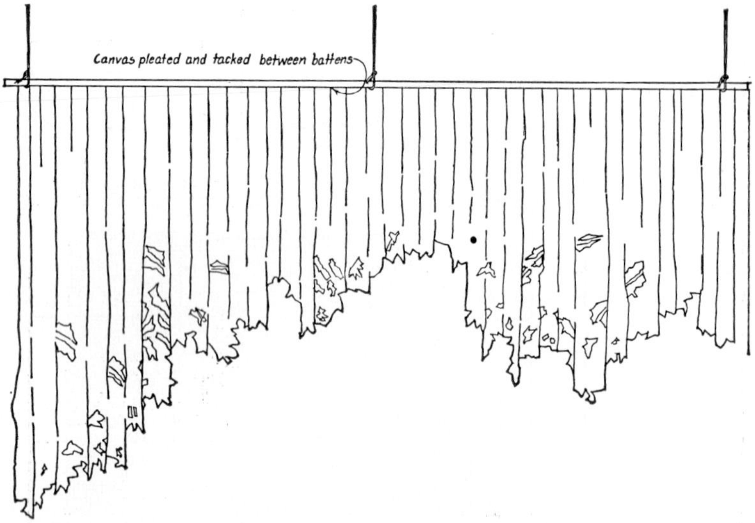

FIG. 30. Cut and pleated foliage border. Interesting effects can be obtained with this type of foliage piece by draping one or both ends of the canvas. Scale ⅛″ = 1′.

If a drop is cut, it should be backed by a large piece of netting or scrim (depending upon whether a clear or a misty effect is desired) which should extend over the entire open space and support the free branches and bits of foliage (or whatever the elements represent) that compose the silhouette. To attach the netting, turn the drop on its face and glue the netting to the back of the drop with some flexible adhesive agent. Rosine, a preparation which is made especially for this purpose and can be secured from any stage hardware company, is generally employed. It is melted for use in the double boiled arrangement which is described in the section on "Covering" (Section 7), and applied with a brush. Some of the cold water pastes are fair substitutes. Whatever the agent is, it should be flexible enough not to crack when the drop is rolled. If the netting used is of the large mesh variety, it will be necessary to attach it to the drop by gluing little strips of cloth over the areas to be fastened.

The *border* is made in the form of a shallow drop, commonly of only one width of 72-inch canvas, with no battens at the bottom. Except as an occasional foliage or masking piece, the border is not used very much now and its name is often appropriated for other service. On a modern stage the simple term *border* is commonly used to refer to a striplight or row of spotlights hanging on a pipe batten overhead (Chapter 17, Section 3). To distinguish it, the canvas border is now commonly called a "cloth border."

The *tab* is made in the form of a narrow drop or border.

Drops, borders, and tabs are flied by attaching sets of lines to their upper battens (Chapter 12, Sections 5–6).

15. CYCLORAMAS

Cycloramas, or *cycs,* are made of a variety of cloth materials hung from U-shaped wood or metal frames. They are commonly wide enough to reach well beyond the tormentors into each wing, and generally high enough to require no masking above, other than that offered by the teaser and perhaps a border. Made in several different forms, they serve a number of purposes.

The most common form is the drapery or curtain cyclorama (Figure 31). The cloth material, usually a dyed fabric with a surface texture that takes stage lighting well—such as velvet, flannel, poplin, monk's cloth, silk, satin, or duvetyn—is put together in vertical seams, reinforced with a strip of webbing at the top, and tied to the cyc frame by short cords which pass through grommeted holes along the webbed edge of the cloth. The grommets are placed 6 to 12 inches apart.

The frame itself is commonly made of three 1″ x 4″ battens, single or double depending on the reach and the weight of the draperies. A long batten supports the material at the rear, and two shorter ones, the *arms,* pivoted to its ends with 5″ to 8″ strap hinges, carry the material downstage and off.

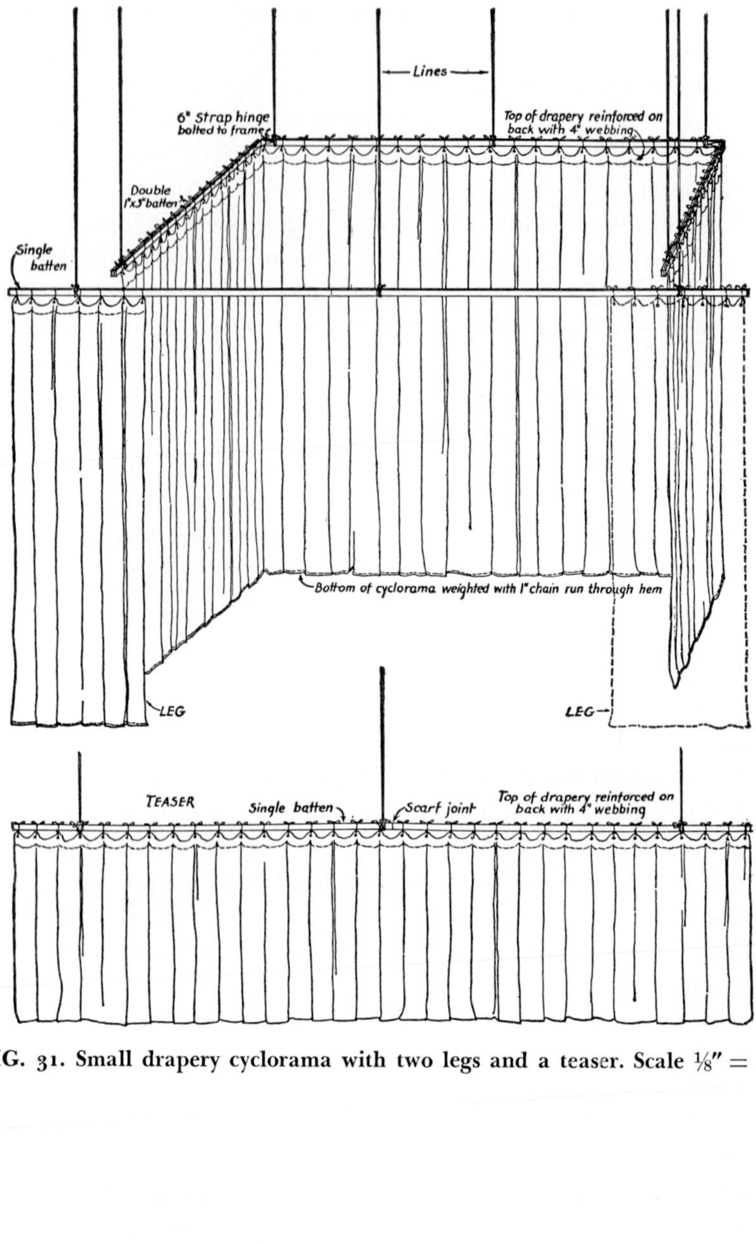

FIG. 31. Small drapery cyclorama with two legs and a teaser. Scale ⅛″ = 1′.

As draperies are nearly always hung in folds, sufficient material must be ordered to allow for the gathering ("fullness")—generally twice the total width of the cyclorama. The bottom should be weighted with about a 1-inch chain run through a strong hem.

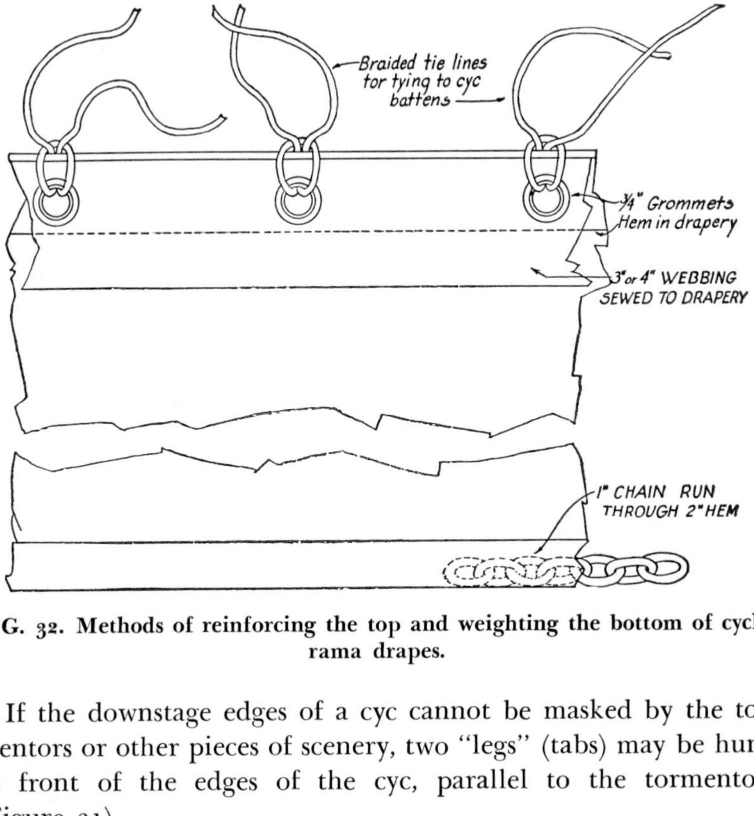

FIG. 32. Methods of reinforcing the top and weighting the bottom of cyclorama drapes.

If the downstage edges of a cyc cannot be masked by the tormentors or other pieces of scenery, two "legs" (tabs) may be hung in front of the edges of the cyc, parallel to the tormentors (Figure 31).

16. PLATFORMS

A platform (Figure 33) must be light and collapsible, but strong enough to support safely the maximum weight for which it is intended. If it is to be large, it is made up of a number of smaller, more portable parts, which may be assembled quickly in a performance to form the larger structure.

In unit form, a platform consists of two parts: a *platform top,* the floor piece on which actors stand and walk; and a *parallel,* the light folding trestle which supports this. The construction of the parallel is illustrated in the drawing. Each of the five sections is made out of 1″ x 3″ wood strips, cut and put together in the pattern shown. The parts are butt jointed, fastened with ¾-inch No. 5 corrugated fasteners, and reinforced with the usual corner blocks. Each frame is made rigid by diagonal 1″ x 2″ braces in its upper corners. (The corrugated fasteners can be omitted.)

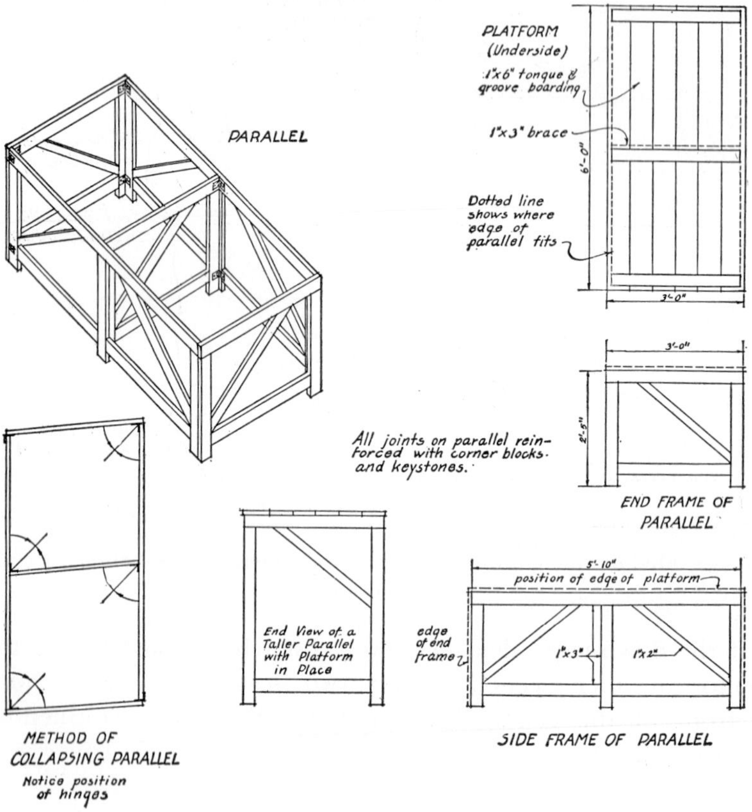

FIG. 33. Platform unit. Scale ¼″ = 1′.

The five sections are fastened together with 2-inch black-flaps, and secured with ¾-inch No. 9 screws, two hinges being placed at each corner. The two end sections overlap the edges of the side sections, in order to make square outside corners. With this arrangement it is important that the hinges be placed as shown, otherwise the parallel will not fold. It should close one way only.

The platform top is made of 1″ x 6″ tongue-and-groove stock, held together by 1″ x 3″ cross battens fastened with 1½-inch No. 9

screws. As the cross braces must fit inside the edge of the parallel, they should be cut so that they will be an inch shorter at each end than the width of the platform. Care must also be taken to see that the center brace clears the edge of the middle section of the parallel.

If one or more sides of a platform are to be in view of the audience, the visible face, or faces, of the parallel may be covered with plywood. This should be attached in such a way that it will not interfere with the folding of the parallel.

The inclined platform, or runway, called a *ramp,* is made similar to the platform just described.

17. STEPS AND STAIRS

The principal parts of a simple flight of stairs are the *stringers,* the parallel planks which support the steps; the *treads,* the horizontal boards that form the steps; and the *risers,* the vertical boards that connect the treads.

Figure 34 shows a common method of construction. Each step is made by nailing a 1″ x 8″ to 12″ tread across two or more stringers cut from 1″ x 10″ stock, in such a way as to allow about an inch of the front edge of the tread to overhang the step below. If the step is over 30 inches wide, one or more additional stringers are placed between the outside two. Risers, because they bear no weight, are made of ¼″ plywood. There is no absolute standard for dimensions of steps. Their height and depth depend on the pitch required of a flight of steps. The amount of 17 inches is frequently employed, however, as a standard over-all measurement of a tread and its adjacent riser; that is, if the tread is to be 12 inches deep, the riser will be 5 inches high, if the tread is to be 9 inches deep, the riser will be 8 inches high, and so on.

A flight of stairs, unless it is supported independently, is made to fasten to the platform to which it leads. A 1″ x 4″ batten is fastened with 1½-inch No. 9 screws across the stringers at the top, under the edge of the last tread, and a similar batten is placed just below its level on the parallel. A couple of brace cleats are screwed to the second batten (on the parallel). To attach the stairs to the platform, the head of the former is lifted and slipped over the cleats of the batten on the parallel. In this position, one batten rests on top of the other. The cleats prevent them from slipping

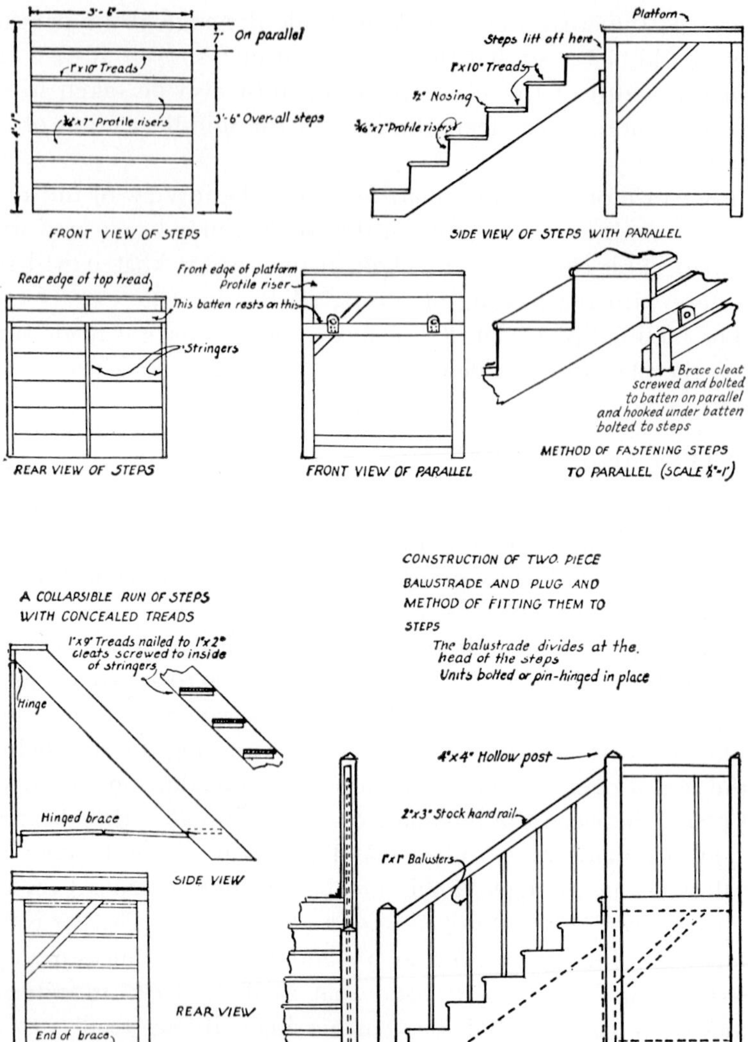

FIG. 34. Stationary and collapsible runs of steps, a balustrade, and a plug. Scale ¼″ = 1′.

apart. The parallel should be well anchored with stage braces to prevent it from tipping over.

If a long flight of steps is to be constructed, it is planned as a number of unit runs and parallels. When assembled, they are fastened together by 2-inch loose-pin hinges or ⅜-inch carriage bolts (Section 8). Balustrades, also, are made separately, attached to the edge of 1″ x 10″ planks, and fastened to the flight of steps with similar hardware. When the side of a staircase is in view of the audience, the entire construction work may be concealed by a triangular flat *(plug)* fastened by loose-pin hinges to the face of the staircase. The balustrade may be constructed as a part of this unit.

A narrow stairway which does not have to reveal its steps from the side may be built without cut stringers. The treads are merely nailed to cleats screwed to the inside of the straight stringers. A small, portable unit, constructed on this plan, is illustrated in the drawing.

Steps should be covered with canvas before being painted. The canvas should be glued with dope to the wood.

18. COLUMNS

A column (Figure 35) is constructed by nailing wide sheets of ¼-inch plywood around a light cylindrical frame. Wooden discs or rings, each made up of several pieces of 1″ x 6″ to 10″ stock fastened together with corrugated fasteners, form the core of the column. They are spaced at intervals equal to the width of the plywood sheets, and held in place by 1″ x 2″ strips running the length of the unit. The plywood sheets are wrapped around this core and nailed to the edge of the discs, or rings, as well as seamed along the strips. The column viewed from one side only needs but one good face. In fact, small columns are often made in halves, that is, formed around half discs, called "half-rounds." This type of column, if it is not held erect by some other structure above, is secured by a brace cleat and stage brace fastened on the blind side (the side away from the spectators). The column should be covered with canvas before it is painted.

Columns are frequently constructed also in the form of simple canvas cylinders stretched between solid bases secured to the floor and wooden discs or frames attached to ropes in the flies. Cloth

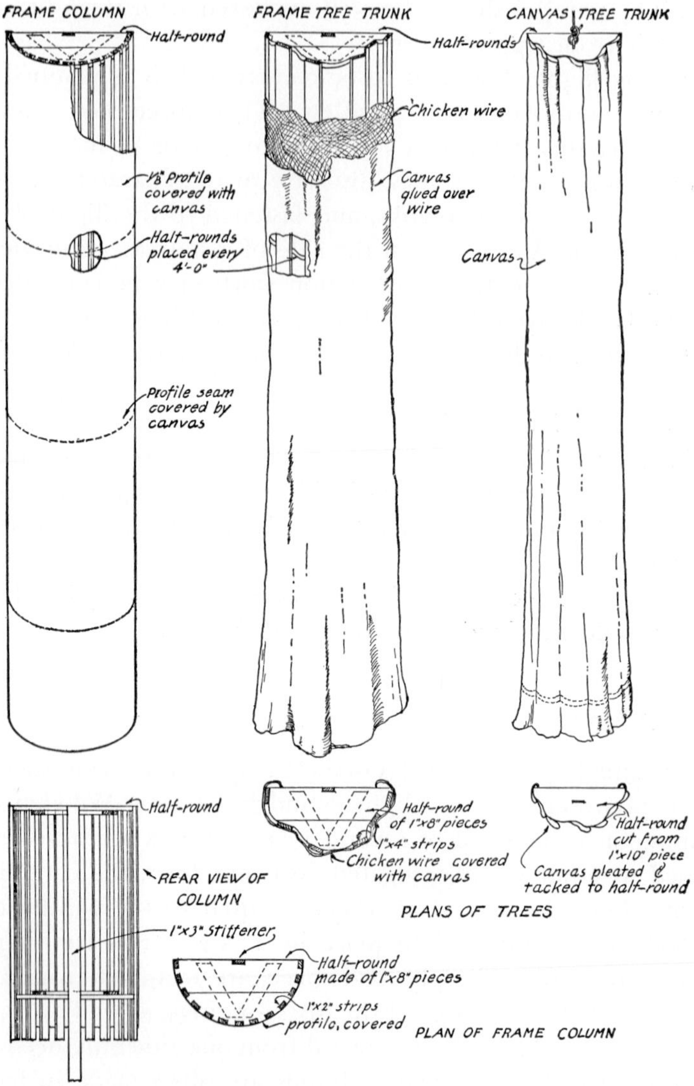

FIG. 35. Frame column, and a frame and a collapsible tree trunk. The "profile" indicated in the drawings of the column is plywood. Scale 1/4" = 1'.

columns are practicable only, of course, in positions where actors are not likely to lean or brush against them.

19. TREE TRUNKS AND FOLIAGE

The construction of a "solid" tree trunk (Figure 35) involves the same principles as those employed in the building of a column, except that a more irregular "core" is often used, and chicken wire and canvas are employed instead of plywood. Irregularities, such as knots and excrescences, are built up on the half-cylindrical frame, then chicken wire is tacked over the whole thing with ½-inch staples. Small pieces of scrap canvas are dipped into the hot glue preparation which is described in Section 7 and pasted, with their edges lapping, in irregular patterns over the wire. When this dries, a hard, uneven surface remains on which can be painted a suggestion of bark. This type of trunk is held erect with the help of a brace cleat and a stage brace on the blind side.

If the tree trunk called for in the design occupies a position on the stage where the audience cannot scrutinize it too closely and where no actor will brush against it, it is possible to substitute a much more easily built collapsible form for the rather elaborate framed kind described above. A wide strip of canvas is tacked in irregular pleats around notched discs at the top and bottom and hung by means of a screw eye to a line in the flies.

Realistic foliage is difficult to create on the stage, except in very expensive ways, and modern scenic artists consequently avoid its use as much as possible. Showing the lower portions of several realistic tree trunks in the foreground, the designer attempts merely to suggest masses of leaves and shrubbery in the background by using well-shadowed cut-out drops kept discretely behind much scrim. Where foliage must be shown downstage, cut-out cloth borders can be hung in silhouette. The canvas is frequently gathered or draped, after it is cut, to add to the depth of the foliage (Figure 30). The effect secured, especially in fairly dim scenes, is sometimes quite convincing.

Bushes and smaller shrubbery units may be constructed out of actual branches or sticks wired together and shaped up with papier-mâché, in accordance with the artist's design. To this skeleton are attached—by means of short lengths of fine wire—pieces of greenery secured from any concern that makes artificial flowers, or leaf and blossom forms cut from glue-stiffened cloth, felt, or crepe paper. The bush is then painted.

Short lengths of vine and little plants can be made best out of artificial foliage materials bought in the five and ten cent store. At twenty cents a sprig, however, their cost precludes their use for quantitative effects.

20. ROCKS AND BUILT-UP GROUND

Rocks and built-up ground (Figure 36) are made by covering light, irregular frames of 1″ x 3″ stock with chicken wire tacked down with ½-inch staples, and covering the wire, in turn, with small pieces of canvas dipped in a mixture of hot glue and whiting, in much the same way as tree trunks are built. If the rock or ground is to be walked on, care must be taken to make the framework strong and rigid. The standard method for building a practical rock is to start with a number of vertical three- or four-sided frames, similar (except that these are irregular) to the sections of a parallel (Section 16). They are of different heights, some straight, some inclined, and some pointed. Placed edge to edge and edge to side, lengthwise and across, they are fastened together with nails, or better, with 1½-inch No. 9 screws. In the parts of the rock that must be practical, additional battens are nailed at short intervals between sections, and these are covered with pieces of planking arranged in different planes. If the rock is large, it should be made in a number of smaller units, pin-hinged or bolted together. Tufts and folds of brown burlap or felt attached to the surface here and there may be made to suggest patches of earth and knots of grass.

21. GROUND ROWS

Ground rows and other silhouette pieces (Figure 37) are made by nailing 3/16- or ¼-inch plywood over flat frames of 1″ x 3″ stock, which are put together with corrugated fasteners and reinforced with corner blocks in the usual way (Section 6). The silhouettes are then painted and the outlines are finally cut out with a compass saw. The unit is made to stand up by hinging a triangular brace, called a *jack,* to its back. Small units may use an angle iron in place of the jack.

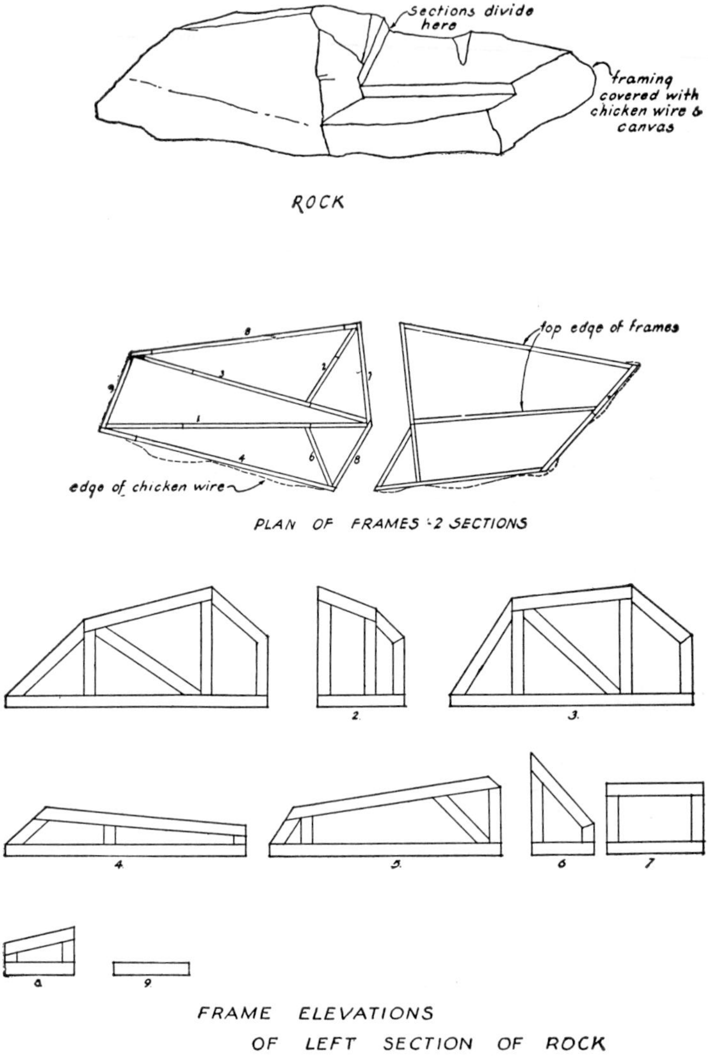

FIG. 36. Frame rock in two sections. Scale ¼″ = 1′.

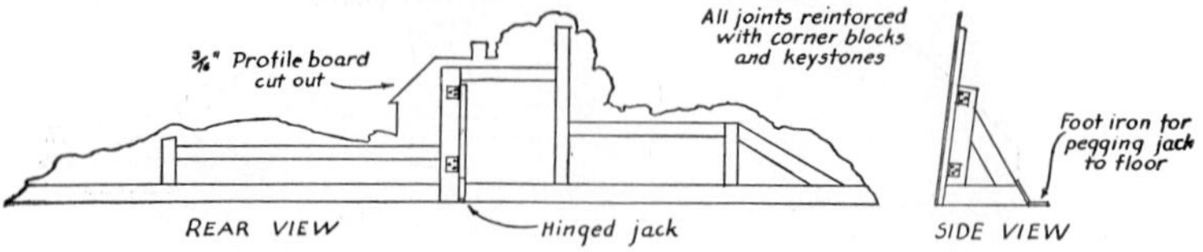

FIG. 37. Ground row, rear and side elevations. (What is designated here as cut-out "profile board" is ¼" plywood.) Scale ¼" = 1′.

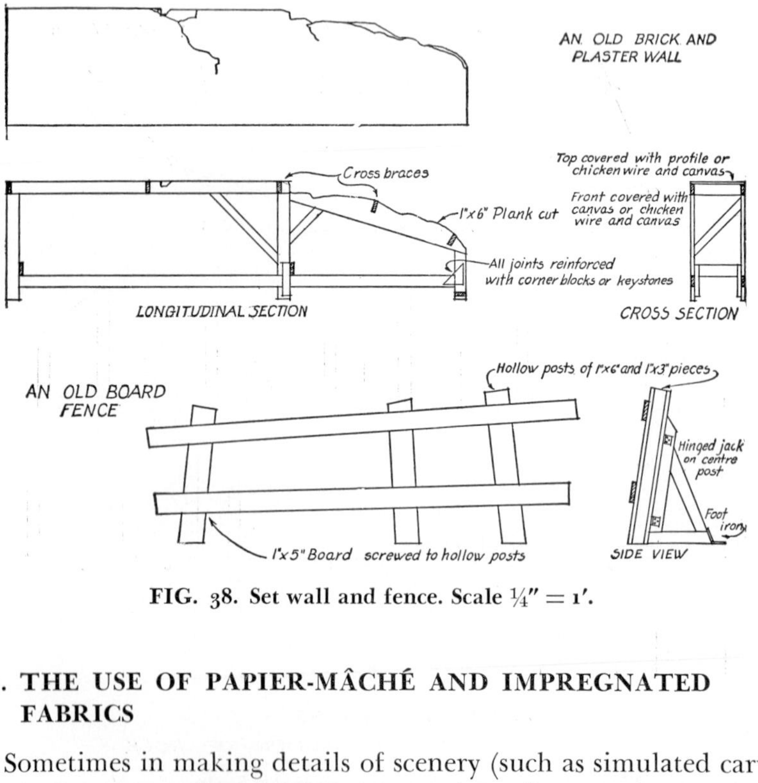

FIG. 38. Set wall and fence. Scale ¼" = 1′.

22. THE USE OF PAPIER-MÂCHÉ AND IMPREGNATED FABRICS

Sometimes in making details of scenery (such as simulated carvings), but more often in the construction of properties (such as statues, urns, ornamented platters, and masks) the shop worker will wish to do some molding which cannot be done with either wood or canvas. In these cases he will find papier-mâché very useful.

Papier-mâché is prepared by cutting or tearing long strips of newspaper from ½ inch to 2 inches wide (depending on the fineness of the molding desired) and soaking these in a mixture of thick *size water* and a little whiting. This mixture is similar to the dope used for gluing down the canvas edges of flats, except that it is a little thinner. In place of this mixture one can use flour paste. The paper strips are torn into easily manageable lengths and pasted on the object to be shaped, one strip crossing the one beneath it to insure strength. Commonly, three or four layers of paper are required. It will take at least twenty-four hours for the papier-mâché to dry, and it may take several days.

If the object to be molded is of any considerable size it should have an armature (interior framework) of wood and chicken wire, worked into a shape approximating the form desired. Unwanted hollows can be filled and desired bulges and projections can be created with twists or clumps of newspaper tied into place. The paper strips are then pasted over all of this.

Such forms as masks cannot have, of course, any underlying framework. They may be made directly on a preliminary molding made of modeling clay (coated with a little Vaseline), allowed to dry, then lifted off. Since the clay itself is moist, however, the coating of paper strips may take a long time to dry. Sometimes it is better first to make a plaster cast of the clay form, to allow this to set and dry, then to cover the inside of it with a thin coating of Vaseline, and to paste the papier-mâché strips in the mold.

Papier-mâché has the advantages of being cheap and easy to work with. It has also certain disadvantages. It is not too strong, it is not waterproof, and when it is stored it is tempting food for rats. A new medium which has none of these disadvantages is an impregnated fabric now being manufactured under several trade names. The best of the products on the market is Celastic, which is extremely rugged, sheds water, and lasts like iron. Celastic may be purchased in sheets of various sizes and various widths. That which is needed is cut off, soaked in a liquid called Box Toe Softener, then applied to the mold and allowed to dry, like papier-mâché. Since Celastic is much stronger than paper, it does not need to be cut into strips pasted one over the other, but it should be applied in small enough pieces to make wrinkling unnecessary. To prevent the Celastic from sticking to the mold, one must coat the mold with Parting Agent before the pieces of the impregnated cloth are put on.

QUESTIONS AND EXERCISES

1. Name and explain six practical requirements which must be kept in mind when scenery is constructed.
2. What kinds of lumber are used in the construction of scenery?
3. What are the most common covering materials for scenery?
4. Name and describe several common pieces of hardware for scenery.
5. Tell how one makes a simple butt joint, and how one may reinforce this with a corner block or keystone. Better still, demonstrate the making of this joint with actual materials in the shop.
6. Tell, or show, how a flat is covered.
7. Tell, or show, how two units of scenery may be fastened together by (*a*) a lash line, (*b*) a loose-pin hinge, and (*c*) a carriage bolt with wing nut.
8. Tell, or show, how one builds (*a*) a simple flat, (*b*) a flat for a door or window, (*c*) a two-fold, (*d*) a three-fold. (Call each separate part by its right name.)
9. Tell, or show, how one builds a typical (*a*) stage door, (*b*) stage window.
10. Tell, or show, how one builds a typical fireplace.
11. Describe standard methods of constructing the following stage units:
    a. ceiling
    b. drop (plain and cut)
    c. border (plain and cut)
    d. cyclorama
12. Described standard methods of constructing platforms, steps, and stairs.
13. Describe standard methods of constructing the following units:
    a. column
    b. tree trunk
    c. rocks and built-up ground
    d. ground rows
14. Select three standard units described in the book, and make a scaled drawing of each, using in each case a scale double the size indicated in the book. That is, if you redraw the diagram of the Plain Flat in Fig. 19 (which has a scale of ½″ = 1′), use for your drawing the scale 1″ = 1′.

CHAPTER 12

Assembling and Shifting Scenery

1. THE STAGE MACHINE

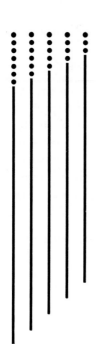

To design a stage for the most effective handling of present-day scenery requires a fine knowledge of engineering principles. The stage must be nicely proportioned and carefully organized in order to give a maximum of mechanical service in a minimum of space. No more complex in structure than some of its predecessors, frequently much less so, the modern stage is considerably better planned for economy and flexibility than the older ones. The degree to which it may be called "modern" clearly does not depend upon its size and complexity, nor the number of scene-shifting tricks it can boast. It depends on something more significant, its adaptibility to the specific technical needs of each new play. Stages in this country are comparatively small. Most of the trick devices about which so much has been written require room which can be ill afforded. For that reason, over-elaborate machinery is apt to defeat its own purpose and become a hindrance rather than a help. Flexibility and expansiveness are the first two essentials of good equipment. In the following sections are described some of the more common methods of assembling and shifting scenery on the adaptable type of stage.

2. METHODS OF LASHING AND BRACING SCENERY

Two flats placed edge to edge are bound together by means of a system of "lashing" (Figures 18 and 39) described in Chapter 11. The lash line, attached to the upper-right-hand corner of the flat on the left as one faces the back of the scenery, is grasped with the right hand, tossed up and over the left upper lash cleat on the flat on the right, back over a cleat on the first flat, then carried down over a lower one on the second, back to the first, and so on down to the last cleat on the right flat. It is carried over this cleat,

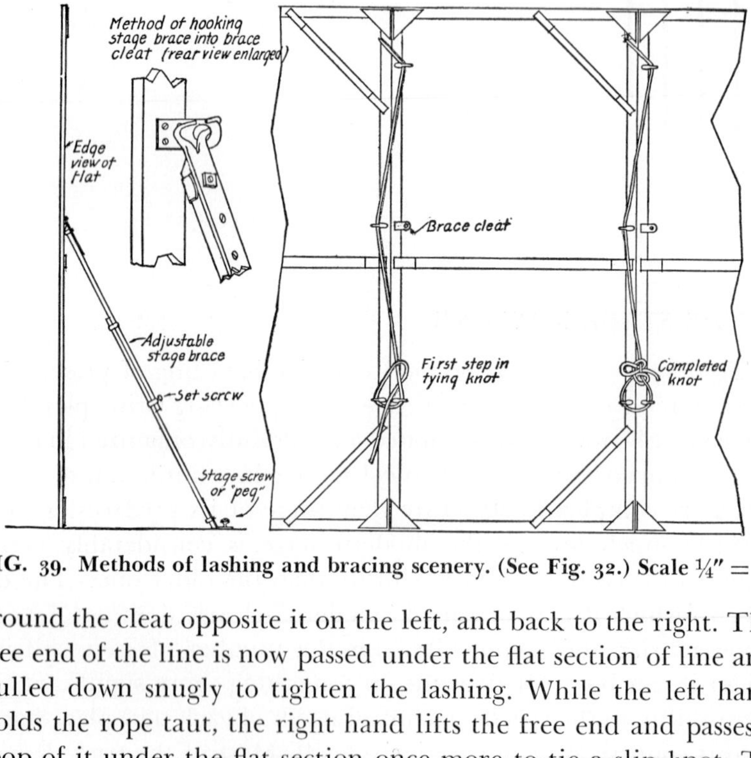

FIG. 39. Methods of lashing and bracing scenery. (See Fig. 32.) Scale ¼″ = 1′.

around the cleat opposite it on the left, and back to the right. The free end of the line is now passed under the flat section of line and pulled down snugly to tighten the lashing. While the left hand holds the rope taut, the right hand lifts the free end and passes a loop of it under the flat section once more to tie a slip knot. To loosen the lashing it is necessary only to pull the free end of the line.

Flats needing special support, such as those on the edge of a set, in the center of a long straight wall, or holding doors or windows, are made secure by propping them from behind with stage braces. In each position where this is necessary the brace (made of two lengths of 1″ x 1″ wood held between clamps, and fitted at one end with a forked iron hook and at the other with an iron heel) is hooked into a brace cleat placed on any convenient part of the flat 8 feet or more from the floor; it is twisted so that its prongs clinch the plate as shown in the enlarged detail Figure 39; and then it is pegged firmly to the floor with a stage screw. The brace, which may be extended open to about twice its closed length, is held at the proper adjustment by means of a set screw placed in one of the clamps. Stage braces can be ordered from any firm dealing in theatrical hardware.

3. METHODS OF BOLTING AND HINGING SCENERY

Heavier units, demanding strength, such as stairs, platforms and other built pieces, and certain lighter units which cannot conveniently be lashed, are fastened together by means of carriage bolts and wing nuts, or loose-pin back flaps and wire pins. The methods of using this attachment hardware are described in Chapter 11, Section 8, and under the construction of the various units which usually require them. On pieces of scenery which have to be put together or taken apart quickly, the bolts or hinges must not only be securely attached but must be in readily accessible places.

4. THE GRIDIRON AND THE FLY FLOOR

In order to fly scenery it is necessary to have some arrangement for hanging ropes from above. Every well-equipped stage has a gridiron (Chapter 10, Section 1) that extends over the entire working space and is built high enough to permit drops to be lifted completely out of view of the audience (Figures 40 and 41). The fly space on some professional stages reaches over 100 feet above the floor. The grid itself is constructed as a skeleton framework of steel I-beams, or wood beams, which is supported by the side walls and often vertical hangers from the roof. It is covered with an open lattice-work of steel strips, and it is slotted from front to back at regular intervals to accommodate the fly ropes. The slots are commonly placed about 15 feet apart. A narrow stage will have four slots, a wider one six or more. Above each of these slots, except one, are bolted large steel protected sheaves called *loft-blocks,* while above the last slot, situated directly over the fly gallery, are set up multiple sheave frames called head blocks.

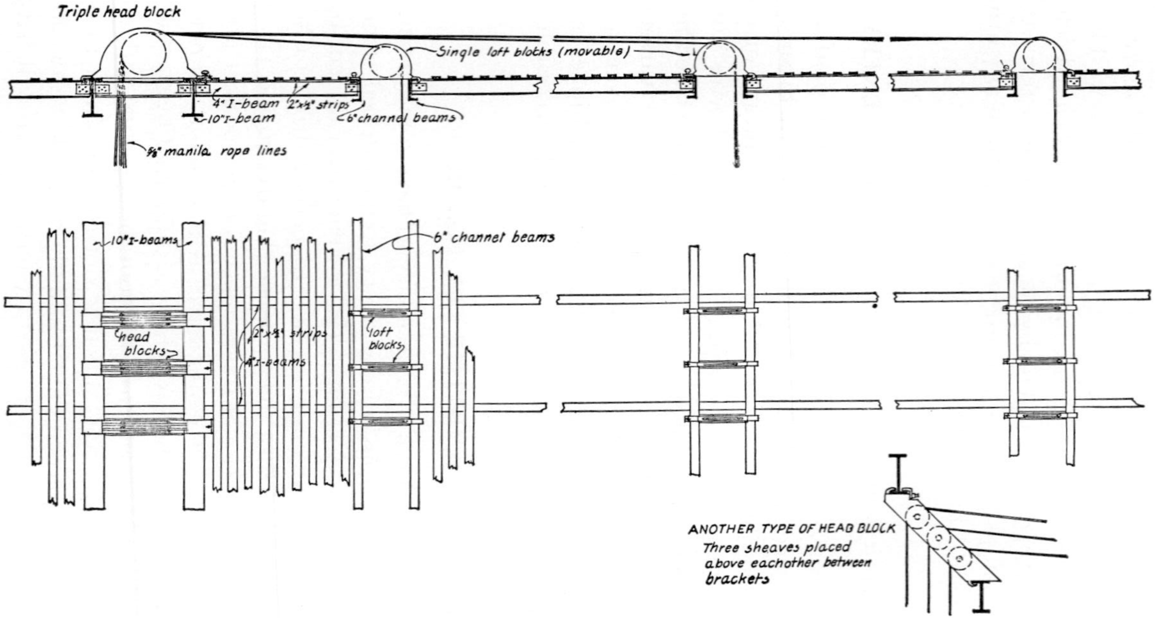

FIG. 40. Construction of the gridiron. Section and plan. Scale $\frac{1}{4}'' = 1'$.

Each set of blocks on an average sized stage (with a proscenium opening 20 to 30 feet wide) generally consists of three loft blocks [1] and one head block arranged in a row at right angles to the slots and parallel to the proscenium wall. A *set of lines,* made up of three or four ½-inch to ⅝-inch manila ropes (depending on the load), is attached to the center and the two ends of a hanging piece of scenery, passed over the three loft blocks directly above and the common head block at the side, then brought down and tied off on the row of belaying pins (the *pin rail*) on the fly floor (Chapter 10, Section 1, and Figure 41).

The fly floor, from which all the fly ropes are controlled, is a narrow floor, sturdily constructed, placed along one of the side walls of the stage, between the proscenium wall and the rear wall, some distance from the floor. It is situated high enough to clear all standing scenery—frequently 20 to 30 feet in the air. The pin rail, to which the fly lines are attached, is a double row of 17- to 21-inch hickory or iron belaying pins—commonly just short pieces of 1″ pipe—stuck through about 8-inch wooden beams or 5-inch iron pipes running the length of the gallery and supported by heavy wood or channel iron posts. The two rows of pins, set on the on-stage side of the gallery, are arranged one above the other.

A well-equipped stage has 15 to 30 or more sets of lines, with corresponding pins, placed about 9 inches apart and numbered from the proscenium back. The complete system of ropes, blocks, and belaying pins is termed the *rigging.*

5. GENERAL METHODS OF FLYING SCENERY

A line is attached to a drop, or other hanging piece, by tying it around the upper batten or into specially attached hanging irons. The three ropes in a set are called respectively the *short, center,* and *long line* as they are fastened to the near end, middle, and far end of the unit of scenery from the point of view of the flyman. The knots (Figure 42) used in making the ropes fast to the scenery must be those which combine absolute security with ease in untying. The bowline is commonly used for straight lifts, and the clove hitch for horizontal and bias pulls. If a quick attachment (*temporary* only) is to be made on a light piece of scenery, the

[1] For a proscenium over 30 feet wide, four or more loft blocks are required in each set. The maximum distance between these blocks is about 15 feet.

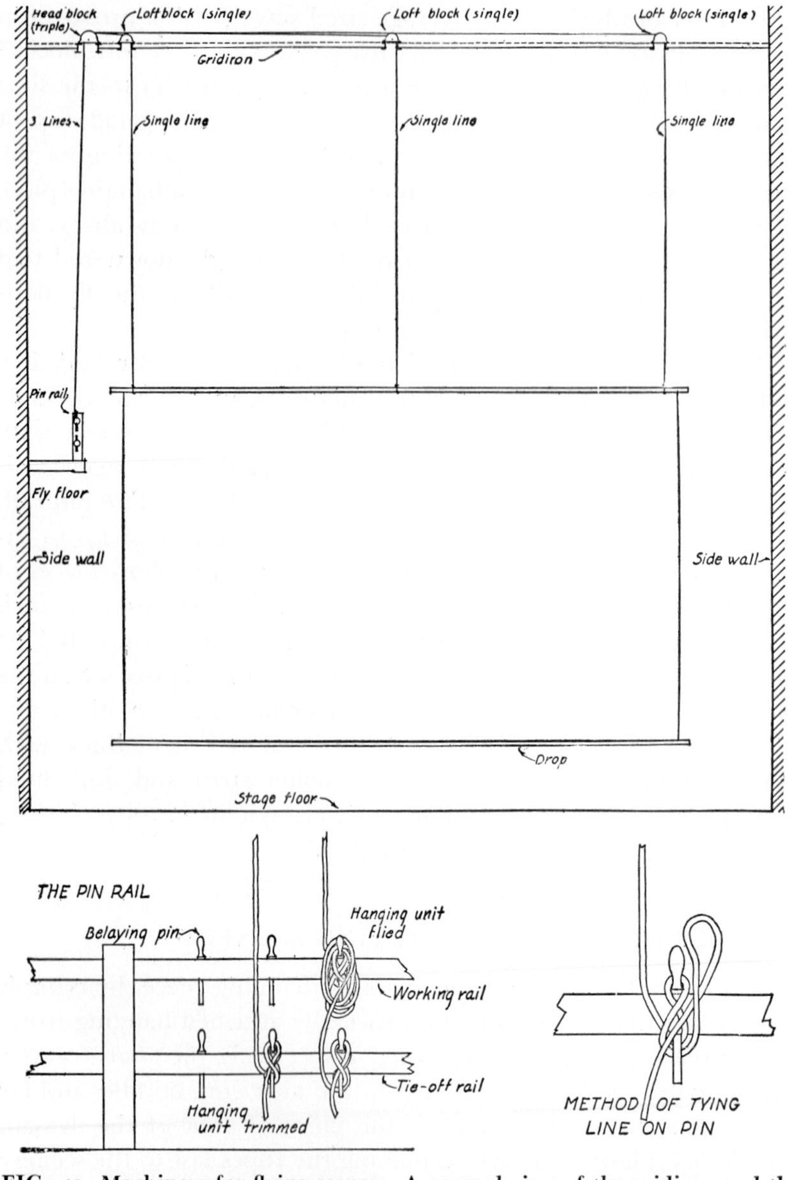

FIG. 41. Machinery for flying scenery. A general view of the gridiron and the fly floor, and a detailed study of the pin rail showing the method of tying off a line. (Usually there would be three lines together.)

slip knot may be employed. This knot, which will not hold well on a batten, is useful only for tying a line into a ring or onto another line.

On units which have no free battens to which the lines can conveniently be attached, hanging irons are used (Figure 43). These are fastened vertically, ring end upwards, to the back of the unit, near the top, by means of $\frac{7}{8}$-inch (or longer) No. 9 screws. If the weight on each iron exceeds 50 pounds, one or more $\frac{3}{16}$-inch stove bolts should be used with the screws.

FIG. 42. Three knots commonly used on hanging scenery. The bowline, left; the clove hitch (plus a half hitch), right; and the slip knot, center.

The unit to which a set of lines has been attached is flied simply by pulling on the ropes. When it has reached the desired height, the ropes are made fast to a belaying pin. The method for *tying-off* is illustrated in Figure 41. The ropes are first carried around the lower end of the pin (from left to right), then up, across and around the upper end (from left to right), down around the lower end and up again, about two and a half times. The set of lines is finally made fast by making a loop, turning it over, bringing it down over the top end of the pin, and pulling it tight, as illustrated. The free ends of the ropes are coiled and hung over the same pin to prevent their getting tangled with other ropes. For the sake of clearness in the drawing only one line in each set is shown.

There are two rows of belaying pins on the pin rail: the lower one for tying the drop, or other unit, at *trim,* that is, when it is in position for the set, and the other pin for tying it when it is raised into the flies. This method of using the rail is found serviceable when a piece of scenery must be lifted and lowered during a performance. Trimming takes time which can be ill afforded during a

FIG. 43. Drop hanger and two types of hanging irons.

quick shift. However, by using the two pins, this can be done beforehand. The lower tie remains permanent. When the appropriate scene arrives the flyman loosens the ropes from the upper pin, lets them slide through his fingers, and when the slack is out he knows the drop or other hanging unit has come automatically to position.

Heavy pieces may be counterweighted by sandbags tied to the lines just below the head blocks (Figure 44). A whole rear wall consisting of three or more flats battened together may be balanced this way. A clamp is often used in place of rope for attaching the heavy sandbag to the lines.

A wide piece of scenery, such as a drop, may, in an emergency, be flied on two lines instead of three by using bridles as illustrated in Figure 44.

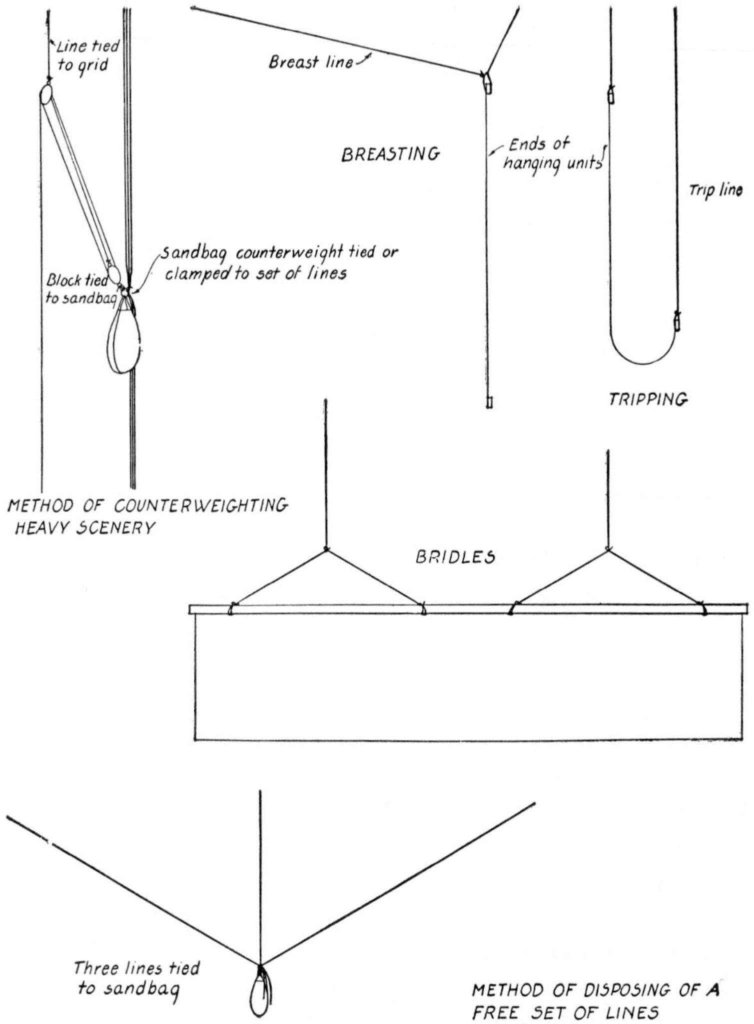

FIG. 44. Methods of maneuvering hanging scenery with lines and counterweights.

On a stage equipped with a low grid a tall drop may be *tripped* out of sight by attaching, from behind, a second, adjacent set of lines to the bottom batten. When both sets of lines are drawn, the drop is folded back and up into a space only half its height (Figure 44).

A small sandbag should be tied into every set of lines not fastened to scenery to prevent the ropes from being pulled through the blocks when they are drawn up out of the way, and to force them to come down again with their own weight when released.

A word of caution. *Be sure that all hardware and knots used in flying are secure.* Some serious accidents have resulted from pulleys or hanging irons or sandbags breaking loose during a performance. Examine ropes from time to time for signs of wear. Safety is the first law of the stage as it is everywhere else.

6. SPECIFIC METHODS OF FLYING SCENERY

A drop or a border is flied by tying a set of three or more lines to its upper batten in the manner described in the preceding section.

A ceiling piece is suspended on two or three sets of lines, and lifted away or lowered to the standing set in the manner explained in Chapter 11, Section 13.

To speed up the setting and striking of a scene a complete back wall is frequently hung on a set of lines and flied like a drop. The several flats (single or hinged—see Chapter 11, Section 9) which compose the wall are first laid flat on the stage, edge to edge, face downwards, and fastened together to make a single rigid panel by placing two or more long battens, called stiffeners, across the back. They are fastened to the stiles of the flats by means of long screws or bolts, never nails. Ropes are tied into hanging irons attached at strong points (the center and two ends) to the back of the combination, and the wall is then raised and lowered as a unit. A side wall, also, may be flied in this way by tying to it single lines from an upstage and a downstage set. A whole box interior, with three walls, can, on occasion, be lifted from the stage as one piece by using one full set of lines which supports the back, and another set of two which supports the two front corners.

Heavy units should be counterweighted by large sandbags tied to each set of lines just below the head block, as described in the preceding section and illustrated in Figure 44. If the wall of an interior which must be placed under the edge of a ceiling is to be balanced in this way, a small auxiliary block and tackle will have to be attached to the sandbag to lift the latter slightly, and so give some slack to the fly ropes when the wall is in position on the floor, in order not to foul the overlapping ceiling.

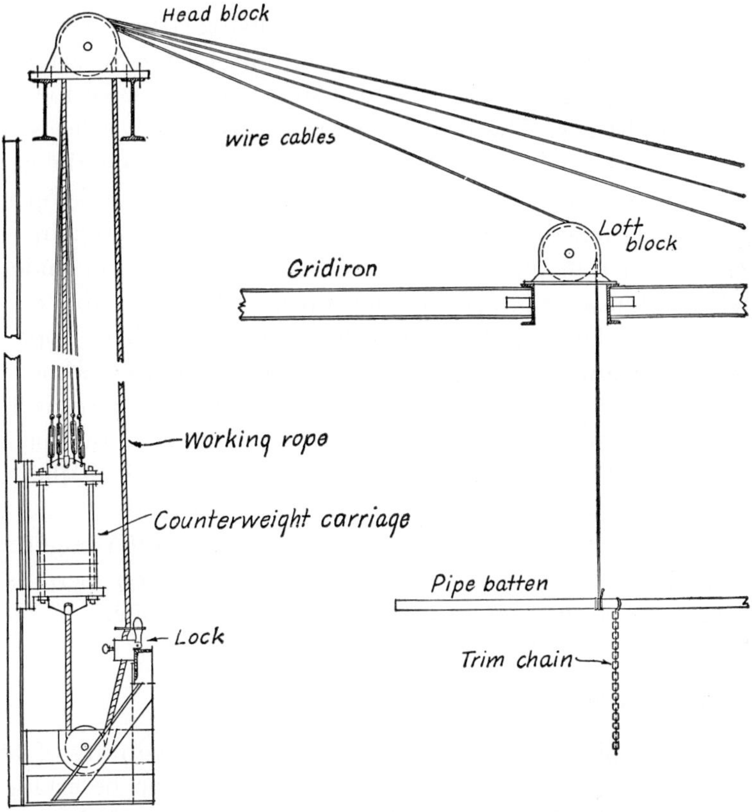

FIG. 45. Counterweight system. By means of this system scenery is handled from the floor of the stage instead of from the fly floor.

Canvas tree trunks and light columns may be suspended on single, independent lines which, in this employment, are termed *spotted* lines.

If the emergency demands it, furniture and other properties may also be flied. As a rule, however, it is not wise to play too many tricks with the fly system. An overloaded grid is not the safest thing under which to perform.

7. THE COUNTERWEIGHT SYSTEM

In many of the newer theatres the fly gallery has been omitted and all flying is handled with a *counterweight system* [2] operated from the stage floor (Figure 45). In the unit form a pipe batten parallel to the proscenium wall and to the floor is attached to small steel cables, which pass over loft blocks in the grid—in the same arrangement as the Manila rope flying system (Section 4)—over a common headblock at the side, and down to a metal carriage with adjustable weights, which slides up and down the wall in a vertical track. The three or more sheaves (pully wheels) for the cables and the one for a Manila rope, which compose the headblock, revolve side by side on a common shaft. The Manila operating rope is fastened to the top of the sliding carriage, passed up and over its sheave in the headblock in the grid, down and under a single block near the stage floor and up again to the bottom of the carriage. The latter, pulled up or down by this "endless" rope, in turn lifts or lowers the pipe batten it counterbalances. Scenery is attached to the pipe by means of trim chains. When a piece is flied to the proper height, the operating rope is fastened with a patent clamp lock. The balance weights are usually placed on the carriage from a narrow loading platform under the grid.

Some stages today are equipped with both a counterweight system and the older rope system. The combination permits a flexibility of control impossible with one system alone.

8. FLYING ON SMALL STAGES

On small platform stages where there is no possibility of constructing a regular gridiron, a makeshift device can be arranged in the form of a few stout pulleys fastened securely to beams in the ceiling. At a minimum, there should be two sets of pulleys to take care of the front and back edges of the ceiling, one to swing the pipe batten holding the front lighting units, and another to support the sky drop upstage. If the scenery is light, the lines may be tied off on a row of common lash hooks fastened to a board bolted to the wall on the side.

[2] The "counterweight system" must not be confused with the use of counterweighting sandbags in the older method of flying scenery (see the two preceding sections and Figure 44).

A little more costly, but a stronger and more generally satisfactory substitute for a grid on a small stage may be had by installing a system of light steel I-beams and underhang blocks (Figure 46). Four beams (about 4-inch), cut long enough to reach the full depth of the stage, are placed against the ceiling and secured to the front and rear walls. One beam extends back from a point above the center of the proscenium opening; two others from points about halfway between that and the side walls; and the fourth from a point near the right or left side wall of the stage.

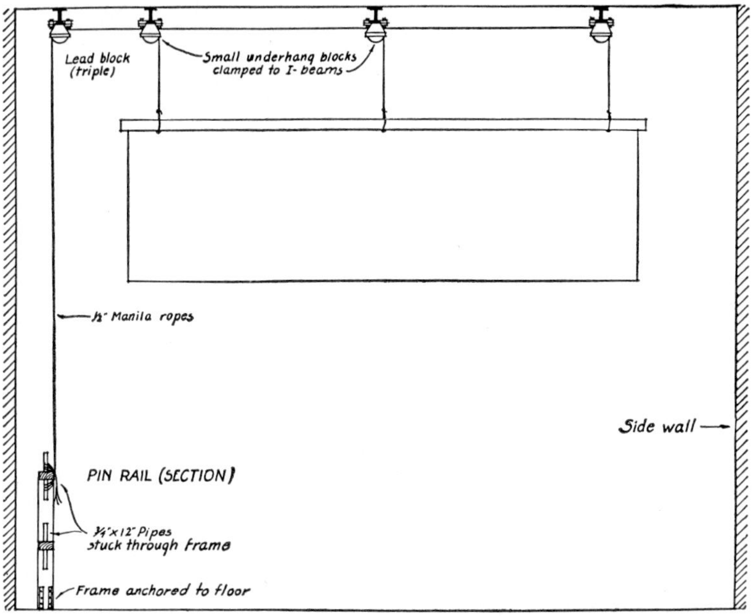

FIG. 46. Method of rigging a small stage with a low ceiling.

Standard steel underhang blocks with 4-inch sheaves are clamped and bolted to the lower flanges of the I-beams in the same general arrangement of parallel "sets" as that employed in the layout of a regular grid (Section 4). Single blocks are attached to the three beams in the center, and triple blocks to the beam at the side.

A modified pin rail may be constructed by sticking 12-inch lengths of ¾-inch pipe through a 2" x 4" wooden framing anchored securely to the floor. This framing should, of course, be placed directly under the beam carrying the triple blocks.

The lines should be ½-inch Manila ropes. Cotton rope can be trusted only for the lightest of loads.

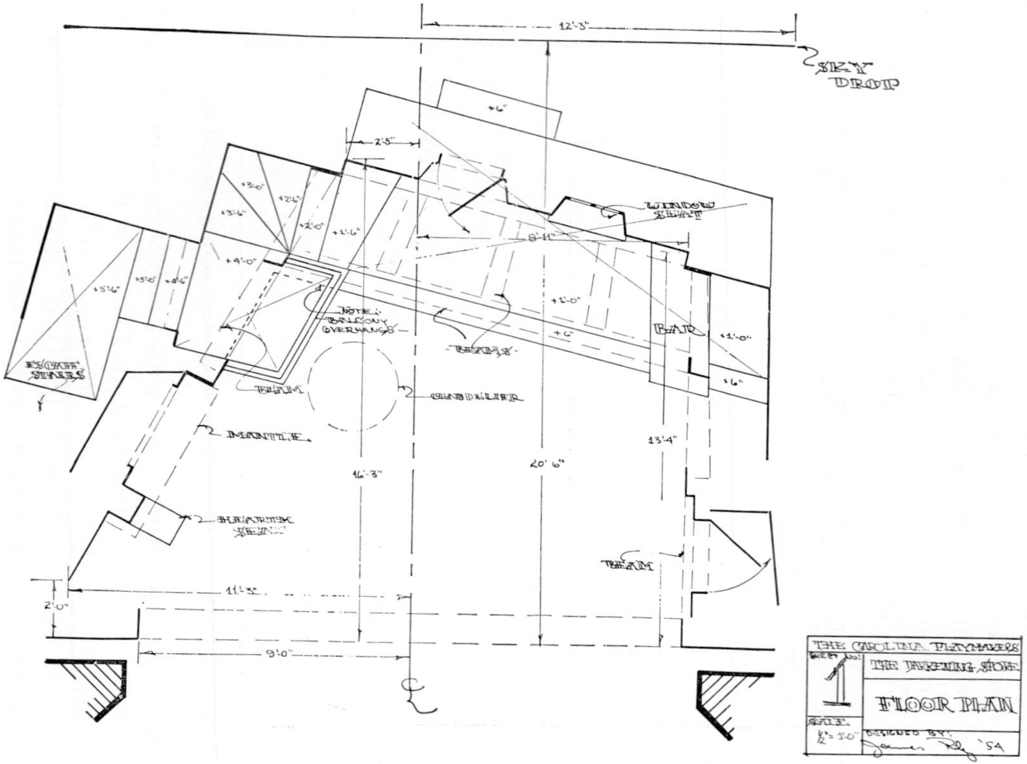

FIG. 47a. Working drawings for *The Darkening Shore:* the floor plan.

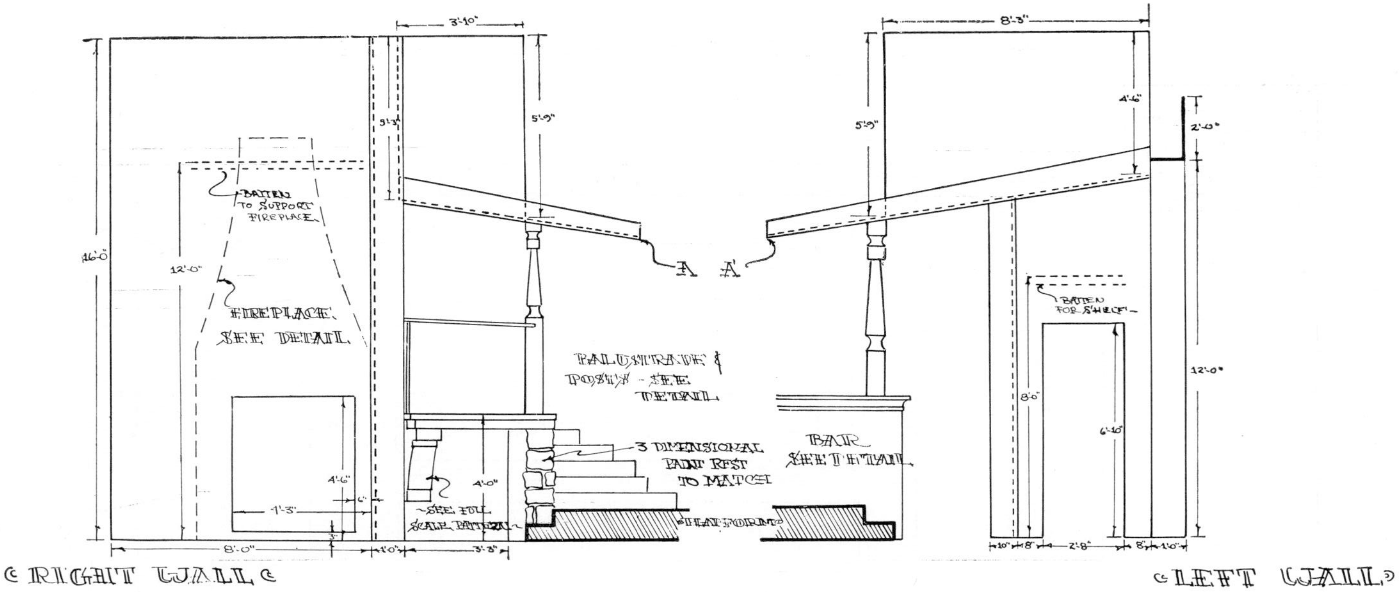

FIG. 47b. Working drawings for *The Darkening Shore:* right and left walls.

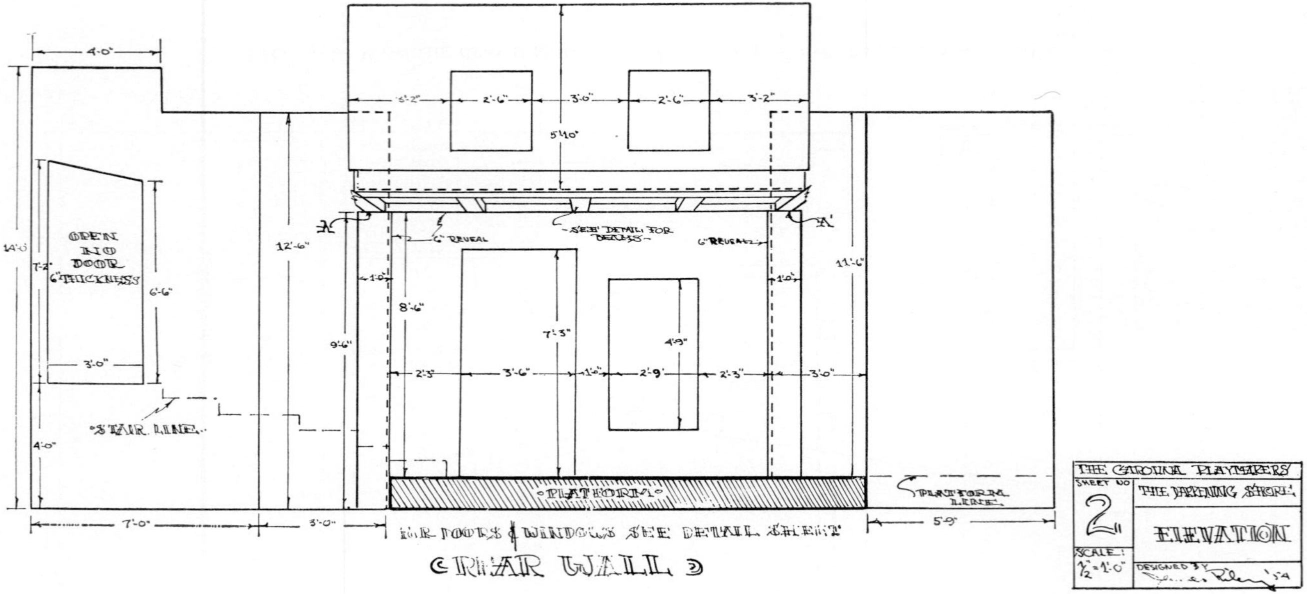

FIG. 47c. Working drawings for *The Darkening Shore:* rear wall.

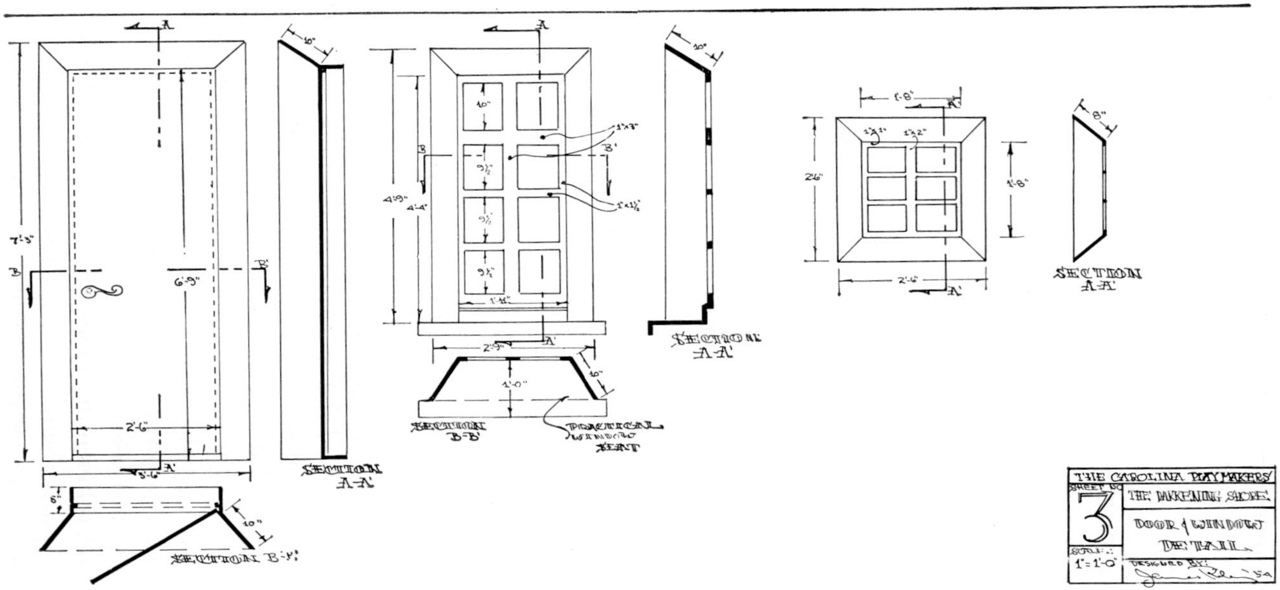

FIG. 47d. Working drawings for *The Darkening Shore:* detail of door and windows.

If the ceiling of the stage is low, a drop may be flied out of sight either by tripping it, as described in Section 5, or by dropping it to the floor, rolling and tying it, and lifting it once more out of the way.

9. SETTING THE SCENE

The exact plan adopted for the assembling of a group of scenic units varies, of course, with each scene. The following, however, is the general procedure for setting (putting together) a simple box interior (Chapter 10, Section 2). After the ground cloth (Chapter 10, Section 1) has been laid, the ceiling is hung and lifted high enough to clear the flats; then the latter are lashed together in position, starting with one downstage end and continuing in order around to the other, stage braces (Section 2) being used where necessary. Door and window frames, if they have not already been bolted to their flats, are put into appropriate openings, and clamped in place with their strap hinges. The ceiling is let down again, trimmed and tied off on the lower pin rail. Lastly, backings are placed behind doorways, and the sky drop or sky cyclorama is lowered. To strike (take apart) the scene, the ceiling is lifted two or three feet and a second tie in its lines made on the upper rail. The process of setting up is then reversed. An exterior scene is set and struck according to the same general plan.

When a group of scenic units is arranged on the stage for the first time, attention must be paid to proper placements and masking for good sight lines (Chapter 14, Section 6). The tormentors at the sides must be brought on far enough to hide the edges of the downstage flats; and the teaser at the top must be lowered to a position where it conceals the flies, the front edge of the ceiling (if there is one), and the overhead lighting units. When the exact arrangement of a scene has been decided upon it is a good plan to mark its position on the floor at the corners by means of a little dark paint (oil if permanent, water color if temporary). This will insure accuracy in reassembling the scene.

All flats and other units should be numbered prominently on the back for quick reference, and be stacked in a definite order before the beginning of the performance. When they are set up and struck during the performance they should be moved strictly according to this order. *Speed* and *efficiency* are two words which should never be forgotten when scenery is handled. Each shift should be plotted out carefully ahead of time and rehearsed until the station of every man and the sequence of his movements becomes absolutely clear. So far as possible, all methods and procedures should be strictly standardized. "A place for everything and everything in its place" is a motto that might well be tacked up prominently on every stage.

QUESTIONS AND EXERCISES

1. What are the general characteristics of an efficient stage, viewed as a machine?
2. How is scenery lashed and braced?
3. How are two units of scenery fastened together by means of bolts and hinges?
4. Describe a standard gridiron and fly floor.
5. Describe, or demonstrate, several standard methods of flying scenery.
6. Show how a set of fly lines should be tied off on a pin rail.
7. Using a border batten, or the top rail of a chair, as the object to be tied, knot a fly line in the form of (*a*) a bowline, (*b*) a clove hitch. Under what circumstances should the first knot be used? the second knot?
8. What is the difference between *trimming, tripping,* and *breasting?*
9. Describe the counterweight system.
10. Describe, or demonstrate, how a set of scenery should be set and struck.

CHAPTER 13

Painting the Scenery

1. INTRODUCTION

THE ART OF SCENE painting was at one time governed by many fixed rules of practice. This no longer is true. Certain tendencies in method, such as those outlined in the present chapter, may still be noted, but ultimate technique today is wholly a personal thing. Only three common requirements regulate the work of all modern scenic artists: (1) to mix and apply their paints carefully, in accordance with the nature of the media; (2) to execute their designs in a bold, free manner, avoiding fussy details, in order to create effects which may be viewed well from a distance; and (3) to paint in such a way as to co-operate to the fullest extent with stage lighting.

A. GENERAL PRACTICE

2. PAINT MATERIALS

The following materials are required for painting:

Scene paints. Distemper, or water color, is employed almost exclusively on the stage, its advantages over oil being that it can be applied more easily and quickly, it dries more rapidly, it does not shine, it is cleaner to handle, it is far cheaper, and it is not inflammable. What is known as *scene paint* is the pure pigment in powdered form. Before it is used it must be mixed with glue and water. It is sold in sixty or more colors. Some of the most serviceable ones are the following:

Light chrome yellow	Magenta
Medium chrome yellow	Venetian red
Hanover green	Raw sienna
Medium chrome green	Yellow ochre
Dark chrome green	Orange mineral
Italian blue	Burnt umber
Ultramarine blue	Drop black

Other useful colors, some of which cost a little more, are: lemon yellow, burnt sienna, vermilion, permanent red, purple lake, light Milori yellow, malachite green, and emerald green.

Because of their cost, ready-made calcimine and other premixed commercial preparations are not recommended except when it is impossible to secure the pure pigments.

Whiting. By far the most useful pigment for the artist is ordinary bolted whiting. He should estimate that he will use as much of this pigment as all of the rest of the pigments put together. Only good grade whiting should be used. Belgian and Danish whitings are standard.

Common flake glue. Flake gelatin glue is preferable to ground glue, though either may be used. These must be cooked. LePage's, which needs no preparation except thinning with cold water, may be employed in an emergency—only in an emergency, however, because not only is it too expensive for general use, but also it has a strong tendency to gray out any pigment mixed with it. Most other cold water glues are to be avoided entirely.

3. PAINTING IMPLEMENTS

For painting scenery, three different types of brushes will be found especially serviceable: one 8-inch and one 6-inch *priming* brush, for priming and covering large surfaces rapidly; one 4-inch *laying-in* brush, for smaller areas; and one 2-inch and one 1-inch *lining* brush for detail. There are a number of other types, such as round *foliage* brushes and special *liners,* which might be mentioned; but the three above will be found to be adequate for most

Arena theatre: A scene from a play produced by Margo Jones at the Dallas Theatre.

purposes. They should all be of the good quality, long-bristle variety used in distempering walls. Brushes deteriorate very rapidly unless they are taken care of. After every painting they should be rinsed, shaken out, and dried in a flat position. Better still, drill a hole in each brush handle and hang the brush up on a nail. Never place a brush in boiling water. Other necessary implements for the artist are:

A yardstick
Charcoal sticks and chalk
A snap line (about 40 feet of heavy braided cotton cord)
A straight-edge beveled liner (for ruling short lines)
A 12-foot batten with a perfectly straight edge for ruling long lines
A large wooden compass (for describing circles and arcs)
Several 2–3 gallon pails and smaller pans
Muffin tins (for holding small amounts of different kinds of color)
A gas, electric, or kerosene stove with at least two burners

4. PREPARING THE PAINT

Paint is prepared by mixing pigment with a solution of glue called *size water,* according to the following procedure: 4 pounds of flake (or ground) glue are placed in a 3-gallon pail of water, allowed to soak for at least an hour (or better, overnight) and then cooked on a stove. This pail is placed inside a larger one, with a little water and a block of wood or a brick in the bottom of the latter to prevent burning. When completely dissolved, the glue is further diluted to make size water. Four pounds of dry flakes will make from 6 to 8 pails of size water. (This is about the proportion of one cup of glue to a pail.) The more concentrated preparation may be kept as stock to be diluted as it is needed. Because time must be taken to remelt it every time it is used, however, it is wise to make up several buckets of size water at a time to prevent delay in painting. If glue is to be kept on hand for any length of time, a couple of teaspoonfuls of carbolic acid may be put in it to keep it from decomposing.

The glue solution should be warm when the pigment is added. Pour the powder into it slowly, stirring it thoroughly to prevent lumping, until the mixture has the consistency of coffee cream. It is difficult to give any more nearly exact proportions for mixing scene paints as both glue and pigments vary. Veteran artists judge largely by the "feel" acquired through experience. If too much glue is used the paint, when dry, will draw and crack on the surface of the canvas; also the paint will have a tendency to look shiny, and dark stains may appear. If too little glue is used, the paint will powder on a hand rubbed across it. If too much pigment is used, the paint will seem stiff and heavy in brushing, and one stroke will pile up on top of the preceding one. If the mixture is too thin it will look transparent on the canvas.

The paint, when applied, should be at least slightly warm. The mixture in the bucket should be stirred from time to time to prevent the powder from precipitating. If the pail is set aside for a while and grows cold, it should be thoroughly stirred and returned to the stove briefly before being used again, care being taken that the glue does not burn.

Certain of the pigments (Prussian blue, ultramarine blue, Van Dyke brown, most of the reds, lampblack, and the anilines) need to be "cut," moistened with a little alcohol, before they are mixed with size water.

5. SOME SUGGESTIONS FOR MIXING PAINTS

It is seldom necessary to use pure colors, except for accents. For most purposes they should be mixed with at least an equal portion of whiting for painting brighter blocks of color, and several times this amount for laying in lighter tones. On the other hand, the use of whiting should be avoided when it is not needed. Whiting exerts a strong influence over other pigments in a mixture; even a small amount dropped by mistake into a pailful of some dark paint (such as burnt umber or black) is apt to destroy its brilliance and make it appear chalky.

The various pigments may be mixed together in any proportion. Only in very unusual circumstances will an artist find just the tone of a color he wants without first blending two or more together.

A word of caution should be given to those experimenting with scene paints for the first time. Water colors invariably look darker when wet than dry, mixtures containing white being especially tricky deceivers in this respect. Those who have trouble in estimating in advance the result of a certain mixture would do well to mix their pigments in a dry state before adding any liquid.

It is difficult to match blends. Before painting a sky drop or the walls of a set, therefore, it is wise to mix enough paint to prevent running short at some critical point. Two 2- or 3-gallon pailfuls will take care of a drop 25′ x 30′, or a set of seven flats of standard width and 12 feet high, very nicely.

6. THE PRIME COAT

The first coat of paint is called the *prime coat.* Its purpose is to close the pores of the canvas and prepare a working surface for the following coats. Because whiting is the cheapest powder, it is commonly the chief ingredient used, but any other pigment may be employed equally well. Left-over scraps from the previous day's painting may be *boxed* together (poured back and forth into each other) and warmed up to prime the new flats. The tendency in professional studios is to prime a set of scenery with the tint of a color approximating the final tone of the scenery if the effect is to be smooth, and with a complementary to this tone if the effect is to be rough. To prepare a foundation for an open texture the priming is often done with several different colors. The only fixed directions for applying this first coat are to use a large brush and to spread the paint evenly, smoothly, and not too thickly over the canvas.

7. THE FOLLOWING COATS

One coat of paint should be allowed to dry thoroughly before another is applied; otherwise the damp pigments will mix and produce muddy spots. If the paints are properly applied, one coat will completely hide the preceding one (unless it is in extreme contrast or is mixed with an aniline dye). If it does not, it is probably too thin. If one coat picks up another, the fault lies in one of three possibilities: the fresh paint is too warm, that beneath it is still damp, or the under paint lacks glue. A little experience will quickly teach one how to avoid such conditions.

8. SURFACE TEXTURES

Irregular surfaces on the stage are, when viewed from a distance, more interesting to look at than perfectly smooth ones. For some reason, flatly painted scenery is never quite convincing; its chalky flatness reveals it to be what it really is, color-washed canvas. Even a slightly varied texture, scarcely recognizable as such from the audience, seems to "carry" where the flat one will not. The theory of *broken color,* which maintains that scintillation is secured by breaking up a desired tone into its simpler elements and placing these side by side in little blocks which the eye, at a distance, will blend into one, finds one of its surest proofs on the stage. A plainly tinted wall painted by spattering, one over the other, three coats—one magenta-gray, one yellow-gray, and one cyan-gray—has a suggestion of life which one painted with the same colors mixed together in a pail and applied flatly most clearly has not.

9. METHODS OF APPLYING PAINT

The following are the most common methods of applying paint to scenery:

Flat Painting. The paint is brushed on smoothly and evenly. This is obviously the most simple method, useful for priming and laying on ground (base) colors. Since the distemper paint used for scenery does not have to be "worked out" like oil paint, it may be applied freely and quickly. But some care must be taken to avoid making puddles.

Scumbling. A fairly wet brush is passed lightly, and with long free strokes, over the surface of the canvas in various directions in such a way as to conceal only partly the surface beneath. Unless an effect of obvious blotchiness or streakiness is desired, care must be taken to lay the strokes on fairly evenly. This method is useful for producing rough surface effects. Scumbling is commonly employed in the painting of plaster walls to produce a variety of textures and hues. Several colors may be used at the same time, one color being brushed into, across, or around the others. Scumbling is employed also in the "laying-in" of foliage. Several tones of green, and some red and dark blue, may be brushed in large, long, curved strokes to suggest clumps of leaves and shadows. (See Section 15). Scumbling is commonly followed by spattering (see below).

Dragging. The technique employed in dragging is similar to that in scumbling except that a drier brush is used, and the strokes are commonly laid in straighter lines. The bristles of the brush are dipped into the pail of paint an inch or less, the surplus liquid is shaken off, and then the brush is swept over the surface of the canvas swiftly and lightly. Dragging is useful for softening shadows, and for suggesting grain markings in wood. Dragging is sometimes called "dry brushing."

Sponging. A large sponge, trimmed to present a flat surface, is dipped into a pail of paint, squeezed out, and patted gently over the canvas. Care must be exercised in using this method to cover evenly and avoid undue spottiness. The textural pattern should be continuous. It will be found helpful to pat in spirals or semicircles and to turn the sponge constantly in the hand. Sponging is useful for producing rough or patterned surfaces.

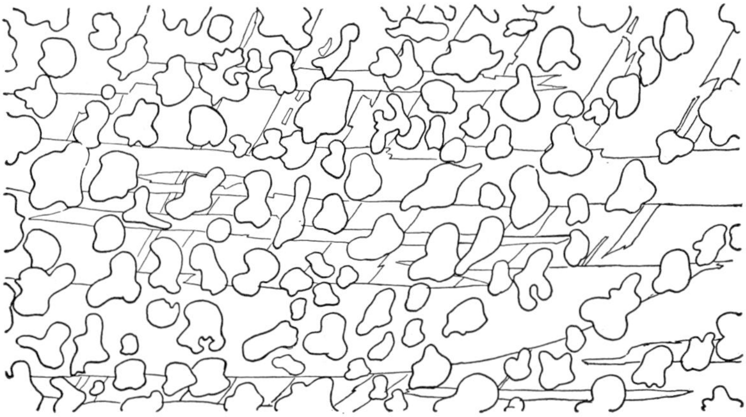

FIG. 48. Full-size spattering for a smooth texture. For a rough texture the spots should be three or four times the size of those shown here. This spattering has been applied over dry brushing.

Rolling. An effect somewhat similar to that obtained by sponging can be secured by dipping and wringing out a ragged piece of coarse linen or burlap and rolling it over the surface to be covered. This is an excellent method to use for imitating old plaster or rock surfaces. Most painters prefer rolling to sponging.

Spattering. A brush full of paint is shaken over the canvas or snapped by the wrist so that the paint falls in little drops. To insure evenness, it is well to start with one end or corner of a piece or group of pieces of scenery and proceed systematically to the opposite one. Be generous with the paint. A few tiny speckles will not be effective. At the same time avoid dribbling from an overwet brush and dropping large spots which the audience will recognize as paint, thus destroying the illusion of texture. If it is difficult for the artist at the start to spatter evenly, he will find it helpful to snap the brush by striking the wrist of the brush hand against the wrist of the other hand at each shake of the brush. One secret of good spattering lies in loading the brush each time with the same amount of color, that is, always dipping the bristles the same distance into the liquid (never more than about three quarters of the way). Spattering is the method most often used for producing broken color impressions. It is often combined with one or more of the other methods (see Figure 48).

Glazing. Sometimes a thin, transparent wash of one color is brushed over another color, or group of colors, for the purpose of blending or softening, or heightening tonal values. A pail of wash for this employment may be prepared by diluting ordinary scene paint with size water, or by dissolving dye crystals in size water.

If a series of flats in a wall, or any other group of pieces which must be set together in a scene, is to be painted by one of the methods indicated here, it is imperative that the pieces be laid side by side in the proper order on the floor as a unit, to ensure their being matched.

There are few really standard ways of painting scenery. The successful artist is an inventor and experimenter. The suggested solutions of the various problems that follow should be appreciated as hints chiefly for beginners. These hints will be modified or disregarded as one discovers better methods.

B. SPECIFIC PRACTICE

10. INTERIOR AND EXTERIOR WALLS

The principles of broken color (Section 8) may be used in developing wall surfaces which are intended to appear either smooth or rough. For the smooth surface, which suits interiors better than it does exteriors, choose two or three colors which are nearly alike, such as blue-gray and yellow-gray, or light-cream, darker cream, and pink. Lay one of the colors on solidly as a ground coat; when it is dry, spatter the second evenly over the first until it nearly conceals it; then spatter over these two the third in the same manner. If the spattering has been properly done, it should present a surface which, from a distance, at first sight will appear perfectly smooth, but upon closer examination will be seen to have just enough texture to prevent it from looking monotonous and uninteresting. If a hard texture is desired, the spattering should be done on a perfectly dry surface; if a soft texture is desired, a wet surface should be used. Avoid working over a partly wet and a partly dry surface, however, or the result will be uneven.

The use of more widely separated colors in spattering will suggest stucco. If two or more colors are cleverly enough applied by the cloth-rolling method, a very convincing effect of old mottled wall paper may be produced. If a more pronounced design is desired, simple figures may be cut in oil paper and stenciled onto the wall. In applying the paint through the stencil use an almost dry brush to keep the paint from running. Avoid any very conspicuous patterns or they will probably refuse to lie at rest on the surface. If the figures appear too vigorous when viewed from a distance, spatter them over lightly with a little of the ground color, to tone them back into the rest of the wall. Remember at all times that good scenery acts as an environment and must not detract from the action of the play.

Old stained plaster, particularly effective for exterior walls, may be suggested by scumbling and blocking in large irregular patches of various light and dark browns, or yellows, reds, and blues, and spattering this all over, while it is still wet, with the same colors. Keep the darker tones near the surface. As dark blue under the prevailing straw and amber lights of the stage looks nearly black, a little of this color may be mixed with a small amount of real black and sprinkled *very lightly* here and there over the plaster, to suggest holes and crevices. Guard against the appearance of large drops or you will give away your secret.

Brick walls should be handled thoughtfully. Rows of regular red rectangles with hard white lines between, seen so often on amateur stages, never look very convincing. Even the most evenly laid walls in actual life show many irregularities and signs of weathering. One good plan to follow in painting is to scumble in first the plaster effect (later to be seen between the bricks) in a full ground coat—not in one tone, but in two or three slightly different ones—then lay the bricks in lightly on top of this with a comparatively dry 2- or 3-inch brush. Vary red with a little neutralized orange, brown, and blue. It is well to keep the bricks in fairly straight lines, of course, but do not attempt to paint them too regularly. Knock off a corner here and there and touch occasional edges with darker blue to suggest stains. After the bricks have been laid in, spatter them all over very lightly with the same colors. Keep in mind that an *impression* is what one is trying to create, and that fussy details are lost on the audience.

11. SHADING AND TONING WALLS

In creating wall surfaces an artist must work constantly for variety. He should give special attention to large plain areas. Unless these are well painted, they are apt to appear bare even under the best lighting. It is not enough simply to suggest texture (see Sections 9 and 10). The artist should work for some difference between illuminated and shadowed areas. The light concentration on a high wall in a night scene, for instance, would naturally be near the bottom where the actors stand and walk in lamplight. In treating such a wall the artist might wisely lay his lightest tints here, and then shade them off gradually into deeper and deeper ones as he proceeds toward the top, until the wall appears to melt into darkness. The outer edges of the wall, away from the light source, might likewise be made to fade into the shadows.

Wall surfaces often seem more interesting when they are *toned* (tinted or grayed) with a light scumble or spatter of aniline dye dissolved in size water. One or more tints or shades may be used. A thin wash of silver may be used in the same way. By this kind of silver treatment, dull-looking walls may be given a remarkable sparkle without appreciably changing their color. The dye and silver powders may be mixed in the same bucket, if so desired, and thrown together.

Both shading and toning, if they are to be at all effective, must be done subtly.

12. IMITATING WOODWORK

Woodwork is very difficult to imitate satisfactorily with canvas and paint. When he is preparing a realistic setting, a professional scenic artist likes to use at least some real lumber on the stage.

This he can do without great difficulty where door frames and moldings are involved; but it is obviously impossible to build a complete wooden interior to represent a shack or a log cabin. Where rough boards must be suggested with paint, lay a ground coat of gray-brown, rule the flats with charcoal to indicate positions of the planks, and scumble in each with shades and tints of brown. blue, and gray, using long strokes and avoiding making one plank exactly like the next. Alternate a couple of darker boards with a lighter one, and vice versa. Vary the ends, or the middles, of boards. Stain the edges of occasional boards. Now take a little yellow ochre, mixed with white, on an almost dry brush with the

FIG. 49. An elevation sketch. Drawn by Samuel Selden for *Wappin' Wharf* by Charles S. Brooks.

bristles spread, and with long sweeps suggest very lightly some pronounced graining here and there. If the pattern of the graining must be made more obvious, mix up a little black aniline dye and sweep it on in the same way, that is, lightly and with an almost dry brush. If the brown and yellow show up too brightly, reduce their intensity with a little gray or blue. Finally, outline the boards lightly with blue accented with black, draw in a few knots, and drag and spatter a little light gray-blue over the entire surface to suggest the rough texture of the wood. A little real lumber seen in beams and supports will carry out the illusion.

In the more pretentious, formal type of interior which must be dressed up with baseboards, dadoes, cornices, wall paneling and shaped door and window trims, strips of molding may be indicated (when the use of real wood is considered impractical) by laying bands of suitable color and drawing on these, with a 1-inch lining brush, thin lines of highlight and shadow. Wherever the light may be presumed to strike an edge of the molding a line of highlight is ruled. In the hollows below this line (or above—depending on the direction of the light) the lines of shadow are placed. The color for the highlighted strip is commonly prepared by mixing the "local tone" (body color of the molding) with a little white, the color for the shadows, by mixing the local tone with a little dark blue or blue-black. If the lightness of the ground on which the lines of highlight and shadow are to be drawn is extreme, pure white and pure pale blue may be substituted for the mixed colors. The pigment should be applied with a full brush in long, clean strokes, the brush being carried the length of the straightedge once only in each position. If the pigment is scrubbed on, the lines of light and shadow will look fuzzy, heavy, and unconvincing. To rule a crisp, thin line, the broader side of a small brush should be placed against the straightedge; to mark a softer line, the flat side should be turned to the canvas.

13. THE SKY

A large drop, high enough and wide enough completely to back up all exterior views, and painted pale blue, is generally used to represent the sky (Chapter 11, Section 14). As it depends chiefly upon lighting for its effect, its own tinting should be very soft. Mix not more than 3 or 4 ounces of Italian blue in a full pail of white, and apply the paint with a large, absolutely clean brush, taking great care not to streak. If it is a big drop, prepare two or three buckets of paint and box them thoroughly (pour them back and forth into each other) before starting. To run short and attempt to match tints in the center of the sky is disastrous. The sky may be given a little texture and a surface which will better reflect different qualities of light which may be thrown on it if it is spattered very carefully and evenly with pale, closely related tints of pink, purple, and blue (a fraction of a degree darker or lighter than the main blue). It may be given added scintilation by mixing into the paint a little aluminum (silver) powder.

The old-fashioned practice of painting a landscape on the sky drop is now frowned upon by the best artists. Besides being difficult to do, it never produces very convincing results, and it limits the use of the drop. A simple sky may be used in every set of a play calling for a glimpse of outdoors, whereas a painted landscape fits the locality of just one scene.

If the drop must be rolled up frequently, the paint on its surface should be flexible. If to each 3-gallon pail of paint one adds ½ cup of glycerin, the paint can be prevented from cracking. Or one can use ready-prepared glycerin glue in place of the hard glue.

14. LANDSCAPE PIECES

The character of an outdoor setting is suggested better by a few plastic *set* and *built* pieces, such as ground rows, silhouette hills, rocks, trees, and fences placed in front of the sky, than by anything painted on the drop. The construction of these is described in a previous chapter (Chapter 11, Sections 19 and 20). When painting them one would do well to keep in mind that, except possibly for the sky on a cloudless day, there are no large masses of flat color in nature. Even a simple tree trunk will show a surprising number of colors—perhaps a dozen or more browns, grays, blues, and greens. Of course it would be impractical to indicate very many of these, but at least two or three tones should be used to indicate that a piece of scenery represents a tree trunk, not a painted post.

Rocks are never a dead gray. For painting the lighted side of a block of granite use warmer colors, perhaps a dull cream varied with a little rose pink, light brown, and pale blue; while in the shadows use cooler colors, blue, bluish-green, and purple. Greenish patches of moss may be added. A sandstone wall would be painted in the same way with the addition of a little yellow. Work freely in large blocks of color. Sprinkle the whole piece lightly, when finished, with a small amount of dark and light blue to break up the smooth surfaces and add texture.

Paint mountain rows in light greens, blues, and purples, and spatter them well with pale violet (ultramarine blue with a little Venetian red and white) to blend their outlines into the sky. Distant banks of earth may be suggested in much the same way by using burnt umber, ultramarine, and Italian blue. Wherever possible run a little of the sky color into the far-away objects.

In planning landscapes, keep colors as light as possible, vary the values of tints, and avoid black shadows. Paint objects in the foreground in purer, brighter colors than those in the background. The shadow colors should go on first, and the painting proceed step by step from dark to light.

Certain colors, also, give the impression of distance. Pale blues and violets are especially helpful in this respect. A little very light ultramarine or Italian blue spattered over a row of hills will make them appear ten miles closer to the horizon.

15. FOLIAGE

To repeat the statement made in Chapter 11, Section 19, thoroughly convincing foliage is very difficult to paint. The tendency now is to avoid the use of definite shrubbery and other leafy pieces as much as possible. In out-of-door scenes calling for the presence of trees, an artist generally tries to design his setting in such a way as to draw the main attention to three or four bare, but convincing, solid-looking trunks rising out of sight behind the teaser in the more brightly lighted foreground, while merely *suggesting* masses of leaves, intertwining branches, and silhouettes of other trees (created by means of dark cut-out drops kept discreetly behind much scrim) in the shadows of the background. If a foliage piece, such as a masking border, must be used in the foreground, paint it in blocks to hint at clumps of leaves, rather than individual ones; then cut the edges and punch holes in the border (according to the characteristics of the foliage represented), and hang it in silhouette as much as possible. Dark chrome green, leaf green lake, and Hanover green are good foliage colors. They may be modified by mixing white into them. A few touches of neutralized red here and there will add roundness to the blocks of green. Some artists prime their foliage pieces with pure ultramarine and paint over it.

C. COLOR PRINCIPLES IN PIGMENTARY PAINTING

16. ELEMENTS OF COLOR AND COLOR MIXTURE

Before the scenic artist attempts to go very far into the methods of painting he should read and familiarize himself with the principles of color discussed in Chapter 18. The application of these principles to the pigments with which the scenic artist deals is, of course, quite different from that required for lighting, but the fundamentals are the same wherever color exists.

Generally speaking, the scenic artist is not concerned with *additive* mixtures (used in the composition of light) in which red, green, and blue are regarded as the primary colors, but with *subtractive* (Chapter 18, Sections 4 to 6) mixtures in which blue-red (magenta), yellow, and blue-green (cyan) are the primaries. Simply, this means that blue-red, yellow, and blue-green are the basic colors for pigmentary schemes and that under ideal conditions they may be mixed to make three other colors. Magenta combined with yellow makes red, yellow with blue-green makes green, blue-green with magenta makes blue. These second three are the secondary colors.[1]

It is easy to see the relationship of these colors if one studies Figure 50. The three primaries occupy the circles. Where any two of them overlap (are mixed in accordance with the subtractive scheme) they produce a secondary color. This is assuming, of course, that the proportions are about equal. If much yellow is mixed with a very little magenta, the product will be orange rather than red. If much yellow is combined with a small amount of blue-green, the result will be yellow-green instead of green, and so on.

If all of these colors are arranged on the circumference of a wheel, such as that indicated in Figure 50, one can see other relationships. Colors adjacent to each other, such as yellow, yellow-green, and green, are *analogous*. Colors directly opposite each other are *complementaries*. Green is the complement of magenta (blue-red), blue is the complement of yellow, and red is the complement of cyan (blue-green). In the center of the wheel is gray, the absolutely neutral point. Colors are brightest when they are related to (nearer to) the outside edge of the wheel and dullest when they are related to the center.

When two colors, represented by two points anywhere on the circumference of the wheel, are mixed, they produce a third color. If this were represented in a diagram, the third color, or blend, would be placed somewhere on a straight line drawn between the two original colors. The position of the blend on this line would depend on whether there was more of one of the original

[1] It will be noted that the secondary colors that result from mixing subtractive primaries are the additive primaries, and vice versa.

colors than the other in its composition. It will be seen that a point on this line (anywhere short of the extremities) is nearer to the hub of the wheel (grayness) than is a point on the circumference. This explains the fact that a mixture is never as intense in tone as a pure pigment. When two colors are combined they lose part of their intensity (saturation). If pure yellow is combined with pure magenta, for instance, a red is produced which, because it is a mixture, is not quite so intense as a pure red of the same hue. The more widely separated on the color wheel are the colors to be combined, the grayer or more nearly neutral will be the blend. When complementaries (directly opposite colors) are mixed

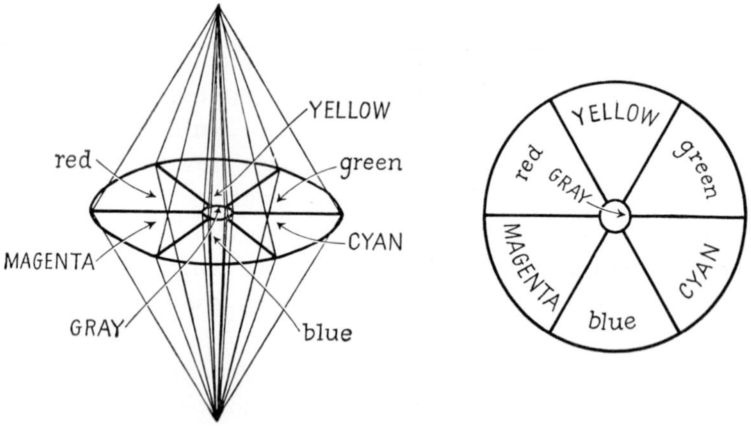

FIG. 50. Color wheel and color solid.

together in correct amounts, they produce a pure gray. This is a useful principle to remember when preparing paint for scenery. A pigment which appears too bright may very easily be toned down or softened (neutralized) by the addition of a little of its complement.

We have just glanced at the color wheel. This, however, is not a complete diagram of the behavior of color. If we place the wheel on edge, we find that it is a cross section of a three-dimensional figure made of two cones with their bases placed together (Figure 50). The end points of the two cones represent white and black respectively and mark the extremities of the gray line passing through the center of the figure. What happens to a color when it is mixed with white or black can now be seen very clearly. Not only is it grayed but lightened or darkened as well. A cross section of the color solid may be taken at any point, between the extremities, to produce a perfectly proportioned color wheel. The only dissimilarity between a cross section taken near an end and one taken near the center would lie in the fact that the colors on the circumference of the wheel sliced near the end would be less widely differentiated than those on the wheel sliced near the center.

A color, then, has three characteristics, which are determined by its position in this figure. Its *hue* is determined by its position in relation to other colors on the circumference of the wheel—that is, by its redness, yellowness, orangeness, blue-greenness, and so on. Its *saturation* is determined by its nearness to the center of the wheel—that is, the amount of gray, or of its complementary, it has in its composition. Its *lightness* is determined by the amount of white or black it has mixed with it. A color of high lightness is called a *tint,* of low lightness, a *shade.*

If we were to list some of the more obvious characteristics of color the following would be included:

Magenta, red, and yellow are warm colors.
Green, cyan, and blue are cool colors.
Analogous colors are harmonious.
Complementary colors offer the greatest contrast.
Colors of high lightness are more "exciting" than those of low lightness.
A low degree of lightness gives a greater impression of dignity than a high degree of lightness.
A little bright color outweighs much grayed color.
Mixing colors always lowers saturation. The more widely separated are the hues, the grayer is the result.
The appearance of a color is always influenced by the colors surrounding it.

17. COLOR HARMONY

Harmony is, to a large extent, the result of good proportion.

Almost any color may be placed next to any other color, providing it is used in a correct amount. Two colors, which clash when combined equally, will usually appear well together in unequal quantities. Proportion involves balance. A little intense (saturated) color, for instance, as we have already noted in the preceding section, will hold its own against a considerable amount of neutral (grayed) color. The following rules for combining colors are founded on principles that operate under most conditions on the stage:

1. Various shades and tints of the same hue may be used together in any proportion.

2. Analogous hues (that is, those adjacent to each other on the color wheel) may be used together in any proportion, if they are used without a third color.

3. Complementaries may be used together in unequal proportion only.

4. Strict neutrals (grays), very light tints, or very dark shades may be used together in their own classes in almost any proportion.

5. Intense (highly saturated) colors may be used with neutral ones in almost any proportion, though balance, especially in the consideration of large designs, generally demands that the neutral colors predominate.

6. A neutral background may be used to tie together smaller masses of bright colors that would otherwise clash.

The greatest encouragement that can be given harmony is to keep the larger areas of the scene fairly neutral, and to sharpen visual interest by building up intensities in certain smaller points only.

18. PRACTICAL MODIFICATIONS

Whatever is said here about color mixtures and color relationships should be regarded as having to do with *principle.* The painter finds in practice that pigments seldom behave just as they should according to the color schemes. The reason for this is that complicating factors which prevent the conditions from being ideal are always present. Theoretically, a mixture of magenta and yellow will make red; practically it may make a dull, unpleasant brown. What the principle of color mixture (in its simplest form) cannot take into account is the effects of chemical reactions between ingredients, the difference of purity in the pigments, and variations in texture.

The fact that magenta, yellow, and blue-green (cyan) are called the three pigment primaries is based on the premise that the pigments being dealt with are transparent. Opaque pigments (such as many of those used in scene painting) tend to behave differently from the others. Since light does not penetrate them, and the effect created by a mixture of two of them depends on the visual blending of tiny spots—color particles of one pigment and color particles of the other—on the outer surface of the painting, the results often fit the *additive* mixture scheme more than they do the *subtractive*.

Backgrounds also influence effects. Painting done on a dark ground tends to be different from one on a light ground. There is a difference also when the pigments are transparent, or when they are applied loosely in spattering or dry-brushing and the ground shows through.

Another complication exists in the nature of surfaces. A shiny surface on one piece of painting may produce an entirely different color effect from a rough one on another, even when the hue, saturation, and lightness in both cases are identical.

Knowledge of how to deal with all these variants comes from practice. Skilled painters use the basic color principles as general guides, but general guides only; they are prepared to adjust proportions and relationships freely in the light of experience. Apprentice painters would do well to use a somewhat limited palette to begin with, and to learn thoroughly all of its idiosyncrasies before experimenting with new pigments.

QUESTIONS AND EXERCISES

1. Describe scene paint.
2. Name several common painting implements.
3. How is scene paint prepared for application? Describe each step carefully.
4. What is the prime coat? What is its purpose, and how is it prepared and applied?
5. Why must the painter of scenery give so much attention to surface texture?
6. Describe, or demonstrate, seven methods of applying scene paint.
7. Tell how you would paint a room with (*a*) plaster walls, (*b*) wall-paper walls, (*c*) wood-paneled walls.
8. What is meant by the "toning" of walls?
9. Tell how you would paint (*a*) a plain sky drop, (*b*) landscape pieces, (*c*) foliage.
10. What are the primary and secondary pigment colors? Tell what happens when you mix together two primaries, or a primary and a secondary.

11. What are (*a*) analogous colors, (*b*) complementary colors? What happens when you mix analogous colors? When you mix complementaries? What effect does proportion—that is, using more of one pigment than another—have on the result?
12. Explain the terms *hue, saturation,* and *lightness* as they are applied to pigment colors.
13. What is the difference between "warm" and "cool" colors?
14. What is color harmony, and how is it achieved?
15. Design, in accordance with principles of good color harmony, a color plot for a set of scenery and the furniture and decorations for it; and describe what costumes and lighting would be suitable in this setting.
16. Compare color in stage pigments with color in stage lighting.

CHAPTER 14

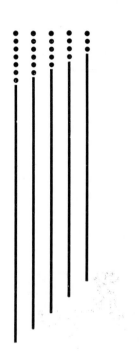

Designing the Scenery

1. INTRODUCTION

IF THE CONSTRUCTING, the painting, and the assembling of a group of scenic units to form the visual environment of a play are to be done effectively and efficiently, they must be carefully planned in advance. The layout may be done in a variety of ways: by making a pencil, ink, or color sketch, by drawing a floor plan, or by building a small model of the proposed set. The process of evolving a scenic idea in the professional studio more often than not includes all three of these steps. The stage picture as seen in elevation through the proscenium arch by the audience is first visualized in a general way in a sketch; then the arrangement of walls, entrances, steps, and other parts is worked out carefully in a floor plan; and finally the complete setting is checked from a three-dimensional point of view by constructing it in miniature form as a scale model of wood or cardboard. The technique of developing scenery through these three steps, and the method of converting the completed plan into working drawings for the carpenter is outlined briefly in the following pages.

A. MEDIA OF DESIGN

2. THE SKETCH

With the general design of his setting in mind, the artist usually attempts to visualize it first in the form of a sketch. Drawn in pencil or ink, and usually developed in water color, the sketch represents an ideal view of the projected scene as the latter would be seen from the front through the proscenium by a member of the audience. Offering, as it does, the best opportunity for the working out of the artist's ideas in line, mass, and color, it is in this step in the evolution of the setting that many designers expend their greatest effort.

FIG. 51. A Preliminary pen-and-ink sketch by Samuel Selden for a setting for *On Dixon's Porch,* by Wilbur Stout and Ellen Lay, as produced by The Carolina Playmakers.

One or two suggestions on the mechanical arrangement of the sketch are offered to those who are in doubt as to just what the drawing should include. Let the outside border of the sketch represent the proscenium opening. Draw the set within this boundary as one would assume it would be seen by a person sitting in about the center of the auditorium, downstairs. Suppose the set to represent a simple box interior. From this position one would see the whole back wall, a little of each side wall (in sharp perspective), a very narrow strip of the floor, and nothing of the ceiling.[1] As the

[1] If the relationship of parts in a design is quite clear without their being shown in perspective, the sketch may be drawn in simple elevation (Figure 53), in which case the floor can be indicated by one straight line.

teaser is always trimmed two or more feet below the edge of the ceiling to accommodate the border light and spotlights (Chapter 17, Sections 2 and 3), the ceiling (unless it is made to slope down at the back) is never seen except by those sitting in the first few rows of the orchestra. This would obviously be a poor spot from which to design a scene. Figure 51 represents a rough pen-and-ink sketch for an interior scene.

One cannot emphasize too strongly the importance of keeping proportions accurate. If the maximum dimensions of the practical proscenium opening of the stage on which the scenery is to be set up are only 20′ x 12′, do not design a layout that would require an opening 50′ x 30′ to show the whole scene. Disappointment in the final staging of the scene, besides an endless amount of annoyance in the process of its creation, can be avoided only by strict honesty in the initial sketching. Never show in the drawing anything that cannot be made thoroughly real in production.

3. THE FLOOR PLAN

After the artist has worked out his inspiration first in the form of a general sketch, he develops his ideas further by making a diagram of them. The most valuable diagram he can use is the floor plan. The floor plan is a skeleton outline which shows the relationship of the walls, doors, windows, platforms, stairways, and other features that enter into the scheme of the scene, as these features would be seen from above, looking down onto the set. The diagraming can be done quite simply in a few lines. Floor plans of different scenes are shown in Figures 9–12.

If a floor plan is to be of practical value, it must be drawn carefully to scale throughout, and it must include the positions and dimensions of not only the main elements of the scene, but also the incidental units, such as backings for the doors, set pieces seen through the windows, and the larger properties, as well. The size and position of the proscenium opening and the placement of the tormentors in relation to the set should likewise be indicated. In this outline the arrangements for lighting the scene may also be blocked in.

An artist frequently plots his first rough ideas, as well as his later more matured ones, in the form of a floor plan. A simple outline helps him to organize his ideas before he works them out in his sketch.

4. THE MODEL

For those persons who possess a creative understanding of scenery, but who cannot draw in perspective, an excellent medium of design is offered in the model. A model is a three-dimensional miniature of a scene built carefully to scale out of wood, cardboard, or other material (Figure 52). Many artists who develop their ideas in sketch form make use of this miniature also, either to check up on their plans before they lay them out in the final working drawing for the carpenter, or to demonstrate their plans to other members of the producing staff. The model is especially valuable to the artist who is required to submit in advance the scheme of a proposed setting to a director for his approval. A model usually presents a setting much more clearly and definitely than does a sketch of the same scene.

The model is constructed most easily out of light cardboard. Two-ply bristol board with a finished surface for painting is excellent for this purpose. Matt board with an eggshell surface makes a better model, but is more difficult to work with. The model described below is of bristol board. The walls are first drawn out carefully to some definite scale such as ¼ inch = 1 foot or ½ inch = 1 foot. A scale of ½ inch = 1 foot indicates that ½ inch in the model represents 1 foot in the actual stage set. When completely outlined, including door and window openings, the walls are cut out. This is done in one piece, if possible, because cardboard can be folded more easily than it can be fastened together. In cutting out the piece, or pieces, leave ¼-inch or ½-inch flaps along all edges which must be joined with glue to other edges. Now, with the back of a knife or razor blade, score all lines along which folds are to be made. In each case score the cardboard on the side opposite to that of the crease. Fold the wall up and mount it on edge, by means of the ¼-inch or ½-inch flaps, on a piece of heavy cardboard or a wooden panel. If the glue does not hold very well, the joints may be temporarily held in place by means of thumb tacks or paper clips. Rubber glue is superior to the ordinary forms of glue for model making. Pieces of gummed paper strips, such as those used for binding packages

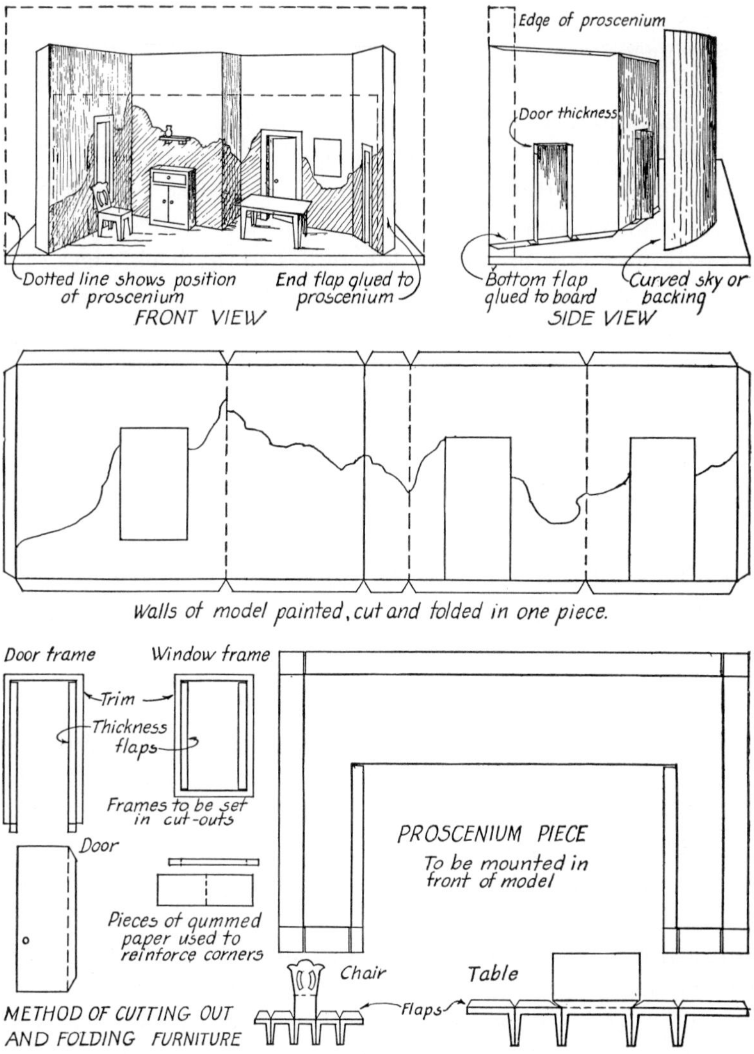

FIG. 52. Construction of a cardboard model. The various pieces are cut out and folded forward on the dotted lines and backward on the heavy black lines.

in stores, or Scotch or masking tape are excellent for making or reinforcing joints.

Usually the walls of the model are decorated before they are folded. Common water-color or show-card paints may be used for this purpose. Door and window openings can be made to look more real by inserting paper thicknesses (Chapter 11, Section 10) into them to represent their door and window frames, then fastening small door shutters or window sashes to the back edges of the thicknesses. Bits of furniture, folded out of paper and painted, add considerably to the effectiveness of the little set.

When the interior of the miniature has been finished, cut out a small proscenium to the same scale, paint it black or gray, and mount it in front of the set as a frame for it. Place a light blue sky piece at the back and add any foliage cutouts or mountain rows called for in the final plan. If the walls of the model are made a little higher than the proscenium opening, no ceiling need be used. In fact, it is a good plan in any case to leave at least part of the top open for lighting.

5. THE WORKING DRAWINGS

The working drawings of a set of scenery are the building plans drafted for the carpenter. Laid out to some selected scale—such as ¼ inch = 1 foot or 1 inch = 1 foot—they show the exact dimensions and construction of each unit, and include indications of materials to be used (if that is not apparent) and written explanations of all points that cannot be made clear by lines and figures alone. As the lines, however, are always more eloquent than the figures, words are employed very sparingly. If more than a dozen phrases are needed on any one sheet the plans may generally be considered poorly done. Details, such as the plan of a difficult joint, an arrangement of molding, or a special placing of hardware, are shown separately in enlarged detail drawings. Three-dimensional units, such as stairs and platforms, are laid out both in plan and elevation. Cross sections of units are added wherever they are necessary for clarity. As building principles on the stage are seldom complicated, it is usually unnecessary to make drawings elaborate.

If the carpenter who is superintending the building of the scenery is a man of experience in the ways and means of the stage,

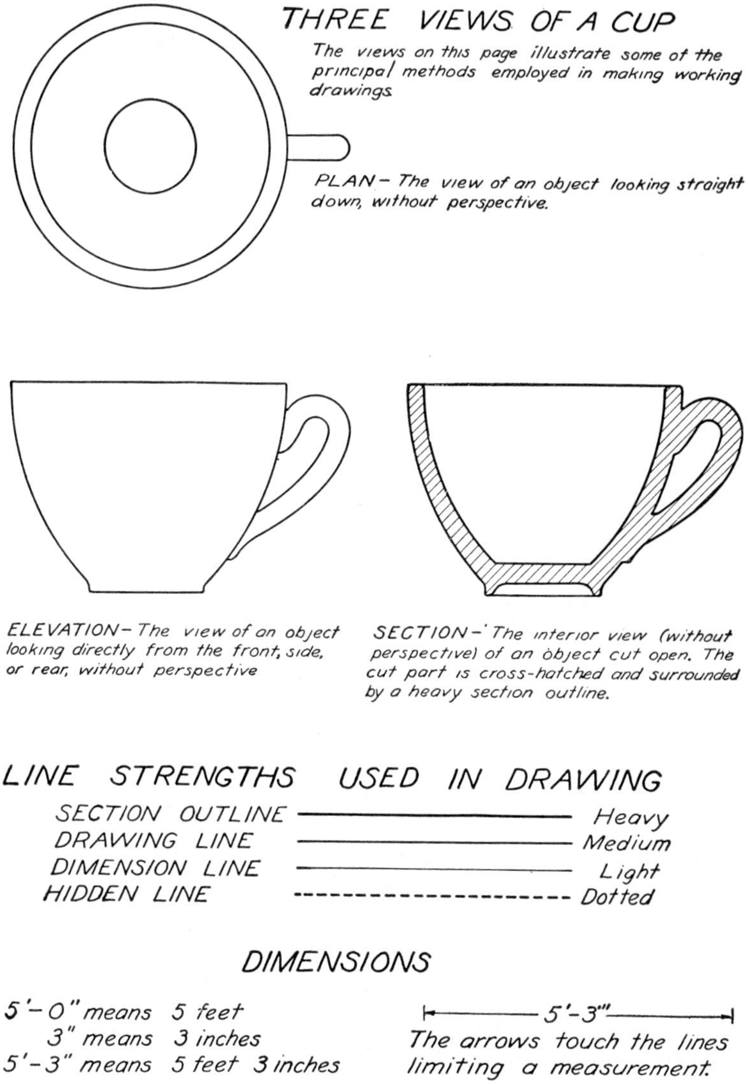
THREE VIEWS OF A CUP
The views on this page illustrate some of the principal methods employed in making working drawings.
PLAN – The view of an object looking straight down, without perspective.
ELEVATION – The view of an object looking directly from the front, side, or rear, without perspective
SECTION – The interior view (without perspective) of an object cut open. The cut part is cross-hatched and surrounded by a heavy section outline.
LINE STRENGTHS USED IN DRAWING
SECTION OUTLINE Heavy
DRAWING LINE Medium
DIMENSION LINE Light
HIDDEN LINE Dotted
DIMENSIONS
5'–0" means 5 feet
3" means 3 inches
5'–3" means 5 feet 3 inches
5'–3"
The arrows touch the lines limiting a measurement.

FIG. 53. Methods and symbols employed in the drafting of working drawings. illustrated in the drawing of a coffee cup.

it is, of course, a waste of effort to include in the working drawings all such details as the standard arrangement of parts in steps and parallels, of frame supports for columns and trees, or of joints and hardware on simple flats. Usually mere outlines of such units, with their widths and heights and the positions and sizes of any special features, like door or window openings, are all that are required.

In general, make the complete drawing accurately to one scale. For this purpose the use of a scale ruler, such as that employed by architectural and mechanical draftsmen, is quite essential. By accuracy we mean that a line on the paper 6 inches long should not vary from 6 inches by more than $\frac{1}{32}$ inch. If an enlarged detail is shown, write the scale immediately under it. The scale for the whole drawing should be placed in the lower right hand corner of the page. Check dimensions carefully several times and be sure that the sum of the dimensions of parts equals the over-all dimensions. If there is a discrepancy, the carpenter will probably toss a coin to decide which is correct. Small errors of less than an inch in the completed set will make it very difficult or impossible to put the set together.

B. OBJECTIVES IN DESIGN

6. MAKING THE STAGE SETTING PRACTICABLE

The effective stage setting fulfills three general requirements: (*a*) it must be practicable, (*b*) it must be attractive, (*c*) it must be expressive.

In the first place, the setting should be planned so that it can be used efficiently and effectively by the actors. The artist must provide for, in the places where they are most needed, the entrances, exits, platforms, steps, chairs, tables, and other means for walking, standing, sitting, and lying demanded by the action. The artist must see that his scenery is also safe and strong. He should make certain, for instance, that a platform which must bear the weight of a number of people is properly reinforced, that a wall, or a door against which an actor is required to fall at some moment in the play is properly braced, and so on. All these points it is his privilege and duty to work out carefully with the director.

The designer must arrange his setting so that all its chief parts will be visible to every member of the audience—the man on the side, the man at the back, the man in the balcony, as well as the man in the ideal center (see Figure 13). In order to obtain good sight lines for the stage action, he should see that his set is not too deep, and that the angles at the sides and at the top are right.

The artist must consider in his design not only the actor and the audience, but also the shop carpenter and the stage crew, and (far from incidentally) the business manager who guards the budget. In accordance, therefore, with the suggestions outlined in Chapter 11, Section 1, the artist should plan scenery so that it may be capable of being:

a. easily and rapidly constructed,
b. economically constructed,
c. quickly and silently shifted,
d. safely exposed to strain and wear,
e. well assembled,
f. readily packed or stored.

The successful designer of stage settings is invariably a person who knows intimately the anatomy of scenery and who is familiar with the usual solutions to all of the fundamental problems related to the placement of that scenery in the theatre. Whether or not he always employs them, he is completely informed regarding the standard methods for building and handling scenery (Chapters 11 and 12)—and improves on them when he can.

The artist of the stage is primarily a dramatist. But he can never hope to fulfill the high duties of his principal function until he has made himself a wise and efficient technician.

7. MAKING THE SETTING ATTRACTIVE

In the second place, as has been said, a stage setting should be *attractive.* By the use of pleasing shapes and colors in the surrounding forms it should set off the action, and make it appear at all times "good to look at." The artist must select for the design of his scenes objects which have interesting and graceful qualities and arrange these in accordance with the principles of good composition.

A well-composed scene has, first, *unity.* All of its parts (the mass, line, and color of the larger units of scenery, the properties, the costumes, and the lighting) should appear to belong together; they should all create an environment particularly appropriate to the action. The environment desired for the first act of Philip Barry's drama, *Holiday,* for example, is that of a "handsome room, and quite a comfortable room, but very, very rich." The idea in a design for the first act of *You and I* by the same author, on the other hand, would be "a huge, uneven, motherly sort of room that pats your hand as you come into it, and tells you to sit down and be comfortable with the rest of us." Securing unity in a design involves, then, (*a*) the selection of only those elements which relate to one another and contribute to the specific environment desired; (*b*) the arrangement of the elements chosen into a plan that emphasizes that feature, or group of features (the "motifs"), which most clearly express the environment; and (*c*) the maintenance of a single style throughout the design. A unified scene may be said to be one that is *well focused.*

Also, a well-composed scene has *variety.* It avoids monotonous repetition. Identical shapes and colors should not appear everywhere. Forms with vertical lines are varied with forms with horizontal lines, round objects are varied with square objects, intense colors are varied with neutral colors, light colors with dark colors (Chapter 13, Sections 16 and 17), and so on. Contrast is introduced to make the design alive and interesting. If, for example, in designing a scene to represent a sitting room the doors and windows are made square, certain other details may be rounded; if one color, somewhat neutral, is selected for the walls, another quite dissimilar one, somewhat brighter than the first, may be chosen for the window hangings, table covers, certain pieces of pottery, lampshades, and other objects that stand in front of the walls. Variety cannot be demanded at the expense of unity. If, however, the primary motif is allowed to dominate at all times, there is little danger of losing unity through contrast and variety in the elements of the design. In fact, by their very difference from the main motif they will have a tendency to call attention to it.

A well-composed scene has *balance.* The prominent architectural features (such as the doors and windows), the larger pieces of furniture, and all the other objects of special pictorial or dramatic interest should be so distributed on the two sides of the stage that they weigh against each other more or less equally. Color, too, must conform to the principle of balance.

Finally, the well-composed scene has *harmony*. In it all of the different elements combine to make an attractive whole. This is the result of successfully applying the first three principles of good composition, namely, unity, variety, and balance.

8. MAKING THE SETTING EXPRESSIVE

In the third place, the stage setting must be *expressive*. The principal function of scenery, as has been observed in Chapter 9, is to serve as an "environment." Through the power of suggestion in the visual forms which surround the action of the play, the setting must help to make clear the thought and the spirit of the play.

A setting rightly designed locates the dramatic action of a scene. It creates a specific home for it. The setting tells the audience whether the action takes place in a doctor's house in Norway, an artist's studio in Italy, a broker's office in New York, or a mountaineer's cabin in North Carolina. Through the use of suggestive shapes, colors, and lighting the audience is informed concerning the conditions surrounding the action—the physical circumstances of the characters, the time of day, the kind of weather, and so on. But, more important still, the audience obtains intimate hints regarding the personalities themselves. The general appearance of a room, for instance, can be made to tell something about the tastes and habits of the people who live in it. The general state of tidiness in which the characters keep the room, the color they paint the walls, the kind of chairs they like to sit in, the kind of tools and utensils they use, the incidental, intimate objects they have lying about—all may be made to indicate personality, just as in real life. There are a hundred ways in which surroundings may be made to describe the thought and behavior of the characters in a play.

Then, too, scenery may create *atmosphere* for the action. For example, it may cause the audience to view the action in a warm, sympathetic frame of mind. Consider, for instance, a setting for the famous little love scene in the avenue to Portia's house in the last act of *The Merchant of Venice,* suggested by Lorenzo's lines to Jessica:

> How sweet the moonlight sleeps upon this bank!
> Here we will sit and let the sounds of music
> Creep in our ears. Soft stillness and the night . . .

A setting designed in the spirit of these lines would itself build up a romantic attitude toward the two lovers even before Lorenzo spoke. It would create the *atmosphere.* It would make each spectator think to himself: "A moonlit garden is a place for love; in such unusually soft and expressive moonlight, in such a beautiful garden, these two young people must be very deeply in love." Atmospheric scenery is what might be called emotional scenery. Its elements, both individually and collectively, convey an emotional impression. Each of these scenic elements symbolically suggests sadness, or loneliness, or weariness, or joy, or laughter, and puts the spectator in the proper mood for the action of the play. In a setting for the scene in the convent park in the last act of *Cyrano de Bergerac,* for example, the soft fall of leaves, the quiet movement of black-gowned nuns, and the light slowly fading through the trees, all help the audience to understand how the old soldier's poetical life is finally drawing to a close. All scenery that suggests in one way or another the thoughts and feelings of the characters that move within it has *atmosphere.* Gordon Craig's mist-covered rock in *Macbeth,* the two contrasting rooms in *Holiday,* as well as the strange surroundings of *The Cabinet of Dr. Caligari*—all are atmospheric. They attune the audience to the proper mood for drama.

9. ART AND THE BUDGET

To conceive perfection in scenic design is one thing; to achieve it, another. Those of us who must labor in the theatre with one hand on the stage and the other stretched to the slim tin box in the business manager's office realize, often only too keenly, the truth of this statement. Under the emergency conditions occasioned by temporary or chronic budgetary depression, wise practice demands, of course, a compromise. It is a compromise, however, not of purpose but of method. The author has often been asked by the directors and technicians of small school and community producing groups what an ambitious artist is expected to do when he is allotted from the treasury for the preparation of scenery, not one or two hundred dollars, but a meager twenty-five! The reply to this troublesome question is contained in one or two general suggestions. Hints only they are, because the ultimate solution of each emergency problem in scenic design is naturally influenced by specific circumstances, and must, therefore, be handled in terms of itself.

Any program of economy related to the stage usually involves some form of initial investment. The particular "money-saver" which is here recommended for purchase or construction by the artist required to provide a quantity of scenic environments on a frail allowance, is a black duvetyn, rep, or velour cyclorama. Hung

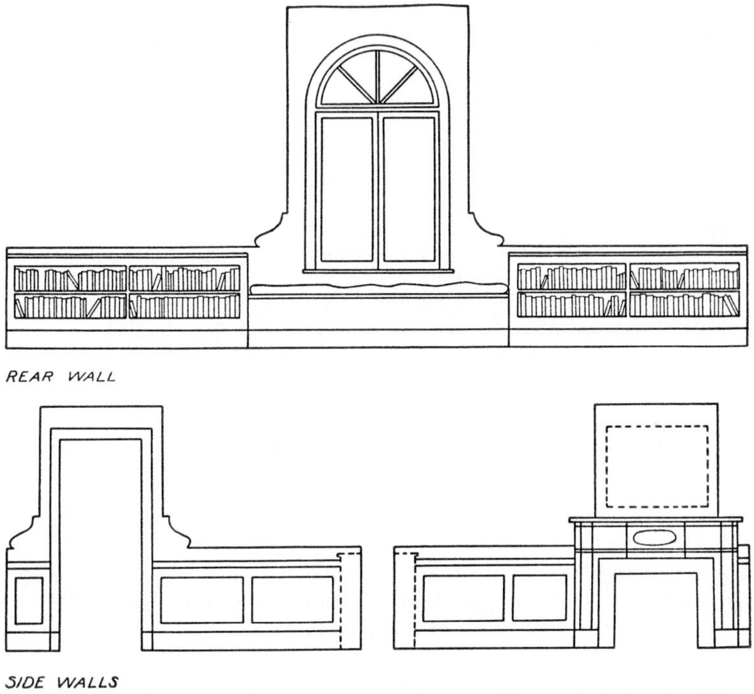

FIG. 54. A design for a set of cut-down scenery. Setting by Samuel Selden for *The Common Gift,* a one-act play by Elwyn de Graffenried, produced by The Carolina Playmakers.

around, and behind, the acting area on the stage, the cyclorama is employed as a neutral background for small screens and other low-cut scenic forms placed in front of it. It is surprising what attractive, dramatically effective, and at the same time inexpensive settings can be produced with this combination of black curtains and painted set pieces. Examples of scenery of the suggestive type are pictured in Figures 54 and 55.

The cyclorama should never, of course, be used by itself alone—except for occasional purely spatial settings. Black, unrelieved by color, is depressing and a view of it soon grows tiresome to the spectator. The "feeling" of a cyclorama setting is almost invariably imparted by the decorative and dramatic objects placed in front of the cyclorama. Black curtains on the stage should, therefore, be regarded purely as contrivances for masking from the audience the sides and top of the stage, and for providing a neutral, or spatial, background for the scenery proper.

If a sky drop (Chapter 11, Section 14) is hung behind the cyclorama and is revealed for outdoor settings by parting the two rear

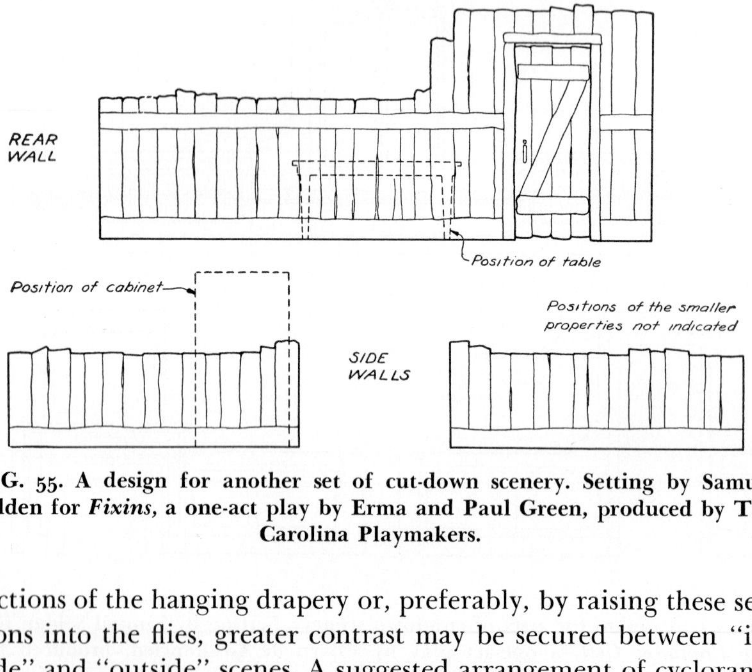

FIG. 55. A design for another set of cut-down scenery. Setting by Samuel Selden for *Fixins*, a one-act play by Erma and Paul Green, produced by The Carolina Playmakers.

sections of the hanging drapery or, preferably, by raising these sections into the flies, greater contrast may be secured between "inside" and "outside" scenes. A suggested arrangement of cyclorama and sky-drop units for the ready accommodation of all kinds of abbreviated scenery is indicated in Figure 56.

Regarding the cost of the initial investment—a duvetyn cyclorama designed for a small stage, consisting of four sections (two for the back and one each for the sides), two borders, two tormentor tabs, tie-lines, and a batten frame, may be made (see Chapter 11, Section 13) at fairly modest cost. Rep and velour curtains are heavier and stronger, but they are also priced a little higher. A muslin sky drop might require the outlay of a few more dollars.

Whatever may be the expense of these two units to the producer, he may rest comforted in the knowledge that he will soon save several times their cost in lowered scenery bills.

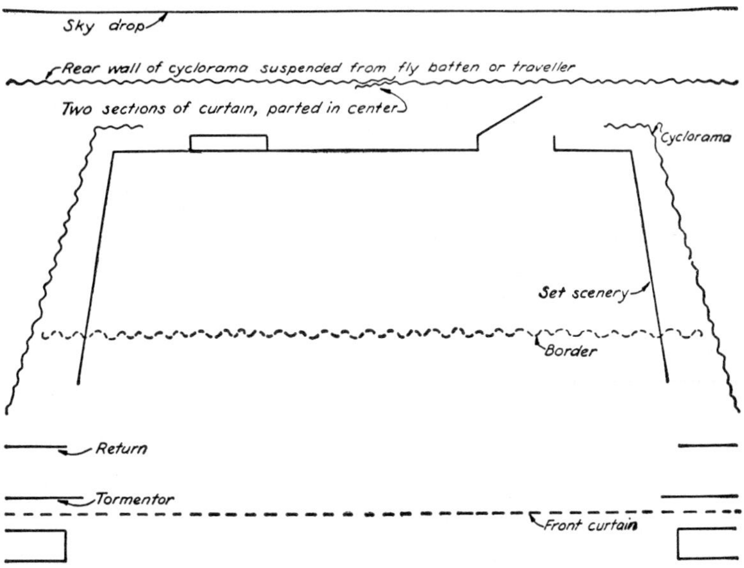

FIG. 56. Stage layout for minimum scenery.

C. SETTINGS FOR SPECIAL CONDITIONS

10. SETTINGS FOR THE ARENA THEATRE

One of the liveliest of theatre developments in recent years has taken place in the *arena,* sometimes called also the *theatre-in-the round.* In arena theatre the acting area, usually square or rectangular, is placed in the center, and the spectators encircle it. Players' entrances and exits are made down aisles between sections of the audience. Sometimes the acting is done on a level with the lowest seats, sometimes it is raised a foot or two. Ideally, the surrounding audience chairs are banked (sloped up) to give the spectators better vision. There are no definite rules about the size and shape of the arena space, or about the relation between the acting and audience areas, except two: the front seats should be close enough to the playing space to keep the feeling intimate, but not so near as to inhibit the actors' freedom of movement; and the rear seats should be so arranged that people sitting in them can hear and see easily every part of the performance, including the entrances and exits.

Generally speaking, arena staging uses no scenery. Occasionally, directors staging plays with multiple locales have found it advantageous to mark off one part of the playing space as a sitting room, another as an office, another as a street corner, and to erect one or two low scenic set pieces to help the spectators visualize the different places. One device that has been used is to give floor areas in the different spaces different colors by means of rugs or painted pieces of canvas. Since, however, this kind of arrangement tends inevitably to corner the action during each of the several scenes, it is usually frowned upon. In arena theatre, the actors are supposed to play equally to every part of the audience, and this cannot be done if their actions are restricted to specific areas.

Sometimes, of course, the whole play may be set outdoors. In this case, the use of a scenic rock, or one or two tree trunks (not so large as to interfere with lighting or sight lines) may help to create a sense of locale. Generally, however, the responsibility for creating a feeling of surroundings rests with the actors, assisted by the lighting director. This does not mean that there is consequently nothing for a designer to do. There is much for him to do in the selection and construction of properties—pieces of furniture, utensils, bits of machinery, and various portable objects, which will *suggest* by their form and style the kind of surroundings which would naturally go with them. Thus the properties help the actors create an illusion of scenery.

And, of course, there are always present the problems of texture and color, and of the composition of the various blocks, lines, and contours of physical objects in relation to the costumes and the movements of the players. All of these details are especially important in arena staging, and the designer will find himself busy attending to them.

11. SETTINGS FOR TELEVISION

Designing for television seldom requires any planning of whole settings; rather it calls for substantial fragments. As one walks through a television studio one is likely to see set up next to each other, part of a wall featuring a large and handsome fireplace, with a chair and stool beside it; the corner of a kitchen, with the stove, icebox, table and, perhaps, one window showing; a glimpse of a street corner with a streetlamp and a bit of a building, a shop window, nothing more; and a garden bench surrounded by shrubbery. None of the settings is very wide—unless the action covered by the cameras will need width—and none is any higher than it is necessary to make it for the camera's eye.

Before the designer of scenery for a television sequence even begins to make any drawings, he must find out from the director just how much space the acting will cover, and how close and how far away the cameras will move to record the action. This knowledge will be necessary for right planning not only with regard to size but also with regard to good toning and the right texture effects.

What the camera eye sees is often very different from what impresses the human eye. For this reason, the designer, as well as the carpenter and painter, should consult the recording technicians and use their advice on how to modify shapes and colors so that the results will be right.

In learning to plan the best kinds of settings for television, as well as for regular and arena theatre, there is nothing more valuable than experience.

QUESTIONS AND EXERCISES

1. Through what steps is a design for a stage setting commonly carried? Describe each.
2. Prepare a freehand pencil or ink sketch for a stage setting for a play of your choice, and develop this with water colors.
3. Carefully draft a set of scaled working drawings for the setting you have already visualized roughly in the sketch.
4. Construct a scaled model of your setting.
5. How, in general, should you plan a stage setting in order to make it (*a*) practical, (*b*) attractive, (*c*) expressive?
6. Select a play (or one scene from this play) and design for it an effective set of scenery on a twenty-five dollar budget. Assume that the play will be produced on your stage. Make the twenty-five dollars you have allotted for your setting cover lumber, covering material, paint, and hardware.

PART IV

STAGE LIGHTING

By HUNTON D. SELLMAN

CHAPTER 15

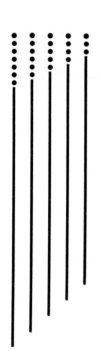

The Meaning of Light on the Stage

1. INTRODUCTION

As WE ALL KNOW, light as a means of revealing the actor and his background is as old as the theatre. Skylight and direct sunlight can do little else. But even when the theatre was indoors, light seldom served other functions than that of visibility until late in the nineteenth century. To be sure, it was known in Renaissance Italy that light should be dimmer in the more serious parts of a play. In succeeding years theatre history records the occasional use of light for mood, and Garrick's scenic artist is said to have made use of the "magic lantern" for some sort of projected effect. For a new concept of light, however, we waited until the late nineteenth century when Adolphe Appia started writing about lighting as an art. In 1898 he wrote of light as design, as a dynamic, mobile means of emotional expression. It is only recently, however, that science and engineering have provided theatres with the technical means of fulfilling a part of Appia's dream. At last a few theatres have equipment for lighting control comparable to electrical and mechanical equipment in an average office building. When this superior equipment for control is supplemented with lighting instruments that are designed and built with the care and precision of common binoculars and both find their way into theatres organized for something besides profit, Appia's conception of stage lighting will be an everyday reality. Indeed, new functions of light will certainly evolve.

2. LIGHT OF TWO KINDS

At present, however, light is of two general kinds. The first is form-revealing or shadow-producing light, which we shall call *specific illumination*. The other is shadowless light, which is commonly called *general illumination*. While the matter will be discussed in some detail later, our whole problem of stage lighting can be reduced to a least common denominator. Stage lighting can be as simple as the proper handling and blending of these two kinds of light, effectively controlled according to their function in the production of each play.

3. THREE CONTROLLABLE PROPERTIES

Continuing, light of either kind can be controlled in three ways which we shall call *quantity, color,* and *distribution*. By changing or controlling these three characteristics of the two kinds of light, all of the functions, and accordingly all of the effects that artificial illumination seems to be capable of, can be accomplished. For example, the *quantity* or the amount of light can be varied between two useful limits: avoiding technical terms, it may be said that the upper limit is glare-producing light, which injures the eye, and the minimum limit is illumination so low that vision is difficult without strain. While one is trying to adapt his eyes to low levels of illumination, he is concentrating his attention on the visual stimulus and does not hear as well. Muscular control of the iris of the eye, part of adaptation, controls the amount of light that falls on the retina. Because adaptation takes time, we must control our changes in illumination accordingly, especially from light to dark. For example, an audience can see a dimly lighted scene much more clearly (and with less strain) if the auditorium lighting is dimmed slowly and if the house is left dark for a few seconds before the curtain rises. This practice is much better than if the auditorium light is snapped off and the curtain opened immediately. The reason for this is that adaptation is much more rapid when light becomes brighter, but it takes from three to thirty minutes for dark adaptation to become complete. Everyone has had the experience of stumbling about for a while upon entering a cinema theatre from bright daylight. A number of quick changes of scene with widely different levels of illumination will tire an audience much more rapidly than lighting slowly changed or kept at a single level of illumination, because in the first case the muscles of the iris have been overworked. It has been proved by experiment that higher levels of illumination make people more alert, and we know by experience in the theatre that an audience enjoys a sophisticated comedy in bright light more than it does under conditions of poor visibility. The maximum quantity of illumination for any scene is determined by the wattage of the lamps, by accessories such as reflectors, and by the density of color media placed in front of the lamp. Changes in the amount of illumination during a scene, however, almost always should be accomplished electrically at the control board.

Color, too, was important in the theatre early in its history. In producing plays in the fifteenth century, not only were higher intensities used for comedy than for tragedy, but different colors were used also. Warm colors were used for comedy and cool ones for tragedy. This conception of color has survived and is in common use today. Less general in its use, but still applicable to stage lighting as well as to costuming is the elaborate color symbolism that has developed through the ages. For example, white is said to be the symbol of light, chastity, truth, purity, peace; black, the symbol of gloom, death, night, mystery, and evil; red is said to suggest murder, fire, blood, health, passion, and shame. These are a mere beginning compared with the hundreds of symbols and ideas associated with one color. Many are contradictory, and few if any have meaning when used abstractly or alone. For example, a setting flooded with red light might mean a dozen things from fire to passion, but if the red light were accompanied by changes in intensity and familiar forms, or if the color were associated with smoke, most people would think of fire, even though a small part of firelight is actually red. In general, then, if one hopes to convey an idea to the audience by means of such symbols, or if he expects to affect the audience emotionally by means of changes in color, he should follow these simple suggestions. Color in costumes, scenery, and light must be directly related to the text of the play. Furthermore, to ensure clarity in the minds of the audience one should choose simple, conventional symbols. Besides these, one must not forget the prejudices, color preferences, former associations in and out of the theatre, and the opportunity for confusion that an audience may bring to the production of a play. Carelessly handled, color for this purpose can be nothing but a plaything for the artist that will confuse and dissatisfy the audience; thoughtfully and clearly presented, it can be an effective means of revealing the emotional and dramatic values in a play.

Color symbolism is probably more important historically than it is now in everyday lighting practice. In the production of modern plays it is seldom considered. Of more importance for the present, however, is the intelligent use of color for variety, composition, and the natural appearance of the actor and his environment. When actually setting up a scene, changes in color are made by changing the color medium in front of the light source and sometimes by changing the source itself.

Distribution means the way in which light of any quantity or color is spread or distributed over the acting area and the background. Obviously then, the three variables are closely interrelated. Distribution depends upon the use of both kinds of light, specific and general, to produce different levels of illumination on the acting area and on the scenery, and upon a variety in color over the same surfaces. The fact that scenery, costumes, properties, and even the actors' faces and make-up vary considerably in their ability to reflect light and in the way they reflect it is a highly important consideration in the lighting distribution for a play. Even when an actor moves about the stage he changes the distribution of light because his body and costume are reflectors like any part of the setting. Thus the controllable properties take their place in an analysis of stage lighting.

4. THE FUNCTIONS OF STAGE LIGHTING

The real functions of stage lighting are pretty well established and agreed upon, but the names and number of them vary with opinion. For purposes of discussion and explanation these functions may be divided into five:

a. Selective visibility
b. Revelation of form
c. Illusion of nature
d. Composition
e. Emotional and psychological effects

a. Selective visibility. It is of primary importance that an audience see comfortably and clearly everything the producer intends it to see. Visibility depends upon the amount of illumination, the size of objects, the amount of light an object reflects, contrast with its background, and the distance between the object and the observer. This is true anywhere, off the stage as well as on. Obviously, light at all times should be sufficiently bright for comfortable vision without strain. The theatre is only a minor offender in this respect, and more often gives the audience too much illumination rather than too little. But everything must not be illuminated to the same degree. Visibility must be selective if the audience is to see only what is intended for it at any moment. For example, in the New York production of Robert Anderson's *Tea and Sympathy* several rooms were visible to the audience at the same time. When a scene was being played in the living room, the hall and bedroom were comparatively dim. When the scene took place in the bedroom, the other two rooms were less bright. This is a matter of having the proper relative amounts of light in the several scenes to produce a pleasing distribution of light without allowing the audience to be pulled away from the most important scene at any moment.

By lowering the level of illumination, visibility can be reduced until an object completely disappears or is left inconspicuously in shade or shadow until one wishes to have it appear. This method of lighting is always effective with a permanent set when changes are made by moving from one part of the stage to another. Color, too, is concerned with visibility. Under ordinary lighting conditions visibility reaches the maximum in yellow and drops off in blue, green, orange, and red. Because of this fact, higher levels of blue light are necessary for a night scene than would be if yellow light were used. On the other hand, monotonous uniform distributions of blue light in large quantities quickly bring fatigue to the eyes of the audience.

b. Revelation of form. This is a function that is easily ignored and overlooked. When plays are lighted with general illumination alone, actors, properties, and pieces of scenery all look flat and uninteresting. There are no highlights, no shadows, no variety in the distribution of light. The walls of a set have as much light on them as the actors' faces have, and in fact every object, every surface, is at the same level of illumination. This is anything but form-revealing light. In order for objects to appear in their natural form, the distribution of light must have a high degree of variety produced by different levels of illumination. In the first place, there must be that form-revealing, shadow-producing light which we call specific illumination. Appia said that shade and shadow are equal in importance to light itself. In one of the notebooks of Leonardo da Vinci there appear some pertinent comments on the subject. He says, "Shadow is the withholding of light. It seems to me that shadows are of supreme importance in perspective, seeing that without them opaque objects and solid bodies will be indistinct both as to what lies within their boundaries and also as to their boundaries themselves. Consequently I treat of shadow and say in this connection that every opaque body is surrounded and has its surface clothed with shadows and light." And again, "Excess of light makes things seem hard; and too much darkness does not admit of our seeing them. The mean is excellent." This function, then, revelation of form, can be accomplished by specific illumination, light from specific directions balanced by shade, shadow, and areas of different degrees of brightness with some variety in color.

c. Illusion of nature. This includes time, locale, season, and the creation of the illusion of special kinds of light. According to the demands of the play, the hard shafts of a tropical sun, a cold northern light, or romantic moonlight can be produced, not with naturalistic accuracy (such accuracy is always unnecessary) but with good taste and sufficient illusion to suggest reality without "stealing the show." Illusion can be improved by a natural angle for the sun or moon, normal shadows of the actors, and shadow foliage patterns on the walls of buildings. Although actual sunlight is white in color, stage sunlight is usually a light amber to add warmth, color, and contrast to the lighting of a scene. Natural moonlight is really yellow, but for the stage we associate moonlight with the blue of the sky and the coolness of the night. The con-

Suggestion and realism at Yale University. Above: Peter Larkin's setting for *American Primitive* by Thomas M. Patterson. Below: Bill Eckhart's setting for *First in Heart* by Betty Smith. Both plays were directed by Frank McMullan.

ventional color of stage moonlight is a tint of blue-green or light blue.

d. Composition. Composition is the use of light as an element of design. If one turns a borderlight and footlights on three walls and a few pieces of furniture, he illuminates a box set and the first function, visibility, may be accomplished. But if one can succeed in creating, according to the principles of good design, a distribution of light, with variations in quantity and color, he is approaching the art of light by means of composition. This requires general illumination of the right tonality and quantity; it requires specific illumination from an angle best suited to each object, so that the highlights are accurately placed and the shadows are massed and formed as a part of the design. Shadow patterns, too, are useful for design as well as for representations of nature. Design in light is not static like a painting in oil or water color, but is a mobile painting in space, changing continually and following the drama as an accompaniment. Lighting should focus the attention of the audience and build a new design with every movement of the actor. Without light, design cannot exist; and without design, lighting is only illumination.

e. Emotional and psychological effects. The last function is probably the most difficult one to accomplish. Training in psychology is useful, but a combination of good judgment and experience with audiences is indispensable. Color for this function was mentioned above (see Section 3), but light and shade are equally important.

Very dim light, or darkness with light on a single figure gives an audience the feeling of mystery, impending disaster, or the presence of the supernatural. Spirits from another world have a way of preferring the darkness, returning to us at night, glowing dimly from "within" by means of fluorescent or phosphorescent pigments in costume and make-up, or they are often followed about by a mysterious dim light. In contemporary productions of *Hamlet,* the ghost of Hamlet's father is sometimes made unearthly by means of fluorescent materials and ultra-violet light. Likewise, by changes in distribution, that is, by difference in light and shade, and by producing certain kinds of shadows, we multiply the opportunity of affecting the audience emotionally. How much more dramatic it is to see the slightly distorted or enlarged shadow of a villain slinking along a wall rather than to see the figure of the villain himself. The shadow of a noose appearing on a prison cell wall just above the head of a prisoner, or the shadow of a cross in a religious play can serve both a pictorial and an emotional purpose. Occasionally when a play calls for a murder or violent death onstage, the scene might be softened and presented in better taste by allowing the audience to see only the shadows of the action. A lynching scene done in this manner could be made less objectionable but sufficiently emotional and terrible for any audience. Audiences are not hard to please in this matter. In attempting to carry out this function errors are more often made in the direction of being too complex rather than too simple.

We have seen with discussion and examples how the broad function of light on the stage can be subdivided into five individual functions: selective visibility, revelation of form, illusion of nature, composition, and emotional and psychological effects. In every case imagination will lead us further because lighting is an art and the possibilities are infinite. Thus, our general analysis is complete and we can sum it up in one sentence. There are two kinds of light (general and specific) that can be controlled in three ways (quantity, color and distribution) in order to accomplish these five functions.

This analysis gives us a basic philosophy about light on the stage. Going further we shall need a plan of action and a discussion of the materials with which to work. In the following chapters a survey of lighting instruments, lighting control, and simple methods of using this equipment to light a play effectively will be found.

QUESTIONS AND EXERCISES

1. What did Appia have to do with our modern conception of the two kinds of light?
2. How is the term *distribution* used in connection with light?
3. How is the term *selective* used in referring to visibility?
4. Why is illumination not a function of stage lighting?
5. How can we make effective use of color symbolism on the stage?
6. Write a paragraph on the relationship of the composition of light to stage direction.

CHAPTER 16

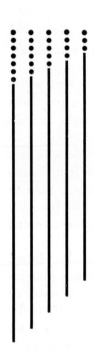

A Lighting Plan

1. INTRODUCTION

To help the reader understand the recommendations in the following chapter on lighting instruments, the general method of lighting a play is presented first. The application of this plan to a specific play will follow the description and use of instruments and their control. While the lighting plan discussed here requires more equipment than many little theatres have, it can be modified or simplified according to the means of any theatre, as will be discussed later. This scheme will serve also as a guide in the selection of lighting instruments to be purchased in the future. Many producing groups buy foolishly and haphazardly because they do not know what they are working toward, but once they have learned effective methods of lighting their plays, they can purchase new instruments from time to time more intelligently.

Although the plan to be explained is not as simple as lighting a set with footlights and borderlights only, the results are so far superior to this antiquated method that comparison would be meaningless. This plan is as simple as a high degree of flexibility will permit and as unpretentious as possible for accomplishing the functions of light for an average production. Although there may be other satisfactory lighting methods, the one discussed here is in common use in many theatres where superior lighting is done.

2. THE BALANCE OF SPECIFIC AND GENERAL ILLUMINATION

The effective lighting of any play or scene depends upon a properly proportioned mixture of the two kinds of illumination, general and specific. As was mentioned in Chapter 15, specific illumination brings variety to the stage, and because it is shadow producing, it is also form revealing. In contrast to this, general illumination softens shade and shadow, modifies excessive contrasts in specific illumination, and creates the general color tonality of the whole area.

If the actor were static, like a piece of sculpture, lighting him effectively would be a comparatively simple problem. After studying a static pose, one would place a source of specific illumination at that ideal horizontal and vertical angle which would cause areas of shade and shadow to contrast most effectively with highlights. Then one would add general illumination of just the right amount to soften the contrast between highlight, shade, and shadow and to produce a desirable color tonality in the areas of less illumination. In this way, a single actor remaining immobile in one area might be effectively lighted; but alas, the problem is not so simple. The actor is in almost constant movement within an area, and he ordinarily uses all of the areas in a setting. Thus a degree of complexity is introduced.

3. INSTRUMENTS FOR SPECIFIC ILLUMINATION

A large number of instruments might seem to be necessary to produce specific illumination from various angles, according to the position of the actor; but this is impracticable for reasons that will soon be obvious. Two instruments separated by a horizontal angle of about 90 degrees (the size of this angle is controlled to considerable extent by physical conditions) will light the actor adequately in a single area. Since the stage is commonly divided into six areas, a total of twelve instruments is needed for the specific illumination on the whole acting area as a basic pattern (see Figure 57). The downstage areas are properly lighted from a position in the auditorium ceiling. Because the instruments for these areas are often placed in false beams that form a part of the auditorium ceiling, they are ordinarily called beam lights or antiproscenium lights. The verticle angle at which the light from these sources strikes the acting area varies from 35 to 60 degrees, but there are a number of circumstances that influence one in choosing the right angle. The building may impose limitations; the distance from the source to the stage may be greater than the efficiency of a spotlight will permit; and an angle as low as 35 degrees may make shadows of the actors on the wall of the set, unless the set is very deep. If, however, no footlights are used, the vertical angle of the beam lights should not be over 40 degrees, because a higher angle will make the shadows and shade too dark in the eye sockets and under the nose and chin. If the set is shallow and footlights are available, an angle of approximately 55 degrees is satisfactory. At this angle shadows on the rear wall are eliminated, and the deep facial shadows can be softened with the general illumination from footlights. On the other hand, a low teaser height may require a very low beam angle. In any case, footlights are necessary when players wear hats with broad brims. Instruments to be used as beam lights should be large conventional spotlights (with 8-inch lenses), sufficiently well ventilated to hold 1000 watt or 1500 watt lamps, or even better, ellipsoidal spotlights with 750 to 1500 watt lamps (see Chapter 17).

Anyone familiar with the technical side of the theatre will have noticed that lighting the downstage areas from the beam position is not common in the commercial theatre in New York City. The road companies from New York follow the same practice of lighting the front of the stage from spotlights hung from frames on the front of the balcony. Some of the commercial theatres in New York supplement this with spotlights partly concealed in boxes fastened to the side walls of the auditorium. The front of the balcony places the spotlight at a much lower angle than the beam position, causing the eye sockets to be more easily illuminated without footlights. This has certain advantages to the mature matinee idol who is desperately trying to look twenty-eight. An important disadvantage of this low vertical angle is in the large shadows of the actors that appear on the wall of an interior, or on the cyclorama in an exterior. The usual method of removing these objectionable shadows is to pile on light from so many angles

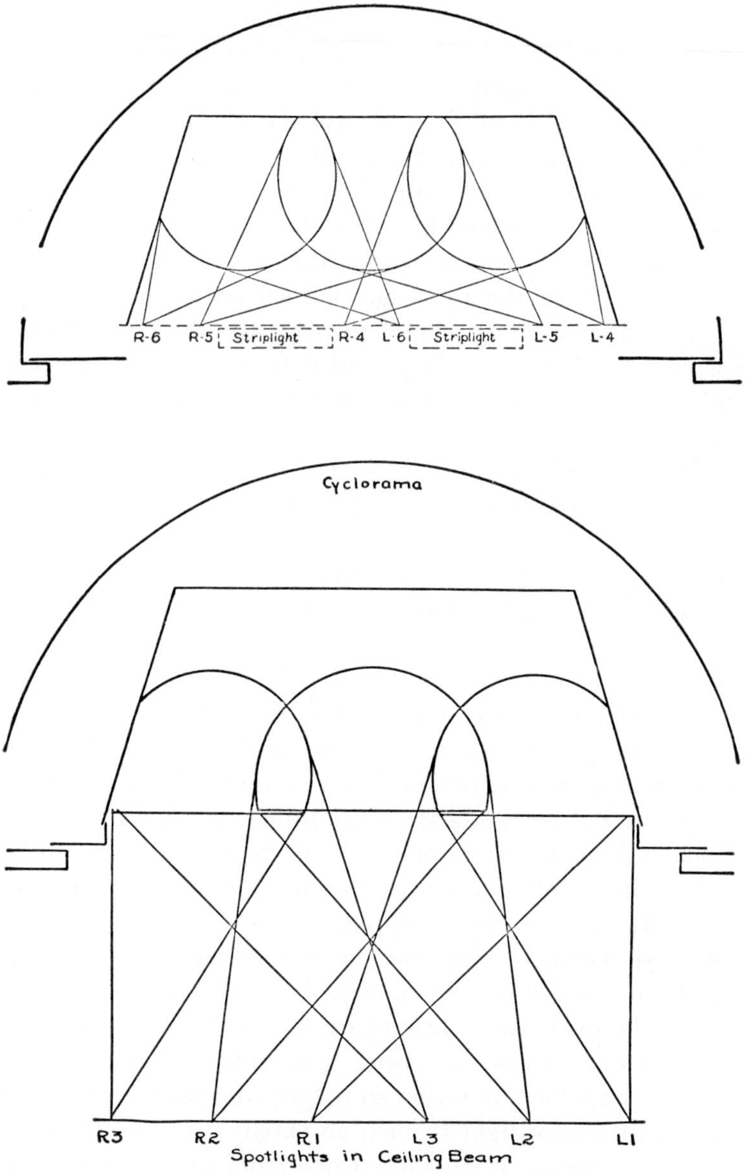

FIG. 57. Diagram of general lighting plan.

that the shadows are at least partly wiped out. In order to accomplish this result, sometimes as many as twenty to thirty balcony front spotlights are used, and the result is not flattering but flattening, giving the actors' faces a washed-out appearance.

In the recent production of *The Little Hut* in New York, where the exterior scene showed most of the lower part of the cyclorama to the audience, Charles Elson had the problem of keeping the actors' shadows off the cyclorama. He accomplished it by carefully cutting down the top edge of each beam and by crossing the beams from extreme angles to place the shadows offstage in the wings. The higher angle provided by spotlights in a "ceiling beam" position is considerably better for lighting the downstage areas.

Similar circumstances obtain in the upstage areas, and six instruments are used to cover these three areas just as they are on the downstage areas. In this case, however, the vertical and horizontal angles are both much larger and the length of throw is considerably shorter. The upper diagram in Figure 57 and the lighting layout in Figure 93 show the two common mounting positions for the instruments covering the upstage areas. In either case, the instruments are mounted on the teaser batten; that is, in the position farthest downstage next to the teaser. This batten ordinarily hangs a little higher than the ceiling of the set. Shadows of the actors and areas of greater brightness on the walls of the set are inevitable if the actors play close to the walls. These shadows, as well as those in the faces of the players, are modified in part by general illumination from striplights on the teaser batten (see Figure 57). General illumination from these same striplights helps also to smooth out the spottiness in the acting area from all twelve of the instruments producing specific illumination.

The current practice of using spotlights with Fresnel lenses (see Chapter 17) has a tendency to reduce contrast and increase the general diffusion of light to such an extent that very little or no general illumination is desirable when from six to twelve Fresnel spotlights are used on the upstage areas.

Separate control of each of these twelve or more instruments allows considerable flexibility and variety of distribution. In this way, any area can be brought into prominence or reduced to obscurity by changes in quantity of illumination. Variety in color is often obtained by having one cool color and one warm one in the two instruments that light a single area. If moonlight is coming through windows on one side, then the instruments covering the acting area from that direction should produce cool light. Pink, illusion pink, orange pink, light violet, and daylight blue are the most useful acting area color media (see Chapter 18, Section 9). Since general illumination from both footlights and the striplights on the teaser batten affects the tonality of the walls of the set, the color of this light must be determined by the color of the set.

4. MOTIVATIONS FOR ACTING AREA LIGHTING

When interiors appear to be illuminated by artificial light from floor lamps, table lamps, candles, and other sources of very low intensity in themselves, they serve as motivation for area instruments of greater illumination and variations in color. Exterior motivations, such as sunlight, can be produced by spotlights or special instruments producing parallel rays. These may add to the visibility at times, but are useful chiefly to produce highlights and to justify the use of certain colors and higher levels of illumination in certain places on the acting area. In this way such sources of light accomplish several functions at the same time.

All visible sources of light, such as table and floor lamps, bracket lamps, candles, lanterns, and torches, should contain small incandescent lamps of a very low wattage. Nothing is more annoying to an audience than to be forced to look at a bright source of light on the stage. Even a wax candle is frequently too bright. Obviously, any lighting instrument must be so masked that it is not visible from any seat in the house.

Around the backings of the set, illumination should be much less than on the acting area; in these locations short compartment striplights are adequate. They can be attached to the offstage side of the set itself. These striplights, moreover, are very useful on the floor to illuminate ground rows.

5. LIGHTING THE WALLS OF A SET

The actual walls of a set should have very little light on them, probably not more than from a twentieth to a twenty-fifth part of the light on the acting area. This keeps the emphasis and the attention of the audience on the actors instead of on the background. More fundamental than the matter of relative emphasis is the fatigue that follows looking at large areas of bright light. In fact, a good play could fail because the set was as bright as the acting area. An important reason why illuminating a play by means of borderlights and footlights alone is wrong is that the background receives the same amount of light as the actors receive. Since a setting that is high in brilliance would probably reflect more light than the average make-up, it would appear brighter than the actors' faces. Sometimes, however, it is necessary to increase the amount of illumination on the wall of a set beyond an appropriate degree. For example, if actors play up against the wall, the specific illumination must be high enough for adequate visibility, and this will cause spottiness on the wall that will have to be smoothed out by increasing the general illumination. The practice of using Fresnel lenses in upstage area spotlights has helped smooth out this difficulty to a large extent. Even if this objectionable increase is necessary, the upper part of the set can be kept darker by directing the striplights down. Then very little illumination other than footlighting will fall on the upper portion of the set. Since this light should be dim, it will add a pleasing color tonality to the set without making it too light. In general, one should always regulate and distribute the light on the setting so that the intensity decreases gradually from the bottom to the top.

6. BACKGROUND LIGHTING

The last element to be considered in the setting is the background. For this discussion the principal background elements are sky cycloramas, drops, borders, and wings. A cyclorama is the most difficult element in the setting to light effectively, probably because stage space is nearly always so limited that instruments have to be placed too close to the surface of the cyclorama. This condition makes an even distribution very difficult to maintain.

While a cyclorama ordinarily extends from an offstage position near one side of the proscenium arch to a similar position on the other side of the stage, seldom must the whole of it be lighted at once. From a half to two thirds of the surface is as much as is commonly used for any one play. The size of the area has little to do with the difficulty or simplicity of the task of lighting a cyclorama. The difference is largely in the number of instruments necessary. The whole problem, then, is that of producing general illumination evenly distributed over a smooth surface. Of course, variations in quantity and color in this distribution are necessary. The base of the cyclorama, including an area extending about 10 or 12 feet up, can be lighted best by short striplights from 6 to 9 feet long. Such instruments, with a maximum wattage in each lamp of 150 with the reflectors on 6-inch centers (see Chapter 17, Section 3), are the right size for all cyclorama base lighting in common practice in an average theatre. Employing an instrument with reflectors on 6-inch centers, one should use 150 watt lamps, although there is much more blue needed than green or red. With such instruments color mixing is close to the instrument, so that an 18-inch ground row is high enough to mask the mixing, and the instrument can be placed within a foot of the cyclorama surface. For a better distribution of light, however, the instruments should be at least 5 or 6 feet from the surface. Larger instruments can be used where greater wattage is necessary, if space allows them to be placed 6 feet from the surface and if taller ground rows are used to mask them. This condition will obtain in large theatres only. The reader is no doubt familiar with the fact that these instruments produce the changes in color necessary for sunsets and sunrises. By the use of the primary colors in three circuits, subtle changes in quantity and color can be made at the control board to produce beautiful sunrises and sunsets of the cloudless variety. The short striplights are connected end to end in an arc-like formation in front of the cyclorama.

The upper part of the cyclorama is lighted by floodlights mounted on a batten or frame, as explained in Chapter 17. To accomplish changes from daylight to night, or vice versa, it is necessary to have these in two circuits. If space is limited and the instruments have to be within 5 or 6 feet of the surface, they must be very close together in a row with every other instrument on the same circuit. A more nearly even distribution can be acquired, however, if the instruments are placed 15 or 20 feet from the surface. Floodlights of 500 watts are large enough for almost any cyclorama.

Again in the case of cycloramas, we find that the errors in lighting fall on the side of too much light rather than too little. The cyclorama needs no more than between a twenty-fifth and a fiftieth of the illumination on the acting area. In color the daylight sky can be produced with light-blue color medium (see Chapter 18). It should be neither toward the green nor toward the violet. A dark blue that transmits no red is hard to obtain in cheap color media, but for a night sky the medium must be neither green-blue nor purple. Only a strictly pure blue, so far as the eye is concerned, will carry the illusion of sky. One rarely sees a stage sky that is dim enough and of the proper hue.

While only sky cycloramas have been discussed above, any surface that partly encloses the acting area of the stage might, generally speaking, be called a cyclorama. In fact, a drapery of monk's cloth, velour, or any other material hung in folds might be considered in this general class. The method of lighting these is much the same as that described above, but much more variety in color is often used over the whole surface, depending on the purpose to which the drapery is put. Floodlights on stands are used as supplementary sources if the height of the material is not more than 12 or 14 feet, and the width 20 feet or less. Flat surfaces of material hung from battens, called drops, are really substitutes for cycloramas. When a drop is used as a sky backing, the lighting is done according to the method described above or by means of a borderlight; striplight sections connected end to end serve the same purpose. On the other hand, in producing plays from the nineteenth century or earlier, painted drops, wings, and borders are often made a part of the setting if the play is done in the style of its original production. These drops and their companions, the wings and the borders, look best in dim general illumination produced with a borderlight placed parallel to the drop and about 6 or 8 feet from it. A row of floodlights is a satisfactory substitute, but spotlights cannot be used because shadows and an uneven distribution distort the painting. Even with borderlighting, however, shadows may appear if the actors are allowed to play very near the drop. Natural shadows produced by light are always incongruent with painted ones. When painted drops must be used, the only satisfactory light for them is general illumination that is as nearly shadowless as possible.

These generalities concerning the method of lighting a play including comments on using certain instruments will not only give perspective but also will motivate an examination of the details of lighting instruments in the following chapter. After continuing with color (Chapter 18) and lighting control (Chapter 19) one should be ready for an amplification of the material of the present chapter and the application of the principles to certain examples in the staging of plays.

QUESTIONS AND EXERCISES

1. At about what vertical angle should beam lighting strike the stage?
2. Why do we use striplights on the acting area?
3. What are the common acting-area colors?
4. What is meant by motivation for light on the stage?
5. In proportion to the light on the acting area, how much light should be on the background? (Assume that actor and scenery reflect the same amount of light.)
6. In what way does the lighting of the upper part of a cyclorama differ from that of the lower part?

CHAPTER 17

Lighting Instruments

1. INTRODUCTION

FORTUNATELY FOR THE directors of college, school, and community theatres, salesmanship in the best manufacturers has become quite ethical. These companies are employing graduates from theatre departments in universities and experienced workers from the commercial theatre who have been of genuine assistance to workers in the educational theatre with technical advice and better catalogue information and a sincere attempt to give the customer an intelligent selection for the money available. On the other hand, everyone knows that a salesman's primary interest is in selling his own product, and only those workers in the theatre who will use the equipment day in and day out should make the final selection. Training, actual experience with lighting equipment and shrewd purchasing ability are still needed, and the only substitute for these three essentials is authoritative and unbiased technical advice. Because one manufacturer makes the best spotlights, it does not follow that his floodlights are equally good. And again, the idea of buying three borderlights instead of one in the hope of multiplying the opportunities for good lighting has about as much basis in fact as the notion that three pills will cure one more quickly than a single pill. Accordingly, the purpose of this chapter is to prevent this sort of mistake and to discuss the best that is available, so that directors and technical workers will be able to select lighting instruments more intelligently and handle them more effectively.

For purposes of discussion we shall classify everything used in stage lighting as (*a*) instruments, (*b*) accessories, (*c*) control equipment. In the present chapter, the first two will be discussed, and in Chapter 19 the third will be considered. Instruments will be analyzed and explained under these headings: spotlights, striplights, floodlights, special instruments, and accessories.

2. SPOTLIGHTS

A good spotlight should consist of several thoughtfully designed and well-fabricated parts. First, it needs a strong, light sheet metal hood, or enclosure, that is well ventilated and properly reinforced with steel. The size of the hood is determined by a number of factors, but it should be as small as is practicable, making it possible to focus sharply a lens of the longest focal length needed for the application of the instrument.

Different manufacturers have placed the access door (for removing or replacing the lamp) on either side, top, bottom, front, or rear of the instrument. For spotlights to be used in the ceiling of the auditorium, the rear access door is preferable; for a teaser spotlight, that is, one hanging from a batten behind the teaser, a front door is much more convenient if the instrument is adjusted from a ladder on the floor. This is an illustration of the difficulties attendant upon building a completely adaptable instrument.

The focusing slide, lamp socket, and reflector should be a unit assembly which will slide easily within the hood and which can be quickly and easily held in any position. Strips of metal that move with this assembly should be placed under the socket to prevent light from spilling through the slot in the bottom of the hood.

Reflectors. The light that falls on the lens is actually a very small part of the total output of a spotlight lamp; so a spherical reflector is mounted directly behind the lamp socket, mentioned above, to increase the efficiency about 40 per cent. This reflector must have a regular reflecting surface, such as polished aluminum,[1] so that light falling upon it will return directly to the center of curvature of the reflector, which should be at the center of the lamp filament. If the reflector mounting is designed and set by the manufacturer to prevent any misplacement when it is returned to the spotlight after necessary removal (for dusting or relamping), many irregularities in the distribution of light will be avoided (see Figure 58).

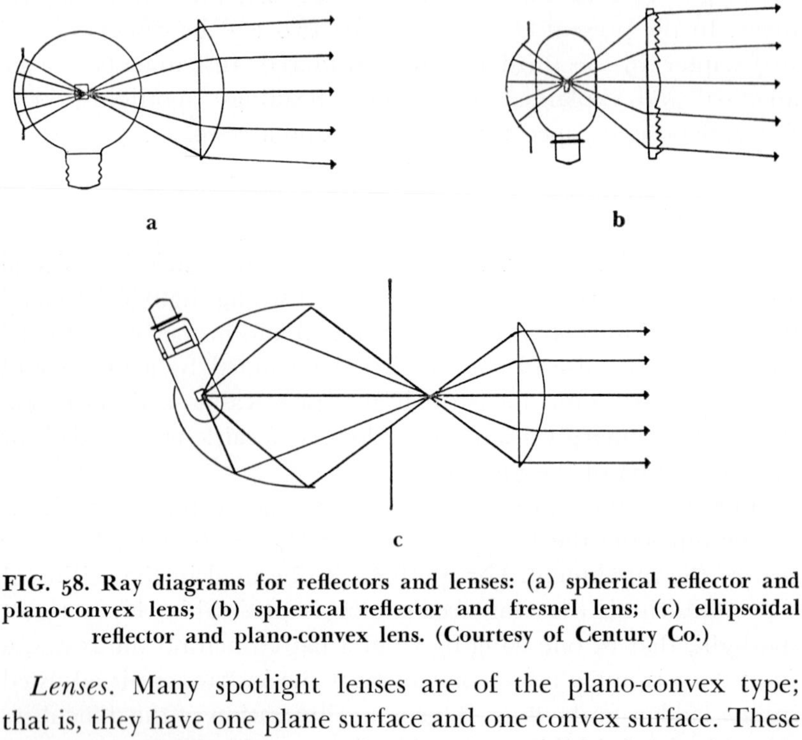

a b

c

FIG. 58. Ray diagrams for reflectors and lenses: (a) spherical reflector and plano-convex lens; (b) spherical reflector and fresnel lens; (c) ellipsoidal reflector and plano-convex lens. (Courtesy of Century Co.)

Lenses. Many spotlight lenses are of the plano-convex type; that is, they have one plane surface and one convex surface. These lenses are designated by their diameter and focal length, such as a 6 x 10 lens (a 6-inch diameter lens of 10-inch focal length). The focal point of a lens is the point to which, after passing through the lens, all parallel rays of light converge. Theoretically, if a point source of light were placed at the focus, the light passing through the lens would go forth in parallel lines. Then the focal length would be the distance from this point of convergence to a point within the lens. The slide range in a spotlight is within

[1] Alzak, a patented process, is the best known method of treating aluminum for long wear and a high reflecting surface.

this distance. The filament of a lamp is much larger than a point, and as soon as a part of the filament gets just beyond the focus, an image of the filament appears on the illuminated surface. This, of course, is undesirable; so the focusing slide should not allow the lamp to go back farther than half an inch in front of the focus. On the other hand, the forward limit of the slide is determined by the size of the lamp, since the bulb of the lamp should approach the lens not closer than approximately three-eights of an inch. For highest efficiency and proper distribution, lens, lamp, and reflector must be in optical alignment. In other words, a line perpendicular to the plane face of the lens and passing through its center must also pass through the center of the lamp filament and the center of the reflector (see Figure 58).

Plano-convex lenses used for spotlights are crude, uncorrected pieces of crown glass, unsatisfactory for optical work but quite adequate for theatrical purposes. The most useful diameters in spotlight lenses are 4½ inches, 6 inches, and 8 inches. Focal lengths depend upon the purpose to which the lens is to be put, but there are practical difficulties in the way of making and using very thick lenses, that is, lenses of short focal length. This eliminates very short focal lengths in the 6- and 8-inch diameters. In general, one should choose short-focal-length lenses for short throws and long-focal-length lenses for long throws. The useful lengths for 4½-inch lenses are 6 inches to 7½ inches, for 6-inch lenses, 7½ inches to 10 inches, and for 8-inch lenses, 10 inches to 12 inches focal length. The longer the focal length, the smaller the illuminated area can be made without producing a filament image, but as focal length increases, efficiency decreases. For example, to produce equally illuminated areas the lamp must be farther from a lens of 12 inches focal length than from one of 10 inches, but as anyone can see, more light goes through the lens when the lamp is close to it than when it is 8 or 10 inches away. For example two 6-inch lens spotlights, identical in every way except that one has an 8-inch focal length and the other has a 12-inch, produce illuminated areas of equal diameter. The lamp in the instrument with the longer focal length is 7 inches behind the lens, and in the shorter, the lamp is 5 inches behind the lens. Because of the relative positions of the lamps, the instrument with the 8-inch focal-length lens is producing about 65 per cent more light than the other.

The loss of light in the lens itself is about 10 to 12 per cent, including both transmission and reflection. The diameter, as well as the focal length, is an important factor in efficiency.

Replacing the plano-convex lens in many spotlights in the last few years is the Fresnel type lens. It is a piece of heat-resistant glass cast with one plane face and one consisting of concentric portions of lenses of different diameters and approximately the same focal length (see Figures 58 and 59). The result of combining these

FIG. 59. 500 watt 6-inch lens Century Fresnelite.

lens elements is a thin lens of short focal length impossible in plano-convex lenses. Focal lengths obtainable in Fresnel lenses are one-half as long or less than those of plano-convex lenses with the same diameter. For equal beam spreads, the lamp can be so much closer to the lens that the efficiency of Fresnel lenses is sometimes two or three times higher. The diffuse-edge (soft-edge) beam, which is unavoidable in Fresnel lenses, is, however, sometimes a disadvantage.

Mounting. All good spotlights are designed for mounting either on a floor stand or with a yoke or suspension arm for mounting on a pipe batten (see Figure 60). Since the suspension arm supports the instrument on one side only, the yoke, which supports the instrument from both sides, is the preferable method of mounting. To fasten the yoke or arm to a pipe batten, either a

"C" type clamp (Figure 61) or a "two part" clamp (Figure 60) is used, but the "C" clamp is much more convenient to attach to a batten when only two hands are available.

Color frame guides. Adequate guides for color frames should be provided on the front of each instrument. By far the best type of color frame is open at the top and closed on the sides and bottom. Side openings may cause frames to fall on actors, crew members, or spectators.

FIG. 60. 500 watt 6-inch Fresnel lens spotlight by Kliegl.

Baby spotlights. The baby spotlight with its 4½- or 5-inch plano-convex lens for 250 watt or 400 watt lamp is still a useful small spotlight for cramped localities, but it has been superseded by the six-inch Fresnel lens 500 watt spotlight because of its higher efficiency and larger lamp. The cost of the Fresnel instrument is only a few dollars more than a well-made baby spotlight and the size is only slightly larger. In fact, this 6-inch instrument has become the most common one for lighting upstage areas on small and medium size stages where the length of throw is less than sixteen feet. Each of the better manufacturers makes such an instrument for approximately thirty dollars. There is even a smaller size for a 3-inch lens and a 100 watt lamp.

Larger spotlights. Instruments for 1000 watt or 1500 watt lamps are made with either 6-inch or 8-inch plano-convex lenses (see Figure 61). These still are common for sunlight from offstage angles and for acting area instruments either upstage or down mounted on a teaser batten or in the auditorium ceiling or on the balcony front. These are the basic instruments for sciopticon and other lens-effect machines of the simpler and cruder type (see Section 5). Several of the best manufacturers of stage light-

FIG. 61. Major 1000 watt spotlight.

ing equipment, including Century and Kliegl, make a complete line of Fresnel lens spotlights beginning with the 3-inch lens and going up to 12 inches and even larger, the lamp size increasing with the lens diameter. The 8-inch lens instrument for a 1000-watt lamp is the most common for a larger stage for the upstage areas. In New York City at the Martin Beck Theatre there were twenty-one of these on the first batten above the teaser and an equal number on the second batten set up for the *The Teahouse of the August Moon.* The lamp receptacle or socket in nearly all spotlights manufactured today is of the prefocus type. With this receptacle a lamp of pre-focus base is used. In this combination the lamp does not screw in but is pushed in and rotated a quarter turn so that the filament will be properly related to the reflector and lens (see Figure 58).

Ellipsoidal spotlights. Like the Fresnel lens, the ellipsoidal reflector came into spotlight design and construction in the early nineteen thirties. The use of this reflector has made it possible to build a more efficient and convenient instrument for long throws such as from the auditorium ceiling beam and balcony

FIG. 62. Ellipsoidal spotlights by Kliegl, 1000–2000 watts.

front. It is useful too, for long throws mounted on battens on stage but this is not as common as the "out front" position for lighting the downstage areas. The sectional drawings (Figure 58) show the fundamental difference in the optical principles involved in the conventional spotlight and the ellipsoidal spotlight.

The ellipsoidal reflector receives a larger part of the light than the spherical reflector in the conventional spotlight. The lamp filament is placed at one focal point of the ellipsoid from which all the rays of light that fall on the reflector are directed to the second focal point. Crossing at the second focal point the rays continue to the lens where they are bent into a narrower beam before reaching the stage. Framing shutters to shape and control the size of the beam are placed near the second focal point. By keeping the focal point of the lens on the lens side of the framing shutters (shutters can be said to be "beyond" the focal point), the ellipsoidal spotlight becomes a projector type of instrument like any lantern-slide projector used for lectures with illustrating slides (see Section 5). The framing shutters shape the opening for the light rays corresponding to the lantern

FIG. 63. Ellipsoidal spotlight by Century 6-inch lens, 500–750 watts.

slide and the lens produces an image of this opening on the acting area. There is an adjustment near the front of the instrument allowing the lens to move a short distance to produce a sharp or a fuzzy out-of-focus edge of the lighted area, whichever is desired.

The efficiency of an ellipsoidal spotlight with its framing shutters wide open is about twenty-eight to thirty per cent compared with efficiencies of from five to fifteen per cent in conventional spotlights. These instruments (ellipsoidal) are made in several sizes, the most useful ones being the 500 watt to 750 watt and the 1000 watt to 2000 watt sizes. In either wattage size the instrument for a wider spread uses a 6-inch diameter lens and for the narrow beam instrument an 8-inch diameter lens is used. An ellipsoidal spotlight costs considerably more than a conventional spotlight but for long throws they are worth it.

For larger outdoor theatres or civic auditoriums, where spotlights are mounted three hundred feet from the stage, there are special ellipsoidal instruments for 3000 watt and 5000 watt lamps, including blowers for cooling, and other accessories. Arc spotlights, too, are common under such conditions.

3. STRIPLIGHTS

Striplight is used here as a general term that includes borderlights, footlights, cyclorama border or footlights, and backing striplights. Older striplights (now obsolete) consisted of an open painted trough, with sockets and wiring compartments below. A few of them still can be found and, although they are inefficient and ineffective in the control of distribution and color, they are not totally useless. If one has unfortunately fallen heir to one or more of these, chances are he will need to consider other purchases before he decides to replace the striplights. If they are properly wired in three or four circuits and used for supplementary lighting of low intensity, they can serve a very useful purpose, even if they are inferior in design. The warning is essentially against purchasing new ones of this class when much better striplights are available. The old ones are still useful as worklights.

One of the two best types of striplight units (Figure 64) consists of a row of individual reflectors, each containing one lamp and a round glass color-medium that completely covers the mouth of the reflector. The reflector should be of Alzak aluminum, with either a specular (polished) or a diffuse reflecting surface. Alzak has a reflectance [2] of at least 80 per cent. The diffuse surface tends to spread the light a little more than the polished surface. The shape of the reflector is a combination of parabolic and spherical, which seems to produce the best distribution in striplights. The reflector with a parabolic shape tends to send out light in parallel lines if the source is placed at the focus. A spherical reflector was explained above (see Section 2). Striplights should be wired in three or four circuits for the three primary colors, blue, green,

[2] The reflectance is the amount of light reflected from a surface, divided by the light falling on that surface. It is usually expressed in per cent.

and red (see Chapter 18), and possibly one for white light. The color roundel, which is placed in the mouth of the reflector, is of heavy heat-resistant glass that is not easily broken in normal use. These color media are readily interchangeable. Reputable dealers carry five or six colors in stock. Variations in distribution are possible by changing the reflector surface (an expensive process), lamp, and color roundel. For a sharp, narrow wedge of light, when the surface to be illuminated is at a considerable distance,

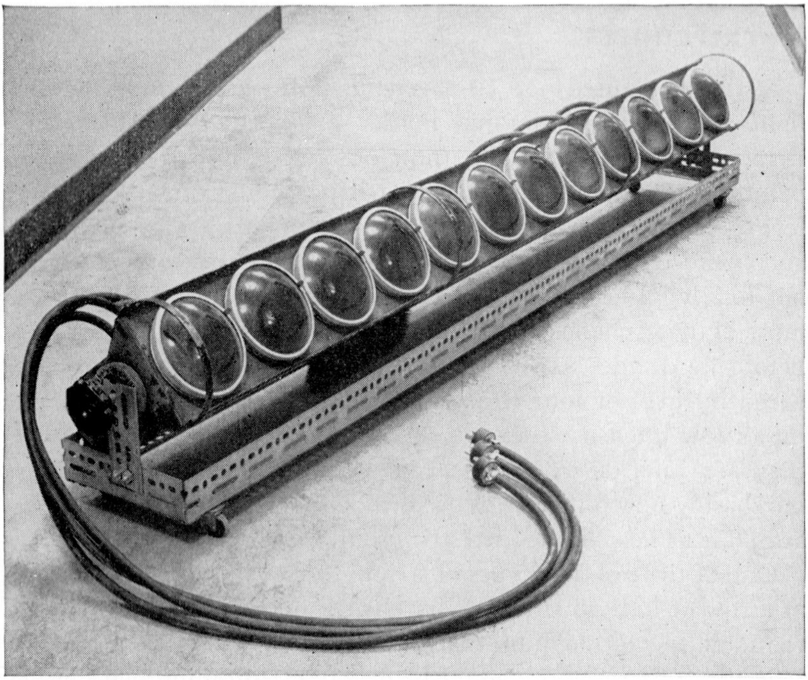

FIG. 64. Three-color reflector striplight section (Major) in punched steel angle iron frame for use as cyclorama footlights.

the specular (polished) reflector, clear lamp, and clear roundel might be indicated. For the maximum spread at close range, one can use the diffuse reflector, inside frost lamp, and the diffusing color roundels. Various other combinations of the three may give better results under special circumstances.

The second satisfactory type of striplight came into common use with the development of the PAR 38 and R40 150 watt spot and floodlamps (see Section 8). Since these lamps have built-in reflectors, the reflectors mentioned above for the first type of strip-light are omitted in this one. This second type consists of the wiring channel, with screw sockets for the lamps, and a sheet-metal housing to protect the lamps and secure the color roundels. Associated with this striplight is a widespread color roundel that allows color mixing near the instrument when it is necessary to place the striplight unusually close to a surface such as the cyclorama. Changes in distribution are made possible with this strip-light by changing from the spot type to the flood type of lamp, or vice versa (Figure 65).

The purpose of striplights, borderlights, and footlights is to produce general illumination; a more wedge-like distribution of light is possible with these two types instead of allowing it to spill over everywhere, as was the case in the earlier models.

Borderlights. A borderlight is just a striplight hanging from a pipe batten overhead to produce general illumination on the acting area from above. Since the new striplights will produce a wedge of light, the light can be restricted in part to certain areas. For example, by tipping the borderlight downward, most of the illumination can be kept off the scenery, or any part of the light can be directed to the set by rotating the instrument on its axis. The usual method of mounting is by means of chains. More accurate manipulation becomes possible, however, when the instrument is attached by short arms and pipe clamps, one at each end, in a similar manner to the arm-and-clamp method of mounting a spotlight. Borderlights with individual reflectors are made for lamps from 75 watts to 500 watts, but 75 watts to 150 watts is sufficiently large for the average theatre. This is true because the three small sizes, 75, 100, and 150 watts, can be placed on 6-inch centers, and it is preferable to have like colors near each other to make the distribution as nearly even as possible. An instrument with 150 watt lamps is composed of reflectors on 6-inch centers, while one with 200 watt lamps is on 8-inch centers. There is exactly the same wattage and illumination per foot, but the units of the same color are 6 inches farther apart in the larger one, and the larger one is more expensive—two definite disadvantages.

In the past it has been the accepted practice to have several borderlights on a stage, extending from one side of the proscenium arch to the other. In other words, a 36-foot proscenium opening would require a 36-foot borderlight. While these are satisfactory for lighting rehearsals, orchestra, and band practice, striplight sections from 6 to 7½ feet long, with line connectors at one end and load connectors at the other, are three times as useful (see section on accessories). If a section is provided with a studbolt extending from each end it can be attached to a batten with hangers (Figure 65), or set on the floor with feet or carriages with casters (Figure 64) for ground row and cyclorama base lighting. These sections are also excellent for direct or indirect footlights.

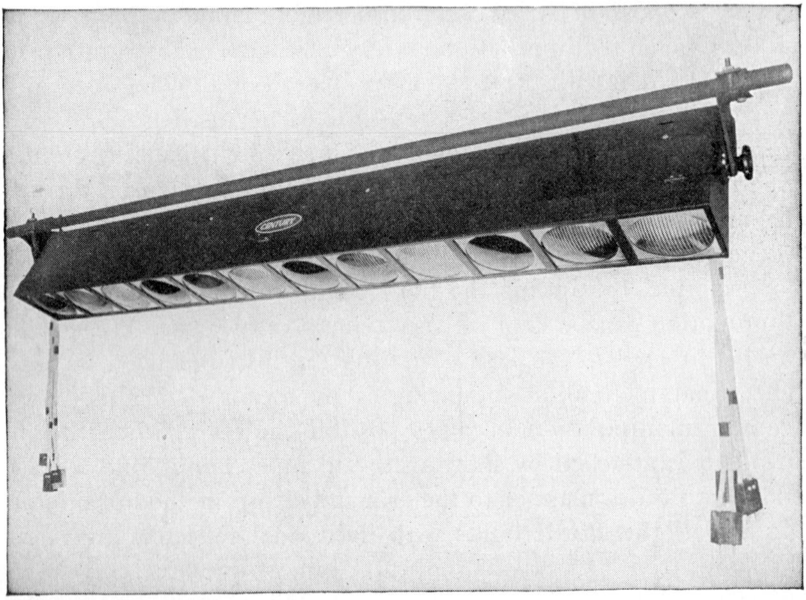

FIG. 65. Century striplight for use with PAR 38 or R40 lamps.

Footlights. Usually footlights consist of a striplight concealed from the house by proper recession near the edge of the stage floor outside the curtain line. They should be of very low wattage and need not be longer than three-fourths the width of the proscenium arch. Footlights should be carefully placed to avoid spilling light on the proscenium arch or on the teaser when it is at its lowest useful position. They should not be placed higher than 3½ inches above the stage floor. Like other striplights, they might well be made in 6- or 7½-foot sections, so that less than the full width can be used when desired. Again, like striplights, they should be wired in three circuits for the primary colors. The same colors should not be farther apart than 18 inches in order that they will blend well and no spottiness will occur when only one color is in use.

Since the illumination from footlights is directed upwards, as well as backstage, large shadows are likely to appear on scenery, because each source of light produces a separate shadow of every object in front of it. This is one of the most objectionable characteristics of ordinary footlights, but the difficulty can be overcome by reversing the striplight to send its illumination in the direction of the audience. To receive this illumination a long trough-like, properly shaped (spherical is a desirable shape) reflector of polished aluminum (with a "broken" or partly diffusing surface) is provided to direct the illumination back to the stage. This reflector acts as a line source of light that does not produce shadows of objects that stand perpendicular to it as the actor does. In this manner, then, indirect footlights solve the problem of annoying footlight shadows.

Most of the epithets hurled at footlights come as a result of their being used as a primary source of light, but this criticism does not apply to footlights of good design that are used for their intended purpose. Color in footlight illumination adds to the general tonality of the setting, but the primary purpose of footlights is to soften facial shadows and to diminish excessive contrasts in the actors' faces caused by illumination from beam spotlights placed in the auditorium ceiling. This function requires illumination of a very low level, and is akin to the function of borderlights and any other source of general illumination—that of blending and reducing contrasts in the distribution of specific illumination from spotlights. One can do very well without footlights if the angle of spotlights in the auditorium ceiling is fairly low, 35 to 40 degrees, except when actors wear broad-brimmed hats. If this angle is about 60 degrees, footlights are necessary in any case. They are, however, more often too bright than too dim.

4. FLOODLIGHTS

The old box type floodlight is now obsolete. While a few of these are still in use, floodlights that are more efficient, lighter, more easily mounted, and more suitable in light distribution to the needs of modern stage lighting, are now preferred by technical workers in most theatres. Figure 66 illustrates one of the best, which consists of a spun-aluminum reflector with a diffuse reflecting surface, guides for a color frame to drop in at the top, a mogul receptacle, and a small yoke with pipe clamp. The shape of this reflector is ellipsoidal,[3] but a parabolic reflector is common also, and equally good. When floodlights are mounted above on battens to light the cyclorama or perhaps a drop, cramped stage conditions may demand that the floodlight batten be four or five feet from the surface to be illuminated. Under such conditions, the ellipsoidal shape will probably produce a smoother distribution. Many of these floodlights are made for 750 or 1000 watt lamps, but the one

FIG. 66. Ellipsoidal floodlight by Century.

illustrated in Figure 66 is smaller, being intended for a 500 watt lamp. The 500 watt size has the advantage of taking less space in mounting and is of ample intensity for college and community theatres.

A floodlight produces general illumination similar to the distribution of only one unit in a striplight; for the same reason, the illumination from a whole row of floodlights is similar to the distribution of one striplight, but probably greater in spread. Floodlights can be used interchangeably with striplights in some cases, one taking the place of a short strip for illuminating backings, several replacing a borderlight to provide the general illumination for the acting area, or most important of all, a number

[3] See discussion of ellipsoidal spotlights, page 461.

of them, on a batten, lighting the cyclorama from above. In this case they are more satisfactory than any other instrument for this purpose. In some cases they are mounted close together in rows on a pipe batten and connected in two circuits, one light blue and one dark blue, for changes from day to night scenes. Perhaps better than a single batten mounting for cyclorama lighting, would be a rectangular pipe frame of several short battens, supporting a large number of floodlights. This frame is hung fifteen or twenty feet from the cyclorama to produce a more even distribution of light over the surface than that produced by a single, longer row, placed closer to the cyclorama. These floodlights are exceedingly useful instruments for many purposes.

5. SPECIAL INSTRUMENTS

Lens projectors. For the projection of clouds, rain, moving objects, and painted or photographed scenes under circumstances in which detail and sharply focused images are wanted, a lens projector is necessary. It consists of an ordinary 1000 watt 6-inch to 1500 watt 8-inch lens spotlight to which are attached an additional condensing lens, effect or lantern slide holder, and an objective

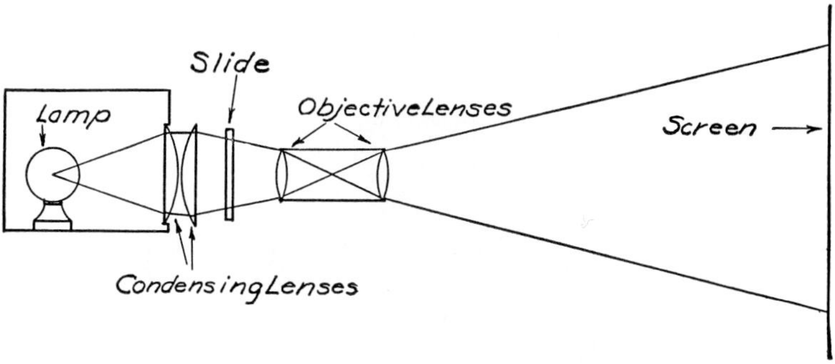

FIG. 67. Elements of a lens projector.

lens (see Figure 67 for a diagrammatic illustration). If one knows the distances and conditions under which the projected effect is to be used, he can calculate the focal length of the objective lens necessary to produce an image of the desired size. The sciopticon is an instrument for the production of moving effects. Within the drum of the sciopticon is a mica or plastic disc which is turned by clockwork or motor. The effect to be projected is painted on this disc. All kinds of moving effects can be rented or purchased from the larger dealers in lighting equipment. If the effect part of the system is replaced with a slide holder, any kind of cutout or painted lantern slide can be made to project a still effect. Flashes of zigzag lightning, stars, photographed scenes, and

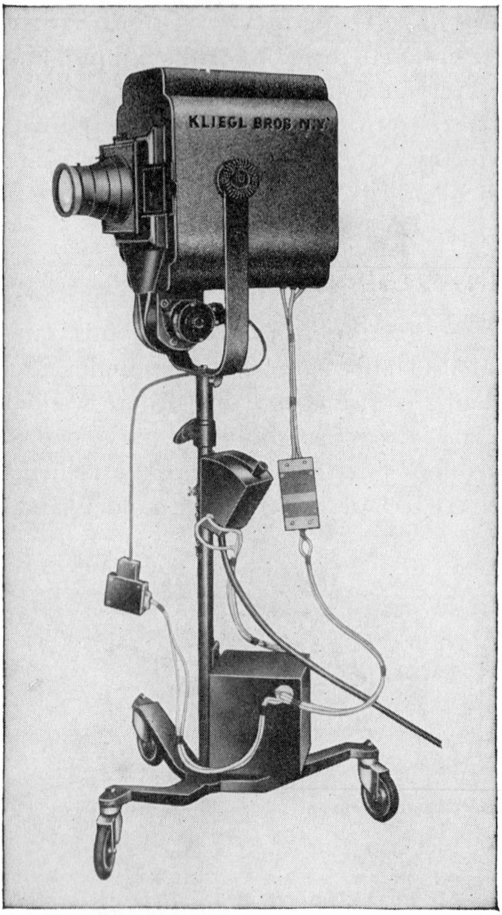

FIG. 68. Lens projector by Kliegl.

foliage patterns are often done in this manner. To select the proper lenses one must be able to make the simple calculations with the lens formulas found in any elementary text in physics.[4]

Linnebach projectors. In projecting broad effects where detail

[4] See Samuel Selden and Hunton D. Sellman, *Stage Scenery and Lighting,* 3rd ed., Chap. 13 (New York, Appleton-Century-Crofts, Inc., 1958).

is unimportant, a Linnebach projector can be used. It consists of a large sheet-metal hood or box with guides for the slide and a lamp receptacle within. The inside surface is painted black to prevent reflections. A spotlight lamp with concentrated filament of fairly high intensity is a necessary part of the instrument, which can be mounted on a batten or stand, or set on the floor. The slide may be made of glass, transparent plastic, or cardboard with the design cut out. Sometimes the instruments are set behind a translucent drop, so that the image is visible from the opposite side, or mounted downstage overhead to project the scene over the heads of the actors. Obviously a place of mounting must be found which will prevent the actor from making a shadow on the projected image. Finding such a place frequently results in a distorted image. This can be corrected or even completely avoided by proper design of Linnebach hood and the slide.

When a plane slide is used to project an image on a flat drop there will be no distortion in the image if the slide and drop are parallel and the lamp and instrument are properly centered in relationship to the drop. In projecting on a semi-cylindrical surface such as a cloth cyclorama, there is no distortion of the image when a semi-cyclindrical slide is used provided that here too the slide and cyclorama surfaces are parallel and the light source is at the center of curvature of both slide and cyclorama. Even if the cyclorama is not a true cylinder, the front of the Linnebach hood where the flexible slide fits and accordingly the slide surface can be made in exactly the same shape as the surface of the cyclorama. That is, the ratio of the slide distance to the image distance (measured from the lamp in each case)—is constant for corresponding points in the slide and image. When and if it becomes necessary to move the Linnebach hood away from the center of curvature of the cyclorama, an undistorted image can be maintained if the lamp is moved a proportional distance within the hood so that the ratio of slide and image distances can be kept constant.

When the image surface (drop or cyclorama) and the slide are not the same shape or not parallel (plane slide projected on a cylindrical surface, for example) the resulting distortion can be corrected by working from the image through the slide to the source with a system of plotted squares. This is tedious and unnecessary since it is easy to build one's own Linnebach projector to suit the drop or cyclorama. For further information on this subject see the book by Thomas Wilfred listed in the bibliography.[5]

6. LIGHTNING AND RAINBOW EFFECTS

A number of effects can be produced, as explained in Section 5, by means of lens projections of painted, photographic, or paper-cutout lantern slides. Examples of these are a zigzag cutout made in a piece of black paper for flashes of stylized lightning, tiny holes punched in a tin slide for stars, or a handpainted slide for a rainbow. Such a rainbow effect can be rented or purchased, but anyone familiar with the physics of light can assemble one for temporary use from parts found in almost any department of physics in a college or university. Lightning more naturalistic than that produced by a projected cutout is created by momentary contacts between a carbon and a metal terminal. This lightning effect, which is offered for sale, is properly enclosed to guard against fire. One type is operated by hand, and another is operated by a magnet so that it can be controlled electrically from a distance.

A Linnebach lightning effect can be convincing, too, under the right circumstances. The writer made one for the storm scene in Maxwell Anderson's *High Tor* in the following manner. The basic instrument was an arc floodlight with the white reflecting surface repainted black. The arc carbons rested against each other and when the switch was closed the carbons separated, striking the arc. Next, a piece of glass was cut to fit the color frame guides of the arc hood, and painted with a coat of thick black paint of a type that will not flake off. With a photograph as a guide, a forked lightning pattern was scratched with a sharp point through the black paint in a thin line. When the switch was closed momentarily, the movement of the carbon in the striking of the arc gave the projected image on the cyclorama enough movement to make the lightning very dramatic.

A Linnebach rainbow is well suited to a romantic folk play, such as Obey's *Noah*. One can cut a curved slot in a cardboard slide, cover the slot with a piece of transparent plastic, and paint the colored stripes with colored lacquer. Craftint transparent

[5] Further information, including calculations, can be found in 1958 edition of *Stage Scenery and Lighting*, Chapter 13.

colors, made for painting on plastic materials, are good for this purpose.

7. FIREPLACE EFFECTS

Fireplaces offer opportunities for variety and beauty in lighting interior settings that are worthy of some consideration. The motivation—that is, the apparent source of light—must be a dimly illuminated, inconspicuous coal grate or set of fire logs, neither of which is difficult to assemble. To produce a coal-grate fire, one can borrow a metal basket and fill it with chunks of amber and black glass. In the bottom of the basket it will be necessary to clamp two receptacles containing lamps of small wattage, which will illuminate the chunks of glass and make them seem like glowing coals. This whole unit can be purchased or borrowed from a department store that uses the grate for window display. Fire logs are expensive to purchase but quite simple and cheap to construct. Taking a board of suitable size and shape as a base, first attach two lamp receptacles, and wire them to illuminate the logs. Then make a form from chicken wire in the shape of a group of logs, coals, and ashes, and attach it to the wooden base. Clearance, of course, must be left to allow the lamps to be placed in the receptacles. The next step is to cover the frame with papier-mâché. Dip strips of newspaper or paper toweling in cold water paste and smoothe it into place over the frame until it is completely covered. When this dries, it forms a durable surface that will stand fairly rough treatment. To complete the logs, punch some holes in appropriate places and cover them with colored cellophane or gelatin, and finally, paint the whole unit to resemble logs. Naturalistic detail is unnecessary, since fire logs are always partly concealed and are never seen at close range. If the fireplace is in a side wall downstage, one or two small spotlights with red and amber color media should be concealed where they can be focused on a chair or sofa to illuminate the actors in this area with the warmth of firelight in contrast, perhaps, to moonlight coming in a window. The amount of illumination from a fireplace should be rather low because of the position and angle of illumination that might produce objectionable shadows on the opposite wall.

8. ACCESSORIES

An incandescent lamp consists of a base (the part that screws into the receptacle or socket), which is made in a number of sizes and shapes, a bulb of glass of various shapes, the lead-in wires, the filament with different forms (Figure 69), and the filament supports. Lamps with pear shaped (PS) bulbs are used in floodlights and striplights; lamps with globe shaped (G) and tubular (T) bulbs are used in spotlights. A small spotlight, such as the

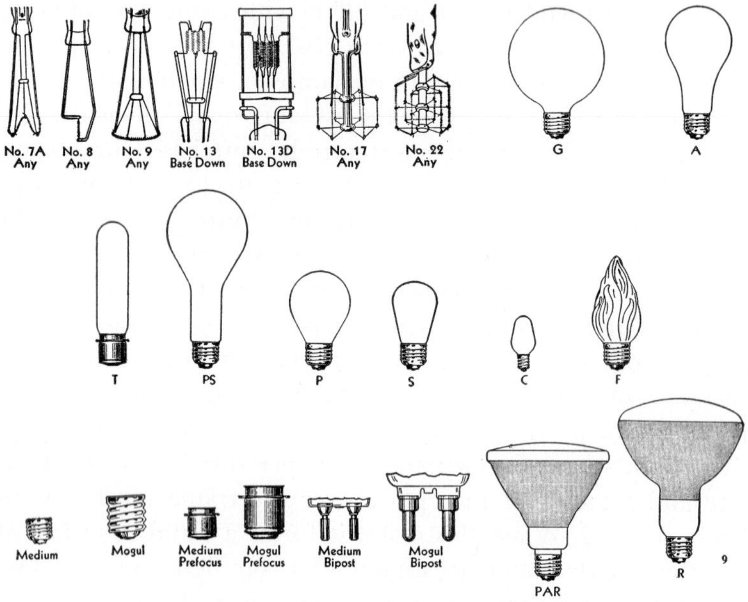

Courtesy General Electric Co.

FIG. 69. Incandescent lamps and their parts.

6-inch Fresnel lens instrument, is equipped with a medium prefocus socket for the 250 or 400 watt G lamps, and the 500 or 750 watt T lamp, each of which is made with a medium prefocus base. As mentioned above in Section 3, lamps for spotlight service ordinarily have a prefocus base that places the filament in the most efficient position in relationship to the reflector and lens, when inserted in the receptacle in the spotlight. Larger lamps for spotlights, such as the 1000 watt with the G bulb, are provided with mogul prefocus bases.

PS lamps of 1000 watts or less can be burned in any position, but G lamps cannot be burned within 45 degrees of vertically base up. Operators must be careful in mounting spotlights to see that the lamps are burning in the proper positions, because G and T lamps will burn out quickly if placed vertically base up. PS lamps have an average life of 1000 hours, while G and T lamps for spotlight service are limited to about two hundred hours. The ellipsoidal spotlight requires a tubular lamp which burns base up. It is made particularly for this instrument.

9. COLOR FRAMES

Frames for supporting color media used on spotlights, floodlights, and striplights are commonly made of sheet metal in two halves, with square or round openings large enough to prevent obstruction of light from the instrument for which the frame is intended. The best frames are those in which the two halves are hinged at one edge, and on the opposite edge there is riveted a fold of metal that clips the two parts together after the color medium has been inserted. Temporary frames can be cut from cardboard and held together with paper clips. One should be careful, when selecting lighting instruments, to reduce the number of color frame sizes necessary to be carried in stock.

10. MASKS AND FUNNELS

A mask is a piece of sheet metal or cardboard placed within the guides of a spotlight to change the shape or size of the illuminated area. A mask may be made of a single piece with a hole cut in it, or of two pieces, to allow an operator to change the size and shape of the illuminated area at will. One expensive professional mask (called an iris) is made like the iris diaphragm of a camera which allows one to change the diameter of a round opening from the full size of the lens down to a pinhole, or "blackout." An approximation of this can be made of two pieces of cardboard, with a triangular notch in one edge of each. Funnels are frequently used to modify or partly eliminate the diffuse or soft edge of the beam of a Fresnel lens. They are fairly successful if long enough. A funnel is a most useful accessory in preventing spill light (caused by reflections from the walls) from appearing outside the illuminated area, such as spill light from beam spotlights falling on the teaser or proscenium arch. The funnel is a cylinder of sheet metal from 12 to 30 inches long, with some arrangement for attaching it to the instrument for which it is intended. It must be painted black inside and out.

11. STAGE CABLE

A stage cable is a flexible twin conductor which consists of two bundles of fine wire, each twisted into a heavier wire like a cotton cord constructed from fine threads. Each of these conductors is covered with insulating material made of rubber or plastic. The two insulated conductors are finally covered together with more insulating material to form a single flexible cable. The safe size for use on stage in connecting spotlights, floodlights, and any other movable instrument whose total wattage is 1500 or less, is No. 14 wire, which safely carries a current of 15 amperes.

All nonprofessional workers should be warned against using cable of current-carrying capacity less than the current through the load. It is both illegal and unsafe. For example, No. 14 wire is unsafe for arc spotlights because they draw from 25 amperes up to 100 amperes, or occasionally even more. Where the wire or cable is subject to heat, asbestos covered wire is essential. Any of the lighting equipment companies listed in the appendix, as well as the electrical wholesalers, can supply all sorts of stage cable.

A short table of wire sizes with corresponding ampere capacities is listed here for convenience. A more complete table can be found in any handbook of wiring practice and in some catalogues of lighting equipment.

Wire Sizes Guage No.	*Maximum Ampere Capacity*
18	3
16	6
14	15
12	20
10	25
8	35
6	50

12. STAGE CABLE CONNECTORS

The common method of connecting stage cable and lighting instruments to a source of electrical energy is by means of connectors used for the stage, called pin connectors or pin plug connectors. They consist of small blocks of fiber with contacts on one edge and a cable entrance on the opposite edge. They belong in pairs, a line connector with a load connector. The line connector has two brass cylindrical openings that receive the brass prongs of the load connector. These connectors are used in splicing lengths of cable together, to connect the short asbestos leads from a spotlight or floodlight to a length of cable, and to make any sort of connection from portable equipment to the source of electrical energy. The line connector should always be on the "live" end (the one connected to electrical energy) of a cable, and the load connector is always placed on the short leads from the lighting instrument.

For school, college, and community theatres these connectors of 15 ampere size are recommended to take the place of stage plugs and plug receptacles ordinarily found in commercial theatres. The connectors are cheaper and their exclusive use in one size throughout the theatre greatly simplifies the handling of cable, because all cable will then be interchangeable. The 15 ampere size is sufficiently large to handle all ordinary incandescent loads.

"Twistlock" connectors, resembling heavy duty convenience plugs except that after they are pressed together they are rotated slightly to prevent their being accidentally pulled apart, are sometimes used in college and university theatres. They are quite satisfactory but are forbidden in theatres by the electrical code requirements in some cities.

13. TELEVISION LIGHTING EQUIPMENT

There are a good many similarities as well as some differences between stage lighting and television lighting. Both general and specific illumination are as common in television lighting practice as they are on the stage, but unlike general illumination on the stage, television's general illumination is sometimes produced by fluorescent lamps. The lamps are arranged in large rectangular "pans" four to five feet long and thirty to forty inches wide. Since

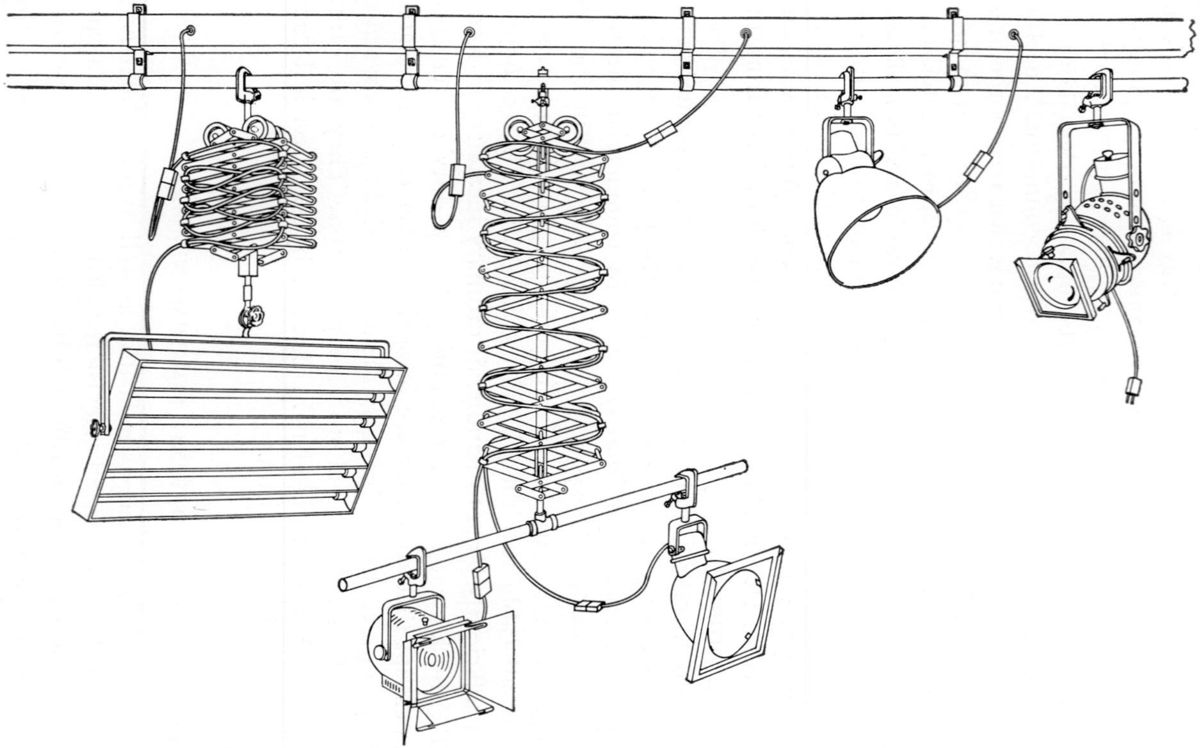

FIG. 70. Lighting instruments for television by Century.

these pans are rather clumsy, an incandescent floodlight called a scoop is usually preferred for this purpose (Figure 70). The scoop is an open reflector with an Alzak matte finish and is available in sizes for 500 watts and even larger lamps. Many of these can be seen hanging overhead in any television studio (see Figure 71).

The other common instrument (for specific illumination) in television lighting is that same Fresnel lens spotlight commonly seen around the stage. Various sizes are used in television from the 3-inch lens for 150 watt lamps (an accent instrument sometimes

FIG. 71. Kliegl lighting equipment for television: WTVJ-TV Miami, Fla.

attached to the front of a camera) up to the 16-inch lens instrument for 5000 watt lamps. Spotlights with the 8-inch lens or the 12-inch lens (1000 to 2000 watts) are probably the most common, hanging from a large pipe grid or battens suspended over the acting area. A few such instruments are on floor stands that roll about on casters, but this practice is discouraged. The floor must be kept free for camera movements, actors, and crew. Some of the instruments are fastened by pipe clamps directly to the grid; others are attached to short lengths of pipe extending from the grid four or five feet toward the floor. These pipes can be adjusted vertically to change the vertical angle of a light beam. Another device for suspending spotlights that can be raised or lowered more rapidly is a counter balanced spring hanger illustrated in Figures 70 and 71.

For controlling the beams of spotlights (in addition to the usual focusing) a "barn door" is a useful accessory. When it is in place in the color frame guides of a spotlight, a portion of the beam of light can be cut down by one or more of the hinged shutters

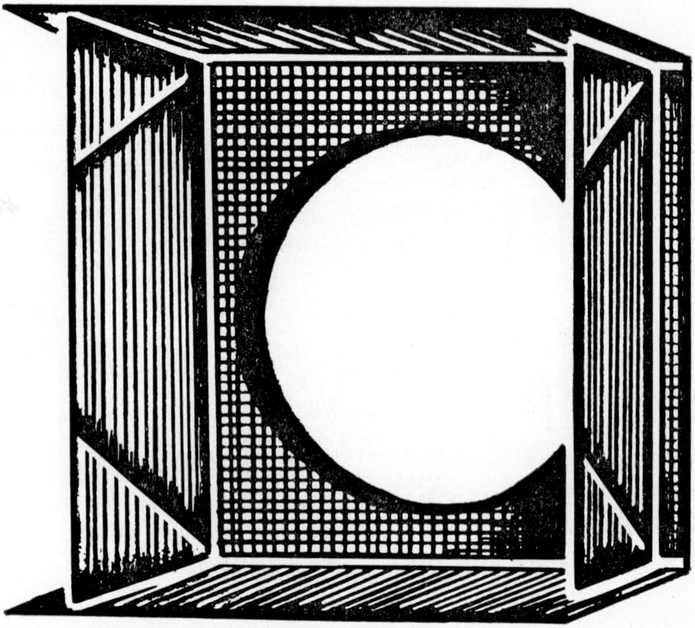

FIG. 72. Four-way barn door by Kliegl.

shown in Figure 72. Instead of color media, sheets of frosted gelatin or plastic and such other diffusers as fibre glass and spun glass are in general use with both scoops and spotlights.

Another fairly common instrument for television lighting is a lens projector similar to those described in Section 5 of this chapter. Those in use in television studios are made for high wattage incandescent sources or carbon arc lights. The expensive wide angle lens system in these projectors will project a large picture at a relatively short throw. For example, the better instruments will project a picture twelve to fourteen feet wide when the projector is about twelve feet from the screen. Projecting background scenes is much more common in television production than it is in stage production.

There is little or no time for scene shifting during most television programs. Scenes move quickly and quietly from one set to another with no time between, and large numbers of lighting instruments must be set up and focused before the dress rehearsals of a complete program. For a brief outline of lighting practice in television the reader should turn to Chapter 20.

QUESTIONS AND EXERCISES

1. What are the limitations of a baby spotlight compared with larger spotlights?
2. On what does the efficiency of a spotlight depend?
3. How does one choose the diameter and focal length of a lens?
4. State the advantages and disadvantages of a Fresnel lens.
5. What are the advantages of an ellipsoidal spotlight over the conventional type? Are there disadvantages?
6. Write the specifications for an adaptable, efficient striplight.
7. How are footlights used correctly? Is their use related to the use of beam lighting? How?
8. Compare the use of direct and indirect footlights.
9. Compare floodlighting with striplighting.
10. Why is an ellipsoidal or parabolic reflector better than an olivette for floodlighting purposes?
11. Discuss the circumstances under which you would choose a lens projector for a projected effect. When would a Linnebach projector be preferred?
12. Name the parts of a lens projector.
13. What is a sciopticon?
14. Compare the life (in hours) and burning positions of spotlight and floodlight lamps.
15. When does one use a T-shaped lamp in lighting instruments?
16. What type and size of stage cable is best for most purposes?

CHAPTER 18

Color

1. INTRODUCTION

EVERYTHING THAT we see is in color. It is as difficult to imagine a colorless world as it is to appreciate sight until we have gone without it. Vision is commonly considered our most useful sense, and the most important attribute of vision is color. Our enjoyment of nature and our preference for one manufactured article over another are concerned with color to a great extent. The color in scene design contributes to the mood and atmosphere, and to the beauty of a whole production. Color in costume and make-up aids immeasurably in our enjoyment of an actor's performance. These contributions to our pleasure both in the theatre and elsewhere come to us by means of light, and light is almost synonymous with color in its broadest sense.

2. THE SPECTRUM

More than three hundred years ago, Sir Isaac Newton succeeded in separating white light into its components by passing a beam of sunlight through a glass prism, demonstrating thereby that white light is really a mixture of colors commonly called violet, blue, blue-green, green, yellow, orange, and red. Physicists refer to this band of colors as the visible spectrum, and to the color regions by their wave lengths measured in milimicrons such as a red between 680 and 700 milimicrons.

3. PROPERTIES (VARIABLE)

It has been said that color could be thought of as being almost synonymous with light, but in a psychophysical sense color must be considered in terms of the observer, in terms of the human eye. This, of course, involves light falling on objects and being reflected to the eye or light coming directly to the eye from a source. Starting with a specific source of light such as sunlight or on the stage an incandescent lamp, radiant energy is emitted and frequently modified by passing through a transparent color medium. The color medium absorbs some of the light and transmits some of it. The transmitted part falls on a colored object where certain wavelengths are absorbed and others are reflected, eventually reaching the retina of the eye. In this way an object is revealed to people in the audience.

When we work with color in the theatre and need to communicate our ideas of reflection, transmission, absorption, and color mixing, we need some common terms to describe color as accurately as possible. It seems best to follow the Committee on Colorimetry of the Optical Society of America [1] and call the three mental variables of color *hue, saturation,* and *brightness* (or *lightness*). The following definitions are similar to those of the Colorimetry Committee.

Brightness (*lightness*). A large number of color systems have been invented to clarify and describe color, two of which are the Munsell System and the Ostwald System. Each of these uses a solid figure to help the explanation. These solid figures have a central axis called a gray scale with white at the top and black at the bottom with a graduated series of grays between. This is a scale of brightness or lightness. By means of white light we can raise a gray in lightness until it would seem to be white or lower it until it would be called black.

Hue. Hue is the property of a color that distinguishes it from

[1] Journal of the Optical Society of America, *Colorimetry Report,* Vols. 43, 44, and 45 (1943, 1944, and 1945).

Above: *Ethan Frome* by Owen and Donald Davis, directed by Nadine Miles. Below: *Women Have Their Way* by Serafin and Joaquin Alvarez Quintero, directed by Ray Smith. Both settings by Henry Kurth. Western Reserve University.

gray. It is the quality that makes us call it green as in one part of the spectrum or red in another part. The human eye is said to be able to distinguish more than one hundred and eighty hues. Hue is the chromatic quality of a color as distinguished from gray, the achromatic.

Saturation. Saturation is the measure of the amount of hue in a color. Stating it another way, saturation indicates the degree of difference from gray that matches the color in brightness. A gray is an unsaturated color; gray-green is a partly saturated color. Pink might be called a color of low saturation but high in lightness.

Thus the three variable properties of color—hue, saturation, and brightness (lightness)—completely describe a color in quality and quantity. These variables have been made the basis of a number of color systems, such as Munsell's and Ostwald's. Munsell used an odd-shaped figure for his color solid and substituted the words *value* for *lightness,* and *chroma* for *saturation,* retaining the term *hue* as used by the Optical Society. His solid has a gray scale as the axis. Wilhelm Ostwald in Germany developed a somewhat different system, but his solid is a double cone (two cones base to base), with a scale of lightness as the central axis, white at the top (upper apex), and black at the bottom (lower apex). The circle at the double base of the cones contains the "full colors," those of highest saturation, although Ostwald does not use the term *saturation.* These color solids are not perfect but they help in the understanding of color principles. For example, we can think of a color becoming less saturated as we move horizontally from the outside toward the central axis in Ostwald's color solid. As we follow a color toward the top, it is becoming higher in lightness and lower in saturation at the same time. Tints are near the top. As a color changes, going toward the lower apex, the color becomes lower in saturation and also in lightness, moving toward the shades and eventually to black.

4. COLOR MIXTURE—ADDITIVE

In Section 2 of this chapter it was said that white light can be separated into the colors of the spectrum; by reversing the process, white light can be produced by putting the colors together. One can produce white light, furthermore, by mixing only three of them: blue, green, and red. In fact, by mixing two or three of these almost any color can be produced synthetically, and accordingly these three colors, blue, green, and red are called the additive primary colors. The simplest way to think of an additive mixture is to visualize two or three spotlights, each with a different color medium projecting the colored light to a white surface, so that the beams of light overlap. Diagramatically, additive mixtures are illustrated by means of an equilateral triangle shown in Figure 73. Imagine that at each apex there is a colored light, one blue, one green, and one red, each a saturated primary color. Mixing red and green results in yellow; red and blue make magenta,

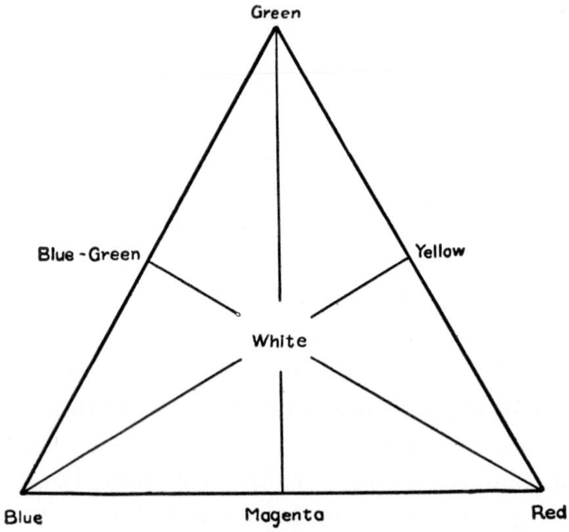

FIG. 73. Additive mixture of color.

and blue and green produce cyan or blue-green. All three produce white. By mixing colors that lie in an apex, and at the mid-point of the opposite side, blue and yellow for example, white light will result. Such pairs of colors are called complements. In fact, complimentary colors might be defined as two colors which, when mixed additively, will produce white light. When there is considerably less of one complement than the other, an unsaturated color or tint is the result. When a small amount of magenta is added to a greater amount of green, we have desaturated the green.

The principle of additive color mixing is applied in striplights or borderlights wired in three circuits, each circuit producing light of a primary color (see Chapter 17, Section 3). Then, by changing the intensity of the lamps in each of the circuits at the control board, various mixtures of color can be made a part of the general illumination. Repeating what was said above, two spotlights covering the same area with two colors in light are producing an additive mixture. When small dots of colored pigment are applied to a surface and the observer is far enough away so that he can no longer see individual dots, the resulting mixture is an additive one. Light from the dots mixes additively before it reaches the eye (see Section 16).

5. REFLECTION, TRANSMISSION, AND ABSORPTION

When light falls on an opaque object, some of the light is reflected and some of it is absorbed. We call this selective reflection and selective absorption. If light falls on a transparent object, such as a color filter, a small part of the light is reflected, part is transmitted, and part is absorbed. We now have a third term called *selective transmission.* While there are no materials that will reflect or transmit only one narrow line in the spectrum, let us start by saying that when a white light falls on a blue color filter, red, yellow, green, etc., are absorbed, and only blue is transmitted. If a blue light falls on a red medium and the red medium transmits only red, the blue will be absorbed and nothing passes through. The behavior is similar when a green light falls on a red object. If there is no green in the object, the green light will be absorbed and the red will appear as black. In actual practice it is not as simple to predict what will happen unless one knows by experience or has a spectral analysis of the materials. For example, the best primary red glass will transmit yellow, orange and red and perhaps a small amount of violet. The best primary blue will transmit violet and blue-green as well as blue. Lighter colored glass filters, such as a daylight blue, will transmit the whole spectrum, but less energy will be transmitted in the red end than in the blue end of the spectrum. Pigments, too, are even less selective than color filters and tend to reflect wide sections of the spectrum rather than narrow bands.

6. COLOR MIXTURE—SUBTRACTIVE

Colors are also mixed by subtraction, by placing one transparent color over another as is done in color printing and color photography and in the mixing of transparent water color painting. It seems best to call the most common subtractive primaries blue-green, magenta, and yellow, to prevent confusion with the additive primaries. The subtractive blue must be a greenish blue, the subtractive red must be a bluish red, and the yellow must be a greenish yellow, for reasons that will be clear below. But first,

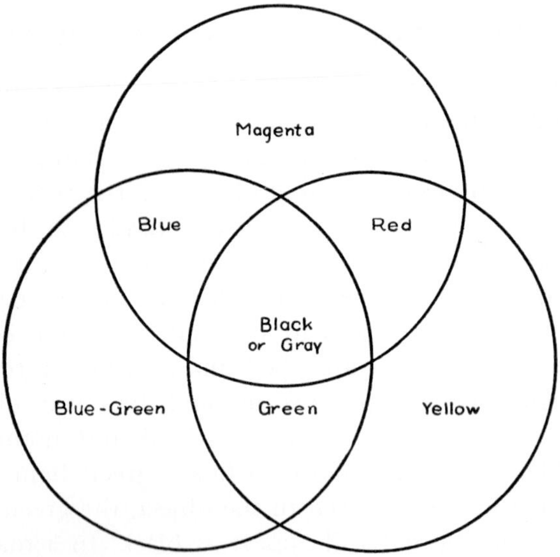

FIG. 74. Subtractive mixture of color.

a look at Figure 74 may help. These superimposed circles should be considered as color media such as gelatin or cellophane. Blue-green over magenta produces blue, yellow over magenta produces red, and blue-green over yellow allows green to pass through. This method of mixing works exactly like selective transmission explained in Section 4. Theoretically, blue could not act as a subtractive primary, because it transmits only blue, and a red could pass only red. Placing one over the other, nothing would be transmitted. Yellow is a satisfactory subtractive primary, because it transmits both green and red: so when it is placed over blue-green, the result will be green, because green is the color they have in common. If a blue that is not greenish is placed over yellow, they will have nothing in common, and the light will not pass through. Artists who use water colors do not limit themselves to a three color palette, but find many useful transparent colors that mix to produce other desirable colors.

When two transparent colors that have nothing in common are mixed, little or no light can pass through and the mixture appears gray or black. This is shown by the mixtures in Figure 74 of the complementary pairs, green and magenta, blue and yellow, and blue-green and red. In each case with saturated colors the result is gray or black. In stage lighting practice, the subtractive principle is sometimes used when a color is out of stock. Needing a piece of red, one could superimpose pieces of magenta and yellow. Or in using lighter tints for the acting area, one might find a blue that was too greenish (cellophane light blue). By superimposing a light tint of magenta (lavender) one could produce a straight blue.

7. COLOR MEDIA

Color filters currently accessible are far from satisfactory. The following sections will show simple comparisons of such qualities as range of color, durability, fading, and cost. Better materials at lower cost would be made in this country if there were greater demand.

Transparent lacquer. Transparent lacquer that can be applied directly to the bulb of an incandescent lamp is available in five or six colors, and these can be mixed to produce others. It fades easily and is burned off rapidly in lamps larger than 50 watts. It is useful in coloring a few lamps for backing striplights and for painting slides for projection.

Glass. Colored glass roundels that fit over individual lamps or reflectors in borderlights, footlights, and striplight sections have been common for many years. They are made of heat-resistant glass in different sizes and shapes, but are limited to a few colors like red, green, blue, yellow, and clear. The so-called primary colors are quite satisfactory for mixing the other colors needed for the cyclorama, including sunsets, and for toning and blending the acting area with general illumination. Although the roundels are expensive, their colors do not fade. Various tints in glass strips, framed in the usual color frame sizes for spotlights, have been available for several years. These are expensive and heavy, but with good care will last a long time. Since they are handled much more than roundels in striplights, breakage is much higher.

Gelatin. Colored sheets of gelatin are still the most popular for use in spotlights and have survived a number of newer materials. Gelatin is available in about one hundred hues and tints in sheets approximately 20″ x 24″. The cost is around 30 cents a sheet. Its only advantages are its low cost, large variety of colors, and flameproof quality. It fades easily, is easily dehydrated in dry climates or in heated storage places. When dry, it is brittle and fragile, its usual condition after a short time in a hot spotlight. All the colors seem to fade, especially the blues and blue-greens, which last no more than six or eight hours when in use.

Cellophane. This cellulose product with which everybody is familiar is a satisfactory color medium in many ways, but it is not approved by fire departments. When a match is touched to gelatin it shrivels, but does not support a flame; but cellophane burns as easily as newsprint. Although the writer has tested it under circumstances hotter than average for stage production (ellipsoidal spotlights with two thousand watt lamps), it still is not approved as a flameproof substance. Cellophane is easy to find in stationery and ten-cent stores, but the better colors for the acting area, such as lavender, pink, and light blue, are sometimes hard to find. Mechanically, cellophane is much superior to gelatin, but its fading qualities are about the same.

Cinabex and cinemoid. Two new color filters, imported from England, have appeared on the American market in recent years. The two are not identical, but they are quite similar in some of their names and numbers. Although the number of colors is perhaps fewer than the number available in gelatin, there are certainly more than most of us need. The material is thicker and stiffer than gelatin, but still not thick enough to use without color frames. The sheets are about 20″ x 24″ and the price is slightly over a dollar a sheet. These materials are flameproof and mechanically strong, but fade about as fast as gelatin.

8. LIGHT AND COSTUME

Although it is rarely done, the color of the light in which the costume will be worn by all means should be considered when the costume is designed. Using colored light in the dye room, or looking at the material through small pieces of color media will help a great deal to prevent re-dyeing after the first dress rehearsal. In general, unsaturated colors in light are much safer than saturated ones for period costumes that are made of several colors, but even with such acting area colors as daylight blue and amber, light colored costumes can be considerably affected. For example, a yellow costume can be grayed or neutralized by daylight blue light, and it will be black in saturated blue light. The reverse is also true. A blue costume is grayed by light amber illumination, and yellow-orange light will make the blue look absolutely black. Generalizing, one can say that light of a complementary hue will make a costume appear gray, but light of a similar hue will enhance the beauty of a piece of fabric and make it more prominent. Blue light on blue velvet or satin makes it seem to glow from within. In dimly illuminated scenes costumes should be of tints if possible, because they need to reflect more light than the background, while in well-lighted scenes saturated hues and shades may also be included. The designer of costumes, all will agree, should have a thorough understanding of color in light as well as color in fabrics.

9. LIGHT AND MAKE-UP

One who is responsible for the lighting of a play is often held responsible for deficiencies in make-up, but make-up is really the actor's problem, and he should include in his training some consideration of the way light affects his appearance. In general, foundation make-up has more red in it than normal flesh color, because much amber light has been common in stage lighting. Heavy foundations now are out of style, because more suitable colors in light, like daylight blue, very light amber, and pink, are in more general stage use. Illusion pink (a highly unsaturated violet) is a flattering color medium that passes all of the spectrum but is low in yellow. For this reason, it takes away sallowness and emphasizes the pink pigment in the actor's complexion.

The following simple suggestions about make-up and colored light may prove useful.

Amber light adds a yellow tonality that tends to make the complexion sallow, and reduces the contrast between rouge and foundation. More rouge, or rouge with less orange in it, is necessary.

Red light is reflected by rouge and foundation equally, leaving the actor apparently with no rouge. More rouge slightly toward the blue is necessary in red light.

Blue light has the opposite effect. Red reflects little or no blue light; therefore in blue light, rouge on the cheeks appears as two black spots. A very light foundation, with only a trace of rouge, is best in blue light.

Green light gives the face an unearthly appearance and should be avoided unless the play demands such an effect.

A common practice that cuts down distortions in make-up is the use of two colors from two spotlights covering the same area. Amber from one direction and light blue from the other, surprise pink from one and light blue from the other, or pink from one and light blue from the other, are examples. By using these additive mixtures the highlights become less saturated and accordingly less distorted, leaving shade and shadow with a variety in color.

10. LIGHT AND SCENERY

The radical lighting artist is of the opinion that scenery is merely one of the reflectors that he needs in making a design in light. While most scenic artists would probably disagree, this is, from a technical view at least, essentially true, and in this way it will be considered for the moment. Ideally, acting area light should be kept off the scenery, but reflections from the floor and spill light influence its appearance to some degree. As in the case of costumes, scenery must be designed and painted for a specific color in lighting. Otherwise it will never look as it was intended. Scenery, as most people in the theatre know, should almost never be painted in a flat color, but by one technique or another several colors should be applied, so that definite spots or small areas of each color lie near each other (see Chapter 13). When light falls on the whole surface, each small area reflects certain parts of the spectrum, and the reflected light mixes additively before it reaches the eye some distance away in the auditorium. If the primaries blue, green, and red were painted on the surface in this way and illuminated with white light, the surface at a distance would appear gray, but very different from one with a uniform gray paint covering the whole surface. The one with the three colors would have texture, variety, and beauty, while the solid color surface would be monotonous. If the three colors were illuminated with red light, the blue and green would reflect no light, and the appearance at a distance would be that of a dark red, uneven surface, uneven because of the areas reflecting no light. By changing the light to blue, the color of the surface would appear as dark blue. Changes in the color of light frequently assist in scene changes, but the painting must be done with this definite intention. It is not, however, so simple as it sounds. The primaries are rarely used, if ever, but several colors more appropriate to the particular design are used, along with a color in the general illumination that will emphasize the dominant color in the paint.

Monk's cloth, hemp, and other neutral (gray) materials used as draperies for the stage are easily colored by means of striplights and floodlights with appropriate color media. Because of their sheen and the interesting highlights and shade when they are hung in folds, silk, satin, and rayon look well in colored light. All of these materials should be hung in folds in order to attain variety in light and shade. If light from opposite directions is of different colors, one can have shadows of two different colors and an additive mixture of these colors in the highlights.

By carefully selecting pigments that have a distinctly different appearance in two or more colors in light, spectacular and comic effects are possible for the right occasion (not usually for drama). As an illustration, one can draw two sketches on white paper, one with blue chalk and one with orange or red chalk. In blue light the blue chalk and the white paper are equally blue because each reflects blue light to about the same degree; so the blue sketch essentially disappears. The orange chalk, reflecting little or no blue light, appears black and stands out boldly. In red light the orange or red chalk disappears and the blue sketch appears. Very amusing cartoons can be made in this way and changed by changing the color of the light. One might paint a drop according to these principles and change a woodland scene from summer to winter. If the sky were light blue and the leaves of the trees green or blue-green, the leaves could be made to disappear by using green or blue-green light. Such things have to be very well done to have any measure of success, and such a drop could not be shown in its entirety. If only a part of it were seen through windows, it might be satisfactory. In general though, such things are too spectacular for drama, and belong to musical comedy and revues, where smart effects are always in demand.

Good designers should know the relationship of light to pigment so thoroughly that they think in terms of light even when using pigments. Sorrowful is he who paints a set for amber light and discovers later that his set will be clothed in daylight blue.

11. CONCLUSION

The foregoing chapter gives a basic outline of the principles and practice of color for the stage, and will serve as a starting point for those who are beginning. Color is probably the most important and difficult of all lighting problems, but it is also the most fascinating and exciting. A little study, sensitivity, and much practice will bring results.

QUESTIONS AND EXERCISES

1. Define *brilliance* or *lightness, hue,* and *saturation.*
2. How does one mix light additively? Subtractively?
3. How are the additive and subtractive mixtures of light accomplished on the stage?
4. Find the results of mixing the following colors, both additively and subtractively: (*a*) blue and yellow, (*b*) blue-green and orange, (*c*) blue and red, (*d*) green and red, (*e*) magenta and yellow, (*f*) violet and yellow-green.
5. How does a tint differ from a shade?
6. Compare cellophane with gelatin, cinabex, or cinemoid as to cost, resistance to fading, and mechanical strength.

CHAPTER 19

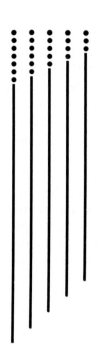

Lighting Control

1. INTRODUCTION

For the present, perfect control of light in the theatre may be defined as complete control of the properties of light—quantity, color, and distribution—from a single position within easy reach of an operator who has a clear view of the result. To approach perfection in ideal control, a place must be provided for the operator somewhere in front of the proscenium, with every element of control as conveniently within his reach as the keys of an organ console are to an organist. Where, then, should this position be? At the Metropolitan Opera House in New York City, at the new theatres at the University of Wisconsin and at Stanford University (there are a number of others) the control board is below the level of the stage floor near the orchestra pit. Much the same position was chosen for the control board in the larger theatre in Rockefeller Center. Viewing the stage from the footlight position gives one a somewhat distorted impression because the operator is too close to see the performance in normal perspective. A better place is farther away from the stage, such as the rear of the auditorium. This is the position of the control board in the University Theatre at the University of Iowa and in the smaller theatre at Stanford University. If the balcony is not too high, a place almost equally good is in the rear of the balcony, where the board is located in the University Theatre at the University of Oregon. From either of these last two positions an excellent view of the stage is presented to the operator, who can follow every change in mood and movement as easily as the audience. The only disadvantage in the "out front" position is the necessity for communication by telephone with the stage manager and head of the light crew. This rarely, if ever, causes any difficulties, however. The more conventional or traditional location for the control board, left or right backstage near the proscenium arch, may be satisfactory for road-show theatres, but for repertory or production theatres, as well as for college, school, and community theatres, a location of complete visibility for the operator greatly multiplies the opportunity for effective lighting.

While many new theatres have been built for colleges and universities and almost all have "out front" positions for their control boards, the commercial theatre seems to be completely backward in this respect. Except when a theatre has been taken over by television, almost no antiquated control equipment has been replaced, and nearly all plays are lighted with rented portable controls that could hardly be called modern. These portable control boards are placed offstage right where it is ordinarily impossible to see the stage. In the television studios control equipment is more modern and is commonly placed where the operator has a good view of the objects and people to be lighted. In some instances the latest electronic and magnetic amplifier control boards are found in television studios.

It is highly important that the location of the control board and its dimensions be known before the final plans for a new theatre are approved. With constant inconvenience to those who work in them, theatres have been built without realization of the depth of a control board and the space behind it necessary for repair.

2. ELECTRICITY

Since this analysis of stage lighting does not contain a chapter on electricity, a few paragraphs inserted here will aid the beginner in understanding the following sections on lighting control and control boards themselves.

Electricity is a natural force which man has learned to control and utilize in his daily living. It behaves according to simple laws that are easily understood. In its simplest form in lighting circuits, electricity is explained by comparing it with water flowing through a pipe. Just as pressure is required to make water flow through a pipe, so pressure is necessary to make electricity move along a wire. This pressure on the wire is called electromotive force or voltage and is measured in units called volts. Water being forced through a pipe is called a current of water; likewise, when electrical pressure, voltage, is applied to a circuit of copper wire, a current of electricity moves along this wire. The rate of flow of current is measured in amperes. Unlike water, electric current will not move along a single wire from source to point of consumption, but a return wire back to the source is always necessary. For example, two wires run into a building and continue to a wall outlet in a room. In order to have light, two wires must lead from a lamp socket to this outlet. Before the lamp is screwed in place, there is electrical pressure or voltage on the wires, but no current will flow until the circuit is complete through the filament of the lamp when the lamp is screwed into the socket. In a similar way, wires go from the street into a theatre building. They branch off to serve many lighting purposes, but for the stage the wires continue to the stage control board. When a lighting instrument including a lamp is plugged into a stage outlet, the circuit is complete from a source of electrical energy outside of the theatre through a wire to the control board, where the current continues to flow through a dimmer and switch out to the lighting instrument, through its lamp and back to the source of energy by way of a second wire, making a complete circuit.

Resistance. All substances can be divided into conductors and nonconductors of electricity. Nonconductors are often called insulators. Common insulating materials used on the stage include fabric, plastic, rubber, fiber, and porcelain. Copper wires are covered with plastic or fabric and rubber to prevent electrical contact with each other, and to prevent fire, and harm to human beings. Copper is the cheapest satisfactory conducting material and consequently is in general use for wiring of all kinds, but no material is a perfect conductor. A perfect conductor would offer no resistance to flow, but just as pipes of different lengths and different diameters offer various degrees of resistance to the flow of water, so do wires of different size, length, and material offer greater or less resistance to electric current. The practical unit of resistance is the ohm. A conductor is said to have a resistance of one ohm if a current of one ampere is forced through the circuit by a pressure of one volt.

Ohm's Law. There is a simple relationship between current in amperes, resistance in ohms, and electromotive force in volts called Ohm's Law which applies to electrical circuits. According to Ohm's Law, the product of the current and resistance equals the voltage.

$$\text{Volts} = \text{Amperes} \times \text{Ohms}$$

Using the symbols E for electromotive force in volts, I for current in amperes, and R for resistance in ohms,

$$E = IR$$

By means of this simple equation it is easy to calculate any one of the three quantities if the other two are known. For example, find the current which will pass through 1000 feet of copper wire with a resistance of two ohms per 100 feet. The voltage is 110. If there are two ohms in 100 feet there will be 20 ohms in 1000 feet.

$$I = \frac{E}{R}$$

$I = \frac{110}{20} = 5.5$ amperes, the amount of current which will pass through the wire.

As stated above, electricity flows only when there is a complete circuit from the source of power through the power-consuming device, such as a spotlight on the stage, and back again to the source. Electrical parts can be connected in two important ways: in series or in parallel. A series circuit is a group of electrical parts, such as lamps, rheostats, and so forth, connected so that the current passes from one to the other and finally back to the source from which it started (see Figure 75). Since series circuits are not common on the stage, they will be omitted from the present discussion. While in a series circuit there is only a single path for the current, in the parallel circuit there are as many paths for the current as there are elements or parts. That is, the current divides and a part of it goes through each element and back to the source. In Figure 76 a number of lamps are in parallel. In fact, each lamp might be considered to have a separate circuit

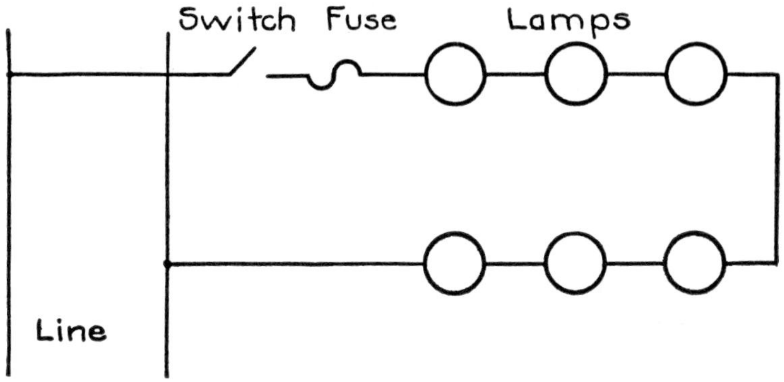

FIG. 75. Series circuit.

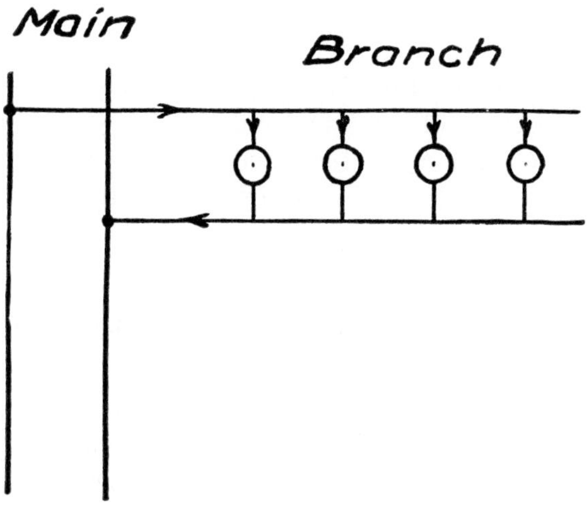

FIG. 76. Parallel circuit. Arrows indicate paths of current.

of its own, since it burns independently of the others. In a series circuit if one lamp burns out, none will burn. In the parallel circuit the current may be different in each part (according to the wattage of each lamp in a lamp circuit), but the voltage is the same in all the parts. The total current is the sum of the current in all the parts.

Power. The watt is the unit of power, and it is equal to the product of amperes and volts.

$$\text{Watts} = \text{Volts} \times \text{Amperes}$$
$$W = EI$$

If the wattage and voltage of a lamp are known, the current can be determined by means of this relationship. When the current is known, the proper wire size for connecting the lamp can be obtained from a table (see Chapter 17, Section 8).

PROBLEM. Find the current and resistance of a 500 watt, 110 volt lamp.

$$EI = W$$
$$110I = 500$$
$$I = 4.54 \text{ amperes passing through the lamp.}$$

Then by Ohm's Law,

$$R = \frac{E}{I}$$

$$R = \frac{110}{4.54} = 24.2 \text{ ohms, the resistance of the lamp.}$$

If it is desirable to dim this lamp completely, a dimmer of 3.5 times the resistance of the lamp will be necessary, that is, about 85 ohms. The dimmer is connected in series with the lamp or group of lamps which are in parallel among themselves (see Figure 76).

3. GENERAL CLASSIFICATION—PERMANENT AND FLEXIBLE

There are two methods of lighting control, permanent and flexible. Permanent control is the one in which the wiring from any outlet on the stage, such as the wiring for a borderlight circuit, to a switch and dimmer on the control board, is permanently fixed with no provision for connecting that outlet or instrument to any other circuit on the board. This method of control has developed out of antiquated lighting practice and the associated tradition of equipping theatres with stock lighting instruments, such as footlights, borderlights, and stage pockets for spotlights or floodlights. In the past, these were thought to be the backbone of all stage lighting, and accordingly were always permanently

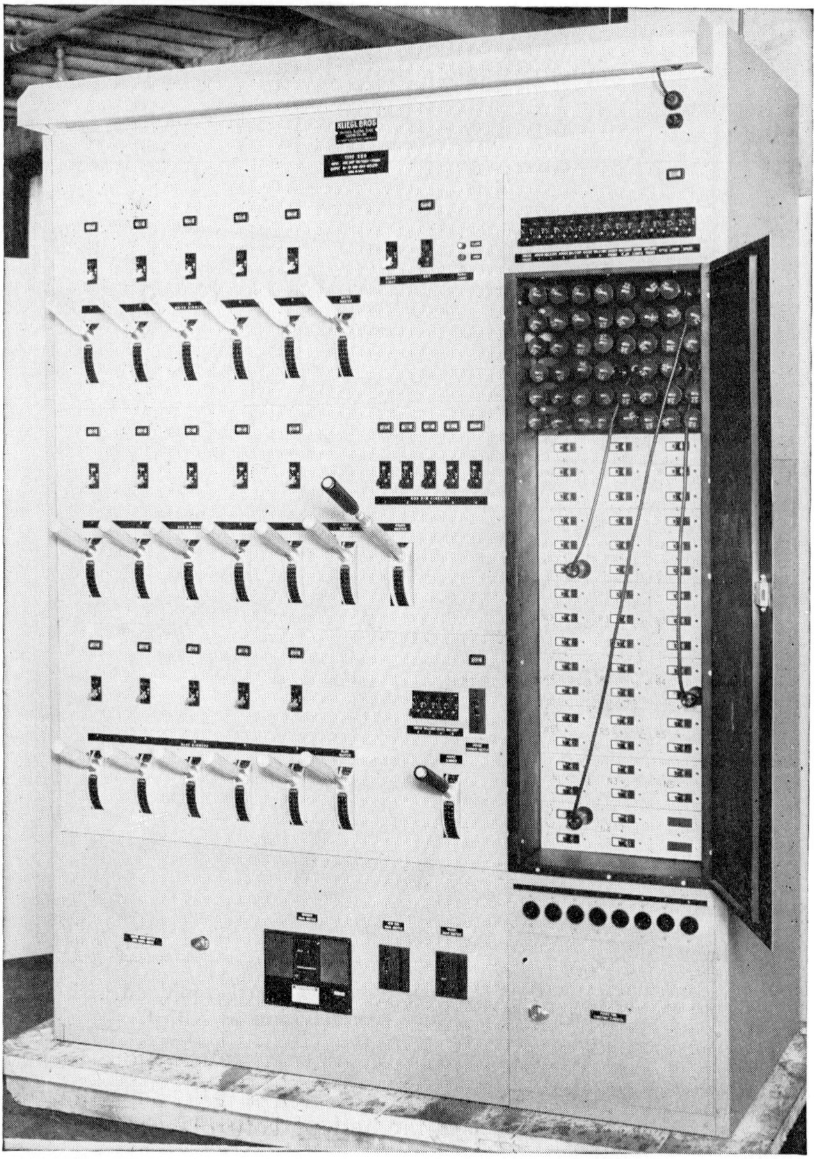

FIG. 77. Interconnecting panel (right) by Kliegl combined with manually operated autotransformer control board.

connected to the control board. As a result, in recent years the majority of road companies have carried their own lighting instruments and portable control boards, and have completely ignored the permanent stage-lighting equipment in the theatres on the road.

FIG. 78. Rotary selector type of interconnecting panel combined with autotransformer control board for television by Kliegl.

Modern practice in stage lighting requires much more variety and flexibility in an equipment layout, especially for experimental theatres, than the permanent method of control affords. For a number of reasons, then, a method of control has come into use that is far better suited to college or community theatres. It is called flexible control, which means that between the control board and the outlets where instruments are connected, there is some means of connecting any outlet to any dimmer and switch on the control board. Furthermore, any number of outlets can be connected to one dimmer if desirable, as it often is.

4. INTERCONNECTING PANELS

This means of connecting dimmer circuit to outlet is known by several other names, including interplugging panel, patch-plug panel, rotary selector panel, push button selector panel, and the bus bar cross-connecting panel. The bus bar type consists of horizontal bars in front connected to the outlets on the stage, and vertical bars in the rear connected to the dimmer circuits on the control board. In order to connect one or more stage outlets (to which spotlights, footlights, or other instruments can be connected) to any one of the dimmer circuits, one moves a sliding connection along the outlet bar until it is directly in front of the desired dimmer bar. Then he pushes the sliding contact forward until it slips over the dimmer bar to make a tight connection between a lighting instrument somewhere onstage and a dimmer circuit on the control board. This particular type is reasonable in price and works well mechanically but is not permitted by most city electrical codes because it is possible to touch the electrical parts that are "hot" and receive a shock. The push button and rotary selector types (Figure 78) automatically open the circuit when they are changed and are "dead front," or free from the possibility of shock. The patch plug type, shown in Figure 79, is perfectly safe because the plug which is handled is not "hot" and carries no electrical energy until it is pushed into the receptacle. A small weight or spring is used to pull the excess cable out of the way when it is released from its outlet.

5. ADVANTAGES OF FLEXIBLE CONTROL

By means of such an interconnecting arrangement, flexible control has the following advantages both for theatre and television.

a. In permanent control some of the dimmers are connected to instruments that are seldom used, while special instruments may be in need of dimmers. Flexible control makes a more efficient use of dimmers possible since every dimmer can be made available to a needed instrument.

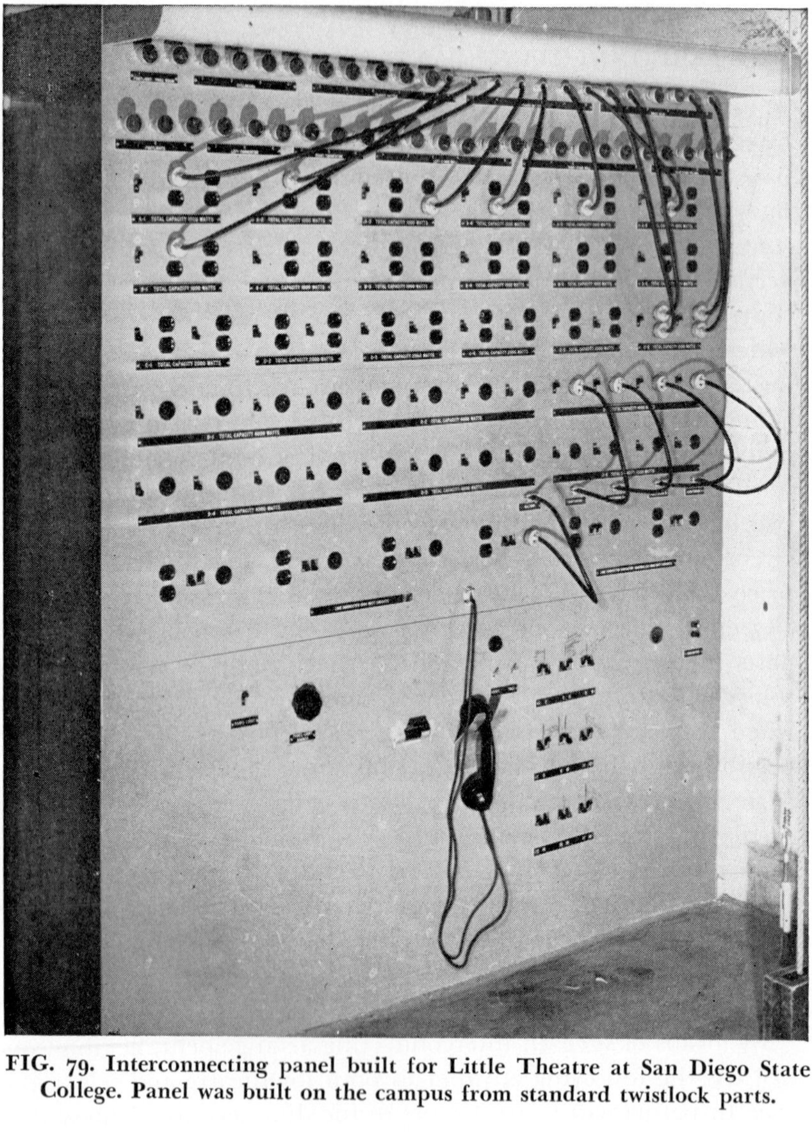

FIG. 79. Interconnecting panel built for Little Theatre at San Diego State College. Panel was built on the campus from standard twistlock parts.

b. If the dimmers are of different wattages, any outlet may be connected to a specific dimmer of appropriate wattage (matched to lamp wattage if necessary).

c. A single dimmer may be connected to more than one outlet. For example, it is desirable to have all of the light blue cyclorama floodlights connected to one large dimmer, but the floodlights for convenience are often plugged into four or more outlets. It is simple in flexible control to connect four or more outlets to a single dimmer. If dimmers are scarce, two spotlights covering one area may be connected to one dimmer, but it may be more convenient to connect the spotlights through two different outlets.

d. Since outlets are not permanently connected to dimmers in flexible control, outlets can be placed in every useful location on the stage. This condition allows shorter lengths of cable between outlet and instrument to be used, reducing confusion and possible accidents caused by actors and crew tripping over long cables. Less cable with fewer accidents and mistakes makes another advantage for flexible control.

e. And last, flexible control allows the operator to arrange the controls into groups according to the needs of each production, so that he can handle the switches and dimmer handles with maximum speed and facility with minimum danger of error.

Interconnecting panels and flexible control are very common in television studios where, with notable exceptions, portable control boards with sixteen or twenty dimmers are quite common. Many instruments are controlled by switches only, and many changes are made through interconnecting panels. A few studios have elaborate systems with large numbers of electronic dimmer controls, but they always have interconnecting panels (flexible control).

6. DIRECT AND REMOTE CONTROL

Control boards are classified, also, as direct or remote control. In direct control, the switches and dimmers which the operator actually handles carry the total current that passes through the lamps. When a single circuit carries a large group of lamps, or a master switch or dimmer handles the whole board, the space occupied by such a switch or dimmer becomes quite large. Dimming under these circumstances is less subtle and not as smooth as it

Arthur Miller's *Death of a Salesman,* designed by Arnold Gillette and directed by Gregory Foley. Produced by the State University of Iowa.

is with small parts. In remote control the large switches and dimmers are placed in some remote place, such as a basement room, where space is not at a premium. These large parts are controlled by small switches and dimmer handles on a compact pilot console (manually operated control board) out front where the operator can see the entire production.

7. PRESET OR MULTI-SCENE CONTROL

For the past twenty-five years a method of setting up the switches, and later the dimmer readings, for several scenes in advance has been developing. Today it has reached a relatively high state of refinement in contemporary electronic control systems, described in Section 12, and more elaborately elsewhere.[1] In plays with a large number of short scenes with only a few seconds between scenes, it is helpful to have all of the scenes set on the board in advance, up to the intermission of ten minutes or so, when the operator can set up another group of scenes. Faders are provided on these control boards to smoothly change the individual readings on a group of instruments to another set of dimmer readings on the second preset, and so forth to the last preset available. In the opinion of some, two presets are sufficient, because after one has faded to the second, an assistant can help reset the first preset readings in time for the fade to the third scene, and so on. This argument falls down if the control board has from fifty to one hundred individual controls to be reset during a 30-second scene. A representative of the Strand Electric Company of London said recently that in England good control boards had at least 144 individual controls. While this sounds like a beautiful dream compared with the average board in an American theatre, it is desirable to have more than the usual twenty-four to sixty controls commonly found in American theatres. Our controls cost about five times as much as those made in England.

Another point of view concerning presets is that at least twenty or more are needed on the assumption that changing the distribution of light from one scene to another is not nearly so important as the use of presets in establishing a large number of specific dis-

[1] See Kliegl, Century, and Ward Leonard catalogues, and Samuel Selden and Hunton D. Sellman, *Stage Scenery and Lighting,* 3rd ed. (New York, Appleton-Century-Crofts, Inc., 1958), Ch. 14.

tributions of light within a scene, then allowing a motor-driven fader to blend slowly from one distribution to another while the scene is in progress. This could be done in an exciting sunset that lasted for ten minutes, while changing continually in color, quantity, and distribution. Control boards of this kind cost from $25,000 to $50,000. A sensitive and interested student can create this effect manually with the individual controls on a much simpler piece of equipment.

8. CONTROL BOARD PARTS

A discussion of the way in which control boards operate is difficult without a brief mention of the essential parts of which these boards are composed. The vital essentials for controlling the intensity of an incandescent lamp are a switch to open and close the circuit, a fuse or circuit breaker to guard against short circuits or excessively high current, and a dimmer for the purpose of changing the amount of illumination.

Switches. The smallest durable switch which is silent in operation, easy to operate manually, and which meets the requirements of the electrical code, is usually the best for stage control boards. Mercury switches are very good but are not common for the stage. Silent mechanical switches seem to be preferred by control board manufacturers. Toggle switches are much too noisy.

Fuses. Either plug or cartridge fuses are satisfactory for stage lighting. The plug type, which screws into place like a lamp, has the advantage of displaying the fact that it is either intact or blown. This fuse, however, is not made in sizes above 30 amperes. Cartridge fuses are small cylinders of fiber with brass contacts on the ends. Their size varies with the current to be carried. Circuits should never be over-fused; in other words, a circuit carrying current for 500 watts should have a 6 ampere fuse, not a 10 ampere one. The 6 ampere fuse will "blow" if a 1000 watt lamp is connected to a 500 watt dimmer, warning the operator that an overload has been placed on the dimmer; the 10 ampere fuse will not give this warning.

Circuit breakers. Replacing fuses in branch circuits (such as individual circuits on a control board) is now done almost entirely by a thermal device that opens the circuit when excessive current overheats an element in the breaker, causing it to separate. This device is provided with a handle to open and close it manually, and many models of this type resemble the common toggle switch. Over a period of time the circuit breaker is cheaper than fuses if the fuses have to be replaced often, and the circuit breaker prevents the dangerous practice of putting pennies behind fuses when they are blown. Either a fuse or a circuit breaker is required by law in each circuit, and anything that interferes with its normal operation is a serious and dangerous matter.

Dimmers. Almost every person actually associated with the production of plays appreciates the supreme importance of being able to change the intensity of light on the stage. Those who need to be convinced are local architects and electrical contractors, school principals, and superintendents. The architect and school administrator are often more concerned with combining the cafeteria with the auditorium than they are with making the stage and its equipment effective for producing plays. In twenty-five years there has been some improvement, but dimming control is all too often neglected.

Dimmers are usually classified according to the electrical principle on which they operate. The ones in common use today are resistance, autotransformer, electronic reactance, electronic, and magnetic amplifier. Since the last four have so many advantages over the resistance dimmer, it might be considered obsolete for permanent installations where alternating current is available. Since the resistance dimmer is the only one that will operate on direct current, the portable control boards used in Broadway productions contain almost no other type. Not only are some Broadway theatres provided with direct current only (in a large number of cases), but each production, unless it is extremely elaborate, plans to tour, either for a "warm up" period preceding its opening in New York, or a road tour following the New York run, or both. In a few places on the road they might run into direct current, and the resistance type operates on both direct and alternating current.

Resistance and autotransformer dimmers are essentially direct control in their operation unless they are motor driven. Since a motor drive with variable speed is impracticable, in the opinion of the writer a motor-driven dimmer is unsatisfactory for stage lighting. Electronic, electronic reactance, and magnetic amplifier dimmers are associated with remote control because the dimmers themselves, and their supplementary parts, are rather large and have no moving parts; in this case it is ideal to place them in a remote place from the stage and have the manually operated part of the system, where parts are small and sensitive, in the rear of the auditorium or some other out-front position. Remote control systems cost from two to four times as much as direct control. For many small schools and colleges a remote control system is too expensive to consider.

9. RESISTANCE DIMMERS

In shape, resistance dimmers are either square or round plates, varying in height from about 12 to 20 inches. The round-plate type (Figure 80) can be interlocking or noninterlocking. Inter-

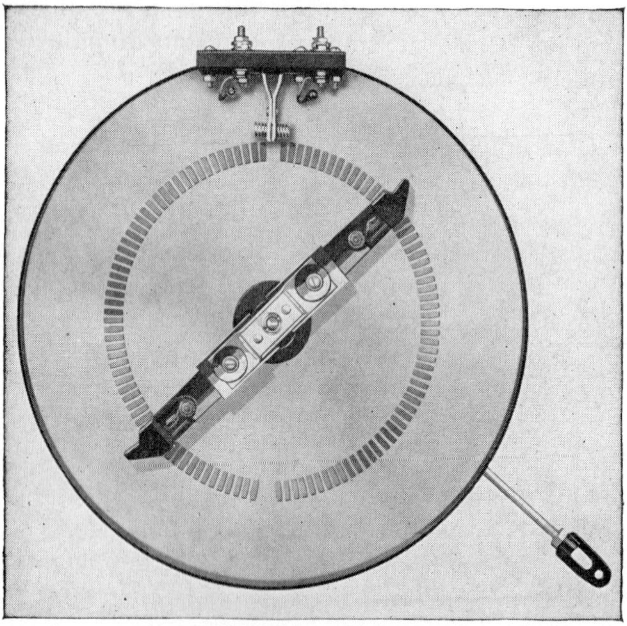

FIG. 80. Ward Leonard resistance dimmer (interlocking type).

locking means that the handles which change the intensity can be connected in such a way that two or more dimmers set in a row can be operated together by a single handle called the interlocking handle. Interlocking dimmers (both resistance and autotransformer types) can be mounted in rows in a steel frame with a large interlocking handle near the end of each row. These dimmers (if resistance) have 110 steps, so that they will dim very gradually, and each handle is provided with a scale of 10, so that the desired quantity of illumination controlled by the dimmer can be noted and recorded for succeeding rehearsals, and for the performance. The noninterlocking dimmers have about 30 or 40 steps only, which does not produce such smooth dimming, and there is no scale provided for noting a dimmer-reading. The price of noninterlocking dimmers, however, is only about half that of the interlocking ones. When the most rigid economy must be practiced even at considerable sacrifice in result, the cheaper ones are recommended if used with master dimmers.

Multicapacity resistance dimmers. For stage outlets into which spotlights or floodlights of various loads are plugged, dimmers of various ratings are needed. This is taken care of somewhat with a flexible control board, but if the circuits are permanently connected, a multicapacity dimmer is needed. These so-called dual or multicapacity dimmers have, for example, resistance enough to dim a 500 watt lamp and will carry enough current for a 1000 watt lamp. They are also made in 250 to 500 watt and 1000 to 2000 watt capacities. The disadvantage, however, is that the control handle will have moved only two-thirds of its travel when it has completely dimmed a lamp of maximum wattage for the dimmer. This restricts gradual dimming to some extent. Nevertheless, some of these, especially those from 250 to 500 watts, are highly recommended for flexible control boards on a small stage provided with direct current, although all of the dimmers on the board should not be of this type.

10. AUTOTRANSFORMER DIMMERS

Some years ago a new dimmer appeared using the autotransformer principle that has been common in electrical engineering practice for many years. It consists of a coil of copper wire surrounding an iron core. At one end of its cylindrical form is a dial (much like a large dial of an early model radio), to which is fastened a carbon brush, or sliding contact, which is manually moved around the coil of wire. In this piece of apparatus there is no heat loss, and practically no energy is used by the dimmer. Its chief advantage, however, is that it has complete variable capacity.

FIG. 81. Autotransformer dimmer with vertical control by Superior Electric Co.

FIG. 82. Autotransformer dimmer with rotary control by General Radio.

That is, a 1000 watt dimmer will dim completely and gradually any wattage, even a 5 watt lamp, up to its maximum capacity (1000 watts).

The large manufacturers of resistance dimmers (and others) soon realized that the autotransformer principle was much superior to resistance for lighting control, and they have designed autotransformers to fit into their standard interlocking frames. The new dimmers are well built and rugged, and have a capacity up to 8000 watts on a single unit. While they have complete variable capacity, they are even more expensive than resistance dimmers, and offer no improvement over these in compactness and subtlety of operation. Autotransformers made by three different manufacturers are shown in Figures 81, 82, and 83. Autotransformers operate on alternating current only, whereas resistance dimmers can be used with either direct or alternating current.

FIG. 83. 6600 watt autotransformer dimmer by Ward Leonard Electric Co.

11. ELECTRONIC REACTANCE DIMMERS [2]

As made by the Ward Leonard Electric Company, the electronic reactance dimming circuit consists of the basic reactance coil and the supplementary controls which they call a Hyster Set. Included are a thyratron electronic tube that produces the direct current, and miscellaneous transformers, potentiometers, and so forth. The reactance coil is in reality two coils, one in series with the lamp to be dimmed, and the other a control coil connected to the direct current produced by the electronic tube. All of this (placed in a remote part of the theatre) is connected by electrical

[2] The latest development in reactance dimmers is called a magnetic amplifier. In this arrangement, the electronic tube is replaced by dry disc rectifiers. Tube difficulties and maintenance are said to be eliminated or reduced. While more expensive than the electronic dimmer, the magnetic amplifier is now its strongest competitor.

cable to the small manually operated parts on a compact pilot control board (console) placed where the operator can see the stage. As is shown in Figures 84 and 85, the parts are small and sensitive, readily lend themselves to subtle operation, and are usually within reach of a single operator. Master and submaster dimming (Section 14) are very simple and are accepted as essen-

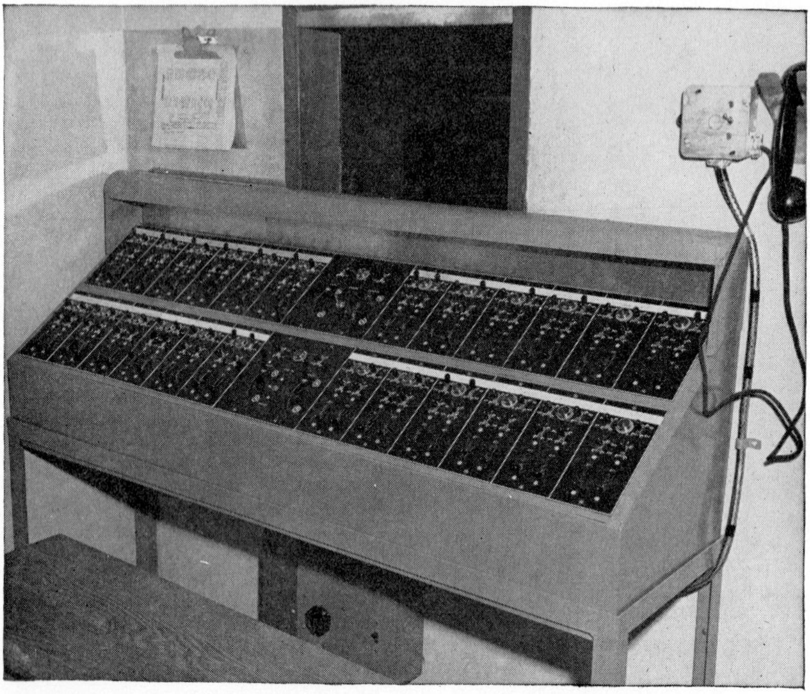

FIG. 84. Electronic reactance control board at San Diego State College (Little Theatre), assembled from Ward Leonard parts.

tial parts of this type of control. Two or more presets are usual, too. The most recent improvement in this system is the quick response noticeable in larger sizes from 4000 watts up. The actual change in brightness corresponds exactly with the movement of the pilot dimmer handle. The lag that was so annoying in earlier models has been eliminated completely. The loading range, or degree of multicapacity, is 80 per cent, that is, a 1000 watt dimmer will completely dim a 200 watt lamp.

12. ELECTRONIC DIMMERS

An electronic dimmer, a more recent development in dimmer design, is one in which the large thyratron tubes themselves act as a dimmer, of course with a number of accessory transformers, potentiometers, and so forth. The more elaborate of the two competing electronic control boards, the Century Izenour board, was invented by George Izenour and is manufactured by Century

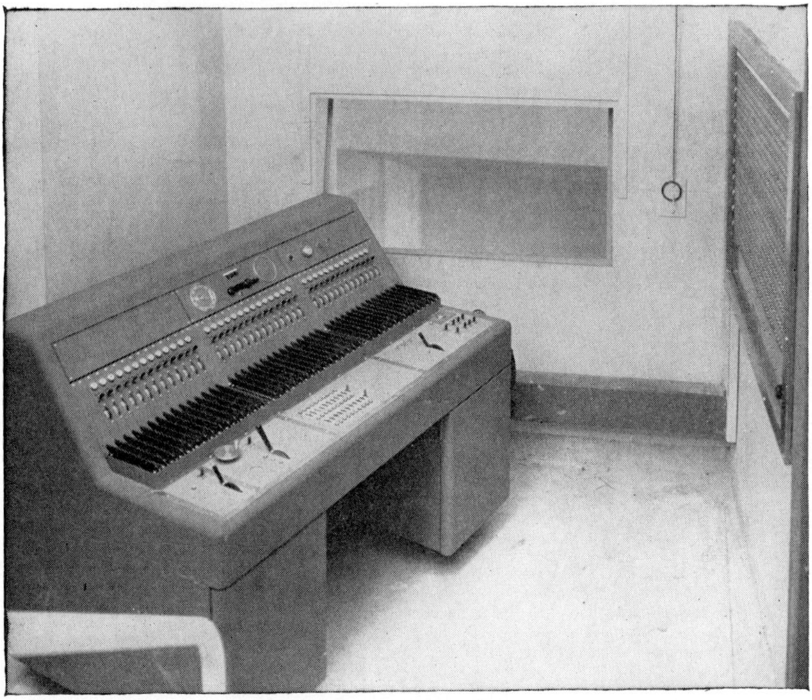

FIG. 85. Ward Leonard electronic reactance control board at Brooklyn College Theatre.

Lighting, Inc. It is illustrated in Figure 88, showing the control console at the center and the preset panel on each side. This model has ten presets for each control, and the fading and master control can be done automatically by motor drive at a pre-selected speed, or by manual operation.

The other electronic control board is manufactured by Kliegl Brothers. It, too, uses a thyratron type tube, which actually consists of three tubes in each circuit that serve as the dimmer along

FIG. 86. Magnetic amplifier dimmers. Latest development in remote control.

FIG. 87. Console for magnetic amplifier control board for NBC-TV made by Metropolitan Electric Co. Notice "draw-bar" type dimmer controls.

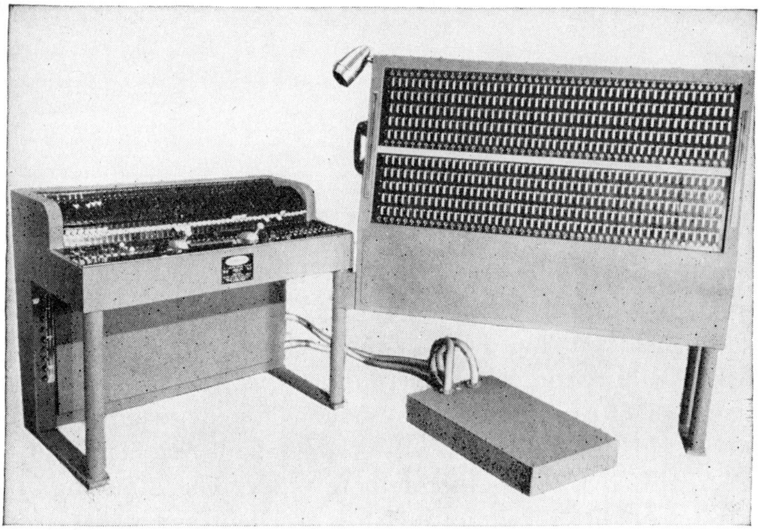

FIG. 88. Century Izenour electronic control board and preset panel at Denver Civic Theatre.

with their supplementary parts. This system has a more conventional console with the presets associated with the individual controls and switches, or they can be arranged in scene groups. The necessary fading devices and master dimmers can be arranged to suit the purchaser, since this, as well as the Izenour board, is a custom made item. Electronic dimmers are completely flexible in their loading range, that is, they have complete multicapacity. A 6000 watt dimmer will completely dim the smallest lamp. The Kliegl board is illustrated in Figure 89.

A dimming control devise has appeared in the last few months that promises to make all methods of remote control obsolete and in time might compete with the autotransformer type of dimmer. The new dimmer is a silicon rectifier, a miniature electronic de-

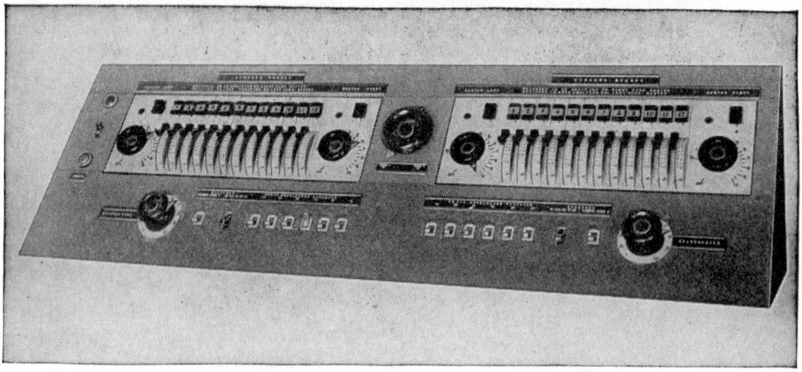

FIG. 89. Kliegl electronic two-scene control board.

vice related to the transistor in that it can control the flow of current. It is already available in 3000, 4000, and 5000 watt sizes and weighs about one and a fourth pounds per kilowatt compared to eight to ten pounds per kilowatt for thyratron electronic dimmers or fifteen to twenty-five pounds for the magnetic amplifier type. The new dimmer will occupy about one eighth of the space required by the other remote types. The dimming characteristics of the silicon rectifier are excellent and it has a dimming range of at least one tenth of its rated capacity; some models have an infinite loading range as in the thyratron and autotransformer dimmers. Both Kliegl and Century are now building control boards with this new dimmer and other companies are planning to bring out similar systems.

13. MASTER DIMMERS

With a master dimmer one can do electrically what is done mechanically by the interlocking mechanism used with interlocking dimmers, and the master dimmer has an additional feature which makes it superior. If one desires to change the intensity of six groups of lamps simultaneously by means of noninterlocking dimmers, three operators would be needed. If there were fifteen or twenty dimmers, quite a large crew would be necessary for this purpose alone. Fortunately, a master dimmer, connected in series with all of the individual dimmers and circuits to be

FIG. 90. The new silicon rectifier dimmer as produced by Kliegl. At the left is the manual control to be placed on the console and at the right the actual dimmer parts to be placed anywhere that is convenient.

controlled, will accomplish this task of dimming all of these circuits together, and it can be operated by one man. This master dimmer must have a wattage capacity equal to the total wattage of all the load connected to it.

A small control board wired for flexible control is sometimes divided into two groups of circuits, each group having a number of individual dimmers controlled by a master. A single operator can manipulate two handles simultaneously, and two masters are superior to one in that one group can be decreased in intensity while the other is being increased. This is possible, however, with a control board wired for flexible control only (see Section 2).

The important feature which makes a master dimmer superior to mechanical interlocking is called proportional dimming. Suppose a master dimmer were connected to four individual dimmers which were set at different readings, "full up," one-fourth dimmed, one-half dimmed, and three-fourths dimmed. With the master dimmer one could dim this group proportionally, that is, change the intensity of the whole group without changing the relative intensities of the lamps controlled by these four individual dimmers. Proportional dimming is useful also when one uses three-color striplights (see Chapter 17). The master can dim the mixture without changing its essential hue.

Although master dimmers for direct control are quite expensive because their size must be equal to the total load connected to them, in remote control the matter is much simpler and the cost very little beyond that of the individual controls. In mastering remote controls, the master dimmer is only mastering the small individual pilot controls on the manually operated console, and may consist of a small autotransformer or variable resistance carrying a very small current like that in all of the parts on the console. No additional parts need to be added to the heavy remote equipment.

14. PORTABLE CONTROL BOARDS

A portable control board is what its name implies—a control board light enough to be either carried about by hand or rolled on casters. It consists of the usual parts associated with stationary boards—dimmers, switches, circuit breakers, wiring, outlets, and sometimes an interconnecting panel. Almost any stage lighting equipment manufacturer will make control boards of the portable variety according to the customer's specifications or can provide certain stock sections. Many theatre groups buy parts and assemble their own portable controls. While the basic function of such a board, by definition, is control that is portable, this type of equipment appeals also to those seeking lighting control that is reasonable in price.

Theatre groups starting with little equipment have accumulated dimmers in small numbers and have assembled them in boxes of wood or steel, planning to add more dimmers later. Both the Ward Leonard Electric Company and the Superior Electric

Company have "packaged dimmer" units, illustrated in Figure 91, in standard "packages" of three, four, five, and six dimmers of the autotransformer type, including circuit breakers, switches, and outlets for plugging lighting instruments directly into the portable board. A larger version on casters built by Kliegl Bros. is shown in Figure 92.

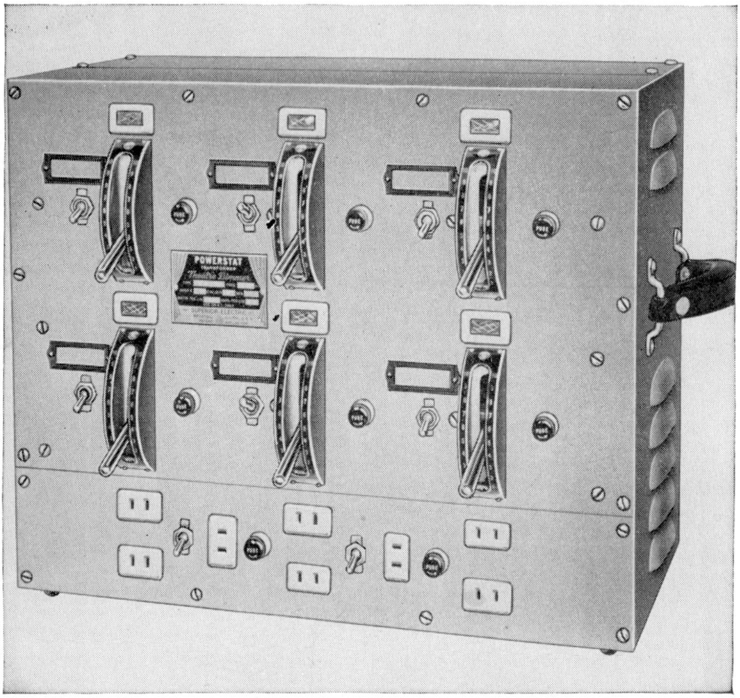

FIG. 91. A portable control board by Superior Electric Co.

An interesting variation built by the Ariel Davis Manufacturing Co. is intended particularly for schools and colleges. This company has designed and is building an autotransformer dimmer with six sliding contacts and six outlets. Each dimmer will control 6000 watts but each slider will dim a separate lighting load (such as a spotlight) of 2400 watts provided that the total on all six does not exceed the 6000 watt maximum. Each multiple dimmer is provided with six outlets and a circuit breaker mounted in a steel box. These can be assembled, of course, into groups for a larger portable control board with master dimmers and other conveniences such as interconnecting arrangements.

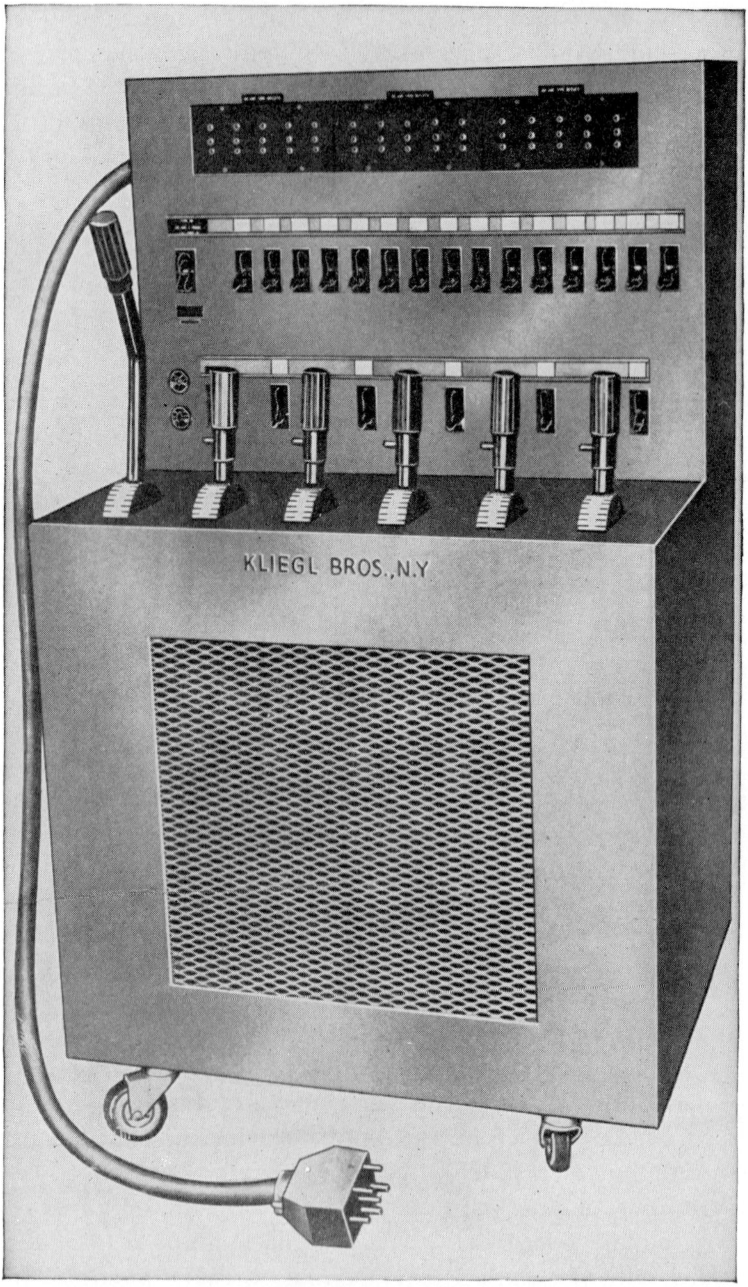

FIG. 92. Portable control board by Kliegl. This type is common in small television studios.

15. TELEVISION LIGHTING CONTROL

Similar to control equipment for stage lighting, television lighting control equipment includes the whole range of possibilities from elaborate electronic controls to the simplest of portable arrangements of dimmers, switches, and outlets. Figure 91 is typical of the simpler portable direct control variety. If the television studio has been adapted from a theatre, the lighting controls have often included the old stage control board, revised or used without modification.

Since television programs often require fairly numerous and elaborate scenes, only a small number of spotlights and floodlights set up for the whole program can be connected to dimmer circuits at any one time. By means of an interconnecting panel (see Section 4), the control operator can change his board quickly from instruments for one scene to instruments for another; or he can change instruments from dimmed to undimmed circuits, and vice versa. As new television studios are built and older ones are revised, the direction in control equipment seems to be toward better quality and a larger number of dimmer circuits. Electronic controls are gaining in favor, but autotransformer and resistance types have been more common in New York.

QUESTIONS AND EXERCISES

1. Define permanent and flexible control.
2. What are the advantages of flexible control for a college or school theatre?
3. What are the requirements of a good switch to be used on the stage? Would a mercury switch be satisfactory?
4. In what respects is an autotransformer dimmer superior to the others for a direct control board?
5. What does mechanical interlocking mean?
6. Why is an electrical master dimmer superior to mechanical interlocking?
7. What are the advantages of electronic and electronic reactance controls?
8. Explain multiscene controls. How are they used?

CHAPTER 20

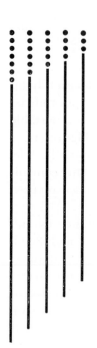

Specific Lighting Practice

1. INTRODUCTION

In the use of terms and designations for various kinds of equipment, it will be assumed that the reader has read the preceding chapters on the functions of light and the general plan for lighting as suggested in Chapter 16, and that he has such familiarity with instruments, color, and lighting control as one might acquire from reading Chapters 17, 18, and 19.

If one is now familiar with the general approach, he is ready to begin planning the lighting in the production of a specific play. The obvious way to begin is with a good knowledge of the text. If one is planning or designing the lighting, he must read the script, first for its general emotional impact and mood, and then again for its detailed requirements that concern light. Before the next step, which is consulting with the director and designers of scenery and costumes, the lighting designer might ask himself several questions. What is the mood; what is the emotional effect of the play? What is the playwright trying to say? Is this a serious play, a comedy, a tragedy, or a melodrama? What is its style? Can these general matters be expressed in terms of quantity, color, and distribution of light? Should the light be evenly distributed, with subtle tints of color, such as one might use in many of Chekhov's plays? What are the time, place, and season in each scene? How is light to be motivated; that is, shall the light on the actor and the set seem to come from the sun or sky? Or should the light seem to come from artificial sources such as table and floor lamps, candles, or gas luminaires? And finally, which functions of light should be emphasized? These questions are a part of the lighting designer's thinking as he studies the play in detail and makes appropriate notes. Some of the answers will be found in the text. Others will

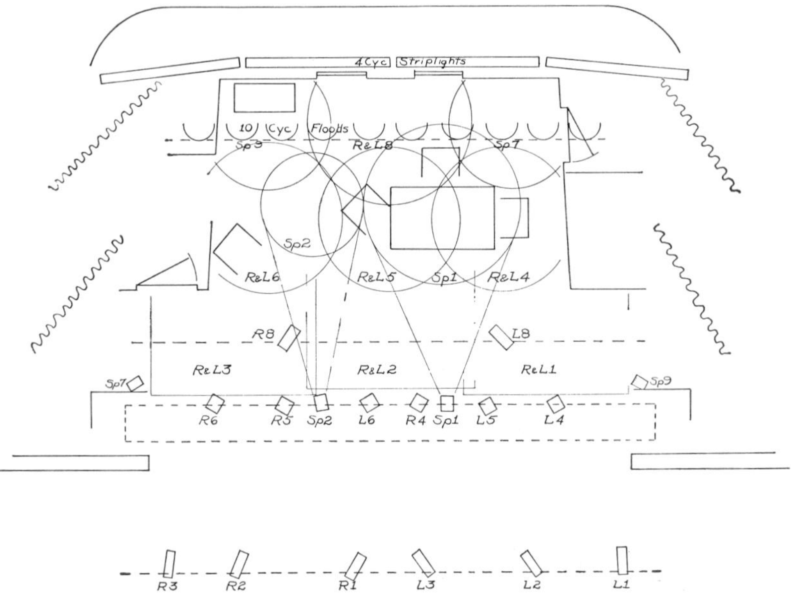

FIG. 93. Light plot for Act I, Scene i and Act II, Scene ii, *The Grass Harp*.

come from the designer's imagination and analytical ability, or from consultations with the director and other designers. If the theatre staff consists of several people, the planning of a production becomes a co-operative matter led by the director. In a one man organization he may have to answer all of these questions alone, but in the educational theatre we can assume that the production of a play is a learning process for students and that those with experience and imagination will have a part in the lighting plans under discussion.

After consultation with his fellow artists and an examination of the scene and costume sketches, the lighting designer is ready to make the detailed plans commonly called the lighting layout, or a light plot. The light plot includes a floor plan of the set (Figures 93 and 94, a section (Figure 95), an instrument schedule (Figure 96), and a control board cue sheet. The plan and section show the position of each instrument and the area lighted by that instrument. The instrument schedule, using the same symbols, shows the type, wattage, outlet, dimmer, color and so forth, for each instrument. While the section is not always necessary, it is helpful in indicating instrument heights above the floor and the vertical

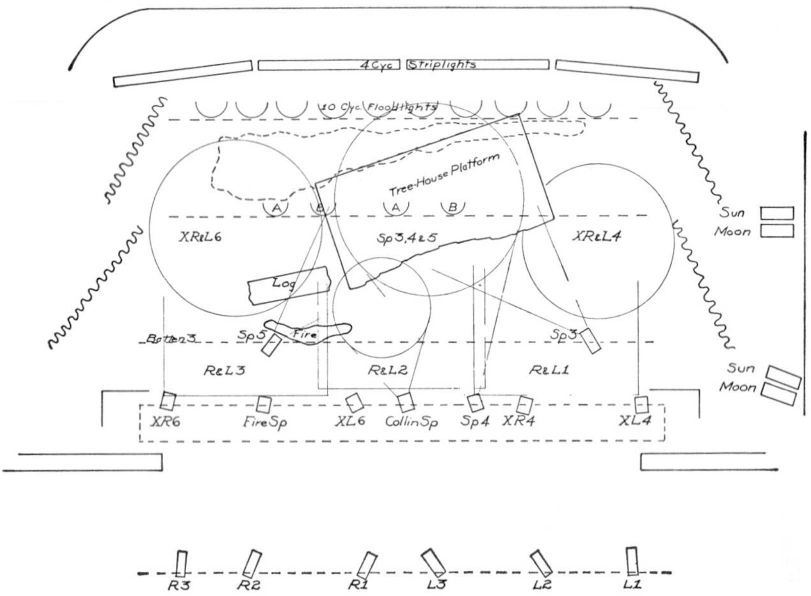

FIG. 94. Light plot for Act I, Scene iii, Act II, Scene i, *The Grass Harp*.

angles of the beams of light. Although the control board cue sheets must be prepared in part before the lighting rehearsals, the dimmer readings may be changed frequently before the final dress rehearsal.

2. LIGHTING A SPECIFIC PLAY

The Grass Harp, by Truman Capote, has been selected for an example because it has both an interior and an exterior scene and because it combines certain elements common to the lighting of many plays, with some interesting special problems of its own.

The scenes of *The Grass Harp* are laid in a small town in the deep South where the atmosphere is quiet and pastoral, far removed from the outside world. The somewhat frustrated characters lead sheltered lives, and the protagonist (Dolly) lives in a childlike fantasy world. The author seems to want us to see the setting through her eyes when he describes the whole house as, "a painted, extremely stylized curtain representing its dull tinted exterior."

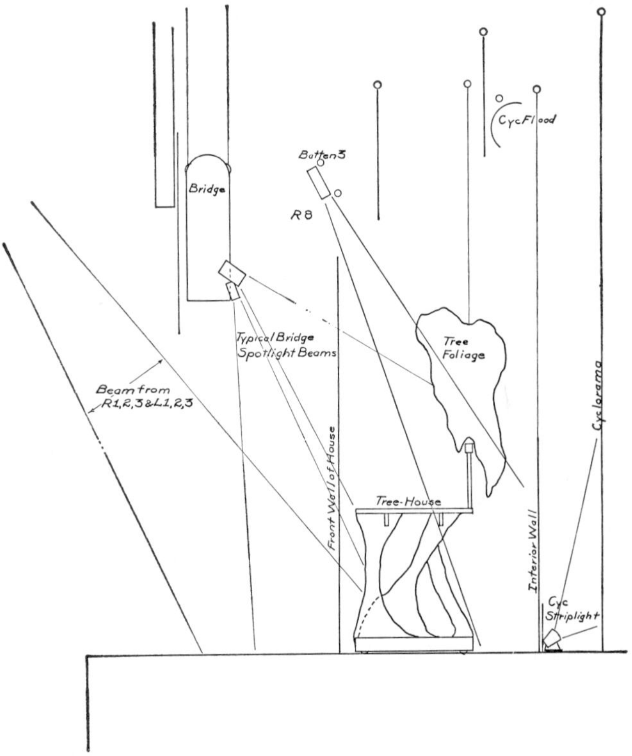

FIG. 95. Section showing both interior and exterior, *The Grass Harp*.

We see the upstairs windows and a "practical" front door. The dining room is our principal acting area—in Capote's words, "it is embedded there, like the scenes inside of sugar Easter eggs." Figure 96 shows the first scene of this production, designed by Don Powell,[1] who supported the somewhat fragile, unreal point of view by covering the frame of the house and the back wall of the dining room with painted gauze through which the sky cyclo-

[1] Associate Professor of Speech Arts, San Diego State College.

INSTRUMENT SCHEDULE - The Grass Harp

Type	Mfr.	Lens or Refl.	Wattage	Position	Outlet	Dimmer	Color	Scene	Location
Ellips.	Cent.	6"	750	L1	Beam 1	B6	Day.Bl	Act I Sc1	Beam
"	"	8"	750	R1	Beam 4	B5	Pink	" "	"
"	"	6"	750	L2	Beam 2	B4	Day.Bl	" "	"
"	"	8"	750	R2	Beam 5	B3	Pink	" "	"
"	"	6"	750	L3	Beam 3	B2	Day.Bl	" "	"
"	"	8"	750	R3	Beam 6	B1	Pink	" "	"
Fresnel	Cent.	6"	500	L4	Br1	A6	Day.Bl	" "	Bridge
"	Kliegl	6"	500	R4	Br6	A5	Pink	" "	"
"	Cent.	6"	500	L5	Br2	A4	Day.Bl	" "	"
"	Kliegl	6"	500	R5	Br7	A3	Pink	" "	"
"	Cent.	6"	500	L6	Br3	A2	Day.Bl	" "	"
"	Kliegl	6"	500	R6	Br8	A1	Pink	" "	"
"	Cent.	6"	500	Sp1	Br4	C2	Lav.	" "	"
"	Kliegl	6"	500	Sp2	Br9	C1	Lav.	" "	"
Major	Plan-o-lens	6"	1000	L8	TorL1	C3	Lav.	" "	
"	"	6"	1000	R8	TorR1	C4	Lav.	" "	
"	"	6"	1000	Sp7	TorR2	C5	Lav.	" "	
"	"	6"	1000	Sp9	TorL2	C6	Day.Bl	" "	
Flood	Cent.	Ellips.	500	1	Cyc B1	D4	Lt.Bl.	All	CycBatten
"	"	"	500	2	Cyc B2	D5	D. Bl.	"	"
"	"	"	500	3	Cyc B1	D4	Lt.Bl.	"	"
"	"	"	500	4	Cyc B2	D5	D. Bl.	"	"
"	"	"	500	5	Cyc B1	D4	Lt.Bl.	"	"
"	"	"	500	6	Cyc B3	D5	D. B.	"	"
"	"	"	500	7	Cyc B4	D4	Lt.B.	"	"
"	"	"	500	8	Cyc B3	D5	D. B.	"	"
"	"	"	500	9	Cyc B4	D4	Lt.B.	"	"

FIG. 96. Instrument schedule for *The Grass Harp.*

rama was visible at all times. There was no ceiling and the scalloped top edge of the walls carried out the "sugar Easter egg" feeling.

The second scene is a tree house in the woods, where Dolly and her companions find refuge from the domination of her unpleasant sister. The tree house has an unrealistic, fantastic quality because it represents Dolly's escape from her sister and from reality. This scene (Figure 98) will be discussed later.

3. THE INTERIOR

As pictured in Figure 97, the first scene is both exterior and interior in the sense that actors walk along a sidewalk in front of the frame of the house and enter the front door at stage right

FIG. 97. Act I, Scene i, *The Grass Harp* designed by Don Powell for San Diego State College production. Direction and lighting by H. D. Sellman.

just beyond the dining room. The actors cross from stage left and go through the exterior door into a hall and enter the dining room up right. The door to the kitchen is up left.

The following description refers to the ground plan in Figure

92. The downstage areas (sidewalk mentioned above) were lighted by six auditorium ceiling beam spotlights (ellipsoidal) that covered an area as wide as the theatre's proscenium opening in order to include the outside door and the full stage width for the following scene. Areas four through nine were entirely within the dining room opening (Figure 92). The midstage areas four, five, and six were lighted by Fresnel spotlights on the bridge.[2] Area eight had to be lighted from a batten upstage of the bridge by two 1000 watt 6-inch spotlights. Faces could not be reached by bridge spotlights when actors were close to the rear wall of the dining room. Areas seven and nine had to be lighted by the same type of instrument from the tormentor positions mounted low enough to get under the inner frame for the dining room. These last two also served as doorway specials. A table special (sp. 1) was useful during Act I, Scene 1, because a considerable part of the movement revolves around the table in this scene. "Special two" covered the area at stage right of the table and was centered on the line between areas five and six where Dolly told her story of receiving the dropsy cure formula from the Gypsies. "Special two" is useful also for the reconciliation scene in Act II, Scene 2. Variety in the dining room lighting was obtained by differences in color indicated in the instrument schedule and variety in brightness by different levels of illumination made possible by different dimmer readings, and also by different vertical angles of illumination. The tormentor spotlights were at the lowest angle, the bridge spotlights at a higher angle and the two spotlights for area eight were at a much higher angle, since their beams went over the top of the frame of the house. Spotlight seven lighted the right hall way sufficiently, and general spill and reflection from the cyclorama lighted the kitchen backing satisfactorily, so no backing striplights were used for this interior.

Since a large part of the walls of this interior setting were nearly transparent, the cyclorama had to be completely lighted at all

[2] In the production shown in the photograph a bridge was used instead of a teaser batten. A bridge is a light steel structure sometimes made of steel pipe which is often used to take the place of a teaser batten. The bridge is usually as long as the proscenium width and is about twenty-four inches wide, so that operators may walk on it in adjusting and mounting instruments. A bridge contains more places for mounting instruments than a single batten and makes adjustments between scenes more convenient. Most bridges are hung from the gridiron by means of steel cables.

times. The upper part was illuminated by ten 500 watt ellipsoidal floodlights, half with daylight blue color media and half with dark blue. From the floor the cyclorama was lighted by four 3 color (blue, green, and red) striplights, six feet in length. Because the stage was quite small, it was necessary to place the striplights just three feet from the cyclorama surface. For this reason, 55° spread, color roundels were an absolute necessity to mix the colors at such close range. Throughout the play the lighting on the cyclorama was in continual change from day to night and night to day, including dawn and sunset. During the first scene, the time is late afternoon, and in the last scene (same set) the time is late at night two days later.

4. LIGHTING AN EXTERIOR

Scene 3 of Act I and Scene 1 of Act II were played in and around a tree house in the woods (see Figures 98 and 94). The tree with its platform seven feet above the stage floor and a ground row behind it to mask the striplights were the principal objects on the stage floor. There was a papier mâché fire effect right center in front of the tree.

The lighting on the cyclorama remained as it was in Scene 1 of Act I except the changes in color and brightness required by this scene (Act I, Scene 3). These changes were adjustments in control board dimmer readings and no back stage activity was involved. The downstage areas had to be lighted exactly as they were in Act I, Scene 1 because color changes and focusing adjustments were not possible for the ceiling beam spotlights in this theatre. Separate dimmers for each instrument, however, made changes in brightness and distribution very simple. The upstage areas four and six were conventionally lighted by two 1000 watt spotlights for each area and designated as XL4, XR4, XL6, and XR6 (refer to Figure 93). In addition to the regular downstage area instruments, two specials were needed, one camp fire special and a "Collin" special, for Collin when he falls after being shot. These two spotlights were 6-inch Fresnels with 500 watt lamps. "Special four," a spotlight of the same type, mounted likewise on the bridge, served as front lighting for people standing and sitting on the tree house platform. Specials "three" and "five" (1000 watt 6-inch lens spotlights) lighted approximately the same area from the sides but from a higher angle. They were mounted on batten three with the two upstage area spotlights for the interior. The higher angle helped give roundness and separation from the background to the people in the tree house and produced less spill on the foliage than if mounted on the bridge (see Figure 94).

Four 200 watt floodlights, A and B, contributed cool (blue-green) or warm (amber) general illumination to the foliage according to the needs of the time of day. For further indicators

FIG. 98. Act I, Scene ii, *The Grass Harp,* designed by Don Powell for San Diego State College production. Direction and lighting by H. D. Sellman.

of the time and for highlights from another angle, two sun spotlights and two moon spotlights (1500 watts, 8-inch lens) were mounted on a batten on the stage left wall of the theatre about fourteen feet above the stage floor.

The opening of Act I, Scene 3, takes place in mid-morning sunlight. After about twenty minutes and the exit of the sheriff's group, the stage directions read, ". . . the set dims to a silvery twilight, music falls, and a transitional time lapse, in the most stylized sense, occurs before our eyes." Twilight fades into night as the little group descends from the tree house, gathers sticks and makes a fire. The remainder of the scene is played around the fire as the tree house specials, the upstage area instruments, and the beam spotlights gradually dim, concentrating the light around the fire area. The light in the fire effect comes up on cue followed by the fire special that adds more pink area light to this scene. The sky, of course, had been changed to dark blue rather more rapidly than it does in nature. The moonlight spotlights are dimmed up later in the scene.

The second exterior scene (Act II, Scene 1) opens at dawn with people sleeping on the ground and in the tree house. The general illumination grows brighter with a slightly pinkish tint in the striplights at the foot of the cyclorama. A little later, the two sun spotlights are added but they must be dimmed out in about twenty-five pages when the Judge comments that it is clouding over. There is no other indication by the author that light is changing until five pages later when the group has gathered in the tree house to defend itself against a second attack by the sheriff and his men. Here, according to the stage directions, "the scene is in complete darkness." Gradually dimming to this point, it was thought more effective to leave a trace of light in the cyclorama striplights to reveal the sheriff's party in faint silhouette. Several members of this party carry flashlights to light the faces of Dolly and Verona, but this scene becomes more effective when the "fire special" with its color changed to daylight blue and the "special" for Collin are added, both with very low dimmer readings. As Collin is carried off, the two beam instruments on area one are brightened one point. With the use of the grand master dimmer, the last traces of light disappear as the curtain falls.

5. COMPARISON

In some respects these two scenes are not typical. Many interior settings have ceiling pieces although they are less common now than they were twenty years ago. With a ceiling in place, the upstage area spotlights and specials have to be placed on a single batten and there is less variety in vertical angles. Without the ceiling one might go further, and, as is common in television production, add back lighting. This can be done from a batten above the back wall of the set where a row of spotlights are hung and directed at a high vertical angle perhaps a foot or two further upstage than directly overhead. This practice gives the actor separation from the background and highlights the shoulders and hair. If the side walls are attached directly to the tormentors (a common practice), tormentor lighting, another way to gain variety in angle, is eliminated. In many interiors the cyclorama lighting problem is much simpler than in the case discussed here because the average interior shows a small expanse of sky behind a window. A drop or even a flat twelve feet square might be all that is needed. If so, it might be lighted by two floods on stands.

Our exterior is more nearly typical since the need for lighting an upper level is its only unusual quality. Nearly every exterior has a part of the acting area covered with scenery so that it is unnecessary to light every square foot of stage area. Levels are common but they are not often as high as the tree house. Tormentor lighting, which was used in *The Grass Harp,* is very common in lighting exteriors.

Basic plans such as the one suggested in Chapter 16 and continued in this Chapter are useful to the lighting designer and technician as guides to complete coverage of the areas used in a scene or play. On the other hand, any such plan of lighting is inclined to be dull unless special instruments are added for specific business and for particular furniture groups. As mentioned above, the variety in the angle of the beams from specials frequently helps the total lighting effect. One danger in using many area and special instruments is that of using them all at the same time and at almost the same brightness level, which leads to flatness and dullness such as that which results from using general illumination alone. This happens frequently when most of the instruments are provided with Fresnel lenses but no funnels. The spill light from many Fresnel lenses blends and smoothes the distribution of light until specific illumination becomes general illumination.

6. USING MORE LIMITED EQUIPMENT

Now all this may be very well for an organization with plenty of equipment, but how will those who have two or three spotlights solve their lighting problems? In the first place, the fewer spotlights one has, the more general illumination he needs. If one had three spotlights, he might use one on each downstage area from the beam position directed at a horizontal angle perpendicular to the proscenium arch. If one had six spotlights, he might add the other three to the upstage areas in the same way. There is another method of using a few spotlights to best advantage. It is to study the play carefully in rehearsals to learn the important focal points of interest or the areas where the most important scenes are played and to use the spotlights on these areas. As these scenes appear during the course of the production, one can decrease the general illumination in order to attract attention to a special area. These suggestions, of course, are for crude simplifications of the recommended plan, and in general will not produce results that are as effective as those in which the complete plan is carried out. The reader is not to infer, however, that a large number of instruments will always contribute to successful or aesthetic lighting. The most beautiful scenes are sometimes lighted with three or four instruments, and occasionally a play with a conventional box set requires all of the instruments one owns and all of the circuits on the control board.

Lack of equipment is no excuse for careless and thoughtless lighting. The more crude the apparatus, the greater challenge for improvement to those who must suffer with it. Crude as a conventional spotlight is, it is quite possible that no one has exhausted the ways in which it might be used effectively. The lighting in many little theatres can be improved by the addition or substitution of two show-window floodlights, but how often have they been tried? The simplest things are often the most beautiful, and one's skill is sometimes judged by his ability to do much with little. Working with little is, indeed, the usual lot of the nonprofessional director and technician, but many are doing superior things in spite of these handicaps.

7. LIGHTING FOR ARENA STAGING

Since there are so many ways of staging a play that could be called arena staging, it will be safer to limit this discussion to the central staging type in which there is a rectangular acting space surrounded by seats on all four sides. It is preferable from both a seeing and lighting point of view to have each row of seats higher than the one in front of it.

Although it may be obvious, the first consideration in arena lighting is to light the actor without lighting the audience. This should be simple, but really the most difficult problem in arena lighting is to light the actor in any place on the acting area so that he can be seen from every direction without spilling light (glare) in the eyes of people on the front row of the audience. When a theatre is built for arena staging this problem can be simplified or eliminated by constructing the ceiling with ports through which the beams pass on their way to the acting area. When a ceiling is high with good mounting arrangements above, almost no glare is produced to annoy the spectators if their attention is on the actors and the play. Since most arena productions are produced in large rooms built for other purposes, one needs to know how to light a central area where overhead conditions are not ideal.

The first requirement is an adequate means of mounting lighting instruments above the acting area. A crude but adequate one can be constructed of pipe in the form of a rectangle somewhat larger than the acting area with cross pipes in both directions in the form of a grid. This grid is attached to the ceiling of the room by means of steel rods or pipe. Steel cable may allow the pipe frame to sway. With such a method for mounting instruments, all of the instruments are completely exposed to view, giving the room an unsatisfactory appearance and contributing considerably to glare and spill light. To improve appearances and reduce spill and glare, one should add to the actual supports for the instruments an "egg crate" arrangement of wood, sheet metal or even drapery material extending twelve to twenty-four inches below the mounting pipes. This baffle or louver masks the spotlights and other instruments and, if the color is black or dark blue, absorbs much of the spill light.

Several types of lighting instruments have been used successfully in arena staging. These include the conventional spotlight with a plano-convex lens, the Fresnel lens spotlight, and the PAR 38 and R40 projector and reflector lamps with built-in reflectors. Common wattages for this purpose are 500 and 1000 in the regular spotlights and either 150 or 300 in the reflector and projector lamps. Sometimes ellipsoidal spotlights are used in arena lighting, but their extra length is against them. In fact, of all spotlights for arena staging, the 500 watt 6-inch Fresnel seems to be preferred because it is the most compact instrument for its wattage. All instruments used in arena lighting, especially those with Fresnel lenses, must be provided with funnels at least six inches long or with "barn doors," a four-way masking device used extensively in television lighting. The projector and reflector lamps can be used in a homemade stovepipe or 6-inch cylinder with a medium screw socket attached to a disc at one end. Several manufacturers have made inexpensive holders for these lamps which include a clamping device, louvers, and color cap retainers. The louvers should be somewhat longer for arena lighting.

Assuming an acting area which is two areas wide and four areas long, it is common to use three or four instruments to the area. The lighting grid (mounting position) should be fifteen to eighteen feet above the floor and the beam angle from forty to fifty degrees above the horizontal. Lower angles will spill more light on the spectators in the front row, and higher ones make long undesirable shadows in the actors' faces. In the discussion above it was assumed that it is undesirable to have any light on the audience while a scene is being played. Although it is usual to keep an audience in semidarkness, there is no valid reason why a small amount of light on the audience is undesirable. Some years ago the writer produced plays in a small arena theatre in which actors and audience both were lighted by six office type "direct-indirect" luminaires provided with 500 watt lamps. The direct portion of the light went through a Fresnel lens in the central part of the fixture. The indirect light was reflected to the ceiling and side walls of the room from a 28-inch indirect reflector surrounding the lens and lamp. The audience, being lighted entirely from the indirect illumination, received about one half as much light as the actor. The actor, too, was lighted in part from the indirect light from ceiling and walls, with some direct highlighting from overhead through the lenses. While the proportion of general illumination to specific lighting was undoubtedly too high, it seemed adequate, and no one complained that the audience on the opposite side of the stage was too brightly lighted. At the present time many commercial lighting installations are designed with all or most of the light coming from luminous ceilings. Below the actual structural ceiling a transluscent ceiling of plastic is supported by light steel or aluminum frames. Fluorescent or incandescent light sources are concealed above. An arena theatre might be built or rebuilt with such a ceiling but with the section over the acting area lighted with four or five times as much light as the part over the audience. The stage light and the audience light should be separately controlled by dimmers. Plastic in an egg-crate pattern might be used over the acting area.

8. TELEVISION LIGHTING PRACTICE

Near the end of Chapter 17 in discussing lighting instruments for television it was mentioned that we are still working with two kinds of light, general and specific, just as is commonly done on the stage. In the early days of developing methods for lighting in television, two opposing points of view developed concerning the relative importance of these two kinds of light. The "engineering" side inclined toward using general illumination alone, an even distribution of light, shadowless and rather monotonous. This was satisfactory in some respects, but the proponents of artistic lighting wanted something better. They insisted on light and shade, sharp spotlight beams, "shafts and pools" of light, accents and emphasis by means of light with much stronger contrasts. In the theatre these points of view were resolved long ago, and it is generally accepted that both kinds of light are needed to light a stage production effectively. Both kinds are needed in television, too.

In the theatre one is dealing directly with the human eye, which is an extremely adaptable optical instrument with the ability to distinguish objects clearly in moonlight producing about half a foot-candle of illumination. At the opposite extreme, the eye can see fairly comfortably in direct sunlight producing ten thousand foot-candles. The television camera tube, however, has a much narrower range, narrower even than motion picture film. Recently the Television Committee of the Illuminating Engineering Society [3] reported a range of illumination levels for television to be from thirty to one hundred foot-candles while light on the stage probably ranged between two foot-candles in quite dim scenes to perhaps as much as fifty foot-candles in very bright ones.

Terminology varies among the lighting supervisors in commercial television, but the following terms seem to be fairly common. Authorities agree that it is of fundamental importance to have *base lighting*. Base lighting is a flat, shadowless, general illu-

[3] "Current Lighting Practice in Television Production," *Illuminating Engineering* (September, 1951).

mination necessary for a good image on the picture tube of television receivers. This illumination is provided by the incandescent scoops (floodlights) and in some cases by fluorescent pans (see Chapter 17, Section 9). *Fill light* might be called a subdivision of base light since it is produced by general illumination too, and a certain amount of "fill" is taken care of by the base light. *Fill light* softens or fills the shadows that are too dark for a good picture; so this must not be a shadow-producing light. Floodlights at a fairly low angle are common for fill light. At times a 3-inch Fresnel lens 150 watt spotlight mounted on the camera helps to fill face shadows in close ups.

The general class corresponding to specific illumination in television is called *accent lighting*. This classification includes modeling light, key lighting, highlighting, and back lighting. The principal instrument for this group is the Fresnel spotlight in lens sizes from 6 inches to 14 inches made for lamps from 500 watts to 5000 watts. The larger commercial studios seem topheavy with dozens of the 1000 watt and 2000 watt instruments hanging above (see Figures 71 & 99). The *modeling* or *key light* is usually from a definite direction motivated by the sunlight or moonlight which may be coming in a window or over a wall. The modeling lights also cast shadows and add highlights, thus contributing to the three-dimensional quality of all good lighting. *Back lighting,* as the name implies, falls on the actor from above and somewhat behind (light directly overhead is undesirable for several reasons). It is produced by spotlights to highlight the shoulders and hair and to "separate" the actor from the background. *Background* lighting can be simple illumination on the walls of a set or draperies, or it can be a projected background. For background scenes it is common to project from the rear to a translucent screen sometimes as large as twelve feet by eighteen feet. As mentioned in the chapter on lighting instruments, large wide-angle lens projectors with carbon arc or high wattage incandescent sources will project to a screen slides of buildings, landscapes, and other backgrounds which are more acceptable in television than they are in the theatre. The projected effects are "tied in" with foliage, special frames, and other scenery to provide realistic or stylized settings. Moving effects on 16 mm. film are projected likewise from the rear, as they are in motion picture film production. Scenes in cabs and other vehicles are shown with

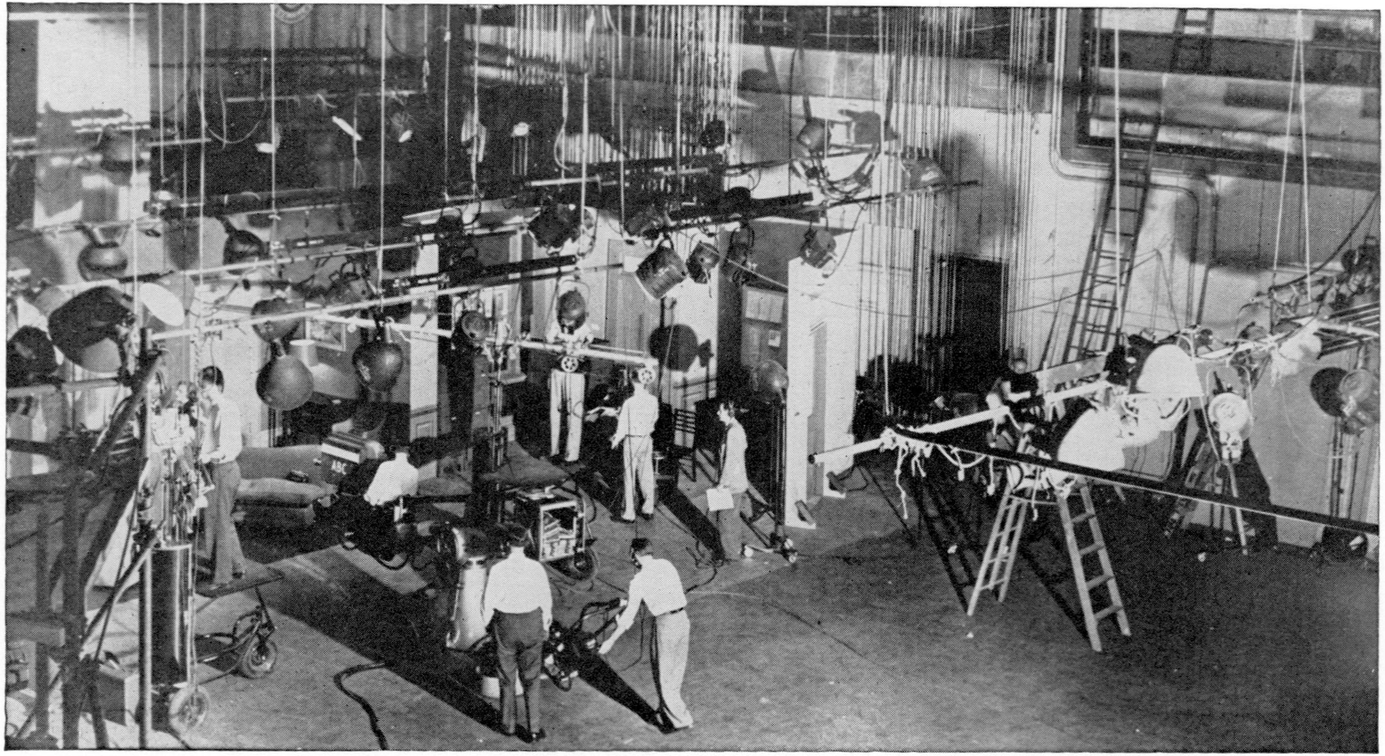

FIG. 99. A television studio with Kliegl lighting equipment.

the street or landscape receding in the distance. The vehicle is set up in front of the screen.

Much time in commercial television production is spent in attempting to remove undesirable shadows, especially those which fall on the actors' faces. The ever-present microphone and boom, just out of camera range but near the actors' heads, is one of the most common objects to cast a shadow across the actor's face.

It should be made clear that this brief section on television lighting is not intended as a complete analysis, but it should show the lighting designer the similarities and differences in lighting for stage and television. In the first place, the sensitivity of the television camera is very different from the sensitivity of the human eye. This variation requires much greater emphasis on general illumination for television. The problem of angles and sight lines in television is similar to that in motion pictures since they each have definite camera angles and the movement of actors is considerably restricted. Masking problems are relatively simple in both of these media, but on the stage we are concerned with sight lines from seats in the front row as well as the back, balcony, and from extreme left and right. Here masking is more difficult. On the stage occasional minor shadows and high contrasts may be ignored momentarily, but in television such things are more noticeable and must be corrected. Experience in stage lighting is an excellent background for television lighting but there are many new problems for the lighting supervisor in the latter field.

QUESTIONS AND EXERCISES

1. What are the essential differences between the lighting of an interior and that of an exterior?
2. Why is a cyclorama more difficult to light than a drop?
3. What is sacrificed when only one spotlight is used on an area instead of two?
4. Plan the lighting for a one-act play, making a complete lighting layout or plot including the ground plan and longitudinal section. Make a list of the instruments used, their location on the plan, wattage, focal length of lenses, and color changes. If possible, indicate where the instruments are to be plugged and connected to the control board. Make a control board sheet with dimmer readings and cues for the control operator.

5. Name and explain two fundamental problems in lighting for arena staging that are not important in conventional stage lighting.
6. How does arena lighting differ from ordinary area lighting for the stage?
7. What are the types of lighting in television production?
8. How are general and specific illumination related to these types?
9. Compare lighting instruments for stage and television.

CHAPTER 21

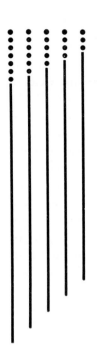

Sound and Music

1. INTRODUCTION

THERE WAS A TIME when every theatre in New York City and in stock throughout the country had an orchestra that played before the curtain opened, during the intermissions, and while the audience left the theatre. When the music was carefully selected for the mood and rhythm of the play, it contributed much toward the total effectiveness of the performance. Unfortunately the entr'act music disappeared with the stock company and the rising costs of commercial theatre productions.

Producers of plays in the noncommercial and educational theatre, where school orchestras and excellent recordings are not such serious financial burdens, should not overlook the opportunities to contribute to the emotional and aesthetic experiences of their audiences with music. A few moments of Lully before the curtain of a Molière production can evoke the spirit of seventeenth century France, or the recorded music of William Boyce played during the intermissions for *She Stoops to Conquer* or *The School for Scandal* can add immeasurably to the pleasure of the spectator and complete the picture of an eighteenth century comedy.

Motion pictures have accustomed audiences to expect complete scores of background music, and awards have been given for the superior quality of this phase of cinematography. In the field of drama and theatre such plays as *Johnny Johnson, Tread the Green Grass, Dark of the Moon,* and *The Grass Harp* (none of which could be called musicals) have had background music written especially for them by well-known composers. There are many other examples, and there are some plays in which sounds that are not strictly musical enhance the rhythm and the mood. The drum beats in *The Emperor Jones* and *Distant Drums* and the storm in Synge's *Dierdre* are integral parts of the emotional impact of these plays. In addition to the sounds that are a part of many playwrights' requirements, there are many incidents in plays which can be heightened emotionally by carefully selected phrases of recorded music. Expressionistic plays like *From Morn 'Til Midnight* and *The Adding Machine* display obvious needs for a background of music and other appropriate sounds. James Bridie's *Tobias and the Angel,* on the other hand, does not seem to lean heavily on sound and music, but when we settled down to a careful study of the play for a recent production, the sound problem included several dog barks, a water splash, archangel theme music, Asmoday theme sounds, accompaniment for a singer and dancers, an offstage orchestra, several bird call cues, thunder, wind, and several short music selections to cover scene changes. Many directors who achieve excellent results with other phases of production are neglecting the opportunities inherent in the subtle use of sound and music.

2. EQUIPMENT

One of the reasons for ignoring the opportunities to improve a production through sound is the lack of effective equipment and competent assistance in assembling and operating it. These difficulties can be overcome, often with little or no expense.

The equipment needed for producing sound and music in the theatre can be divided into three groups: (*a*) the *source,* (*b*) the *amplifier,* and (*c*) the *loudspeaker system.*

a. The source can be a microphone into which an actor or a group of actors speak, or through which "live" sounds are recorded for later use in the theatre. A good dynamic microphone with a frequency response [1] of 60 to 8000 c.p.s. is moderately priced (thirty to eighty dollars) and very satisfactory for the preparation of sound and music cues.

The source may be disc records of music or a disc-recorded sound effect from one of the commercial organizations listed at the end of this book. Radio and television stations, college departments of dramatic art or radio and television usually maintain a large library of these effect records as well as a good selection of music records. Common record players, often called transcription playbacks, can be used in assembling sound and music, but a professional turntable is better because it has a more powerful and accurately controlled motor. To be of greatest service it must run at all three speeds—78 R.P.M., 33⅓ R.P.M., and 45 R.P.M. In fact it is well to have access to a variable-speed turntable in order to distort certain sounds and to create new and unusual ones. In assembling sounds, two or three turntables and three or four pickup arms are useful in blending sounds for a composite effect. The working part of the pickup arm containing the needle is called a cartridge. The best types are "ceramic" or "variable reluctance." The most useful needles are of the "permanent jewel" type. The turntables and pickup combinations with appropriate controls are found in every radio department.

After acquiring our source of elements from disc records and "live" sounds picked up through a microphone, we must assemble them on magnetic tape through a tape recorder. The tape recorder is used both in recording live and disc-recorded sound and also as the playback for rehearsals and performances. Since

[1] There is an audible spectrum, comparable to the visual spectrum mentioned in Chapter 18 in which the frequencies of vibration of the sound waves are measured in cycles per second. A normal person has the ability to hear sounds that vibrate in the range of about 16 cycles per second (low bass) to 16,000 cycles per second (high treble). Age and disease change this range considerably. In middle to old age, auditory acuity is reduced to 12000 c.p.s. or less. The average radio receiver (excluding FM) covers a range of 125 c.p.s. to 5000 c.p.s. Old phonograph records seldom produced frequencies above 4000 c.p.s. because the material from which they were pressed had such a coarse grain that loud scratching sounds were produced at higher frequencies. The substitution of vinylite for record material has eliminated most of the scratch, and frequencies have gone much higher. Some high fidelity records are recorded as high as 15000 or 16000 c.p.s., but only the best record players will bring these high frequencies to the ear.

the best tape recorders with frequency response of approximately 40 to 15,000 cycles per second are expensive and bulky, we shall mention the cheaper ones costing less than $350. They are made by Web-Cor, Wilcox Gay, and Pentron and are fairly rugged and portable. While their frequency response is considerably narrower than that of expensive tape recorders, they are entirely satisfactory for our purpose and are easy to locate on a college campus or in any community. Some have two speeds, but a speed of 7½ inches per second is all that one needs.

b. The amplifier is the electronic means of expanding (amplifying) the minute amount of energy from the microphone, disc, or tape to the level of the original source, or in some cases, to higher levels. The amplifier also controls and balances the energy from the source. While there is an amplifier in each tape recorder, its power is insufficient to supply large speakers on the stage, and a booster amplifier of from 10 to 20 watts will be needed. The 5-inch by 7-inch or 6-inch speakers built into these tape recorders are too small for theatre sounds, but the controls for loudness and frequency on the average tape recorder will be found to be entirely satisfactory. Most of these recorders have an outlet for a plug and shielded cable to connect them to larger speakers. The most economical way to acquire the booster amplifier is to purchase one of the Heathkit amplifier kits for about sixty or seventy dollars. The directions for assembling these kits are quite simple, and considerable money can be saved with a few hours of labor.

c. The loudspeaker system may be composed of a single speaker or a combination of several speakers and an acoustical baffle, box, horn, or other element that converts the energy into sound waves. The 12-inch speakers made by RCA, Electro-Voice, and a few others with a frequency range of 50 to 11,000 c.p.s. have sufficient loudness and will work well with the equipment mentioned above. They, too, can be borrowed ordinarily from the audio-visual or radio and television department.

3. LOCATION OF EQUIPMENT

One or two tape recorders with their booster amplifier should be placed in a booth, possibly in the lighting control booth, where the sound technician can see the stage and can hear clearly the cues from the actors. Shielded cable must be run from the recorders to the speakers on the stage. The speaker or speakers should be placed several feet above the stage floor, if possible, out of the way of actors, scenery, and crew. Cable, too, should be above and away from harm and interference with other stage activities. Two or more speakers are used sometimes to give direction to sounds; even placing speakers in the auditorium will assist in getting certain effects. To give the effect of a plane passing overhead, one can fade from one speaker to another or even to one in the auditorium to give the illusion of the plane disappearing over the heads of the audience.

4. SOLVING THE SOUND PROBLEM OF A PLAY

Tobias and the Angel, mentioned above, will be used as a typical sound problem. Two students with a small amount of experience in radio production classes were selected to handle the sound for this play. After reading and marking their script with the sound cues, a conference with the director was the next step. Simple sounds, like the dog bark, the bleating of the kid, the water splash, and the bird calls, the sound technicians knew were in the sound effects record library. It was easy to play these for the director and get his approval of the nature and duration of each sound.

The music cues for this play turned out to be somewhat more difficult. Published sheet music is available for the "Jackal Song" and the dance which introduce the garden scene in Act II. It is arranged for oboe and pot drum as an accompaniment for a singer and several dancers who are the slave girls of Sara, Tobias' future wife. After the musicians had been assembled and rehearsed with the singer and dancers to establish the rhythm and tempo, the oboe and drum music was recorded by means of a tape recorder.

Searching for recorded music for the offstage orchestra in the same scene is typical of this problem in many plays. We must consider the time, the instrumentation, and the occasion which suggests the mood, nationality, and cultural background. *Tobias and the Angel* is based on the *Book of Tobit* from the Old Testament Apocrypha. While the book was written much later, it is concerned with a Hebrew family in Ninevah probably about

Two views of America's first Elizabethan theatre: the Oregon Shakespearean Festival, in Ashland. In this performance shot, the audience is watching the 1957 production of *As You Like It,* directed by the Theatre's founder and producing director, Angus L. Bowmer.

750 B.C. In this story Tobias goes on a journey to collect a debt for his father. While on the journey he stops in Persia to visit an old friend of his father and falls in love with the daughter, Sara, and marries her. From this we know that the music must sound Oriental, the instrumentation must be simple with the effect of fairly primitive instruments, and the mood must be suitable for a marriage celebration. Of course there are many sources, such as record libraries, private collections, the music stores with large stocks of classical records and all of the catalogues of recorded music, but perhaps the best place to start is with Katzman's *Recorded Bridges, Moods, and Interludes,*[2] a valuable reference book with many classifications and cross references to aid in running down all sorts of music for radio and television. By using such sources as these, the sound crew found six or eight disc recordings of good possibilities to suggest to the director. A final selection came from these and was recorded on a length of tape.

For the short fight scene between the Archangel Raphael and the fiend, Asmoday, we encountered the most difficult sound problems in the production. The author's directions are helpful in suggesting that Asmoday appear accompanied by thunder and wind. There are a number of good disc recordings of wind and thunder; so, as in the other similar cases, the length of the cue was timed and a mixture of thunder and wind was recorded on tape with an extra thirty seconds allowed for possible change in movement that might happen later. Since these two sounds were placed on a single tape, the loudness level of the two different sounds was varied as the recording was being done. The level of the combination, of course, would be controlled on the playback recorder as this effect was used in rehearsal and performance.

Although the author, James Bridie, does not suggest it, there developed during the discussion of the sound problems of this play the thought that if Asmoday had an accompanying sound, the Archangel should have one also. Theme music for an archangel was one of the most difficult sounds to locate. Dozens of records were tried, including harp records, and chords on an autoharp were recorded and played in rehearsals, but nothing seemed appropriate. Finally we settled for an ethereal abstract section from a piece of modern music. With the angel music on one tape and

[2] Henry M. Katzman, *Recorded Bridges, Moods, and Interludes* (New York, Broadcast Music, Inc., 1953).

the Asmoday sounds on another it was possible not only to play them separately, but also to play them in opposition during the fight, making each more prominent as each character seemed to be ahead, until the archangel triumphs with his music dominating at the end of the scene.

One of the cue sheets for Act II, the one for the fight scene, has been included below to indicate how the sound crew members plan their cue sheets and work during rehearsal and performance. In this case we used an operator for each of the two tape recorders.

General suggestions—preparation. When taking music from disc records, one should use new records if possible and handle them so that no fingerprints are added to the grooves. To get the best from records one must keep them clean, and fingerprints are as bad as dirt. If one must use an old or scratched record, it should be recorded in a radio department where the scratch can be filtered out.

Music and sound effects should be recorded at a constant level, and the variations can be added effectively by the sound technician in rehearsals and performances. It is satisfactory to play records on a playback of good quality and to record from the playback speaker to a microphone connected to a tape recorder. By watching the "electronic eye" and by ear one can control the loudness level that is being recorded on the tape. If one takes the tape recorder out to record a "live" sound directly, it is usually advisable to plug in some earphones to help in controlling the loudness of the recording. One should keep the microphone a proper distance from the sound source and watch for extraneous sounds.

When the properly timed and approved sounds have been recorded satisfactorily on lengths of tape, they must be assembled with pieces of white "leader tape" two feet long before and after each sound tape. Each sound should have a tab that sticks up and can be seen when the whole reel of tape is on the recorder which is being used as the final playback.

If one sound cue follows another very rapidly, it is better to place the second one on a separate tape to be played by another tape machine which probably should be controlled by a different operator. If the same sound is repeated, the director must not expect the operator to roll back his tape to repeat the cue. This causes confusion and mistakes that can be eliminated by adding another piece of tape in proper sequence each time the cue is needed.

Miscellaneous suggestions—rehearsals and performance. When the tape or tapes are completely edited with leaders and tabs, placed on reels, and the reels have been mounted on the tape recorders that are being used as playbacks for the production, we are ready for rehearsal. We are assuming, of course, that the speaker or speakers have been mounted and connected in effective positions on stage. We are also assuming that shielded cable

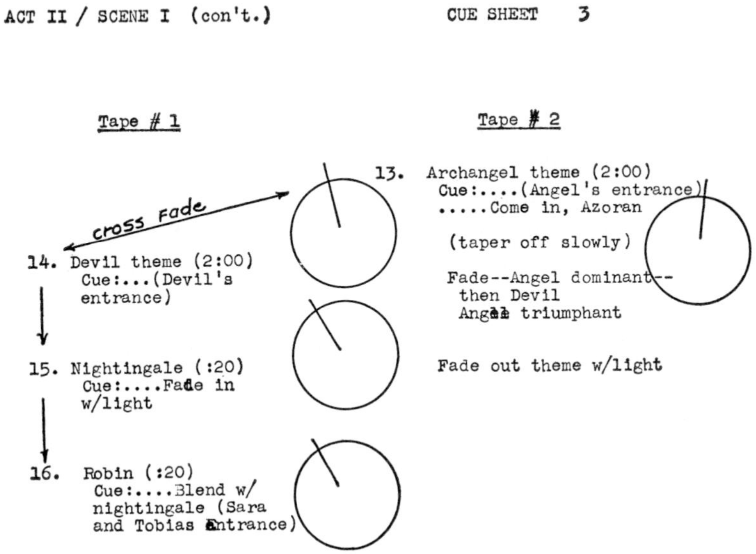

FIG. 100. Cue sheet for *Tobias and the Angel*.

joins the speakers to the booster amplifier and the tape recorders. If the sound operators are to do an effective job of cueing and controlling the loudness levels, they must be placed in an enclosure (if possible) where they can see and hear as well as people in the audience. The page from the *Tobias and the Angel* cue sheets may help to guide the beginner into a satisfactory method of making cue sheets for any production. The circles with the pointer lines is a rough indication of loudness level when there are no calibrated lines on the volume control.

Sound effects and background music should be added to the rehearsals about a week before performance, not only for accurate cueing but also to be certain to find the right sound level in relationship to the loudness of actors' voices. There is nothing more annoying to an audience than sounds that interfere with the voice of the actor.

5. A SHORT GLOSSARY OF SOUND EFFECTS

Thousands of sound effects are now available on transcription discs. Many of them are excellent, and new ones of better quality and higher fidelity are being added regularly. The catalogues of these effects, listed in the bibliography, should be in the collection of every director and technical director. More elaborate and complete glossaries of sound effects can be found in books on radio production. Robert Turnbull's *Radio and Television Sound Effects* contains very good chapters on "Improvised Sounds" and "Constructing Sound Effects." This is one of the best books on sound for the theatre as well as for radio and television. A glossary may be no more than an historical record. It is evident that there are several ways of producing each sound, and experience and imagination will lead one to the best solution.

Airplanes: A great variety of airplane effects are available on records. A poor substitute is an electromagnetic vibrator with the vibrating arm held against the head of a drum. Records are better.

Animal sounds: Many animal sounds are recorded by the companies listed in the bibliography. In some cases vocal effects are fairly good when performed by clever imitators.

Automobiles: There is a great variety of records of automobiles of different makes and models, moving, idling, and even crashing and skidding.

Battle sounds: (see also *Shots* and *Machine guns*) Records of distant artillery, machine gun fire, rifles, and so on are effective when properly synchronized; that is, when several of these are recorded on tape simultaneously. Very close shots and explosions can be added by firing blank cartridges of various calibers backstage. Kettle drum and thunder screens are helpful additions.

Bells, gongs, and chimes: Various effects used in orchestras, such as triangles, bells, cylindrical pipes of various lengths and diameters, old brake drums, and pieces of bar iron which vibrate with a variety of frequency and quality when struck with mallets of different materials. Church and cathedral bells, school bells, and locomotive bells are fairly well recorded on discs. Actual bells and gongs of different sizes and types are frequently useful. A set of electric bells and buzzers of various tones and qualities is a necessity for every theatre. It should contain five or six different bells and two or three buzzers to take care of telephones and several kinds of doorbell signals. Since most of these operate on 6 volts, it is more convenient to provide a 6 volt transformer and mount all of this equipment in a partly open box. Batteries can be substituted for the transformer. Recording a real telephone bell on tape may be preferable.

Chopping (see *Wood*).

Clock sounds: Authentic clock sounds are best. If they are not loud enough, they can be operated in front of a microphone. A few excellent clock sounds are recorded on discs.

Door slams: Although door slams are recorded, they can be co-ordinated better and are usually more convincing if a real door is used. A door somewhat smaller than normal may be used but the hardware, as well as the door frame, should be heavy. Real automobile doors are frequently placed in frames and used for car door slams.

Explosions (see *Battle sounds* and *Thunder*): Explosion records played on equipment capable of great loudness are sometimes useful. They can be supplemented with shotguns, explosive charges, drums, and thunder screens. Boiler explosions necessitate the addition of a hissing sound which can be added to the total effect by gradually discharging a small cylinder of compressed air.

Fighting: Fist fighting is sometimes effected by real fists striking a padded surface before a microphone and amplifies in the usual way. The sound of a body being struck with a rod or stick is made by striking a melon. Fighting with swords and sabres can be simulated offstage by clashing strips of metal three or four feet long, or even by swords themselves. Foil blades are too light. The clashes should not be too frequent if a duel is being represented. Continuous clashing is unnatural and spoils the illusion for anyone who is familiar with swordplay.

Fire: Twisting and crushing cellophone or a similar material near a microphone is the usual method. One might try recording a real crackling fire composed of partly damp wood.

Glass crashing: A useful glass crash can be made with a wooden frame covered with wire screen about 16 inches square and 3 feet high. The bottom and top are solid wood but the bottom is covered with a tray or drawer to catch the broken glass. An inch or so below the lid is a narrow frame to support the piece of glass which will be broken by a steel stud (as a ¼ inch bolt) projecting down from the center of the lid. Forcing the lid down brings the stud in contact with the sheet of glass and breaks it. The sound is further improved by steel strips projecting from the sides into the space through which the glass must pass. In striking the steel strips the sound continues until it falls on other pieces of glass in the tray at the bottom.

Hoofbeats: The well-known coconut shells are satisfactory when struck against appropriate materials. Radio sound-effects men sometimes use suction cups on their own chests or in damp sand for horses on turf or a dirt road. There are good disc recordings of hoofbeats, but they often have the wrong gait or the wrong number of horses.

Horns (automobile): A collection of automobile horns mounted and connected to push-buttons and battery terminals is a valuable addition to a theatre's sound department. Such horns operate on direct current and will not work with transformers and alternating current. A variety of these sounds is included with automobile sounds on records.

Machine guns: The old method of slapping an automobile cushion with two bamboo sticks is a rather crude machine gun effect. Now, there are many good recordings of nearly every type and make of machine gun.

Machinery and construction sounds: Stagecraft shop machinery is sometimes operated and recorded when woodworking sounds are needed. Hand sawing and hammering contribute to the effect of a workshop. Clanking of small pieces of metal and the operation of small electric motors and mechanical toys near a microphone help in the illusion of a machine shop. A few good records are available.

Rain: Rain has not been recorded very effectively. The old offstage effect of rain produced by dried beans or small shot in a thin plywood cylinder is still better than most records. Water from a sprinkling can poured on various materials near a microphone is good.

Roaring sounds: Certain types of roaring sounds can be made with a simple device consisting of a large metal can with a cord knotted through a small hole in the bottom. When the cord, covered with rosin, is held taut and rubbed with the hands, several kinds of roars and vibrating sounds come forth. Loud roaring sounds have been produced by introducing a mixture of brickbats, rocks, gravel, and miscellaneous objects at the end of a long wooden chute, irregular in shape and surface, set up so that one end is considerably higher than the other. This apparatus will create the effect of a landslide. Recordings are fairly good.

Shots (see also *Battle sounds*): Individual shots, while available on recordings, can be produced more convincingly with revolvers and blank cartridges. The different calibers available give one a good range of loudness.

Squeaks: Squeaky hinges can be imitated effectively by a device that is simple to make according to the following directions (see Figure 101). Drill a hole in a rectangular block of wood to fit a half-inch dowel. With a saw, cut a slot to the hole from the side of the block. Drill another hole perpendicular to the first one (and also perpendicular to the slot) through the slot, so that with a bolt and thumb nut inserted through this second hole the degree of tension on the dowel may be changed. Put a handle on the dowel and twist it in the hole as you adjust the tension. All kinds of squeaks will result. Another kind of squeak can be obtained from pushing a drinking glass, top down, across a pane of glass.

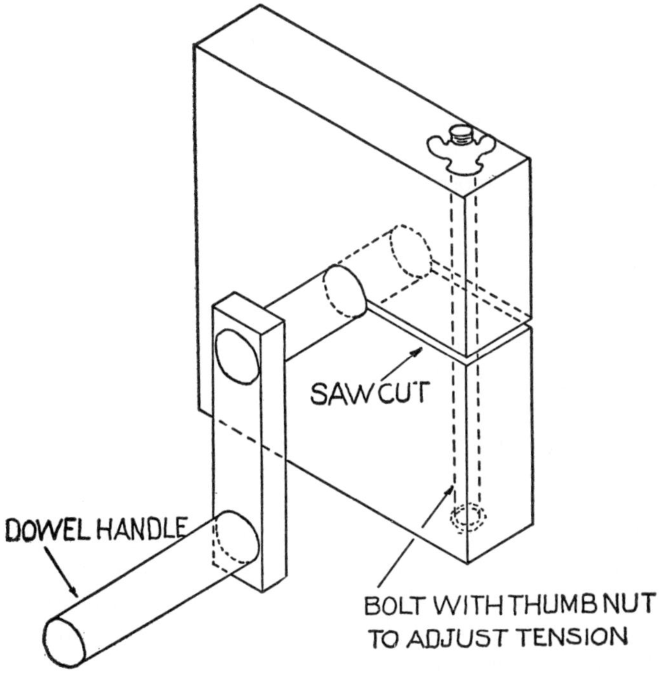

FIG. 101. The squeak device.

Thunder: The old-fashioned thunder sheet, while metallic and none too convincing, is still in use to some extent. It is a thin piece of sheet metal about 2½ by 5 feet, suspended by a rope at one end. The other end, provided with a wood handle, is shaken manually. It may also be struck with a padded mallet. An electrical thunder screen which is much more effective can be made in the following way. A piece of wire screen about 30 by 40 inches is held in a frame with a clamping device at one end to regulate its tension. To the wood frame is fastened an old magnetic phonograph pickup, and somewhere near the center of the screen is bolted a stiff piece of wire, several inches long, reaching into the opening for the needle in the pickup. (The wire is sometimes twisted into a spiral.) When the screen is vibrated by means of a soft drumstick, human fingers, or other objects, the vibrations are transmitted to the pickup, where they are changed into electrical impulses and sent along wires to the amplifier and speaker. A variety of thunderous and rumbling sounds can be brought forth in this manner.

Good thunder effects are available on records, some with effective thunderclaps that are hard to manufacture otherwise. Cueing disc-recorded peaks or claps of thunder is difficult. It is easier if the electrical thunder screen, bass drums, and tympani are used.

Trains: There are many good recorded train and locomotive effects that are rather difficult to equal with mechanical devices.

Water effects: Gurgling and rippling sounds can be produced by blowing through a straw into a glass of water near a microphone. The basic machine for most water sounds in radio studios is a tank, such as a square laundry tub lined with cloth (to dampen the metallic effect) and filled with water. Then a paddle wheel of four blades is mounted horizontally in the water and turned by a crank. Many water effects originate in this apparatus placed near a microphone.

Whistles: Sound technicians need a great variety of small whistles, such as those used in sports as well as the cheaper ten-cent-store variety. Steamboat whistles can be imitated with the organ-pipe type of wood whistle found among the sound apparatus in a physics department. Blowing across bottles and sections of pipe makes whistling sounds that are sometimes useful.

Wind: Very good wind effects are available on recordings, but the old revolving drum with a piece of canvas attached to the frame and allowed to hang over the revolving surface is still worth using. Variety is achieved by varying the speed of rotation and the tension on the canvas. The surface of the drum may be a series of slats whose sharp edges scrape the canvas and make the desired sound. Some of the drums are covered with wire screen.

Wood crashes: Breaking wood can be done with thin pieces such as berry boxes placed in front of a microphone; or heavier material such as orange crates can be broken offstage without amplification. Larger crates are sometimes suspended in the flies and dropped to the stage floor. Records of various crashes are available too. Chopping has been recorded adequately, and real chopping is simple to perform offstage, or best of all, add it to the taped material recorded for the production to be played back on the tape recorder.

6. CONCLUSION

Good sound effects and music are valuable additions to the production. Most of us have the means close at hand and are not taking advantage of them. In this chapter there is insufficient space to define and explain every technical term. It is wiser for a director to engage the assistance of a student with some background in audio engineering and who will enjoy relating his background to a new and interesting application—sound and music in the theatre.

APPENDIX

COSTUME AND MAKE-UP

I. THE RELATION OF COSTUME AND MAKE-UP TO PRODUCTION

A. The Place of Costume and Make-up

COSTUME and make-up constitute the outward and visible appearance of the actor. As such, they aid in focusing attention on the player, they enhance his appearance and they intensify his stage personality. Costume and make-up include not only period styles and character make-up but also modern dress and straight make-up. In considering the production of a modern play, the costume and make-up should be as carefully planned and as effectively rendered as are the period styles.

1. *Subordinate to the Actor and Production*

The actor, however, should not be dominated by the costume or the make-up. Costume and make-up are dramatic elements in a production, but they are subordinate to the actor and to the production as a whole.

2. *Harmonious Elements in the Production*

The importance of maintaining the balance of a production should always be borne in mind. In order that costume and make-up shall constitute harmonious elements in the over-all production, they should reflect sympathetically, and also give dramatic emphasis to, the characterization of the individual actor and type of production as a whole. They should register effectively in the setting, and blend with its color range. They should be planned in relation to the lighting of the production, scene by scene and act by act.

B. The Purpose of Costume and Make-up

3. *To Give Visual Emphasis to the Actor*

The purpose of costume and make-up is to give visual emphasis to the player. The actor is, in physical size, a not very considerable unit on a stage of ordinary proportions. The line and color of his costume and the accentuation of his features with make-up aid in identifying him to the audience, and intensify his actions and his speech.

4. *To Reflect the Actors' Characterization and Its Changes*

Make-up and costume not only identify the actor, but they also reflect his characterization. There has been many Hamlets and there will be many more. Every good actor not only creates his own interpretation of the role, but also assumes an outward semblance of dress and features expressive of his individual conception. Great actors, indeed, set traditions of costume and make-up, as well as traditions of interpretation, which less creative actors copy.

If the character grows older, or his disposition changes for better or worse, or if some accident or chain of events strongly affect him or his health, these changes should be reflected in the costume, make-up, and accessories.

5. *To Identify Characters to the Audience and to Other Actors*

The audience more easily follows the action of the plot when the various persons in the play are dressed and made up suitably for their parts. Especially is this true of plays with complicated plots, such as the *Comedy of Errors,* or of plays with unusual, exaggerated character types, such as *Dr. Jekyll and Mr. Hyde.*

The intensification of the character, through the use of costume and make-up, makes him more readily acceptable also to his fellow actors. Their reaction is quickened and the emotional value of the scene is heightened. Anecdotes are told of fellow actors swooning away at the all-too convincing appearance of a Richard III. Care must be taken, however, to avoid the bizarre, the startling, or the shocking.

6. *To Submerge the Actor's Personality in That of the Role*

In supplementing the art of acting with the visual artistry of dress and facial make-up, the actor disguises his own personality in that of the part he is portraying. Self-consciousness, the bane of most new actors, and a serious handicap to many older and more experienced actors, can be lessened and often eliminated, by the complete identification, in outward appearance, with the assumed role. This transition of personality lessens the actor's nervous tension and adds to the energy and vitality given to the role.

C. Methods of Preparation

7. *Costumes Can Be Borrowed*

If the group of players cannot afford to rent or to make costumes, these must be borrowed from persons friendly to the organization and willing to co-operate in the project. If the play deals with the life and times of the late nineteenth or early twentieth century, it is preferable to borrow authentic costumes. Trunks and attics yield treasures of bygone days which the owners may be persuaded to loan, if they are assured that the garments will receive proper handling. Proper handling of such costumes means precautions against tearing, soiling, or altering the garments. It also means pressing and mending with careful consideration of the delicate fabrics.

Borrowed costumes should be collected from the various lenders and returned promptly after using. Before being returned, each garment should be carefully inspected, mended, and cleaned as thoroughly as the material will allow.

If a series of costume plays is given over a period of time, borrowing enough costumes for the players will become a problem. Therefore, it is wise to alternate costume plays with modern plays.

8. *Costumes Can Be Rented*

If the group relies on rental organizations for its costumes, the expense will mount up during the year, unless the modern plays outnumber the costume plays. It is advisable that the person in charge of renting costumes for the group send to the costumer's a complete set of costume work sheets. Each one shows the measurements of the actor, the desired color of the costume and the preferred materials. (See Figure 102, for illustration of Costume Work Sheet.) Alternate colors of materials should be noted on these, in case the required type of costume is not available and a substitution must be made. Measurement blanks provided by costume houses may be used to advantage.

Rental costumes, like borrowed costumes, should be collected and returned promptly, as an additional charge is made for tardy return. The garments do not have to be cleaned, but they should be mended if minor tears occur, and should be neatly packed.

9. *Costumes Can Be Made by the Group*

If the group has its costumes made, the initial cost will seem large, but the final cost will be less. This is because the garments can be used over and over again, with small changes. Judicious buying in large quantities can reduce the initial cost of the materials, and other economies will suggest themselves.

If the costumes are to be made, there should be a sewing committee, headed by a chairman. The committee may be composed of volunteer workers, students, or paid helpers, but they should be reliable, and capable of understanding stage dress. Sometimes the Home Economics Department in schools and colleges co-operates in designing and making

COSTUME WORK SHEET

COSTUME WORK SHEET (Male) ______________________________

Character

______	______	______	______	______
Date	Production	Act-Scene	Costume-No.	Designer

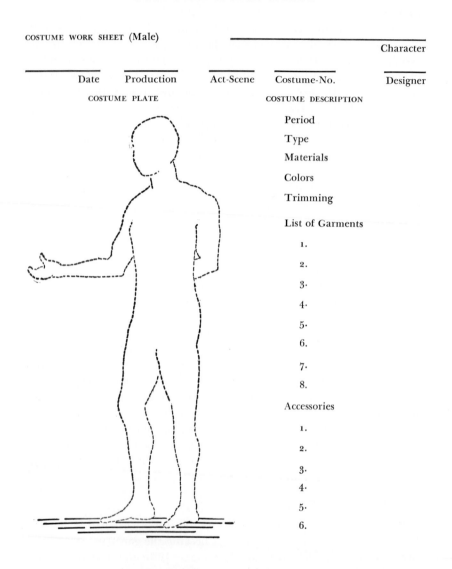

COSTUME PLATE

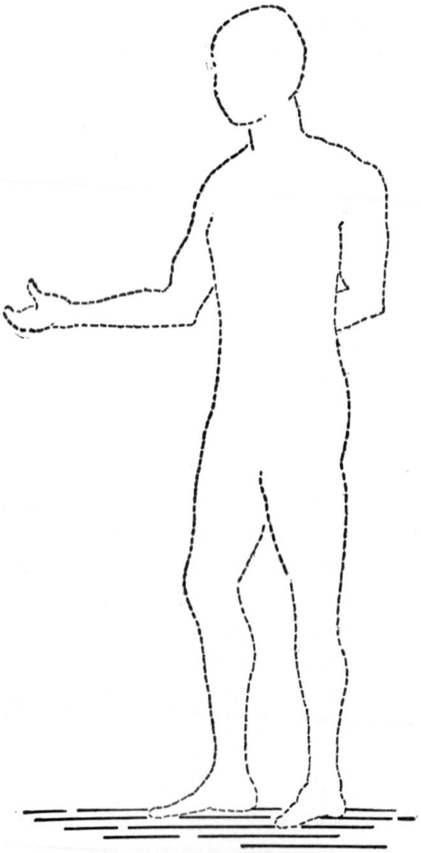

COSTUME DESCRIPTION

Period

Type

Materials

Colors

Trimming

List of Garments

1.
2.
3.
4.
5.
6.
7.
8.

Accessories

1.
2.
3.
4.
5.
6.

FIG. 102. From a plan suggested by Dr. Charles W. Cooper, Director of Dramatics, Whittier College, California, and arranged by his assistant, Paul Camp.

the costumes. This greatly aids the production and, in addition, gives valuable practical experience to the students.

The value to the organization of having costumes made lies in the steady accumulation of garments for future production use. Most important, however, is the fact that the costumes can be carefully planned to suit the production.

10. *The Make-up Artist Can Be Engaged*

If the acting group can afford to hire a make-up artist for each play and each performance of that play, it is assured of professional work. However, the services of a make-up artist are expensive, and his task of making up all the individual actors in a cast will necessitate much time.

The make-up artist is not necessarily acquainted with all plays, and may not always create the correct effect.

11. *Actors Can Apply Make-up under Supervision*

The actors can make themselves up under the supervision of a make-up instructor. This method has several advantages. The actor will learn the craft under expert direction, his mistakes can be quickly rectified, and his confidence will be strengthened so that, in time, he can handle his make-up unaided.

Where the make-up artist supervises the make-up, work sheets should be drawn up for each member of the cast (see Figure 103). The make-up work sheet should show the proper bases, color, powder, liner, and other materials to be used for each actor. In addition, if lines of age or suffering must be shown, these also are indicated on the chart.

The actor, under this method, not only learns the art of make-up by practical application, but he can express his conception of the part through facial portraiture.

D. The Actor's Use of Costume and Make-up

12. *Correct Wearing of Costume*

Actors should be trained to wear period costumes. Historic dress should be worn with an accustomed air, which dates further back than dress rehearsal. Practice should be given in wearing and handling the long, swirling medieval or Renaissance dress, the stiff, full, Elizabethan farthingale, the dainty, bouffant Marie Antoinette gown. Accessories, such as fans and snuffboxes, should also be rehearsed with until they can be handled with an ease that seemingly comes of long usage. Not only will this pre-performance training give an air of verity to the production, but it will assist in setting the actors at ease in their parts.

MAKE-UP WORK SHEET

CHARACTER ________________ PROD. ________________

DATE ________________

GENERAL DESCRIPTION: Age ________ Type ________ Comp. ________

____

Foundation		
High light		
Shadow		
Under rouge		
Eye shadow		
Eye liner		
Eyebrow pencil		
Eyelash		
Lip rouge		
Liner		
High light liner		
Powder		
Dry rouge		

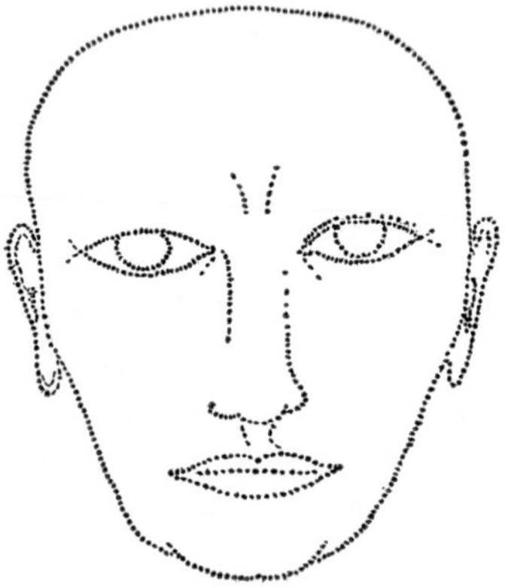

HAIR TREATMENT ________________________________

____

SPECIAL INSTRUCTIONS ________________________________

____

PRODUCTION NOTES ________________________________

____

DESIGNER ________________ APPROVED BY ________________

director

____

art director

FIG. 103. From a plan suggested by Dr. Charles W. Cooper, Director of Dramatics, Whittier College, and arranged by his assistant, Paul Camp.

It is said that a costume play is better for amateurs than a modern play, as the period dress and make-up hide the personality of the actor more completely than the modern dress. However, if the period dress is not worn convincingly, this advantage is lost.

If the period play calls for the wearing of a farthingale, hoop petticoat, or hoop skirt, the actor should be trained to walk and sit while wearing it and to handle it while entering and making an exit through stage doors. In entering and making an exit, the hoop, or farthingale, should be lightly lifted with the hand which is away from the audience; this will flatten the hoop, and will not lift the skirt on the side which is toward the audience. In walking, the steps should be short and carefully spaced and the feet should be held close to the floor with the knees slightly bent, as vigorous strides will sway the hoops unbecomingly. In sitting, the farthingale or the hoop should be lightly lifted up behind, to avoid embarrassing exposure in front. Comedies can use these obvious situations to advantage. Men actors should have the same training in the wearing and handling of cloaks, swords, plumed hats, handkerchiefs, gloves, snuffboxes and other details of period dress. They should learn to drape the classic Greek and Roman robes with ease and to wear them with an air of accustomed familiarity and dignity. Nothing is so disconcerting or disillusioning to an audience as the sight of a noble Roman senator nervously stumbling over his ill-draped toga. Medieval tights should be properly rolled and twisted about the waist (the old actors traditionally used pennies for the twisting). This will prevent bagging and wrinkling of the garment.

In general, it should be emphasized that entering, making an exit, walking, sitting, bowing, standing, and the handling of accessories should be part of the training of the actor for the role.

Underclothes should be carefully considered. The general effect of a costume may be ruined by the actor's neglecting to use the correct type of underclothing. Long, shadowproof slips should be worn by women with the classic Greek and Roman dress, so that the silhouette of the body is not revealed. With the Elizabethan farthingale, a roll or pad about the hips should be worn, with several petticoats underneath. With the Marie Antoinette type of dress, the bodice should be carefully fitted over a corset, or stiff lining, reinforced with stays, in order to give the properly rounded form to the waist and bust. The late nineteenth-century styles also call for a corseted form with a high bustline, and for many gored and ruffled underskirts beneath, with small or large bustles superimposed. Without these foundational layers, the effect of the period fashion is lost. No matter how much the modern woman rebels, a sufficiency of correct underclothing must be insisted upon. A single gored muslin skirt, with eight-inch crinoline ruffle around the bottom, will suffice for fullness; crinoline ruffles at waist, center back, will supply required bustle effect.

The exigencies of the play may demand that the actor underdress; this means he must put on one costume, or the major portion of it, and another costume over it. The top costume is used first, then quickly discarded, uncovering the costume below for the next scene. An actor may have to overdress, that is, quickly put on another costume or part of a costume over the first costume without removing the first costume. These changes are only resorted to when the time between appearances is too short for complete changes. A long cape or loose robe is a valuable garment for such occasions.

Nothing betrays the amateur more quickly than an ill-fitting, carelessly adjusted costume. The audience is quick to detect any discrepancies of toilette. In putting on the costume, therefore, the man or woman should take care that all fastenings are secure. In the woman's case, no petticoat must sag below the top skirt, no plackets must gape, the waist must not fail to meet the skirt. Men should take care that there is no gap between the vest and the trousers, that the trousers are securely held up, that the collar fits and that the tie is arranged neatly and in place.

13. *Correct Wearing of Make-up*

As much care should be taken in wearing period make-up as in wearing period costume. It is not enough to know what the correct make-up is for a certain historic period; the actor should accustom himself to wearing this make-up as if it were part of his ordinary self. To accomplish this end, the actor should first acquaint himself with the correct historic appearance of the character; this he can obtain from portraits, historic sketches, and other authentic data. Then he should practice putting on a make-up which reflects the likeness as closely as possible. Beards, moustaches, wigs, including powdered wigs for the men, and powdered headdresses, "puffs," "Psyches," pompadours for the women, are some of the accessories of make-up which should be worn with assurance and practiced ease. When the actor has attained the proper make-up, he should practice using expressions which were characteristic of the personage he portrays. Research in books, periodicals, and historic novels will reveal certain tricks of expression which were associated with the historic character. Finger-nail polish should never be worn with period make-up.

14. *Proper Care of Wardrobe and Make-up*

The actor should take the best care of his costumes and accessories—wigs included—for the same reason that any artist takes care of his materials. While the actor is making up, a cloth should be placed about the shoulders to protect the costume from powder and paint. Minor repairs should be attended to promptly, so that the wardrobe presents a neat appearance. Paints and powders and other make-up should be neatly stored after using, with the tops to cans, tubes, and bottles carefully replaced.

An actor should take pride in keeping his dressing room in immaculate order. Visitors receive their first impressions from his surroundings. When time is an element, and "the show must go on" without waiting for the actor to find misplaced belongings, it is most important that all make-up and other stage appurtenances be kept in order and easily accessible.

Costumes should be picked up and hung in their appointed places on hooks or on racks, in order that they may not become unduly wrinkled or mussed. They should be hung in the order in which they are used.

The floor of the dressing room should be kept as clean as possible, in order that costumes may not be soiled. Each actor in a dressing room which is shared with one or several companions should keep his own belongings in a compact area. This will preserve harmony and prevent loss and misplacement of articles.

Questions

1. What is the place of costume and make-up in the production?
2. How can costume and make-up aid the actor's characterization?
3. How do costume and make-up affect the actor's self-consciousness?
4. What essential points should be recorded on a costume work sheet?
5. What essential points should be recorded on a make-up work sheet?
6. What are the essentials of the correct wearing of costume and make-up?
7. What is necessary to the proper care of wardrobe and make-up?

II. PLANNING THE COSTUMES AND MAKE-UP

A play represents the projection of the author's creation through the medium of actors. The value of costume and make-up in a production may be considered from three viewpoints. The director values make-up and costumes as important pictorial aids to the production as a whole. The designer values them as reflections of his creative imagination and skill. The actor values them for their wearability and adaptability to the role.

Costume and make-up should be planned with all three viewpoints taken into consideration. Unless this is done, the resulting stage picture will lack balance.

A. Principal Points to Be Considered

1. *Costume and Make-up Should Suit the Mood, Atmosphere, and Style of the Production*

Since the mood and atmosphere of a play influence costuming and make-up, it is important that these aspects of the play be clearly understood by the costume designer. The costumes in *Hamlet* can be very rich and splendid for those characters connected with the court of the king; but they should be subdued in tone, in harmony with the fateful mood of the play and with the gloomy atmosphere of the Danish country. On the other hand, *Othello,* although it is also tragic in tone, should be costumed in the flamboyant, baroque style of the Venetian Renaissance. The quaint, tongue-in-cheek flavor of Barrie's *Quality Street* should be suggested in every line of the costumes and make-up.

Some plays are dominantly masculine in tone, others are dominantly feminine. This should be borne in mind in the designing of the actors' clothes. An instance of a play dominantly masculine is Shakespeare's *Julius Caesar* or Romain Rolland's *The Wolves.* Plays dominantly feminine in tone are Aristophanes' *Lysistrata* or Helen Jerome's adaptation of *Pride and Prejudice.*

The style of the production is equally important to the designer. *Amphitryon* can be costumed realistically in the classic Graeco-Roman style, or the designer can modernize the costumes and make-up and stylize it, as the Lunts did in *Amphitryon 38.* The symbolic, fantastic, expressionistic, or other treatment may be employed by the director, in which event the designer must follow the trend in his costumes and make-up.

2. *Costume and Make-up Should Reflect the Characterization and Its Changes*

Each costume should reflect the economic and social position as well as the taste of the character who wears it. In the case of a modern realistic play such as O'Neill's *Ah Wilderness!,* the costuming and make-up should be so true to the parts portrayed that each actor could walk off the stage and on to the street and—allowing for a certain exaggeration of grease paint—would appear to be the very character he represented on the stage.

If the character undergoes a change during the play, costume and make-up should reflect this change. If, for instance, he ages twenty years, the color and texture of his skin should be toned down, the lines of the face should be more definitely marked and his hair should be grayed or thinned. The dress should be subdued in line, cut, and color; accessories should be those appropriate to an older person, with the additional items suggested by his age or infirmities.

3. *Costume and Make-up Should Be Planned to Suit the Physical Theatre*

Costumes designed for small, intimate stages, where the audience is fairly close to the actors, should be planned with careful detail. The line and style of the costume, whether it is of a historic or modern period, should be accurately fashioned (and true to the character portrayed). The materials should be real silk, velvet, or other required fabric, or should approximate closely these materials. Colors should be chosen to blend well in a small area; accessories and trimmings should stand close inspection. The make-up should be finely shaded, lines should be few and carefully blended, crepe hair should be convincingly put on. Poorly arranged false hair and moustaches betray the amateur.

On a large, indoor stage, where the greater part of the audience is at a distance from the actors, the lines of the costumes should be characteristic of the period style, but not necessarily minutely accurate as to detail. In fact, stage costume should usually be simplified to some extent, as multiplicity of detail, even when quite true to the period, is in large measure lost to the audience. It interferes with the general effect of the costume if it attracts too much attention. Colors must be definite, and sparingly combined. Not over three colors should usually be combined in one costume, unless a definite patchwork effect is desired. Accessories and trimmings should be reduced to a minimum or discarded altogether. Materials can be imitated or "faked"—that is, unbleached muslin can be used for brocade, canton flannel or duvetyn for velvet; other effective substitutes will suggest themselves. This point will be discussed further in Section III.

In a pageant, or any play given out of doors, with limited lighting and a considerable distance between the spectators and the actors, the treatment of costumes and make-up should be broad. Color is the first consideration; line and material are subordinate. Warm colors, in saturated tones, such as scarlet, orange, and similar hues, should predominate. The fundamental characteristic and significant lines of dress should be retained, but these should be exaggerated. Detail should be eliminated, and pattern and design in the materials should be very large and cleverly defined. When costumes are designed, those that appear in groups in the various scenes should be planned as a whole, rather than as individual garments. Even the costumes of the principals should be planned in color and design with the background of the ensemble, or mob, in mind. This is especially true of pageants, where massed groups are used constantly to further the action of the play.

The various scene-shifting devices of modern staging, such as the jack-knife, wagon, and revolving stages, speed up the changing of sets to such an extent that costume and make-up must be adjustable to the quicker schedule. When the newer type of staging is used, elaborate changes of costume and make-up should be planned for act changes rather than scene changes, if possible, in order to avoid long waits between scenes. When costume changes between scenes are absolutely necessary to the plot, it is wise to assign a helper to assist the actor in his changes.

On the space stage, in which a scene or a series of scenes are shown on a dark stage, with very little setting, or none, the scene is revealed by concentrated specific illumination on small areas. Properties, as well as setting, are reduced to the minimum. Costume and make-up should also be simplified, even stylized, so that neither the costume nor the make-up attracts undue attention.

4. *Costume and Make-up Should Reflect Good Period Style*

Accuracy in design means good style in any period, ancient or modern. Any good history of costume can supply the range of types for the various historical eras; any good fashion magazine can supply the best styles for modern dress. The costume designer for the stage, however, should always keep the audience in mind and should choose the more familiar characteristics of an historical period that will be identified easily by the spectator. In this way, the costuming and make-up will assist in building the authenticity of the production without straining the credulity of the audience. For this reason, the fundamental, characteristic, and significant lines should be retained. The designer can profit by a study of the silhouettes of the different periods. Unduly complicated fashions or patterns should be eschewed; trimmings or designs be chosen sparingly and effectively used.

The fundamental, characteristic, and significant lines in make-up for the various historical periods, and for modern times, can best be learned, as has previously been stated, through the study of authentic portraits, statues, and word pictures. The hair arrangement is most important in establishing the verity of the character, and should receive careful consideration.

5. *Color and Lighting Should Be Considered in Planning Costume and Make-up*

Color is an important element in costume and make-up. When it is properly used, it builds up the interest in the character, or group of characters. Color is a strong visual stimulus, even when it is stationary; when it is in motion—on a character moving about on the stage—it compels the interest and directs the attention of the audience. This rhythmic flow of line and color builds up the tempo of a scene, and contributes to the success of the production. Color grouping should, however, be correctly used—the colors should be rightly chosen and the groupings of colors harmonious. The graduations in color have to be considered; the principals should be clothed in the more saturated [1] hues, the ensemble, or mob, in more subdued hues. The only exception to this general rule occurs when the mob, or chorus, is used for the specific purpose of building up the action and tempo of the production; in this instance, the mob can be costumed in saturated and variegated hues also, presenting a kaleidoscopic effect. An instance of this use of color by the mob is seen in the large chorus groups of ballets and spectacles.

The color schemes for each principal should be worked out with reference to the other principals with whom he plays in the majority of scenes. This will obviate the unpleasant situation in which several of the principals are clothed in costumes of similar, but unharmonious, hues. A designer can play with color as with the notes of a musical instrument; the principal character should sound a dominant note of color, the other characters should echo this note, to some extent, but also blend into the general harmony. This will prevent two or more characters appearing in red or purple or a similar color in the same scene.

If the mood of the play demands that the principal character be costumed in a dull gray, or other neutral shade, the characters surrounding the principal should be clothed in subdued shades also; the colors can be rich, but neither brilliant nor saturated. Ibsen's plays usually present this problem; ingenious shading, however, can produce striking and dramatic effects.

Care should also be taken that the groupings of colors on the stage should not be spotty; the colors worn by principals should be blended, and the mob or ensemble kept to a low range of color tone and shade (except, as has been stated, in the case of productions like ballets, pageants, and spectacles).

The style of the production influences the color arrangement; bizarre, fantastic productions demand striking and unusual combinations of colors. Color is, in these types of productions, a very vital element in building up the required effect.

The poor lighting of the early theatres before the nineteenth century

[1] For the explanation of "saturated" and other terms used in reference to color, see Part III, Chapter 13, Section C; also Part IV, Chapter 18.

led to the lavish use of tinsel and spangles on the actors' costumes. These, though often incongruous to the character, helped to reflect every scant gleam of the feeble lighting, and served to focus attention on the actors, who were often lost in the dim expanses of the large stage. Today, however, the use of glass, jewels, or metallic trimmings and cloth on the modern, well-lighted stage is fraught with danger. The surfaces reflect the least particle of light, and the glitter distracts attention from the actor and his lines. Any costuming and make-up is bad that unduly distracts attention from the actor or the play. Costume and make-up are subordinate factors in the production, and should be emphasized above the value of the spoken line only when the plot or action so demands, as in comedies, farces, or spectacles.

The many possible effects obtainable with modern lighting equipment are important to consider in connection with costume and make-up. As stated previously (see page 435), there was little stage lighting in the modern sense until the nineteenth century; before then, the acting area was lit by the sun, candles, or lamps of simple design. Lighting was used only to make the actors visible to the audience. The use of color media was by no means as general as it is today. The invention of the incandescent lamp and its control revolutionized theatre lighting. Intensity of light and greater variety and control of color became possible. This complicated the designer's problems and he had to experiment with fabrics, color combinations, and significant lines, to achieve new and interesting effects. Modern lighting instruments, effectively controlled and capable of producing interesting and dramatic distributions of light and color, assure the designer that costume and make-up can be seen by an audience to good advantage. Early consultations with the director of lighting, however, are necessary to co-ordinate lighting with costume and make-up. This precautionary measure will prevent the use of certain ranges of color in the costumes which will not be effective in lighting planned by the lighting director, or will prevent the use of color in light undesirable for certain necessary colors in dress and make-up. An ideal method is to test the colored fabrics under an approximation of the stage lighting.

B. The Use of Research Materials

6. *Source of Material*

The greatest care should be taken to insure the accuracy of costume and make-up in plays of other days and manners. The designer should visit libraries for available material concerning the period and the background of the play. Any librarian will co-operate in assembling a bibliography of the best material available on its shelves. This bibliography should then be accessible not only to the designer but to the various persons working on costume and make-up.

In assembling research material, reputable costume books should first be consulted. The best ones include the proper treatment of hair, features and the like. Books specializing in make-up can also be studied.

If the play is of ancient or medieval times, the background of the times can be learned through the use of history books (preferably illustrated), encyclopedias, biographies, art magazines, novels, and pictures. The last are most helpful. Not only pictures of people and places but also pictures of statues are most enlightening.

For Elizabethan and modern plays there are, in addition to these sources of material, commentaries by well-known authorities, notes, diaries, other plays of the same period, and sundry authentic source material invaluable to the searcher. In the case of Shakespeare's plays and certain other famous plays in constant use over a period of years, there exist several versions of the texts which vary in many particulars. It is well to consult the several versions if there is any important question of authenticity or historicity which affects costume or make-up.

Late nineteenth- and twentieth-century plays are discussed in the current magazines of the time, and pictures of the original casts can frequently be found in the files. These original pictures are especially valuable for make-up purposes.

Maps and geographies are important source material, where the location of the story affects the type of costume, the weight and colors of the materials.

Frequently there is interesting material concerning local costumes and customs in recreation and travel guides, and in other pamphlets distributed for publicity purposes. Trade books, mail-order catalogues, tailors' advertisements, and sample books of various kinds contain much excellent data for costumes and make-up.

7. *Procedure*

When the designer has assembled all the available material, he first makes notes on the general background of the period in which the play is written. This includes notes on the manners and customs, sports, religion, trades, and other points connected with daily living. For instance, if the play is laid in Holland in the seventeenth century, the notes should include the types of persons—fishermen, tradesmen, and the like—and their habits of living. Details from pictures by Vermeer and other Little Dutch Masters should be noted. If the picture is laid in England in the early seventeenth century, the general notes should include special notes concerning the religious controversy between Puritans and Cavaliers, and its consequent effect on customs and costumes.

After the general notes have been compiled, the designer should assemble specific information concerning the principal characters, if these are historical. Biographies, portraits, diaries, and literary sketches and anecdotes will furnish valuable items. If the characters are fictional, they reflect certain types of the times, for which material, as suggested above, can be found.

With the notes and sketches thus assembled, the designer is ready to create his costumes and make-up so that they truly reflect the characters and the times.

Questions

1. In what ways may costume and make-up be adapted to the mood, atmosphere, and style of the production?
2. What general rules should be followed in planning costume and make-up for a small, intimate stage? For a large indoor stage? For a large outdoor stage? For a modern jackknife, wagon, or revolving stage? For a space stage?
3. In period plays, what points must be kept in mind in choosing costumes and make-up?
4. What points must be considered in planning the color range of costumes?
5. Why must lighting be considered in choosing colors and fabrics?
6. Name three primary sources of research for material on costume. Name three secondary sources.

III. THE EXECUTION OF COSTUMES AND MAKE-UP

A. The Selection and Purchase of Materials

1. *Consideration of the Budget*

Schools, colleges, universities, and little theatres usually undertake a series of plays during a season. The budget should, therefore, be carefully considered. There should be no overexpenditure on one costume or on one play, if the season's repertory is to be carried out successfully.

2. *The Selection and Purchase of Materials*

It is not generally necessary to use fine materials for stage dress. Substantial materials of standard quality are easy to cut and sew and are economical in the long run, as they will withstand wear and tear by many actors, and can be dyed and made over, again and again. Cheap, showy materials should only be used for costuming fantastic, unusual types of plays; as the costumes would probably not be used again, it would be an unnecessary extravagance to make them of durable, more expensive materials.

Some of the materials which are useful for costume construction are unbleached muslin, in different weights, duvetyn (cotton broadcloth), desert cloth, monk's cloth, canton flannel, sateen, terry cloth, cotton crepe, corduroy, and voile. It is economical to purchase such materials in large quantities, even by the bolt, if the production calls for many costumes. With a little ingenuity, these materials can assume the appearance of gorgeous fabrics. Unbleached muslin, with stenciled designs outlined with cord, colored or gilded, gives the effect of brocade. Duvetyn, with the folds highlighted, resembles velvet. Sateen, lined and weighted, is similar to heavy satin, monk's cloth, dyed a dark shade, and judiciously shadowed with touches of paint, gives the effect of heavy woolen cloth.

The purchasing of materials should not be limited to what the dry-goods department offers. Visits should be paid to bargain basements, ten-cent stores, curtain and drapery departments, thrift shops, furniture, Salvation Army, and second-hand stores. Remnants, old curtains, discarded fur coats, samples of tapestries, old beaded evening gowns, broken costume jewelry and ornaments are valuable materials for the designer's deft fingers.

There are several well-established firms dealing in theatrical materials and accessories. It is well to consult their catalogues for certain unusual costume fabrics, difficult, if not impossible, to duplicate—fabrics such as glazed tarlatan, iridescent jewel cloth, lastex net and satin, cellophane sparkle cloth, imitation leather, and animal cloth.

For accessories—jewels, laces, and flowers—there is no better shopping place than the ten-cent store. Furs and fur trimmings, for which there is no good substitute, are frequently to be found on discarded garments in stores dealing in second-hand clothing.

In purchasing unbleached muslin, canton flannel, or other standard materials, it is advisable to purchase the cloth in white, cream, or some neutral shade, especially if purchasing a large amount of yardage. Individual costume lengths can be dyed separately, in various colors, to suit the designer's color scheme. The dyeing should be done for each costume in the piece, before the garment is made up. This allows for shrinking and redyeing, if necessary.

It is not necessary to purchase such items as trimmings and accessories, if the acting group can make the proper appeals to friends and acquaintances. Outmoded hats, gloves, shoes, shawls, and the like may thus be added to the wardrobe, without reducing the budget. Ballet slippers are welcome gifts, as they can be used with many costumes.

3. *Selection and Purchase of Make-up Materials*

Make-up cannot be purchased in wholesale quantities, as the make-up kit for each person varies due to age, coloring, and facial contour. Moreover, in some acting groups, each player provides his own make-up.

Time and money, however, can be saved if the director has a work sheet made, preferably by the make-up instructor, as has been suggested (see Figure 102). This will indicate the physical type and the make-up items needed. The order can then be filled as a unit, and even if no money is saved, there will be less confusion in assembling and distributing the material.

Make-up should be bought from a standard firm, such as Max Factor's, Stein's, etc., for poor, cheap make-up can ruin the skin. The expense of corrective skin treatments will be far greater than the initial cost of good make-up.

B. The Equipment for Construction of Costumes and Make-up

4. *Necessary Aids to Construction*

The successful construction of the costumes depends on the sewing committee's skill, enthusiasm, and faithfulness to the task. The director should choose the committee and its chairman carefully, and provide a convenient, well-equipped workroom.

In most colleges and high schools, the space and equipment for such extracurricular activities are limited. If, in the case of school or college productions, the Home Economics Department co-operates, the additional space and facilities of this department can be advantageously used.

The necessary equipment for the construction of garments is not extensive, nor costly. Large organizations, with generous budgets, may elaborate on the number and quality of the items, but the following list will be adequate for an ordinary amateur production:

(a) *Sewing machine.* The most necessary article is the sewing machine. If the group cannot afford to buy one, they will have to borrow or rent one. The latter course is preferable, for a borrowed machine may be old or out of order, while a rented machine is presumably in good condition. It should be motor-driven, if possible, as much theatrical material is heavy and difficult to sew without a motor-driven machine. For this reason, also, heavy-duty machines are preferable.

(b) *Lights.* There should be a sufficient number of electrical outlets for irons, sewing machines, and the like. If possible, from 20 to 30 foot-candles of illumination (fluorescent lights are best), so arranged as to eliminate glare, should be provided on all working surfaces, and additional specific sources of light should be placed on sewing machines. If the general illumination is much below recommended practice, additional direct specific sources should be added when close work is being done. Always provide additional light when sewing with dark thread on dark materials.

(c) *Cutting and basting tables.* There should be one cutting table, about 4 by 7 feet, covered with unbleached muslin. Another table, about the same size, but uncovered, can be used for basting and sewing.

(d) *Ironing board and iron.* The ironing board should be placed close to the sewing table. It can be hinged to the wall, with a near-by outlet for the iron.

(e) *Mirror.* For fitting, a full-length mirror should be placed at one end of the sewing room.

(f) *Garment racks.* One or more racks should be kept in the sewing room on which to hang garments in the process of being fashioned, as well as the finished garments. These racks can be made economically of one-inch pipe. A double-tiered rack will give extra storage space. Cards should be on hand to pin on each garment at the time it is hung on the rack.

(g) *Dress form.* A dress form is an excellent aid to the fitting of garments. After the preliminary measuring and fitting has been done on the human figure, most of the remaining work can be done with the aid of the dress form. This saves the time and energy of the actors and also of the person making the garment, as she does not have to suspend operations until the person to be fitted arrives. A skirt hemmer is a valuable time saver.

(h) *Sewing supplies.* There should always be on hand an adequate supply of needles (hand and machine), pins, thread, scissors, tape, thimbles, snaps, hooks and eyes, razor blades, yard sticks, tape measures, large cutting shears, buttons, and other items necessary to the making of garments. A supply of sewing baskets should be available, in which to store the individual work. A large box of scraps, containing cutting-scraps and left-over bits, will be found useful for providing scarfs, belts, sashes, and ties.

(i) *Patterns.* For the execution of the costumes, there should be a stock of basic patterns on hand. If the group cannot afford to pay for the drafting of a set of basic patterns by a good tailor, it can purchase certain stock patterns which will serve as basic patterns. A further discussion of these patterns will follow.

(j) *Costume work sheets* (see Figure 101). It is important that the sewing committee be given a complete set of costume work sheets for the play. If they are not acquainted with the play (and, of course, they should be, if possible), the costume work sheets will provide an acceptable working plan. The director or stage manager usually makes out a costume plot also, and delivers it to the chairman of the sewing committee.

(k) *The costume plot,* as shown in Figure 104, divides the play into acts and scenes, and lists each actor, with a description of his costume and accessories for each scene in every act. Various symbols can be used to indicate headdress, gloves, and cane. This plot presents a complete picture of the costume problems, grouping the color combinations in the various scenes.

5. *Dyeing and Spraying Equipment*

The dyeing and spraying of garments or materials should be done in a place close to the sewing room. A stationary tub is necessary for this work, also movable aluminum and enamel tubs for holding the material to be dyed, a gas plate for heating, and a sink for cleaning brushes and other items. The amount of equipment must be governed by the budget.

For dyeing, there should be on hand cold dyes, also boiling dyes, in most used shades, salt, vinegar, and stain remover. For the making of wigs, armor, and other unusual accessories, there should be a supply of old newspapers, paper tape, cord, paint brushes, paints (including metallic), plaster of paris, head forms (on which to make wigs), soap flakes, yard stick, and other related items.

6. *Make-up Supplies*

When the organization does not furnish the make-up, each actor must have his own supplies. The first requisite is an adequate supply of cold cream and cleansing tissues. If cold cream is too expensive, mineral oil, vegetable oil, or cooking grease with a cottonseed oil foundation can be used. For very tender skins, baby oil is soothing and will not irritate the skin. Any of these suggested alternatives to cold cream is better than a cheap cold cream, which may seriously injure the texture of the skin.

All make-up must be removed after each performance. If the actress wishes to change to street make-up, she must first remove the stage make-up and then, after thoroughly cleansing the skin, apply street make-up.

Cleansing tissues are handier than towels or soft cloths for removing grease paint and cold cream, and are also more economical. As cleansing tissues are easily disposed of, the actor can keep his dressing table tidier than when greasy, discolored cloths are left lying about. As cleansing tissues are used only once and discarded, they are also more hygienic than towels, which collect dust and dirt.

COSTUME PLOT

PROD. Emma DATE

APPROVED director art director

Cast	1-1 Oct. 1814 Wedding Recept. Late aft.	1-2 Nov. 1814 Morning	1-3 Dec. 25, 1814 X'mas Party Late morning	2-1 Feb. 1, 1815 Early aft.	Additional Costumes and Accessories
Emma	Yellow [B] [P] [G]	Yellow (C) (sleeves)	Green	Yellow	B-Bonnet G-Gloves C-Lace cap P-Pelisse-blue
Harriet	Blue [B] [P] [G]	Blue (A)	Blue	(Honey Dew) (P) (B)	B-Bonnet, P-Pelisse } Rose G-Gloves A-Apron
Miss Bates	Lavender [B]		Lavender (C)	Lavender (B) (S)	B-Bonnet S-Spencer C-Lace collar Sh-Shawl
Mrs. Bates	Black [B] [C]		Black (Sh)	Black	B-Bonnet C-Lace cap Sh-Shawl
Mrs. Weston	Buff (B)		Buff		B-Bonnet G-Gloves
Jane Fairfax				Dk. Green (C) (Sc)	C-cap Sc-Scarf G-Gloves
Mrs. Elton					G-Gloves T-Turban F-Fan
Robert	Mat Green (taupe)	Mat Green (taupe)		Mat Green (taupe)	Boots
Elton	Black	Black			
Woodhouse	Henna	Henna (S)	Henna	Henna	S-Shawl Cane
Perry	Royal Blue				
Knightley	Green (D. Brown)	D. Brown	D. Brown	D. Brown	Green Coat
Weston	Military Blue		Military Blue	Military Blue	
Churchill				Lt. Grey	

FIG. 104. (Explanation below.)

Explanation of Fig. 104. Read the costume plot horizontally to analyze each character's costume problem for each scene. The costume changes and color sequences can also be checked. Read the costume plot vertically to sum up the color combinations in each scene. The symbols B (bonnet), G (gloves), show the costume accessories to be used by the actors in each scene. The B in a square means that the bonnet is removed during the scene; the B in a circle means that it is left on during the scene.

In addition to these aids to the putting on of make-up, each actor should have an adequate supply of the following items, of recognized standard make—materials that are backed by the integrity of the maker. The items include at least three shades of base, or foundation, grease paint, from light to dark; brown and black dermatograph eye pencils; proper shades of lip rouge and cheek rouge, moist and dry; several shades of eye shadow and liner; powder of various shades; crepe hair, and spirit gum, as required. To these basic requirements may be added other items, from time to time. The colors, shades, and therefore the number of the items vary with the individual coloring. The system of numbering and classifying make-up items varies with the different manufacturers.

7. *Make-up Plots*

The make-up plot is of great help to the make-up artist, to the actor, and, most of all, to the director of the production. Like the costume plot, it divides the play into acts and scenes, and lists each actor, with a brief description of his make-up for each scene in every act (see Figure 105). For brevity, symbols can be used to indicate beards and mous-

MAKE-UP PLOT

PROD. ______________________ DATE ______________________

APPROVED ______________________ ______________________

director art director

Cast	Class	Type	Age	Complexion	Hair	Special

FIG. 105. This plot analyzes each member of the cast as to the class of person, the physical type, age, and other individual items, with special notes, if needed. It gives a picture of the make-up problem, and emphasizes special requirements in materials and in technique.

taches of the several types, wigs, and the like. This plot presents a complete picture of the make-up problem, and should be considered by the director in determining the time element and other fine points of production.

8. *Procedure of Handling Finished Costumes*

A production usually takes about four weeks to assemble. This gives time for costumes to be made, and for make-up to be practiced.

After the costumes are finished, and before the production goes on, they are hung on the racks and ticketed, as has been suggested. Each card bears the name of the actor, the notation of the act and the scene, and also of the accessories, if any. The accessories, such as wigs, scarfs, ties, are pinned or fastened to the costume they accompany. This same process, it may be noted, is carried out with rented or borrowed costumes.

Just before dress rehearsal, the racks can be taken to a place adjacent to the dressing rooms. Here the costumes and accessories can be distributed to the actors. One person should be assigned to check on cards each item for each actor, and recheck at end of the performance. This will prevent confusion and loss.

The make-up artist or instructor should check on all make-ups under the lighting setup for the production. Changes or alterations are noted on the individual work sheets and explained later to the actor.

During the performance it is advisable that one of the sewing committee, if not the chairman, be accessible for minor repairs on garments, if any are torn or ripped.

After the final performance, the same person who was in charge of distribution collects and checks all costumes, and sees that they are returned to the proper storage place. Necessary repairs, cleaning, and washing of garments should be done before they are stored. This will preserve them in good condition.

C. The Execution of Costumes

9. *Cutting from Patterns*

The cutting of the garments should be assigned to the most adept and experienced member of the group, as much of the success of the finished product depends on the cut of the material. Sometimes it is advisable to let one person carry through the making of a garment from cutting to the sewing on of fastenings. Sometimes it is wiser to let certain ones baste, others sew up the garment, others fit, others press, and so on. This is usually decided according to the talents and adaptabilities of the group.

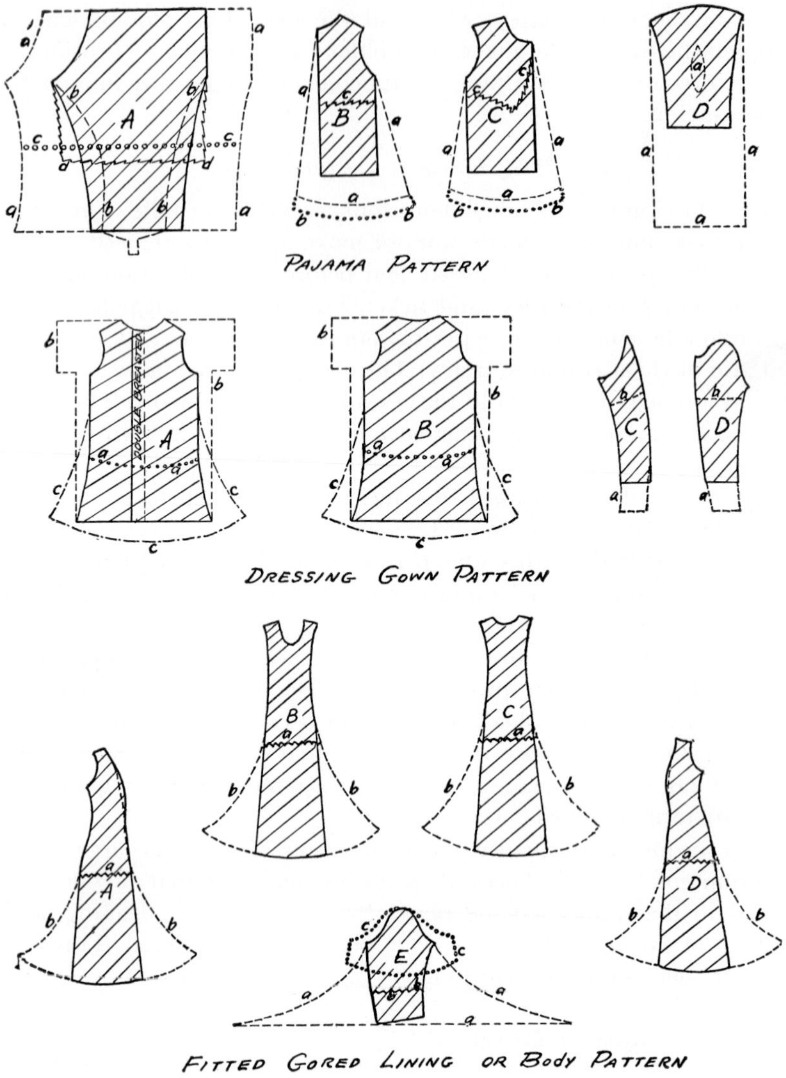

FIG. 106. Basic patterns (explanation at right).

The costumes for the principal characters are cut first. First choice of materials and accessories is also allowed to the principals. The less important characters come next; lastly, the mob, or ensemble. If the ensemble is a large one, it is wise to choose a simple pattern for both the man's type of garment and the woman's. They can then be dyed and cut at one time, and made up alike. Variations can be obtained by dyeing the pieces different shades, by the addition of collars, shawls, sashes, and other simple accessories.

In cutting costumes, the design for each should be translated into the basic pattern most closely approximating its lines. In cutting, always leave large seams; fittings are more easily made, if this is done; also the costume can be altered later for another wearer.

The basic patterns will be found to approximate the general lines of the various historic period styles (see Figure 106 and Figure 107). These patterns are based on standard patterns, obtainable in any pattern department, and therefore can be used by amateur seamstresses with a minimum of effort. The medium size (38 for men, 36 or 20 for women) was used in preparing the drawings for Figures 105 and 106.

(a) *Pajama pattern.* (Figure 106.) Pajama trousers can be used for Persian trousers, and for Celtic, Saxon, Anglo-Saxon, Frankish, and other trousers of the Dark Ages; when made a bit fuller, for modern Oriental trousers; for Indian and trapper's trousers, fringed or unfringed; for sixteenth-, seventeenth-, and eighteenth-century knee-length

Explanation of Figure 106:

1. PAJAMA PATTERN: A, pajama-breeches pattern; Aa, full Oriental breeches; Ab, tight 19th-C. trousers; Ac, full 16th-C. breeches; Ad, snug 18th-C. breeches.
   B, coat-back pattern (½); Ba, 15th-C. coat; Bb, long Tudor coat; Bc, back of vest.
   C, coat-front pattern; Ca, 15th-C. coat; Cb, long Tudor coat; Cc, front of vest.
   D, sleeve pattern; Da, 15th- and 16th-C. sleeve.
2. DRESSING-GOWN PATTERN: A, front, dressing-gown pattern; Aa, Roman colobium, also Viking, Goth tunic; Ab, Roman dalmatic, also cassock; Ac, medieval robe, also 16th-C. gown.
   B, back, dressing-gown pattern; Ba, Roman colobium, also Viking, Goth tunic; Bb, Roman dalmatic, also cassock; Bc, medieval robe, also 16th-C. gown.
   C, D, coat-sleeve pattern; CaDa, long Anglo-Saxon wrinkled sleeve; CbDb, short sleeve, many styles.
3. FITTED GORED LINING OR BODY PATTERN: ABCD, fitted gored lining or body pattern; AaBaCaDa, 14th-C. cote-hardie; AbBbCbDb, medieval gown.
   E, plain sleeve, for many styles; Ea, medieval long, pointed sleeve; Eb, short puff sleeves, for many styles; Ec, short, full sleeve, for ca. 1810.

breeches, cut fuller or scantier than the basic pattern, as the historic style requires. This pattern, with the proper alterations, can be used for nineteenth- and twentieth-century trousers, and for women's slacks and overalls. The shirt pattern to the pajamas can be used for men's shirts, vests, and coats, from the fifteenth century on, with changes to suit the period. The pajama pattern as a whole is a good basic pattern for Chinese costumes for men and for women, for Balinese, Siamese, and other Oriental costumes. Other uses for this pattern will suggest themselves to the thoughtful designer.

(b) *The dressing-gown pattern.* (Figure 106.) The simplest type of tunic is cut from a man's dressing-gown pattern, in two pieces, front and back, with rounded neck, slightly gored sides, and cut-out armhole. The tunic may be cut with straight sides and a sleeve may be added. It may be cut long to the ground, or shortened to the calf or to the knee. This pattern can be used for the Egyptian priest, the Mesopotamian, Roman, or Persian tunic, the Roman colobium and dalmatica. The short tunic can be used for the costume of different barbarian groups in the Dark Ages. The long tunic, cut with more flare at the bottom, can be used for the long medieval robe, and the sixteenth-century gowns for clerks, judges, and other dignitaries.

(c) *Fitted gored lining or body pattern.* (Figure 106.) This pattern is useful for all fitted tunics and bodices, especially for the fourteenth-century cote-hardie for men and women; a separate circular skirt may be attached to it at hip length to form a type of medieval gown. Another good medieval style can be achieved with the gored lining pattern by continuing the gores to the ground length and flaring them out in typical princess style. With the addition of puffed drapings over the hips, the princess style can be used for the middle and late seventeenth-century dress. The fitted gored lining can be used for bodices, with or without a pointed waistline in front or back. Men's doublets and other items can also be cut from this pattern with minor variations. The plain, fitted sleeve (or sleeve lining) pattern that comes with the gored lining pattern is a good basic design for all fitted sleeves, from the Dark Ages to the present day.

(d) *Fitted gored skirt.* (Figure 107.) This pattern can be used for many types of skirts, particularly those of the seventeenth century, the nineteenth century, and the early twentieth century.

(e) *The straight, gathered-skirt pattern.* (Figure 106.) This can be used for many styles, from the early barbarian dress to the latest beach costume or peasant street dress. With the addition of an underpropping such as the sixteenth-century farthingale, the eighteenth-century hoop petticoat, or the nineteenth-century hoop skirt, interesting period styles can be achieved. Hip panniers can be added to the eighteenth-century hoop petticoats. Deep ruffles can be added to the nineteenth-century hoop-skirt.

(f) *Circular-skirt pattern.* (Figure 106.) This can be used for the full circular skirt of the Middle Ages and the fourteenth and fifteenth centuries. It can also be used for circular capes. If trimmed down to narrower proportions, it can serve for the skirts of Tudor times, and for certain Elizabethan dresses. If the full circle is used, or even two or more circles sewed together, and gathered into a band, it can be used for a dancer's skirt, of Spanish, Oriental, or other fanciful types.

(g) *The Russian blouse.* (Figure 106.) This is useful for any type of loose, full tunic and coat, especially for the nineteenth-century dropped-sleeve bodice, and the Henry VIII loose coat.

Other patterns valuable to have handy in the sewing room are the following: a dressing gown or hostess gown pattern; princess slip; men's vest and coat pattern; fancy dress patterns, such as a "milkmaid" or "shepherdess," "Colonial," "Uncle Sam," "Santa Claus," and "George Washington"; union suit for tights of the long medieval and Renaissance hose. *Vogue, McCall, Simplicity,* and *Butterick* have a series of period patterns, which are excellent, and also animal-suit patterns which can be used for tights and fantastic styles of dress. The Pictorial Review Pattern Company has a series of "Gay Nineties" patterns which approximate satisfactorily the styles of this difficult era. Dazian also puts out a series of basic patterns, including the leotard, blouse, and circular skirt, which are practical and inexpensive. Masquerade-group patterns (six or seven costumes in one) are issued by Dazian, New York Pattern, and other companies.

Patterns which are used over and over again should be cut out of unbleached muslin or other durable material, as paper patterns tear and are easily lost. Each piece of the muslin pattern should be marked and numbered, to prevent parts of the pattern becoming separated.

10. *Basting and Fitting*

After the garment is cut, it should be basted, allowing large seams, as has been stated. The garment should then be fitted. Since rehearsal time is usually limited, the costume should be ready to fit when the actor is called into the fitting room. He usually takes time off for this purpose between scenes, and becomes fearful of missing his cue if kept too long. The fitting, though quickly done, should be careful and accurate, as the actor, however impatient at fittings, expects a perfect costume for the production. So does the director.

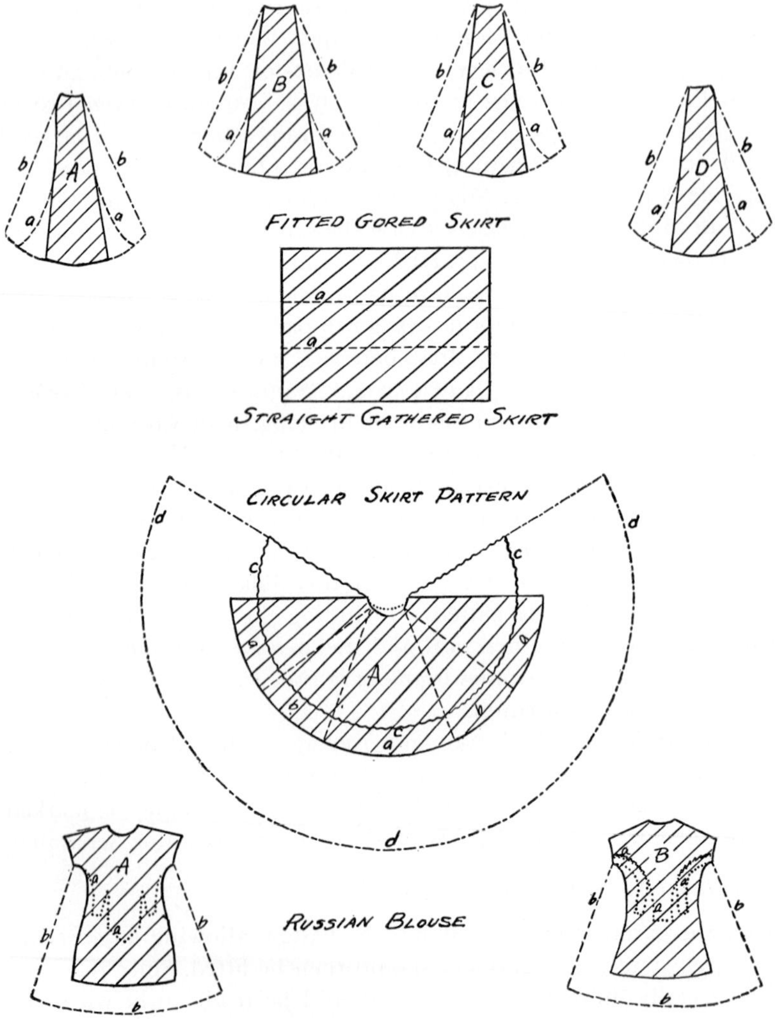

FIG. 107. Basic patterns (explanation at right).

11. *Finishing*

When the garment is satisfactorily fitted, the sewing can be completed. Good, stout thread and firm stitches should be used in sewing. Time and effect are lost with poor, loose sewing which rips and tears at the first strain on the stage.

The garment should be pressed carefully at each stage of its construction. This will produce a smooth, neat, workmanlike article. After the costume is made, the addition of accessories and trimmings should follow. These should never be attached too firmly until the effect has been approved by the director or the chairman of the committee.

When everything is in order, the completed costume should be hung on the rack with the identification card, properly made out, pinned upon it.

In judging the finished product, the director and the actor must consider the effect of the garment on the stage, rather than close-up appearance and perfection of workmanship. Costumes are for stage use, and are not intended to be models of exquisite dressmaking. Fine needlework seldom registers on the stage, where broad effects are more desired.

12. *Collecting Certain Types of Costumes*

Any dramatic organization which produces a regular program of plays will find it of value to design and keep costumes of certain types, as they may be used over and over again. There are costumes of no definite period-style, such as the princess dress, the smock, the full skirt, which can be rendered available for period plays by the addition of certain characteristic accessories or trimmings. For instance, the dress consisting of plain bodice and full skirt can be transformed into an

Explanation of Figure 107:

1. Fitted gored skirt: A, side front; B, center front; C, center back; D, side back. ABCD, fitted gored skirt for 17th C., 18th C., 19th C., 20th C.; Aa, Ba, Ca, Da, bell-shaped skirt, 1898–1905; AbBbCbDb, cone-shaped Tudor skirt, also 1860 skirt.
2. Straight gathered skirt. A, straight gathered skirt, for many styles (section only); Aa, lines for ruffles, 1860, also Spanish style.
3. Circular skirt pattern. A, front half of circular skirt. The back waist line is shown dotted. Aa, 16th-C. skirt (minus dotted segments b, b); Ac, short cape, 16th C.; Ad, long, circular cape, 17th C., 18th C., 19th C.
4. Russian blouse. A, B, front and back of Russian blouse, used for many styles of loose tunics; Aa, Ba, front and back of 19th-C. dropped-sleeve bodice; AbBb, front and back of Henry VIII loose coat. Saw-tooth line is the back seam to bodice.

Elizabethan costume by the addition of a ruff and a small roll placed underneath the skirt about the hips to simulate a farthingale. The same dress, with deep Vandyke collar and cuffs, can be used for a Cavalier lady; the same dress, with panniers or puffs over the hips, and a fichu about the shoulders, can be used for an eighteenth-century play.

The typical mob dress for women consists of a full skirt, either short or long; a full blouse, with full sleeves, short and long. For men, the mob costume consists of loose, baggy trousers, knee-length or long; a loose shirt with or without open collar, with sleeves cut full and long, open at the cuff, or cut off short above the elbow. The women's skirts should be made of durable, unbleached muslin or cheap sateen, dyed in the duller shades. The blouses should be of beige, gray, off-white, or of colors that will harmonize with the skirts. The men's trousers should be of dull shades, darker in tone than the women's skirts. The men's shirts should be of the same range of colors, but not matching the trousers. Men in the ensemble should not wear white shirts except in certain types of Spanish plays, or in Cavalier plays, during dueling scenes, and on certain other occasions. White is a difficult color to wear on the stage, as it reflects light to the detriment of the actor's expression. It should rarely be used for the ensemble costumes, as it draws too much attention to these lesser characters. If used, it should be an offshade of white. Dipping in tea or ecru dye will help.

A good costume of a distinctive historic period—such as Louis XV court dress, Empire, 1880 style, should never be made over, but should be carefully preserved for plays of these periods only. All original models of the late nineteenth century should be left intact, as the dress-making is intricate and elaborate, and remodeling is difficult.

D. The Application of Make-up

13. *Procedure of Making Up*

Each actor, having received his make-up chart (see Figure 102), should check with the make-up artist and with the director. Frequently the director wishes the actor to accentuate certain facial characteristics for the sake of the performance.

Each actor must check carefully the time it takes to put on the complete make-up for his part, including the laying out of materials. If the make-up is a complicated one, it is a wise plan for the actor to practice putting on the make-up several days in advance, and noting the time it takes; then, for dress rehearsal and for opening night, he should allow himself more than the regular time for making up, as due allowance must be made for the nervousness which usually accompanies dress rehearsals and first-night performances. An actor who puts on make-up for the first time at dress rehearsal, and does not allow plenty of time for the process, may find himself, if he is inexperienced in the art, dashing on the stage at the rise of the curtain with but half a moustache!

If one side of the face is more difficult than the other for the actor to make up, it is a good plan to finish the difficult side first.

The procedure in applying a straight make-up is as follows: After cleansing the face with cold cream or oil, the base or foundation is applied to all parts of the face and neck visible to the audience. The foundation should be applied thinly and smoothly. Then shape the face by the application of rouge to the proper places. Next, apply the proper shade of eye shadow and lining to accentuate the eyes, which are the most important features to an actor. Then rouge the lips. A light foundation paint may be used, then the rouge. The lips should be shaped to suit the character, but must not be exaggerated beyond the natural outlines. Last of all, powder generously all over the make-up, powdering from the neck up to the forehead. Then dust off surplus powder with a very soft brush or cotton.

The procedure in applying a character make-up is as follows: After the foundation is applied, of the proper shade to suit the character, block out the natural features by means of high lights, shadows, and lines, accentuating those features that are a characteristic of the person the actor is portraying. Next, add lines to bring out certain features. Exaggerate the eyes, mouth, and other features, as called for by the part. Then, having put on all the necessary make-up, apply powder of a lighter shade than the foundation, in order to preserve the high lights and shadows. Dust off as before. If any unusual tricks are used, such as scars or other facial blemishes, these can be applied either before or after the face is made up.

Wigs are expensive items to rent, and sometimes an actor can create the desired effect with crepe hair. However, crepe hair is very difficult to handle, and not many actors are proficient in the art. The right kind of hair and beard are so important to the characterization that it is better for the actor to rent the proper hair equipment than to risk spoiling his entire stage appearance with makeshift equipment. Wigs can usually be rented more cheaply if several are engaged for a performance, and also if the rental extends over a period of several days or for the run of the play instead of for just one performance. One wig may be used for several minor characters in the same play, provided, of course, that they do not appear together in the same scene. For instance, a powdered "Colonial" type wig may be used for several of the soldiers and lesser characters, when they appear on the stage at different times.

Wigs should be adjusted after the costume and make-up are on. The wig should be adjusted from the front of the head to the back, the center front of the wig being held firmly between two fingers while the adjustment to the back of the head is made. Make-up should be worked into the wig from the forehead so that the line of demarcation is completely hidden. A bald wig demands especial care of this detail.

If no wig is used, and a young actor is impersonating an old man, statue white—a thick body white—can be made into a paste and smoothed into the hair in streaks to suggest middle age or old age. Clown white, aluminum powder, or white masque, or mascara, can be used with the same effect. Powder can also be applied to the hair, to simulate old age, or to give the effect of eighteenth-century wigs, but the use of powder is dangerous, as the least movement of the actor may send clouds of powder out around him, some of which is sure to settle on his shoulders and person, to the detriment of his art and the amusement of the audience. If white, aluminum, or other powders are used, the hair should be oiled, to prevent occurrences like the one just mentioned. Light hair can be darkened by the application of black mascara or a dark body paint.

If wigs are to be made for the actors—the kind that are made of cable cord glued on to a foundation of gummed-paper strips—the actor must be fitted as to head size, his name written inside the wig, and his hairline carefully marked. All wigs should be set up on racks especially made for this purpose and returned to the racks every night after the performance. This will preserve their shape, and safeguard them from being misplaced or lost.

Questions and Exercises

1. Name three standard materials that may be used to make inexpensive stage costumes.
2. How may these materials be treated to give a richer appearance?
3. Name five items necessary to a good costume work room.
4. Name five items ordinarily included in every make-up kit.
5. Name three basic patterns used in creating period-style garments.
6. Describe the procedure in applying straight make-up.

IV. ORGANIZATION

A. The Organization of a Costume Staff

1. *Staff for a School, College, or Little-Theatre Group*

THE proper organization of a costume staff is the first step toward a successful production. In addition to the costume director, who is the over-all head of costumes and designer-in-chief, there should be an assistant to the costume director, who supervises the making of costumes. Depending on the size of the organization, the assistant may also be in charge of the wardrobe, and may serve as assistant designer; in a large organization, other assistants would be assigned to these duties. The assistant to the costume director usually makes out the various costume plots, work sheets, and individual costume cards for checking costumes in and out during the run of the show. The assistant also arranges with the actors and the sewing committee for all fittings; these should be posted promptly in a conspicuous place near the rehearsal area. To make the costumes, there should be a sewing committee headed by a chairman. The committee may be composed of volunteer workers, drama students, paid employees, or Home Economics students. The sewing committee may be chosen from the dramatic club, or from sororities, one or more persons being elected from each sorority. Faculty wives may be interested in joining the group. To acquaint this group with the play, and render their work more interesting, there should be planned one or more talks on the play with accompanying illustrative material. The sewing committee should also be allowed to visit one or more rehearsals.

The sewing committee follows the instructions of the costume director, who, in turn, is responsible to the director of the production. Sometimes the stage manager or technical director, working under the supervision of the director, arranges with the actors and the sewing committee chairman for all fittings; usually, however, this work is done by the assistant to the costume director.

2. *Staff for Large Group of Players*

In a large organization (or a group producing a pageant, spectacle, or other elaborate show), the costume director may assign additional assistants to the costume staff. These may include the assistant to the costume director, supervisor for the making of costumes, assistant designer, purchaser of all materials and rental agent, and co-ordinator between the costume department and the director, art director, and technical director. In the larger organizations, there is usually a head seamstress who cuts all garments and supervises the actual fitting and sewing of more intricate costumes. The wardrobe mistress usually keeps the wardrobe in order, and sees that the sewing area is kept neat and clean.

B. The Organization of a Make-up Staff

3. *Staff for School, College, or Little-Theatre Group*

The make-up artist is usually also the instructor of make-up. In this capacity, he usually functions under the supervision of the director of the production, or he may have a position independent of the producing group. He is assisted by one or more trained helpers, but, as make-up is an individual item for each actor, the make-up staff is primarily for advice and assistance, rather than for active duty during the performance.

4. *Staff for Large Group of Players*

A large organization may hire a make-up artist who functions with the director and the art director. In some cases, the organization may have such a person on the permanent staff. Whatever the plan, the make-up artist, or make-up director, works along with the art director and under the supervision of the director of the production.

C. Planning the Work Rooms and Storage Space

5. *The Sewing Room*

The sewing room, or rooms, should be easily accessible to the rehearsal group. This will expedite the fitting of costumes.

The dimensions of the sewing room will depend, of course, on the amount of space available. There should be room for the cutting, basting, pressing, and sewing of garments. A room rectangular or square in shape with a good north light will be found adaptable to these needs. The sewing machine should be placed under the north window and the mirror should be on a side wall. The two tables, mentioned in Section III, should be placed close to the machine and to the ironing board.

Along the walls should be shelves and cupboards for the storing of accessories and sewing materials.

There should be one or more racks, on castors, so that they can be moved from place to place as desired. These should be placed in the sewing room, to receive the garments in the process of being fashioned, and also to hold the finished garments, duly ticketed. These racks can be made economically of one-inch pipe.

These minimum requirements may be augmented by a larger organization to suit its needs. More space, more machines, more racks and shelves, will be needed; but the general plan will be the same.

6. *The Storage Room*

Adjoining the sewing room and accessible to the stage, should be the storage room for costumes and accessories. A limited space can best be utilized by lining the walls with shelves and cupboards and by filling the center space with racks similar to those described above, but made in double tiers, so that they can hold twice as many garments. A folding ladder should then be added to the equipment. Each shelf should be devoted to a certain type of accessory or garment not easily hung on racks, such as shirts, aprons, shawls, fans, and the like.

Hats and headdresses should be stored on wooden racks with upright pegs, or on narrow shelves (top shelves will serve). Below these should be stored the shoes, in small bins, sorted according to styles—for men, for women, high shoes, low shoes, and so on. Parasols and other items, difficult to store, should have special bins, or boxes, large enough to hold them without crowding.

As with the sewing room, the space and size of equipment increases with the size and facilities of the organization. The storage room should be kept clean. All garments, especially fur-trimmed garments, should be inspected frequently, and demothed at intervals. Covers should be put on the more fragile garments.

7. *The Dye Room*

A dye room, however small, is indispensable to a production group. It should be close to the sewing room, adjoining it if possible, and have adequate ventilation, as the steam and fumes from the dye are not pleasant in a close room. The dye room should have sufficient space for two tubs, a drying line or clothes horse, table, shelves and cupboards for storing the dyes and other materials. The room can be used also for making masks, papier-mâché props, and other crafts connected with the production. A larger organization will, of necessity, need a larger dye room with more elaborate equipment. This will include more tubs, gas plates, racks, drying lines, storage space, tables, and materials.

8. *The Make-up Room*

Although each dressing room has in it certain make-up equipment, such as mirrors and a wash stand, there should also, if possible, be a make-up room for demonstration purposes by the make-up artist; this room can be used as a dressing room for choruses or ensemble groups during production.

The shape of this make-up room should be rectangular, or square, with wall space for the mirrors. These mirrors should be fastened against the wall, with strong light above, below, and on the sides, so that all angles of the face are illuminated. Below the mirrors there should be a shelf on which to lay out the make-up equipment—grease paint, rouge, powder, and the like.

There should be room below the make-up shelf for the actor to keep his small personal belongings, make-up box, wigs, and other accessories. This storage space should not be directly below the mirror, but to the side, in order that the actor have adequate seating space in front of the mirror.

Questions and Exercises

1. Draw a diagram for a costume-staff organization for a small theatre group.
2. Draw a diagram for a costume work room, 30′ x 40′.
3. Draw a diagram for a make-up room, 12′ x 15′.
4. Identify the following: crinoline, Vandyke beard, farthingale, redingote, passementerie, chignon.

GLOSSARIES

STAGE SCENERY AND LIGHTING TERMS

(For more elaborate definitions and descriptions of the following terms and others in the text, see the index.)

Acting Area: That portion of the stage enclosed by scenery which is used by the actors during a performance.

Alzak: A patented method of processing aluminum reflecting surfaces to increase reflectance and to prevent deterioration. It is now used in many lighting instruments.

Ampere: The common unit of current or rate of flow of electricity.

Apron: A slight outward curve of the stage floor in front of the curtain line. (In past periods the apron was often quite large.)

Autotransformer: A transformer in which a single coil of wire wound around an iron core is used as both primary and secondary. As used in the theatre for a dimmer, it has a brush that can be rotated around the coil, thus changing the voltage applied to the lamps.

Baby Spotlight: A small spotlight intended for a 100 watt, 250 watt, or 400 watt lamp. Its lens is ordinarily 5 inches, 4½ inches, or smaller, in diameter.

Backing: A flat, a series of flats, a drop, a border, or a tab used to limit the view of the audience through an opening (e.g. a doorway or window) in a set of scenery. (See Figure 9.)

Backing Striplight: A short, light striplight about three feet long or less, wired in one circuit and used to light backings behind doors, and so on. It is sometimes used between ground rows.

Balcony Spotlight: A spotlight mounted somewhere in the balcony of the auditorium, frequently on a railing or in a box at the front of the balcony.

Base: (1) The part of an incandescent lamp that screws into, or is fastened in, the socket or receptacle. (2) A cast-iron disc that can be attached to the yoke of a spotlight to make the spotlight sit on a flat surface.

Batten: A length of rigid material, usually wood. The 1″ x 3″ lumber strips used to construct scenery are battens. The strips of wood fastened to the top and bottom of a drop are battens. The length of wood or iron pipe on a set of lines, to which scenery is often fastened for flying, is a batten.

Beam: The cone of light from a lens or a parabolic reflector.

Beam Light: A spotlight mounted in a false beam, or otherwise concealed in the auditorium ceiling for the purpose of lighting the downstage acting areas from above. Antiproscenium light is a synonym.

Blackout: A rapid change in illumination produced by opening a switch, usually a master switch, to control all or nearly all of the illumination on the stage.

Board: See *Control Board.*

Boomerang: A box attached to a lighting instrument to hold color frames. Its purpose is to make color changes convenient, and frequently the frames can be changed electrically or mechanically at a distance.

Border: An abbreviated drop, used to represent overhead foliage or to mask the flies. (See Figures 29 and 30.)

Borderlight: A striplight, usually as long as the width of the proscenium arch, hung overhead from the gridiron to produce general illumination on the stage. Many older theatres have three or four of them hung at intervals of 10 or 12 feet.

Brace Cleat: A small metal plate attached to the frame of a flat. Into it a stage brace is hooked to prop up the flat. (See Figures 14 and 39.)

Bridge: A narrow platform, as long or longer than the width of the proscenium arch, hung from the gridiron or sometimes supported from the side walls or on legs. Various kinds of lighting instruments are mounted on the upstage side of the bridge, and an operator can adjust them or change color frames from the platform just behind the instruments. If a theatre has only one bridge it is usually hung just upstage from the teaser.

Brilliance: Brilliance is that property of any color that allows the color to be classified according to a series of grays ranging from black to white. Lightness is used as a synonym.

Bulb: The glass part of an incandescent lamp containing the filament, supports, and so on.

Cable: An electrical conductor (two wires in each cable is the usual practice on the stage) containing one or more copper wires properly insulated with cotton and rubber or plastic and further protected on the outside with a very tough rubber or neoprene sheath to withstand rough treatment.

Ceiling: A large, horizontal, canvas-covered frame hung on two or three sets of lines, used to close in the top of an interior set. (See Figure 27.)

Ceiling Plate: A metal plate with a ring, used in bolting together and flying ceiling frames. (See Figure 27.)

Circuit: A complete path of good conductors leading from the source of electrical energy to a useful device, such as a lighting instrument, and back again to the source.

Circuit Breaker: A more modern device for opening a circuit automatically, taking the place of a fuse.

Clamp, or Pipe Clamp: A brass, aluminum, or steel device that connects the yoke or pipe arm of a spotlight or other instrument to a pipe batten. (Two kinds are shown in Figures 59 and 60.)

Code: Refers to the National Electrical Code, or to the city electrical code that has been enacted into law and based on the National Electrical Code.

Color: In general, refers to all sensations arising from activity of the retina. Color may be chromatic or achromatic, the latter including white, grays, and black.

Color Frame: A metal, wood, or cardboard holder to keep the color filter rigid and to protect it when placed in a lighting instrument.

Color Medium or Filter: A transparent material such as glass, gelatin, or sheet plastic used to obtain color from incandescent light by a process called selective transmission.

Complements, or Complementary Colors: Two colors possessing hue that may be mixed to produce white light. Transparent complementary pigments mixed together produce gray.

Connector: A small block of insulating material with metallic contacts connected to the ends of cable or to lighting instruments, so that power may be conducted from an outlet on the stage through one or more cables to a lighting instrument. Connectors are of two kinds, the *line* connector, which is at the "hot" or power end, and the *load* connector, which is fastened to an instrument or the instrument end of a cable. The twistlock connector is now common.

Contactor: A magnetically operated switch, located in a remote place to save space and to keep the noise of closing the contactor from being heard on the stage. A small switch on the manually operated pilot control board is used to energize the magnet that closes the contactor.

Control Board: The distribution point of electrical energy where the amount of energy, going to the various lighting instruments on the stage, may be controlled. It is composed of switches and dimmers, as well as necessary wiring for the proper distribution of power.

Corner Block: A small piece of ¼-inch 3-ply veneer board, cut in the shape of a triangle and used to reinforce joints in scenery. (See Figure 16.)

Counterweight System: A mechanical system for flying scenery with a counterweight that runs up and down a track at the side of the stage.

In contrast with the pin rail system, which is usually operated from the fly floor, the counterweight system is operated from the stage floor. (See Figure 45.)

Cue Sheet: A record of the dimmer readings and changes for each scene of the play, placed on the control board where the operator can see it during the progress of a performance.

Current: Rate of flow of electricity is called current of electricity. It is expressed in amperes.

Curtain Line: The line across the stage behind the proscenium which marks the position of the front curtain when it is closed.

Cyclorama: A large curtain of canvas, or other material—single or in sections—hung from a horizontal U-shaped wood or metal frame suspended by sets of lines from the gridiron. (See Figure 31.)

Diffuse Reflection: Reflection in all directions.

Dim: To change the amount of illumination, either by increasing it or decreasing it.

Dimmer: Any means for changing the amount of light, but usually an electrical device operating on the principle of resistance, reactance, autotransformer, electronic tube, or magnetic amplifier.

Door Frame Unit: A solid wood door frame made to fit into a flat. (See Figure 22.)

Dope: A mixture of glue and whiting that sticks to canvas.

Downstage: Any position on the stage near the footlights.

Draw Curtain: A type of curtain suspended from sliding or rolling carriers running in a track overhead. The curtain is opened by being drawn off to the sides. (See Figure 5.)

Drop: A large sheet of canvas, fastened to a batten at top and bottom and hung on a set of lines from the gridiron. It is commonly used to represent the sky. (See Figure 29.)

Effect Machine: See *Sciopticon.*

Electrician: A name applied in the professional theatre to a union stagehand who is capable of operating the control board and of making connections between instruments and the electrical outlets. The term is correctly applied to one who is capable of wiring buildings and of making and repairing various kinds of electrical apparatus.

Ellipsoidal Reflector: A reflector used in spotlights and floodlights that has two focal points. When a light source is placed at one focal point, light falling on the surface of the reflector converges to the other focal point.

Fireplace Unit: A fireplace frame made to fit into a flat. (See Figure 26.)

Flat: A unit section of flat scenery. A tall screen made of wood and canvas. (See Figure 19.)

Flies: The space above the stage occupied by sets of lines and hanging scenery.

Flipper: A small piece of flat scenery hinged to a larger piece of flat scenery.

Floodlight: A lighting instrument composed chiefly of a large reflector and a fairly high wattage lamp. It is used to produce general illumination. (See Figure 66.)

Floor Pocket: A metal box in the stage floor, its top flush with the floor surface, in which the stage electrical outlets are placed.

Fluorescence: Some substances have the property of absorbing invisible light and emitting visible light. This property is called fluorescence. Because the emitted light is very dim it can be noticed only in dark surroundings.

Fly: To lift scenery up above the level of the stage floor (usually out of view of the audience) by means of lines run from the gridiron.

Fly Foor, or Fly Gallery: A narrow gallery extending along a side wall of the stage some distance above the stage floor. The ropes used in flying scenery are operated from this gallery.

Flyman: A man employed to fly scenery.

Focus: The point to which parallel rays of light converge after passing through a lens. As a verb it is frequently used on the stage to refer to the adjustment of a spotlight to make the illuminated area larger or smaller, or to change the position of the area.

Foot-Candle: A unit of illumination. The illumination on a surface when there is a luminous flux of one lumen on an area of one square foot. It is also the illumination on a surface one foot from a source of one candle.

Foot Iron: A piece of hardware used to secure scenery to the floor. (See Figure 14.)

Footlights: One or more striplights placed in a recess or trough outside of the curtain line to produce general illumination from below. (See Figure 65.)

Funnel: A sheet metal hood, circular or square in section, from 1 to 3 feet long, intended to absorb spill or stray light that would otherwise fall outside the illuminated area. The funnel is fastened to the front of a spotlight.

Fuse: A protective device used in main circuits and branch circuits to prevent overloads and short circuits that might damage electrical equipment. When an overload happens, the small strip of fusable metal (within the fuse) melts and breaks the circuit.

Gelatin: The most common color medium. It is made of ordinary gelatin in thin sheets with an aniline dye producing the color.

Glare: The cause of the sensation of discomfort experienced when observing a surface or light source that is very bright. It depends on contrasts as well as the intrinsic brightness of a source or surface.

Grand Master: A term applied to a switch or dimmer that controls all of the individual switches or dimmers. It is used in contrast to a group master which may master a smaller number of individual controls.

Gridiron, or Grid: The framework of steel or wooden beams above the stage which supports the rigging employed in flying scenery. (See Figures 40 and 41.)

Ground Cloth, or Floor Cloth: A large piece of waterproof duck canvas frequently used to cover the stage floor.

Ground Row: A low, flat profile of ground foilage, a bank of earth, a distant mountain range, or the like, designed to stand up independently on the stage. (See Figure 37.)

Hanger Iron: A piece of hardware attached to the frame of a hanging flat, or other unit, for flying purposes. It has a ring at one end into which the line from the gridiron is tied.

Head Block: See *Lead Block.*

House Lights: Auditorium lighting.

Hue: That property of any color that distinguishes it from gray of the same brilliance.

Illumination: Strictly, it is the density of the luminous flux on a surface and is expressed in foot-candles. In a general way it is often used as a synonym for lighting.

Illuminometer, or Illumination Meter: A meter that measures illumination, usually read in foot-candles.

Instrument, or Lighting Instrument: A synonym for lighting unit, as a spotlight, striplight, floodlight, and so on.

Insulation: Materials, such as fabric, rubber, fiber, porcelain, and so forth, that are very poor conductors of electricity and are used to prevent conductors of opposite polarity from coming in contact with each other, and to prevent contact with individuals who must handle the conductors.

Intensity: The power of a light source, which is measured in candles.

Interlock: To move several dimmer handles up or down together. The usual method is to have a catch that temporarily connects each handle to a single shaft. A single handle permanently fastened to the shaft will then control any of the individual handles connected to it.

Jack: A triangular device made of wood, which is hinged to the back of a ground row or other set piece for the purpose of propping up the scenery from behind. The end of the jack is fastened to the floor by means of a foot iron and a stage screw. (See Figure 37.)

Keystone: A small piece of ¼-inch 3-ply veneer board, cut in the shape of a keystone and used to reinforce joints in scenery. (See Figure 16.)

Lamp, or Incandescent Lamp: Refers to the complete unit, including bulb, base, filament, lead-in wires, and so forth.

Lamp Dip, or Colored Lacquer: A colored transparent or frosted lacquer used on clear or frosted incandescent lamps when it is difficult to place color media in front of them.

Lash Cleat: A small metal hook on the frame of a flat over which a lash line is thrown to bind the flat to the edge of another flat. (See Figures 14 and 18.)

Lash Line Eye: The metal eye on the frame of a flat to which the lash line is attached. (See Figures 14 and 18.)

Lead Block, or Head Block: Three or more sheaves framed together and attached to the gridiron directly above the outer edge of the fly floor. The sheaves may be framed in a line, or parallel to each other on a single shaft. The ropes from the three or more loft blocks in a set come together at the lead block and pass on down together to the pin rail. (See Figures 40 and 41.)

Left Stage: Any position on the stage to one's left when facing the audience. (See Figure 2.)

Lens: A piece of transparent material, such as glass, frequently having one or two spherical surfaces and sometimes having cylindrical surfaces. Lenses are used on the stage to converge the rays of light from a small source and concentrate the light to a narrow beam. They are used also to produce an image from a lantern slide or of moving objects. The latter are called objective or projection lenses; the former, condensing lenses.

Lighting Unit: See *Instrument.*

Linnebach Projector, or Shadowgraph Projector: A sheet metal hood painted black inside, using a concentrated source of light and a painted or cut-out slide.

Loft Block: A sheave (pulley wheel) in a steel frame bolted to the gridiron, used to run a fly rope. There is one block for each line in a set. (See Figures 40 and 41.)

Louvers, or Spill Shields: A series of thin cylindrical sections of sheet metal or parallel strips, placed in front of a reflector to eliminate spill light or direct emanation that would fall outside the beam produced by the reflector.

Lumen: The unit of luminous flux. The flux through a unit solid angle (steradian) from a source of one candle. It is also the flux on a surface, one square foot in area, one foot from a source of one candle.

Mask: To conceal a lighting instrument from the audience, usually by means of scenery.

Masking, or Masking Piece: A piece of scenery used to cut off from the view of the audience any part of the stage space which should not be seen. (See *Backing.*)

Master Dimmer, or Switch: See *Grand Master.*

Multiple, or Parallel Circuit: A circuit in which there are several paths through which the current may flow, as in all stage lighting circuits, and in fact, nearly all lighting circuits except street lighting.

Objective Lens: See *Lens.*

Offstage: Any position on the stage outside of the acting area.

Olivette: A box floodlight that can be mounted on a stand or hung by means of chains from a pipe batten.

Onstage: Any position on the stage within the acting area.

Operating Light: Usually a work light built into the control board to illuminate the handles and the cue sheet.

Operator: Any person who handles lighting instruments and equipment on the stage, or changes color frames between scenes. A person in charge of the control board for a production is frequently called the control board operator.

Outlet: A receptacle into which a plug or connector is inserted in order to connect a lighting instrument to the source of electrical energy. A floor pocket or wall pocket may contain one or more outlets.

Parabolic Reflector: A concave reflector whose surface is in the form of a paraboloid. When a source of light is placed at the focus, reflected rays of light tend to go out in straight lines. It is used in floodlights and striplights.

Parallel: The collapsible frame support for a stage platform. (See Figure 33.)

Parallel Circuit: See *Multiple Circuit.*

Phosphorescence: A substance is said to exhibit the property of phosphorescence if, after exposure to light, it continues to give off visible light when the stimulating source has been removed.

Picture-Frame Hook and Socket: Small pieces of hardware used to hang a lightweight unit of scenery, or a property, on another unit. (See Figure 14.)

Pilot Light: A small incandescent lamp, frequently covered with a colored cap, placed in the face of a control board to indicate that a circuit is turned on. One is frequently placed beside the switch and dimmer handle of each individual circuit.

Pin Rail: The double rail holding belaying pins on which fly ropes (sets of lines) are tied. The pin rail is generally located along the outer edge of a fly floor. (See Figure 41.)

Pipe Clamp: See *Clamp.*

Pipe Batten: A length of pipe suspended on a set of lines. Flied scenery is frequently attached to a pipe batten by means of snatch lines instead of being tied directly to a set of lines. A pipe batten is a standard part in a unit of the counterweight system. (See Figure 66.) It is also used to carry lighting instruments.

Platform: A collapsible and portable frame platform constructed in unit sections. (See Figure 33.)

Plug: A standard stage plug is a fiber block with heavy copper contacts rated for 50 amperes. It fits into a standard stage outlet. Especially in the nonprofessional theatre these plugs and outlets are being replaced by 15 or 30 ampere stage connectors or twistlock connectors.

Plywood: Veneer board in three or more plies, made from basswood, whitewood, fir, or other soft wood. Sometimes called *profile board.*

Pocket: See *Floor Pocket.*

Portable Control Board: A control board intended to be moved about, especially from one theatre to another. (See Figures 90 and 91.)

Practical: Practicable—capable of being used by the actor. A door with a swinging shutter, or a window with movable sashes, is "practical."

Primary Colors: The primary colors in light are usually called blue, green, and red. The primary colors in pigments are commonly considered to be blue-green, yellow, and magenta.

Profile Board: See *Plywood.*

Projector: A floodlight with a polished parabolic reflector and concentric louvers producing a beam of light is often called a floodlight projector, or sometimes a spot flood. See also *Lens* or *Linnebach Projector.*

Proscenium: The wall which divides the stage from the auditorium. The opening through which the spectator views the stage is termed the Proscenium Opening. (See Figure 2.)

Quality: In light it is sometimes used as a synonym for color.

Rail: A cross piece in the frame of a flat. In a flat 12 feet or less there are a *top rail,* a *bottom rail,* and one *toggle rail* (which braces the center of the flat). In a flat over 12 feet there are two or more *toggle rails.* (See Figure 19.)

Ramp: An inclined platform, sloping up from the level of the floor.

Receptacle: See *Outlet.* Frequently used as a synonym for socket.

Reflectance: The reflected light divided by the incident light, usually expressed in per cent.

Reflector: Any surface that reflects light, but this term usually refers to a definite piece of equipment, such as a spotlight reflector.

Regular Reflection: Reflection in which the angle of incidence is equal to the angle of reflection. Examples are highly polished metals and glass mirrors.

Remote Control: Control in which the current through the lamps does not pass through the manually operated control board, but through dimmers and switches in some remote place such as the basement of the theatre. Its purpose is to make possible the use of small and compact parts in the manually operated pilot control board.

Resistance: A characteristic of materials concerned with their ability to conduct electricity. Insulating materials are said to have very high resistance, and conductors very low resistance.

Rheostat: A variable resistance. Sometimes a synonym for resistance dimmer.

Right Stage: Any position on the stage to one's right when facing the audience.

Saddle Iron: A narrow strip of iron used to brace the bottom of a door-flat across the the door opening. (See Figure 21.)

Saturation: That property of any color possessing hue which determines its degree of difference from gray of the same brilliance. A measure of amount of hue.

Sciopticon: A spotlight to which has been added a supplementary condensing lens, moving effect holder, and an objective lens. Such moving effects as clouds, rain, rippling water, and so on, are accomplished with this instrument.

Series Circuit: A circuit with a single path in which the same current passes through every element. (See Figure 75.)

Set: A group or series of scenery units which suggests a single locale.

Set: To put up or assemble scenery for use. This word is generally combined with other words in a phrase—to *set the stage,* or to *set the scene.*

Set of Lines: A unit group of ropes hanging from the gridiron, used to fly (lift) scenery. There are commonly three or four lines in a set. (See Figures 40 and 41.)

Shade: In reference to color, a shade is a color below median gray in brilliance and frequently, but not necessarily low in saturation.

Sheave: A grooved pulley wheel.

Shift: To change scenery and properties from one setting to another.

Short Circuit: When two wires of opposite polarity and low resistance come in contact, the current tends to become excessive and dangerous, possibly causing fire or damage to electrical equipment and wiring. Fuses or circuit breakers are used to prevent damage when this accidental condition obtains.

Size Water: A thin solution of glue which is mixed with pigment powders to make paint for scenery.

Spherical Reflector: A concave reflector that has the property of sending light back to the center of curvature when a source of light is placed at this center. It is used in spotlights and, combined with a parabolic shape, in striplights.

Spill, or Spill Light: Stray light outside a beam, or any light that is misplaced on scenery or other objects on the stage.

Spot Line: A single line specially rigged from the gridiron to fly a piece of scenery which cannot be handled by the regular lines.

Spotlight: A lighting instrument with a condensing lens producing a beam of light; used for specific illumination. (See Figures 59, 60, 61, 62, and 63.)

Stage Brace: An adjustable device made of two lengths of 1″ x 1″ wood held between clamps, used to prop up scenery from behind. A forked iron hook fastened to one end of the brace is hooked into a brace cleat attached to the unit requiring support, and an iron heel at the other end of the brace is secured to the floor by means of a stage screw. (See Figure 39.)

Stage Screw, or Peg: A large, tapered screw with a handle, used to secure foot irons and stage braces to the floor. (See Figures 14 and 39.)

Stand: A heavy round iron base to which is attached a vertical telescoping pipe and rod. Spotlights and floodlights can be attached to the end of the rod and directed toward the acting area from a position five or ten feet above the floor.

Stile: The long side piece in the frame of a flat. (See Figure 19.)

Strap Hinge: A hinge with long tapered flaps, used principally for hanging door shutters in their frames and for locking door and window frames into flats. (See Figure 23.)

Strike: To take apart and remove a set of scenery from the acting area after it has been used—generally at the end of an act.

Striplight: A long trough-like reflector with sockets for lamps of small wattage, or a row of individual reflectors properly housed in a rigid sheet metal structure. Striplights are made in any length from a few feet to 30 or 40 feet long. They are used for borderlights, footlights, and for cyclorama lighting to produce general illumination. (See *Backing Striplight* and Figures 64 and 65.)

Switch: A device used to open and close an electrical circuit. In modern stage lighting practice, switches are placed behind the face of a control board with the handle extending through to the front. A remote control switch is called a contactor.

Tab: A sheet of canvas or other material, framed or unframed, narrower than a drop but suspended like it—used chiefly for masking offstage spaces. (See Figure 29.)

Template: A special type of work bench used in the construction of flats.

Thickness: A width of lumber, or other material, attached to the edge of an opening (a doorway, an archway, or a window) to give the edge the effect of depth or thickness. (See Figure 25.)

Three-Fold: Three flats hinged together to fold inward, face to face.

Throw: Indicates the distance from a lighting instrument to the illuminated area.

Tint: A color higher in brilliance than median gray and of various degrees of saturation.

Toggle Rail or *Toggle Bar:* The cross piece in the frame of a flat. (See Figure 19.)

Tormentor Light: A spotlight mounted on a vertical pipe batten just offstage from either tormentor.

Traveller: A slotted steel or wooden track, used to hang draw curtains. (See Figure 5.)

Trim: The wooden facing, about 4 or 6 inches wide, which surrounds a door or window opening. It is usually ornamented with molding. (See Figure 25.)

Trim: To level off a flied piece of scenery at the right height for use during a performance.

Trip: To elevate the bottom of a drop, or other flied scenery, with an auxiliary set of lines in such a way as to make it occupy a space approximately half its height. Tripping is resorted to on stages where there is not sufficient fly space to get a unit out of sight by taking it straight up with one set of lines only. (See Figure 44.)

Two-Fold: Two flats hinged together to fold inward, face to face. A two-fold is also called a *wing.*

Upstage: Any position on the stage away from the footlights.

Veneer Board: See *Plywood.*

Volt: A volt is the unit of electromotive force or electrical pressure. Electrical pressure is often referred to as voltage.

Wagon: A low, rolling platform on which a section of a set may be mounted to expedite scene changes.

Watt: The unit of electrical power. Since it is a small unit, the term kilowatt, meaning 1000 watts, is in common use.

Window Frame Unit: A solid wooden window made to fit into a flat. (See Figure 24.)

Wing: Two or three flats hinged together to fold inward, face to face. On the old-fashioned stage a "wing" was a painted, and usually profiled, screen, which was pushed onstage in a groove to represent part of the side wall of a set. Hence arose the practice of calling the offstage spaces to the right or left of the acting area the "wings." (See Figures 2 and 20.)

Wing Nut: A special type of nut which may be tightened with the fingers, without the aid of a wrench. (See Figure 18.)

Work Light: Illumination for the stage used for rehearsals, scene shifting and building. Work light is controlled ordinarily by a wall switch instead of a switch on the control board.

COSTUME TERMS

Alb: Long, close-fitting ecclesiastical garment, originally white.

Alpaca: Thin, wiry material, wool (from the alpaca) sometimes mixed with silk; 19th century.

Bandoleer: Strap worn across shoulders to hold weapon or ammunition; 16th and 17th centuries.

Baudekin: Medieval silk, first manufactured at Baldac (Bagdad), stiff texture, shot with gold, used for canopies. *Baldachin* is an alternative form of this word.

Bliau: Dress with close-fitting bodice, full, rippling skirt; medieval.

Bracae: Men's trousers, sometimes tied with thongs about ankles; Dark Ages.

Breeches-hose: Puffed or padded top part of leg covering, used with tight leg hose; 16th century.

Brocade: Patterned silk, frequently with gold or silver threads woven into pattern; 15th century.

Buff Jerkin: Rather long, semi-fitting jacket, with or without sleeves, of leather; 17th century.

Buskin: Soft, low shoe, Greek and Roman, associated with comedy.

Camlet: Mixture of wool and silk; 16th century.

Cashmere: Light-weight wool cloth; 19th century.

Caul: Wired, cylindrical part of headdress; 14th and 15th centuries.

Cendal: Silk cloth, similar to modern taffeta, woven in rich colors; medieval.

Chapeau Bras: Three-cornered hat carried under the arm; 17th and 18th centuries.

Chaperon: Wrap-around headdress, coxcomb effect at side; 14th and 16th centuries.

Chatelaine: Medieval pouch or bag, hung from girdle.

Chausses: Fitted leg covering, laced up behind, of linen or wool; medieval.

Chignon: Low knot at back of head, frequently encased in net; 1860.

Chintz: Figured cotton material, sometimes glazed.

Chiton: Greek dress, folded and draped about the figure.

Chopine: Venetian-type shoe with thick soles; 16th century.

Commode: Stiff, tall headdress, of lace, ribbons, etc.; 17th century.

Cothurnus: Tall boot, Greek and Roman, associated with tragedy.

Crinoline: A fine, horsehair weave, combined with linen; applied also to garment made of this material, and to hoop skirt; 1840–60.

Cyclas: Sleeveless overdress, cut out low under arms; 14th century.

Damask: Patterned linen or silk; medieval or later.

De Medici Collar: Stiff, upstanding collar, frequently wired; 16th century.

Doublet: Close-fitting upper garment, usually of double thickness, quilted or padded; 15th to 17th century.

Farthingale: 16th-century skirt, also applied to the frame of the skirt; bell- or wheel-shaped.

Ferroniere: Headdress, ribbon or chain, with pendant over forehead; Renaissance.

Fibula: Ornament, like safety pin; Dark Ages.

Fichu: Neckwear of lace draped about neck, folds in front; 17th and 18th centuries.

Fillet: Band about head; Greek, Roman, medieval.

Fustian: Coarse, cotton cloth, used by peasants and clergy; medieval and later.

Gambeson: Quilted garment, long sleeves of leather, wool or linen; medieval.

Gorget: Chin on throatpiece of armor, also cloth draped about woman's chin; medieval.

Greaves: Leg guards, Greek and Roman and later.

Hennin: Tall, cone-shaped headdress; medieval.

Hessian Boots: Boots, calf-length behind, higher in front; 19th century.

Himation: Greek mantle, draped about figure.

Hoop Skirt: Wired frame with full skirt over it; 1850–60.

Hose: Upper or trunk hose were knee-length or shorter, full, puffed and slashed, or tight-fitting; nether hose resembled tights; 16th and 17th centuries.

Houppelande: Long, lined garment, like dressing gown, high neck; 14th and 15th centuries.

Incroyable: Dandy of the Directory period, France.

Jabot: Frilled and gathered neckwear; 18th century.

Kirtle: Skirt, usually full, sometimes looped up about waist; 16th century.

Leg-of-Mutton Sleeve: 1895 sleeve, full top, tight at wrist.

Linsey-Woolsey: Coarse, woolen stuff, first manufactured at Linsey, Suffolk; 16th century.

Liripipe: Rat-tail appendage to hood; 14th and 15th centuries.

Lovelocks: Curls at side of face, worn by Cavaliers; 17th century.

Mackintosh: Waterproof coat; 19th century.

Manches Volantes: Oversleeves, frequently fur-trimmed; 16th century.

Mantilla: Lace scarf; 18th and 19th centuries.

Milan Bonnet: Soft, tam-o'-shanter type, with feather, or jeweled; 16th century.

Mobcap: Soft linen or lawn cap, gathered, with frill about face; 18th and 19th centuries.

Mohair: Material similar to alpaca, from the Angora goat, mixed with silk or cotton; 19th century.

Nankeen: Cotton cloth, originally from Nanking, China, yellow or buff in color, much favored in 19th century for trousers.

Paile or Pall: Stiff, medieval silk fabric, used for canopies. *Pall* derives from this word.

Pallium: Ecclesiastical bishop's scarf worn about neck, with pendant in front and behind.

Pannier: Soft puffs over skirt, at hips, and behind; 18th century.

Pantalettes: Long, frilled leg coverings, worn by women; 18th century.

Passementerie: Elaborate trimming, appliquéd to dress; 19th century.

Patten: Type of overshoe; 19th century.

Pelisse: 14th-century, circular cape garment frequently trimmed with fur, slit up the side; also a 19th-century cloak, snug-fitting, with high neck and long sleeves.

Petasos: Greek traveling hat, wide-brimmed, tied on with cords; fore-runner of the crimson Cardinal's hat.

Petticoat Breeches: Short skirt with knee breeches attached, worn by men of fashion about 1660.

Phrygian Cap: Grecian headdress, shaped like a stocking cap with the rounded bulge curved forward over the forehead; Romans adopted it, colored red, as mark of freedman; in 1789, French Revolutionists adopted it, with tricolor, as *Cap of Liberty.*

Piccadilly: Wire frame used in 16th century to prop up the ruff, or collar; later the name was given to the wide Cavalier collar; the street where these were sold came to be called Piccadilly.

Points: Laces tipped with pointed metal caps, used in 15th and 16th centures to fasten nether to upper garments, also to fasten sleeves to body of garment.

Poke Bonnet: Hood with curved brim extending over face; 19th century.

Poleyns: 15th-century pointed shoes, sometimes 22 inches long.

Polonaise: 18-century dress with fitted back, panniers over back and sides; also late 19th-century dress with panniers, buttoned down front.

Pomander: A spherical perforated scent ball, for perfumes or medica-ments; 14th century.

Pompadour: Flowered and brocaded material, named after Mme. Pom-padour, 18th century; also type of hair dressing, puffed over fore-head, 20th century.

Redingote: Long-tailed coat, copied after English riding-coat; Directory and later 19th century.

Reticule: Small bag suspended on ribbons or chains from belt, used in 16th century and later.

Roundlet: 15th-century hat, with rounded roll about crown.

Ruff: A ruffle of lawn, from 1 to 12 inches wide, gathered, starched, and pleated in layers; trimmed with lace and otherwise adorned; 16th century.

Sagum: Mantle of the Dark Ages, about 3 by 5 feet, fastened on right shoulder or in front.

Sarcenet: Thin silk (from Saracen), of pale colors, used for veils and linings.

Samite: Closely woven, heavy silk of Chinese origin; medieval.

Sark: Shirt worn by Vikings.

Spencer: Short fitted jacket, buttoned up the front, with high collar, and with or without skirt or peplum; 19th century.

Steinkirk: Neck scarf, of linen or lace, twisted loosely about neck, named after the battle of Steinkirk; 17th century.

Stephane: Greek crown, worn by women.

Stomacher: Stiffened front to bodice, usually ornamented with lace, jewels, etc., worn from 16th century to late 19th century, with variations.

Surcoat: Sleeveless tunic, or overgarment, worn over chain mail, also long sleeveless overtunic, worn by older men; medieval.

Tabard: 14th-century sleeveless garment, oblong in shape with hole for head, worn by workmen, also lawyers and others; "Tabard Inn" derives name from this garment.

Tippet: Narrow piece of cloth, plain, tasseled or variously edged, fastened above the elbow with long pendant, 14th century; also narrow fur neckpiece, late 19th century.

Toga: Roman mantle, segment of arc in shape, wrapped about body.

Torque: Neckband of twisted or plain metal; Dark Ages.

Tricorne: Three-cornered hat; 18th and early 19th centuries.

Vandyke Beard: Pointed beard with pointed moustache, of the type often seen in portraits by the Flemish painter Van Dyck; 17th century.

Vandyke Collar: Wide, deep collar, rounded or square front edges, trimmed with deep point lace, frequently worn in Van Dyck portraits.

Vandyke Cuff: Deep cuff, similarly trimmed; 17th century.

Vizard: Mask worn by ladies; 16th and 17th centuries.

Watteau Sacque: Dress with low-cut bodice, square-necked, with pleats in back, draped in panniers, or puffs, over hips and behind; 18th century.

Wimple: Rectangular piece of cloth, usually white, worn draped over woman's head; medieval period through 16th century.

Woad: Blue stain used by early Britons on bodies during battle.

MAKE-UP TERMS

Foundation Grease Paint: Basic color which is applied to all parts of the face; the color is dependent upon nationality, race, environment, age, health, etc.

Under Rouge: A basic rouge which is applied to the cheeks; a moist lip rouge, indelible when applied to the cheeks.

Hair Whitening: Liquid whitening which is used for whitening the hair; corn starch, aluminum polish, or white mascara may be used.

Spirit Gum: Glue which is used for the fastening of beards or crepe hair to the face.

Crepe Hair or Wool: Used for the making of beards.

Nonflexible Collodion: Because of its drawing qualities, this is used for the creation of scars.

Nose Putty: A waxlike substance which is used for building up the nose and other features of the face. (Mortician's wax may also be used for the same purpose.)

Lining Colors: Used as eye shadow, high lighting, and low lighting; colors are many and varied.

Low Lights in Terms of Grease Paint: Colors darker than the foundation paint, which are applied to the parts of the face and features that are to be sunken.

High Lights in Terms of Grease Paint: A color lighter than the foundation grease paint, which is applied to the features or parts of the face to be accentuated.

Dermatograph Pencil: Pencil used for marking the skin; made in black, brown and blue; used for lining eye and eyebrows.

Dry Rouge: Applied after the grease-paint make-up has been completed and *powdered,* and used for touching up.

Tooth Enamel: White, light, medium, and dark; dark or black is used for the blocking out of teeth; the three light shades are used for covering gold teeth.

Cosmetique: Black and brown; used for beading the eyelashes.

Masque or Mascara: Black, brown, and white; used for touching up eyelashes and hair.

Liquid Body Make-up: Used for covering the neck, arms, and all exposed parts of the body; made in a variety of colors which correspond to the grease paint; is semi-waterproof, but can easily be removed by soap and water.

Pancake Make-up: Variety of colors; most favorable for photography and used in motion pictures.

BIBLIOGRAPHY*

AMERICAN PUBLISHERS OF PLAYS

WALTER H. BAKER COMPANY, 178 Tremont Street, Boston 11, Mass.

DRAMATIC PUBLISHING COMPANY, 59 East Van Buren Street, Chicago 5, Ill.; 448 S. Hill St., Los Angeles, Calif.

DRAMATISTS PLAY SERVICE, Inc., 6 East 39th Street, New York 16, N.Y.

ROW, PETERSON & COMPANY, 1911 Ridge Avenue, Evanston, Ill.

SAMUEL FRENCH, Inc., 25 West 45th Street, New York 19, N.Y.; 811 West 7th Street, Los Angeles, Calif.

BIBLIOGRAPHIES, PLAY LISTS, AND REFERENCE WORKS

An extensive selection of bibliographies of bibliography, play lists, and reference works is included in this section in order that the references included under succeeding headings may be kept to a minimum.

AMERICAN EDUCATIONAL THEATRE ASSOCIATION, *Educational Theatre Journal,* Vol. I (October, 1949). Two issues only were published in 1949. Since then it has appeared quarterly. Extensive bibliographies and articles on all aspects of theatre and drama are included. The May issue contains lists of theses and dissertations and "Projects in Progress." Extensive listings of college and university productions.

AMERICAN LIBRARY ASSOCIATION, *Subject-Index to Children's Plays* (Chicago, American Library Association, 1940). Very helpful to the teacher and to the director of children's plays seeking plays for specific occasions or specific subjects.

BAKER, Blanch M., *Dramatic Bibliography, An Annotated List of Books on the History and Criticism of the Drama and the Stage and on the Allied Arts of the Theatre* (New York, H. W. Wilson Company, 1933). This work is still a very useful guide for the director and teacher.

———, *Theatre and Allied Arts* (New York, H. W. Wilson Company, 1952).

BATES, Mary E., and SUTHERLAND, Anne C., eds., *Dramatic Index,* 1915, etc. (annual) (Boston, F. W. Faxon & Company, Inc.). Since its first

* This bibliography follows the style set forth in Skillin and Gay's *Words into Type* (New York, Appleton-Century-Crofts, Inc., 1948).

appearance in 1915, this *Index,* published each year, has been the standard guide to current theatrical literature and to articles and books on the drama.

BATESON, F. W., ed., *The Cambridge Bibliography of English Literature,* 4 vols. (New York, The Macmillan Company, 1941). This is the scholar's standard bibliography of English literature compiled by outstanding authorities in England and America. Each of the first three volumes contains bibliographies on the theatre and the drama in the periods to which it is devoted, Volume IV is an index to the whole.

BRITISH DRAMA LEAGUE, *The Player's Library. The Catalogue of the Library of the British Drama League* (London, Faber and Faber, Ltd., 1950).

———, *First Supplement to the Player's Library* (London, Faber and Faber, Ltd., 1951).

———, *Second Supplement to the Player's Library* (London, Faber and Faber, Ltd., 1954).

CROSS, Tom Peete, *Bibliographical Guide to English Studies,* 8th rev. ed. (Chicago, University of Chicago Press, 1943). A guide for the graduate student in English studies. Contains a section on the drama.

DINGWELL, Wilbur, ed., *The Handbook Annual of the Theatre, May 1940–May 1941.* (New York, Coward-McCann, Inc., 1941). Despite the promise of its title, this *Handbook* seems to have appeared only once.

DRUMMOND, A. M., *Plays for the Country Theatre* (Ithaca, N.Y., Cornell University Press, 1922). This is an excellent example of the university-compiled play lists and, even though this list is now somewhat out of date, its wise compilation by an able editor makes it still useful. Another example of the university list is *Lists of Plays for the School and Community* (Topeka, Kansas, University of Kansas Extension Division, 1926).

GASSNER, John, *Masters of the Drama,* 3rd rev. and enl. ed. (New York, Dover Publications, Inc., 1954). In addition to the history of drama, the book contains extensive bibliographies.

EBISCH, Walther, and SCHÜCKING, Levin L., eds., *A Shakespeare Bibliography* (Oxford, The Clarendon Press, 1931). Supplement for the years 1930–35. *Ibid.,* 1937. This is a select bibliography, a standard guide to scholarly works on Shakespeare, his plays, and his theatre. It is especially useful to the mature director and teacher engaged in the production of a Shakespeare play.

FIRKINS, Ina Ten Eyck, *Index to Plays, 1800–1926* (New York, H. W. Wilson Company, 1927). *Index to Plays; Supplement. Ibid.,* 1935. These are the standard library reference guides to plays after 1800.

Every mature director, especially in the academic theatre, should be acquainted with them.

GAMBLE, Willima Burt, *Development of Scenic Art and Stage Machinery* (New York, New York Public Library, 1928). A valuable bibliography for the technician and artist in the theatre, compiled from the extensive collections in the New York Public Library. Valuable also for the director and theatre historian.

GILDER, Rosamond, *A Theatre Library: A Bibliography of One Hundred Books Relating to the Theatre* (New York, Theatre Arts, Inc., 1932). Limited in scope but valuable to the student director.

———, and FREEDLEY, George, *Theatre Collections in Libraries and Museums.* An International Handbook (New York, Theatre Arts, Inc., 1936). An invaluable aid to the graduate student engaged in research. Tells where the important collections in libraries and museums on theatre and drama are located.

GRANVILLE, Wilfred, *A Dictionary of Theatrical Terms* (London, Andre Deutsch, 1952). This useful glossary, compiled and published in England, naturally emphasizes English rather than American usage.

HARSH, Philip Whaley, *A Handbook of Classical Drama* (Stanford, Calif., Stanford University Press, 1944). The best one-volume guide to the drama of Greece and Rome. Contains excellent bibliographies.

HARTNOLL, Phyllis, ed., *The Oxford Companion to The Theatre* 2nd ed. (London, New York, Toronto, Oxford University Press, 1957). In addition to historical materials, the volume contains a select bibliography.

HILER, Hilaire, and HILER, Meyer, *Bibliography of Costumes: A Dictionary Catalog of about Eight Thousand Books and Periodicals* (New York, H. W. Wilson Company, 1939). The best bibliographical guide to the literature on costume.

LAWSON, Hilda Josephine, *The Negro in American Drama* (Urbana, Ill., University of Illinois Press, 1939). A list of contemporary American Negro plays.

LIBRARY ASSOCIATION, *Modern Drama, 1900–1938* (London, Library Association, 1939). A select list of plays published since 1900. See also the *Index* compiled by Firkins listed above.

LOGASA, Hannah, and VER NOOY, Winifred, *An Index to One-Act Plays, 1900–1924* (Boston, F. W. Faxon & Company, 1924). *An Index to One-Act Plays. Supplement, 1924–1932. Ibid.,* 1932. *An Index to One-Act Plays. Second Supplement, 1932–1940. Ibid.,* 1941. These volumes are the standard guides to modern one-act plays.

MANTLE, Burns, and SHERWOOD, Garrison P., *The Best Plays of 1899–1909* (New York, Dodd, Mead & Company, 1944).

MANTLE, Burns, and SHERWOOD, Garrison P., *The Best Plays of 1909–1919* (*Ibid.*, 1933).

MANTLE, Burns, *The Best Plays of 1919–1920* (Boston, Small, Maynard & Company, 1920–25. New York, Dodd, Mead & Company, 1926, etc.) (annual). Each year since 1920 this outstanding critic and his successors have continued to issue a volume devoted to the plays of the year. They have selected the ten best plays of each season and given a condensed outline of each. A complete list of all plays produced on the New York stage is included, with casts, length of run, and other pertinent information; with a review of the season in New York and other important theatrical cities of the nation. Small, Maynard published the first six volumes and Dodd, Mead have published the remaining volumes. Here the director can find through these volumes a complete list of the professionally produced plays that have appeared on the American stage since 1899. These volumes are a valuable asset to any director. Since the death of Burns Mantle, these have been edited successively by John Chapman and by Louis Kronenberger.

MAYORGA, Margaret, *The Best One-Act Plays for 1937* (New York, Dodd, Mead & Company, 1938, etc.) (annual). This is a companion work to the Burns Mantle *Best Plays* but differs from those volumes in that each volume contains the full text of the best one-act plays as selected by Margaret Mayorga. Each volume contains lists and bibliographies. A volume has been published for the succeeding years since 1937. These are definite aids to teachers and directors.

MERSAND, Joseph, ed., *Guide to Play Selection,* 2nd ed. (New York, Appleton-Century-Crofts, Inc., 1958). An excellent descriptive guide to full-length, one-act, radio and television plays from classical times to the present. Short descriptions are given of the plots of individual plays, settings, number of characters, costuming, together with book sources and royalty fees. The book also contains bibliographies of general theatre interest.

MONRO, Isabel, and COOK, Dorothy E., *Costume Index: A Subject Index to Plates and Illustrated Text* (New York, H. W. Wilson Company, 1937). A valuable index to be used in connection with the Hiler and Hiler *Bibliography of Costume* mentioned above. Especially important for its listing of plates and pictures.

NAGLER, A. M., ed., *Sources of Theatrical History* (New York, Theatre Annual, Inc., 1952). An anthology of the chief documents from the Greeks to the present day on theatre and theatre arts.

NATHAN, George Jean, *The Theatre Book of the Year* (New York, Alfred A. Knopf, Inc., 1950). This is the eighth volume in Nathan's series of "Records and Interpretations." It contains keen criticisms of the various Broadway productions, as well as records of the current seasons covered.

NATIONAL ASSOCIATION OF TEACHERS OF SPEECH, *Speech Monographs.* A volume devoted to research in the speech and drama fields and published annually (after 1950, four more issues per year) by the National Association of Teachers of Speech. Each year this publication carries a list, "Graduate Theses—An Index of Graduate Work in the Field of Speech," compiled by Franklin H. Knower. In this list can be found the author and the title of each important research thesis presented in the field of theatre and drama.

OTTERMILLER, John H., *Index to Plays in Collections* (New York, H. W. Wilson Company, 1943). This is the guide that aids the director and the teacher to find the plays that have been reprinted in various volumes and collections. Very helpful to the student.

PARKER, John, *Who's Who in the Theatre,* 9th ed., rev. (New York, Pitman Publishing Corp., 1939). A biographical record of the contemporary stage.

QUINN, Arthur Hobson, *A History of the American Drama,* 2 vols. *From the Beginning to the Civil War* and *From the Civil War to the Present Day,* 2nd ed. (New York, Appleton-Century-Crofts, Inc., 1943). These two volumes are the standard history of the American drama by the foremost scholar in the field. The commentary on the contemporary playwrights and the bibliographies and play lists are very useful to the director. Quinn's collection of *Representative American Plays* (7th ed., same publisher) contains an excellent select bibliography as well as texts of outstanding American plays down to the contemporary period.

SHIPLEY, Joseph T., ed., *Dictionary of World Literature: Criticism—Forms—and Technique* (New York, Philosophical Library, Inc., 1943). A very helpful reference book with a large number of articles on theatre and especially on drama, its various forms, types, and techniques.

SOBEL, Bernard, ed., *The Theatre Handbook and Digest of Plays,* 2nd ed., rev. (New York, Crown Publishers, Inc., 1943). Another helpful reference book for the student of the theatre and the director. Contains bibliographies.

SPARGO, John Webster, *A Bibliographical Manual,* rev. ed. (Chicago, Packard & Company, Publishers, 1941). This is primarily a guide for research students in language and literature and speech, but the sections on theatre and drama are useful to the director as well as to the graduate student.

THONSSEN, Lester, FATHERSON, Elizabeth, and THONSSEN, Dorothea, *Bibliography of Speech Education* (New York, H. W. Wilson Company, 1939). This is the outstanding and most complete bibliography in the field. Section III is devoted to "Dramatics." It includes in that major section subsections on general drama, play production, children's drama, community drama, religious drama, radio drama, pageantry, puppetry, shadow plays, pantomime, technique in dramatics (including direction, production, acting, scenic design, lighting, costume, make-up), and play lists. The bibliography included under each of these subsections is extensive. Every teacher and director should know this excellent index. Because it is available, the bibliography included in this book can be kept to a select list of references. Fuller references on all subjects included in this present index will be found in *Bibliography of Speech Education.*

———, Robb, Mary Margaret, and Thonssen, Dorothea, *Bibliography of Speech Education Supplement: 1939–1948* (New York, H. W. Wilson Co., 1950).

Whetstone, Harvey A., Jr., *Plays for Schools and Little Theatres* (Chapel Hill, University of North Carolina Library, 1955).

DIRECTION AND PRODUCTION

Albright, H. D., Halstead, William P., and Mitchell, Lee, *Principles of Theatre Art* (Boston, Houghton Mifflin Company, 1955).

Alekseev, Konstantin Sergeevich, *Stanislavsky Produces Othello,* translated by Helen Nowak (London, G. Bles, 1948).

Andrews, Harry Lee, and Weirick, Bruce, *Acting and Play Production* (New York, Longmans, Green & Company, Inc., 1925). An elementary general treatment now partially out of date.

Banke, Cecile de, *Shakespearean Stage Production: Then & Now* (New York, McGraw-Hill Book Company, Inc., 1953).

Bax, Peter, *Stage Management* (London, Lovat Dickson, Ltd., 1936). A book on directing and production.

Bosworth, Halliam, *Technique in Dramatic Art,* rev. ed. (New York, The Macmillan Company, 1934). A useful book for both the director and the actor.

Brandon-Thomas, Jevan, *Practical Stagecraft for Amateurs,* edited by David C. Keir (London, 1936).

Bricker, Herschel, ed., *Our Theatre Today: Art, Craft, and Management* (New York, Samuel French, Inc., 1936). A book of essays or chapters by thirteen different contemporary workers in the American theatre, including Arthur Hopkins and Brock Pemberton. Various aspects of production and direction are treated.

Boyle, Walden P., *Central and Flexible Staging* (Berkeley, Calif., University of California Press, 1956).

Brown, Gilmore, and Garwood, Alice, *General Principles of Play Direction* (New York, Samuel French, Inc., 1936). A good general treatment of the elements of directing.

BROWN, Hubert Sydney, *Success in Amateur Opera* (London, William Reeves, Ltd., 1939). Instructions on auditions, the organization of an amateur opera society, hints to the conductor, casting, rehearsals, training soloists, including a section on stage management by H. G. Toy.

BROWNE, Elliot Martin, and others, *Putting On a Play* (London, Lovat Dickson, Ltd., 1936). This is a composite work by various English theatre workers, and includes a chapter on acting by E. M. Browne, one on production by John Fernald, one on presentation by F. Sladen Smith, and one on the choice of a play by John Browne.

CLARK, Barrett H., *How to Produce Amateur Plays,* rev. ed. (Boston, Little, Brown & Company, 1925). This book, first published in 1917, was one of the first American works on the subject. Elementary and practical.

COLE, Toby, and CHINOY, Helen Krich, eds., *Directing the Play* (Indianapolis, The Bobbs-Merrill Company, Inc., 1953). A compilation of articles and essays on directing and the history of directing.

COOPER, Charles W., and CAMP, Paul A., *Designing the Play* (New York, Appleton-Century-Crofts, Inc., 1942). A handbook on the analysis of plays for production, containing essays on the problems with assignments and work forms.

CRAFTON, Allen, *Play Directing* (Englewood Cliffs, N.J., Prentice-Hall, Inc., 1938).

———, and ROYER, Jessica, *The Process of Play Production: A Book for the Nonprofessional Theatre Worker* (New York, F. S. Crofts & Company, 1926). A general treatment of the whole problem of directing and production.

CRUMP, Leslie, *Directing for the Amateur Stage* (New York, Dodd, Mead & Company, 1935).

DEAN, Alexander, *Fundamentals of Play Directing* (New York, Farrar & Rinehart, 1941). The most extensive single work devoted entirely to the problems of directing. The theories and exercises were developed by the late Alexander Dean in courses which he taught at Northwestern and Yale Universities. A valuable and helpful book, especially for advanced students.

DIETRICH, John E., *Play Direction* (Englewood Cliffs, N.J., Prentice-Hall, Inc., 1953).

DOLMAN, John, *The Art of Play Production,* rev. ed. (New York, Harper & Brothers, 1946). A good book based to a considerable extent upon theoretical and aesthetic considerations. Students in directing should read it.

DOWNS, Harold, ed., *Theatre and Stage,* 2 vols. (London, Sir Isaac Pitman & Sons, Ltd., 1934). An illustrated work on the whole range of directing and production. It consists of short articles by various writers, some of a very elementary nature.

DRUMMOND, A. M., *Play Production for the Country Theatre* (Ithaca, N.Y., Cornell University Extension Division, 1924). A brief and practical manual; revised by the author in 1930.

———, *A Manual of Play Production* (Ithaca, N.Y., Cornell Co-operative Society, 1939). A very useful manual by one of the great teachers in the field.

ENGEL, Lehman, *Music for Classical Tragedy* (New York, Harold Flammer, Inc., 1953).

EWER, Monica, *Play Production for Everyone* (London, Labour Publishing Company, 1924). A widely used elementary monograph.

GASSNER, John, *Producing the Play, with New Scene Technician's Handbook by Philip Barber,* rev. ed. (New York, The Dryden Press, Inc., 1953).

GRUVER, Bert, *The Stage Manager's Handbook* (New York, Harper & Brothers, 1953).

HEWITT, Barnard, *The Art and Craft of Play Production* (Philadelphia, J. B. Lippincott Company, 1940). This book applies the "problem" or "solution" approach to play production. It includes material on the type and structure of drama and a chapter on staging period plays.

———, FOSTER, J. F., and WOLLE, Muriel Sibell, *Play Production: Theory and Practice* (Philadelphia, J. B. Lippincott Company, 1952). A statement of the basic theories and techniques of theatre arts, similar to Bernard Hewitt's earlier work, *The Art and Craft of Play Production.*

HUGHES, Glenn, *The Penthouse Theatre: Its History and Technique* (New York, Samuel French, Inc., 1942). The story of the development of this "center-staging" idea at the University of Washington and the building of the interesting theatre to house the productions. It includes a discussion of the technique of production without a stage by an outstanding teacher who made a great success with this method.

HUNT, Hugh, *The Director in the Theatre* (London, Routledge and Kegan Paul, 1954). An excellent book on directing by one of England's foremost modern directors. The chapters were originally delivered as lectures before the Department of Drama at the University of Bristol.

JONES, Charles T. H., and WILSON, Don, *Musico-Dramatic Producing* (Chicago, Gamble Hinged Music Company, Inc., 1930). A useful work on the staging of the musical show.

JONES, Margo, *Theatre-in-the-Round* (New York, Farrar & Rinehart, Inc., 1951).

KELLY, Mary, *How to Make a Pageant* (New York, Pitman Publishing

Corp., 1937). A useful guide for the teacher or director who is called upon to prepare and produce pageants.

KNIGHT, George Wilson, *Principles of Shakespearian Production with Especial Reference to the Tragedies* (New York, The Macmillan Company, 1936). This book contains many good hints on the staging of Elizabethan plays in general.

KROWS, Arthur Edwin, *Play Production in America* (New York, Henry Holt & Company, Inc., 1916). Front-of-the-house and backstage methods in the commercial theatre of the period before the First World War.

LEES, C. Lowell, *Play Production and Direction* (Englewood Cliffs, N.J., Prentice-Hall, Inc., 1948).

MATHER, Charles Chambers, SPAULDING, Alice H., and SKILLEN, Melita H., *Behind the Footlights: A Book on the Technique of Dramatics* (Morristown, N.J., Silver Burdett Company, 1935). A work especially devoted to school dramatics.

MITCHELL, Roy E., *Shakespeare for Community Players* (New York, E. P. Dutton & Company, Inc., 1929). A very helpful work on producing Shakespearian plays. It contains useful references and bibliographies.

NAPIER, Frank, *Curtains for Stage Settings* (London, Frederick Muller, Ltd., 1937). A very good aid to the director who, from choice or necessity, produces a show in drapes. The illustrations are especially helpful.

———, *Noises Off: A Handbook of Sound Effects* (London, Frederick Muller, Ltd., 1936).

NELMS, Henning, *Play Production* (New York, Barnes & Noble, Inc., 1950). A presentation of basic materials on directing and production in concise form similar to that employed in the Barnes and Noble outlines of other college subjects.

PARSONS, Charles S., *Amateur Stage Management and Production* (London, Sir Isaac Pitman & Sons, Ltd., 1931). A helpful work on directing and production.

PURDOM, Charles B., *Producing Plays* (New York, E. P. Dutton & Company, Inc., 1930).

RAINE, James Watt, *Bible Dramatics* (New York, D. Appleton–Century Company, 1927). Very helpful for the church drama leader and for the director in a church school.

RICKETT, Edmond W., and HOOGLAND, Benjamin T., *Let's Do Some Gilbert and Sullivan* (New York, Coward-McCann, Inc., 1940). A practical production handbook with illustrations.

RUSSELL, Mary M., *Producing Your Own Plays* (New York, R. R. Smith, Inc., 1931).

Schonberger, Emanuel D., *Play Production for Amateurs* (New York, Thomas Nelson & Sons, 1938).

Selden, Samuel, *First Principles of Play Direction* (Chapel Hill, University of North Carolina Press, 1937). A very good brief treatment by an outstanding teacher and director. This manual supersedes the one prepared by F. H. Koch in 1922, listed above.

———, *The Stage in Action* (New York, Appleton-Century-Crofts, Inc., 1941). One of the most mature treatments of acting and directing that we have. Both actor and director will profit from reading it.

Shay, Frank, *The Practical Theatre* (New York, D. Appleton–Century Company, 1926).

Smith, Milton, *Play Production: For Little Theatres, Schools, and Colleges* (New York, Appleton-Century-Crofts, Inc., 1948). A thoroughly practical and well-illustrated elementary book on direction and stage production.

Stratton, Clarence, *Producing in Little Theatres* (New York, Henry Holt & Company, Inc., 1921). An early general work on direction and production.

Taylor, Emerson Gifford, *Practical Stage Directing for Amateurs* (New York, E. P. Dutton & Company, Inc., 1916). One of the earliest guides for the director published in America. Still useful because it was written on the basis of sound practical experience.

Volbach, Walther R., *Problems of Opera Production* (Fort Worth, Texas, Texas Christian University Press, 1953).

Watkins, Ronald, *On Producing Shakespeare* (New York, W. W. Norton & Company, Inc., 1951). A discussion of practical problems in the staging of Shakespeare's plays.

Whanslaw, H. W., *Everybody's Theatre* (London, Wells Gardner, Darton & Company, Ltd., 1923). A brief general guide to direction and production.

———, *Bankside Stage-Book* (London, Wells Gardner, Darton & Company, Ltds., 1924). Hints on staging Shakespeare.

Whiting, Frank M., *An Introduction to the Theatre* (New York, Harper & Brothers, 1954).

HISTORY AND ART OF THE THEATRE

Altman, George, Freud, Ralph, and Macgowan, Kenneth, *Theatre Pictorial* (Berkeley and Los Angeles, University of California Press, 1953). A history of theatre and stage production in pictures.

Appia, Adolphe, *Die Musik und die Inscenierung* (München, F. Bruckmann, 1899). This book, now out of print, was a very important work in forwarding the "New Movement" in the theatre on the Continent.

Appia and Gordon Craig were two of the foremost prophets of this new theatre.

BOWERS, Faubion, *Japanese Theatre* (New York, Hermitage House, 1952). Chapter V deals with the staging of Kabuki—design of costumes, make-up, settings, dance movements, and "poses." See Earle Ernst entry following.

BURTON, Elizabeth, *The Pageant of Elizabethan England,* ill'd. by Felix Kelly (New York, Charles Scribner's Sons, 1958). With its excellent text and profuse illustrations of houses, furniture, clothing, and other aspects and accessories of Elizabethan life, this is a most valuable book for the director and designer.

CARTER, Huntly, *The New Spirit in Drama and Art* (London, F. Palmer, 1912). An early and important statement of the "New Movement" presented in English.

———, *The New Spirit in the European Theatre, 1914–1924* (New York, George H. Doran Company, 1926). A further elaboration of the above work applied specifically to the theatre.

CHANDLER, Frank W., *Modern Continental Playwrights* (New York, Harper & Brothers, 1931). This book is by all odds the best one-volume study of the modern continental European drama and dramatists in print. Its extensive bibliographies of plays and their English translations, of works on the various playwrights, and of general works on the modern theatre and drama make it an invaluable tool.

CHENEY, Sheldon, *Modern Art and Theatre* (Scarborough-on-the-Hudson, N.Y., The Sleepy Hollow Press, 1921). Cheney was one of the first apostles of the "New Movement" in America.

———, *Stage Decoration* (New York, The John Day Company, 1928).

———, *The New Movement in the Theatre* (New York, Mitchell Kennerley, 1914). An early and provocative work.

———, *The Art Theatre* (New York, Alfred A. Knopf, Inc. 1925). Written back in that period when it seemed important to try to make distinctions between the "art theatre" and the commercial. This book should be read along with Lee Simonson's *The Stage Is Set.* Simonson holds that Cheney, like other prophets and apostles of the "new theatre," theorizes without facts. Nevertheless, Cheney's books are stimulating to the director.

———, *The Theatre* (New York, Longmans, Green & Company, Inc., 1929). A one-volume outline history from its beginning to the present time, now published in an inexpensive reprint. Not accurate enough for scholarly work, but helpful to the beginning student.

———, *The Theatre, Three Thousand Years of Drama, Acting and Stagecraft,* rev. and enl. ed. (New York, Longmans, Green & Company, Inc., 1952).

CLARK, Barrett H., *A Study of the Modern Drama,* rev. ed. (New York, D. Appleton–Century Company, 1938). A standard handbook on the modern drama, European and American. An excellent aid for the director and for students. The bibliographies are extensive.

CRAIG, Gordon, *Towards a New Theatre* (New York, J. M. Dent & Sons, Ltd., 1913). An early work setting forth the ideas and theories of one of the chief prophets of the "New Movement." Craig's works are often incoherent and frequently entirely impractical, but they have had a stimulating influence on the art of the modern theatre. For a searching criticism of Craig's theories, see Simonson's *The Stage Is Set.*

———, *The Theatre Advancing* (Boston, Little, Brown & Company, 1919).

———, *Scene* (London, Humphrey Milford, Oxford University Press, 1923).

———, *On the Art of the Theatre* (New York, Dodd, Mead & Company, 1925). These four books by one of the most widely discussed insurgents in the modern theatre are illustrated by himself. They are stimulating to the mature and experienced theatre worker, but are not books for beginners.

DICKINSON, Thomas H., *An Outline of Contemporary Drama* (Boston, Houghton Mifflin Company, 1927). A good handbook for the student. Helpful to teachers and directors.

———, *The Insurgent Theatre* (New York, B. W. Huebsch, 1917). An early American study of the "free theatre movement."

DOWNER, Alan, *The Art of the Play* (New York, Henry Holt & Company, Inc., 1955). Valuable for its introductory interpretations of nine plays included in the volume.

DRINKWATER, John, *Theatre-Going* (Boston, Houghton Mifflin Company, 1927). An essay on the theatre and the enjoyment of the theatre by an outstanding modern English poet and playwright.

DUKES, Ashley, *Drama* (New York, Henry Holt & Company, 1927). A study of drama as written for the theatre by a student of the modern drama.

———, *Modern Dramatists* (Chicago, C. H. Sergel & Company, 1912). An early study by an American of the modern dramatists who had appeared in Europe. Stimulating essays on the chief dramatists from Ibsen to Shaw.

———, *The Youngest Drama* (Chicago, C. H. Sergel & Company, 1924). A continuation of the above volume to include the newer drama and the more recent playwrights.

ERNST, Earle, *The Kabuki Theatre* (New York, Oxford University

Press, 1956). A history and a full discussion of staging in this famous form of Japanese theatre. The best account available. See entry on Faubion Bowers.

FREEDLEY, George, and REEVES, John A., *A History of the Theatre* (New York, Crown Publishers, 1941). This volume is by all odds the best single-volume history of the theatre in English. It is written with discrimination by two accomplished students of the theatre and is copiously and well illustrated. It has an excellent select bibliography on theatre history. Playwrights and plays are discussed in connection with the theatre of their respective periods.

GOLDBERG, Isaac, *The Drama of Transition* (Cincinnati, Stewart & Kidd Company, 1922). A thoughtful treatment of the new forms, types, and themes appearing in the modern drama and theatre.

GREGOR, Joseph, ed., *Monumenta Scenica: Denkmäler des Theaters,* Twelve portfolios (Vienna, Piper & Company, 1925–30). These beautifully reproduced pictures of theatre settings and decorations, in black and white and in color, assembled and edited by Joseph Gregor, are invaluable for the historian of the theatre and especially for designers.

———, *Monumenta Scenica: The Art of the Theatre,* New Series I, (Vienna, Giuseppe Galli-Bibiena, 1954). This new series contains an "Introduction" by Joseph Gregor. A set of the original *Monumenta Scenica,* now out of print, and the New Series may be secured from Samuel J. Hume, Book Dealer, Berkeley, California. Of course the original twelve portfolios are not always available.

GUTHRIE, Tyron, DAVIES, Robertson, and MACDONALD, Grant, *Renown at Stratford* (Toronto, Clarke, Irwin and Company, Ltd., 1953).

——, *Twice Have the Trumpets Sounded* (Toronto, Clarke, Irwin and Company, Ltd., 1954). These two books comprise a record of the first two years of Shakespearian productions at Stratford, Ontario.

HENDERSON, Archibald, *The Changing Drama* (Cincinnati, Stewart & Kidd Company, 1919). An excellent study of the changes that have occurred in the modern drama since Ibsen, by the biographer of George Bernard Shaw.

HEWITT, Barnard, *Theatre U.S.A., 1668–1957* (New York, McGraw-Hill Book Company, 1959). A comprehensive survey of the operations of the American theatre by a leader in the academic theatre and a well-known scholar.

HUGHES, Glenn, *The Story of the Theatre* (New York, Samuel French, Inc., 1928). An elementary history of the theatre from the beginnings to the present day.

ISAACS, Edith J. R., ed., *Theatre* (Boston, Little, Brown & Company,

1927). A series of thought-provoking essays on the theatre by outstanding authorities edited by the well-known former editor of *Theatre Arts.*

JAMESON, M. Storm, *Modern Drama in Europe* (New York, Harcourt, Brace & Company, 1920). The backgrounds of the modern drama and its development from the time of Ibsen.

JONES, Robert Edmond, *Drawings for the Theatre* (New York, Theatre Arts, Inc., 1925). A collection of designs by one of the leading stage artists of this country. A director will derive profit from studying these.

KOMISARJEVSKY, Theodore, and SIMONSON, Lee, *Settings and Costumes of the Modern Stage* (London, The Studio, Ltd.; New York, Studio Publications, Inc., 1933). Another stimulating collection of illustrations with good introductions and commentaries.

KOMISSARZHEVSKII, Fedor Fedorovich, *Myself and the Theatre* (New York, E. P. Dutton & Company, Inc., *c.* 1930). An autobiography from which the director may learn much about what not to do in the theatre and perhaps something about what to do.

LANGNER, Lawrence, *The Magic Curtain* (New York, E. P. Dutton & Company, Inc., 1951). An account of The Theatre Guild by one of its organizers.

LEWISOHN, Ludwig, *The Modern Drama* (New York, The Viking Press, Inc., 1915). An early study by a foremost student of the modern drama and theatre.

———, *The Drama and the Stage* (New York, Harcourt, Brace & Company, 1922).

MACGOWAN, Kenneth, *The Theatre of Tomorrow* (New York, Boni & Liveright, 1921). An interpretation of the modern movement in the theatre that had considerable influence in the development of the contemporary stage in this country. Beautifully illustrated.

———, and JONES, Robert Edmond, *Continental Stagecraft* (New York, Harcourt, Brace & Company, 1922). Another book that helped to open American eyes as to what could be accomplished in the theatre.

MANTZIUS, Karl, *A History of Theatrical Art,* translated from the German by Louise von Cossel, 6 vols. (London, Gerald Duckworth and Company, 1903–1921). An extended history of the theatre, including the oriental and the occidental. Many of the short histories are really based on this work and reproduce its inaccuracies. Reissued in the United States around 1936.

MILLER, Anna Irene, *The Independent Theatre in Europe, 1887 to the Present* (New York, Ray Long & Richard R. Smith, Inc., 1931). An extremely valuable work for the director, teacher, and student. A thorough study of the independent theatres, their organizations and management, their creeds and theories, their programs and repertories, and their successes and failures. An example of a well-written and interesting scholarly study. The extensive bibliographies in the Appendix are very valuable.

MODERWELL, H. K., *The Theatre of Today* (New York, Dodd, Mead & Company, 1927). A comprehensive account of the modern movement in the theatre. Contains discussions of scenery and lighting now somewhat out of date but still useful. Well illustrated.

MOODY, Richard, *America Takes the Stage: Romanticism in American Drama and Theatre, 1750–1900* (Bloomington, Indiana University Press, 1955).

MOREHOUSE, Ward, *Matinee Tomorrow: Fifty Years of Our Theatre* (New York, Whittlesey House, McGraw-Hill Book Company, Inc., 1949). An informal and entertaining account of American theatre during the first half of the present century.

NICOLL, Allardyce, *The Development of the Theatre,* new rev. ed. (New York, Harcourt, Brace & Company, 1937). An authoritative and scholarly discussion of the development of the physical theatre in Europe from the time of the Greeks to the present day. Beautifully and effectively illustrated.

———, *World Drama: From Aeschylus to Anouilh* (London, George G. Harrap & Company, Ltd., 1949). A comprehensive treatment of the history of theatre and drama from the Greeks to the present day.

PALMER, John Leslie, *Studies in the Contemporary Theatre* (Boston, Little, Brown & Company, 1927). A stimulating book on the theatre and the drama in France after the First World War.

———, *The Future of the Theatre* (London, G. Bell & Sons, Ltd., 1913). Not all of the prophecies and predictions herein presented have been fulfilled.

PHELPS, William Lyon, *The Twentieth Century Theatre* (New York, The Macmillan Company, 1918). Another book that helped to make the modern European drama and dramatists more widely known in this country.

SELDEN, Samuel, and SPHANGOS, Mary Tom, *Frederick Henry Koch: Pioneer Playmaker* (Chapel Hill, University of North Carolina Press, 1954). A biography of a leader in the American academic theatre.

SIMONSON, Lee, *The Stage Is Set* (New York, Harcourt, Brace & Company, 1932). A sane and well-written work on the theory of stage design and art of the theatre by one of America's foremost professional designers, who is at the same time a thinking man widely acquainted with the findings of modern scholarly research usually unknown to some theorizers in the theatre. Every director and theatre artist should read this book carefully.

SMITH, Cecil, *Musical Comedy in America* (New York, Theatre Arts Inc., 1950). An historical survey of the type from *The Black Crook* to *South Pacific.*

STANISLAVSKY, Constantine, *My Life in Art* (Boston, Little, Brown & Company, 1927). The autobiography of the cofounder and director of the Moscow Art Theatre. A helpful general work for directors, despite all the nonsense talked and written about "the Stanislavsky system."

SPRAGUE, Arthur Colby, *Shakespeare and the Actors: The Stage Business in His Plays, 1660–1905* (Cambridge, Harvard University Press, 1944). A scholarly examination of the stage business used by the great actors in the interpretation of Shakespeare's plays since the time of Betterton.

STRATTON, Clarence, *Theatron: An Illustrated Record* (New York, Henry Holt & Company, Inc., 1928). A record of artistic productions in the professional and nonprofessional theatre of this country.

VARDAC, A. Nicholas, *Stage to Screen: Theatrical Method from Garrick to Griffith* (Cambridge, Harvard University Press, 1949). An excellent discussion of the staging of nineteenth-century plays.

WALLACE, Karl R., ed., *A History of Speech Education in America* (New York, Appleton-Century-Crofts, Inc., 1954). Part III deals with the background and growth of the educational theatre.

WEBSTER, Margaret, *Shakespeare without Tears* (New York, McGraw-Hill Book Company, Inc., 1942). An eminent contemporary director's interpretation of Shakespeare's plays as she sees them presented on the stage. Among numerous other productions Miss Webster directed the Evans production of *Richard II* and the full-length *Hamlet,* and the Paul Robeson production of *Othello.* Her book is a stimulating aid to the advanced director.

WISNER, Payne Kinne, *George Pierce Baker and the American Theatre* (Cambridge, Harvard University Press, 1954). A biography of the founder of the American academic theatre.

YOUNG, Stark, *Theatre Practice* (New York, Charles Scribner's Sons, 1926). A highly theoretical but stimulating work for advanced directors.

———, *The Flower in Drama and Glamour: Theatre Essays and Criticisms.* Rev. ed. (New York, Charles Scribner's Sons, 1955).

ZUNG, Cecelia S. L., *Secrets of the Chinese Drama* (Shanghai, Kelly and Walsh, Ltd., 1937). Probably the best book in English on the technique and structure of the Chinese drama. Detailed analysis of the stylized technique of the actor, as well as of the other features of Chinese stage production.

ACTING

ALBERTI, Madame Eva, *A Handbook of Acting* (New York, Samuel French, Inc., 1932).

ALBRIGHT, H. D., *Working Up A Part: A Manual for the Beginning Actor* (Boston, Houghton Mifflin Company, 1947).

ANDERSON, Virgil A., *Training the Speaking Voice* (New York, Oxford University Press, 1942).

BARRY, Philip Beaufroy, *99 Points for Amateur Actors* (London, Samuel French, Inc., 1936).

BATTYE, Marguerite, *Stage Movement* (London, Herbert Jenkins, 1954).

BOLESLAVSKY, Richard, *Acting: The First Six Lessons* (New York, Theatre Arts, Inc., 1933).

BOSWORTH, Halliam, *Technique in Dramatic Art* (New York, The Macmillan Company, 1934).

BRIDGE, William H., *Actor in the Making: A Handbook on Improvization and Other Techniques of Development* (Boston, The Expression Company, 1936).

CALVERT, Louis, *Problems of the Actor* (New York, Henry Holt & Company, 1918).

CAMPBELL, Wayne, *Amateur Acting and Play Production* (New York, The Macmillan Company, 1931).

CARROLL, Sidney W., *Acting for the Stage,* Foreword by St. John Ervine (New York, Pitman Publishing Corp., 1939).

CARTMELL, Van H., *A Handbook for the Amateur Actor* (Garden City, N.Y., Doubleday & Company, Inc., 1936).

CHALMERS, Helena, *Modern Acting* (New York, D. Appleton–Century Company, 1930).

CHEKHOV, Michael, *To the Actor: On the Technique of Acting* (New York, Harper & Brothers, 1953).

COLE, Toby, and CHINOY, Helen Krich, eds., *Actors on Acting: Theories, Techniques, and Practices of the World's Great Actors* (New York, Crown Publishers, Inc., 1949). A collection of essays and articles by actors on acting and by critics on the art of the actor.

COLVAN, E. B. (Zeke), *Face the Footlights! A New and Practical Approach to Acting* (New York, McGraw-Hill Book Company, Inc., 1940).

COSGROVE, Frances, ed., *Scenes for Student Actors; Dramatic Selections from New Plays,* 5 vols. (New York, Samuel French, Inc., 1934–44).

CRAFTON, Allen, and ROYER, Jessica, *Acting: A Book for Beginners* (New York, F. S. Crofts & Co., 1928).

CRAUFORD, Lane, *Acting: Its Theory and Practice; with Illustrative*

Examples of Players Past and Present (New York, R. R. Smith, Inc., 1930).

CROCKER, Charlotte, FIELDS, Victor Alexander, and BROOMALL, Will, *Taking the Stage: Self Development through Dramatic Art* (New York, Pitman Publishing Corp., 1939).

D'ANGELO, Aristide, *The Actor Creates* (New York, Samuel French, Inc., 1939).

DILLON, Josephine (Gable), *Modern Acting* (Englewood Cliffs, N.J., Prentice-Hall, Inc., 1940).

EUSTIS, Morton, *Players at Work* (New York, Theatre Arts, Inc., 1937).

FRANKLIN, Miriam A., *Rehearsal: The Principles and Practice of Acting for the Stage,* rev. ed. (Englewood Cliffs, N.J., Prentice-Hall, Inc., 1942).

GILDER, Rosamond, *John Gielgud's Hamlet* (New York, Oxford University Press, 1937).

HANES, Ernest, and TALLMAN, Raymond J., *The Laboratory Stage* (New York, Dramatists Play Service, Inc., 1940).

HARDEN, Edwin Lyle, *Practice in Dramatics: Selections for Study of Dramatic Values* (Boston, Walter H. Baker Company, 1936).

HORNBLOW, Arthur, *Training for the Stage* (Philadelphia, J. B. Lippincott Company, 1916).

HUTCHINSON, Ann, *Labanotation* (New York, New Directions, 1954). A system of notation for the purpose of recording dance movement.

IRVINE, Harry, *The Actor's Art and Job* (New York, E. P. Dutton & Company, Inc., 1942).

JAMES, Henry, *The Scenic Art: Notes on Acting and the Drama.* Edited with an Introduction and Notes by Alan Wade (New Brunswick, Rutgers University Press, 1948). Essays and articles by the great novelist, who also wrote plays, on actors, acting, and the art of the drama. Useful also for its discussions of the techniques of drama.

KESTER, Katherine, *Problem-Projects in Acting* (New York, Samuel French, Inc., 1937).

KJERBULL-PETERSEN, Loving, *Psychology of Acting: A Consideration of Its Principles as an Art.* Translated from the German by Sarah T. Barrows (Boston, The Expression Company, 1935).

LATHAM, Jean Lee, *Do's and Don'ts of Drama: Five Hundred and Fifty-five Pointers for Beginning Actors and Directors* (Chicago, Dramatic Publishing Company, 1935).

LEES, C. Lowell, *A Primer of Acting* (Englewood Cliffs, N.J., Prentice-Hall, Inc., 1940).

LEWES, George Henry, *On Actors and the Art of Acting* (New York, Brentano's, 1875). One of the older books, especially useful in the staging of eighteenth- and nineteenth-century plays.

Lowther, James B., *Dramatic Scenes from Athens to Broadway* (New York, Longmans, Green & Company, Inc., 1937).

Lutz, Florence, *The Technique of Pantomime* (Berkeley, Calif., Sather Gate Book Shop Publishers, 1927).

McGaw, Charles, *Acting Is Believing* (New York, Rinehart & Company, Inc., 1955).

Mackay, Edward, and Mackay, Alice, *Elementary Principles of Acting* (New York, Samuel French, Inc., 1934).

Mackenzie, Frances, *The Amateur Actor* (London and New York, Thomas Nelson and Sons, Ltd., 1935).

Morosco, Selma Paley, and Lounsbury, Athea, *Stage Technique Made Easy* (New York, M. S. Mill Company, Inc., 1942).

Pratt, Harriett, comp., *Notes on Acting with Maria Ouspenskaya* (Hollywood, California, American Repertory Theatre Magazine, 1954).

Rosenstein, Sophie, Haydon, Larrae A., and Sparrow, Wilbur, *Modern Acting: A Manual* (New York, Samuel French, Inc., 1936).

Selden, Samuel, *First Steps in Acting* (New York, Appleton-Century-Crofts, Inc., 1947).

———, *The Stage in Action* (New York, Appleton-Century-Crofts, Inc., 1940).

Shawn, Ted, *Every Little Movement* (Pittsfield, Mass., Privately Printed, 1954).

Silverthorne, Carolyn, *The Actor's Handbook* (Boston, The Expression Company, 1939).

Southwick, Frank Townsend, *Elocution and Action* (Belmar, N.J., Edgar S. Werner & Company, 1924).

Speight, Robert, *Acting: Its Idea, Tradition, Technique* (London, Cassell & Company, 1939).

Stanislavski, Constantin, *An Actor Prepares,* translated by Elizabeth Reynolds Hapgood (New York, Theatre Arts Inc., 1936).

Strickland, F. Cowles, *The Technique of Acting* (New York, McGraw-Hill Book Company, Inc., 1956).

Todd, Mabel Ellsworth, *The Thinking Body* (New York, Paul B. Hoeber, Inc., 1937).

Watkins, Dwight Everett, and Karr, Harrison M., *Stage Fright and What to Do about It* (Boston, The Expression Company, 1940).

White, Edwin C., *Problems of Acting and Play Production* (New York, Pitman Publishing Corp., 1938).

Woolbert, Charles H., and Nelson, Severina E., *Art of Interpretative Speech: Principles and Practices of Effective Reading,* 4th ed. (New York, Appleton-Century-Crofts, Inc., 1956).

STRUCTURE AND TECHNIQUE OF DRAMA

ANDERSON, Maxwell, *The Essence of Tragedy and Other Footnotes and Capers* (Washington, D.C., Anderson House, 1937). This book contains a number of essays by the famous American dramatist. His essay "The Essence of Tragedy" should be read by all prospective playwrights and directors.

ANDREWS, Charlton, *The Technique of Play Writing* (Springfield, Mass., The Home Correspondence School, 1915).

ARCHER, William, *Play-Making: A Manual of Craftsmanship* (Boston, Small, Maynard & Company, 1912). Despite the fact that Archer tends to disregard any other form or style of drama than the "well-made play," this is an informative and worthwhile book.

ARISTOTLE, *Poetics* (*De Poetica*), translated by Ingram Bywater and republished in *The Basic Works of Aristotle,* edited by Richard McKeon (New York, Random House, 1941). There are, of course, many translations of Aristotle's *Poetics.* Perhaps the one most often consulted is that by Butcher, which is in certain respects more Butcher than Aristotle. See the reference under Lane Cooper and John Gassner below.

BAKER, George Pierce, *Dramatic Technique* (Boston, Houghton Mifflin Company, 1919). This is the standard book in the field; it is used, or at least consulted, by most teachers of playwriting. Like Archer's *Play-Making,* it perhaps overemphasizes the "well-made" technique and structure.

BENTLEY, Eric, *The Playwright As Thinker* (New York, Reynal & Company, 1953).

———, *In Search of Theatre* (New York, Alfred A. Knopf, Inc., 1953).

BUSFIELD, Roger M., Jr., *The Playwright's Art, Stage, Radio, Television, Motion Pictures* (New York, Harper & Brothers, *c.* 1958).

BURTON, Richard, *How to See a Play* (New York, The Macmillan Company, 1929).

CANNON, Fanny, *Writing and Selling a Play* (New York, Henry Holt & Company, Inc., 1915). An old and superficial treatment.

CLARK, Barrett H., *European Theories of the Drama, with a Supplement on the American Drama,* rev. ed. (New York, Crown Publishers, 1947). The best comprehensive collection of theory and criticism of drama available. Contains historical and biographical notes and extensive bibliographical materials.

COOPER, Lane, *Aristotle on the Art of Poetry* (Boston, Ginn & Company, 1913). This work is called "an amplified version with supplementary illustrations for students of English." It is Aristotle through the eyes of Lane COOPER.

CRANE, R. S., *The Language of Criticism and the Structure of Poetry* (Toronto, University of Toronto Press, 1953). The most adequate and complete exposition of the Aristotelian theory of tragedy available.

DIXON, William Macneile, *Tragedy* (New York, Longmans, Green & Company, Inc., 1924). A helpful work to the student seeking to understand the meaning and significance of tragedy. Treats especially the three great writers of Greek tragedy and Shakespeare.

EASTMAN, Max, *Enjoyment of Laughter* (New York, Simon & Schuster, Inc., 1936).

EGRI, Lojos, *How to Write a Play* (New York, Simon & Schuster, Inc., 1942).

ELIOT, T. S., *Poetry and Drama* (Cambridge, Harvard University Press, 1951).

FERGUSSON, Francis, *The Idea of a Theatre* (Princeton, N.J., Princeton University Press, 1949). Reprinted in a paper-back edition by Doubleday Anchor Books, Garden City, N.Y., Doubleday & Company, Inc., 1953.

GASSNER, John, ed., *Aristotle's Theory of Poetry and Fine Art.* Critical Text and Translation by S. H. Butcher, prefatory essay, "Aristotelian Literary Criticism." 4th ed., (New York, Dover Publications, 1951). Often Butcher, rather than Aristotle.

———, *The Theatre in Our Times* (New York, Crown Publishers, Inc., 1954).

HAMILTON, Clayton, *So You're Writing a Play!* (Boston, Little, Brown & Company, 1935).

———, *The Theory of the Theatre* (New York, Henry Holt & Company, Inc., 1939). This combined edition includes four of Clayton Hamilton's previously published studies: *The Theory of the Theatre,* first published in 1910; *Studies in Stagecraft,* 1914; *Problems of the Playwright,* 1917; and *Seen on the Stage,* 1920. The essays are very helpful for the beginning student in theatre and drama.

HENDERSON, Archibald, *The Changing Drama* (New York, Henry Holt & Company, Inc., 1914).

HENNEQUIN, Alfred, *The Art of Playwriting* (Boston, Houghton Mifflin Company, 1890).

HILLEBRAND, Harold Newcomb, *Writing the One-Act Play: A Manual for Beginners* (New York, Alfred A. Knopf, Inc., 1925). One of the most useful books in the field by an eminent scholar and teacher.

HOARE, John, *The Psychology of Playwriting* (New York, Dramatists Play Service, Inc., 1949). Aimed at the young playwright who is just beginning.

HOPKINS, Arthur, *How's Your Second Act?* (New York, Philip Goodman Company, 1918). Useful to the director as well as the playwright.

HUNT, Elizabeth R., *The Play of Today* (London, John Lane Company, 1913).

JONES, Henry Arthur, *The Renascence of the English Drama* (London, The Macmillan Company, 1895). An interesting study by a famous playwright.

KOZLENKO, William, ed., *The One-Act Play Today* (New York, Harcourt, Brace & Company, 1938). This book is made up of a series of provocative and stimulating essays by various critics, playwrights, and other authorities on the one-act play. Part I deals with technique and forms; Part II deals with scope; and Part III is an historical survey.

KRONENBERGER, Louis, *The Thread of Laughter* (New York, Alfred A. Knopf, Inc., 1952).

KRUTCH, Joseph Wood, *The American Drama since 1918,* rev. ed. (New York, Random House, 1957). Probably the best single study of the contemporary American playwrights and their plays.

———, *"Modernism" in Modern Drama* (Ithaca, N.Y., Cornell University Press, 1953).

LAWSON, John Howard, *Theory and Technique of Playwriting* (New York, G. P. Putnam's Sons, 1936). A very good and useful book by a well-known American playwright. Despite the undue influence of Marxian dialectics upon the author, much of his theorizing is sound.

LEWIS, B. Roland, *The Technique of the One-Act Play* (Boston, John W. Luce & Company, 1918).

MACEWAN, Elias J., *Freytag's Technique of the Drama: An Exposition of Dramatic Composition and Art* (Chicago, S. C. Griggs & Company, 1895). This is a translation of the famous German work written by Gustav Greytag in 1863, and widely influential in this country and in England.

MACGOWAN, Kenneth, *A Primer of Playwriting* (New York, Random House, 1951). A text designed to aid the beginner in playwriting but valuable for the director as well.

MARX, Milton, *The Enjoyment of Drama* (New York, F. S. Crofts & Co., 1940). Written especially to enhance the appreciation of drama.

MATTHEWS, Brander, *The Short Story* (New York, American Book Company, 1907). Useful for its treatment of story and plot.

———, *A Study of the Drama* (Boston, Houghton Mifflin Company, 1910). An interesting and very useful study for the beginning student.

———, *The Development of the Drama* (New York, Charles Scribner's Sons, 1914). Another useful work for the beginning student.

———, *The Principles of Playmaking* (New York, Charles Scribner's Sons, 1919). An important study for the director and the playwright.

MEREDITH, George, *Essay on the Idea of Comedy and the Uses of the Comic Spirit* (New York, Charles Scribner's Sons, 1918). This famous essay by the eminent English novelist was first delivered as a lecture at the London Institution, February 1, 1877. It was published in London in 1903 by Constable and was republished in 1918 in The Modern Student's Library, edited with notes by Lane Cooper. The theory of comedy herein expressed is much too narrow, but the essay is nevertheless stimulating and useful.

MILLETT, Fred B., and BENTLEY, Gerald E., *The Art of the Drama* (New York, Appleton-Century-Crofts, Inc., 1935). A work written especially to aid students in the understanding and analysis of drama.

NICOLL, Allardyce, *Theory of Drama* (New York, Thomas Y. Crowell Company, 1931). A very useful book for all drama and theatre students.

OWEN, Harrison, *The Playwright's Craft* (London and New York, Thomas Nelson & Sons, 1940).

OWENS, Dale, comp., *Scenarists' Reference and Handy Book* (Hollywood, Calif., Select Press, 1940).

PAGE, Brett, *Writing for Vaudeville* (Springfield, Mass., The Home Correspondence School, 1915).

PRICE, W. T., *The Analysis of Play Construction and Dramatic Principle* (New York, Published by the author, 1908).

———, *The Philosophy of Dramatic Principle and Method* (New York, published by the author, 1911).

———, *The Technique of the Drama* (New York, Brentano's, 1905).

PRIOR, Moody E., *The Language of Tragedy* (New York, Columbia University Press, 1947).

QUILLER-COUCH, Sir Arthur, *On the Art of Writing* (New York, G. P. Putnam's Sons, 1916). Interesting materials by an eminent scholar and writer.

———, *Shakespeare's Workmanship* (New York, The Macmillan Company, 1931).

RAPHAELSON, Samuel, *The Human Nature of Playwriting* (New York, The Macmillan Co., 1949). Conversations with student on playwriting by the author of various plays and of *An Actor Prepares,* also aimed at the playwright.

ROWE, Kenneth Thorpe, *Write That Play* (New York and London, Funk & Wagnalls Company, 1939). Probably the best book in the field for the beginning student of playwriting and directing. The discussions are clear and well presented. The book contains several plays with analysis of the structure on pages opposite the text.

SCHEYER, Betty, *So You Want to Be a Playwright* (New York, Exposition Press, 1954).

SELDEN, Samuel, *An Introduction to Playwriting* (New York, Appleton-Century-Crofts, Inc., 1946).

SHAFTEL, George Armin, *Dynamics of Drama: Fundamentals of Writing Craftsmanship* (St. Louis, Comfor Press, 1942).

SOURIAU, Etienne, *Les Deux Cent Mille Situations Dramatique* (Paris, Bibliothèque d'Esthetique, Flammarion, 1950). A discussion by a philosopher of the basic structure of drama.

STUART, Donald Clive, *Development of Dramatic Art* (New York, D. Appleton–Century Company, 1928). A work on the development of dramatic structure from the days of the Greeks to the present time which no student of drama can afford to overlook.

THOMPSON, Alan Reynolds, *The Anatomy of Drama* (Berkeley, Calif., University of California Press, 1942). A book on structure and analysis by an outstanding teacher.

VAN DRUTEN, John, *Playwright at Work* (New York, Harper & Brothers, 1953).

VAUGHAN, Charles E., *Types of Tragic Drama* (New York, The Macmillan Company, 1924). A series of lectures delivered at the University of Leeds in 1906 and first printed in 1908. Deals with differences and similarities between classic and romantic tragedy.

WHITFIELD, G J. Newbold, *Introduction to Drama* (London and New York, Oxford University Press, 1940).

WILDE, Percival, *The Craftsmanship of the One-Act Play* (Boston, Little, Brown & Company, 1923). A guide for the playwright by a successful writer of one-act plays. The most extensive treatment of the one-act play yet written.

WOODBRIDGE, Elisabeth, *The Drama, Its Law and Technique* (Boston and Chicago, Allyn and Bacon, Inc., 1898). A widely used and helpful book.

ORGANIZATION, THEATRE MANAGEMENT, THE PROFESSION

BERNHEIM, Alfred L., *The Business of the Theatre* (New York, Actors Equity Association, 1932). Somewhat out of date but still contains valuable information.

DEAN, Alexander, *Little Theatre Organization and Management* (New York, D. Appleton–Century Company, 1926). Contains much of value to the director as well as the manager.

EUSTIS, Morton, *B'way, Inc!* (New York, Dodd, Mead & Company, 1934).

FLANAGAN, Hallie Ferguson, *Arena* (New York, Duell, Sloan & Pearce, Inc., 1940). The story of the Federal Theatre Project.

———, *Dynamo* (New York, Duell, Sloan & Pearce, Inc., 1943). An account of the history and activities of the Vassar Experimental Theatre.

HINSDELL, Oliver, *Making the Little Theatre Pay* (New York, Samuel French, Inc., 1925).

HUGHES, Glenn, *The Penthouse Theatre: Its History and Technique* (New York, Samuel French, Inc., 1942). An account of this well-known institution at the University of Washington.

MCCLEARY, Albert, and GLICK, Carl, *Curtains Going Up* (New York and Chicago, Pitman Publishing Corp., 1939). An account of some of the nonprofessional theatres in America. Not so well done as MacGowan's *Footlights across America.*

MACGOWAN, Kenneth, *Footlights across America* (New York, Harcourt, Brace & Company, c. 1929). This study was subsidized by the Rockefeller Foundation and done by an outstanding authority. A solid history of the nonprofessional theatre in America to 1925. Contains very valuable information for the director. See Anna Irene Miller's *The Independent Theatre in Europe* for a comparable study of the European nonprofessional theatre movement. Along with MacGowan's book one should read Helen Deutsch and Stella Hanau's *The Provincetown: A Story of the Theatre* (New York: Farrar & Rinehart, 1931); Susan Glaspell's *The Road to the Temple* (New York and Toronto, Frederick A. Stokes Company, 1941); and Walter Prichard Eaton's *The Theatre Guild: The First Ten Years* (New York, Brentano, 1929).

PERRY, Clarence Arthur, *The Work of the Little Theatre* (New York, Russell Sage Foundation, 1933).

SELDEN, Samuel, ed., *Organizing a Community Theatre* (Cleveland, Ohio, National Theatre Conference, 1945).

STANTON, Sanford E., *Theatre Management* (New York, D. Appleton–Century Company, 1929). Though somewhat out of date, this work is still a valuable account of professional practice.

TRAUBE, Shepard, *So You Want to Go into the Theatre* (New York, Little, Brown & Company, 1940). Every student who is contemplating a professional career in the theatre should read this book.

WELLS, Charles, *Drama Clubs Step by Step* (Boston, Walter H. Baker Company, 1933).

SCENERY

ADAMS, John Cranford, *The Globe Playhouse: Its Design and Equipment* (Cambridge, Mass., Harvard University Press, 1942).

ALBRIGHT, H. D., HALSTEAD, William P., and MITCHELL, Lee, *Principles of Theatre Art* (Boston, Houghton Mifflin Company, 1955). Has nine valuable chapters dealing with the organization of the theatre structure, the nature and function of design, and the practical solution of various problems in staging.

Altman, George, Freud, Ralph, Macgowan, Kenneth, and Melnitz, William, *Theater Pictorial* (Los Angeles, University of California Press, 1953).

Appia, Adolphe, *Adolphe Appia: A Portfolio of Reproductions* (Zurich, Orell-Fussli, 1929).

Architectural Forum, Theatre Reference Number (September, 1932).

Ashworth, Bradford, *Notes on Scene Painting,* Donald Oenslager, ed. (New Haven, Whitlock's, Inc., 1952). A small but valuable manual by a professional scenic artist of long experience.

Barber, Philip, *The New Scene Technician's Handbook* (see Gassner, John, *Producing the Play*).

Bel Geddes, Norman, Cole, Edward C., Lauterer, Arch, Chermayeff, Serge, and McCandless, Stanley, "Theatre Planning: A Symposium," *Educational Theatre Journal,* Vol. II, No. 1 (March, 1950), pp. 1–7. Several controversial and stimulating ideas.

Boyle, Walden P., *Central and Flexible Staging* (Los Angeles, University of California, 1956).

Buerki, F. A., *Stagecraft for Nonprofessionals,* rev. ed. (Madison, University of Wisconsin Press, 1956). A brief but very helpful guide.

Burris-Meyer, Elizabeth, *Color and Design in the Decorative Arts* (Englewood Cliffs, N.J., Prentice-Hall, Inc., 1935).

Burris-Meyer, Harold, and Cole, Edward C., *Scenery for the Theatre* (Boston, Little, Brown & Company, 1938). Unquestionably the most complete and detailed professional book on the construction and handling of scenery. Contains chapters on the organization of the professional and nonprofessional theatre, scenery planning and construction, stage machinery, rigging, properties, sound effects, the assembling and running of the show. Exceptionally well illustrated.

———, *Theatres and Auditoriums* (New York, Reinhold Publishing Corporation, 1949).

Cheney, Sheldon, *Stage Decoration* (New York, The John Day Company, Inc., 1928).

Cole, Wendell, "Some Contemporary Trends in Theatre Architecture," *Educational Theatre Journal,* Vol. VII, No. 1 (March, 1955), pp. 16–21.

Cornberg, Sol, and Gebauer, Emanuel L., *A Stage Crew Handbook* (New York, Harper & Brothers, 1941). A handy, easily understood manual on scenery and lighting, using the question-and-answer method of presentation. Contains many good drawings and a glossary of technical terms.

Crafton, Allen, and Royer, Jessica, *The Complete Acted Play: From*

Script to Final Curtain (New York, Appleton-Century-Crofts, Inc., 1943). Contains several good chapters on scenery.

CRAIG, Edward Gordon, *Scene* (New York, Oxford University Press, 1923).

EVANS, Ralph M., *An Introduction to Color* (New York, John Wiley & Sons, Inc., 1948). A thoroughly practical discussion of color theories as they apply to both light and pigment colors.

FRIEDERICH, Willard J., and FRASER, John H., *Scenery Design for the Amateur Stage* (New York, The Macmillan Company, 1950). A useful, practical manual.

FRY, Roger, *Vision and Design* (London, Chatto & Windus, 1920).

FUERST, Walter R., and HUME, Samuel J., *Twentieth Century Stage Decoration,* 2 vols. (New York, Alfred A. Knopf, Inc., 1928).

GASSNER, John, *Producing the Play,* rev. ed. (New York, The Dryden Press, Inc., 1953). The last part of this encyclopedic volume is given over to the first publication in book form of Philip Barber's *New Scene Technician's Handbook,* formerly available only as a mimeographed syllabus. A detailed and excellently illustrated treatment of scenery and property construction, sound effects, and lighting. In addition, Gassner's book contains many useful chapters on all phases of theatre production, including styles of drama, acting, directing, theatre organization, stage management, costuming, lighting, make-up, the dance, and radio production, by some of the foremost authorities in the theatre.

GRAVES, Maitland, *The Art of Color and Design* (New York, McGraw-Hill Book Company, Inc., 1941). Line, direction, shape, proportion, texture, value, color, analyzed according to repetition, harmony, gradation, and contrast. Good illustrations.

GREENBERG, Edward M., and RUBIN, Joel E., "Production Aspects of the Music Circus," *Educational Theatre Journal,* Vol. IV, No. 1 (March, 1952), pp. 26–32. Technical information for the larger arena.

HALSTEAD, William Perdue, *Stage Management for the Amateur Theatre* (New York, F. S. Crofts & Co., 1937). Contains valuable information on backstage organization, scene shifting, handling of properties and costumes, lighting, and sound effects.

HEFFNER, Hubert C., SELDEN, Samuel, and SELLMAN, Hunton D., *Modern Theatre Practice,* 4th ed. (New York, Appleton-Century-Crofts, Inc., 1959).

ISAACS, Edith J. R., ed., *Architecture for the New Theatre* (New York, Theatre Arts, Inc., 1935). Illuminating and stimulating articles on new trends in theatre design. Illustrated.

JACOBSON, Egbert, *The Science of Color* (Chicago, American Photo-Engravers Association, 1937).

JONES, Leslie Allen, *Scenic Design and Model Building* (Boston, Walter H. Baker Company, 1939).

JONES, Margo, *Theatre-in-the-Round* (New York, Rinehart & Company, Inc., 1951).

JONES, Robert Edmond, *Drawings for the Theatre* (New York, Theatre Arts, Inc., 1925).

KEPES, Gyorgy, *Language of Vision* (Chicago, P. Theobold, 1944).

KOMISARJEVSKY, Theodore, and SIMONSON, Lee, *Settings and Costumes of the Modern Stage* (London, The Studio, Ltd., 1933).

LEEPER, Janet, *Edward Gordon Craig: Designs for the Theatre* (London, Penguin Books, Ltd., 1948).

LUCKIESH, Matthew, *Light and Shade and Their Application* (New York, D. Van Nostrand Company, Inc., 1916).

MACGOWAN, Kenneth, *The Theatre of Tomorrow* (New York, Boni & Liveright, 1921).

———, and JONES, Robert Edmond, *Continental Stagecraft* (New York, Harcourt, Brace & Company, Inc., 1922).

National Theatre Conference, *Are You Going to Build a Theatre? A Bibliography* (Cleveland, National Theatre Conference, 1946).

NELMS, Henning, *A Primer of Stagecraft* (New York, Dramatists Play Service, 1941). One of the best handbooks available. Concise and accurate discussions of all technical matters. Especially well illustrated. Easy for beginners to use.

NICOLL, Allardyce, *The Development of the Theatre,* rev. ed. (New York, Harcourt, Brace & Company, Inc., 1947).

OENSLAGER, Donald, *Scenery Then and Now* (New York, W. W. Norton & Company, Inc., 1936).

PHILIPPI, Herbert, *Stagecraft and Scene Design* (Boston, Houghton Mifflin Company, 1953).

POPE, Arthur, *The Language of Drawing and Painting* (Cambridge, Mass., Harvard University Press, 1949).

ROBINSON, Horace W., "An Approach to Theatre Planning," *Educational Theatre Journal,* Vol. I, No. 2 (December, 1949), pp. 96–99.

SCHOLZ, Janos, ed., *Baroque and Romantic Stage Design* (New York, Herbert Bittner & Co., 1950).

SELDEN, Samuel, and SELLMAN, Hunton D., *Stage Scenery and Lighting: A Handbook for Nonprofessionals.* 3rd ed. (New York, Appleton-Century-Crofts, Inc., 1959). A thorough, detailed treatment of both scenery and lighting, containing many drawings and photographs.

SHERINGHAM, George, and LAVER, James, *Design in the Theatre* (London, The Studio, Ltd., 1927).

SIMONSON, Lee, *The Art of Scenic Design* (New York, Harper & Brothers, 1950).

SMITH, Milton M., *The Book of Play Production: For Little Theatres, Schools and Colleges* (New York, D. Appleton–Century Company, Inc., 1926). A good elementary book on amateur stagecraft. Practical, well illustrated.

Stanley Tool Guide (New Britain, Conn., Stanley Tools, Inc., 1942). Loose-leaf sheets fitting 8½″ x 11″ binder. Complete directions for the use of all common woodworking tools. Splendid illustrations. This company also publishes a handbook entitled *How to Work with Tools and Wood,* a useful guide for the scenery technician.

TEAGUE, Walter Dorwin, *Design This Day* (New York, Harcourt, Brace & Company, Inc., 1940).

WATKINS, Charles Law, *The Language of Design* (Washington, D.C., Phillips Memorial Gallery, 1946).

WILFRED, Thomas, "The Projected Setting," *Educational Theatre Journal,* Vol. VI, No. 2 (May, 1954), pp. 136–144.

LIGHTING

BENTHAM, Frederick, *Stage Lighting* (London, Sir Isaac Pitman & Brothers, 1957).

BOWMAN, Wayne, *Modern Theatre Lighting* (New York, Harper & Sons, 1950). A British text, particularly good on equipment.

Color as Light, International Printing Ink Corp., 1935. An elementary monograph on the physics of color.

ENGEL, Alfred von, *Bühnenbeleuchtung* (Leipzig, Hachmeister, 1926). Profusely illustrated.

EVANS, Ralph M., *An Introduction to Color* (New York, John Wiley & Sons, Inc., 1948). A thorough, well written discussion of the physics and psycho-physics of color.

FUCHS, Theodore, *Home-Built Lighting Equipment* (New York, Samuel French, Inc., 1939).

———, *Stage Lighting* (Boston, Little, Brown & Company, 1929). A comprehensive treatment of the subject with special emphasis on equipment.

GASSNER, John, *Producing the Play,* rev. ed. (New York, The Dryden Press, Inc., 1953). Several chapters on stage lighting.

HARTMAN, Louis, *Theatre Lighting: A Manual of the Stage Switchboard* (New York, D. Appleton–Century Company, Inc., 1930). Interesting reminiscences of the manner in which Belasco and Hartman achieved their effects.

HEWITT, Barnard, FOSTER, J. F., and WOLLE, Muriel S., *Play Production: Theory and Practice* (Philadelphia, J. B. Lippincott Co., 1952).

KNAPP, Jack Stuart, *Lighting the Stage with Homemade Equipment* (Boston, Walter H. Baker Company, 1933).

KRANICH, Frederick, *Buhnentechnik der Gegenwart* (Berlin, 1929 and 1933). Profusely illustrated. One can learn much about German theatre practice from the illustrations in this and the Engel volume, even if he cannot read German. This volume covers every aspect of theatre engineering, including large sections on lighting.

Light Sources Past and Present, G. E. Bulletin, LS 139 (General Electric Co., 1956). Useful for those interested in lamp history and recent design.

LUCKIESH, Matthew, *Color and Its Application* (New York, D. Van Nostrand Company, Inc., 1921). Good general background material.

———, *Color and Its Application,* 2d ed. (New York, D. Van Nostrand Company, Inc., 1921).

MCCANDLESS, Stanley R., *A Method of Lighting the Stage,* 3rd ed. (New York, Theatre Arts, Inc., 1947).

———, *A Syllabus of Stage Lighting,* 9th ed. (New Haven, Conn., Yale University Press, 1958). A sound, thorough text.

MOYER, Jas. A., and WOSTREH, John F., *Industrial Electricity and Wiring* (New York, McGraw-Hill Book Company, Inc., 1943).

RIDGE, C. Harold, and ALDRED, F. S., *Stage Lighting Principles and Practice* (London, Sir Isaac Pitman & Sons, 1940). A good British text, interesting largely for British terminology.

RUBIN, Joel E., and WATSON, Leland H., *Theatrical Lighting Practice* (New York, Theatre Arts Books, 1954). Covers arena, outdoor production, and television as well as stage lighting.

SELDEN, Samuel, and SELLMAN, Hunton D., *Stage Scenery and Lighting: A Handbook for Nonprofessionals,* 3rd ed. (New York, Appleton-Century-Crofts, Inc., 1958).

STURROCK, Walter, and STALEY, K. A., *Fundamentals of Light and Lighting,* G. E. Bulletin LD-2 (General Electric Co., 1956). Contains a useful discussion of the physics of light.

WEITZ, C. E., *Lamp Bulletin,* GE Bulletin LD 1 (General Electric Co., 1956). Characteristics and applications of various incandescent lamps and other light sources.

WILFRED, Thomas, *Projected Scenery* (Nyack, New York, Art Institute of Light, 1954).

WILLIAMS, R. Gillespie, *The Technique of Stage Lighting* (London, Sir Isaac Pitman & Sons, 1952). A British text, good on color and British practice.

———, *Lighting for Color and Form: Principles, Equipment and Applications* (London, Sir Isaac Pitman & Sons, 1954).

DESIGNING

BISHOP, A. Thornton, *Composition and Rendering* (New York, John Wiley & Son, Inc., 1933). Chapters on composition and rendering by a master draftsman. Part IV deals with composition in the theatre. Illustrated.

CLIFFORD, C. R., *Period Furnishings,* 4th ed. rev. and amend. (New York, Clifford & Lawton, Inc., 1927). An encyclopedia of historic decorations and furnishings. Fully illustrated.

DOW, Arthur Wesley, *Composition,* rev. and enl. (Garden City, New York, Doubleday, Doran & Company, Inc., 1924). A standard treatise on art structure. Illustrated.

EBERLEIN, Harold Donaldson, MCCLURE, Abbot, and HOLLOWAY, Edward Stratton, *The Practical Book of Interior Decoration* (Philadelphia, J. B. Lippincott Company, 1919). Probably the most comprehensive single book on the subject of room design. Includes an outline of the principal periods. Illustrated.

FIELD, Wooster Bard, *Architectural Drawing* (New York, McGraw-Hill Book Company, 1922). One of the best books on drafting. Includes, among others, chapters on the use of instruments, geometric methods, perspective, rendering, scale drawing, the orders, and lettering. Illustrated.

FLETCHER, Sir Banister, *A History of Architecture on the Comparative Method* (New York, Charles Scribner's Sons, 1929). A full and standard history of architectural styles in the principal countries of the world, with about 3500 illustrations.

FLORAN, Erle, *Cezanne's Composition* (Berkeley, University of California Press, 1943). A remarkable analysis, of particular interest to the scene designer who is concerned with similar problems of composition in depth. Paintings and photographs of the same scenes are compared.

GILMAN, Roger, *Great Styles of Interior Architecture* (New York, Harper & Brothers, 1924). A study of historic Italian, French, and English interiors, with their decoration and furnishing. Well illustrated.

GLASS, Frederick J., *Drawing, Design and Craft Work* (New York, Charles Scribner's Sons, 1927). A general guide. Illustrated.

GOULD, Mr. and Mrs. G. G., *The Period Furniture Handbook* (New York, Dodd, Mead & Company, Inc., 1928). A standard reference book. Some of the illustrations in this book offer suggestions of a fresh and dramatic nature.

PRICE, Charles Matlack, *The A B C of Architecture* (New York, E. P. Dutton & Company, Inc., 1927). A good primer of architecture. In addition to the chapters on history, it contains material on drafting. Very helpfully illustrated.

RICHMOND, L., and LITTLEJOHNS, J., *The Technique of Water-Colour Painting* (London, Isaac Pitman and Sons, 1925). A good book on water-color painting. Includes instruction in various techniques. Illustrated.

RINES, Frank M., *Drawing in Lead Pencil* (Pelham, N.Y., Bridgman Publishers, 1929). Another good book on freehand sketching. Illustrated.

SMITH, André, *The Scenewright* (New York, The Macmillan Company, 1926). A helpful handbook on practical model-making. The part on full-sized scenery is, however, rather elementary. Attractively illustrated.

WRIGHT, Richardson, and MCELROY, Margaret, eds., *House and Garden's Book of Color Schemes* (Greenwich, Conn., Condé Nast, 1929). An excellent book of suggestions for the designer and decorator. Profusely illustrated.

Periodicals of help to the scenic designer:

American Home
Architectural Forum, The
Architectural Record, The
Art and Archeology
Art and Decoration
Good Housekeeping
House Beautiful
House and Garden
National Geographic Magazine, The
Pencil Points
Studio, The
Theatre Arts Monthly
Travel

COSTUME AND MAKE-UP

ASHDOWN, Mrs. Charles H., *British Costume during Nineteen Centuries* (London, T. C. and E. C. Jack, 1910).

BAIRD, John F. *Make-up* (New York, Samuel French, Inc., 1930).

BARTON, Lucy, *Historic Costume for the Stage* (Boston, Walter H. Baker Company, 1935).

BOEHN, Max von, *Modes and Manners*, translated by Joan Joshua, 4 vols. (London, George G. Harrap & Company, Ltd., 1932–35).

BRADLEY, Carolyn G., *Western World Costume: An Outline History* (New York, Appleton-Century-Crofts, Inc., 1954).

BROOKE, Iris, *English Costume* (London, A. & C. Black, Ltd., 1930–35).

Calthrop, D. C., *English Costume* (London, A. & C. Black, Ltd., 1923).

Chalmers, Helena, *The Art of Make-up* (New York, D. Appleton and Company, 1925).

———, *Clothes On and Off the Stage: A History of Dress from the Earliest Times to the Present Day* (New York, D. Appleton-Century Company, 1928).

Corson, Richard, *Stage Makeup,* 2nd ed. (New York, Appleton-Century-Crofts, Inc., 1949).

Dabney, Edith, and Wise, C. M., *A Book of Dramatic Costume* (New York, F. S. Crofts & Co., 1930).

Exmouth, Charles Ernest Pellew, *Dyes and Dyeing* (New York, Robert M. McBride & Company, Inc., 1928).

Factor, Max, *Hints on the Art of Make-up* (Hollywood, Max Factor Make-up Studios, 1936). A set of nine pamphlets, subject matter tersely and ably presented and illustrated.

Fischel, Oscar, and von Boehn, Max, *Die Mode,* 7 vols. (Munich, F. Bruckmann, 1909–23). This work treats costume from the Middle Ages to 1878. The volumes concerning the nineteenth century have been translated into English by Marian Edwardes and published by Dutton. One of the most useful, well-illustrated works on source material for theatrical costumes.

Gorsline, Douglas, *What People Wore* (New York, The Viking Press, Inc., 1953). Illustrations of the trends in Western fashions by means of 1800 line drawings, 12 color plates, and 50 pages of text.

Grimball, E., and Wells, R., *Costuming a Play* (New York, Appleton-Century-Crofts, Inc., 1925).

Hartley, D., and Elliott, M., *Life and Work of the People of England* (New York, W. W. Norton & Company, Inc., 1929).

Hope, Thomas, *The Costume of the Ancients,* 2 vols. (London, Chatto and Windus, 1875).

Hottenroth, F., *Le Costume chez les peuples anciens et modernes* (Paris, A. Guerinet, N.D.).

Houston, Mary G., and Hornblower, F. S., *Ancient Egyptian, Assyrian, and Persian Costumes and Decorations* (London, A. & C. Black, Ltd., 1920).

Kelly, F., and Schwabe, R., *Historic Costume: A Chronicle of Fashion in Western Europe, 1490–1790* (London, B. T. Batsford, Ltd., 1925).

Koehler, C., and von Sichart, E., *A History of Costume* (London, G. H. Watt, 1928).

Laver, James, ed., *Costume of The Western World,* Vol. III (London, George C. Harrap and Company, 1951). This series in six volumes, edited by the well-known Keeper of Prints and Drawings at the Victoria and Albert Museum in London, represents the most complete source for information on historic costume available.

McClellan, Elisabeth, *History of American Costume, 1607–1870* (New York, Tudor Publishing Company, 1937).

Norris, Herbert, *Costume and Fashion,* 3 vols. (London, J. M. Dent and Sons, Ltd., 1924).

Parsons, Charles S. A., *Guide to Theatrical Make-up* (London, Sir Isaac Pitman & Sons, Ltd., 1932).

Planche, James R., *A Cyclopedia of Costume; or Dictionary of Dress,* 2 vols. (London, Chatto and Windus, 1876–79).

Racinet, Albert C. A., *Le Costume Historique,* 6 vols. (Paris, Firmin-Didot et Cie, 1888).

Strauss, Ivard, *Paint, Powder and Make-up* (New Haven, Sweet and Son, 1936).

Strenkovsky, Serge, *The Art of Make-up* (New York, E. P. Dutton & Company, Inc., 1937).

Uzanne, Louis Octave, *Fashion in Paris* (London, William Heinemann, Ltd., 1901).

Walkup, Fairfax P., *Dressing the Part,* rev. ed. (New York, Appleton-Century-Crofts, Inc., 1950).

Wilcox, R. T., *The Mode in Costume* (New York, Charles Scribner's Sons, 1942).

Wolters, N E. B., *Modern Make-up for Stage and Screen* (London, Lovat Dickson & Thompson, Ltd.; Toronto, The Macmillan Company of Canada, Ltd., 1935).

Zur Geschichte der Kostume, edited by Louis Braun, W. Diez, Ernst Frohlich, I. Gehrts, C. Haberlin, M. Heil, A. Muller, and F. Rothbart (Munich, Braun und Schneider, 1909).

INDEX